VALUES
IN
CONFLICT

VALUES IN CONFLICT:
LIFE, LIBERTY, AND THE RULE OF LAW

BURTON M. LEISER

Drake University

MACMILLAN PUBLISHING CO., INC.
New York
COLLIER MACMILLAN PUBLISHERS
London

Copyright © 1981, Burton M. Leiser

Printed in the United States of America

Macmillan Publishing Co., Inc.
866 Third Avenue, New York, New York 10022

Collier Macmillan Canada, Ltd.

Library of Congress Cataloging in Publication Data

Leiser, Burton M.
Values in conflict.

    Includes bibliographical references.
    1. Civil rights—United States—Addresses, essays, lectures. 2. Rule of law—United States—Addresses, essays, lectures. 3. Civil rights—Addresses, essays, lectures. 4. Social values—Addresses, essays, lectures. I. Leiser, Burton M.
JC599.U5V28   323.4′0973   80-22448
ISBN 0-02-369520-X

Printing: 1 2 3 4 5 6 7 8   Year: 1 2 3 4 5 6 7

To all the philosophers
who helped me along the way,
and most especially to

Paul Edwards

Sidney Hook

Richard Taylor

and

Vincent Tomas

PREFACE

This book was originally conceived as a companion to my volume *Liberty, Justice, and Morals: Contemporary Value Conflicts*. As work progressed on it, however, and as my colleagues at other institutions communicated with me, it became apparent that an anthology dealing with some of the less conventional moral issues that face our society at this time, as well as with those that have engaged the attention of philosophers over the last decade or so, would be a welcome addition to the options available to those who teach courses in applied philosophy, normative ethics, or contemporary moral problems. The present volume, therefore, may be used either independently or in combination with one or more other texts. Many of the articles included in this volume are published here for the first time. Other articles were first published in respected journals or in books within the last few years. In addition, relevant excerpts from a number of pertinent legal decisions, including some from lower courts as well as from the United States Supreme Court, help to round out the collection and to introduce both the legal issues and judicial arguments on philosophical issues.

Among the more "traditional" topics the reader will find in this volume are abortion, euthanasia, and questions of free speech and freedom of the press. Less frequently does one find in a philosophy anthology such issues, included here, as the rights of distant peoples (including those who are temporally as well as geographically remote), espionage, and terrorism. The right of privacy, homosexual rights, and affirmative action are other areas of great immediate and long-range concern and are therefore accorded separate sections of their own. The collection is introduced by a new essay by Richard Taylor on "The Meaning of Human Existence," a subject that students often expect to discuss in introductory philosophy courses, but one that instructors often feel is not quite respectable, at least from the point of view of a professional philosopher. Professor Taylor's beautifully written and provocative essay should fill a long-neglected need.

Many people have helped to make this book possible. It goes without saying, of course, that I am most grateful to all the authors of the articles included herein, and to their publishers (in those cases where the articles were published previously), for permitting me to include their work in this collection. In addition, I should like to record here my deep gratitude to the many colleagues and friends whose fine articles I was unable to use because considerations of space and economy compelled us to omit several entire chapters as well as a number of other articles.

Finally, a note of appreciation to Rachel Buckles, whose diligence and attention to detail are indispensable not only to me, but to a number of other faculty members who rely upon her invaluable services as secretary, mother confessor, and memory; to the fine staffs at

Cowles Library and the Law Library of Drake University, who are always ready to track down the most obscure reference at any hour and with truly unbelievable speed; and to Hurd Hutchins, Susan Greenberg, and Kenneth E. Scott, whose editorial assistance was invaluable.

Some court decisions and a few previously published articles have been edited to meet space limitations. In court decisions, most citations have been deleted without ellipses. Ellipses have been employed to indicate deletions of text, as opposed to citations. Wherever footnotes have been deleted, that fact has been noted in a footnote at the beginning of the article, and the remaining notes have been renumbered.

Many excellent bibliographical references may be found in the notes to individual articles. For extensive bibliographies to parts II, V, VI, VII, and IX, see *Liberty, Justice, and Morals*, Second Edition (Macmillan, 1979). Bibliographies on the other parts are readily available in standard reference sources.

B.M.L.

CONTENTS

VALUES
IN
CONFLICT

I
THE
MEANING
OF
LIFE

INTRODUCTION

Students who enroll for a first course in philosophy often expect to hear something about the meaning of life—whatever that may be—and are just as often disappointed. Instead, depending upon the professor's preferences, they are more likely to find that the course is devoted to epistemology, metaphysics, philosophy of science, ethics, or linguistic analysis, or perhaps to the history of philosophy. But philosophers often have discussed the meaning of life in their philosophical writings, and their conclusions on that important subject often have an important bearing upon the conclusions they may draw on other topics in more specialized areas of philosophy, including ethics. It therefore seems appropriate to begin with a rather unusual article dealing with a subject that most philosophers in recent years have chosen to ignore as if it were somehow disreputable to discuss it.

Consider Richard Taylor's observation that there is a threat in discovering, too late, that one's life is meaningless. It is easy to recognize "the utter insignificance in the fact that a leaf withers and falls from a tree, or that a housefly perishes," but it is very difficult indeed to think of ourselves—or even of human fetuses—in quite the same way. Is it not precisely because we believe, perhaps without ever having tried to figure out why, that human life is meaningful and not trivial, that we are so adamantly opposed to its destruction and so utterly dedicated to its preservation?

In discussing whether life has any meaning, Taylor recalls the myth of Sisyphus, the man condemned by the gods to everlasting toil—forever pushing a giant boulder to the summit of a mountain, only to lose his grip and have it roll to the bottom from where he would have to start all over again. The ancient Greeks described other imaginative penalties that were perhaps even more appalling. For having given man the gift of fire, Prometheus was chained to a rocky crag where each morning a giant vulture would attack him, gnawing at his liver, which would grow back at night in time for the next morning's attack. And Tantalus, who served his dinner guests his broiled son, was condemned to remain forever in a beautiful pool, whose waters rose up to his neck. Above him were the branches of a tree from which the most succulent fruits dangled just within his reach. As he grew ever more hungry and thirsty, the fruit and the water became more and more tantalizing. But whenever he would reach for a fruit, the branch would swing away just out of his grasp; and if he attempted to cup his hands so as to refresh himself with a few drops of the clear waters in which he was immersed, they fell away from him, remaining forever just beyond his reach. Each of these myths has to do with the punishment of a wrongdoer. They suggest that the worst punishment of all might be to render a person's life meaningless, that is, not merely to torment him or to cause him physical pain, but to consume his days and years with utterly meaningless tasks. Taylor carries this suggestion still further, asking

whether all human life might not ultimately be as meaningless as that
of Sisyphus, whether we are not all condemned to endless toil that in
the end has no real purpose.

RICHARD TAYLOR I

THE MEANING OF HUMAN EXISTENCE

Arthur Schopenhauer, in a comment on human existence that is somber
even for this philosopher, wrote

> It is really incredible how meaningless and void of significance when
> looked at from without, how dull and unenlightened by intellect when felt
> from within, is the course of the life of the great majority of men. It is a
> weary longing and complaining, a dream-like staggering through the four
> ages of life to death, accompanied by a series of trivial thoughts. Such
> men are like clockwork, which is wound up, and goes it knows not why;
> and every time a man is begotten and born, the clock of human life is
> wound up anew, to repeat the same old piece it has played innumerable
> times before, passage after passage, measure after measure, with insigni-
> ficant variations. Every individual, every human being and his course of
> life, is but another short dream of the endless spirit of nature, of the
> persistent will to live; is only another fleeting form, which it carelessly
> sketches on its infinite page, space and time; allows to remain for a time
> so short that it vanishes into nothing in comparison with these, and then
> obliterates to make new room. And yet, and here lies the serious side of
> life, every one of these fleeting forms, these empty fancies, must be paid
> for by the whole will to live, in all its activity, with many and deep
> sufferings, and finally with a bitter death, long feared and coming at last.
> This is why the sight of a corpse makes us suddenly so serious.

What Schopenhauer was calling attention to here was not, of course,
some malady that might be corrected by modifying the structure of
government, or by a new economic order, or even by philosophical enlightenment. Nor was he claiming that human existence cannot be, at
least in some cases, happy. Nor was he calling attention to the familiar
evils that beset life. These themes belong to political and economic
theory, or to ethics. Schopenhauer, instead, was suggesting that this
meaninglessness of our existence is metaphysical, unavoidable, or part

of the very nature of life. He accordingly offered no program for overcoming it.

I am going to pursue this Schopenhauerian claim, but without any special reference to Schopenhauer. I believe that his perception was basically correct, that human life, in spite of its joys and in spite of the tenacity with which we cling to it, does have the character that led Schopenhauer to deem it meaningless. I also believe, however, that this is not the final verdict on life and that, having conceded to pessimism the facts that it claims are there, we can find another, to which both philosophy and religion have hitherto given little attention, that will at least partly redeem the otherwise forlorn description.

LIFE AND MEANING

Life is not self-authenticating, any more in a person than in an animal. That a given thing—a housefly, a horse, a man, whatever—should be living is a fact, but not as such a meaningful one; for a life just considered by itself can be quite devoid of significance. Meaningfulness does not follow automatically on the mere occurrence of a heartbeat.

Thus the efforts, so commonly made, to sustain a fading and flickering life at all costs are entirely misguided. Here the potentiality for meaning has usually evaporated, and the effort at a mere prolongation of bodily processes can only rest upon the absurd idea that life itself, as a mere fact, is something precious. The life of a breathing but comatose and dying person has no more value than does that of an expiring insect. Its meaning is gone, and, more important, its potentiality of achieving meaning is gone.

Nor does the fact that a given life is *human* automatically invest it with meaning. To be a living person may—and, indeed, certainly does —enhance the possibility of meaningfulness; but it is still only a possibility. Being human, as distinct from being something else, such as canine, ursine, or whatever, is not by itself a quality possessed of worth. Life's meaning for a dying person lies entirely in the life that has been lived, not in anything that exists any longer, even though that person is undeniably still possessed of his or her humanity. And the same, alas, is true of many whose mundane lives are still far from over and even, sometimes, only just beginning. For, while they have the gift of life, and even the quality of personality, that is, of being *persons,* circumstances still will never allow them to give their lives the slightest meaning or, at least, any meaning that is not as easily possessed by any animal. A person's life can be long, quite free from pain, and even enjoyed and clung to, yet bereft of meaning; for the life of any animal can have all these characteristics. Still the extinction of that life can be without the slightest significance anywhere in the world, as meaningless as the autumn withering and falling of a leaf from a tree.

People want to deny this, to claim that the life of every person has exactly the same value as that of any other, as though one needed only to be born and to draw breath from one day to another to have a meaningful existence. There is a challenge in the claim that a person's life can be meaningless—the challenge, namely, to make it otherwise—

and not everyone feels that he or she can rise to it. Indeed, rather few persons have a very clear idea of what they would need to do to meet that challenge. They accordingly reject the challenge by declaring, in effect, that it has already been met—met by the simple expedient of being born and continuing to draw breath!

There is, moreover, a threat in what has been said, the threat of discovering, too late, that one's own life is quite meaningless. We can all recognize the utter insignificance in the fact that a leaf withers and falls from a tree, or that a housefly perishes. It is not so easy to view our own existence in the same light, to think of our own decay as the culmination of a life that never had any significance to begin with. Our conceit forbids it.

Thus we are tempted to say, in desperation, that every individual's life is meaningful *to him* or *to her*, quite regardless of any other consideration, thinking that we have thereby made some sort of point. All this actually means, however, is that people normally cling to their lives, no matter what. Which is certainly true. There are exceptions, as in the cases of suicide, or sometimes a weariness with life that comes with very advanced age, but normally, the threat to life is regarded by anyone as supremely terrible. Who can on reflection suppose, however, that one's own or any other life can be made meaningful just by the fact of being clung to? This anxious concern for one's own being might be, and in fact clearly is, quite blind, that is, without any rational conviction of life's worth. Even animals flee from danger and try with their most desperate efforts to ward off every threat to their existence. No one can suppose that this is because they have *chosen* to, after rationally balancing life's good and evils. They still cling to life even when the balance seems clearly tipped in favor of evil, for they do so from blind impulse. And it is no different in the case of a person. One may claim, if one likes, that in our case the blessings of life do greatly outweigh its evils, which certainly seems doubtful, but whether this is true or not, it is irrelevant. For a person normally clings to existence with the same tenacity as an animal even without balancing these things or making any rational choice at all. Like any animal, a person's craving for existence, sometimes called an "instinct" for self-preservation, is the blindest, least enlightened craving there is. The most worthless things are sometimes desperately sought and grasped. Indeed, actual evils, even things destructive of what one cherishes most deeply, are sometimes fervently sought and held—in ignorance of their true nature, perhaps (perhaps not), but clung to none the less. Nothing, accordingly, can be made good or significant just by the fact of its being thus fervently grasped; and to say that every person's life is meaningful *to that person,* meaning only that every person does cling to it, is really to say nothing at all to the point.

THE IMAGE OF MEANINGLESSNESS

We need, then, to get before us some clear idea of meaningfulness, to avoid entanglement in epigrams having to do with human worth and the quality of personality that are nothing more than slogans. And the best way to do this will be by creating a picture of meaninglessness. Thus, if we can portray a kind of existence that is clearly meaningless, and then see just what makes it so, we can certainly give content to the claim that human life is meaningless—for we can say that it is such, to just the extent that it resembles that picture. And then we can proceed to say what a meaningful existence would be; for life will, by these criteria, be meaningful just to the extent that these ingredients of meaninglessness are abolished. By going about things in this way, we will, it is hoped, avoid the kind of banality that characterizes so much of the discussions of questions such as these. We will not, for example, think of meaningful existence in terms of the mere attainment of ambitions and goals; for if those should happen to be of only illusory value, then whatever meaning they would appear to give to one's life would be no less illusory.

Probably no clearer image of meaninglessness can be found in literature than in the ancient myth of Sisyphus. Sisyphus, it will be recalled, was condemned by the gods to this fate: that he should roll a stone to the top of a hill, whereupon it would at once roll back down, and Sisyphus would then have the task of again rolling it to the top, and it would once more roll to the bottom, and so on, and so on throughout eternity.

This myth has always haunted men, like a bad dream that we cannot awaken from. We are moved by pity for the condemned Sisyphus, yet that is not all of it; there is something deeper to it than his suffering. We are struck by both the stupidity of what he is doing—moving a stone, the commonest and least worthwhile object on the face of the earth—and by his inability ever to stop. If it were a jewel that he were moving, or perhaps a lovely picture that he was condemned endlessly to be painting, or the infinite stars that he was to try counting, then his existence would not be quite so pathetic. Then besides this is the element of a rhythmic recurrence of what he does, as though his life were divided into uniform cycles of rising and falling, with nothing ever becoming finally settled, either for good or for bad.

The more important things to note about the picture, however, are that Sisyphus's labors are purposeless and endlessly repetitive. It is this combination that is unique to the picture, and haunting. The pathos of it does not lie in the thought that Sisyphus is condemned to great toil but, rather, that nothing ever comes of his efforts that must, nevertheless, be repeated, forever. Not even the minimal achievement that the picture warrants, the mere coming to rest of the stone, is ever reached. It has always to be moved once again, endlessly, pointlessly, meaninglessly. These elements of pointlessness and repetitiveness would remain even if we were to suppose that the stone was not even heavy, that it could be transported almost effortlessly. Toilsome or not, the work would still fit the pattern of endless pointlessness.

But we need not go to mythology or even to fiction to find exactly the same image. There is, for example, a convent in Quebec in which the following scene is enacted every day: About a dozen nuns enter a barren room and, standing in a circle, chant prayers, in Latin and in perfect unison, for several hours. Having finished, they are replaced by another similar group of nuns who do exactly the same thing for several hours, these to be replaced by still another group. Thus does the chant rise from this bleak and dreary room, without variation, day after day and year after year, unendingly. The nuns who participate in this repetitive ritual have no other life; they are either in their places, chanting in unison, or resting, to resume exactly that behavior when their turn comes around again, very shortly. They go on and off in shifts. Nightfall brings no rest, nor do any holy days, nor does anything whatsoever except ultimately, of course, death. But even then a replacement, trained for the role, steps into it. The prayers chanted, being in Latin and delivered in a fixed and highly ritualized manner, are virtually meaningless to any hearer, aesthetically worthless, and probably without meaning any longer to the nuns who pronounce them.

Here, in the life of such a nun, is precisely the image contained in the myth of Sisyphus. Nothing ever gets completed, for a prayer is uttered, at length and at considerable speed, only to be commenced again, from the same beginning as before. Nor does anything count as bringing the agent of this labor closer to achieving her purpose, for that purpose simply is to repeat, over and over, what has already been done, over and over.

Consider now another picture, an imaginative one this time, but sufficiently like what is common to be recognizable. Imagine, that is, a man, totally innocent of any wrongdoing, who is nevertheless, by an appalling miscarriage of justice, condemned to a lifetime of hard labor. Suppose further that his sentence is beyond appeal and irrevocable, and beyond all hope of mitigation. And suppose further that the labor contrived for him, to engage all his remaining days, is this: that he shall start by digging an immense hole in the barren prison yard, this to occupy him for an entire day. On the next day he will fill it up again, restoring everything to its original condition. Then on the day after that he will dig another huge hole, this one to be filled up again like the first, on the day following. And so on, for every day—he shall be bending his back to the shovel, either in creating a large hole in the ground or in refilling the very such hole that he made the day before, this work to continue without rest or modification through every day of his life. Thus looking back, at the end of his life, to assess his life's work, he will find that it consists either of a large and meaningless hole in the ground or of a hole just filled in, nothing more.

The resemblance of this picture to the image of Sisyphus, or of the chanting nuns, is obvious. The element of meaninglessness is similarly obvious in all three pictures. And that element is not simply that of gross injustice, or onerous toil, or frustration, or pain, or hopes dashed, even though all these things are clearly contained in the pictures. It is not hard, for example, to find instances of injustice that, however evil, do not convert the lives of their victims to meaninglessness. And it is similarly not hard, and in fact very easy, to find in typical life examples of lifelong toil more onerous than what has been portrayed here; yet lives in which such toil is an ingredient are not thereby made meaningless. Indeed, the most seemingly meaningful lives may sometimes be the hardest, in terms of the sheer work that is exacted from their possessors. Similarly, the pictures we have before us, though they are obviously not portrayals of pleasure, are also not strong images of pain, either. If our purpose were to illustrate a life of pain, we could easily do much better than this, by describing almost any slum, for example, or terminal ward of a hospital. Nor again do we have before us the clearest images of frustrated hope. In the case of the nuns, it is even possible to suppose that their strange existence is the fulfillment of their hope, this having been ignited and fueled by a religious conviction.

The meaninglessness in these portrayals is something different from all these things and is perhaps captured by the following supposition. Suppose someone, quite capable of understanding what he was being told, were informed that his whole life would be spent in the manner of those illustrated. It is not hard to imagine the condemned man hearing, and completely believing, such a pronouncement, for example. What, then, exactly, would be the cause of his despair? Simply this: that his life would thus be divested of all purpose, including even the minimal purpose of somehow avoiding total boredom from one hour to the next. That a lifetime should be spent to no purpose is, however common, tragic enough. That it should in addition be deprived even of that minimal sort of variety that enables the hours and the days to pass by one more or less unnoticed, as his attention is drawn to other things, is totally appalling. We have here, in this combination of things, the very essence of meaningless existence.

MEANING AND CONTENTMENT

Our next undertaking will be to see to what extent life itself resembles the pictures of meaninglessness that have just been sketched. Are those pictures aberrations? Do they express the rare, exceptional, the somewhat bizarre deviations from the normal course of life? Or do they, on the contrary, typify it?

We cannot in a straightforward manner answer this question with respect to human life, for we are too close to it, and we tend, moreover, to interpret it through the reflections of hope and optimism, so that we are in danger of not seeing what is really there. This is sometimes clear enough with respect to certain individual lives. Thus we sometimes see someone whose life so perfectly resembles the pictures just drawn, and is so patently without meaning, that this verdict is forced upon us—yet that very individual may rejoice in his or her meaningless existence. Consider, for example, the employee of the slaughterhouse whose lifelong work is to wield a huge sledgehammer against the skulls of beef cattle as they are conveyed before him, hanging terrified by their hind legs. One after another, in a steady procession, for a full working day, day in and day out, through the weeks, years, through the major part of a lifetime, the work goes on, blow after blow after blow, never varying. Of course this portrayal is revolting and filled with horror, but that is not to the point. The agent of this endless infliction of suffering and death has long since ceased to be troubled by the nature of his work. Like anyone else, he delights after the day's work in playing with his dog or his kitteń, putting his children to bed, listening to soft music, whatever. And that *is* just the point; namely, that he rejoices in life, in spite of its meaninglessness. And it is especially at this point that one must suppress the impulse to say, "Then how can anyone say that his life is without meaning?" True, the individual rejoices. And true, the slaughterer's work is by normal standards valuable to humanity, possibly even necessary. And true, he does it well. Yet it would be difficult to find a life that more exactly resembles these pictures of meaninglessness. So the lesson that should be drawn is not that a life that is lived with contentment is by virtue of that fact made meaningful but, rather, that even a meaningless life can be filled with contentment. And that is, of course, the great danger—that the inner satisfactions of our lives can blind us to their meaninglessness.

We may all be like the slaughterer, not in the sense that our lives are lived in the ambience of horror and death, but in the sense that they are ultimately without meaning and that we are blinded to this by our inner satisfaction.

THE MEANINGLESSNESS OF ANIMAL LIFE

Instead, then, of looking directly at human existence at this point, we will have a much better chance of seeing things as they are if we look first upon the life that surrounds us, at the whole of living nature excepting human beings. We shall thereby avoid not only the misrepresentation of things arising from our own contentments, as the life we describe is not our own, but also the kind of fatuous investment of life with such qualities as dignity, nobility, and inherent worth that philosophers so delight in when humanity is the object of their inquiry. Whatever else one might say about insects and rodents, for example, the temptation is never to ascribe to them inherent worth.

Consider, then, the life of any animal whatever, and note its perfect resemblance to the pictures of meaninglessness that have been sketched. We can begin anywhere, with whatever living thing next catches our attention. Consider the ground mole. This pathetic and innocuous little animal has settled into the most forbidding environment imaginable, into the dark and abrasive earth itself, and there each generation lives out its life in unredeeming toil. This animal has vestigial eyes, capable only of distinguishing light from darkness, and it instinctively knows that the moment light appears, it is vulnerable to whatever preying animal is about. Its huge shovel-like claws get it with incredible labor from one point to another, and this is how it spends its life, digging. And to what end? Only that it may find a worm or grub that will nourish it and give it strength to dig farther to yet another worm or grub, and then on to still another, day after day, endlessly. The resemblance to Sisyphus is perfect. And is there no further purpose to all this? There is, of course—but that is where the irony of this animal's existence becomes complete. For its purpose is simply and solely to beget others exactly like itself, and having exactly the same destiny, to inch along through the hard ground in search of a worm, and then another, and another—throughout eternity. Nothing ever comes of this pointless endeavor, except more pointless endeavor that is its exact replication.

This animal epitomizes all animal life. An insect spends its whole existence feeding, for no other end than that another generation of insects may do the same again. Sometimes the preparations for this are staggering, as in the case of the seventeen-year locust. It is so called because this animal spends that great period of time burrowing deep in the darkness of the earth, only then finally to emerge into the light of day, spend a few days in the sun, and lay eggs, just so that this long and meaningless cycle can begin once more, to be repeated again and again, endlessly. The bee that emerges today is no different from the one that took wing ten million years ago, and its destiny is no different. It toils only that others exactly like it may do exactly the same, for another million years, then a million more, and, indeed, forever. The birds that move north and south, back and forth, with the cycles of the seasons, often over unbelievable distances, do so only that the same pointless behavior will be repeated again and again. At no point is a signal ever given to stop. At no point can one find that even the slightest beginning has been made in anything at all, beyond the sheer perpetuation of repetitive toil. What, one wants to ask, is it all *for*? And the answer is perfectly obvious: It is all for nothing, it just goes on and on, to no end whatever.

THE MEANINGLESSNESS OF HUMAN LIFE

Do we, then, find ourselves at a new level when we move from animal to human existence? Can we accept the obvious meaninglessness of all the life that surrounds us, assured that our lives are essentially different, that there is some unique meaning to human life that is denied to everything else?

Most people simply take for granted that there is, without feeling the least need to support that conviction. They assume that a human life is precious just because it is human and that no matter how closely its pattern may resemble the pictures of meaninglessness we have drawn, we are nevertheless spared the obvious inference. And there have, of course, always been plenty of philosophers and theologians to add their own comforting assurances, as though what is here in question should be perfectly obvious to all. Thus theologians and clergy claim man to be the very image of God, and their hearers nod their automatic assent, without even knowing what might be meant by this, beyond the implication that human life is not without meaning. It is the comfort conveyed by these words, and not their truth, that elicits assent. And philosophers, for their part, speak of the human dignity, absolute worth, and autonomy that are shared by no other living things. Again, the declarations are comforting, however meaningless to the mind. Some have turned with great hope to man's supposed rational nature, even calling this the divine element, after the manner of Plato and Aristotle.

Thus are philosophers able to join with the theologians and to speak with one voice of man's kinship with God, utterly oblivious to the obscurity of this fond idea, and equally oblivious to our most manifest kinship with the whole of living nature.

It is all very well to proclaim that human nature has some unique value and meaning, but to give that declaration credibility, one must somehow show that human life is not like the image of meaninglessness that we have before us. And that is not an easy thing to do. For if we actually look at mankind, at human history or at the typical life of an individual, what we find is every ingredient of meaninglessness that was carefully inserted into the pictures of Sisyphus, the nuns, or the hole-digging convict. Schopenhauer's description is apt. Our lives are lived out like clockwork, accompanied by trivial thoughts and impulses. Their whole meaning, by whatever lofty words we may choose to describe it, appears to arise solely from the intensity with which we cling to this clockwork existence, forever vainly supposing that what seems to be of the very essence of life is instead some sort of accident, a temporary aberration, that will surely disappear in another day or so. We are like aging parents who nourish the hope that their child, long since lost, is still living after all and will come back any day, or someone who still lives in the fantasy of a love long dead, imagining that it will now be revived and go on as before, yet inwardly knowing that it really is dead. We hope that the banality of our lives and the speciousness of our satisfactions will at any moment be converted to lasting triumphs and that we will be able to say, finally, that it really was worth it after all. But inwardly we know better. We partially conceal the truth even from ourselves, in order not to overwhelm hope; and in this we are again assisted by philosophers, who declare that our very humanity is enough to make our existence utterly good and meaningful. We need not, they say, in effect, look any further; what we seek has already been conferred.

It is a pleasant notion. It may even be a necessary one, once the alternatives are seriously considered.

Consider the life of any individual person—someone who says, with the utmost sincerity, that he or she is happy, someone filled with the zest for life—for the question is not whether anyone is happy, but rather, whether human existence, in an individual or in the race as a whole, has any meaning. We find that each day simply duplicates the one that went before, with only insignificant variations. The person you meet after a year is the same, doing what he or she was doing then, responding to the same things in the same ways, saying much the same things, and thinking much the same things, most of them unworthy of thought to begin with. Hardly a thing has changed. A child has been born, a business venture undertaken, some purchases made, a trip completed, a few games watched or played—all about the same as the year before, and the year forthcoming. And what, besides the pleasure of the moment or, more likely, the momentary escape from boredom, is the purpose of it all? Rarely is it anything beyond the accumulation of possessions. The similarity to Sisyphus is still inescapable as is the similarity to the nuns, who simply add one meaningless chant to another, the total swelling, but never being anything but more of the same.

THE EVIL OF INACTION

How much of life is spent in the sheer escape from boredom? A person who rises in the morning knowing that his day will be about the same as the one before will nevertheless undertake it with zest, provided that it will deliver him from the otherwise unbearable boredom. Thus he will engage in his familiar routine—corresponding, making decisions of the same sort that he made yesterday and a year ago, realizing a profit here and a loss there, along with the usual breaks for lunch or whatever, relating and hearing anecdotes such as are by now familiar, then finally to dinner and bed, to repeat the same tomorrow. The picture is perfectly familiar, wherever you turn—to the postal worker making the same rounds each day; the truck driver moving hither and thither, filling the long hours, diverted only by such things as he sees along the way though he has already seen them a hundred times; the dentist; the physician; the teacher. Do not ask, "Are they happy?" Very likely they are, for they manage to escape the greatest evil of the world, which is boredom. Ask instead, Do their lives resemble the image of Sisyphus?" And then, without shifting the subject to one of happiness, human worth, or other pleasant things, give an honest answer.

When we think of evil, we are likely to think of pain and death, but these are not the greatest evils. The greatest evil that can be inflicted upon anyone is unrelieved boredom, and the escape from it is therefore necessarily good, though only in a negative sense. It is good in the way in which an animal's *not* being caught in a trap, or a child's *not* being hit by a truck, is good. But negative though this good is, it is absolutely essential to have it, for the alternative, boredom, is such an unmitigated evil. It is not hard to see this if one looks closely at the picture of it. Thus suppose that you were told, by someone having the power to carry out this threat, that you were going to be strapped in a fixed position, that henceforth you would not be able to move any muscle, and that you would be sustained like this for years by a means of nourishment and the maintenance of other vital functions without your participation at all. And suppose that what you were thus condemned to look at the rest of your life was sheer nothingness—the blank sky, for instance, or perhaps an illuminated expanse of white. There would, in short, be nothing for you ever to do again, nothing to claim your attention. Surely the most tormented sufferer in the terminal ward of a hospital, struggling against unbearable pain, is lucky in comparison to this. There is a rare affliction, in which the victim is likely to awaken and realize that he or she is unable to move a single muscle, not even to speak or otherwise convey his or her plight to anyone. Suppose one were to thus awaken and then, however painlessly, remain in that state for years! I have seen a man, very young and a few years ago faced with every blessing and good fortune, who as the result of a sudden brain injury was left unable to move anything but his eyes. He languishes in a nursing home, amidst the sick and the old who have been sent there to die, but with this difference: that he, being still young, is condemned to quite a long life. What does he think of all day, week after week? Perhaps his overwhelming boredom has by now deadened his power of thought, so that his mind is slowly becoming as helpless as the rest of him. Surely, one hopes so. For otherwise, no greater evil can be imagined.

HUMAN ANIMALITY

We noted that it is the destiny of every animal simply to beget more of its kind, these in turn struggling against all odds to achieve the very same thing again, a succession of identical generations never ceasing. Is mankind different? Superficially, yes. The world changes at our hands and a human history unfolds, the chapters of which are not all exactly alike, as they are in the case of other living things. Yet basically, we are the same. We respond to the urge to beget as blindly as does everything else. And it is, in our case as in theirs, a blind and irrational urge, not a goal. Many living things never see their offspring, and it is not really for them that they copulate and bring them forth. They do this because they are impelled to, by an irrational force.

We are not basically different. At the basis of our own lives is the same mindless urge, though our inventive intellects have imposed variations that distinguish the expression of this urge from that of other creatures and superficially lead us to think that it is something quite different. For we have found ways to avoid the natural outcome of this impulse in its primary expression, namely, the begetting of children, and we have also found numberless ways of diverting it into totally novel modes of expression. That we go through all the motions of begetting children and yet avoid that result by numerous clever means, shows clearly enough that we have no such goal in mind. In fact, we have no goal other than the sheer indulgence of an appetite, imposed on us by nature and never intellectually chosen at all. Moreover, we differ from the animals in that we have a culture. We are not merely the product of external nature; we are also the product of human acculturation. And an enormous part of that acculturation, what in fact seems sometimes to lie at the very basis of it, is the suppression of the sexual impulse. Everywhere it is hedged about by rules, imposed at such a tender age that they seem eventually to be part of our natures. The result is that we seek "other outlets," as it is aptly expressed. That is, people throw themselves into careers, the pursuit of glory, office-seeking, honors. Every bit of this behavior belongs in the same genre as that of a bird, spreading and preening itself before an intended mate, making itself glorious. In the case of the bird, the point of it all is copulation—not to create offspring, for it really cares nothing for these things, perhaps never to be seen anyway, but simply for its own sake—in response to the promptings of nature. We are not that different. What it comes to is simply this: that we feel *alive* when we are doing things, especially when we are preening ourselves and making ourselves, as it seems to us, glorious. The most natural way of doing this, the way that more than anything else makes us feel alive, is in sexual intimacy. It is the only thing for which nothing is too great to sacrifice. With it goes the passion of loving and the total sense of fulfillment that comes from feeling loved, the only thing that the world offers that comes even close to being truly good. But when the barriers erected by culture and custom, reinforced by religion and law and every instrument on which humans can lay their hands, stand in the way of this most obvious expression of *eros,* then we find other things to do, that is, other ways of glorifying ourselves and seeming, even if only for a while, to come alive. Because they are substitutes, we have to hurl ourselves into them with that much more energy, to get anything resembling the intended result. And thereby do we escape boredom. To be barred from sexual intimacy and genuine, deeply felt affection is indeed hard, but not impossible if we are still allowed to come alive otherwise. But to be denied *this,* to be so placed that we have nothing to do, to be placed in unremitting boredom and allowed no hope of escape, is to suffer the ultimate evil. Better to be simply running in circles, which is what the lives of most persons consist in, than languishing in inaction, that is, in utter boredom.

Behold, then, the life of any individual. If you select someone who is happy and by every ordinary measure successful, so much the better, for you will then not need to ask whether he is happy or successful. You can ask instead whether his existence has any meaning. His life, you will find, consists of a perpetual running in circles, with periods of rest that serve only to revitalize him for more of exactly the same running in circles. These circles are defined by things undertaken and done—a business venture consummated here, a love affair there, a trip to this place or that for novel sights and sounds, an occasional victory for some trivial reward, a little applause here, praise there, reassuring words, and bits of self-glorification. And these circles, instead of leading on to something different and perhaps nobler, for the most part overlap, such that the creator of them tends very much to be recreating the same circle over and over. Viewed from within, that is, from the standpoint of the person himself, his existence can quite truly be said to be happy. At least it is not one either of pain or boredom—which is quite enough to satisfy the demands of happiness. But viewed from without it has exactly the pattern of Sisyphus.

THE INDIVIDUAL AND THE SPECIES

Do we, then, move to some new level of meaningfulness when we pass from such an individual to the race as a whole? Other animals, we found, simply replicate in each generation the generations that went before, as exactly as does each journey of Sisyphus up the hill repeat his preceding ones. No variation is introduced at all. What, then, of mankind?

Here we could be reassured if it could be shown that, although the life of each individual may be without ultimate purpose or meaning, the individual is nevertheless part of a greater being, or the whole of humanity, whose existence does have meaning. And there is no doubt that most persons deem their own lives in some sense meaningful if they can view their efforts, or sometimes their life's work, as having made some sort of contribution to mankind. But, if we look at it more closely, that kind of meaning is as specious as the others we have considered. The conditions of life change, to be sure, from one generation to another, and no doubt some of them get better, in some sense, just as others get worse. Life gets longer. For many it becomes less onerous. Disease is in some sense conquered. Changes of this sort are familiar and need no review. We can even say, though it is not obviously true, that life has for most people become happier; in any case, they have become less vulnerable to some of the ancient evils, even though new evils may now threaten. But even granting all this, it can hardly be said that there is any clear meaning to human existence that is lacking in the existence of the individual. On the contrary, the life of the species here resembles exactly the life of the individual, and both resemble the pattern of meaninglessness embodied in the pictures with which we began.

For what do we actually find here? Generation following upon generation, all in response to the all-powerful urge to beget, but to no purpose whatever. No sooner has one generation of men arisen, passed across the stage of life, then sunk into oblivion, than another is seen following in its steps, repeating exactly what went before, with only minor variations in the externals. The spectacle is like a play, in which the lines of each act simply paraphrase the preceding ones and in which there is no real story, no theme, no point. From time to time stage hands appear to rearrange the settings, and the actors themselves, instead of repeating verbatim what was said in the previous acts, find different ways to say the very same things. Otherwise, all goes on as before, and any observer knows ahead of time how things will unfold, the surprises, such as they are, being confined to the stage settings. The thing builds up to no point, no redeeming theme comes across, no meaning is even hinted at, only endless banality. A metaphysician contemplating this, and noting that the players seem sometimes to rejoice, sometimes to suffer, always moving about, mostly in circles, determined above all to lay the conditions for another episode to follow, would be led to wonder: But what is this all about? Why all this trouble, the elaborate preparations, this prodigious expenditure of effort? In what does it all culminate, what is its meaning, what is its point? And certainly he would have to conclude that it has no point, that these things are all done, over and over in about the same way, just because that is the way the thing has been written, and it is the sad lot of the actors to have been cast in that dismal production. Of course someone might point out that each act does, after all, constitute the foundation for the next, that the actors play their parts well, even that they enjoy them, that they are happy in what they are doing, and that it is, in any case, far better than just standing there doing nothing at all, all of which is obvious and true. And all of which is, of course, beside the point.

THE CONCEPT OF MEANING

So far we have dwelt only on life's meaninglessness, construing this as the repetitive pointlessness that was illustrated at the outset. It is time now to consider the more positive side of life, if there is one, to determine what a positively meaningful existence would be, and whether it is attainable.

To do this we must revert to the pictures of meaninglessness with which we began, to see how they might be modified in order for a conception of meaningful existence to emerge.

Consider once more, then, the nuns, whose whole lives are spent repeating exactly the same chanted prayers and adorations, over and over. That all life, human as well as animal, bears a resemblance to this is, I think, unquestionable. Yet our own lives, as we live them, do not seem to us like that—otherwise we could not declare ourselves to be happy, while at the same time pitying the nuns. There are differences, and we need to see first what these are, and then see whether any of them confer the kind of meaningfulness we are seeking.

With respect, then, to the nuns, we can consider four possibilities, each of which, while leaving the picture exactly what it was insofar as it is a picture, nevertheless alters its significance.

For the first possibility, let us suppose, with rather cruel imagination, that the nuns are in effect enslaved persons and that their vocation was in no way chosen by them. We can imagine, for example, that arrangements have been made with some orphanage to deliver over infant female children from time to time and that these children are then raised up, more or less as animals might be, to perform this strange role throughout their lives, no attempt at explanation or justification being offered to them or to anyone. We are not, in other words, supposing now that the nuns are motivated by religious zeal or by any conviction at all; rather, we are saying that they are virtual automata, simply trained and brainwashed, like so much clockwork, to behave in the way that they do, and never to stop. Their behavior is in no sense voluntary, for they are, due to the conditions of their lives from infancy on, psychologically so degenerate that they have no power of choice, no purposes or goals of their own.

Second, varying this extreme image a bit, we can suppose that these nuns have in fact chosen this vocation but that their choice was essentially irrational. We can suppose, for example, that they were simply subjected to severe and constant indoctrination during childhood, the effect of which was to plant in their minds the conviction that such a life was the finest and noblest that could be offered to anyone. Thus coming to value such a life above any other that they could envisage, they vied with others for the chance to be chosen for it and rejoiced when they were chosen. Eventually, we can imagine, they began to have doubts and misgivings, but by then it was too late, their vows were irrevocable, and in any case they still take pride in having been chosen and in being able to fulfill their deepest wish, born in them at a tender age. We are not, by this second supposition, imagining that these nuns are motivated by faith in any significant way; rather, they are driven by a desire that was implanted in them by others, and their religious faith, which is of course unquestioned by them, is the product, rather than the source, of that desire.

Third, we can significantly modify this last image by supposing that the nuns are in fact moved by religious faith, that they are deeply and unshakably convinced of the reality of God and of the truth of the religion that they have received, and that they completely believe that by their life of prayer, lived in exactly the way in which it is lived, they glorify God in the noblest way possible. We need not here suppose that these religious convictions are in fact true; what we are supposing is, rather, that they are unshakably held and that it is because of those convictions that the nuns have embarked upon the severe and demanding vocations we have described. Unlike our second supposition, then, we here suppose that the nuns' religious faith is the source, not the mere product, of their behavior.

And finally, for our fourth and final image, let us make exactly the same supposition as we just did, but with the qualification that (we are supposing) the religious beliefs of these nuns are in fact *true;* that is, that God does exist, that He created heaven and earth, that the creed of the nuns is true in every detail, and, most important of all, that the nuns do in fact glorify God by their prayers or, if this is unclear, that they do without doubt thus carry out His will, and that their lives are accordingly, not just in their eyes but in the eyes of God as well, noble beyond measure.

MEANING AND PURPOSE

Now let us look at this image of the chanting nuns in these four quite different contexts, to see what distinguishes a meaningless from a meaningful existence.

That the picture of the nuns within the first context is a picture of total meaninglessness is obvious. The most fertile imagination could not construct a better image of meaninglessness. Here we have not only the elements of pointlessness and endlessness, but the absence of anything that could in any way redeem the life portrayed. There is no hint that this endless toil either accomplishes anything or is meant to do so, and the nuns themselves are deprived even of the personal satisfaction, however illusory it would be, that they are engaged in a noble or even worthwhile vocation. All they do is chant, meaninglessly, forever, and to no purpose.

Then what of the second image, wherein we suppose that the nuns have, however irrationally, at least chosen this life for themselves? Does the presence of choice confer meaning on their lives? Hardly, for what they have chosen is precisely a meaningless existence, and the choice is irrational in just the sense that no justification can be given for it.

Their desire for it was planted in their minds by others, and their choice was nothing more than a response to this desire. If we were to suppose that their desire to chant endlessly, and to do nothing else, were nothing but the effect of some hormonal imbalance in their endocrinal systems, to emphasize its irrational source, then the failure of this to confer meaningfulness on their lives would be perfectly manifest. It is hardly less obvious on the supposition we have made. The lives of the nuns, considered in either of the first two contexts that we have imagined, are as meaningless as the behavior of a clock running on and on, but without hands.

What, then, of our third context? Here we supposed that the nuns have chosen their extraordinary vocations, their choice being not simply the effects of some groundless conditioning but, instead, a deliberate and considered commitment of their faith. Do we finally have here the element that gives their lives meaning?

Not really, for those beliefs that governed their choice might, however firmly held, be illusory. Mere strength of convictions does not convert an illusion to truth, even though the things believed might be lofty and inspiring. To suppose otherwise would be to beg the very question we are raising by saying, in effect, that any life is meaningful given only that it is believed to be so. The plainly meaningless lives of the nuns considered in our first imaginary context could, no doubt, be made to appear meaningful to their possessors, and, while this might make their fate seem less cruel, it would certainly not make it more genuinely meaningful. Similarly, the convict of our other example might somehow be led to believe, quite falsely, that he was gradually achieving some great purpose by his hole digging, but from this it would certainly not follow that he was. His hole digging would still be nothing but pointless hole digging, whatever might be his own distorted conception of it.

Here it is important to avoid a locution that seems almost spontaneously to rise to people's lips considering this kind of example, namely, that the lives described are meaningful "to them." For this only repeats what has been said, that is, that they do have that conviction and that they do, in the light of it, believe their lives to be meaningful. That very belief can be totally false. Human beings are not, to be sure, quite so much an object of pity when governed by such grand illusion, for they are thus made content with their meaningless existence. But that kind of contentment, far from implying that their existence is after all meaningful, certainly entails that it is not. And the ingredients of meaningfulness still elude our search.

What, then, of our fourth context? Here, finally, we have one of the elements of meaningful existence, but only one; for we can at least say that the repetitive labor of the nuns is not utterly lacking in purpose. On the contrary, on the supposition we are making, it achieves a purpose that is the noblest imaginable: the very glorification of God. If one doubts this claim, it is only because one has not really made the supposition required by this fourth context, namely, that the religious conviction of the nuns is in fact *true*. If anyone's labors did in some real and unmistakable sense tend to the glorification of the *earth,* then no one would suggest that they were without purpose, for no one doubts the reality of the earth. But what could this purpose be in comparison with that of glorifying the very creator of the earth, and of everything else, assuming, as we must here, that this creator exists and that these labors do in some perhaps mysterious way achieve this purpose?

This point can perhaps be made more convincingly with reference to the example of Sisyphus. Let us suppose that Sisyphus does not, as the ancient myth presents it, simply roll the same stone over and over, accomplishing nothing. Instead, suppose that he rolls a succession of stones, one after another, and that each, instead of rolling back to the bottom of the hill, remains at the top, as intended. And suppose, further, that this task is unending or, in other words, that no matter how many stones Sisyphus moves to the top of the hill, presumably with dreadful labor, there will always be another that he must move, so that his work is never completed. So far, these modifications in the original story constitute no significant change, for if we actually contemplate what Sisyphus does, his work is virtually indistinguishable from that in the original story—he moves a rock over and over to the top of the hill— except in this case he moves a different rock each time. But now suppose that these rocks, which we said remain on the hill, do not merely accumulate there in a meaningless pile of rubble but instead become the foundation for a vast and beautiful and indestructible temple and then, gradually, the materials for its walls and all its many parts, with this construction going on and on, endlessly, and the temple gradually becoming ever more beautiful and inspiring and capable of enduring to the end of time. Can we still say that Sisyphus's existence is without meaning? Surely not! For one of the two ingredients of meaningfulness now appears in this picture. Namely, his efforts are not purposeless or pointless—something does result from them—and what results is of great and lasting significance.

SUBJECTIVE MEANINGFULNESS

Here we must be careful to avoid a tempting error. And that is to suppose that the question, whether or not Sisyphus's labors are meaningful, depends on how he feels about them and about their effect—that is, whether he really wants to build this temple badly enough to devote an endless life to it. That does not really matter. For the temple was described as beautiful and everlasting, and if it really is such, then it does not matter whether Sisyphus appreciates that fact or not. Our question was not whether Sisyphus enjoys his existence or approves of the purpose to which it is put but rather, whether his existence has meaning. And in the picture before us, it certainly has an end or purpose, and (we are supposing) a significant one, and that was one of the two elements of meaningfulness. Putting this point otherwise, we can say that just as someone's enjoyment of a meaningless life does not convert that life to meaningfulness, so one's failure to appreciate true meaningfulness does not obliterate that meaningfulness.

THE MEANINGLESSNESS OF ENDLESS PURSUIT

But what of the other ingredient? The lives sketched earlier were meaningless, we noted, in two ways, one being the lack of purpose and the other their quality of repetitive toil. And while we have, in our last examples, eliminated the first, by endowing these lives with great purpose, the element of repetitiveness remains. The nuns, we suppose, do indeed glorify God, but in a sense, they never get anywhere. They are on a treadmill that turns a great wheel and performs a great task, but the task is unending, and the purpose is never really fulfilled. So it is with Sisyphus. Even though his mission now is to erect an everlasting temple of great beauty, and he can be said actually to be doing that, he is nevertheless doomed to the frustration of never completing the work, thus never really fulfilling his purpose. Every pursuit of a goal is animated by the hope of achieving it. If the very goal of one's existence is impossible to attain, if the purpose is there but the fulfillment of it always elusive, then life is merely a betrayal—like that of a dog in pursuit of a stuffed rabbit that hangs from a pole in front of it, the pole being fixed to the dog itself, so that the increased frenzy of pursuit only results in the accelerated elusiveness of the dog's already illusory prey. Our goals, unlike the dog's, may be real enough, but if the hope of attaining them is as illusory as in this simile, if there is no possibility of fulfilling them, then in a very real sense they are false goals after all, and the same falseness is imparted to our lives. At some point it must be possible to rest. Life cannot be *just* a pursuit; and making the thing pursued something real and worthwhile, although it gives the pursuit itself meaning, does not really give meaning to life if the goal is forever unattainable. The resemblance to Sisyphus is still too painfully clear. At some point Sisyphus must be able finally to stop and reflect: There, I *did* it. If his final truth is that he is doing it, will forever be doing it, with no possibility of stopping, then the goal becomes after all a basis for eternal frustration—the very element that is most conspicuous in the story of Sisyphus as it was originally told.

MEANING AND CREATIVITY

If, then, a meaningless existence is one spent in pointless and repetitive toil, is a meaningful existence simply one in which these elements are replaced by their opposites? Can we say, in other words, that a fully meaningful life will be one in which some truly worthwhile goal is sought and achieved? Or, in terms of some of our examples, if we suppose that Sisyphus's labors do culminate in the creation of a lasting and beautiful temple, or that the adoration of the nuns does in fact in some real and theologically significant sense tend to the glory of God, then can we pronounce those lives meaningful? And generalizing, can we say that if human existence has or can be given these ingredients, then human existence is to that extent meaningful after all?

Not quite, I think. For even if we suppose these conditions to be fulfilled, the pictures we have drawn can still fall short of meaningfulness. To see this, let us suppose that Sisyphus, for example, by his labors erects a beautiful and lasting temple that he had no part whatever in creating. His only role, by this supposition, was to pile stone upon stone in a preconceived way, as might be done by some mindless machine that had been programmed to such behavior. We can, for example, suppose that Sisyphus is a slave, bereft of any autonomy or power of choice, whose work from moment to moment is entirely under the direction and within the control of someone having complete power over him. The temple he builds is, therefore, really the work of another, even though the building of it is entirely his. We can even suppose that the purpose or goal is his as well, in the sense that he does want to achieve it and sincerely proclaims it to be his life's purpose. Here we have an image wherein the ingredients of meaningfulness elicited before are clearly present. That is, Sisyphus's existence is not without purpose and, of equal significance, that purpose is of genuine significance, and it is finally and lastingly achieved. What is lacking is that the goal of his life is not of his own creation. It is simply imposed upon him from without.

The same conclusion would emerge from our image of the prisoner, condemned to a lifetime of hole digging. We can, with a bit of imagination, suppose that his labor results in something of lasting beauty and worth, and even that he is aware of this and can entirely comprehend it in his own mind. But still, if that goal, whatever it is, was itself conceived by someone else, so that his role is simply to be the instrument for the realization of what someone else has created, then his existence is still significantly lacking in meaningfulness. What he does, and everything that he does, could as well be done by an unthinking engine.

And similarly in the case of the nuns: if they are merely trained to do what they do, and themselves have no hand in the creation of their goal, then their lives are still essentially meaningless, even though we may suppose this goal to be of great or even supreme worth and to be actually attained by them. For whatever else can be said in justification of their existence, they are still automata, the mere tools to the realization of an end, however noble, rather than the creators of that end.

We do then now have, it seems, all the basic ingredients of meaningless existence before us and, by their negation, all the basic ingredients of meaningful existence. Life is meaningless if it is lacking in a real, not merely illusory, purpose—one that is genuinely significant and not merely believed to be so; capable of attainment, and not forever eluding its pursuer; created and chosen by him whose goal is to achieve it, and not imposed from without. Or, putting the whole matter positively, we can say that life is truly meaningful only if it is directed to goals of one's own creation and choice and if those goals are genuinely noble, beautiful, or otherwise lastingly worthwhile and attained.

THE WILL TO LIVE

Having said that, however, we must not casually dismiss the dismal portrayal of human existence with which we began and blithely declare life to be meaningful after all. For what still needs to be done is to set human existence, as we find it, against these standards and see whether it is meaningful after all. The conception of meaningfulness at which we have now arrived, is one thing; but the discovery of it in our own lives is something else. And what we might discover instead is the mere illusion of it. That possibility cannot just be waved aside. Even a bright and totally convincing illusion is, after all, an illusion still, and it is all the harder to banish if it is metaphysical in character rather than the mere product of prejudice or ignorance.

What is human existence, typically? What, that is, do we actually find if we look objectively at the expression of life in any ordinary individual? We have already described it. It is what Schopenhauer, in the passage with which we began, described as a clockworklike thing, without purpose or meaning. Looked at from without, the typical life of an ordinary person perfectly resembles each of the images of meaninglessness that we have set forth, the main ingredient of these being repetitive routine that culminates in nothing but more of the same.

Why, then, do people cling to it? Why do people cherish life above everything else, consider the loss of it the ultimate calamity, and ward off any threat to their existence at any cost? And why, above all, do people rejoice in it? For, if you look about you, you will find a strange paradox, namely, that the happiest people, the ones who find least to complain of in their lot, are precisely those whose lives are the most totally meaningless. The people whose days have hardly varied from an accustomed routine through their entire lives, and who now, toward the end, pursue exactly the same routines, with no different results from before, that is to say, no more effect than the enlargement of some senseless objective that they have already reached a thousand times, nevertheless declare with total honesty that they are happy, that life has been good, and that they look with pride upon what they have brought about—some considerable accumulation of possessions, or the notice of their peers, or sometimes nothing more than a great number of years of walking a treadmill. The sheer magnitude of the labor is sometimes a source of deep contentment, even though at the end of it nothing has been changed.

Why is this what we actually find when at the same time the image of Sisyphus, or of the prisoner, filled with the zest of life, laughing and singing as they plod year in and year out at their meaningless labor, would seem to be the height of incongruity and absurdity?

We can find the answer to this if we look once more at the chanting nuns in the context of the second of our four suppositions. Suppose, that is, that these nuns, instead of being reluctantly driven to their task, have been somehow conditioned to embrace it, so that their behavior is the expression of a strong and deep urge. In this case their lives, however meaningless, will be nevertheless joyous. Or consider Sisyphus once more. Suppose that the gods, when they condemned him to an eternity of stone rolling, had at the same time imbued him with an intense and insatiable desire to roll stones. Perhaps we can make this possibility seem more real if we imagine Sisyphus to have had injected into his veins some hormonal substance designed to rouse in him just that kind of intense and irrational urge. In that case, of course,·Sisyphus would not have viewed his fate as a condemnation at all, but as a fulfillment, the fulfillment of his deepest and strongest desires. Or varying the image once more, consider a sensualist, whose desire for sexual indulgence is, let us suppose, constant and recurring and, moreover, so strong as to dominate every other desire and to govern his entire activity, so that he is completely undiscriminating in his choice of persons and quite heedless of the effects of his behavior. And now let us place beside it the image of our prisoner, in the earlier example, who was condemned to a lifetime of digging holes. But let us add to it the supposition that this prisoner has exactly the same kind of intense, insatiable, and overwhelming desire to dig holes as does the sensualist's desire for eroticism. Now the convict, like Sisyphus, will view his life, not as one of hard labor, certainly not one of meaninglessness, but as good! He will be in exactly the same position as the sensualist who is surprised to discover himself "condemned" to a lifetime of erotic stimulus, wherein all his fantasies and dreams find fulfillment.

Or in other words, he will find himself in a position much like that of all of us. For the impulses that govern the lives of most people are no more rational than this and have as little to justify them in their outcome. What is to be said for them is that they are strong, sometimes insatiable, and always recurring. So long, then, as we are free to respond to them, free to pursue our ends and goals as we imagine them, we deem our lives to be good and declare ourselves to be happy. The picture of the person devoted entirely to the accumulation of property, daily enlarging this until by life's end it has assumed grotesque proportions—and the achiever of this result has become the envy of all—this picture resembles exactly that of a prisoner who has spent his entire working life digging one immense hole. If such a prisoner had been conditioned to seek such an end, to regard it as a means of self-glorification, and if the rest of us had similarly been so conditioned, then he would by no means think of himself as a prisoner but rather as the most blessed of men, and we would look upon him with the same envy with which the rich are typically viewed. We can say, if we like, that there is no point to digging a vast hole, but neither is there any point to creating a vast pile of rocks, or anything else. And the point to be made is that such prodigious achievements do not *become* meaningful merely because the agents of them find them fulfilling and declare themselves happy in the pursuit of them. If you were to learn that the rest of your life would be spent digging an enormous hole, then it would perhaps be a reassurance of sorts to be told that you were actually going to enjoy doing it. If, further, you were born with, or at any early age conditioned to, a strong desire to do this, then you would not need to have such a task assigned to you—you would go to great lengths to gain the opportunity and consider yourself lucky if you got it. And you would someday view the great hole you had dug with a deep sense of fulfillment. And therein does each of us find, in varying degrees, the very picture of his or her own life.

CREATIVE EXISTENCE

Does it have to be so? The first thing, of course, is to see that it *is* so, that really the main feature of all existence is its meaninglessness, and to see that this meaninglessness does not evaporate under the supposition that we somehow find it fulfilling. Having done that, we have hope of describing a meaningful life, without being blinded by the idea that we need not seek any further, having already found it.

If the ingredients of meaninglessness are what we have described, namely, existence that is repetitive and without purpose, or whose purposes are illusory in the sense described, then we can say what a genuinely meaningful life would be. It would be a life that has a purpose—not just any sort of purpose that we happen to find satisfying, but one that is truly noble and good. And it must be one that is in fact achieved and not just endlessly pursued; and it must be lasting; and finally, it must be our *own* rather than just something imbibed. In short, the only genuinely meaningful existence is one that is *creative*. That one word sums it up, and, if really understood, discloses entirely what is missing, not only in all the animate and inanimate existence that surrounds us but in the lives of the vast majority of human beings. It is also what philosophers have always sought as godlike or what makes man, in the ancient metaphor, the image of God. For what is godlike is not blind power, or aimless knowledge, or unguided reason, but simply creative power. It is the primary attribute in the very conception of God. It is what makes the concept of God awesome.

To see this, let us return one last time to the image of Sisyphus, radically revising it so that it becomes the image, not of meaninglessness, but rather of genuinely meaningful life. It is not enough, as we have seen, merely to make Sisyphus an object of envy rather than of pity, by supposing him to fulfill his deepest desires, as the rest of us desire to fulfill ours. For the desire itself might be worthless.

Suppose, then, that Sisyphus, in rolling stones day after day, is not carrying out a sentence, but rather a plan. Suppose, further, that the plan is his own, totally the fruit of his creative mind rather than something that has been handed to him. And suppose that his plan is to build a great and everlasting temple, not merely beautiful to his eyes, but truly beautiful, in the eyes of every future generation of mortals and, let us suppose, of the gods as well. And let us finally suppose that Sisyphus succeeds in this. Here we have, finally, the perfect image of meaningfulness, albeit an extreme one. Every element of meaninglessness that we inserted into our earlier images has been replaced in this one by its opposite, so that as those conveyed, in extreme and exaggerated form, the idea of meaninglessness, this one conveys, once it is grasped, the idea of meaningfulness, though in similarly exaggerated form.

If we now apply what has been said to life as we actually find it, rather than to extreme and imaginary cases, we can discover the difference between a meaningful and a meaningless life, quite unmistakably. A person who does actually succeed in creating something genuinely good, perhaps even beautiful or noble, has lived meaningfully. And we need not ask whether this person is happy, whether what he or she has done receives any acclaim or is even noticed; for we are not asking what is required to become happy or noteworthy, but rather, what is required for an individual life to have meaning. Some persons might not, to be sure, seek such a meaningful existence, even if it were pointed out to them. Indeed, probably most persons would not. But that, too, is beside the point. We have been concentrating on two quite specific ideas, namely, meaninglessness and its opposite; and this has nothing to do with what the majority of persons happen to seek, or even what they would seek if the world were different.

THE MEANING OF CREATION

Does all this mean, then, that the only meaningful life is one devoted to the creation of some *object,* some great work of art, of whatever kind? It does not. But at the same time, a perfectly clear idea of a meaningful existence is just that. Just as not all of us spend our lives digging holes, rolling rocks, or chanting meaningless words, nevertheless our lives do greatly resemble those pictures. And similarly, just as not everyone's life is that of a genuine creator, one's life *can* resemble that.

For creation is not just the creation of things. Creativity is a state of mind, which sometimes expresses itself in small and otherwise insignificant ways. Great or small, it is precious, and it is the only thing that finally converts life to meaning. No animal, for example, can look at nature, or at any object of nature, creatively, but a person can. A person can contemplate the simplest, and otherwise least significant, thing creatively—can thus consider a blade of grass, a hill, a thunderstorm, a snowflake, virtually anything. Similarly, the creation of such a work as Plato's *Republic* is certainly meaningful. It would be laughable for anyone, from whatever ideology, to suggest that Plato's life had no meaning. Yet meaningful thought need not be thought that has such a result as this or, indeed, any result whatever beyond itself. One's very thoughts can be poems, even if unuttered, in contrast to being trivial or banal or imitative, as most thought is most of the time. Consider two persons looking, say, at a meadow. One sees it for its size, its possible value, the use to which it might be put. He sees it, in short, only in terms of his own conditioned desires, rather as an animal would see it. The other, we can suppose, considers none of these things but is instead drawn to a tiny and insignificant flower at her feet and looks at it in a way that the other person is incapable of viewing it, in a way that no animal can view it. She looks at it creatively, not merely *finding* it meaningful, but investing it with meanings, by her own creative power. This is not the creation of an object, but it is creation just the same.

It is quite possible to go through life this way, more or less—more in the case of true genius, less, but in the same mode, for others, but not at all for the most foresaken of persons, who are totally bereft of creative thought and feeling and simply replicate, as animals do, what others have already thought and felt and done. Thus one can be creative in his or her relationships with other persons, infusing into these much more thought and feeling than would simply be elicited by passive encounter; or one can simply respond, unthinkingly and uncreatively, as he or she feels prompted. Most human relationships are, of course, of this second kind. For some persons they are all that is really possible. But that more is possible is perfectly apparent to anyone of a creative spirit.

And so it is with everything under the sun, with the entire earth and all it contains, and even the heavens too. God, we are taught, did not merely come upon all this and decide to make it his own through sheer power. Instead, he created it all, as we are told, and really is for this reason alone thought to be God. We are not gods, but we are not just animals either. We need not stagger dreamlike through the four stages of life to death, accompanied by a series of trivial thoughts, as Schopenhauer expressed it. We can instead—or, at least, some can—live meaningfully, by creating our own meanings, whether great or small, and then literally glorying in them, caring not in the least what we "get" from it all. We will already have gotten all that is meaningful.

POINTS TO PONDER

1. In light of Taylor's analysis, consider what it is that makes prison so appalling. Is it the degradation of the physical surroundings, the filth, the stench, the idea that men and women are enclosed in cages like animals in a zoo? Or is it, perhaps, the fact that cut off from the rest of humanity, except for brief visits and such communication as they are permitted to enjoy via radio and television, they are unable to do anything that anyone, including themselves, would regard as meaningful? What moral justification might there be (or is there any) for such penalties?

2. Do Taylor's descriptions ring true? When he says, for example, that a person is the same from one year to the next, what is the content of the word *same?* When he asks what the purpose of life might be, what kind of purpose can he be seeking? Does it make sense to ask for a single purpose of life, or do we merely have purposes for particular actions? If there is no single purpose for life in general, does life thereby become meaningless? Is there no difference between the person whose child has been born, who has undertaken a business venture, made some purchases, completed a trip, and played some games—and Sisyphus or the ground mole?

3. Taylor suggests that a task, however noble it might be, adds no meaning to a person's life if it might have been done by a robot or if it was imposed upon him by someone else. Is this necessarily so? If

Michelangelo had produced his paintings and sculptures in obedience to the command of a master whose slave he was, would his life thereby have been rendered meaningless? If so, in what sense? If a mechanical device could be constructed that could compose a symphony equal in majesty and power to Beethoven's *Ninth,* or an opera as moving as Puccini's *Tosca,* would its invention have rendered the lives of Beethoven and Puccini meaningless?

4. Is Taylor correct in asserting that the nuns are mere tools to the realization of an end rather than the creators of that end—and if he is, does that fact thereby render their lives meaningless? Is it not conceivable that one might adopt another's ends as one's own, out of love, devotion, or loyalty—or perhaps merely a sense of duty—and still do what one does creatively and therefore (by Taylor's test) meaningfully?

5. What else, besides works of art, might one create, so as to make life less meaningless than it might otherwise be? Taylor's illustrations all resemble aesthetic creations or aesthetic contemplation. But consider the very things he listed in his catalogue of meaningless occupations— bearing and raising children, doing one's job well, carrying on one's business, doing the day-to-day tasks that ordinary people believe are the things that make life worthwhile and meaningful. Must they be rejected as not fitting the creative pattern that alone Taylor feels makes life meaningful?

II
ABORTION

INTRODUCTION

Throughout the history of philosophy, there has been general agreement that the right to life is fundamental. Such social contract theorists as Hobbes and Locke (whose general approach assumed that men emerged from a state of nature and formed an artificial union designed to protect them from harm against one another and to further their mutual interests) argued that the right to life was fundamental, a right of nature, a right guaranteed by God himself. They often went further, asserting that it was inalienable—a right that no person could give up, one for which people gave up other liberties, the principal purpose of all government. The authors of the American Declaration of Independence expressed it well when they wrote:

> We hold these Truths to be self-evident, that all Men are created equal, that they are endowed by their Creator with certain unalienable Rights, that among these are Life, Liberty, and the Pursuit of Happiness—That to secure these Rights, Governments are instituted among Men, deriving their just Powers from the Consent of the Governed, that whenever any Form of Government becomes destructive of these Ends, it is the Right of the People to alter or to abolish it. . . .

In recent years, a great debate has arisen over the right of human fetuses to life. On the one hand, there are those who claim that a fetus in its mother's womb is a small child, a particularly helpless and vulnerable human being, fully deserving of the protection of the law against anyone who would destroy it. On the other are those who argue that fetuses are not children, that they are not persons, and that they are therefore not entitled to legal protections such as those conferred upon persons by the Constitution, or even to such moral rights as the right to life. Connected with this is the contention that people in general should not be subject to unnecessary interference in their private lives by the forces of government and that pregnant women in particular ought to be left alone, to decide, together with their physicians, whether they should carry their pregnancies to term or procure abortions. The controversy is a complex one, and an exceedingly emotional one as well. Philosophers, theologians, politicians, and the general public have entered into it with perhaps more heat than any other public controversy of recent years, with the possible exception of the war in Vietnam. Political campaigns have been won and lost over the abortion issue. Millions of dollars are spent in lobbying Congress and state legislatures to press them to pass or refrain from passing legislation designed to thwart or overturn the U.S. Supreme Court's decision of 1973 (*Roe* v. *Wade*) that declared, for the first time, that during the first trimester of pregnancy, at least, women had a virtually unqualified right to abortions.

The Court's reasoning centered essentially upon two propositions: The first, that a fetus is not a *person* as that term is used in the law. That is, that only *persons* are entitled to the protection of the law and of the Bill of Rights and that because fetuses are not persons, the law ought not to interfere with their destruction except under very special circumstances. The second had to do with the right to privacy. The Court argued that the constitutionally guaranteed right of privacy entitled women to make choices affecting their own bodies (in this case, whether they should carry their pregnancies to term) without undue interference from the state. The right to privacy itself is a matter of considerable controversy. Not too many years ago, it was not recognized in law at all. In the latter part of the nineteenth century, an article by Louis Brandeis and Charles Warren in the *Harvard Law Review* urged its acceptance by legislatures and courts. As the twentieth century wore on, courts came to accept the notion that there is such a right—and in *Griswold* v. *Connecticut* (1965), the Supreme Court "discovered" it in the Constitution.

But the justices of the Court could not agree on the precise location of the right that they asserted was in the Constitution. Justice Douglas found it in the "penumbras" (shadows) and "emanations" of portions of the Bill of Rights. Justice Goldberg found it implicit in other amendments. And other justices discovered it in still other phrases. No matter that the word was never mentioned in the Constitution: Its presence was somehow perceived to be there, somewhere between the lines. Justice Black, the great literalist, dissented vigorously, arguing that the Court had no business digging up nonexistent rights out of the shadows and emanations of the clear and unambiguous words of the Constitution. But he did not prevail, and ever since 1965, the right of privacy, which will be considered in greater detail in Part VI, has been expanded and extended to ever-wider areas of human conduct.

The various opinions in *Roe* v. *Wade* contain a wealth of philosophically interesting material. The excerpts included here provide only a sample of the extensive arguments employed by the members of the court in their opinions. First, of course, is the notion of privacy itself. Clearly, the right of privacy enunciated by Brandeis and Warren had little if any relationship to the right to procure or perform an abortion. It concerned the right not to have one's features employed by others for commercial purposes or to prevent others from snooping about to discover and publish facts about one's private life.

Second, the majority opinion argues that new medical procedures and techniques have advanced to the point where old laws are obsolete.

Third, the majority focuses upon the use of "person" in the Constitution and in state laws and finds that in the Constitution, at least, the word invariably refers to human beings who have already been born, whereas state laws clearly differentiate between fetuses and persons who have been born.

Finally, the Court turns to what concerns the state may legitimately consider in its legislation in this area and concludes that these include the life and health of the pregnant woman and protecting the potentiality of human life. But it goes further and concludes that prior to viability (another troublesome concept), the state's interest in the potential life of the fetus is less "compelling" than is its interest in preserving the life and health of the mother. Indeed, even after viability, the Court concludes that the life and health of the mother must take precedence over the life of the fetus.

In his concurring opinion, Justice Stewart suggested that the word *liberty* as understood in the Constitution's Fourteenth Amendment includes more than those liberties that are specifically enumerated in the Constitution itself. Quoting Justice Harlan, he argued that liberty "is a rational continuum which . . . includes a freedom from all substantial arbitrary impositions and purposeless restraints . . . and which also recognizes . . . that certain interests require particularly careful scrutiny of the state needs asserted to justify their abridgment." Certain fundamental rights, though nowhere mentioned in the Constitution, are nevertheless protected by it, he said.

Justice Douglas agreed, on the ground that some rights are far older than the Constitution itself. He went further, enumerating certain broad categories of rights that fall under the concept of "liberty" as he read that term in the Fourteenth Amendment: "autonomous control over the development and expression of one's intellect, interests, tastes, and personality," "freedom of choice in the basic decisions of one's life respecting marriage" and related matters, and "freedom to care for one's health and person, freedom from bodily restraint or compulsion, freedom to walk, stroll, or loaf." Nevertheless, he agreed that where the state has a compelling interest, it may abridge some of these freedoms—though it must meet very exacting standards if it is to do so.

In his dissenting opinion, Justice Rehnquist completely rejected the intrusion of the right of privacy into the case. Focusing upon the ordinary usage of the word *privacy,* he concluded that it has nothing to do with the right of a woman to have an abortion or with searches and seizures, from which the Court derived its concept. He agreed with Justice Stewart's broad conception of liberty but insisted that states have the right to exercise reasonable discretion in limiting certain liberties. And he concluded that there was nothing unreasonable in a state's imposing limits upon a woman's right to have an abortion. Moreover, he doubted whether women have a *right* to an abortion.

In the *Planned Parenthood* case, the Court elaborated upon the concept of viability. Justice Blackmun, speaking for the Court, concluded that it is a medical term that must remain flexible, its application to each case to be determined by the medical experts who are immediately concerned. The Court went on to reject any requirement for consent by the father of the fetus, by the spouse of the mother, or by the parents of the mother if she is an unmarried minor, at least during the first trimester of pregnancy. The mother's rights are held to be paramount, and the Court held that the father should not have a right to veto a decision made by the person "who is the more directly and immediately affected by the pregnancy."

In his dissenting opinion, Justice White attacked the majority's decision by pointing out that a minor unmarried woman's decision is likely to be a better informed decision if she has first consulted with and received the consent of her parents. The state, he said, has a legitimate interest in protecting children from their own "immature and improvident decisions." Justice Stevens's opinion indicated his agreement with this judgment, arguing that it is not inappropriate to use chronological age as a basis upon which to impose restraints upon a minor's freedom of choice, even in such major decisions as those having to do with bearing children.

U.S. SUPREME COURT 2

ROE V. WADE
410 U.S. 113, 93 S.Ct. 705, 35 L.Ed.2d 147 (1973)

Mr. Justice BLACKMUN delivered the opinion of the Court.

This Texas federal appeal and its Georgia companion, Doe v. Bolton, 410 U.S. 179, 93 S.Ct. 739, 35 L.Ed.2d 201, present constitutional challenges to state criminal abortion legislation. The Texas statutes under attack here are typical of those that have been in effect in many States for approximately a century. The Georgia statutes, in contrast, have a modern cast and are a legislative product that, to an extent at least, obviously reflects the influences of recent attitudinal change, of advancing medical knowledge and techniques, and of new thinking about an old issue.

We forthwith acknowledge our awareness of the sensitive and emotional nature of the abortion controversy, of the vigorous opposing views, even among physicians, and of the deep and seemingly absolute convictions that the subject inspires. One's philosophy, one's experiences, one's exposure to the raw edges of human existence, one's religious training, one's attitudes toward life and family and their values, and the moral standards one establishes and seeks to observe, are all likely to influence and to color one's thinking and conclusions about abortion.

In addition, population growth, pollution, poverty, and racial overtones tend to complicate and not to simplify the problem.

Our task, of course, is to resolve the issue by constitutional measurement, free of emotion and of predilection. We seek earnestly to do this, and, because we do, we have inquired into, and in this opinion place some emphasis upon, medical and medical-legal history and what that history reveals about man's attitudes toward the abortion procedure over the centuries. We bear in mind, too, Mr. Justice Holmes' admonition in his now-vindicated dissent in Lochner v. New York, 198 U.S. 45, 76 (1905):

> [The Constitution] is made for people of fundamentally differing views, and the accident of our finding certain opinions natural and familiar, or novel, and even shocking, ought not to conclude our judgment upon the question whether statutes embodying them conflict with the Constitution of the United States.

I

The Texas statutes that concern us . . . make it a crime to "procure an abortion," as therein defined, or to attempt one, except with respect to "an abortion procured or attempted by medical advice for the purpose of saving the life of the mother." Similar statutes are in existence in a majority of the States. . . .

II

Jane Roe, a single woman who was residing in Dallas County, Texas, instituted this federal action in March 1970 against the District Attorney of the county. She sought a declaratory judgment that the Texas criminal abortion statutes were unconstitutional on their face, and an injunction restraining the defendant from enforcing the statutes.

Roe alleged that she was unmarried and pregnant; that she wished to terminate her pregnancy by an abortion "performed by a competent, licensed physician, under safe, clinical conditions"; that she was unable to get a "legal" abortion in Texas because her life did not appear to be threatened by the continuation of her pregnancy; and that she could not afford to travel to another jurisdiction in order to secure a legal abortion under safe conditions. She claimed that the Texas statutes were unconstitutionally vague and that they abridged her right of personal privacy, protected by the First, Fourth, Fifth, Ninth, and Fourteenth Amendments. By an amendment to her complaint Roe purported to sue "on behalf of herself and all other women" similarly situated. . . .

. . . On the merits, the District Court held that the "fundamental right of single women and married persons to choose whether to have children is protected by the Ninth Amendment, through the Fourteenth Amendment," and that the Texas criminal abortion statutes were void on their face because they were both unconstitutionally vague and constituted an overbroad infringement of the plaintiffs' Ninth Amendment rights. . . .

V

The principal thrust of appellant's attack on the Texas statutes is that they improperly invade a right, said to be possessed by the pregnant woman, to choose to terminate her pregnancy. Appellant would discover this right in the concept of personal "liberty" embodied in the Fourteenth Amendment's Due Process Clause; or in personal, marital, familial, and sexual privacy said to be protected by the Bill of Rights or its penumbras, or among those rights reserved to the people by the Ninth Amendment. . . .

VII

Three reasons have been advanced to explain historically the enactment of criminal abortion laws in the 19th century and to justify their continued existence.

It has been argued occasionally that these laws were the product of a Victorian social concern to discourage illicit sexual conduct. Texas, however, does not advance this justification in the present case, and it appears that no court or commentator has taken the argument seriously. The appellants and *amici* contend, moreover, that this is not a proper state purpose at all and suggest that, if it were, the Texas statutes are overbroad in protecting it since the law fails to distinguish between married and unwed mothers.

A second reason is concerned with abortion as a medical procedure. When most criminal abortion laws were first enacted, the procedure was a hazardous one for the woman. This was particularly true prior to the development of antisepsis. Antiseptic techniques, of course, were based on discoveries by Lister, Pasteur, and others first announced in 1867, but were not generally accepted and employed until about the turn of the century. Abortion mortality was high. Even after 1900, and perhaps until as late as the development of antibiotics in the 1940's, standard modern techniques such as dilation and curettage were not nearly so safe as they are today. Thus, it has been argued that a State's real concern in enacting a criminal abortion law was to protect the pregnant woman, that is, to restrain her from submitting to a procedure that placed her life in serious jeopardy.

Modern medical techniques have altered this situation. Appellants and various *amici* refer to medical data indicating that abortion in early pregnancy, that is, prior to the end of the first trimester, although not without its risk, is now relatively safe. Mortality rates for women undergoing early abortions, where the procedure is legal, appear to be as low as or lower than the rates for normal childbirth. Consequently, any interest of the State in protecting the woman from an inherently hazardous procedure, except when it would be equally dangerous for her to forgo it, has largely disappeared. Of course, important state interests in the areas of health and medical standards do remain. The State has a legitimate interest in seeing to it that abortion, like any other medical procedure, is performed under circumstances that insure maximum safety for the patient. This interest obviously extends at least to the performing physician and his staff, to the facilities involved, to the availability of after-care, and to adequate provision for any complication or emergency that might arise. The prevalence of high mortality rates at illegal "abortion mills" strengthens, rather than weakens, the State's interest in regulating the conditions under which abortions are performed. Moreover, the risk to the woman increases as her pregnancy continues. Thus, the State retains a definite interest in protecting the woman's own health and safety when an abortion is proposed at a late stage of pregnancy.

The third reason is the State's interest—some phrase it in terms of duty—in protecting prenatal life. Some of the argument for this justification rests on the theory that a new human life is present from the moment of conception. The State's interest and general obligation to protect life then extends, it is argued, to prenatal life. Only when the life of the pregnant mother herself is at stake, balanced against the life she carries within her, should the interest of the embryo or fetus not prevail. Logically, of course, a legitimate state interest in this area need not stand or fall on acceptance of the belief that life begins at conception or at some other point prior to live birth. In assessing the State's interest, recognition may be given to the less rigid claim that as long as at least *potential* life is involved, the State may assert interests beyond the protection of the pregnant woman alone.

Parties challenging state abortion laws have sharply disputed in some courts the contention that a purpose of these laws, when enacted, was to protect prenatal life. Pointing to the absence of legislative history to support the contention, they claim that most state laws were designed solely to protect the woman. Because medical advances have lessened this concern, at least with respect to abortion in early pregnancy, they argue that with respect to such abortions the laws can no longer be justified by any state interest. There is some scholarly support for this view of original purpose. The few state courts called upon to interpret their laws in the late 19th and early 20th centuries did focus on the State's interest in protecting the woman's health rather than in preserving the embryo and fetus. Proponents of this view point out that in many States, including Texas, by statute or judicial interpretation, the pregnant woman herself could not be prosecuted for self-abortion or for cooperating in an abortion performed upon her by another. They claim that adoption of the "quickening" distinction through received common law and state statutes tacitly recognizes the greater health hazards inherent in late abortion and impliedly repudiates the theory that life begins at conception.

It is with these interests, and the weight to be attached to them, that this case is concerned.

VIII

The Constitution does not explicitly mention any right of privacy. In a line of decisions, however, going back perhaps as far as 1891, the Court has recognized that a right of personal privacy, or a guarantee of certain areas or zones of privacy, does exist under the Constitution. In varying contexts, the Court or individual Justices have, indeed, found at least the roots of that right in the First Amendment, in the Fourth and Fifth Amendments, in the penumbras of the Bill of Rights, in the Ninth Amendment, or in the concept of liberty guaranteed by the first section of the Fourteenth Amendment. These decisions make it clear that only personal rights that can be deemed "fundamental" or "implicit in the concept of ordered liberty" are included in this guarantee of personal privacy. They also make it clear that the right has some extension to activities relating to marriage, procreation, contraception, family relationships, and child rearing and education.

This right of privacy, whether it be founded in the Fourteenth Amendment's concept of personal liberty and restrictions upon state action, as we feel it is, or, as the District Court determined, in the Ninth Amendment's reservation of rights to the people, is broad enough to encompass a woman's decision whether or not to terminate her pregnancy. The detriment that the State would impose upon the pregnant woman by denying this choice altogether is apparent. Specific and direct harm medically diagnosable even in early pregnancy may be involved. Maternity, or additional offspring, may force upon the woman a distressful life and future. Psychological harm may be imminent. Mental and physical health may be taxed by child care. There is also the distress, for all concerned, associated with the unwanted child, and there is the problem of bringing a child into a family already unable, psychologically and otherwise, to care for it. In other cases, as in this one, the additional difficulties and continuing stigma of unwed motherhood may be involved. All these are factors the woman and her responsible physician necessarily will consider in consultation.

On the basis of elements such as these, appellant and some *amici* argue that the woman's right is absolute and that she is entitled to terminate her pregnancy at whatever time, in whatever way, and for whatever reason she alone chooses. With this we do not agree. Appellant's arguments that Texas either has no valid interest at all in regulating the abortion decision, or no interest strong enough to support any limitation upon the woman's sole determination, are unpersuasive. The Court's decisions recognizing a right of privacy also acknowledge that some state regulation in areas protected by that right is appropriate. As noted above, a State may properly assert important interests in safeguarding health, in maintaining medical standards, and in protecting potential life. At some point in pregnancy, these respective interests become sufficiently compelling to sustain regulation of the factors that govern the abortion decision. The privacy right involved, therefore, cannot be said to be absolute. In fact, it is not clear to us that the claim asserted by some *amici* that one has an unlimited right to do with one's body as one pleases bears a close relationship to the right of privacy previously articulated in the Court's decisions. The Court has refused to recognize an unlimited right of this kind in the past. Jacobson v. Massachusetts, 197 U.S. 11, 25 S.Ct. 358, 49 L.Ed. 643 (1905) (vaccination); Buck v. Bell, 274 U.S. 200, 47 S.Ct. 584, 71 L.Ed. 1000 (1927) (sterilization).

We, therefore, conclude that the right of personal privacy includes the abortion decision, but that this right is not unqualified and must be considered against important state interests in regulation. . . .

IX

The District Court held that the appellee [Wade, the Dallas County District Attorney] failed to meet his burden of demonstrating that the Texas statute's infringement upon Roe's rights was necessary to support a compelling state interest, and that, although the appellee presented "several compelling justifications for state presence in the area of abortions," the statutes outstripped these justifications and swept "far beyond any areas of compelling state interest." Appellant [Roe] and appellee both contest that holding. Appellant, as has been indicated, claims an absolute right that bars any state imposition of criminal penalties in the area. Appellee argues that the State's determination to recognize and protect prenatal life from and after conception constitutes a compelling state interest. As noted above, we do not agree fully with either formulation.

A. The appellee and certain *amici* argue that the fetus is a "person" within the language and meaning of the Fourteenth Amendment. In support of this, they outline at length and in detail the well-known facts of fetal development. If this suggestion of personhood is established, the appellant's case, of course, collapses, for the fetus' right to life would then be guaranteed specifically by the Amendment. The appellant conceded as much on reargument. On the other hand, the appellee conceded on reargument that no case could be cited that holds that a fetus is a person within the meaning of the Fourteenth Amendment.

The Constitution does not define "person" in so many words. Section 1 of the Fourteenth Amendment contains three references to "person." The first, in defining "citizens," speaks of "persons born or naturalized in the United States." The word also appears both in the Due Process Clause and in the Equal Protection Clause. "Person" is used in other places in the Constitution: in the listing of qualifications for Representatives and Senators, Art. I, § 2, cl. 2, and § 3, cl. 3; [1] in the Migration and Importation provision, Art. I, § 9, cl. 1; in the Emolument Clause, Art. I, § 9, cl. 8; in the Electors provisions, Art. II, § 1, cl. 2, and the superseded cl. 3; in the provision outlining qualifications for the office of President, Art. II, § 1, cl. 5; in the Extradition provisions, Art. IV, § 2, cl. 2, and the superseded Fugitive Slave Clause 3; and in the Fifth, Twelfth, and Twenty-second Amendments, as well as in §§ 2 and 3 of the Fourteenth Amendment. But in nearly all these instances, the use of the word is such that it has application only postnatally. None indicates, with any assurance, that it has any possible prenatal application. [2]

[1] We are not aware that in the taking of any census under this clause, a fetus has ever been counted.
[2] When Texas urges that a fetus is entitled to Fourteenth Amendment protection as a person, it faces a dilemma. Neither in Texas nor in any other State are all abortions

All this, together with our observation, *supra,* that throughout the major portion of the 19th century prevailing legal abortion practices were far freer than they are today, persuades us that the word "person," as used in the Fourteenth Amendment, does not include the unborn. . . .

This conclusion, however, does not of itself fully answer the contentions raised by Texas, and we pass on to other considerations.

B. The pregnant woman cannot be isolated in her privacy. She carries an embryo and, later, a fetus, if one accepts the medical definitions of the developing young in the human uterus. The situation therefore is inherently different from marital intimacy, or bedroom possession of obscene material, or marriage, or procreation, or education, with which *Eisenstadt* and *Griswold, Stanley, Loving, Skinner* and *Pierce* and *Meyer* were respectively concerned. As we have intimated above, it is reasonable and appropriate for a State to decide that at some point in time another interest, that of health of the mother or that of potential human life, becomes significantly involved. The woman's privacy is no longer sole and any right of privacy she possesses must be measured accordingly.

Texas urges that, apart from the Fourteenth Amendment, life begins at conception and is present throughout pregnancy, and that, therefore, the State has a compelling interest in protecting that life from and after conception. We need not resolve the difficult question of when life begins. When those trained in the respective disciplines of medicine, philosophy, and theology are unable to arrive at any consensus, the judiciary, at this point in the development of man's knowledge, is not in a position to speculate as to the answer.

It should be sufficient to note briefly the wide divergence of thinking on this most sensitive and difficult question. There has always been strong support for the view that life does not begin until live birth. This was the belief of the Stoics. It appears to be the predominant, though not the unanimous, attitude of the Jewish faith. It may be taken to represent also the position of a large segment of the Protestant community, insofar as that can be ascertained; organized groups that have taken a formal position on the abortion issue have generally regarded abortion as a matter for the conscience of the individual and her family. As we have noted, the common law found greater significance in quickening. Physicians and their scientific colleagues have regarded that event with less interest and have tended to focus either upon con-

---

prohibited. Despite broad proscription, an exception always exists. The exception contained in Art. 1196, for an abortion procured or attempted by medical advice for the purpose of saving the life of the mother, is typical. But if the fetus is a person who is not to be deprived of life without due process of law, and if the mother's condition is the sole determinant, does not the Texas exception appear to be out of line with the Amendment's command?

There are other inconsistencies between Fourteenth Amendment status and the typical abortion statute. It has already been pointed out [n. 49], *supra,* that in Texas the woman is not a principal or an accomplice with respect to an abortion upon her. If the fetus is a person, why is the woman not a principal or an accomplice? Further, the penalty for criminal abortion specified by Art. 1195 is significantly less than the maximum penalty for murder prescribed by Art. 1257 of the Texas Penal Code. If the fetus is a person, may the penalties be different?

ception, upon live birth, or upon the interim point at which the fetus becomes "viable," that is, potentially able to live outside the mother's womb, albeit with artificial aid. Viability is usually placed at about seven months (28 weeks) but may occur earlier, even at 24 weeks. The Aristotelian theory of "mediate animation," that held sway throughout the Middle Ages and the Renaissance in Europe, continued to be official Roman Catholic dogma until the 19th century, despite opposition to this "ensoulment" theory from those in the Church who would recognize the existence of life from the moment of conception. The latter is now, of course, the official belief of the Catholic Church. As one brief *amicus* discloses, this is a view strongly held by many non-Catholics as well, and by many physicians. Substantial problems for precise definition of this view are posed, however, by new embryological data that purport to indicate that conception is a "process" over time, rather than an event, and by new medical techniques such as menstrual extraction, the "morning-after" pill, implantation of embryos, artificial insemination, and even artificial wombs.

In areas other than criminal abortion, the law has been reluctant to endorse any theory that life, as we recognize it, begins before live birth or to accord legal rights to the unborn except in narrowly defined situations and except when the rights are contingent upon live birth. For example, the traditional rule of tort law denied recovery for prenatal injuries even though the child was born alive. That rule has been changed in almost every jurisdiction. In most States, recovery is said to be permitted only if the fetus was viable, or at least quick, when the injuries were sustained, though few courts have squarely so held. In a recent development, generally opposed by the commentators, some States permit the parents of a stillborn child to maintain an action for wrongful death because of prenatal injuries. Such an action, however, would appear to be one to vindicate the parents' interest and is thus consistent with the view that the fetus, at most, represents only the potentiality of life. Similarly, unborn children have been recognized as acquiring rights or interests by way of inheritance or other devolution of property, and have been represented by guardians *ad litem*. Perfection of the interests involved, again, has generally been contingent upon live birth. In short, the unborn have never been recognized in the law as persons in the whole sense.

X

In view of all this, we do not agree that, by adopting one theory of life, Texas may override the rights of the pregnant woman that are at stake. We repeat, however, that the State does have an important and legitimate interest in preserving and protecting the health of the pregnant woman, whether she be a resident of the State or a nonresident who seeks medical consultation and treatment there, and that it has still *another* important and legitimate interest in protecting the potentiality of human life. These interests are separate and distinct. Each grows in substantiality as the woman approaches term and, at a point during pregnancy, each becomes "compelling."

With respect to the State's important and legitimate interest in the health of the mother, the "compelling" point, in the light of present medical knowledge, is at approximately the end of the first trimester. This is so because of the now-established medical fact that until the end of the first trimester mortality in abortion may be less than mortality in normal childbirth. It follows that, from and after this point, a State may regulate the abortion procedure to the extent that the regulation reasonably relates to the preservation and protection of maternal health. Examples of permissible state regulation in this area are requirements as to the qualifications of the person who is to perform the abortion; as to the licensure of that person; as to the facility in which the procedure is to be performed, that is, whether it must be a hospital or may be a clinic or some other place of less-than-hospital status; as to the licensing of the facility; and the like.

This means, on the other hand, that, for the period of pregnancy prior to this "compelling" point, the attending physician, in consultation with his patient, is free to determine, without regulation by the State, that, in his medical judgment, the patient's pregnancy should be terminated. If that decision is reached, the judgment may be effectuated by an abortion free of interference by the State.

With respect to the State's important and legitimate interest in potential life, the "compelling" point is at viability. This is so because the fetus then presumably has the capability of meaningful life outside the mother's womb. State regulation protective of fetal life after viability thus has both logical and biological justifications. If the State is interested in protecting fetal life after viability, it may go so far as to proscribe abortion during that period, except when it is necessary to preserve the life or health of the mother.

Measured against these standards, Art. 1196 of the Texas Penal Code, in restricting legal abortions to those "procured or attempted by medical advice for the purpose of saving the life of the mother," sweeps too broadly. The statute makes no distinction between abortions performed early in pregnancy and those performed later, and it limits to a single reason, "saving" the mother's life, the legal justification for the procedure. The statute, therefore, cannot survive the constitutional attack made upon it here. . . .

Mr. Justice STEWART, concurring.

"In a Constitution for a free people, there can be no doubt that the meaning of 'liberty' must be broad indeed." The Constitution nowhere mentions a specific right of personal choice in matters of marriage and family life, but the "liberty" protected by the Due Process Clause of the Fourteenth Amendment covers more than those freedoms explicitly named in the Bill of Rights.

As Mr. Justice Harlan once wrote: "[T]he full scope of the liberty guaranteed by the Due Process Clause cannot be found in or limited by the precise terms of the specific guarantees elsewhere provided in the Constitution. This 'liberty' is not a series of isolated points pricked out in terms of the taking of property; the freedom of speech, press, and religion; the right to keep and bear arms; the freedom from unreasonable searches and seizures; and so on. It is a rational continuum which, broadly speaking, includes a freedom from all substantial arbitrary impositions and purposeless restraints . . . and which also recognizes, what a reasonable and sensitive judgment must, that certain interests require particularly careful scrutiny of the state needs asserted to justify their abridgment." In the words of Mr. Justice Frankfurter, "Great concepts like . . . 'liberty' . . . were purposely left to gather meaning from experience. For they relate to the whole domain of social and economic fact, and the statesmen who founded this Nation knew too well that only a stagnant society remains unchanged."

Several decisions of this Court make clear that freedom of personal choice in matters of marriage and family life is one of the liberties protected by the Due Process Clause of the Fourteenth Amendment. As recently as last Term, in Eisenstadt v. Baird, 405 U.S. 438, 453, we recognized "the right of the *individual,* married or single, to be free from unwarranted governmental intrusion into matters so fundamentally affecting a person as the decision whether to bear or beget a child." That right necessarily includes the right of a woman to decide whether or not to terminate her pregnancy. "Certainly the interests of a woman in giving of her physical and emotional self during pregnancy and the interests that will be affected throughout her life by the birth and raising of a child are of a far greater degree of significance and personal intimacy than the right to send a child to private school protected in Pierce v. Society of Sisters, 268 U.S. 510, or the right to teach a foreign language protected in Meyer v. Nebraska, 262 U.S. 390.

Clearly, therefore, the Court today is correct in holding that the right asserted by Jane Roe is embraced within the personal liberty protected by the Due Process Clause of the Fourteenth Amendment.

It is evident that the Texas abortion statute infringes that right directly. Indeed, it is difficult to imagine a more complete abridgment of a constitutional freedom than that worked by the inflexible criminal statute now in force in Texas. The question then becomes whether the state interests advanced to justify this abridgment can survive the "particularly careful scrutiny" that the Fourteenth Amendment here requires.

The asserted state interests are protection of the health and safety of the pregnant woman, and protection of the potential future human life within her. These are legitimate objectives, amply sufficient to permit a State to regulate abortions as it does other surgical procedures, and perhaps sufficient to permit a State to regulate abortions more stringently or even to prohibit them in the late stages of pregnancy. But such legislation is not before us, and I think the Court today has thoroughly demonstrated that these state interests cannot constitutionally support the broad abridgment of personal liberty worked by the existing Texas law. Accordingly, I join the Court's opinion holding that that law is invalid under the Due Process Clause of the Fourteenth Amendment.

Mr. Justice DOUGLAS, concurring.

While I join the opinion of the Court, I add a few words.

I

The questions presented in the present cases . . . involve the right of privacy, one aspect of which we considered in Griswold v. Connecticut, 381 U.S. 479, when we held that various guarantees in the Bill of Rights create zones of privacy.

The *Griswold* case involved a law forbidding the use of contraceptives. We held that law as applied to married people unconstitutional:

> We deal with a right of privacy older than the Bill of Rights—older than our political parties, older than our school system. Marriage is a coming together for better or for worse, hopefully enduring, and intimate to the degree of being sacred. . . .

The Ninth Amendment obviously does not create federally enforceable rights. It merely says, "The enumeration in the Constitution, of certain rights, shall not be construed to deny or disparage others retained by the people." But a catalogue of these rights includes customary, traditional, and time-honored rights, amenities, privileges, and immunities that come within the sweep of "the Blessings of Liberty" mentioned in the preamble to the Constitution. Many of them, in my view, come within the meaning of the term "liberty" as used in the Fourteenth Amendment.

First is the autonomous control over the development and expression of one's intellect, interests, tastes, and personality.

These are rights protected by the First Amendment and, in my view, they are absolute, permitting of no exceptions. The Free Exercise Clause of the First Amendment is one facet of this constitutional right. The right to remain silent as respects one's own beliefs is protected by the First and the Fifth. The First Amendment grants the privacy of first-class mail. All of these aspects of the right of privacy are rights "retained by the people" in the meaning of the Ninth Amendment.

Second is freedom of choice in the basic decisions of one's life respecting marriage, divorce, procreation, contraception, and the education and upbringing of children.

These rights, unlike those protected by the First Amendment, are subject to some control by the police power. Thus, the Fourth Amendment speaks only of "unreasonable searches and seizures" and of "probable cause." These rights are "fundamental," and we have held that in order to support legislative action the statute must be narrowly and precisely drawn and that a "compelling state interest" must be shown in support of the limitation.

The liberty to marry a person of one's own choosing, the right of procreation, the liberty to direct the education of one's children, and the privacy of the marital relation, are in this category. Only last Term . . . we expanded the concept of *Griswold* by saying:

> It is true that in *Griswold* the right of privacy in question inhered in the marital relationship. Yet the marital couple is not an independent entity with a mind and heart of its own, but an association of two individuals each with a separate intellectual and emotional make up. If the right of

privacy means anything, it is the right of the *individual,* married or single, to be free from unwarranted governmental intrusion into matters so fundamentally affecting a person as the decision whether to bear or beget a child.

This right of privacy was called by Mr. Justice Brandeis the right "to be let alone." That right includes the privilege of an individual to plan his own affairs, for, " 'outside areas of plainly harmful conduct, every American is left to shape his own life as he thinks best, do what he pleases, go where he pleases.' "

Third is the freedom to care for one's health and person, freedom from bodily restraint or compulsion, freedom to walk, stroll, or loaf.

These rights, though fundamental, are likewise subject to regulation on a showing of "compelling state interest." We stated that walking, strolling, and wandering "are historically part of the amenities of life as we have known [them]." As stated in Jacobson v. Massachusetts:

> There is, or course, a sphere within which the individual may assert the supremacy of his own will and rightfully dispute the authority of any human government,—especially of any free government existing under a written constitution, to interfere with the exercise of that will.

· · ·

In Meyer v. Nebraska, the Court said:

> Without doubt, [liberty] denotes not merely freedom from bodily restraint but also the right of the individual to contract, to engage in any of the common occupations of life, to acquire useful knowledge, to marry, establish a home and bring up children, to worship God according to the dictates of his own conscience, and generally to enjoy those privileges long recognized at common law as essential to the orderly pursuit of happiness by free men.

The Georgia statute is at war with the clear message of these cases— that a woman is free to make the basic decision whether to bear an unwanted child. Elaborate argument is hardly necessary to demonstrate that childbirth may deprive a woman of her preferred lifestyle and force upon her a radically different and undesired future. For example, rejected applicants under the Georgia statute are required to endure the discomforts of pregnancy; to incur the pain, higher mortality rate, and after-effects of childbirth; to abandon educational plans; to sustain loss of income; to forgo the satisfactions of careers; to tax further mental and physical health in providing child care; and, in some cases, to bear the lifelong stigma of unwed motherhood, a badge which may haunt, if not deter, later legitimate family relationships.

II

Such a reasoning is, however, only the beginning of the problem. The State has interests to protect. Vaccinations to prevent epidemics are one example. The Court held that compulsory sterilization of imbeciles afflicted with hereditary forms of insanity or imbecility is another. Abortion affects another. While childbirth endangers the lives of some women, voluntary abortion at any time and place regardless of medical standards would impinge on a rightful concern of society. The woman's health is part of that concern; as is the life of the fetus after quickening. These concerns justify the State in treating the procedure as a medical one.

. . . Georgia's enactment has a constitutional infirmity because, as stated by the District Court, it "limits the number of reasons for which an abortion may be sought." I agree with the holding of the District Court, "This the State may not do, because such action unduly restricts a decision sheltered by the Constitutional right to privacy."

The vicissitudes of life produce pregnancies which may be unwanted, or which may impair "health" in the broad *Vuitch* sense of the term, or which may imperil the life of the mother, or which in the full setting of the case may create such suffering, dislocations, misery, or tragedy as to make an early abortion the only civilized step to take. These hardships may be properly embraced in the "health" factor of the mother as appraised by a person of insight. Or they may be part of a broader medical judgment based on what is "appropriate" in a given case, though perhaps not "necessary" in a strict sense.

The "liberty" of the mother, though rooted as it is in the Constitution, may be qualified by the State for the reasons we have stated. But where fundamental personal rights and liberties are involved, the corrective legislation must be "narrowly drawn to prevent the supposed evil," and not be dealt with in an "unlimited and indiscriminate" manner. Unless regulatory measures are so confined and are addressed to the specific areas of compelling legislative concern, the police power would become the great leveler of constitutional rights and liberties.

There is no doubt that the State may require abortions to be performed by qualified medical personnel. The legitimate objective of preserving the mother's health clearly supports such laws. Their impact upon the woman's privacy is minimal. But the Georgia statute outlaws virtually all such operations—even in the earliest stages of pregnancy. In light of modern medical evidence suggesting that an early abortion is safer healthwise than childbirth itself,[3] it cannot be seriously urged that so comprehensive a ban is aimed at protecting the woman's health. Rather, this expansive proscription of all abortions along the temporal spectrum can rest only on a public goal of preserving both embryonic and fetal life.

[3] Many studies show that it is safer for a woman to have a medically induced abortion than to bear a child. In the first 11 months of operation of the New York abortion law, the mortality rate associated with such operations was six per 100,000 operations. Abortion Mortality, 20 Morbidity and Mortality 208, 209 (June 1971) (U.S. Dept. of HEW, Public Health Service). On the other hand, the maternal mortality rate associated with childbirths other than abortions was 18 per 100,000 live births. Tietze, Mortality with Contraception and Induced Abortion, 45 Studies in Family Planning 6 (1969). See also Tietze & Lehfeldt, Legal Abortion in Eastern Europe, 175 J.A.M.A. 1149, 1152 (Apr. 1961); Kolblova, Legal Abortion in Czechoslovakia, 196 J.A.M.A. 371 (Apr. 1966); Mehland, Combating Illegal Abortion in the Socialist Countries of Europe, 13 World Med.J. 84 (1966).

The present statute has struck the balance between the woman's and the State's interests wholly in favor of the latter. I am not prepared to hold that a State may equate, as Georgia has done, all phases of maturation preceding birth. We held in *Griswold* that the States may not preclude spouses from attempting to avoid the joinder of sperm and egg. If this is true, it is difficult to perceive any overriding public necessity which might attach precisely at the moment of conception. As Mr. Justice Clark has said:

> To say that life is present at conception is to give recognition to the potential, rather than the actual. The unfertilized egg has life, and if fertilized, it takes on human proportions. But the law deals in reality, not obscurity—the known rather than the unknown. When sperm meets egg life may eventually form, but quite often it does not. The law does not deal in speculation. The phenomenon of life takes time to develop, and until it is actually present, it cannot be destroyed. Its interruption prior to formation would hardly be homicide, and as we have seen, society does not regard it as such. The rites of Baptism are not performed and death certificates are not required when a miscarriage occurs. No prosecutor has ever returned a murder indictment charging the taking of the life of a fetus. This would not be the case if the fetus constituted human life.

In summary, the enactment is overbroad. It is not closely correlated to the aim of preserving prenatal life. In fact, it permits its destruction in several cases, including pregnancies resulting from sex acts in which unmarried females are below the statutory age of consent. At the same time, however, the measure broadly proscribes aborting other pregnancies which may cause severe mental disorders. Additionally, the statute is overbroad because it equates the value of embryonic life immediately after conception with the worth of life immediately after birth. . . .

Mr. Justice REHNQUIST, dissenting.

The Court's opinion brings to the decision of this troubling question both extensive historical fact and a wealth of legal scholarship. While the opinion thus commands my respect, I find myself nonetheless in fundamental disagreement with those parts of it that invalidate the Texas statute in question, and therefore dissent. . . .

II

Even if there were a plaintiff in this case capable of litigating the issue which the Court decides, I would reach a conclusion opposite to that reached by the Court. I have difficulty in concluding, as the Court does, that the right of "privacy" is involved in this case. Texas, by the statute here challenged, bars the performance of a medical abortion by a licensed physician on a plaintiff such as Roe. A transaction resulting in an operation such as this is not "private" in the ordinary usage of that word. Nor is the "privacy" that the Court finds here even a distant relative of the freedom from searches and seizures protected by the Fourth Amendment to the Constitution, which the Court has referred to as embodying a right to privacy.

If the Court means by the term "privacy" no more than that the claim of a person to be free from unwanted state regulation of consensual transactions may be a form of "liberty" protected by the Fourteenth Amendment, there is no doubt that similar claims have been upheld in our earlier decisions on the basis of that liberty. I agree with the statement of Mr. Justice STEWART in his concurring opinion that the "liberty," against deprivation of which without due process the Fourteenth Amendment protects, embraces more than the rights found in the Bill of Rights. But that liberty is not guaranteed absolutely against deprivation, only against deprivation without due process of law. The test traditionally applied in the area of social and economic legislation is whether or not a law such as that challenged has a rational relation to a valid state objective. The Due Process Clause of the Fourteenth Amendment undoubtedly does place a limit, albeit a broad one, on legislative power to enact laws such as this. If the Texas statute were to prohibit an abortion even where the mother's life is in jeopardy, I have little doubt that such a statute would lack a rational relation to a valid state objective. . . . But the Court's sweeping invalidation of any restrictions on abortion during the first trimester is impossible to justify under that standard, and the conscious weighing of competing factors that the Court's opinion apparently substitutes for the established test is far more appropriate to a legislative judgment than to a judicial one. . . .

. . . The decision here to break pregnancy into three distinct terms and to outline the permissible restrictions the State may impose in each one, for example, partakes more of judicial legislation than it does of a determination of the intent of the drafters of the Fourteenth Amendment.

The fact that a majority of the States reflecting, after all the majority sentiment in those States, have had restrictions on abortions for at least a century is a strong indication, it seems to me, that the asserted right to an abortion is not "so rooted in the traditions and conscience of our people as to be ranked as fundamental." Even today, when society's views on abortion are changing, the very existence of the debate is evidence that the "right" to an abortion is not so universally accepted as the appellant would have us believe. . . .

3 U.S. SUPREME COURT

PLANNED PARENTHOOD OF CENTRAL MISSOURI V. DANFORTH

428 U.S. 52, 96 S.Ct. 2831, 49 L.Ed.2d 788 (1976)

Mr. Justice BLACKMUN delivered the opinion of the Court.

This case is a logical and anticipated corollary to *Roe* v. *Wade,* for it raises issues secondary to those that were then before the Court. Indeed, some of the questions now presented were forecast and reserved in *Roe* and *Doe.* . . .

I

In June 1974, somewhat more than a year after *Roe* and *Doe* had been decided, Missouri's 77th General Assembly, in its Second Regular Session, enacted House Committee Substitute for House Bill No. 1211 (hereinafter referred to as the "Act"). . . . It imposes a structure for the control and regulation of abortion in Missouri during all stages of pregnancy.

II

Three days after the Act became effective, the present litigation was instituted in the United States District Court for the Eastern District of Missouri. . . .

The particular provisions of the Act that remained under specific challenge at the end of trial were § 2(2), defining the term "viability"; § 3(2), requiring from the woman, prior to submitting to abortion during the first 12 weeks of pregnancy, a certification in writing that she consents to the procedure and "that her consent is informed and freely given and is not the result of coercion"; § 3(3), requiring, for the same period, "the written consent of the woman's spouse, unless the abortion is certified by a licensed physician to be necessary in order to preserve the life of the mother"; § 3(4), requiring, for the same period, "the written consent of one parent or person in loco parentis of the woman if the woman is unmarried and under the age of eighteen years, unless the abortion is certified by a licensed physician as necessary in order to preserve the life of the mother"; § 6(1), requiring the physician to exercise professional care "to preserve the life and health of the fetus" and, failing such, deeming him guilty of manslaughter and making him liable in an action for damages; § 7, declaring an infant, who survives "an attempted abortion which was not performed to save the life or health of the mother," to be "an abandoned ward of the state under the jurisdiction of the juvenile court," and depriving the mother, and also the father if he consented to the abortion, of parental rights; § 9, the legislative finding that method of abortion known as saline amniocentesis "is deleterious to maternal health," and prohibiting that method after the first 12 weeks of pregnancy; and §§ 10 and 11, imposing reporting and maintenance of record requirements for health facilities and for physicians who perform abortions.

The case was presented to a three-judge District Court. . . .

For convenience, we shall usually refer to the plaintiffs as "appellants" and to both named defendants as "appellees." . . .

IV

. . . Our primary task, then, is to consider each of the challenged provisions of the new Missouri abortion statute in the particular light of the opinions and decisions in *Roe* and in *Doe*. To this we now turn, with the assistance of helpful briefs from both sides and from some of the *amici*.

A

The Definition of Viability. Section 2(2) of the Act defines "viability" as "that stage of fetal development when the life of the unborn child may be continued indefinitely outside the womb by natural or artificial life-supportive systems." Appellants claim that this definition violates and conflicts with the discussion of viability in our opinion in *Roe*. In particular, appellants object to the failure of the definition to contain any reference to a gestational time period, to its failure to incorporate and reflect the three stages of pregnancy, to the presence of the word "indefinitely," and to the extra burden of regulation imposed. It is suggested that the definition expands the Court's definition of viability, as expressed in *Roe*, and amounts to a legislative determination of what is properly a matter for medical judgment. It is said that the "mere possibility of momentary survival is not the medical standard of viability."

In *Roe*, we used the term "viable," properly we thought, to signify the point at which the fetus is "potentially able to live outside the mother's womb, albeit with artificial aid," and presumably capable of "meaningful life outside the mother's womb." We noted that this point "is usually placed" at about seven months or 28 weeks, but may occur earlier.

We agree with the District Court and conclude that the definition of viability in the Act does not conflict with what was said and held in *Roe*. In fact, we believe that § 2(2), even when read in conjunction with § 5 (proscribing an abortion "not necessary to preserve the life or health of the mother . . . unless the attending physician first certifies with reasonable medical certainty that the fetus is not viable), the constitutionality of which is not explicitly challenged here, reflects an attempt on the part of the Missouri General Assembly to comply with our observations and discussion in *Roe* relating to viability. Appellant Hall, in his deposition, had no particular difficulty with the statutory definition. As noted above, we recognized in *Roe* that viability was a matter of medical judgment, skill, and technical ability, and we preserved the flexibility of the term. Section 2(2) does the same. Indeed, one might argue, as the appellees do, that the presence of the statute's words "continued indefinitely" favor, rather than disfavor, the appellants, for, arguably, the point when life can be "continued indefinitely outside the womb" may well occur later in pregnancy than the point where the fetus is "potentially able to live outside the mother's womb."

In any event, we agree with the District Court that it is not the proper function of the legislature or the courts to place viability, which essentially is a medical concept, at a specific point in the gestation period. The time when viability is achieved may vary with each pregnancy, and the determination of whether a particular fetus is viable is, and must be, a matter for the judgment of the responsible attending physician. The definition of viability in § 2(2) merely reflects this fact. The appellees do not contend otherwise, for they insist that the determination of viability rests with the physician in the exercise of his professional judgment.

We thus do not accept appellants' contention that a specified number of weeks in pregnancy must be fixed by statute as the point of viability.

We conclude that the definition in § 2(2) of the Act does not circumvent the limitations on state regulation outlined in *Roe*. We therefore hold that the Act's definition of "viability" comports with *Roe* and withstands the constitutional attack made upon it in this litigation.

C

The Spouse's Consent. Section 3(3) requires the prior written consent of the spouse of the woman seeking an abortion during the first 12 weeks of pregnancy, unless "the abortion is certified by a licensed physician to be necessary in order to preserve the life of the mother."

The appellees defend § 3(3) on the ground that it was enacted in the light of the General Assembly's "perception of marriage as an institution," and that any major change in family status is a decision to be made jointly by the marriage partners. Reference is made to an abortion's possible effect on the woman's childbearing potential. It is said that marriage always has entailed some legislatively imposed limitations: reference is made to adultery and bigamy as criminal offenses; to Missouri's general requirement that for an adoption of a child born in wedlock the consent of both parents is necessary; to similar joint consent requirements imposed by a number of States with respect to artificial insemination and the legitimacy of children so conceived; to the laws of two States requiring spousal consent for voluntary sterilization; and to the long-established requirement of spousal consent for the effective disposition of an interest in real property. It is argued that "[r]ecognizing that the consent of both parties is generally necessary . . . to begin a family, the legislature has determined that a change in the family structure set in motion by mutual consent should be terminated only by mutual consent," and that what the legislature did was to exercise its inherent policymaking power "for what was believed to be in the best interests of all people of Missouri."

The appellants on the other hand, contend that § 3(3) obviously is designed to afford the husband the right unilaterally to prevent or veto an abortion, whether or not he is the father of the fetus, and that this not only violates *Roe* and *Doe* but is also in conflict with other decided cases. They also refer to the situation where the husband's consent cannot be obtained because he cannot be located. And they assert that § 3(3) is vague and overbroad.

In *Roe* and *Doe* we specifically reserved decision on the question whether a requirement for consent by the father of the fetus, by the spouse, or by the parents, or a parent, of an unmarried minor, may be constitutionally imposed. We now hold that the State may not constitutionally require the consent of the spouse, as is specified under § 3(3) of the Missouri Act, as a condition for abortion during the first 12 weeks of pregnancy. . . . The State cannot "delegate to a spouse a veto power which the state itself is absolutely and totally prohibited from exercising during the first trimester of pregnancy." Clearly, since the State cannot regulate or proscribe abortion during the first stage, when the physician and his patient make that decision, the State cannot delegate authority to any particular person, even the spouse, to prevent abortion during that same period.

We are not unaware of the deep and proper concern and interest that a devoted and protective husband has in his wife's pregnancy and in the growth and development of the fetus she is carrying. Neither has this Court failed to appreciate the importance of the marital relationship in our society. Moreover, we recognize that the decision whether to undergo or to forego an abortion may have profound effects on the future of any marriage, effects that are both physical and mental, and possibly deleterious. Notwithstanding these factors, we cannot hold that the State has the constitutional authority to give the spouse unilaterally the ability to prohibit the wife from terminating her pregnancy, when the State itself lacks that right.[1]

---

[1] As the Court recognized in *Eisenstadt v. Baird,* "the marital couple is not an independent entity with a mind and heart of its own, but an association of two individuals each with a separate intellectual and emotional makeup. If the right of privacy means anything, it is the right of the *individual,* married or single, to be free from unwarranted governmental intrusion into matters so fundamentally affecting a person as the decision whether to bear or beget a child." 405 U.S., at 453, 92 S.Ct., at 1038 (emphasis in original).

The dissenting opinion of our Brother WHITE appears to overlook the implications of this statement upon the issue whether § 3(3) is constitutional. This section does much more than insure that the husband participate in the decision whether his wife should have an abortion. The State, instead, has determined that the husband's interest in continuing the pregnancy of his wife always outweighs any interest on her part in terminating it irrespective of the condition of their marriage. The State, accordingly, has granted him the right to prevent unilaterally, and for whatever reason, the effectuation of his wife's and her physician's decision to terminate her pregnancy. This state determination not only may discourage the consultation that

It seems manifest that, ideally, the decision to terminate a pregnancy should be one concurred in by both the wife and her husband. No marriage may be viewed as harmonious or successful if the marriage partners are fundamentally divided on so important and vital an issue. But it is difficult to believe that the goal of fostering mutuality and trust in a marriage, and of strengthening the marital relationship and the marriage institution, will be achieved by giving the husband a veto power exercisable for any reason whatsoever or for no reason at all. Even if the State had the ability to delegate to the husband a power it itself could not exercise, it is not at all likely that such action would further, as the District Court majority phrased it, the "interest of the state in protecting the mutuality of decisions vital to the marriage relationship."

We recognize, of course, that when a woman, with the approval of her physician but without the approval of her husband, decides to terminate her pregnancy, it could be said that she is acting unilaterally. The obvious fact is that when the wife and the husband disagree on this decision, the view of only one of the two marriage partners can prevail. Since it is the woman who physically bears the child and who is the more directly and immediately affected by the pregnancy, as between the two, the balance weighs in her favor. . . .

D

Parental Consent. Section 3(4) requires, with respect to the first 12 weeks of pregnancy, where the woman is unmarried and under the age of 18 years, the written consent of a parent or person *in loco parentis* unless, again, "the abortion is certified by a licensed physician as necessary in order to preserve the life of the mother." It is to be observed that only one parent need consent.

The appellees defend the statute in several ways. They point out that the law properly may subject minors to more stringent limitations than are permissible with respect to adults. . . . Certain decisions are considered by the State to be outside the scope of a minor's ability to act in his own best interest or in the interest of the public. . . . It is pointed out that the record contains testimony to the effect that children of tender years (even ages 10 and 11) have sought abortions. Thus, a State's permitting a child to obtain an abortion without the counsel of an adult "who has responsibility or concern for the child would constitute an irresponsible abdication of the State's duty to protect the welfare of minors." Parental discretion, too, has been protected from unwarranted or unreasonable interference from the State. Finally, it is said that § 3(4) imposes no additional burden on the physician because even prior to the passage of the Act the physician would require parental consent before performing an abortion on a minor.

---

might normally be expected to precede a major decision affecting the marital couple but also, and more importantly, the State has interposed an absolute obstacle to a woman's decision that *Roe* held to be constitutionally protected from such interference.

The appellants, in their turn, emphasize that no other Missouri statute specifically requires the additional consent of a minor's parent for medical or surgical treatment, and that in Missouri a minor legally may consent to medical services for pregnancy (excluding abortion), venereal disease, and drug abuse. The result of § 3(4), it is said, "is the ultimate supremacy of the parents' desires over those of the minor child, the pregnant patient." It is noted that in Missouri a woman who marries with parental consent under the age of 18 does not require parental consent to abort, and yet her contemporary who has chosen not to marry must obtain parental approval. . . .

We agree with appellants . . . that the State may not impose a blanket provision, such as § 3(4), requiring the consent of a parent or person *in loco parentis* as a condition for abortion of an unmarried minor during the first 12 weeks of her pregnancy. Just as with the requirement of consent from the spouse, so here, the State does not have the constitutional authority to give a third party an absolute, and possibly arbitrary, veto over the decision of the physician and his patient to terminate the patient's pregnancy, regardless of the reason for withholding the consent.

Constitutional rights do not mature and come into being magically, only when one attains the state-defined age of majority. Minors, as well as adults, are protected by the Constitution and possess constitutional rights. The Court indeed, however, long has recognized that the State has somewhat broader authority to regulate the activities of children than of adults. It remains, then, to examine whether there is any significant state interest in conditioning an abortion on the consent of a parent or person *in loco parentis* that is not present in the case of an adult.

One suggested interest is the safeguarding of the family unit and of parental authority. It is difficult, however, to conclude that providing a parent with absolute power to overrule a determination, made by the physician and his minor patient, to terminate the patient's pregnancy will serve to strengthen the family unit. Neither is it likely that such veto power will enhance parental authority or control where the minor and the nonconsenting parent are so fundamentally in conflict and the very existence of the pregnancy already has fractured the family structure. Any independent interest the parent may have in the termination of the minor daughter's pregnancy is no more weighty than the right of privacy of the competent minor mature enough to have become pregnant.

We emphasize that our holding that § 3(4) is invalid does not suggest that every minor, regardless of age or maturity, may give effective consent for termination of her pregnancy. The fault with § 3(4) is that it imposes a special consent provision, exercisable by a person other than the woman and her physician, as a prerequisite to a minor's termination of her pregnancy and does so without a sufficient justification for the restriction. It violates the strictures of *Roe* and *Doe*. . . .

Mr. Justice WHITE, with whom The CHIEF JUSTICE and Mr. Justice REHNQUIST join, concurring in the judgment in part and dissenting in part. . . .

I

Roe v. *Wade* holds that until a fetus becomes viable, the interest of the State in the life or potential life it represents is outweighed by the interest of the mother in choosing "whether or not to terminate her pregnancy." Section 3(3) of the Act provides that a married woman may not obtain an abortion without her husband's consent. The Court strikes down this statute in one sentence. It says that "since the State cannot . . . proscribe abortion . . . the State cannot delegate authority to any particular person, even the spouse, to prevent abortion. . . ." But the State is not—under § 3(3)—delegating to the husband the power to vindicate the *State's* interest in the future life of the fetus. It is instead recognizing that the husband has an interest of his own in the life of the fetus which should not be extinguished by the unilateral decision of the wife. It by no means follows, from the fact that the mother's interest in deciding "whether or not to terminate her pregnancy" outweighs the *State's* interest in the potential life of the fetus, that the husband's interest is also outweighed and may not be protected by the State. A father's interest in having a child—perhaps his only child—may be unmatched by any other interest in his life. It is truly surprising that the majority finds in the United States Constitution, as it must in order to justify the result it reaches, a rule that the State must assign a greater value to a mother's decision to cut off a potential human life by abortion than to a father's decision to let it mature into a live child. Such a rule cannot be found there, nor can it be found in *Roe* v. *Wade*. These are matters which a State should be able to decide free from the suffocating power of the federal judge, purporting to act in the name of the Constitution.

In describing the nature of a mother's interest in terminating a pregnancy, the Court in *Roe* v. *Wade* mentioned only the post-birth burdens of rearing a child, and rejected a rule based on her interest in controlling her own body during pregnancy. Missouri has a law which prevents a woman from putting a child up for adoption over her husband's objection. This law represents a judgment by the State that the mother's interest in avoiding the burdens of child rearing do not outweigh or snuff out the father's interest in participating in bringing up his own child. That law is plainly valid, but no more so than § 3(3) of the Act now before us, resting as it does on precisely the same judgment.

II

. . . The Court rejects the notions that the *State* has an interest in strengthening the family unit or that the *parent* has an "independent interest" in the abortion decision, sufficient to justify the statute and apparently concludes that the statute is therefore unconstitutional. But the purpose of the parental consent requirement is not merely to vindicate any interest of the parent or of the State. The purpose of the requirement is to vindicate the very right created in *Roe* v. *Wade, supra*— the right of the pregnant woman to decide "whether *or not* to terminate her pregnancy." The abortion decision is unquestionably important and has irrevocable consequences whichever way it is made. Missouri is entitled to protect the minor unmarried woman from making the decision in a way which is not in her own best interests, and it seeks to achieve this goal by requiring parental consultation and consent. This is the traditional way by which States have sought to protect children from their own immature and improvident decisions; and there is absolutely no reason expressed by the majority why the State may not utilize that method here. . . .

IV

Section 6(1) of the Act provides:

> No person who performs or induces an abortion shall fail to exercise that degree of professional skill, care and diligence to preserve the life and health of the fetus which such person would be required to exercise in order to preserve the life and health of any fetus intended to be born and not aborted. Any physician or person assisting in the abortion who shall fail to take such measures to encourage or to sustain the life of the child, and the death of the child results, shall be deemed guilty of manslaughter. . . . Further, such physician or other person shall be liable in an action for damages.

If this section is read in any way other than through a microscope, it is plainly intended to require that, where a "fetus . . . [may have] the capability of meaningful life outside the mother's womb," the abortion be handled in a way which is designed to preserve that life notwithstanding the mother's desire to terminate it. Indeed, even looked at through a microscope the statute seems to go no further. It requires a physician to exercise "*that* degree of professional skill . . . to preserve the life and health of the fetus," which he would be required to exercise if the mother wanted a live child. Plainly, if the pregnancy is to be terminated at a time when there is no chance of life outside the womb, a physician would not be required to exercise any care or skill to preserve the life of the fetus during abortion no matter what the mother's desires. The statute would appear then to operate only in the gray area after the fetus *might* be viable but while the physician is still able to certify "with reasonable medical certainty that the fetus is not viable." See § 5 of the Act which flatly prohibits abortions absent such a certification. Since the State has a compelling interest, sufficient to outweigh the mother's desire to kill the fetus, when the "fetus . . . has the capability of meaningful life outside the mother's womb," the statute is constitutional.

Incredibly, the Court reads the statute instead to require "the physician to preserve the life and health of the fetus, whatever the stage of pregnancy," thereby attributing to the Missouri Legislature the strange intention of passing a statute with absolutely no chance of surviving constitutional challenge under *Roe* v. *Wade*. . . .

Mr. Justice STEVENS, concurring in part and dissenting in part.

In my opinion, . . . the parental consent requirement is consistent with the holding in *Roe*. The State's interest in the welfare of its young citizens justifies a variety of protective measures. Because he may not foresee the consequences of his decision, a minor may not make an enforceable bargain. He may not lawfully work or travel where he pleases, or even attend exhibitions of constitutionally protected adult motion pictures. Persons below a certain age may not marry without parental consent. Indeed, such consent is essential even when the young woman is already pregnant. The State's interest in protecting a young person from harm justifies the imposition of restraints on his or her freedom even though comparable restraints on adults would be constitutionally impermissible. Therefore, the holding in *Roe* v. *Wade* that the abortion decision is entitled to constitutional protection merely emphasizes the importance of the decision; it does not lead to the conclusion that the state legislature has no power to enact legislation for the purpose of protecting a young pregnant woman from the consequences of an incorrect decision.

The abortion decision is, of course, more important than the decision to attend or to avoid an adult motion picture, or the decision to work long hours in a factory. It is not necessarily any more important than the decision to run away from home or the decision to marry. But even if it is the most important kind of a decision a young person may ever make, that assumption merely enhances the quality of the State's interest in maximizing the probability that the decision be made correctly and with full understanding of the consequences of either alternative.

The Court recognizes that the State may insist that the decision not be made without the benefit of medical advice. But since the most significant consequences of the decision are not medical in character, it would seem to me that the State may, with equal legitimacy, insist that the decision be made only after other appropriate counsel has been had as well. Whatever choice a pregnant young woman makes—to marry, to abort, to bear her child out of wedlock—the consequences of her decision may have a profound impact on her entire future life. A legislative determination that such a choice will be made more wisely in most cases if the advice and moral support of a parent play a part in the decision-making process is surely not irrational. Moreover, it is perfectly clear that the parental consent requirement will necessarily involve a parent in the decisional process.

If there is no parental consent requirement, many minors will submit to the abortion procedure without ever informing their parents. An assumption that the parental reaction will be hostile, disparaging or violent no doubt persuades many children simply to bypass parental counsel which would in fact be loving, supportive and, indeed for some indispensable. It is unrealistic, in my judgment, to assume that every parent-child relationship is either (a) so perfect that communication and accord will take place routinely or (b) so imperfect that the absence of communication reflects the child's correct prediction that the parent will exercise his or her veto arbitrarily to further a selfish interest rather than the child's interest. A state legislature may conclude that most parents will be primarily interested in the welfare of their children, and further, that the imposition of a parental consent requirement is an appropriate method of giving the parents an opportunity to foster that welfare by helping a pregnant distressed child to make and to implement a correct decision.

The State's interest is not dependent on an estimate of the impact the parental consent requirement may have on the total number of abortions that may take place. I assume that parents will sometimes prevent abortions which might better be performed; other parents may advise abortions that should not be performed. Similarly, even doctors are not omniscient; specialists in performing abortions may incorrectly conclude that the immediate advantages of the procedure outweigh the disadvantages which a parent could evaluate in better perspective. In each individual case factors much more profound than a mere medical judgment may weigh heavily in the scales. The overriding consideration is that the right to make the choice be exercised as wisely as possible.

The Court assumes that parental consent is an appropriate requirement if the minor is not capable of understanding the procedure and of appreciating its consequences and those of available alternatives. This assumption is, of course, correct and consistent with the predicate which underlies all State legislation seeking to protect minors from the consequences of decisions they are not yet prepared to make. In all such situations chronological age has been the basis for imposition of a restraint on the minor's freedom of choice even though it is perfectly obvious that such a yardstick is imprecise and perhaps even unjust in particular cases. The Court seems to assume that the capacity to conceive a child and the judgment of the physician are the only constitutionally permissible yardsticks for determining whether a young woman can independently make the abortion decision. I doubt the accuracy of the Court's empirical judgment. Even if it were correct, however, as a matter of constitutional law I think a State has power to conclude otherwise and to select a chronological age as its standard.

In short, the State's interest in the welfare of its young citizens is sufficient, in my judgment, to support the parental consent requirement.

INTRODUCTION

In "Abortion and Infanticide," Michael Tooley attempts to provide a criterion by which some rational cutoff point—one that is not arbitrary—might be set for distinguishing those human organisms (such as fetuses) that are not entitled to protection against destruction from those that are. Tooley finds that there is at least one characteristic that persons, to the exclusion of all creatures, have and that it is the possession of this characteristic that entitles them to the right to life: the organism's "concept of a self as a continuing subject of experiences and other mental states" and its belief that it is itself such a continuing entity. On the basis of this consideration, as well as certain others that he develops in the course of his article, Tooley concludes that abortion is permissible. Even more, he argues that infanticide too is permissible, since early in their lives, infants possess no more of this "concept of a self" than do fetuses.

Jane English takes a rather different point of view. She too is concerned about the concept of "person," but she rejects what she calls the "straightjacket of necessary and/or sufficient conditions," concluding instead that "person" is a "cluster of features." Because fetuses are in "the penumbra region" of the concept of "person," she rejects the use of "person" to resolve the abortion controversy. Even if the fetus is a person, she says, abortion would still be permissible under certain circumstances. And if it is not, there are other circumstances in which abortion would nevertheless be morally impermissible. She observes that even animals have rights and that if it is wrong to torture them or to cause them needless suffering, it is surely wrong to cause human fetuses needless suffering. Moreover, she suggests that certain psychological facts lead to conclusions that are rather different from those that are typically held by those who adopt a liberal position on the abortion controversy.

It should be noted that none of these cases or articles approaches the abortion question from a theological point of view. This is not because religious values and opinions are unimportant. They have clearly played an important role in setting public policy on the abortion question for many years and are likely to continue to do so. But this volume, devoted to philosophical discussions of various moral issues, is necessarily limited in the scope of materials that can be included.

MICHAEL TOOLEY 4

ABORTION AND INFANTICIDE

This essay deals with the question of the morality of abortion and infanticide.[1] The fundamental ethical objection traditionally advanced against these practices rests on the contention that human fetuses and infants have a right to life. It is this claim which will be the focus of attention here. The basic issue to be discussed, then, is what properties a thing must possess in order to have a serious right to life. My approach will be to set out and defend a basic moral principle specifying a condition an organism must satisfy if it is to have a serious right to life. It will be seen that this condition is not satisfied by human fetuses and infants, and thus that they do not have a right to life. So unless there are other substantial objections to abortion and infanticide, one is forced to conclude that these practices are morally acceptable ones. In contrast, it may turn out that our treatment of adult members of other species—cats, dogs, polar bears—is morally indefensible. For it is quite possible that such animals do possess properties that endow them with a right to life.

I. ABORTION AND INFANTICIDE

One reason the question of the morality of infanticide is worth examining is that it seems very difficult to formulate a completely satisfactory liberal position on abortion without coming to grips with the infanticide issue. The problem the liberal encounters is essentially that of specifying a cutoff point which is not arbitrary: at what stage in the development of a human being does it cease to be morally permissible to destroy it? It is important to be clear about the difficulty here. The conservative's objection is not that since there is a continuous line of development from a zygote to a newborn baby, one must conclude that if it is seriously wrong to destroy a newborn baby it is also seriously wrong to destroy a zygote or any intermediate stage in the development of a human being. His point is rather that if one says it is wrong to destroy a newborn baby but not a zygote or some intermediate stage in the development of a human being, one should be prepared to point to a

Michael Tooley, "Abortion and Infanticide," *Philosophy & Public Affairs* 2, no. 1 (Fall 1972). Copyright © 1972 by Princeton University Press. "Abortion and Infanticide: A Postscript," *The Rights and Wrongs of Abortion*, ed. Cohen, Nagel, Scanlon. Copyright © 1974 by Princeton University Press. Reprinted by permission of Princeton University Press.
1 I am grateful to a number of people, particularly the Editors of *Philosophy & Public Affairs*, Rodelia Hapke, and Walter Kaufmann, for their helpful comments. It should not, of course, be inferred that they share the views expressed in this paper.

morally relevant difference between a newborn baby and the earlier stage in the development of a human being.

Precisely the same difficulty can, of course, be raised for a person who holds that infanticide is morally permissible. The conservative will ask what morally relevant differences there are between an adult human being and a newborn baby. What makes it morally permissible to destroy a baby, but wrong to kill an adult? So the challenge remains. But I will argue that in this case there is an extremely plausible answer.

Reflecting on the morality of infanticide forces one to face up to this challenge. In the case of abortion a number of events—quickening or viability, for instance—might be taken as cutoff points, and it is easy to overlook the fact that none of these events involves any morally significant change in the developing human. In contrast, if one is going to defend infanticide, one has to get very clear about what makes something a person, what gives something a right to life.

One of the interesting ways in which the abortion issue differs from most other moral issues is that the plausible positions on abortion appear to be extreme positions. For if a human fetus is a person, one is inclined to say that, in general, one would be justified in killing it only to save the life of the mother.[2] Such is the extreme conservative position.[3] On the other hand, if the fetus is not a person, how can it be seriously wrong to destroy it? Why would one need to point to special circumstances to justify such action? The upshot is that there is no room for a moderate position on the issue of abortion such as one finds, for example, in the Model Penal Code recommendations.[4]

Aside from the light it may shed on the abortion question, the issue of infanticide is both interesting and important in its own right. The theoretical interest has been mentioned: it forces one to face up to the question of what makes something a person. The practical importance

[2] Judith Jarvis Thomson has argued with great force and ingenuity that this conclusion is mistaken. I will comment on her argument later. [See Judith Jarvis Thomson, "A Defense of Abortion," *Philosophy and Public Affairs* 1 (1971): 47–66. Reprinted in Marshall Cohen *et al.* ed., *The Rights and Wrongs of Abortion*. Princeton, N.J.: Princeton University Press, 1974, pp. 3–22. Page references are to the reprint.]

[3] While this is the position conservatives tend to hold, it is not clear that it is the position they ought to hold. For if the fetus is a person it is far from clear that it is permissible to destroy it to save the mother. Two moral principles lend support to the view that it is the fetus which should live. First, other things being equal, should not one give something to a person who has had less rather than to a person who has had more? The mother has had a chance to live, while the fetus has not. The choice is thus between giving the mother more of an opportunity to live while giving the fetus none at all and giving the fetus an opportunity to enjoy life while not giving the mother a further opportunity to do so. Surely fairness requires the latter. Secondly, since the fetus has a greater life expectancy than the mother, one is in effect distributing more goods by choosing the life of the fetus over the life of the mother.

The position I am here recommending to the conservative should not be confused with the official Catholic position. The Catholic Church holds that it is seriously wrong to kill a fetus directly even if failure to do so will result in the death of *both* the mother and the fetus. This perverse value judgment is not part of the conservative's position.

[4] Section 230.3 of the American Law Institute's *Model Penal Code* (Philadelphia, 1962). There is some interesting, though at times confused, discussion of the proposed code in *Model Penal Code—Tentative Draft No. 9* (Philadelphia, 1959), 146–162.

need not be labored. Most people would prefer to raise children who do not suffer from gross deformities or from severe physical, emotional, or intellectual handicaps. If it could be shown that there is no moral objection to infanticide the happiness of society could be significantly and justifiably increased.

Infanticide is also of interest because of the strong emotions it arouses. The typical reaction to infanticide is like the reaction to incest or cannibalism, or the reaction of previous generations to masturbation or oral sex. The response, rather than appealing to carefully formulated moral principles, is primarily visceral. When philosophers themselves respond in this way, offering no arguments, and dismissing infanticide out of hand, it is reasonable to suspect that one is dealing with a taboo rather than with a rational prohibition.[5] I shall attempt to show that this is in fact the case.

II. TERMINOLOGY: "PERSON" VERSUS "HUMAN BEING"

How is the term "person" to be interpreted? I shall treat the concept of a person as a purely moral concept, free of all descriptive content. Specifically, in my usage, the sentence "X is a person" will be synonymous with the sentence "X has a (serious) moral right to life."

This usage diverges slightly from what is perhaps the more common way of interpreting the term "person" when it is employed as a purely moral term, where to say that X is a person is to say that X has rights. If everything that had rights had a right to life, these interpretations would be extensionally equivalent. But I am inclined to think that it does not follow from acceptable moral principles that whatever has any rights at all has a right to life. My reason is this. Given the choice between being killed and being tortured for an hour, most adult humans would surely choose the latter. So it seems plausible to say it is worse to kill an adult human being than it is to torture him for an hour. In contrast, it seems to me that while it is not seriously wrong to kill a newborn kitten, it is seriously wrong to torture one for an hour. This *suggests* that newborn kittens may have a right not to be tortured without having a serious right to life. For it seems to be true that an individual has a right to something wherever it is the case that, if he wants that thing, it would be wrong for others to deprive him of it. Then if it is wrong to inflict a certain sensation upon a kitten if it doesn't want to experience that sensation, it will follow that the kitten has a right not to have sensation inflicted upon it.[6] I shall return to this

---

[5] A clear example of such an unwillingness to entertain seriously the possibility that moral judgments widely accepted in one's own society may nevertheless be incorrect is provided by Roger Wertheimer's superficial dismissal of infanticide on pages 25–26. [See Roger Wertheimer, "Understanding the Abortion Argument," *Philosophy and Public Affairs* 1 (1971): 67–95. Reprinted in Marshall Cohen *et al.* ed., *The Rights and Wrongs of Abortion*. Princeton, N.J.: Princeton University Press, 1974, pp. 23–51. Page references are to the reprint.]
[6] Compare the discussion of the concept of a right offered by Richard B. Brandt in his *Ethical Theory* (Englewood Cliffs, N.J., 1959), pp. 434–441. As Brandt points out,

example later. My point here is merely that it provides some reason for holding that it does not follow from acceptable moral principles that if something has any rights at all, it has a serious right to life.

There has been a tendency in recent discussions of abortion to use expressions such as "person" and "human being" interchangeably. B. A. Brody, for example, refers to the difficulty of determining "whether destroying the fetus constitutes the taking of a human life," and suggests it is very plausible that "the taking of a human life is an action that has bad consequences for him whose life is being taken." [7] When Brody refers to something as a human life he apparently construes this as entailing that the thing is a person. For if every living organism belonging to the species Homo sapiens counted as a human life, there would be no difficulty in determining whether a fetus inside a human mother was a human life.

The same tendency is found in Judith Jarvis Thomson's article, which opens with the statement: "Most opposition to abortion relies on the premise that the fetus is a human being, a person, from the moment of conception." [8] The same is true of Roger Wertheimer, who explicitly says: "First off I should note that the expressions 'a human life' 'a human being,' 'a person' are virtually interchangable in this context." [9]

The tendency to use expressions like "person" and "human being" interchangeably is an unfortunate one. For one thing, it tends to lend covert support to antiabortionist positions. Given such usage, one who holds a liberal view of abortion is put in the position of maintaining that fetuses, at least up to a certain point, are not human beings. Even philosophers are led astray by this usage. Thus Wertheimer says that "except for monstrosities, every member of our species is indubitably a person, a human being, at the very latest at birth." [10] Is it really *indubitable* that newborn babies are persons? Surely this is a wild contention. Wertheimer is falling prey to the confusion naturally engendered by the practice of using "person" and "human being" interchangeably. Another example of this is provided by Thomson: "I am inclined to think also that we shall probably have to agree that the fetus has already become a human person well before birth. Indeed, it comes as a surprise when one first learns how early in its life it begins to acquire human characteristics. By the tenth week, for example, it already has a face, arms and legs, fingers and toes; it has internal organs, and brain activity is detectable." [11] But what do such physiological characteristics have to do with the question of whether the organism is a person? Thomson, partly, I think, because of the unfortunate use of terminology, does not even raise this question. As a

---

some philosophers have maintained that only things that can *claim* rights can have rights. I agree with Brandt's view that "inability to claim does not destroy the right" (p. 440).
[7] B. A. Brody, "Abortion and the Law," *Journal of Philosophy*, LXVIII, no. 12(17 June 1971): 357–369. See pp. 357–358.
[8] P. 3.
[9] P. 25
[10] *Ibid.*
[11] Pp. 3–4.

result she virtually takes it for granted that there are some cases in which abortion is "positively indecent." [12]

There is a second reason why using "person" and "human being" interchangeably is unhappy philosophically. If one says that the dispute between pro- and antiabortionists centers on whether the fetus is a human, it is natural to conclude that it is essentially a disagreement about certain facts, a disagreement about what properties a fetus possesses. Thus Wertheimer says that "if one insists on using the raggy fact-value distinction, then one ought to say that the dispute is over a matter of fact in the sense in which it is a fact that the Negro slaves were human beings." [13] I shall argue that the two cases are not parallel, and that in the case of abortion what is primarily at stake is what moral principles one should accept. If one says that the central issue between conservatives and liberals in the abortion question is whether the fetus is a person, it is clear that the dispute may be either about what properties a thing must have in order to be a person, in order to have a right to life—a moral question—or about whether a fetus at a given stage of development as a matter of fact possesses the properties in question. The temptation to suppose that the disagreement must be a factual one is removed.

It should now be clear why the common practice of using expressions such as "person" and "human being" interchangeably in discussions of abortion is unfortunate. It would perhaps be best to avoid the term "human" altogether, employing instead some expression that is more naturally interpreted as referring to a certain type of biological organism characterized in physiological terms, such as "member of the species Homo sapiens." My own approach will be to use the term "human" only in contexts where it is not philosophically dangerous.

III. THE BASIC ISSUE: WHEN IS A MEMBER OF THE SPECIES HOMO SAPIENS A PERSON?

Settling the issue of the morality of abortion and infanticide will involve answering the following questions: What properties must something have to be a person, i.e., to have a serious right to life? At what point in the development of a member of the species Homo sapiens does the organism possess the properties that make it a person? The first question raises a moral issue. To answer it is to decide what basic [14] moral principles involving the ascription of a right to life one ought to accept. The second question raises a purely factual issue, since the properties in question are properties of a purely descriptive sort.

Some writers seem quite pessimistic about the possibility of resolving the question of the morality of abortion. Indeed, some have gone so far as to suggest that the question of whether the fetus is a per-

---

[12] P. 21.
[13] P. 34.
[14] A moral principle accepted by a person is *basic for him* if and only if his acceptance of it is not dependent upon any of his (nonmoral) factual beliefs. That is, no change in his factual beliefs would cause him to abandon the principle in question.

son is in principle unanswerable: "we seem to be stuck with the in-determinateness of the fetus' humanity." [15] An understanding of some of the sources of this pessimism will, I think, help us to tackle the problem. Let us begin by considering the similarity a number of people have noted between the issue of abortion and the issue of Negro slavery. The question here is why it should be more difficult to decide whether abortion and infanticide are acceptable than it was to decide whether slavery was acceptable. The answer seems to be that in the case of slavery there are moral principles of a quite uncontroversial sort that settle the issue. Thus most people would agree to some such principle as the following: No organism that has experiences, that is capable of thought and of using language, and that has harmed no one, should be made a slave. In the case of abortion, on the other hand, conditions that are generally agreed to be sufficient grounds for ascribing a right to life to something do not suffice to settle the issue. It is easy to specify other, purportedly sufficient conditions that will settle the issue, but no one has been successful in putting forward considerations that will convince others to accept those additional moral principles.

I do not share the general pessimism about the possibility of re-solving the issue of abortion and infanticide because I believe it is possible to point to a very plausible moral principle dealing with the question of *necessary* conditions for something's having a right to life, where the conditions in question will provide an answer to the question of the permissibility of abortion and infanticide.

There is a second cause of pessimism that should be noted before proceeding. It is tied up with the fact that the development of an organism is one of gradual and continuous change. Given this continuity, how is one to draw a line at one point and declare it permissible to destroy a member of Homo sapiens up to, but not beyond, that point? Won't there be an arbitrariness about any point that is chosen? I will return to this worry shortly. It does not present a serious difficulty once the basic moral principles relevant to the ascription of a right to life to an individual are established.

Let us turn now to the first and most fundamental question: What properties must something have in order to be a person, i.e., to have a serious right to life? The claim I wish to defend is this: An organism possesses a serious right to life only if it possesses the concept of a self as a continuing subject of experiences and other mental states, and believes that it is itself such a continuing entity.

My basic argument in support of this claim, which I will call the self-consciousness requirement, will be clearest, I think, if I first offer a simplified version of the argument, and then consider a modification that seems desirable. The simplified version of my argument is this. To ascribe a right to an individual is to assert something about the prima facie obligations of other individuals to act, or to refrain from acting, in certain ways. However, the obligations in question are conditional ones, being dependent upon the existence of certain desires of the in-dividual to whom the right is ascribed. Thus if an individual asks one

[15] Wertheimer, p. 44.

to destroy something to which he has a right, one does not violate his right to that thing if one proceeds to destroy it. This suggests the following analysis: "A has a right to X" is roughly synonymous with "If A desires X, then others are under a prima facie obligation to refrain from actions that would deprive him of it." [16]

Although this analysis is initially plausible, there are reasons for thinking it not entirely correct. I will consider these later. Even here, however, some expansion is necessary, since there are features of the concept of a right that are important in the present context, and that ought to be dealt with more explicitly. In particular, it seems to be a conceptual truth that things that lack consciousness, such as ordinary machines, cannot have rights. Does this conceptual truth follow from the above analysis of the concept of a right? The answer depends on how the term "desire" is interpreted. If one adopts a completely behavioristic interpretation of "desire," so that a machine that searches for an electrical outlet in order to get its batteries recharged is described as having a desire to be recharged, then it will not follow from this analysis that objects that lack consciousness cannot have rights. On the other hand, if "desire" is interpreted in such a way that desires are states necessarily standing in some sort of relationship to states of consciousness, it will follow from the analysis that a machine that is not capable of being conscious, and consequently of having desires, cannot have any rights. I think those who defend analyses of the concept of a right along the lines of this one do have in mind an interpretation of the term "desire" that involves reference to something more than behavioral dispositions. However, rather than relying on this, it seems preferable to make such an interpretation explicit. The following analysis is a natural way of doing that: "A has a right to X" is roughly synonymous with "A is the sort of thing that is a subject of experiences and other mental states, A is capable of desiring X, and if A does desire X, then others are under a prima facie obligation to refrain from actions that would deprive him of it."

The next step in the argument is basically a matter of applying this analysis to the concept of a right to life. Unfortunately the expression "right to life" is not entirely a happy one, since it suggests that the right in question concerns the continued existence of a biological organism. That this is incorrect can be brought out by considering possible ways of violating an individual's right to life. Suppose, for example, that by some technology of the future the brain of an adult human were to be completely reprogrammed, so that the organism wound up with memories (or rather, apparent memories), beliefs, attitudes, and personality traits completely different from those associated with it before it was subjected to reprogramming. In such a case one would surely say that an individual had been destroyed, that an adult human's rights to life had been violated, even though no biological organism had been killed. This example shows that the expression "right to life" is misleading, since what one is really concerned about is not just the continued existence of a biological organism,

---

[16] Again, compare the analysis defended by Brandt in *Ethical Theory*, pp. 434–441.

but the right of a subject of experiences and other mental states to continue to exist.

Given this more precise description of the right with which we are here concerned, we are now in a position to apply the analysis of the concept of a right stated above. When we do so we find that the statement "A has a right to continue to exist as a subject of experiences and other mental states" is roughly synonymous with the statement "A is a subject of experiences and other mental states, A is capable of desiring to continue to exist as a subject of experiences and other mental states, and if A does desire to continue to exist as such an entity, then others are under a prima facie obligation not to prevent him from doing so."

The final stage in the argument is simply a matter of asking what must be the case if something is to be capable of having a desire to continue existing as a subject of experiences and other mental states. The basic point here is that the desires a thing can have are limited by the concepts it possesses. For the fundamental way of describing a given desire is as a desire that a certain proposition be true.[17] Then, since one cannot desire that a certain proposition be true unless one understands it, and since one cannot understand it without possessing the concepts involved in it, it follows that the desires one can have are limited by the concepts one possesses. Applying this to the present case results in the conclusion that an entity cannot be the sort of thing that can desire that a subject of experiences and other mental states exist unless it possesses the concept of such a subject. Moreover, an entity cannot desire that it itself *continue* existing as a subject of experiences and other mental states unless it believes that it is now such a subject. This completes the justification of the claim that it is a necessary condition of something's having a serious right to life that it possess the concept of a self as a continuing subject of experiences, and that it believe that it is itself such an entity.

Let us now consider a modification in the above argument that seems desirable. This modification concerns the crucial conceptual claim advanced about the relationship between ascription of rights and ascription of the corresponding desires. Certain situations suggest that there may be exceptions to the claim that if a person doesn't desire something, one cannot violate his right to it. There are three types of situations that call this claim into question: (i) situations in which an individual's desires reflect a state of emotional disturbance; (ii) situations in which a previously conscious individual is temporarily unconscious; (iii) situations in which an individual's desires have been distorted by conditioning or by indoctrination.

As an example of the first, consider a case in which an adult human

---

[17] In everyday life one often speaks of desiring things, such as an apple or a newspaper. Such talk is elliptical, the context together with one's ordinary beliefs serving to make it clear that one wants to eat the apple and read the newspaper. To say that what one desires is that a certain proposition be true should not be construed as involving any particular ontological commitment. The point is merely that it is sentences such as "John wants it to be the case that he is eating an apple in the next few minutes" that provide a completely explicit description of a person's desires. If one fails to use such sentences one can be badly misled about what concepts are presupposed by a particular desire.

falls into a state of depression which his psychiatrist recognizes as temporary. While in the state he tells people he wishes he were dead. His psychiatrist, accepting the view that there can be no violation of an individual's right to life unless the individual has a desire to live, decides to let his patient have his way and kills him. Or consider a related case in which one person gives another a drug that produces a state of temporary depression; the recipient expresses a wish that he were dead. The person who administered the drug then kills him. Doesn't one want to say in both these cases that the agent did something seriously wrong in killing the other person? And isn't the reason the action was seriously wrong in each case the fact that it violated the individual's right to life? If so, the right to life cannot be linked with a desire to live in the way claimed above.

The second set of situations are ones in which an individual is unconscious for some reason—that is, he is sleeping, or drugged, or in a temporary coma. Does an individual in such a state have any desires? People do sometimes say that an unconscious individual wants something, but it might be argued that if such talk is not to be simply false it must be interpreted as actually referring to the desires the individual *would* have if he were now conscious. Consequently, if the analysis of the concept of a right proposed above were correct, it would follow that one does not violate an individual's right if one takes his car, or kills him, while he is asleep.

Finally, consider situations in which an individual's desires have been distorted, either by inculcation of irrational beliefs or by direct conditioning. Thus an individual may permit someone to kill him because he has been convinced that if he allows himself to be sacrificed to the gods he will be gloriously rewarded in a life to come. Or an individual may be enslaved after first having been conditioned to desire a life of slavery. Doesn't one want to say that in the former case an individual's right to life has been violated, and in the latter his right to freedom?

Situations such as these strongly suggest that even if an individual doesn't want something, it is still possible to violate his right to it. Some modification of the earlier account of the concept of a right thus seems in order. The analysis given covers, I believe, the paradigmatic cases of violation of an individual's rights, but there are other, secondary cases where one also wants to say that someone's right has been violated which are not included.

Precisely how the revised analysis should be formulated is unclear. Here it will be sufficient merely to say that, in view of the above, an individual's right to X can be violated not only when he desires X, but also when he *would* now desire X were it not for one of the following: (i) he is in an emotionally unbalanced state; (ii) he is temporarily unconscious; (iii) he has been conditioned to desire the absence of X.

The critical point now is that, even given this extension of the conditions under which an individual's right to something can be violated, it is still true that one's right to something can be violated only when one has the conceptual capability of desiring the thing in question. For example, an individual who would now desire not to be a slave if he weren't emotionally unbalanced, or if he weren't temporarily un-conscious, or if he hadn't previously been conditioned to want to be a slave, must possess the concepts involved in the desire not to be a slave. Since it is really only the conceptual capability presupposed by the desire to continue existing as a subject of experiences and other mental states, and not the desire itself, that enters into the above argument, the modifi-cation required in the account of the conditions under which an in-dividual's rights can be violated does not undercut my defense of the self-consciousness requirement.[18]

To sum up, my argument has been that having a right to life presupposes that one is capable of desiring to continue existing as a subject of experiences and other mental states. This in turn presup-poses both that one has the concept of such a continuing entity and that one believes that one is oneself such an entity. So an entity that lacks such a consciousness of itself as a continuing subject of mental states does not have a right to life.

It would be natural to ask at this point whether satisfaction of this requirement is not only necessary but also sufficient to ensure that a thing has a right to life. I am inclined to an affirmative answer. How-ever, the issue is not urgent in the present context, since as long as the requirement is in fact a necessary one we have the basis of an adequate defense of abortion and infanticide. If an organism must satisfy some other condition before it has a serious right to life, the result will merely be that the interval during which infanticide is morally permissible may be somewhat longer. Although the point at which an organism first achieves self-consciousness and hence the capacity of desiring to continue existing as a subject of experiences and other mental states may be a theoretically incorrect cutoff point, it is at least a morally safe one: any error it involves is on the side of caution.

IV. SOME CRITICAL COMMENTS ON ALTERNATIVE PROPOSALS

I now want to compare the line of demarcation I am proposing with the cutoff points traditionally advanced in discussions of abortion. My fundamental claim will be that none of these cutoff points can be de-fended by appeal to plausible, basic moral principles. The main sug-gestions as to the point past which it is seriously wrong to destroy

---

[18] There are, however, situations other than those discussed here which might seem to count against the claim that a person cannot have a right unless he is conceptually capable of having the corresponding desire. Can't a young child, for example, have a right to an estate, even though he may not be conceptually capable of wanting the estate? It is clear that such situations have to be carefully considered if one is to arrive at a satisfactory account of the concept of a right. My inclination is to say that the correct description is not that the child now has a right to the estate, but that he will come to have such a right when he is mature, and that in the meantime no one else has a right to the estate. My reason for saying that the child does not now have a right to the estate is that he cannot now do things with the estate, such as selling it or giving it away, that he will be able to do later on.

something that will develop into an adult member of the species Homo sapiens are these: (a) conception; (b) the attainment of human form; (c) the achievement of the ability to move about spontaneously; (d) viability; (e) birth.[19] The corresponding moral principles suggested by these cutoff points are as follows: (1) It is seriously wrong to kill an organism, from a zygote on, that belongs to the species Homo sapiens. (2) It is seriously wrong to kill an organism that belongs to Homo sapiens and that has achieved human form. (3) It is seriously wrong to kill an organism that is a member of Homo sapiens and that is capable of spontaneous movement. (4) It is seriously wrong to kill an organism that belongs to Homo sapiens and that is capable of existing outside the womb. (5) It is seriously wrong to kill an organism that is a member of Homo sapiens that is no longer in the womb.

My first comment is that it would not do *simply* to omit the reference to membership in the species Homo sapiens from the above principles, with the exception of principle (2). For then the principles would be applicable to animals in general, and one would be forced to conclude that it was seriously wrong to abort a cat fetus, or that it was seriously wrong to abort a motile cat fetus, and so on.

The second and crucial comment is that none of the five principles given above can plausibly be viewed as a *basic* moral principle. To accept any of them as such would be akin to accepting as a basic moral principle the proposition that it is morally permissible to enslave black members of the species Homo sapiens but not white members. Why should it be seriously wrong to kill an unborn member of the species Homo sapiens but not seriously wrong to kill an unborn kitten? Difference in species is not per se a morally relevant difference. If one holds that it is seriously wrong to kill an unborn member of the species Homo sapiens but not an unborn kitten, one should be prepared to point to some property that is morally significant and that is possessed by unborn members of Homo sapiens but not by unborn kittens. Similarly, such a property must be identified if one believes it seriously wrong to kill unborn members of Homo sapiens that have achieved viability but not seriously wrong to kill unborn kittens that have achieved that state.

What property might account for such a difference? That is to say, what *basic* moral principles might a person who accepts one of these five principles appeal to in support of his secondary moral judgment? Why should events such as the achievement of human form, or the achievement of the ability to move about, or the achievement of viability, or birth serve to endow something with a right to life? What the liberal must do is to show that these events involve changes, or are associated with changes, that are morally relevant.

Let us now consider reasons why the events involved in cutoff points (b) through (e) are not morally relevant, beginning with the last two: viability and birth. The fact that an organism is not physiologically

[19] Another frequent suggestion as to the cutoff point not listed here is quickening. I omit it because it seems clear that if abortion after quickening is wrong, its wrongness must be tied up with the motility of the fetus, not with the mother's awareness of the fetus' ability to move about.

dependent upon another organism, or is capable of such physiological independence, is surely irrelevant to whether the organism has a right to life. In defense of this contention, consider a speculative case where a fetus is able to learn a language while in the womb. One would surely not say that the fetus had no right to life until it emerged from the womb, or until it was capable of existing outside the womb. A less speculative example is the case of Siamese twins who have learned to speak. One doesn't want to say that since one of the twins would die were the two to be separated, it therefore has no right to life. Consequently it seems difficult to disagree with the conservative's claim that an organism which lacks a right to life before birth or before becoming viable cannot acquire this right immediately upon birth or upon becoming viable.

This does not, however, completely rule out viability as a line of demarcation. For instead of defending viability as a cutoff point on the ground that only then does a fetus acquire a right to life, it is possible to argue rather that when one organism is physiologically dependent upon another, the former's right to life may conflict with the latter's right to use its body as it will, and moreover, that the latter's right to do what it wants with its body may often take precedence over the other organism's right to life. Thomson has defended this view: "I am arguing only that having a right to life does not guarantee having either a right to the use of or a right to be allowed continued use of another person's body—even if one needs it for life itself. So the right to life will not serve the opponents of abortion in the very simple and clear way in which they seem to have thought it would." [20] I believe that Thomson is right in contending that philosophers have been altogether too casual in assuming that if one grants the fetus a serious right to life, one must accept a conservative position on abortion.[21] I also think the only defense of viability as a cutoff point which has any hope of success at all is one based on the considerations she advances. I doubt very much, however, that this defense of abortion is ultimately tenable. I think that one can grant even stronger assumptions than those made by Thomson and still argue persuasively for a semiconservative view. What I have in mind is this. Let it be granted, for the sake of argument, that a woman's right to free her body of parasites which will inhibit her freedom of action and possibly impair her health is stronger than the parasite's right to life, and is so even if the parasite has as much right to life as an adult human. One can still argue that abortion ought not to be permitted. For if A's right is stronger than B's, and it is impossible to satisfy both, it does not follow that A's should be satisfied rather than B's. It may be possible to compensate A if his right isn't satisfied, but impossible to compensate B if his right isn't satisfied. In such a case the best thing to do may be to satisfy B's claim and to compensate A. Abortion may be a case in point. If the fetus has a right to life and the right is not satisfied, there is certainly no way the fetus

[20] P. 12.
[21] A good example of a failure to probe this issue is provided by Brody's "Abortion and the Law."

can be compensated. On the other hand, if the woman's right to rid her body of harmful and annoying parasites is not satisfied, she can be compensated. Thus it would seem that the just thing to do would be to prohibit abortion, but to compensate women for the burden of carrying a parasite to term. Then, however, we are back at a (modified) conservative position.[22] Our conclusion must be that it appears unlikely there is any satisfactory defense either of viability or of birth as cut-off points.

Let us now consider the third suggested line of demarcation, the achievement of the power to move about spontaneously. It might be argued that acquiring this power is a morally relevant event on the grounds that there is a connection between the concept of an agent and the concept of a person, and being motile is an indication that a thing is an agent.[23]

It is difficult to respond to this suggestion unless it is made more specific. Given that one's interest here is in defending a certain cutoff point, it is natural to interpret the proposal as suggesting that motility is a necessary condition of an organism's having a right to life. But this won't do, because one certainly wants to ascribe a right to life to adult humans who are completely paralyzed. Maybe the suggestion is rather that motility is a sufficient condition of something's having a right to life. However, it is clear that motility alone is not sufficient, since this would imply that all animals, and also certain machines, have a right to life. Perhaps, then, the most reasonable interpretation of the claim is that motility together with some other property is a sufficient condition of something's having a right to life, where the other property will have to be a property possessed by unborn members of the species Homo sapiens but not by unborn members of other familiar species.

The central question, then, is what this other property is. Until one is told, it is very difficult to evaluate either the moral claim that motility together with that property is a sufficient basis for ascribing to an organism a right to life or the factual claim that a motile human fetus possesses that property while a motile fetus belonging to some other species does not. A conservative would presumably reject motility as a cutoff point by arguing that whether an organism has a right to life depends only upon its potentialities, which are of course not changed by its becoming motile. If, on the other hand, one favors a liberal view of abortion, I think that one can attack this third suggested cutoff point, in its unspecified form, only by determining what properties are necessary, or what properties sufficient, for an individual to have a right to life. Thus, I would base my rejection of motility as a cutoff point on my claim, defended above, that a necessary condition of an organism's possessing a right to life is that it conceive of itself as a continuing subject of experiences and other mental states.

The second suggested cutoff point—the development of a recognizably human form—can be dismissed fairly quickly. I have already re-

22 Admittedly the modification is a substantial one, since given a society that refused to compensate women, a woman who had an abortion would not be doing anything wrong.
23 Compare Wertheimer's remarks, p. 35.

marked that membership in a particular species is not itself a morally relevant property. For it is obvious that if we encountered other "rational animals," such as Martians, the fact that their physiological makeup was very different from our own would not be grounds for denying them a right to life.[24] Similarly, it is clear that the development of human form is not in itself a morally relevant event. Nor do there seem to be any grounds for holding that there is some other change, associated with this event, that is morally relevant. The appeal of this second cutoff point is, I think, purely emotional.

The overall conclusion seems to be that it is very difficult to defend the cutoff points traditionally advanced by those who advocate either a moderate or a liberal position on abortion. The reason is that there do not seem to be any basic moral principles one can appeal to in support of the cutoff points in question. We must now consider whether the conservative is any better off.

V. REFUTATION OF THE CONSERVATIVE POSITION

Many have felt that the conservative's position is more defensible than the liberal's because the conservative can point to the gradual and continuous development of an organism as it changes from a zygote to an adult human being. He is then in a position to argue that it is morally arbitrary for the liberal to draw a line at some point in this continuous process and to say that abortion is permissible before, but not after, that particular point. The liberal's reply would presumably be that the emphasis upon the continuity of the process is misleading. What the conservative is really doing is simply challenging the liberal to specify the properties a thing must have in order to be a person, and to show that the developing organism does acquire the properties at the point selected by the liberal. The liberal may then reply that the difficulty he has meeting this challenge should not be taken as grounds for rejecting his position. For the conservative cannot meet this challenge either; the conservative is equally unable to say what properties something must have if it is to have a right to life.

Although this rejoinder does not dispose of the conservative's argument, it is not without bite. For defenders of the view that abortion is always wrong have failed to face up to the question of the basic moral principles on which their position rests. They have been content to assert the wrongness of killing any organism, from a zygote on, if that organism is a member of the species Homo sapiens. But they have overlooked the point that this cannot be an acceptable *basic* moral principle, since difference in species is not in itself a morally relevant difference. The conservative can reply, however, that it is possible to defend his position—but not the liberal's—*without* getting clear about the pro-

[24] This requires qualification. If their central nervous systems were radically different from ours, it might be thought that one would not be justified in ascribing to them mental states of an experiential sort. And then, since it seems to be a conceptual truth that only things having experiential states can have rights, one would be forced to conclude that one was not justified in ascribing any rights to them.

perties a thing must possess if it is to have a right to life. The conservative's defense will rest upon the following two claims: first, that there is a property, even if one is unable to specify what it is, that (i) is possessed by adult humans, and (ii) endows any organism possessing it with a serious right to life. Second, that if there are properties which satisfy (i) and (ii) above, at least one of those properties will be such that any organism potentially possessing that property has a serious right to life even now, simply by virtue of that potentiality, where an organism possesses a property potentially if it will come to have that property in the normal course of its development. The second claim—which I shall refer to as the potentiality principle—is critical to the conservative's defense. Because of it he is able to defend his position without deciding what properties a thing must possess in order to have a right to life. It is enough to know that adult members of Homo sapiens do have such a right. For then one can conclude that any organism which belongs to the species Homo sapiens, from a zygote on, must also have a right to life by virtue of the potentiality principle.

The liberal, by contrast, cannot mount a comparable argument. He cannot defend his position without offering at least a partial answer to the question of what properties a thing must possess in order to have a right to life.

The importance of the potentiality principle, however, goes beyond the fact that it provides support for the conservative's position. If the principle is unacceptable, then so is his position. For if the conservative cannot defend the view that an organism's having certain potentialities is sufficient grounds for ascribing to it a right to life, his claim that a fetus which is a member of Homo sapiens has a right to life can be attacked as follows. The reason an adult member of Homo sapiens has a right to life, but an infant ape does not, is that there are certain psychological properties which the former possesses and the latter lacks. Now, even if one is unsure exactly what these psychological properties are, it is clear that an organism in the early stages of development from a zygote into an adult member of Homo sapiens does not possess these properties. One need merely compare a human fetus with an ape fetus. What mental states does the former enjoy that the latter does not? Surely it is reasonable to hold that there are no significant differences in their respective mental lives—assuming that one wishes to ascribe any mental states at all to such organisms. (Does a zygote have a mental life? Does it have experiences? Or beliefs? Or desires?) There are, of course, physiological differences, but these are not in themselves morally significant. *If* one held that potentialities were relevant to the ascription of a right to life, one could argue that the physiological differences, though not morally significant in themselves, are morally significant by virtue of their causal consequences: they will lead to later psychological differences that are morally relevant, and for this reason · the physiological differences are themselves morally significant. But if the potentiality principle is not available, this line of argument cannot be used, and there will then be no differences between a human fetus and an ape fetus that the conservative can use as grounds for ascribing a serious right to life to the former but not to the ·latter.

It is therefore tempting to conclude that the conservative view of abortion is acceptable if and only if the potentiality principle is acceptable. But to say that the conservative position can be defended if the potentiality principle is acceptable is to assume that the argument is over once it is granted that the fetus has a right to life, and, as was noted above, Thomson has shown that there are serious grounds for questioning this assumption. In any case, the important point here is that the conservative position on abortion is acceptable *only if* the potentiality principle is sound.

One way to attack the potentiality principle is simply to argue in support of the self-consciousness requirement—the claim that only an organism that conceives of itself as a continuing subject of experiences has a right to life. For this requirement, when taken together with the claim that there is at least one property, possessed by adult humans, such that any organism possessing it has a serious right to life, entails the denial of the potentiality principle. Or at least this is so if we add the uncontroversial empirical claim that an organism that will in the normal course of events develop into an adult human does not from the very beginning of its existence possess a concept of a continuing subject of experiences together with a belief that it is itself such an entity.

I think it best, however, to scrutinize the potentiality principle itself, and not to base one's case against it simply on the self-consciousness requirement. Perhaps the first point to note is that the potentiality principle should not be confused with principles such as the following: the value of an object is related to the value of the things into which it can develop. This "valuation principle" is rather vague. There are ways of making it more precise, but we need not consider these here. Suppose now that one were to speak not of a right to life, but of the value of life. It would then be easy to make the mistake of thinking that the valuation principle was relevant to the potentiality principle— indeed, that it entailed it. But an individual's right to life is not based on the value of his life. To say that the world would be better off if it contained fewer people is not to say that it would be right to achieve such a better world by killing some of the present inhabitants. *If* having a right to life were a matter of a thing's value, then a thing's potentialities, being connected with its expected value, would clearly be relevant to the question of what rights it had. Conversely, once one realizes that a thing's rights are not a matter of its value, I think it becomes clear that an organism's potentialities are irrelevant to the question of whether it has a right to life.

But let us now turn to the task of finding a direct refutation of the potentiality principle. The basic issue is this. Is there any property J which satisfies the following conditions: (1) There is a property K such that any individual possessing property K has a right to life, and there is a scientific law L to the effect that any organism possessing property J will in the normal course of events come to possess property K at some later time. (2) Given the relationship between property J and property K just described, anything possessing property J has a right to life. (3) If property J were not related to property K in the way indicated, it would not be the case that anything possessing property J thereby had a right to life. In short, the question is whether there is a property J that bestows a right to life on an organism *only because* J stands in a certain causal relationship to a second property K, which is such that anything possessing that property ipso facto has a right to life.

My argument turns upon the following critical principle: Let C be a causal process that normally leads to outcome E. Let A be an action that initiates process C, and B be an action involving a minimal expenditure of energy that stops process C before outcome E occurs. Assume further that actions A and B do not have any other consequences, and that E is the only morally significant outcome of process C. Then there is no moral difference between intentionally performing action B and intentionally refraining from performing action A, assuming identical motivation in both cases. This principle, which I shall refer to as the moral symmetry principle with respect to action and inaction, would be rejected by some philosophers. They would argue that there is an important distinction to be drawn between "what we owe people in the form of aid and what we owe them in the way of non-interference," [25] and that the latter, "negative duties," are duties that it is more serious to neglect than the former, "positive" ones. This view arises from an intuitive response to examples such as the following. Even if it is wrong not to send food to starving people in other parts of the world, it is more wrong still to kill someone. And isn't the conclusion, then, that one's obligation to refrain from killing someone is a more serious obligation than one's obligation to save lives?

I want to argue that this is not the correct conclusion. I think it is tempting to draw this conclusion if one fails to consider the motivation that is likely to be associated with the respective actions. If someone performs an action he knows will kill someone else, this will usually be grounds for concluding that he wanted to kill the person in question. In contrast, failing to help someone may indicate only apathy, laziness, selfishness, or an amoral outlook: the fact that a person knowingly allows another to die will not normally be grounds for concluding that he desired that person's death. Someone who knowingly kills another is more likely to be seriously defective from a moral point of view than someone who fails to save another's life.

If we are not to be led to false conclusions by our intuitions about certain cases, we must explicitly assume identical motivations in the two situations. Compare, for example, the following: (1) Jones sees that Smith will be killed by a bomb unless he warns him. Jones's reaction is: "How lucky, it will save me the trouble of killing Smith myself." So Jones allows Smith to be killed by the bomb, even though he could easily have warned him. (2) Jones wants Smith dead, and therefore shoots him. Is one to say there is a significant difference between the wrongness of Jones's behavior in these two cases? Surely not. This shows the mistake of drawing a distinction between positive duties and negative duties and holding that the latter impose stricter obligations than the former. The difference in our intuitions about situations that involve

25 Philippa Foot, "The Problem of Abortion and the Doctrine of the Double Effect," *The Oxford Review* 5 (1967): 5–15. See the discussion on pp. 11ff.

giving aid to others and corresponding situations that involve not interfering with others is to be explained by reference to probable differences in the motivations operating in the two situations, and not by reference to a distinction between positive and negative duties. For once it is specified that the motivation is the same in the two situations, we realize that inaction is as wrong in the one case as action is in the other.

There is another point that may be relevant. Action involves effort, while inaction usually does not. It usually does not require any effort on my part to refrain from killing someone, but saving someone's life will require an expenditure of energy. One must then ask how large a sacrifice a person is morally required to make to save the life or another. If the sacrifice of time and energy is quite large it may be that one is not morally obliged to save the life another in that situation. Superficial reflection upon such cases might easily lead us to introduce the distinction between positive and negative duties, but again it is clear that this would be a mistake. The point is not that one has a greater duty to refrain from killing others than to perform positive actions that will save them. It is rather that positive actions require effort, and this means that in deciding what to do a person has to take into account his own right to do what he wants with his life, and not only the other person's right to life. To avoid this confusion, we should confine ourselves to comparisons between situations in which the positive action involves minimal effort.

The moral symmetry principle, as formulated above, explicitly takes these two factors into account. It applies only to pairs of situations in which the motivations are identical and the positive action involves minimal effort. Without these restrictions, the principle would be open to serious objection; with them, it seems perfectly acceptable. For the central objection to it rests on the claim that we must distinguish positive from negative duties and recognize that negative duties impose stronger obligations than positive ones. I have tried to show how this claim derives from an unsound account of our moral intuitions about certain situations.

My argument against the potentiality principle can now be stated. Suppose at some future time a chemical were to be discovered which when injected into the brain of a kitten would cause the kitten to develop into a cat possessing a brain of the sort possessed by humans, and consequently into a cat having all the psychological capabilities characteristic of adult humans. Such cats would be able to think, to use language, and so on. Now it would surely be morally indefensible in such a situation to ascribe a serious right to life to members of the species Homo sapiens without also ascribing it to cats that have undergone such a process of development: there would be no morally significant differences.

Secondly, it would not be seriously wrong to refrain from injecting a newborn kitten with the special chemical, and to kill it instead. The fact that one could initiate a causal process that would transform a kitten into an entity that would eventually possess properties such that anything possessing them ipso facto has a serious right to life does not mean that the kitten has a serious right to life even before it has been subjected to the process of injection and transformation. The possibility of transforming kittens into persons will not make it any more wrong to kill newborn kittens than it is now.

Thirdly, in view of the symmetry principle, if it is not seriously wrong to refrain from initiating such a causal process, neither is it seriously wrong to interfere with such a process. Suppose a kitten is accidentally injected with the chemical. As long as it has not yet developed those properties that in themselves endow something with a right to life, there cannot be anything wrong with interfering with the causal process and preventing the development of the properties in question. Such interference might be accomplished either by injecting the kitten with some "neutralizing" chemical or simply by killing it.

But if it is not seriously wrong to destroy an injected kitten which will naturally develop the properties that bestow a right to life, neither can it be seriously wrong to destroy a member of Homo sapiens which lacks such properties, but will naturally come to have them. The potentialities are the same in both cases. The only difference is that in the case of a human fetus the potentialities have been present from the beginning of the organism's development, while in the case of the kitten they have been present only from the time it was injected with the special chemical. This difference in the time at which the potentialities were acquired is a morally irrelevant difference.

It should be emphasized that I am not here assuming that a human fetus does not possess properties which in themselves, and irrespective of their causal relationships to other properties, provide grounds for ascribing a right to life to whatever possesses them. The point is merely that if it is seriously wrong to kill something, the reason cannot be that the thing will later acquire properties that in themselves provide something with a right to life.

Finally, it is reasonable to believe that there are properties possessed by adult members of Homo sapiens which establish their right to life, and also that any normal human fetus will come to possess those properties shared by adult humans. But it has just been shown that if it is wrong to kill a human fetus, it cannot be because of its potentialities. One is therefore forced to conclude that the conservative's potentiality principle is false.

In short, anyone who wants to defend the potentiality principle must either argue against the moral symmetry principle or hold that in a world in which kittens could be transformed into "rational animals" it would be seriously wrong to kill newborn kittens. It is hard to believe there is much to be said for the latter moral claim. Consequently one expects the conservative's rejoinder to be directed against the symmetry principle. While I have not attempted to provide a thorough defense of that principle, I have tried to show that what seems to be the most important objection to it—the one that appeals to a distinction between positive and negative duties—is based on a superficial analysis of our moral intuitions. I believe that a more thorough examination of the symmetry principle would show it to be sound. If so, we should reject the potentiality principle, and the conservative position on abortion as well.

VI. SUMMARY AND CONCLUSIONS

Let us return now to my basic claim, the self-consciousness requirement: An organism possesses a serious right to life only if it possesses the concept of a self as a continuing subject of experiences and other mental states, and believes that it is itself such a continuing entity. My defense of this claim has been twofold. I have offered a direct argument in support of it, and I have tried to show that traditional conservative and liberal views on abortion and infanticide, which involve a rejection of it, are unsound. I now want to mention one final reason why my claim should be accepted. Consider the example mentioned in section II—that of killing, as opposed to torturing, newborn kittens. I suggested there that while in the case of adult humans most people would consider it worse to kill an individual than to torture him for an hour, we do not usually view the killing of a newborn kitten as morally outrageous, although we would regard someone who tortured a newborn kitten for an hour as heinously evil. I pointed out that a possible conclusion that might be drawn from this is that newborn kittens have a right not to be tortured, but do not have a serious right to life. If this is the correct conclusion, how is one to explain it? One merit of the self-consciousness requirement is that it provides an explanation of this situation. The reason a newborn kitten does not have a right to life is explained by the fact that it does not possess the concept of a self. But how is one to explain the kitten's having a right not to be tortured? The answer is that a desire not to suffer pain can be ascribed to something without assuming that it has any concept of a continuing self. For while something that lacks the concept of a self cannot desire that a self not suffer, it can desire that a given sensation not exist. The state desired—the absence of a particular sensation, or of sensations of a certain sort—can be described in a purely phenomenalistic language, and hence without the concept of a continuing self. So long as the newborn kitten possesses the relevant phenomenal concepts, it can truly be said to desire that a certain sensation not exist. So we can ascribe to it a right not to be tortured even though, since it lacks the concept of a continuing self, we cannot ascribe to it a right to life.

This completes my discussion of the basic moral principles involved in the issue of abortion and infanticide. But I want to comment upon an important factual question, namely, at what point an organism comes to possess the concept of a self as a continuing subject of experiences and other mental states, together with the belief that it is itself such a continuing entity. This is obviously a matter for detailed psychological investigation, but everyday observation makes it perfectly clear, I believe, that a newborn baby does not possess the concept of a continuing self, any more than a newborn kitten possesses such a concept. If so, infanticide during a time interval shortly after birth must be morally acceptable.

But where is the line to be drawn? What is the cutoff point? If one maintained, as some philosophers have, that an individual possesses concepts only if he can express these concepts in language, it would be a matter of everyday observation whether or not a given organism possessed the concept of a continuing self. Infanticide would then be permissible up to the time an organism learned how to use certain expressions. However, I think the claim that acquisition of concepts is dependent on acquisition of language is mistaken. For example, one wants to ascribe mental states of a conceptual sort—such as beliefs and desires—to organisms that are incapable of learning a language. This issue of prelinguistic understanding is clearly outside the scope of this discussion. My point is simply that *if* an organism can acquire concepts without thereby acquiring a way of expressing those concepts linguistically, the question of whether a given organism possesses the concept of a self as a continuing subject of experiences and other mental states, together with the belief that it is itself such a continuing entity, may be a question that requires fairly subtle experimental techniques to answer.

If this view of the matter is roughly correct, there are two worries one is left with at the level of practical moral decisions, one of which may turn out to be deeply disturbing. The lesser worry is where the line is to be drawn in the case of infanticide. It is not troubling because there is no serious need to know the exact point at which a human infant acquires a right to life. For in the vast majority of cases in which infanticide is desirable, its desirability will be apparent within a short time after birth. Since it is virtually certain that an infant at such a stage of its development does not possess the concept of a continuing self, and thus does not possess a serious right to life, there is excellent reason to believe that infanticide is morally permissible in most cases where it is otherwise desirable. The practical moral problem can thus be satisfactorily handled by choosing some period of time, such as a week after birth, as the interval during which infanticide will be permitted. This interval could then be modified once psychologists have established the point at which a human organism comes to believe that it is a continuing subject of experiences and other mental states.

The troubling worry is whether adult animals belonging to species other than Homo sapiens may not also possess a serious right to life. For once one says that an organism can possess the concept of a continuing self, together with the belief that it is itself such an entity, without having any way of expressing that concept and that belief linguistically, one has to face up to the question of whether animals may not possess properties that bestow a serious right to life upon them. The suggestion itself is a familiar one, and one that most of us are accustomed to dismiss very casually. The line of thought advanced here suggests that this attitude may turn out to be tragically mistaken. Once one reflects upon the question of the *basic* moral principles involved in the ascription of a right to life to organisms, one may find himself driven to conclude that our everyday treatment of animals is morally indefensible, and that we are in fact murdering innocent persons.

A POSTSCRIPT

June 1973

The key to the question of the moral permissibility of abortion is, I think, the insight that there is a conceptual connection between the possession of a particular right and the capacity to have the corresponding desire. The claim that there is such a conceptual connection was supported by an analysis of the concept of a right and an account of the conditions under which an individual's right to something can be violated. The simplest suggestion as to the nature of this conceptual connection is that an action cannot violate an individual's right to something unless he has, at the time the action is performed, a desire for that thing. This account is, however, exposed to obvious counter-examples, and as a result I suggested that "an individual's right to X can be violated not only when he desires X, but also when he *would* now desire X were it not for one of the following: (i) he is in an emotionally unbalanced state; (ii) he is temporarily unconscious; (iii) he has been conditioned to desire the absence of X."

I believe that the basic contentions and the supporting arguments advanced in my defense of abortion and infanticide are essentially correct. However, it may be helpful to indicate very briefly the more important changes and additions I would make if I were revising the essay. A more detailed discussion of these points can be found in my response to criticisms in the Summer 1973 issue of *Philosophy & Public Affairs* ["Michael Tooley Replies," Vol. 2, 419–432.].

The clauses dealing with emotionally unbalanced individuals and with individuals who have been subjected to conditioning which has "distorted" their desires are perhaps fair enough, for these are clearly exceptional cases, and it is not obvious exactly what account they should receive. But in the case of the temporarily unconscious individual one feels that it is an *ad hoc* modification simply to add a clause which says that an action can violate such an individual's right to something, even though he does not at the time have any desire for the thing. It would seem that a satisfactory account of rights should make clear the underlying rationale. If one fails to do this, a critic may well ask why one should make an exception of temporarily unconscious adults, but not of infants and fetuses.

I think that this problem can be dealt with by setting out a slightly more subtle account of the conditions under which an individual's rights can be violated. Such an account differs from that offered above by incorporating explicit reference to past and future desires. Leaving aside cases in which an individual's desires have been affected by lack of relevant information, or by emotional imbalance, or by his being subjected to abnormal physiological or psychological factors, one could then say that an individual's rights can be violated either by violating a corresponding desire which he now has, or, in appropriate circumstances, by violating a corresponding desire which he had at some time in the past, or will have at some time in the future.

The need to take into account past and future desires is shown by the fact that some present actions may violate, on the one hand, the rights of a dead person, and, on the other, the rights of future generations. For not only do these individuals fail to have the corresponding desire at the time the action is performed; they do not even exist.

Given this more complex but, I think, very natural account of the conceptual connection between rights and desires, the case of the temporarily unconscious individual becomes clear. If one kills such an individual one violates his right to life because one violates a desire he had before becoming unconscious: the desire to continue to exist as a subject of experiences and other mental states. The temporarily unconscious adult thus contrasts sharply with a human fetus or newborn infant, since the latter has not had, at any time past or present, a desire to continue to exist as a subject of experiences and other mental states. Consequently abortion and infanticide do not involve the violation of anyone's right to life.

The above revision also necessitates a slight change in the self-consciousness requirement which something must satisfy in order to have a right to life. In revised form, the self-consciousness requirement will state that an organism cannot have a serious right to life unless it either now possesses, or did possess at some time in the past, the concept of a self as a continuing subject of experiences and other mental states together with the belief that it is itself such an entity.

The other main revisions involve my discussion of the conservative position on abortion. First, there is a slight inaccuracy in my argument against the conservative position. I contended that the conservative position on abortion is defensible only if the potentiality principle is correct. The potentiality principle states that if there are properties possessed by normal adult human beings that endow any organism possessing them with a serious right to life, then at least one of those properties is such that any organism potentially possessing it has a serious right to life, simply by virtue of that potentiality. This conflicts with the account of rights offered earlier. A fertilized human egg cell has never had a desire to continue to exist as a subject of experiences and other mental states, nor is it the case that it would have had such a desire had it not been deprived of relevant information or subjected to abnormal influences. Therefore on the account of rights, it has no right to life, but on the potentiality principle, it appears to have such a right.

This problem can be avoided by revising the potentiality principle slightly. The principle should say, not that an organism that potentially possesses the relevant property has a right to life, but merely that in virtue of its potentiality, to kill such an organism is seriously wrong. (It is true that many people might be unwilling to accept this modification, since it implies that some actions are seriously wrong even though they do not violate anyone's right. This makes the question of *why* it is seriously wrong to kill a fetus a pressing one.)

This change does not substantially affect my objection to the conservative position. For the argument that I offer against the original version of the potentiality principle, based upon the moral symmetry principle, can easily be modified so that it is also an argument against the revised version.

It should be mentioned, however, that the original statement of my argument against the potentiality principle was somewhat imprecise at one point. Let me briefly restate the initial stages of the argument. Suppose that one has a special chemical that will, when injected into a kitten, slowly change its brain into one that is comparable to a human brain, and hence transform the kitten into an animal with all the psychological capabilities characteristic of normal adult human beings. It then follows from the moral symmetry principle that if one has a kitten which has been injected with the special chemical, but which has not had the time to develop the relevant psychological properties, it is no more seriously wrong to inject the kitten with some "neutralizing" chemical that will interfere with the process and thus prevent the kitten from developing the properties in question, than it would be to intentionally refrain from injecting a kitten with the special chemical.

What deserves emphasis is that it is not being assumed here that neither action is seriously wrong. What follows from the moral symmetry principle is simply that one action is no more wrong than the other. My original formulation of the argument was unclear and potentially misleading on this point.

The argument now proceeds as follows. Compare a kitten that has been injected with the special chemical, and then had the chemical neutralized before it could take effect, with a kitten that has not been injected with the special chemical. It is clear that it is no more seriously wrong to kill the former than to kill the latter. For although their bodies have undergone different processes in the past, this difference is morally irrelevant, and there need be no other differences between them, with respect either to present properties or potentialities.

Next, consider two kittens, one of which has been injected with the chemical, but has not yet developed those properties that in themselves would give it a right to life, and the other of which has not been injected with the chemical. It follows from the previous two steps in the argument that the combined action of injecting the first kitten with a neutralizing substance and then killing it is no more seriously wrong than the conbined action of intentionally refraining from injecting the second kitten with the chemical, and then killing it. From this point on the argument will proceed as originally set out.

Finally, let me propose a second objection to the potentiality principle both in its original and revised versions. I believe that if one accepts the potentiality principle, one ought also to accept a generalized version of it. The generalized potentiality principle states that it is not only wrong to destroy *organisms* which have the appropriate potentialities, it is also seriously wrong to prevent *systems of objects,* which would normally develop the morally relevant properties in question, from doing so. For the contention would be that whether the potentialities reside in a single organism or in a system of interrelated objects is morally irrelevant. What matters is only that one is dealing with something that will, if not interfered with, develop the morally significant properties in question. To accept either the original or the revised version of the potentiality principle, while rejecting the generalized version of it, would seem to be an indefensible position.

If, however, one accepts the generalized potentiality principle, one will be forced to conclude that some methods of contraception are seriously wrong. It is true that some people who defend an extreme conservative position on abortion will find this a cheering conclusion.

But I think that there are many more people who are conservatives on abortion who would want to reject, as completely unacceptable, the view that artificial contraception is seriously wrong. If my second argument is correct, such a combination of positions cannot successfully be defended. One must either accept the claim that some methods of contraception are seriously wrong, or else abandon the conservative position on abortion.

JANE ENGLISH 5

ABORTION AND THE CONCEPT OF A PERSON

The abortion debate rages on. Yet the two most popular positions seem to be clearly mistaken. Conservatives maintain that a human life begins at conception and that therefore abortion must be wrong because it is murder. But not all killings of humans are murders. Most notably, self-defense may justify even the killing of an innocent person.

Liberals, on the other hand, are just as mistaken in their argument that since a fetus does not become a person until birth, a woman may do whatever she pleases in and to her own body. First, you cannot do as you please with your own body if it affects other people adversely.[1] Second, if a fetus is not a person, that does not imply that you can do to it anything you wish. Animals, for example, are not persons, yet to kill or torture them for no reason at all is wrong.

At the center of the storm has been the issue of just when it is between ovulation and adulthood that a person appears on the scene. Conservatives draw the line at conception, liberals at birth. In this paper I first examine our concept of a person and conclude that no single criterion can capture the concept of a person and no sharp line can be drawn. Next I argue that if a fetus is person, abortion is still justifiable in many cases; and if a fetus is not a person, killing it is still wrong in many cases. To a large extent, these two solutions are in agreement. I conclude that our concept of a person cannot and need not bear the weight that the abortion controversy has thrust upon it.

This article is reprinted from the *Canadian Journal of Philosophy* 5, no. 2 (October 1975) by permission of the Canadian Association for Publishing in Philosophy.

I am deeply indebted to Larry Crocker and Arthur Kuflik for their constructive comments.
[1] We also have paternalistic laws which keep us from harming our own bodies even when no one else is affected. Ironically, anti-abortion laws were originally designed to protect pregnant women from a dangerous but tempting procedure.

I

The several factions in the abortion argument have drawn battle lines around various proposed criteria for determining what is and what is not a person. For example, Mary Anne Warren [2] lists five features (capacities for reasoning, self-awareness, complex communication, etc.) as her criteria for personhood and argues for the permissibility of abortion because a fetus falls outside this concept. Baruch Brody [3] uses brain waves. Michael Tooley [4] picks having-a-concept-of-self as his criterion and concludes that infanticide and abortion are justifiable, while the killing of adult animals is not. On the other side, Paul Ramsey [5] claims a certain gene structure is the defining characteristic. John Noonan [6] prefers conceived-of-humans and presents counterexamples to various other candidate criteria. For instance, he argues against viability as the criterion because the newborn and infirm would then be non-persons, since they cannot live without the aid of others. He rejects any criterion that calls upon the sorts of sentiments a being can evoke in adults on the grounds that this would allow us to exclude other races as non-persons if we could just view them sufficiently unsentimentally.

These approaches are typical: foes of abortion propose sufficient conditions for personhood which fetuses satisfy, while friends of abortion counter with necessary conditions for personhood which fetuses lack. But these both presuppose that the concept of a person can be captured in a straightjacket of necessary and/or sufficient conditions.[7] Rather, "person" is a cluster of features, of which rationality, having a self-concept and being conceived of humans are only part.

What is typical of persons? Within our concept of a person we include, first, certain biological factors: descended from humans, having a certain genetic make-up, having a head, hands, arms, eyes, capable of locomotion, breathing, eating, sleeping. There are psychological factors: sentience, perception, having a concept of self and of one's own interests and desires, the ability to use tools, the ability to use language or symbol systems, the ability to joke, to be angry, to doubt. There are rationality factors: the ability to reason and draw conclusions, the ability to generalize and to learn from past experience, the ability to sacrifice present interests for greater gains in the future. There are social factors: 'the ability to work in groups and respond to peer pressures, the ability to recognize and consider as valuable the interests of others, seeing oneself as one among "other minds," the ability to sympathize, encourage, love, the ability to evoke from others the responses of sympathy, encourage-

[2] Mary Anne Warren, "On the Moral and Legal Status of Abortion," *Monist* 5 (1973), p. 55.
[3] Baruch Brody, "Fetal Humanity and the Theory of Essentialism," in Robert Baker and Frederick Elliston (eds.), *Philosophy and Sex* (Buffalo, N. Y., 1975).
[4] Michael Tooley, "Abortion and Infanticide," *Philosophy and Public Affairs* 1 (1971).
[5] Paul Ramsey, "The Morality of Abortion," in James Rachels, ed., *Moral Problems* (New York, 1971).
[6] John Noonan, "Abortion and the Catholic Church: a Summary History," *Natural Law Forum* 12 (1967), pp. 125–131.
[7] Wittgenstein has argued against the possibility of so capturing the concept of a game, *Philosophical Investigations* (New York, 1958), §66–71.

ment, love, the ability to work with others for mutual advantage. Then there are legal factors: being subject to the law and protected by it, having the ability to sue and enter contracts, being counted in the census, having a name and citizenship, the ability to own property, inherit, and so forth.

Now the point is not that this list is incomplete, or that you can find counterinstances to each of its points. People typically exhibit rationality, for instance, but someone who was irrational would not thereby fail to qualify as a person. On the other hand, something could exhibit the majority of these features and still fail to be a person, as an advanced robot might. There is no single core of necessary and sufficient features which we can draw upon with the assurance that they constitute what really makes a person; there are only features that are more or less typical.

This is not to say that no necessary or sufficient conditions can be given. Being alive is a necessary condition for being a person, and being a U.S. Senator is sufficient. But rather than falling inside a sufficient condition or outside a necessary one, a fetus lies in the penumbra region where our concept of a person is not so simple. For this reason I think a conclusive answer to the question whether a fetus is a person is unattainable.

Here we might note a family of simple fallacies that proceed by stating a necessary condition for personhood and showing that a fetus has that characteristic. This is a form of the fallacy of affirming the consequent. For example, some have mistakenly reasoned from the premise that a fetus is human (after all, it is a human fetus rather than, say, a canine fetus), to the conclusion that it is a human. Adding an equivocation on "being," we get the fallacious argument that since a fetus is something both living and human, it is a human being.

Nonetheless, it does seem clear that a fetus has very few of the above family of characteristics, whereas a newborn baby exhibits a much larger proportion of them—and a two-year-old has even more. Note that one traditional anti-abortion argument has centered on pointing out the many ways in which a fetus resembles a baby. They emphasize its development ("It already has ten fingers . . .") without mentioning its dissimilarities to adults (it still has gills and a tail). They also try to evoke the sort of sympathy on our part that we only feel toward other persons ("Never to laugh . . . or feel the sunshine?"). This all seems to be a relevant way to argue, since its purpose is to persuade us that a fetus satisfies so many of the important features on the list that it ought to be treated as a person. Also note that a fetus near the time of birth satisfies many more of these factors than a fetus in the early months of development. This could provide reason for making distinctions among the different stages of pregnancy, as the U.S. Supreme Court has done.[8]

Historically, the time at which a person has been said to come into existence has varied widely. Muslims date personhood from fourteen

[8] Not because the fetus is partly a person and so has some of the rights of persons but rather because of the rights of person-like non-persons. This I discuss in part III below.

days after conception. Some medievals followed Aristotle in placing ensoulment at forty days after conception for a male fetus and eighty days for a female fetus.[9] In European common law since the Seventeenth Century, abortion was considered the killing of a person only after quickening, the time when a pregnant woman first feels the fetus move on its own. Nor is this variety of opinions surprising. Biologically, a human being develops gradually. We shouldn't expect there to be any specific time or sharp dividing point when a person appears on the scene.

For these reasons I believe our concept of a person is not sharp or decisive enough to bear the weight of a solution to the abortion controversy. To use it to solve that problem is to clarify *obscurum per obscurius*.

II

Next let us consider what follows if a fetus is a person after all. Judith Jarvis Thomson's landmark article, "A Defense of Abortion," [10] correctly points out that some additional argumentation is needed at this point in the conservative argument to bridge the gap between the premise that a fetus is an innocent person and the conclusion that killing it is always wrong. To arrive at this conclusion, we would need the additional premise that killing an innocent person is always wrong. But killing an innocent person is sometimes permissible, most notably in self-defense. Some examples may help draw out our intuitions or ordinary judgments about self-defense.

Suppose a mad scientist, for instance, hypnotized innocent people to jump out of the bushes and attack innocent passers-by with knives. If you are so attacked, we agree you have a right to kill the attacker in self-defense, if killing him is the only way to protect your life or to save yourself from serious injury. It does not seem to matter here that the attacker is not malicious but himself an innocent pawn, for your killing of him is not done in a spirit of retribution but only in self-defense.

How severe an injury may you inflict in self-defense? In part this depends upon the severity of the injury to be avoided: you may not shoot someone merely to avoid having your clothes torn. This might lead one to the mistaken conclusion that the defense may only equal the threatened injury in severity; that to avoid death you may kill, but to avoid a black eye you may only inflict a black eye or the equivalent. Rather, our laws and customs seem to say that you may create an injury somewhat, but not enormously, greater than the injury to be avoided. To fend off an attack whose outcome would be as serious as rape, a severe beating or the loss of a finger, you may shoot; to avoid having your clothes torn, you may blacken an eye.

---

[9] Aristotle himself was concerned, however, with the different question of when the soul takes form. For historical data, see Jimmye Kimmey, "How the Abortion Laws Happened," *Ms.* 1 (April, 1973), pp. 48ff and John Noonan, *loc. cit.*
[10] J. J. Thomson, "A Defense of Abortion," *Philosophy and Public Affairs* 1 (1971).

Aside from this, the injury you may inflict should only be the minimum necessary to deter or incapacitate the attacker. Even if you know he intends to kill you, you are not justified in shooting him if you could equally well save yourself by the simple expedient of running away. Self-defense is for the purpose of avoiding harms rather than equalizing harms.

Some cases of pregnancy present a parallel situation. Though the fetus is itself innocent, it may pose a threat to the pregnant woman's well-being, life prospects or health, mental or physical. If the pregnancy presents a slight threat to her interests, it seems self-defense cannot justify abortion. But if the threat is on a par with a serious beating or the loss of a finger, she may kill the fetus that poses such a threat, even if it is an innocent person. If a lesser harm to the fetus could have the same defensive effect, killing it would not be justified. It is unfortunate that the only way to free the woman from the pregnancy entails the death of the fetus (except in very late stages of pregnancy). Thus a self-defense model supports Thomson's point that the woman has a right only to be freed from the fetus, not a right to demand its death.[11]

The self-defense model is most helpful when we take the pregnant woman's point of view. In the pre-Thomson literature, abortion is often framed as a question for a third party: do you, a doctor, have a right to choose between the life of the woman and that of the fetus? Some have claimed that if you were a passer-by who witnessed a struggle between the innocent hypnotized attacker and his equally innocent victim, you would have no reason to kill either in defense of the other. They have concluded that the self defense model implies that a woman may attempt to abort herself, but that a doctor should not assist her. I think the position of the third party is somewhat more complex. We do feel some inclination to intervene on behalf of the victim rather than the attacker, other things equal. But if both parties are innocent, other factors come into consideration. You would rush to the aid of your husband whether he was attacker or attackee. If a hypnotized famous violinist were attacking a skid row bum, we would try to save the individual who is of more value to society. These considerations would tend to support abortion in some cases.

But suppose you are a frail senior citizen who wishes to avoid being knifed by one of these innocent hypnotics, so you have hired a bodyguard to accompany you. If you are attacked, it is clear we believe that the bodyguard, acting as your agent, has a right to kill the attacker to save you from a serious beating. Your rights of self-defense are transferred to your agent. I suggest that we should similarly view the doctor as the pregnant woman's agent in carrying out a defense she is physically incapable of accomplishing herself.

Thanks to modern technology, the cases are rare in which a pregnancy poses as clear a threat to a woman's bodily health as an attacker brandishing a switchblade. How does self-defense fare when more subtle, complex and long-range harms are involved?

To consider a somewhat fanciful example, suppose you are a highly

11 *Ibid.*, p. 52.

trained surgeon when you are kidnapped by the hypnotic attacker. He says he does not intend to harm you but to take you back to the mad scientist who, it turns out, plans to hypnotize you to have a permanent mental block against all your knowledge of medicine. This would automatically destroy your career which would in turn have a serious adverse impact on your family, your personal relationships and your happiness. It seems to me that if the only way you can avoid this outcome is to shoot the innocent attacker, you are justified in so doing. You are defending yourself from a drastic injury to your life prospects. I think it is no exaggeration to claim that unwanted pregnancies (most obviously among teenagers) often have such adverse life-long consequences as the surgeon's loss of livelihood.

Several parallels arise between various views on abortion and the self defense model. Let's suppose further that these hypnotized attackers only operate at night, so that it is well known that they can be avoided completely by the considerable inconvenience of never leaving your house after dark. One view is that since you could stay home at night, therefore if you go out and are selected by one of these hypnotized people, you have no right to defend yourself. This parallels the view that abstinence is the only acceptable way to avoid pregnancy. Others might hold that you ought to take along some defense such as Mace which will deter the hypnotized person without killing him, but that if this defense fails, you are obliged to submit to the resulting injury, no matter how severe it is. This parallels the view that contraception is all right but abortion is always wrong, even in cases of contraceptive failure.

A third view is that you may kill the hypnotized person only if he will actually kill you, but not if he will only injure you. This is like the position that abortion is permissible only if it is required to save a woman's life. Finally we have the view that it is all right to kill the attacker, even if only to avoid a very slight inconvenience to yourself and even if you knowingly walked down the very street where all these incidents have been taking place without taking along any Mace or protective escort. If we assume that a fetus is a person, this is the analogue of the view that abortion is always justifiable, "on demand."

The self-defense model allows us to see an important difference that exists between abortion and infanticide, even if a fetus is a person from conception. Many have argued that the only way to justify abortion without justifying infanticide would be to find some characteristic of personhood that is acquired at birth. Michael Tooley, for one, claims infanticide is justifiable because the really significant characteristics of person are acquired some time after birth. But all such approaches look to characteristics of the developing human and ignore the relation between the fetus and the woman. What if, after birth, the presence of an infant or the need to support it posed a grave threat to the woman's sanity or life prospects? She could escape this threat by the simple expedient of running away. So a solution that does not entail the death of the infant is available. Before birth, such solutions are not available because of the biological dependence of the fetus on the woman. Birth is the crucial point not because of any characteristics the fetus gains, but because after birth the woman can defend herself by a means less drastic than killing the infant. Hence self-defense can be used to justify abortion without necessarily thereby justifying infanticide.

III

On the other hand, supposing a fetus is not after all a person, would abortion always be morally permissible? Some opponents of abortion seem worried that if a fetus is not a full-fledged person, then we are justified in treating it in any way at all. However, this does not follow. Non-persons do get some consideration in our moral code, though of course they do not have the same rights as persons have (and in general they do not have moral responsibilities), and though their interests may be overridden by the interests of persons. Still, we cannot just treat them in any way at all.

Treatment of animals is a case in point. It is wrong to torture dogs for fun or to kill wild birds for no reason at all. It is wrong Period, even though dogs and birds do not have the same rights persons do. However, few people think it is wrong to use dogs as experimental animals, causing them considerable suffering in some cases, provided that the resulting research will probably bring discoveries of great benefit to people. And most of us think it all right to kill birds for food or to protect our crops. People's rights are different from the consideration we give to animals, then, for it is wrong to experiment on people, even if others might later benefit a great deal as a result of their suffering. You might volunteer to be a subject, but this would be supererogatory; you certainly have a right to refuse to be a medical guinea pig.

But how do we decide what you may or may not do to non-persons? This is a difficult problem, one for which I believe no adequate account exists. You do not want to say, for instance, that torturing dogs is all right whenever the sum of its effects on people is good—when it doesn't warp the sensibilities of the torturer so much that he mistreats people. If that were the case, it would be all right to torture dogs if you did it in private, or if the torturer lived on a desert island or died soon afterward, so that his actions had no effect on people. This is an inadequate account, because whatever moral consideration animals get, it has to be indefeasible, too. It will have to be a general proscription of certain actions, not merely a weighing of the impact on people on a case-by-case basis.

Rather, we need to distinguish two levels on which consequences of actions can be taken into account in moral reasoning. The traditional objections to Utilitarianism focus on the fact that it operates solely on the first level, taking all the consequences into account in particular cases only. Thus Utilitarianism is open to "desert island" and "lifeboat" counterexamples because these cases are rigged to make the consequences of actions severely limited.

Rawls' theory could be described as a teleological sort of theory, but with teleology operating on a higher level.[12] In choosing the principles

---

[12] John Rawls, *A Theory of Justice* (Cambridge, Mass., 1971), §§ 3–4.

to regulate society from the original position, his hypothetical choosers make their decision on the basis of the total consequences of various systems. Furthermore, they are constrained to choose a general set of rules which people can readily learn and apply. An ethical theory must operate by generating a set of sympathies and attitudes toward others which reinforces the functioning of that set of moral principles. Our prohibition against killing people operates by means of certain moral sentiments including sympathy, compassion and guilt. But if these attitudes are to form a coherent set, they carry us further: we tend to perform supererogatory actions, and we tend to feel similar compassion toward person-like non-persons.

It is crucial that psychological facts play a role here. Our psychological constitution makes it the case that for our ethical theory to work, it must prohibit certain treatment of non-persons which are significantly person-like. If our moral rules allowed people to treat some person-like non-persons in ways we do not want people to be treated, this would undermine the system of sympathies and attitudes that makes the ethical system work. For this reason, we would choose in the original position to make mistreatment of some sorts of animals wrong in general (not just wrong in the cases with public impact), even though animals are not themselves parties in the original position. Thus it makes sense that it is those animals whose appearance and behavior are most like those of people that get the most consideration in our moral scheme.

It is because of "coherence of attitudes," I think, that the similarity of a fetus to a baby is very significant. A fetus one week before birth is so much like a newborn baby in our psychological space that we cannot allow any cavalier treatment of the former while expecting full sympathy and nurturative support for the latter. Thus, I think that anti-abortion forces are indeed giving their strongest arguments when they point to the similarities between a fetus and a baby, and when they try to evoke our emotional attachment to and sympathy for the fetus. An early horror story from New York about nurses who were expected to alternate between caring for six-week premature infants and disposing of viable 24-week aborted fetuses is just that—a horror story. These beings are so much alike that no one can be asked to draw a distinction and treat them so very differently.

Remember, however, that in the early weeks after conception, a fetus is very much unlike a person. It is hard to develop these feelings for a set of genes which doesn't yet have a head, hands, beating heart, response to touch or the ability to move by itself. Thus it seems to me that the alleged "slippery slope" between conception and birth is not so very slippery. In the early stages of pregnancy, abortion can hardly be compared to murder for psychological reasons, but in the latest stages it is psychologically akin to murder.

Another source of similarity is the bodily continuity between fetus and adult. Bodies play a surprisingly central role in our attitudes toward persons. One has only to think of the philosophical literature on how far physical identity suffices for personal identity or Wittgenstein's remark that the best picture of the human soul is the human body. Even after death, when all agree the body is no longer a person, we still observe elaborate customs of respect for the human body; like people who torture dogs, necrophiliacs are not to be trusted with people.[13] So it is appropriate that we show respect to a fetus as the body continuous with the body of a person. This is a degree of resemblance to persons that animals cannot rival.

Michael Tooley also utilizes a parallel with animals. He claims that it is always permissible to drown newborn kittens and draws conclusions about infanticide.[14] But it is only permissible to drown kittens when their survival would cause some hardship. Perhaps it would be a burden to feed and house six more cats òr to find other homes for them. The alternative of letting them starve produces even more suffering than the drowning. Since the kittens get their rights secondhand, so to speak, *via* the need for coherence in our attitudes, their interests are often overridden by the interests of full-fledged persons. But if their survival would be no inconvenience to people at all, then it is wrong to drown them, *contra* Tooley.

Tooley's conclusions about abortion are wrong for the same reason. Even if a fetus is not a person, abortion is not always permissible, because of the resemblance of a fetus to a person. I agree with Thomson that it would be wrong for a woman who is seven months pregnant to have an abortion just to avoid having to postpone a trip to Europe. In the early months of pregnancy when the fetus hardly resembles a baby at all, then, abortion is permissible whenever it is in the interests of the pregnant woman or her family. The reasons would only need to outweigh the pain and inconvenience of the abortion itself. In the middle months, when the fetus comes to resemble a person, abortion would be justifiable only when the continuation of the pregnancy or the birth of the child would cause harms—physical, psychological, economic or social—to the woman. In the late months of pregnancy, even on our current assumption that a fetus is not a person, abortion seems to be wrong except to save a woman from significant injury or death.

The Supreme Court has recognized similar gradations in the alleged slippery slope stretching between conception and birth. To this point, the present paper has been a discussion of the moral status of abortion only, not its legal status. In view of the great physical, financial and sometimes psychological costs of abortion, perhaps the legal arrangement most compatible with the proposed moral solution would be the absence of restrictions, that is, so-called abortion "on demand."

So I conclude, first, that application of our concept of a person will not suffice to settle the abortion issue. After all, the biological development of a human being is gradual. Second, whether a fetus is a person or not, abortion is justifiable early in pregnancy to avoid modest harms and seldom justifiable late in pregnancy except to avoid significant injury or death.

---

[13] On the other hand, if they can be trusted with people, then our moral customs are mistaken. It all depends on the facts of psychology.
[14] *Op. cit.,* pp. 40, 60–61.

POINTS TO PONDER

1. The cases and materials included here make much of the right of privacy. Just what is (or ought to be) included in the notion of privacy? How far ought the right of privacy to extend? Is the extension of that right from the right not to have public officials or private persons spy upon one's intimate affairs to the area of autonomy over one's personal decisions justifiable?

2. Is the Supreme Court's enumeration of passages in the Constitution a convincing demonstration of the meaning of the word "person"? How ought the meaning of that term in moral or legal contexts to be determined? Is it a purely descriptive term or is it normative (i.e., having moral or evaluative overtones and implications)? What are defining characteristics of a *person*? And when does a human organism begin to be a person—or, for that matter, cease to be one?

3. The majority of the Court in *Roe* v. *Wade* argued that old laws are rendered obsolete by technological advances. Can technological advances make a difference where moral principles are concerned? If a fetus is a human person possessing the right to life, does the greater ease and safety of operative procedures for abortions (for the mother, of course, not for the fetus) justify depriving the fetus of its right to live—assuming that it has such a right?

4. Does the Court's analysis in *Roe* contain hidden moral assumptions that ought to be given more careful scrutiny? If so, what are they?

5. In the *Roe* decision, Justice Stewart assumed that the Constitution protects rights that are nowhere mentioned in it. Indeed, the majority seems to make the same assumption, as the right to privacy was found only in the "penumbras" and "emanations" of various provisions in the Bill of Rights. If this is so, what is the point of entering into such detailed exegeses of the Constitution's wording? More important, where does the Court discover these unwritten constitutional protections? Are they truly based upon reason, as Stewart and Harlan suggest, or are they subjective value judgments prone to constant change, as the justices grow older and as the composition of the Court changes over time? Does this approach give the Court the status of a superlegislature, unelected, unaccountable to the people, and with life tenure? If that is the case, then what becomes of the separation of powers and the democratic ideal?

6. If you approve of the Court's decision, explain *why* you approve of it. If you believe that the Court should have the power to overrule state legislatures in such matters, suppose that the Court had reached the opposite decision: that the Constitution confers upon fetuses the right to life and that no state law permitting women to have abortions would be consonant with the Constitution. What would your reaction be? Upon what political or philosophical principles would you base your judgment?

7. Justice Douglas suggested that the concept of liberty itself includes

or implies the conclusion "that a woman is free to make the basic decision whether to bear an unwanted child." If this is correct, what kind of implication is it? What is the logic behind this argument, and how sound is it?

8. Questions on the meaning of "privacy" and judicial legislation that are raised by Justice Rehnquist's opinion have already been considered. But there is a corollary that ought to be raised: If the courts were deprived of their power to pass on the constitutionality of legislation that came before them for review, what would the consequences be? Is such review the same as judicial legislation, or is "judicial legislation" merely an emotive, judgmental expression used by opponents of a particular decision to express their disapproval?

9. Is "viability" properly considered to be a purely medical concept, as the court in the *Planned Parenthood* case held it to be, or should it be defined in some other way? Does this definition confer upon physicians a mantle of authority in an area in which they are no more expert that anyone else?

10. When the Court describes some minors as "competent" and "mature," are those terms used descriptively or normatively? In the context of its opinion, is its use of those terms fully consistent with its other statements? Does its conclusion leave any room for the state to pass legislation to protect "incompetent" and "immature" minors—or are those terms rendered meaningless by the manner in which the Court uses them?

11. How persuasive is the dissenters' argument that the husband has an interest that deserves to be protected?

12. If Justice White's argument—that a woman's right to have an abortion does not imply a right to demand that the fetus be born dead or to be killed after it is born—prevailed, could physicians who failed to exercise due care to preserve the lives of aborted fetuses be brought to trial on criminal charges? Should such a view prevail? On what grounds?

13. Michael Tooley's argument is strongly dependent upon his theory as to what characteristics distinguish persons from all other creatures. How persuasive are his arguments in favor of that position? Is there a certain intellectual bias underlying his assumption that only the "concept of a self as a continuing subject of experiences and other mental states" and a belief that one is such a continuing entity qualifies an organism as a person worthy of protection by the law? Do sleeping or unconscious persons cease to be persons while they are sleeping or unconscious? If a person is in a reversible but complete coma over a period of months, does he or she lose all claims to the right to life? If an individual is so severely retarded as to be unable to formulate such sophisticated concepts as those described by Tooley, does that individual fail to qualify, legally or morally, as a person? On the other hand, if it could be demonstrated that some animals (say, porpoises, monkeys, or cows) had some vague concept of self similar to that which Tooley describes, would they thereupon acquire a right to life equal to that which is currently enjoyed by moral philosophers? Does one have to be aware of this concept of self to qualify, or is a mere inchoate, unformu-

lated, potential concept sufficient? (Does it make sense to talk about inchoate, unformulated, potential concepts? Does this lead to something akin to the theory of innate ideas?)

14. Is infanticide always wrong? If, for example, an infant is born with an irreversible, disabling, ultimately fatal congenital condition, is it wrong for its parents or the physician to withhold treatment so as to assure its early demise?

15. How persuasive is Tooley's analogy to the potentially rational kitten? Would a rational kitten possess a right to life not possessed by nonrational kittens? On what grounds can one make such a decision?

16. Jane English asserts that animals have rights. Is this correct? Is it merely a shorthand way of saying that people have imposed upon other people certain duties with regard to animals? For example, it is a fact that it is unlawful to pick wildflowers in national parks. Does it follow that wildflowers have the right not to be picked? Or is it more accurate to say that persons have a duty, imposed by the law, not to pick wildflowers and that that duty is owed to the people of the state, not to the wildflowers? Is a similar analysis applicable to laws concerning cruelty to animals? Are moral rules subject to the same analysis as legal rules? Is there a logical difference between these statements: (a) It is wrong to kill (or torture) moral philosophers; and (b) It is wrong to kill (or torture) cattle.

17. Is Professor English correct in asserting that there is no possibility of conclusively determining whether or not a fetus is a person? Is she correct in concluding that the meaning of *person* is not crucial to a resolution of the abortion controversy?

18. How persuasive are her analogies between pregnant women and persons who are attacked by highwaymen under various circumstances?

19. English asserts that if the survival of kittens would inconvenience no one, it is wrong to drown them, *contra* Tooley. But she offers no justification to support that judgment. Is there one? If there is, what is its derivation? Does this reveal anything about the manner in which English draws her conclusions about abortion?

20. English seems to put a great deal of weight upon the physical continuity of fetuses with children and, at the other extreme, upon the physical continuity of people and their corpses as a partial explanation of our moral attitudes concerning the treatment to be accorded fetuses and corpses. Physical resemblances, too, seem to have an important role to play. In making ultimate moral judgments, are such considerations relevant? If so, how? And if not, why not?

III
EUTHANASIA

INTRODUCTION

Euthanasia, or mercy killing, is often said to take two very different forms: active and passive. In active euthanasia, one person kills another by shooting, administering a drug, or in some other manner to "put him (or her) out of his (or her) misery." That is, the homicide is committed, not with any selfish aim on the part of the killer, but with a desire to spare the victim any further suffering. Passive euthanasia, on the other hand, consists of withholding treatment from a person who (it is believed) will very likely die soon after the treatment is terminated and who is suffering from what is believed to be a painful or dehumanizing malady.

A long moral and legal tradition against any form of homicide has often been invoked in prosecuting individuals who have committed acts of euthanasia. Generally speaking, although some forms of euthanasia appear to be widely accepted, both among the public and among members of the medical profession, the law does not sanction it. It has sometimes been argued that we are more merciful to suffering dogs and horses than we are to our own loved ones and that it is not rational to permit putting dumb animals to sleep while we threaten anyone who does the same for (or to) a person with the most dire penalties.

Some religious and moral arguments have been adduced on the other side. The Roman Catholic Church has taken a particularly interesting stand on the issue, holding that it is not necessary, under religious law, for anyone to administer heroic treatments to preserve the life of a patient who is dying of an incurable disease. Such treatments may be regarded as a kind of interference in the natural scheme of things.

The case of Karen Ann Quinlan, which is described and discussed in selection 6, constituted an important breakthrough, for a state court held, for the first time, that it was permissible to take a (seemingly) dying patient off the machines that were sustaining her biological functions. Some earlier cases had determined that where brain death has occurred, the patient may be regarded as legally dead and treatment may cease; but Karen Quinlan did *not* qualify as dead under that test. Nevertheless, the court seems to have held that the extraordinary measures that were being employed to keep her alive could be terminated, as there was no hope of her recovering the use of her cognitive faculties.

The *Saikewicz* case followed the *Quinlan* case. but *Saikewicz* concerned a resident of a home for the severely retarded who was dying of a fatal, incurable form of cancer. The question put to the court was whether the authorities at the home were obliged to treat him for his cancer or could legally withhold treatment so that he could die in peace. That is, the question was whether they could practice passive euthanasia in such a case.

Yale Kamisar wrote his article against mercy killing just a few years after World War II came to an end. The world was horrified by the revelations that came out of the Nazi extermination camps and the war crimes trials. Among Hitler's policies was a systematic program of euthanasia of various types of unfit persons—the mentally retarded, homosexuals, and Jews, as well as those who were suffering from incurable cancers and other diseases. Although it is clear that Kamisar was deeply affected by those revelations, his arguments are not merely emotional reactions to them. He considers what it means to say that a person *voluntarily* submits to enthanasia, when it is questionable whether anyone can be sufficiently rational to make such a momentous choice when he or she is wracked with pain. And he raises other questions, too, that must be considered by anyone who is concerned about this difficult moral problem: What does it mean to say that one is incurable? Who should make the final judgment? Are there no other solutions to the problem of pain?

Philippa Foot contends that in some cases, at least, it is better for a person to die earlier rather than later. To elucidate this notion, she subjects the word *beneficial* to a searching philosophical analysis. And she goes on to ask whether a person might not be mistaken as to his or her own prospects, and when it is appropriate or inappropriate to say that life itself is a benefit to a person. Finally, after a further analysis of the notion of a right to life, she turns to the distinction between active and passive euthanasia and the moral differences between them, and to the application of the principles she adduces to such cases as that of Karen Quinlan. But Professor Foot, too, is disturbed (though she writes nearly a quarter of a century after Professor Kamisar's article appeared) by Hitler's program of euthanasia and its implications for the legalization of such practices.

John A. Robertson considers two arguments in favor of the involuntary euthanasia of defective newborns: that they are not persons and that there is no obligation to treat when the costs of maintaining life greatly outweigh the benefits. Like others in Part III, Robertson analyzes Michael Tooley's arguments (in Part II) in favor of infanticide. He considers not only the infant's rights, but those of others who will be affected by its continued existence, including its family, the health professionals who must treat it, and society as a whole.

6

SUPERINTENDENT OF BELCHERTOWN
STATE SCHOOL V. SAIKEWICZ

370 N.E.2d 417 (Mass. 1977)

[Joseph Saikewicz was 67 years of age when this action was brought to court in April 1976. At the time of the hearing, he had an I.Q. of 10 and a mental age of about two years and eight months. He had been living in mental institutions, or in institutions for the mentally retarded, since 1923. He was physically strong and well built, well nourished, and ambulatory, but he was unable to communicate verbally, resorting to gestures and grunts to make his wishes known; and he was able to respond only to gestures or physical contacts. He was unable even to respond intelligibly to inquiries as to whether he was experiencing pain.

[Saikewicz was diagnosed as suffering from acute myeloblastic monocytic leukemia, a fatal form of cancer of the blood that is usually accompanied by enlargement of such organs as the spleen, lymph glands, and bone marrow, internal bleeding, weakness, severe anemia, and high susceptibility to infection. Standard treatment of the disease is chemotherapy, which not only affects the cancerous cells, but normal cells as well, causing, among other things, destruction of the bone marrow, and thus leading to still further effects, such as pronounced anemia, bleeding, susceptibility to infections, loss of hair, and other undesirable symptoms. Only 30 to 50 per cent of the patients who have chemotherapy have remissions—that is, a temporary return to a clinically normal state; but even in such cases, the remission typically lasts for between two and thirteen months—and then usually only when the patient is younger than Saikewicz. The doctors estimated that if he were left untreated, Saikewicz would probably live for a matter of weeks or possibly several months, with no pain, and have a reasonably comfortable death.

[The superintendent of the hospital in which Saikewicz had been confined for the previous forty-eight years petitioned the probate court of the county in which the hospital was located for the appointment of a temporary guardian who would represent Saikewicz's interests. That guardian then concluded that it was in Saikewicz's best interests *not* to be treated with chemotherapy, both for the reasons just mentioned and because such treatment would not only cause Saikewicz considerable pain and fear, but also offer him a very limited prospect of an extension of his life for a short period. Having determined that the liabilities outweighed the potential benefits of such treatment, he asked the court to withhold medical treatment from Saikewicz. The court agreed, and that decision was appealed.

[The Supreme Judicial Court upheld the lower court's ruling, and

Saikewicz died "without pain or discomfort" a few months later in the hospital of the state school in which he had resided.

[Excerpts from the court's opinion, delivered some time later by Justice Liacos, follow.]

II

We recognize at the outset that this case presents novel issues of fundamental importance that should not be resolved by mechanical reliance on legal doctrine. Our task of establishing a framework in the law on which the activities of health care personnel and other persons can find support is furthered by seeking the collective guidance of those in health care, moral ethics, philosophy, and other disciplines. . . . The principal areas of determination are:

A. The nature of the right of any person, competent or incompetent, to decline potentially life-prolonging treatment.

B. The legal standards that control the course of decision whether or not potentially life-prolonging, but not life-saving, treatment should be administered to a person who is not competent to make the choice.

C. The procedures that must be followed in arriving at that decision.

For reasons we develop in the body of this opinion, it becomes apparent that the questions to be discussed in the first two areas are closely interrelated. We take the view that the substantive rights of the competent and the incompetent persons are the same in regard to the right to decline potentially life-prolonging treatment. The factors which distinguish the two types of persons are found only in the area of how the State should approach the preservation and implementation of the rights of an incompetent person and in the procedures necessary to that process of preservation and implementation. We treat the matter in the sequence above stated because we think it helpful to set forth our views on (A) what the rights of all persons in this area are and (B) the issue of how an incompetent person is to be afforded the status in law of a competent person with respect to such rights. Only then can we proceed to (C) the particular procedures to be followed to ensure the rights of the incompetent person.

A

1. It has been said that "[t]he law always lags behind the most advanced thinking in every area. It must wait until the theologians and the moral leaders and events have created some common ground, some consensus." We therefore think it advisable to consider the framework of medical ethics which influences a doctor's decision as to how to deal with the terminally ill patient. While these considerations are not controlling, they ought to be considered for the insights they give us.

Advances in medical science have given doctors greater control over the time and nature of death. Chemotherapy is, as evident from our previous discussion, one of these advances. Prior to the development of such new techniques the physician perceived his duty as that of making every conceivable effort to prolong life. On the other hand, the context in which such an ethos prevailed did not provide the range of options available to the physician today in terms of taking steps to postpone death irrespective of the effect on the patient. With the development of the new techniques, serious questions as to what may constitute acting in the best interests of the patient have arisen.

The nature of the choice has become more difficult because physicians have begun to realize that in many cases the effect of using extraordinary measures to prolong life is to "only prolong suffering, isolate the family from their loved one at a time when they may be close at hand or result in economic ruin for the family."

Recognition of these factors led the Supreme Court of New Jersey to observe "that physicians distinguish between curing the ill and comforting and easing the dying; that they refuse to treat the curable as if they were dying or ought to die, and that they have sometimes refused to treat the hopeless and dying as if they were curable." *In re Quinlan,* 70 N.J. 10, 47, 355 A.2d 647, 667 (1976).

The essence of this distinction in defining the medical role is to draw the sometimes subtle distinction between those situations in which the withholding of extraordinary measures may be viewed as allowing the disease to take its natural course and those in which the same actions may be deemed to have been the cause of death. Recent literature suggests that health care institutions are drawing such a distinction, at least with regard to respecting the decision of competent patients to refuse such measures.

The current state of medical ethics in this area is expressed by one commentator who states that: "we should not use *extraordinary* means of prolonging life or its semblance when, after careful consideration, consultation and the application of the most well conceived therapy it becomes apparent that there is no hope for the recovery of the patient. Recovery should not be defined simply as the ability to remain alive; it should mean life without intolerable suffering."

Our decision in this case is consistent with the current medical ethos in this area.

2. There is implicit recognition in the law of the Commonwealth, as elsewhere, that a person has a strong interest in being free from nonconsensual invasion of his bodily integrity. In short, the law recognizes the individual interest in preserving "the inviolability of his person." One means by which the law has developed in a manner consistent with the protection of this interest is through the development of the doctrine of informed consent. . . . As previously suggested, one of the foundations of the doctrine is that it protects the patient's status as a human being.

Of even broader import, but arising from the same regard for human dignity and self-determination, is the unwritten constitutional right of privacy found in the penumbra of specific guaranties of the Bill of Rights. As this constitutional guaranty reaches out to protect the freedom of a woman to terminate pregnancy under certain conditions, so it encompasses the right of a patient to preserve his or her right to privacy against unwanted infringements of bodily integrity in appropriate circumstances. In the case of a person incompetent to assert this constitutional right of privacy, it may be asserted by that person's guardian in conformance with the standards and procedures set forth in sections II(B) and II(C) of this opinion.

3. The question when the circumstances are appropriate for the exercise of this privacy right depends on the proper identification of State interests. It is not surprising that courts have, in the course of investigating State interests in various medical contexts and under various formulations of the individual rights involved, reached differing views on the nature and the extent of State interests. We have undertaken a survey of some of the leading cases to help in identifying the range of State interests potentially applicable to cases of medical intervention.

In a number of cases, no applicable State interest, or combination of such interests, was found sufficient to outweigh the individual's interests in exercising the choice of refusing medical treatment. . . .

Subordination of State interests to individual interests has not been universal, however. In a leading case, *Application of the President & Directors of Georgetown College, Inc.,* 118 U.S.App.D.C. 80, 331 F.2d 1000 (1964), a hospital sought permission to perform a blood transfusion necessary to save the patient's life where the person was unwilling to consent due to religious beliefs. The court held that it had the power to allow the action to be taken despite the previously expressed contrary sentiments of the patient. The court justified its decision by reasoning that its purpose was to protect three State interests, the protection of which was viewed as having greater import than the individual right: (1) the State interest in preventing suicide, (2) a parens patriae interest in protecting the patient's minor children from "abandonment" by their parent, and (3) the protection of the medical profession's desire to act affirmatively to save life without fear of civil liability. . . .

As distilled from the cases, the State has claimed interest in: (1) the preservation of life; (2) the protection of the interests of innocent third parties; (3) the prevention of suicide; and (4) maintaining the ethical integrity of the medical profession.

It is clear that the most significant of the asserted State interests is that of the preservation of human life. Recognition of such an interest, however, does not necessarily resolve the problem where the affliction or disease clearly indicates that life will soon, and inevitably, be extinguished. The interest of the State in prolonging a life must be reconciled with the interest of an individual to reject the traumatic cost of that prolongation. There is a substantial distinction in the State's insistence that human life be saved where the affliction is curable, as opposed to the State interest where, as here, the issue is not whether but when, for how long, and at what cost to the individual that life may be briefly extended. Even if we assume that the State has an additional interest in seeing to it that individual decisions on the prolongation of life do not in any way tend to "cheapen" the value which is placed in the concept of living, we believe it is not inconsistent to recognize a right to decline medical treatment in a situation of incurable illness. The constitutional right to privacy, as we conceive it, is an expression of the sanctity of individual free choice and self-determination as fundamental constituents of life. The value of life as so perceived is lessened not by a decision to refuse treatment, but by the failure to allow a competent human being the right of choice.

A second interest of considerable magnitude, which the State may have some interest in asserting, is that of protecting third parties, particularly minor children, from the emotional and financial damage which may occur as a result of the decision of a competent adult to refuse life-saving or life-prolonging treatment. Thus, in *Holmes* v. *Silver Cross Hosp. of Joliet, Ill.,* 340 F. Supp. 125 (D.Ill.1972), the court held that, while the State's interest in preserving an individual's life was not sufficient, by itself, to outweigh the individual's interest in the exercise of free choice, the possible impact on minor children would be a factor which might have a critical effect on the outcome of the balancing process. Similarly, in the *Georgetown* case the court held that one of the interests requiring protection was that of the minor child in order to avoid the effect of "abandonment" on that child as a result of the parent's decision to refuse the necessary medical measures. We need not reach this aspect of claimed State interest as it is not in issue on the facts of this case.

The last State interest requiring discussion is that of the maintenance of the ethical integrity of the medical profession as well as allowing hospitals the full opportunity to care for people under their control. The force and impact of this interest is lessened by the prevailing medical ethical standards. Prevailing medical ethical practice does not, without exception, demand that all efforts toward life prolongation be made in all circumstances. Rather, as indicated in *Quinlan,* the prevailing ethical practice seems to be to recognize that the dying are more often in need of comfort than treatment. Recognition of the right to refuse necessary treatment in appropriate circumstances is consistent with existing medical mores; such a doctrine does not threaten either the integrity of the medical profession, the proper role of hospitals in caring for such patients or the State's interest in protecting the same. It is not necessary to deny a right of self-determination to a patient in order to recognize the interests of doctors, hospitals, and medical personnel in attendance on the patient. Also, if the doctrines of informed consent and right of privacy have as their foundations the right to bodily integrity, and control of one's own fate, then those rights are superior to the institutional considerations.

Applying the considerations discussed in this subsection to the decision made by the probate judge in the circumstances of the case before us, we are satisfied that his decision was consistent with a proper balancing of applicable State and individual interests. Two of the four categories of State interests that we have identified, the protection of third parties and the prevention of suicide, are inapplicable to this case. The third, involving the protection of the ethical integrity of the medical profession was satisfied on two grounds. The probate judge's decision was in accord with the testimony of the attending physicians of the patient. The decision is in accord with the generally accepted views of the medical profession, as set forth in this opinion. The fourth State interest—the preservation of life—has been viewed with proper regard for the heavy physical and emotional burdens on the patient if a vigorous regimen of drug therapy were to be imposed to effect a brief and uncertain delay in the natural process of death. To be balanced against these State interests was the individual's interest in the freedom to choose to reject, or refuse to consent to, intrusions of his bodily integrity and privacy. We cannot say that the facts of this case required a result contrary to that reached by the probate judge with regard to the right of any person, competent or incompetent, to be spared the deleterious consequences of life-prolonging treatment. We therefore turn to consider the unique considerations arising in this case by virtue of the patient's inability to appreciate his predicament and articulate his desires.

B

The question what legal standards govern the decision whether to administer potentially life-prolonging treatment to an incompetent person encompasses two distinct and important subissues. First, does a choice exist? That is, is it the unvarying responsibility of the State to order medical treatment in all circumstances involving the care of an incompetent person? Second, if a choice does exist under certain conditions, what considerations enter into the decision-making process?

We think that principles of equality and respect for all individuals require the conclusion that a choice exists. For reasons discussed at some length in subsection A, *supra*, we recognize a general right in all persons to refuse medical treatment in appropriate circumstances. The recognition of that right must extend to the case of an incompetent, as well as a competent, patient because the value of human dignity extends to both.

This is not to deny that the State has a traditional power and responsibility, under the doctrine of parens patriae, to care for and protect the "best interests" of the incompetent person. Indeed, the existence of this power and responsibility has impelled a number of courts to hold that the "best interests" of such a person mandate an unvarying responsibility by the courts to order necessary medical treatment for an incompetent person facing an immediate and severe danger to life.

Whatever the merits of such a policy where life-saving treatment is available—a situation unfortunately not presented by this case—a more flexible view of the "best interests" of the incompetent patient is not precluded under other conditions. . . . Even in the exercise of the parens patriae power, there must be respect for the bodily integrity of the child or respect for the rational decision of those parties, usually the parents, who for one reason or another are seeking to protect the bodily integrity or other personal interest of the child.

The "best interests" of an incompetent person are not necessarily served by imposing on such persons results not mandated as to competent persons similarly situated. It does not advance the interest of the State or the ward to treat the ward as a person of lesser status or dignity than others. To protect the incompetent person within its power, the State must recognize the dignity and worth of such a person and afford to that person the same panoply of rights and choices it recognizes in competent persons. If a competent person faced with death may choose to decline treatment which not only will not cure the person but which substantially may increase suffering in exchange for a possible yet brief prolongation of life, then it cannot be said that it is always in the "best interests" of the ward to require submission to such treatment. Nor do statistical factors indicating that a majority of competent persons similarly situated choose treatment resolve the issue. The significant decisions of life are more complex than statistical determinations. Individual choice is determined not by the vote of the majority but by the complexities of the singular situation viewed from the unique perspective of the person called on to make the decision. To presume that the incompetent person must always be subjected to what many rational and intelligent persons may decline is to downgrade the status of the incompetent person by placing a lesser value on his intrinsic human worth and vitality.

The trend in the law has been to give incompetent persons the same rights as other individuals. Recognition of this principle of equality requires understanding that in certain circumstances it may be appropriate for a court to consent to the withholding of treatment from an incompetent individual. This leads us to the question of how the right of an incompetent person to decline treatment might best be exercised so as to give the fullest possible expression to the character and circumstances of that individual.

The problem of decision-making presented in this case is one of first impression before this court, and we know of no decision in other jurisdictions squarely on point. The well-publicized decision of the New Jersey Supreme Court in *In re Quinlan* provides a helpful starting point for analysis, however.

Karen Ann Quinlan, then age twenty-one, stopped breathing for reasons not clearly identified for at least two fifteen-minute periods on the night of April 15, 1975. As a result, this formerly healthy individual suffered severe brain damage to the extent that medical experts characterized her as being in a "chronic persistent vegetative state." Although her brain was capable of a certain degree of primitive reflex-level functioning, she had no cognitive function or awareness of her surroundings. Karen Quinlan did not, however, exhibit any of the signs of "brain death" as identified by the Ad Hoc Committee of the Harvard Medical School. She was thus "alive" under controlling legal and medical standards. Nonetheless, it was the opinion of the experts and conclusion of the court that there was no reasonable possibility that she would ever be restored to cognitive or sapient life. Her breathing was assisted by a respirator, without which the experts believed she could not survive. It was for the purpose of getting authority to order the disconnection of the respirator that Quinlan's father petitioned the lower New Jersey court.

The Supreme Court of New Jersey, in a unanimous opinion authored by Chief Justice Hughes, held that the father, as guardian, could, subject to certain qualifications, exercise his daughter's right to privacy by authorizing removal of the artificial life-support systems. The court thus recognized that the preservation of the personal right to privacy against bodily intrusions, not exercisable directly due to the incompetence of the right-holder, depended on its indirect exercise by one acting on behalf of the incompetent person. The exposition by the New Jersey court of the principle of substituted judgment, and of the legal standards that were to be applied by the guardian in making this decision, bears repetition here.

"If a putative decision by Karen to permit this non-cognitive, vegetative existence to terminate by natural forces is regarded as a valuable incident of her right of privacy, as we believe it to be, then it should not be discarded solely on the basis that her condition prevents her conscious exercise of the choice. The only practical way to prevent destruction of the right is to *permit the guardian and family of Karen to render their best judgment,* subject to the qualifications [regarding consultation with attending physicians and hospital 'Ethics Committee'] hereinafter stated, *as to whether she would exercise it in these circumstances.* If their conclusion is in the affirmative this decision should be accepted by a society the overwhelming majority of whose members would, we think, in similar circumstances, exercise such a choice in the same way for themselves or for those closest to them. It is for this reason that we determine that Karen's right of privacy may be asserted in her behalf, in this respect, by her guardian and family under the particular circumstances presented by this record" (emphasis supplied).

The court's observation that most people in like circumstances would choose a natural death does not, we believe, detract from or modify the central concern that the guardian's decision conform, to the extent possible, to the decision that would have been made by Karen Quinlan herself. Evidence that most people would or would not act in a certain way is certainly an important consideration in attempting to ascertain the predilections of any individual, but care must be taken, as in any analogy, to ensure that operative factors are similar, or at least to take notice of the dissimilarities. With this in mind, it is profitable to compare the situations presented in the *Quinlan* case and the case presently before us. Karen Quinlan, subsequent to her accident, was totally incapable of knowing or appreciating life, was physically debilitated, and was pathetically reliant on sophisticated machinery to nourish and clean her body. Any other person suffering from similar massive brain damage would be in a similar state of total incapacity, and thus it is not unreasonable to give weight to a supposed general, and widespread, response to the situation.

Karen Quinlan's situation, however, must be distinguished from that of Joseph Saikewicz. Saikewicz was profoundly mentally retarded. His mental state was a cognitive one but limited in his capacity to comprehend and communicate. Evidence that most people choose to accept the rigors of chemotherapy has no direct bearing on the likely choice that Joseph Saikewicz would have made. Unlike most people, Saikewicz had no capacity to understand his present situation or his prognosis. The guardian ad litem gave expression to this important distinction in coming to grips with this "most troubling aspect" of withholding treatment from Saikewicz: "If he is treated with toxic drugs he will be involuntarily immersed in a state of painful suffering, the reason for which he will never understand. Patients who request treatment know the risks involved and can appreciate the painful side effects when they arrive. They know the reason for the pain and their hope makes it tolerable." To make a worthwhile comparison, one would have to ask whether a majority of people would choose chemotherapy if they were told merely that something outside of their previous experience was going to be done to them, that this something would cause them pain and discomfort, that they would be removed to strange surroundings and possibly restrained for extended periods of time, and that the advantages of this course of action were measured by concepts of time and mortality beyond their ability to comprehend.

To put the above discussion in proper perspective, we realize that an inquiry into what a majority of people would do in circumstances that truly were similar assumes an objective viewpoint not far removed from a "reasonable person" inquiry. While we recognize the value of this kind of indirect evidence, we should make it plain that the primary test is subjective in nature—that is, the goal is to determine with as much accuracy as possible the wants and needs of the individual involved. This may or may not conform to what is thought wise or prudent by most people. The problems of arriving at an accurate substituted judgment in matters of life and death vary greatly in degree, if not in kind, in different circumstances. For example, the responsibility of Karen Quinlan's father to act as she would have wanted could be discharged by drawing on many years of what was apparently an affectionate and close relationship. In contrast, Joseph Saikewicz was profoundly retarded and noncommunicative his entire life, which was spent largely in the highly restrictive atmosphere of an institution. While it may thus be necessary to rely to a greater degree on objective criteria, such as the supposed inability of profoundly retarded persons to conceptualize or fear death, the effort to bring the substituted judgment into step with the values and desires of the affected individual must not, and need not, be abandoned. . . .

The decision in cases such as this should be that which would be made by the incompetent person, if that person were competent, but taking into account the present and future incompetency of the individual as one of the factors which would necessarily enter into the decision-making process of the competent person. Having recognized the right of a competent person to make for himself the same decision as the court made in this case, the question is, do the facts on the record support the proposition that Saikewicz himself would have made the decision under the standard set forth. We believe they do.

The two factors considered by the probate judge to weigh in favor of administering chemotherapy were: (1) the fact that most people elect chemotherapy and (2) the chance of a longer life. Both are appropriate indicators of what Saikewicz himself would have wanted, provided that due allowance is taken for this individual's present and future incompetency. We have already discussed the perspective this brings to the fact that most people choose to undergo chemotherapy. With regard to the second factor, the chance of a longer life carries the same weight for Saikewicz as for any other person, the value of life under the law having no relation to intelligence or social position. Intertwined with this consideration is the hope that a cure, temporary or permanent, will be discovered during the period of extra weeks or months potentially made available by chemotherapy. The guardian ad litem investigated this possibility and found no reason to hope for a dramatic breakthrough in the time frame relevant to the decision.

The probate judge identified six factors weighing against administration of chemotherapy. Four of these—Saikewicz's age, the probable side effects of treatment, the low chance of producing remission, and the certainty that treatment will cause immediate suffering—were clearly established by the medical testimony to be considerations that any individual would weigh carefully. A fifth factor—Saikewicz's inability to cooperate with the treatment—introduces those considerations that are unique to this individual and which therefore are essential to the proper exercise of substituted judgment. The judge heard testimony that Saikewicz would have no comprehension of the reasons for the severe disruption of his formerly secure and stable environment occasioned by the chemotherapy. He therefore would experience fear without the understanding from which other patients draw strength. The inability to anticipate and prepare for the severe side effects of the drugs leaves room only for confusion and disorientation. The possibility that such a naturally uncooperative patient would have to be physically restrained to allow the slow intravenous administration of drugs could only compound his pain and fear, as well as possibly jeopardize the ability of his body to withstand the toxic effects of the drugs.

The sixth factor identified by the judge as weighing against chemotherapy was "the quality of life possible for him if the treatment does bring about remission." To the extent that this formulation equates the value of life with any measure of the quality of life, we firmly reject it. A reading of the entire record clearly reveals, however, the judge's concern that special care be taken to respect the dignity and worth of Saikewicz's life precisely because of his vulnerable position. The judge, as well as all the parties, were keenly aware that the supposed ability of Saikewicz, by virtue of his mental retardation, to appreciate or experience life had no place in the decision before them. Rather than reading the judge's formulation in a manner that demeans the value of the life of one who is mentally retarded, the vague, and perhaps ill-chosen, term "quality of life" should be understood as a reference to the continuing state of pain and disorientation precipitated by the chemotherapy treatment. Viewing the term in this manner, together with the other factors properly considered by the judge, we are satisfied that the decision to withhold treatment from Saikewicz was based on a regard for his actual interests and preferences and that the facts supported this decision.

C.

. . . We take a dim view of any attempt to shift the ultimate decision-making responsibility away from the duly established courts of proper jurisdiction to any committee, panel or group, ad hoc or permanent. Thus, we reject the approach adopted by the New Jersey Supreme Court in the *Quinlan* case of entrusting the decision whether to continue artificial life support to the patient's guardian, family, attending doctors, and hospital "ethics committee." One rationale for such a delegation was expressed by the lower court judge in the *Quinlan* case, and quoted by the New Jersey Supreme Court: "The nature, extent and duration of care by societal standards is the responsibility of a physician. The morality and conscience of our society places this responsibility in the hands of the physician. What justification is there to remove it from the control of the medical profession and place it in the hands of the courts?" For its part, the New Jersey Supreme Court concluded that "a practice of applying to a court to confirm such decisions would generally be inappropriate, not only because that would be a gratuitous encroachment upon the medical profession's field of competence, but because it would be impossibly cumbersome. Such a requirement is distinguishable from the judicial overview traditionally required in other matters such as the adjudication and commitment of mental incompetents. This is not to say that in the case of an otherwise justiciable controversy access to the courts would be foreclosed; we speak rather of a general practice and procedure."

We do not view the judicial resolution of this most difficult and awesome question—whether potentially life-prolonging treatment should be withheld from a person incapable of making his own decision—as constituting a "gratuitous encroachment" on the domain of medical expertise. Rather, such questions of life and death seem to us to require the process of detached but passionate* investigation and decision that forms the ideal on which the judicial branch of government was created. Achieving this ideal is our responsibility and that of the lower court, and is not to be entrusted to any other group purporting to represent the "morality and conscience of our society," no matter how highly motivated or impressively constituted.

III

Finding no State interest sufficient to counterbalance a patient's decision to decline life-prolonging medical treatment in the circumstances of this case, we conclude that the patient's right to privacy and self-determination is entitled to enforcement. Because of this conclusion, and in view of the position of equality of an incompetent person in Joseph Saikewicz's position, we conclude that the probate judge acted appropriately in this case. For these reasons we issued our order of July 9, 1976, and responded as we did to the questions of the probate judge.

* [The correct reading should probably be "compassionate." Ed.]

SOME NONRELIGIOUS VIEWS AGAINST PROPOSED "MERCY-KILLING" LEGISLATION

[Professor Kamisar's article was in response to a book by Glanville Williams, *The Sanctity of Life and the Criminal Law,* which advocated legislation that would permit euthanasia under certain circumstances. The excerpts that follow give the essence of Kamisar's arguments against such legislation.]

As an ultimate philosophical proposition, the case for voluntary euthanasia is strong. Whatever may be said for and against suicide generally, the appeal of death is immeasurably greater when it is sought not for a poor reason or just any reason, but for "good cause," so to speak; when it is invoked not on behalf of a "socially useful" person, but on behalf of, for example, the pain-racked "hopelessly incurable" cancer victim. *If* a person is *in fact* (1) presently incurable, (2) beyond the aid of any respite which may come along in his life expectancy, suffering (3) intolerable and (4) unmitigable pain and of a (5) fixed and (6) rational desire to die, I would hate to have to argue that the hand of death should be stayed. But abstract propositions and carefully formed hypotheticals are one thing; specific proposals designed to cover everyday situations are something else again.

In essence, Williams' specific proposal is that death be authorized for a person in the above situation "by giving the medical practitioner a wide discretion and trusting to his good sense." This, I submit, raises too great a risk of abuse and mistake to warrant a change in the existing law. That a proposal entails risk of mistake is hardly a conclusive reason against it. But neither is it irrelevant. Under any euthanasia program the consequences of mistake, of course, are always fatal. As I shall endeavor to show, the incidence of mistake of one kind or another is likely to be quite appreciable. If this indeed be the case, unless the need for the authorized conduct is compelling enough to override it, I take it the risk of mistake *is* a conclusive reason against such authorization. I submit too, that the possible radiations from the proposed legislation, *e.g.,* involuntary euthanasia of idiots and imbeciles (the typical "mercy-killings" reported by the press) and the emergence of the legal precedent that there are lives not "worth living," give additional cause to pause.

I see the issue, then, as the need for voluntary euthanasia versus (1)

These excerpts are reprinted by permission of the author and the *Minnesota Law Review.* First published in the *Minnesota Law Review* 42 (1958): 969ff. Copyright 1958 by *Minnesota Law Review.* Many footnotes were deleted, and those remaining were renumbered.

the incidence of mistake and abuse; and (2) the danger that legal machinery initially designed to kill those who are a nuisance to themselves may someday engulf those who are a nuisance to others.

The "freedom to choose a merciful death by euthanasia" may well be regarded . . . as "a special area of civil liberties far removed from the familiar concerns with criminal procedures, race discrimination and freedom of speech and religion." The civil liberties angle is definitely a part of Professor Williams' approach:

> If the law were to remove its ban on euthanasia, the effect would merely be to leave this subject to the individual conscience. This proposal would . . . be easy to defend, as restoring personal liberty in a field in which men differ on the question of conscience. . . .
> On a question like this there is surely everything to be said for the liberty of the individual.

I am perfectly willing to accept civil liberties as the battlefield, but issues of "liberty" and "freedom" mean little until we begin to pin down *whose* "liberty" and "freedom" and for *what* need and at *what* price. This paper is concerned largely with such questions.

> It is true also of journeys in the law that the place you reach depends on the direction you are taking. And so, where one comes out on a case depends on where one goes in.

So it is with the question at hand. Williams champions the "personal liberty" of the dying to die painlessly. I am more concerned about the life and liberty of those who would needlessly be killed in the process or who would irrationally choose to partake of the process. Williams' price on behalf of those who are *in fact* "hopeless incurables" and *in fact* of a fixed and rational desire to die is the sacrifice of (1) some few, who, though they know it not, because their physicians know it not, need not and should not die; (2) others, probably not so few, who, though they go through the motions of "volunteering", are casualties of strain, pain or narcotics to such an extent that they really know not what they do. My price on behalf of those who, despite appearances to the contrary, have some relatively normal and reasonably useful life left in them, or who are incapable of making the choice, is the lingering on for awhile of those who, if you will, *in fact* have no desire and no reason to linger on. . . .

B. The "Choice"

Under current proposals to establish legal machinery, elaborate or otherwise, for the administration of a quick and easy death, it is not enough that those authorized to pass on the question decide that the patient, in effect, is "better off dead." The patient must concur in this opinion. Much of the appeal in the current proposal lies in this so-called "voluntary" attribute.

But is the adult patient really in a position to concur? Is he truly able to make euthanasia a "voluntary" act? There is a good deal to be said, is there not, for Dr. Frohman's pithy comment that the "voluntary" plan is supposed to be carried out "only if the victim is both sane and crazed by pain."

By hypothesis, voluntary euthanasia is not to be resorted to until narcotics have long since been administered and the patient has developed a tolerance to them. *When,* then, does the patient make the choice? While heavily drugged? Or is narcotic relief to be withdrawn for the time of decision? But if heavy dosage no longer deadens pain, indeed, no longer makes it bearable, how overwhelming is it when whatever relief narcotics offer is taken away, too?

"Hypersensitivity to pain after analgesia has worn off is nearly always noted." Moreover, "the mental side-effects of narcotics, unfortunately for anyone wishing to suspend them temporarily without unduly tormenting the patient, appear to outlast the analgesic effect" and "by many hours." The situation is further complicated by the fact that "a person in terminal stages of cancer who had been given morphine steadily for a matter of weeks would certainly be dependent upon it physically and would probably be addicted to it and react with the addict's response."

The narcotics problem aside, Dr. Benjamin Miller, who probably has personally experienced more pain than any other commentator on the euthanasia scene, observes:

> Anyone who has been severely ill knows how distorted his judgment became during the worst moments of the illness. Pain and the toxic effect of disease, or the violent reaction to certain surgical procedures may change our capacity for rational and courageous thought.

If, say, a man in this plight were a criminal defendant and he were to decline the assistance of counsel would the courts hold that he had "intelligently and understandingly waived the benefit of counsel?"

Undoubtedly, some euthanasia candidates will have their lucid moments. How they are to be distinguished from fellow-sufferers who do not, or how these instances are to be distinguished from others when the patient is exercising an irrational judgment is not an easy matter. Particularly is this so under Williams' proposal, where no specially qualified persons, psychiatrically trained or otherwise, are to assist in the process.

Assuming, for purposes of argument, that the occasion when a euthanasia candidate possesses a sufficiently clear mind can be ascertained and that a request for euthanasia is then made, there remain other problems. The mind of the pain-racked may occasionally be clear, but is it not also likely to be uncertain and variable? . . .

The concept of "voluntary" in voluntary euthanasia would have a great deal more substance to it if, as is the case with voluntary admission statutes for the mentally ill, the patient retained the right to reverse the process within a specified number of days after he gives written notice of his desire to do so—but unfortunately this cannot be. The choice here, of course, is an irrevocable one. . . .

Professor Williams states that where a pre-pain desire for "ultimate euthanasia" is "reaffirmed" under pain, "there is the best possible proof of full consent." Perhaps. But what if it is alternately renounced and reaffirmed under pain? What if it is neither affirmed or renounced? What if it is only renounced? Will a physician be free to go ahead on the ground that the prior desire was "rational," but the present desire "irrational"? Under Williams' plan, will not the physician frequently "be walking in the margin of the law"—just as he is now? Do we really accomplish much more under this proposal than to put the euthanasia principle on the books?

Even if the patient's choice could be said to be "clear and incontrovertible," do not other difficulties remain? Is this the kind of choice, assuming that it can be made in a fixed and rational manner, that we want to offer a gravely ill person? Will we not sweep up, in the process, some who are not really tired of life, but think others are tired of them; some who do not really want to die, but who feel they should not live on, because to do so when there looms the legal alternative of euthanasia is to do a selfish or a cowardly act? Will not some feel an obligation to have themselves "eliminated" in order that funds allocated for their terminal care might be better used by their families or, financial worries aside, in order to relieve their families of the emotional strain involved?

It would not be surprising for the gravely ill person to seek to inquire of those close to him whether he should avail himself of the legal alternative of euthanasia. Certainly, he is likely to wonder about their attitude in the matter. It is quite possible, is it not, that he will not exactly be gratified by any inclination on their part—however noble their motives may be in fact—that he resort to the new procedure? At this stage, the patient-family relationship may well be a good deal less than it ought to be:

> Illness, pain and fear of death tend to activate the dependent longings
> [for the family unit]. Conflict can easily arise, since it may be very difficult
> for the individual to satisfy his need for these passive dependent needs
> and his previous concept of the necessity for a competitive, constructive
> individuality. Our culture provides few defenses for this type of stress
> beyond a suppression of the need. If the individual's defenses break down,
> he may feel angry toward himself and toward the members of his family.

And what of the relatives? If their views will not always influence the patient, will they not at least influence the attending physician? Will a physician assume the risks to his reputation, if not his pocketbook, by administering the *coup de grace* over the objection—however irrational—of a close relative? Do not the relatives, then, also have a "choice"? Is not the decision on their part to do nothing and say nothing *itself* a "choice"? In many families there will be some, will there not, who will consider a stand against euthanasia the only proof of love, devotion and gratitude for past events? What of the stress and strife if close relatives differ . . . over the desirability of euthanatizing the patient?

At such a time, . . . members of the family are not likely to be in the best state of mind, either, to make this kind of decision. Financial stress and conscious or unconscious competition for the family's estate aside:

> The chronic illness and persistent pain in terminal carcinoma may place
> strong and excessive stresses upon the family's emotional ties with the

patient. The family members who have strong emotional attachment to start with are most likely to take the patient's fears, pains and fate personally. Panic often strikes them. Whatever guilt feelings they may have toward the patient emerge to plague them.

If the patient is maintained at home, many frustrations and physical demands may be imposed on the family by the advanced illness. There may develop extreme weakness, incontinence and bad odors. The pressure of caring for the individual under these circumstances is likely to arouse a resentment and, in turn, guilt feelings on the part of those who have to do the nursing

. . .

C. The "Hopelessly Incurable" Patient and the Fallible Doctor

[Professor Kamisar goes on to discuss the fallibility of physicians—their inability to diagnose accurately every case that comes before them and the likelihood that, in at least some instances, their incorrect diagnoses might lead to the deaths of patients whose cases were not as hopeless as they might have appeared to be.

[Turning to the "hopelessly incurable" patient, he notes that before the discovery of insulin, many a diabetic was doomed. And before more recent treatments for certain diseases of the liver, and the development of the so-called wonder drugs, many patients' cases were regarded as hopeless, while today they are treated and cured routinely. He suggests that the same might be true of seemingly hopeless cancer cases as well, concluding that the term "incurable" should be dropped altogether.]

D. "Mistakes Are Always Possible"

. . . A relevant question . . . is what is the need for euthanasia which leads us to tolerate the mistakes, the very fatal mistakes, which will inevitably occur? What is the compelling force which requires us to tinker with deeply entrenched and almost universal precepts of criminal law?

Let us first examine the qualitative need for euthanasia:

Proponents of euthanasia like to present for consideration the case of the surgical operation, particularly a highly dangerous one: risk of death is substantial, perhaps even more probable than not; in addition, there is always the risk that the doctors have misjudged the situation and that no operation was needed at all. Yet it is not unlawful to perform the operation.

The short answer is the witticism that whatever the incidence of death in connection with different types of operations "no doubt, it is in all cases below 100 per cent, which is the incidence rate for euthanasia." But this may not be the full answer. There are occasions where the law permits action involving about a 100 per cent incidence of death, for example, self-defense. There may well be other instances where the law should condone such action, for example, the "necessity" cases illustrated by the overcrowded lifeboat, the starving survivors of a ship-wreck, and—perhaps best of all—by Professor Lon Fuller's penetrating and fascinating tale of the trapped cave explorers.

In all these situations, death for some may well be excused, if not justified, yet the prospect that some deaths will be unnecessary is a real one. He who kills in self-defense may have misjudged the facts. They who throw passengers overboard to lighten the load may no sooner do so than see "masts and sails of rescue . . . emerge out of the fog." But no human being will ever find himself in a situation where he knows for an absolute certainty that one or several must die that he or others may live. "Modern legal systems . . . do not require divine knowledge of human beings."

Reasonable mistakes, then, may be tolerated if as in the above circumstances and as in the case of the surgical operation, these mistakes are the inevitable by-products of efforts to save one or more human lives.

The need the euthanasiast advances, however, is a good deal less compelling. It is only to ease pain. . . .

[Turning to the quantitative need for euthanasia, Professor Kamisar suggests that in view of the many palliative measures that are available, including psychotherapy and drugs, as well as others, relief from the pain that often accompanies cancer might well be achieved so that its victims would not desire to die. Further, he expresses his doubt as to whether many of those who are suffering intense pain really desire death, even though they may desire it at particular times.

[He then moves on to consider the distinctions between voluntary and involuntary euthanasia, observing that, among those advocating legalized euthanasia for voluntary cases, there are some who also advocate involuntary euthanasia for "elderly persons—individuals who had reached a degenerative stage of life." There are also some who advocate involuntary euthanasia of the "deaf, dumb, and crippled," as a member of the House of Lords indicated he would do in the debate on the subject, and of imbeciles and mindless idiots as well as hopelessly defective infants.

[Acknowledging that all of this is a "wedge" (or "slippery slope") objection, Kamisar continues:]

It is true that the "wedge" objection can always be advanced, the horrors can always be paraded. But it is no less true that on some occasions the objection is much more valid than it is on others. One reason why the "parade of horrors" cannot be too lightly dismissed in this particular instance is that Miss Voluntary Euthanasia is not likely to be going it alone for very long. Many of her admirers, as I have endeavored to show in the preceding section, would be neither surprised nor distressed to see her joined by Miss Euthanatize the Congenital Idiots and Miss Euthanatize the Permanently Insane and Miss Euthanatize the Senile Dementia. And these lasses—whether or not they themselves constitute a "parade of horrors"—certainly make excellent majorettes for such a parade:

> Some are proposing what is called euthanasia; at present only a proposal for killing those who are a nuisance to themselves; but soon to be applied to those who are a nuisance to other people.

Another reason why the "parade of horrors" argument cannot be too lightly dismissed in this particular instance, it seems to me, is that the parade *has* taken place in our time and the order of procession has been headed by the killing of the "incurables" and the "useless":

Even before the Nazis took open charge in Germany, a propaganda barrage was directed against the traditional compassionate nineteenth-century attitudes toward the chronically ill, and for the adoption of a utilitarian, Hegelian point of view. . . . Lay opinion was not neglected in this campaign. Adults were propagandized by motion pictures, one of which, entitled 'I Accuse', deals entirely with euthanasia. This film depicts the life history of a woman suffering from multiple sclerosis; in it her husband, a doctor, finally kills her to the accompaniment of soft piano music rendered by a sympathetic colleague in an adjoining room. Acceptance of this ideology was implanted even in the children. A widely used high-school mathematics text. . . included problems stated in distorted terms of the cost of caring for and rehabilitating the chronically sick and crippled. One of the problems asked, for instance, how many new housing units could be built and how many marriage-allowance loans could be given to newly wedded couples for the amount of money it cost the state to care for 'the crippled, the criminal and the insane. . . .' The beginnings at first were merely a subtle shift in emphasis in the basic attitude of the physicians. *It started with the acceptance of the attitude, basic in the euthanasia movement, that there is such a thing as life not worthy to be lived.* This attitude in its early stages concerned itself merely with the severely and chronically sick. Gradually the sphere of those to be included in this category was enlarged to encompass the socially unproductive, the ideologically unwanted, the racially unwanted and finally all non-Germans. But it is important to realize that the infinitely small wedged-in lever from which this entire trend of mind received its impetus was the attitude toward the non-rehabilitatable sick.[1]

[1] Alexander, *Medical Science Under Dictatorship,* 241 New England Journal of Medicine 39, 44, 40 (1949) (emphasis added). To the same effect is Ivy, *Nazi War Crimes of a Medical Nature,* 139 J.A.M.A. 131, 132 (1949), concluding that the practice of euthanasia was a factor which led to "mass killing of the aged, the chronically ill, 'useless eaters' and the politically undesirable," and Ivy, *Nazi War Crimes of a Medical Nature,* 33 Federation Bulletin 133, 142 (1947), noting that one of the arguments the Nazis employed to condone their criminal medical experiments was that "if it is right to take the life of useless and incurable persons, which as they point out has been suggested in England and the United States, then it is right to take the lives of persons who are destined to die for political reasons."

Doctors Leo Alexander and A. C. Ivy were both expert medical advisors to the prosecution at the Nuremberg Trials.

See also the November 25, 1940 entry to Shirer, *Berlin Diary* 454, 458–59 (1941): I have at last got to the bottom of these "mercy killings." It's an evil tale. The Gestapo, with the knowledge and approval of the German government, is systematically putting to death the mentally deficient population of the Reich. . . . X, a German told me yesterday that relatives are rushing to get their kin out of private asylums and out of the clutches of the authorities. He says the Gestapo is doing to death persons who are merely suffering temporary derangement or just plain nervous breakdown.

What is still unclear to me is the motive for these murders. Germans themselves advance three:

∙ ∙ ∙

3. That they are simply the result of the extreme Nazis deciding to carry out their eugenic and sociological ideas.

∙ ∙ ∙

The third motive seems most likely to me. For years a group of radical Nazi sociologists who were instrumental in putting through the Reich's sterilization laws have pressed for a national policy of eliminating the mentally unfit. They

The apparent innocuousness of Germany's "small beginnings" is perhaps best shown by the fact that German Jews were at first excluded from the program. For it was originally conceived that "the blessing of euthanasia should be granted only to [true] Germans."

Relatively early in the German program, Pastor Braune, Chairman of the Executive Committee of the Domestic Welfare Council of the German Protestant Church, called for a halt to euthanasia measures "since they strike sharply at the moral foundations of the nation as a whole. The inviolability of human life is a pillar of any social order." And the pastor raised the same question which euthanasia opponents ask today, as well they might, considering the disinclination of many in the movement to stop at voluntary "mercy killings": Where do we, how do we, draw the line? The good pastor asked:

> How far is the destruction of socially unfit life to go? The mass methods used so far have quite evidently taken in many people who are to a considerable degree of sound mind. . . . Is it intended to strike only at the utterly hopeless cases—the idiots and imbeciles? The instruction sheet, as already mentioned, also lists senile diseases. The latest decree by the same authorities requires that children with serious congenital disease and malformation of every kind be registered, to be collected and processed in special institutions. This necessarily gives rise to grave apprehensions. Will a line be drawn at the tubercular? In the case of persons in custody by court order euthanasia measures have evidently already been initiated. Are other abnormal or anti-social persons likewise to be included? Where is the borderline? Who is abnormal, antisocial, hopelessly sick?

Williams makes no attempt to distinguish or minimize the Nazi Germany experience. Apparently he does not consider it worthy of mention in a euthanasia discussion. There are, however, a couple of obvious arguments by which the Nazi experience can be minimized.

One goes something like this: It is silly to worry about the prospects

---

say they have disciples among many sociologists in other lands, and perhaps they have. Paragraph two of the form letter sent the relatives plainly bears the stamp of the sociological thinking: "In view of the nature of his serious, incurable ailment, his death, which saved him from a lifelong institutional sojourn, is to be regarded merely as a release."

This contemporaneous report is supported by evidence uncovered at the Nuremberg Medical Trial. Thus, an August, 1940 form letter to the relatives of a deceased mental patient states in part: "Because of her grave mental illness life was a torment for the deceased. You must therefore look on her death as a release." This form letter is reproduced in Mitscherlich and Mielke, Doctors of Infamy 103 (1949). Dr. Alexander Mitscherlich and Mr. Fred Mielke attended the trial as delegates chosen by a group of German medical societies and universities.

According to the testimony of the chief defendant at the Nuremberg Medical Trial, Karl Brandt, Reich Commissioner for Health and Sanitation and personal physician to Hitler, the Fuhrer has indicated in 1935 that if war came he would effectuate the policy of euthanasia since in the general upheaval of war the open resistance to be anticipated on the part of the church would not be the potent force it might otherwise be.

Certain petitions to Hitler by parents of malformed children requesting authority for "mercy deaths" seem to have played a part in definitely making up his mind.

of a dictatorship utilizing euthanasia "as a pretext for putting inconvenient citizens out of the way. Dictatorships have no occasion for such
subterfuges. The firing squad is less bother." One reason why this counter argument is not too reassuring, however, if again I may be permitted
to be so unkind as to meet speculation with a concrete example to the
contrary, is that Nazi Germany had considerable occasion to use just
such a subterfuge.

Thus, Dr. Leo Alexander observes:

> It is rather significant that the German people were considered by their
> Nazi leaders more ready to accept the exterminations of the sick than
> those for political reasons. It was for that reason that the first exterminations
> of the latter group were carried out under the guise of sickness. So-called
> "psychiatric experts" were dispatched to survey the inmates of camps
> with the specific order to pick out members of racial minorities
> and political offenders from occupied territories and to dispatch them
> to killing centers with specially made diagnoses such as that of "inveterate
> German hater" applied to a number of prisoners who had been active in
> the Czech underground.
>
> . . .
>
> A large number of those marked for death for political or racial reasons
> were made available for medical experiments involving the use of
> involuntary human subjects.

The "hunting season" in Germany officially opened when, Hitler signed
on his own letterhead, a secret order dated September 1, 1939, which
read:

> Reichsleiter Bouhler and Dr. Brandt, M.D., are charged with the
> responsibility of enlarging the authority of certain physicians, to be
> designated by name, in such a manner that persons who, according to
> human judgment, are incurable can, upon a more careful diagnosis of their
> condition of sickness, be accorded a mercy death.

Physicians asked to participate in the program were told that the
secrecy of the order was designed to prevent patients from becoming "too
agitated" and that it was in keeping with the policy of not publicizing
home front measures in time of war.

About the same time that aged patients in some hospitals were being
given the "mercy" treatment, the Gestapo was also "systematically putting to death the mentally deficient population of the Reich."

The courageous and successful refusal by a Protestant pastor to deliver up certain cases from his asylum well demonstrates that even the
most totalitarian governments are not always indifferent to the feelings
of the people, that they do not always feel free to resort to the firing
squad. Indeed, vigorous protests by other ecclesiastical personalities and
some physicians, numerous requests of various public prosecutors for investigation of the circumstances surrounding the mysterious passing
away of relatives, and a generally aroused public opinion finally caused

Hitler to yield, if only temporarily, and in August of 1941 he verbally ordered the discontinuance of the adult euthanasia program. Special gas chambers in Hadamar and other institutions were dismantled and shipped to the East for much more extensive use of Polish Jews.

Perhaps it should be noted, too, that even dictatorships fall prey to the inertia of big government:

> It is . . . interesting that there was so much talk against euthanasia in certain areas of Germany, particularly in the region of Wiesbaden, that Hitler in 1943 asked Himmler to stop it. But, it had gained so much impetus by 1943 and was such an easy way in crowded concentration camps to get rid of undesirables and make room for newcomers, that it could not be stopped. The wind had become a whirlwind.

Another obvious argument is that it just can't happen here. I hope not. I think not.

But then, neither did I think that tens of thousands of perfectly loyal native-born Americans would be herded into prison camps without proffer of charges and held there for many months, even years, because they were of "Japanese blood" and, although the general who required these measures emitted considerable ignorance and bigotry, his so-called military judgment would be largely sustained by the highest court of the land. The Japanese American experience of World War II undoubtedly fell somewhat short of first-class Nazi tactics, but we were getting warm. I venture to say it would not be too difficult to find American citizens of Japanese descent who would maintain we were getting very warm indeed.

In this regard, some of Justice Jackson's observations in his *Korematsu* dissent seem quite pertinent:

> All who observe the work of courts are familiar with what Judge Cardozo described as "the tendency of a principle to expand itself to the limit of its logic." [Nature of the Judicial Process, p. 51.] A military commander may overstep the bounds of constitutionality, and it is an incident. But if we review and approve, that passing incident becomes the doctrine of the Constitution. There it has a generative power of its own, and all that it creates will be in its own image. Nothing better illustrates this danger than does the Court's opinion in this case.
>
> It argues that we are bound to uphold the conviction of Korematsu because we upheld one in *Hirabayashi v. United States,* 320 U.S. 81, when we sustained these orders in so far as they applied a curfew requirement to a citizen of Japanese ancestry. I think we should learn something from that experience.
>
> In that case we were urged to consider only the curfew feature, that being all that technically was involved, because it was the only count necessary to sustain Hirabayashi's conviction and sentence. We yielded, and the Chief Justice guarded the opinion as carefully as language will do. . . . However, in spite of our limiting words we did validate a discrimination on the basis of ancestry for mild and temporary deprivation of liberty. Now the principle of racial discrimination is pushed from

support of mild measures to very harsh ones, and from temporary deprivations to indeterminate ones. And the precedent which it is said requires us to do so is *Hirabayashi*. The Court is now saying that in *Hirabayashi* we did decide the very things we there said we were not deciding. Because we said that these citizens could be made to stay in their homes during the hours of dark, it is said we must require them to leave home entirely; and if that, we are told they may also be taken into custody for deportation; and if that, it is argued they may also be held for some undetermined time in detention camps. How far the principle of this case would be extended before plausible reasons would play out, I do not know.[2]

It can't happen here. Well, maybe it cannot, but no small part of our Constitution and no small number of our Supreme Court opinions stem from the fear that *it can happen here unless we darn well make sure that it does not* by adamantly holding the line, by swiftly snuffing out what are or might be small beginnings of what we do not want to happen here. To flick off, as Professor Williams does, the fears about legalized euthanasia as so much nonsense, as a chimerical "parade of horrors," is to sweep away much of the ground on which all our civil liberties rest.

Boyd,[3] the landmark search and seizure case which paved the way for the federal rule of exclusion, a doctrine which now prevails in over twenty state courts as well, set the mood of our day in treating those accused of crime:

> It may be that it is the obnoxious thing in its mildest and least repulsive form; but illegitimate and unconstitutional practices get their first footing in that way, namely, by silent approaches and slight deviations from legal modes of procedure. . . . It is the duty of courts to be watchful for the constitutional rights of the citizen, and against any stealthy encroachments thereon. Their motto should be *obsta principiis*... ...[4]

Recent years have seen the Supreme Court sharply divided on search and seizure questions. The differences, however, have been over *application,* not over the *Boyd-Weeks* "wedge principle"; not over the view, as the great Learned Hand, hardly the frightened spinster type, put it in an oft-quoted phrase, "that what seems fair enough against a squalid huckster of bad liquor may take on a very different face, if used by a

---

2 323 U.S. at 246–47.

3 Boyd v. United States, 116 U.S. 616 (1886).

4 116 U.S. 616, 635. The search and seizure cases contain about as good an articulation of the "wedge principle" as one can find anywhere, except, perhaps if one turns to the recent *Covert* and *Krueger* cases, where Mr. Justice Black quotes the *Boyd* statement with approval and applies it with vigor:

> It is urged that the expansion of military jurisdiction over civilians claimed here is only slight, and that the practical necessity for it is very great. The attitude appears to be that a slight encroachment on the Bill of Rights and other safeguards in the Constitution need cause little concern. But to hold that these wives could be tried by the military would be a tempting precedent. Slight encroachments create new boundaries from which legions of power can seek new territory to capture. Reid v. Covert, 354 U.S. 1, 39–40 (1957).

government determined to suppress political opposition under the guise of sedition." [5] And when the dissenters have felt compelled to reiterate the reasons for the principle, lest its force be diminished by the failure to apply it in the particular case, and they have groped for the most powerful arguments in its behalf, where have they turned, what have they done? Why, they have employed the very arguments Glanville Williams dismisses so contemptuously. They have cited the Nazi experience. They have talked of the police state, the Knock at the Door, the suppression of political opposition under the guise of sedition. They have trotted out, if you will, the "parade of horrors." [6]

The lengths to which the Court will go in applying the "wedge principle" in the First Amendment area is well demonstrated by instances where those who have labeled Jews "slimy scum" and likened them to "bedbugs" and "snakes" or who have denounced them "as all the garbage that . . . should have been burnt in the incinerators" have been sheltered by the Court so that freedom of speech and religion would not be impaired. Perhaps the supreme example is the *Barnette* case.

There, in striking down the compulsory flag salute and pledge, Justice Jackson took the position that "those who begin coercive elimination of dissent soon find themselves exterminating dissenters. Compulsory unification of opinion achieves only the unanimity of the graveyard." [7] "The First Amendment," he pointed out, "was designed to avoid these ends by avoiding these beginnings." Justices Black and Douglas kept in step in their concurring opinion by advancing the view that "the ceremonial, when enforced against conscientious objectors . . . is a handy implement for disguised religious persecution."

What were these pernicious "beginnings" again? What was this danger-laden ceremonial again? Why, requiring public school pupils "to par-

---

[5] United States v. Kirschenblatt, 16 F.2d 202, 203 (2d Cir. 1926).
[6] Thus, in Brinegar v. United States, 338 U.S. 160 (1949), it was Jackson the Chief Counsel of the United States at the Nuremberg Trials as well as Jackson the Supreme Court Justice who warned (338 U.S. at 180–81):
> Among deprivations of rights, none is so effective in cowing a population, crushing the spirit of the individual and putting terror in every heart. Uncontrolled search and seizure is one of the first and most effective weapons in the arsenal of every arbitrary government. And one need only briefly to have dwelt and worked among a people possessed of many admirable qualities but deprived of these rights to know that the human personality deteriorates and dignity and self-reliance disappear where homes, persons and possessions are subject at any hour to unheralded search and seizure by the police.

In United States v. Rabinowitz, 339 U.S. 56, 82 (1950), Justice Frankfurter cautioned:
> By the Bill of Rights the founders of this country subordinated police action to legal restraints, not in order to convenience the guilty but to protect the innocent. Nor did they provide that only the innocent may appeal to these safeguards. They know too well that the successful prosecution of the guilty does not require jeopardy to the innocent. The knock at the door under the guise of a warrant of arrest for a venial or spurious offense was not unknown to them . . . We have had grim reminders in our day of their experience. Arrest under a warrant for a minor or a trumped-up charge has been familiar practice in the past, is a commonplace in the police state of today, and too well known in this country. . . . The progress is too easy from police action unscrutinized by judicial authorization to the police state.

[7] Board of Education v. Barnette, 319 U.S. 624 (1943), at 641.

ticipate in the salute honoring the Nation represented by the Flag." Talk about "parades of horror"! This one is an extravaganza against which anything euthanasia opponents can muster is drab and shabby by comparison. After all, whatever else Williams and his allies make "mercy-killings" out to be, *these* beginnings are not "patriotic ceremonies."

The point need not be labored. If the prospects of the police state, the knock on Everyman's door, and wide-spread political persecution are legitimate considerations when we enter "opium smoking dens," when we deal with "not very nice people" and "sordid little cases" then why should the prospects of the police state and the systematic extermination of certain political or racial minorities be taken any less seriously when we enter the sickroom or the mental institution, when we deal with not very healthy or not very useful people, when we discuss "euthanasia" under whatever trade name?

If freeing some rapist or murderer is not too great a price to pay for the "sanctity of the home", then why is allowing some cancer victim to suffer a little longer too great a price to pay for the "sanctity of life"? If the sheltering of purveyors of "hateful and hate-stirring attacks on races and faiths" may be justified in the name of a transcendent principle, then why may not postponing the death of the suffering "incurable" be similarly justified?

A FINAL REFLECTION

There have been and there will continue to be compelling circumstances when a doctor or relative or friend will violate The Law On The Books and, more often than not, receive protection from The Law In Action. But this is not to deny that there are other occasions when The Law On The Books operates to stay the hand of all concerned, among them situations where the patient is in fact (1) presently incurable, (2) beyond the aid of any respite which may come along in his life expectancy, suffering (3) intolerable and (4) unmitigable pain and of (5) fixed and (6) rational desire to die. That any euthanasia program may only be the opening wedge for far more objectionable practices, and that even within the bounds of a "voluntary" plan such as Williams' the incidence of mistake or abuse is likely to be substantial, are not much solace to one in the above plight.

It may be conceded that in a narrow sense it is an "evil" for such a patient to have to continue to suffer—if only for a little while. But in a narrow sense, long-term sentences and capital punishment are "evils," too. If we can justify the infliction of imprisonment and death by the state "on the ground of the social interests to be protected" then surely we can similarly justify the postponement of death by the state. The objection that the individual is thereby treated not as an "end" in himself but only as a "means" to further the common good was, I think, aptly disposed of by Holmes long ago. "If a man lives in society, he is likely to find himself so treated."

8 PHILIPPA FOOT

EUTHANASIA

The widely used *Shorter Oxford English Dictionary* gives three meanings for the word "euthanasia": the first, "a quiet and easy death"; the second, "the means of procuring this"; and the third, "the action of inducing a quiet and easy death." It is a curious fact that no one of the three gives an adequate definition of the word as it is usually understood. For "euthanasia" means much more than a quiet and easy death, or the means of procuring it, or the action of inducing it. The definition specifies only the manner of death, and if this were all that was implied a murderer, careful to drug his victim, could claim that his act was an act of euthanasia. We find this ridiculous because we take it for granted that in euthanasia it is death itself, not just the manner of death, that must be kind to the one who dies.

To see how important it is that "euthanasia" should not be used as the dictionary definition allows it to be used, merely to signify that a death was quiet and easy, one has only to remember than Hitler's "euthanasia" programme traded on this ambiguity. Under this programme, planned before the War but brought into full operation by a decree of 1 September 1939, some 275,000 people were gassed in centres which were to be a model for those in which Jews were later exterminated. Anyone in a state institution could be sent to the gas chambers if it was considered that he could not be "rehabilitated" for useful work. As Dr. Leo Alexander reports, relying on the testimony of a neuropathologist who received 500 brains from one of the killing centres,

> In Germany the exterminations included the mentally defective psychotics (particularly schizophrenics), epileptics and patients suffering from infirmities of old age and from various organic neurological disorders such as infantile paralysis, Parkinsonism, multiple sclerosis and brain tumors. . . . In truth, all those unable to work and considered nonrehabilitable were killed.[1]

These people were killed because they were "useless" and "a burden on society": only the manner of their deaths could be thought of as relatively easy and quiet.

Philippa Foot, "Euthanasia," *Philosophy & Public Affairs* 6, no. 2 (Winter 1977). Copyright © 1977 by Philippa Foot. Reprinted by permission of the author and Princeton University Press.
    I would like to thank Derek Parfit and the editors of *Philosophy & Public Affairs* for their very helpful comments.
1 Leo Alexander, 'Medical Science under Dictatorship', *New England Journal of Medicine*, 14 July 1949, p. 40.

Let us insist, then, that when we talk about euthanasia we are talking about a death understood as a good or happy event for the one who dies. This stipulation follows etymology, but is itself not exactly in line with current usage, which would be captured by the condition that the death should *not* be an evil rather than that it *should* be a good. That this is how people talk is shown by the fact that the case of Karen Ann Quinlan and others in a state of permanent coma is often discussed under the heading of "euthanasia." Perhaps it is not too late to object to the use of the word "euthanasia" in this sense. Apart from the break with the Greek origins of the word there are other unfortunate aspects of this extension of the term. For if we say that the death must be supposed to be a good to the subject we can also specify that it shall be for his sake that an act of euthanasia is performed. If we say merely that death shall not be an evil to him, we cannot stipulate that benefiting him shall be the motive where euthanasia is in question. Given the importance of the question, For whose sake are we acting? it is good to have a definition of euthanasia which brings under this heading only cases of opting for death for the sake of the one who dies. Perhaps what is most important is to say either that euthanasia is to be for the good of the subject or at least that death is to be no evil to him, thus refusing to talk Hitler's language. However, in this paper it is the first condition that will be understood, with the additional proviso that by an act of euthanasia we mean one of inducing or otherwise opting for death for the sake of the one who is to die.

A few lesser points need to be cleared up. In the first place it must be said that the word 'act' is not to be taken to exclude omission: we shall speak of an act of euthanasia when someone is deliberately allowed to die, for his own good, and not only when positive measures are taken to see that he does. The very general idea we want is that of a choice of action or inaction directed at another man's death and causally effective in the sense that, in conjunction with actual circumstances, it is a sufficient condition of death. Of complications such as overdetermination, it will not be necessary to speak.

A second, and definitely minor, point about the definition of an act of euthanasia concerns the question of fact versus belief. It has already been implied that one who performs an act of euthanasia thinks that death will be merciful for the subject since we have said that it is on account of this thought that the act is done. But is it enough that he acts with this thought, or must things actually be as he thinks them to be? If one man kills another, or allows him to die, thinking that he is in the last stages of a terrible disease, though in fact he could have been cured, is this an act of euthanasia or not? Nothing much seems to hang on our decision about this. The same condition has got to enter into the definition whether as an element in reality or only as an element in the agent's belief. And however we define an act of euthanasia culpability or justifiability will be the same: if a man acts through ignorance his ignorance may be culpable or it may not.[2]

2 For a discussion of culpable and nonculpable ignorance see Thomas Aquinas, *Summa Theologica*, First Part of the Second Part, Question 6, article 8, and Question 19, articles 5 and 6.

These are relatively easy problems to solve, but one that is dauntingly difficult has been passed over in this discussion of the definition, and must now be faced. It is easy to say, as if this raised no problems, that an act of euthanasia is by definition one aiming at the *good* of the one whose death is in question, and that it is *for his sake* that his death is desired. But how is this to be explained? Presumably we are thinking of some evil already with him or to come on him if he continues to live, and death is thought of as a release from this evil. But this cannot be enough. Most people's lives contain evils such as grief or pain, but we do not therefore think that death would be a blessing to them. On the contrary, life is generally supposed to be a good even for someone who is unusually unhappy or frustrated. How is it that one can ever wish for death for the sake of the one who is to die? This difficult question is central to the discussion of euthanasia, and we shall literally not know what we are talking about if we ask whether acts of euthanasia defined as we have defined them are ever morally permissible without first understanding better the reason for saying that life is a good, and the possibility that it is not always so.

If a man should save my life he would be my benefactor. In normal circumstances this is plainly true; but does one always benefit another in saving his life? It seems certain that he does not. Suppose, for instance, that a man were being tortured to death and was given a drug that lengthened his sufferings; this would not be a benefit but the reverse. Or suppose that in a ghetto in Nazi Germany a doctor saved the life of someone threatened by disease, but that the man once cured was transported to an extermination camp; the doctor might wish for the sake of the patient that he had died of the disease. Nor would a longer stretch of life always be a benefit to the person who was given it. Comparing Hitler's camps with those of Stalin, Dmitri Panin observes that in the latter the method of extermination was made worse by agonies that could stretch out over months.

> Death from a bullet would have been bliss compared with what many millions had to endure while dying of hunger. The kind of death to which they were condemned has nothing to equal it in treachery and sadism.[3]

These examples show that to save or prolong a man's life is not always to do him a service: it may be better for him if he dies earlier rather than later. It must therefore be agreed that while life is normally a benefit to the one who has it, this is not always so.

The judgement is often fairly easy to make—that life is or is not a good to someone—but the basis for it is very hard to find. When life is said to be a benefit or a good, on what grounds is the assertion made?

The difficulty is underestimated if it is supposed that the problem arises from the fact that one who is dead has nothing, so that the good someone gets from being alive cannot be compared with the amount he would otherwise have had. For why should this particular comparison

---

[3] Dmitri Panin, *The Notebooks of Sologdin* (London, 1976), pp. 66-7.

be necessary? Surely it would be enough if one could say whether or not someone whose life was prolonged had more good than evil in the extra stretch of time. Such estimates are not always possible, but frequently they are; we say, for example, "He was very happy in those last years," or, "He had little but unhappiness then." If the balance of good and evil determined whether life was a good to someone we would expect to find a correlation in the judgements. In fact, of course, we find nothing of the kind. First, a man who has no doubt that existence is a good to him may have no idea about the balance of happiness and unhappiness in his life, or of any other positive and negative factors that may be suggested. So the supposed criteria are not always operating where the judgment is made. And secondly the application of the criteria gives an answer that is often wrong. Many people have more evil than good in their lives; we do not, however, conclude that we would do these people no service by rescuing them from death.

To get around this last difficulty Thomas Nagel has suggested that experience itself is a good which must be brought in to balance accounts.

> . . . life is worth living even when the bad elements of experience are plentiful, and the good ones too meager to outweigh the bad ones on their own. The additional positive weight is supplied by experience itself, rather than by any of its contents.[4]

This seems implausible because if experience itself is a good it must be so even when what we experience is wholly bad, as in being tortured to death. How should one decide how much to count for this experiencing; and why count anything at all?

Others have tried to solve the problem by arguing that it is a man's desire for life that makes us call life a good: if he wants to live then anyone who prolongs his life does him a benefit. Yet someone may cling to life where we would say confidently that it would be better for him if he died, and he may admit it too. Speaking of those same conditions in which, as he said, a bullet would have been merciful, Panin writes,

> I should like to pass on my observations concerning the absence of suicides under the extremely severe conditions of our concentration camps. The more that life became desperate, the more a prisoner seemed determined to hold onto it.[5]

One might try to explain this by saying that hope was the ground of this wish to survive for further days and months in the camp. But there is nothing unintelligible in the idea that a man might cling to life though he knew those facts about his future which would make any charitable man wish that he might die.

The problem remains, and it is hard to know where to look for a solution. Is there a conceptual connexion between *life* and *good?* Be-

4 Thomas Nagel, "Death," in James Rachels, ed., *Moral Problems* (New York, 1971), p. 362.
5 Panin, *Sologdin,* p. 85.

cause life is not always a good we are apt to reject this idea, and to think that it must be a contingent fact that life is usually a good, as it is a contingent matter that legacies are usually a benefit, if they are. Yet it seems not to be a contingent matter that to save someone's life is ordinarily to benefit him. The problem is to find where the conceptual connexion lies.

It may be good tactics to forget for a time that it is euthanasia we are discussing and to see how *life* and *good* are connected in the case of living beings other than men. Even plants have things done to them that are harmful or beneficial, and what does them good must be related in some way to their living and dying. Let us therefore consider plants and animals, and then come back to human beings. At least we shall get away from the temptation to think that the connexion between life and benefit must everywhere be a matter of happiness and unhappiness or of pleasure and pain; the idea being absurd in the case of animals and impossible even to formulate for plants.

In case anyone thinks that the concept of the beneficial applies only in a secondary or analogical way to plants, he should be reminded that we speak quite straightforwardly in saying, for instance, that a certain amount of sunlight is beneficial to most plants. What is in question here is the habitat in which plants of particular species flourish, but we can also talk, in a slightly different way, of what does them good, where there is some suggestion of improvement or remedy. What has the beneficial to do with sustaining life? It is tempting to answer, "everything," thinking that a healthy condition just is the one apt to secure survival. In fact, however, what is beneficial to a plant may have to do with reproduction rather than survival of the individual member of the species. Nevertheless there is a plain connexion between the beneficial and the life-sustaining even for the individual plant; if something makes it better able to survive in conditions normal for that species it is ipso facto good for it. We need go no further, and could go no further, in explaining why a certain environment or treatment is good for a plant than to show how it helps this plant to survive.[6]

This connexion between the life-sustaining and the beneficial is reasonably unproblematic, and there is nothing fanciful or zoomorphic in speaking of benefiting or doing good to plants. A connexion with its survival can make something beneficial to a plant. But this is not, of course, to say that we count life as a good to a plant. We may save its life by giving it what is beneficial; we do not benefit it by saving its life.

A more ramified concept of benefit is used in speaking of animal life. New things can be said, such as that an animal is better or worse off for something that happened, or that it was a good or bad thing for it that it did happen. And new things count as benefit. In the first place, there is comfort, which often is, but need not be, related to health. When loosen-

---

[6] Yet some detail needs to be filled in to explain why we should not say that a scarecrow is beneficial to the plants it protects. Perhaps what is beneficial must either be a feature of the plant itself, such as protective prickles, or else must work on the plant directly, such as a line of trees which give it shade.

ing a collar which is too tight for a dog we can say, "That will be better for it." So we see that the words "better for it" have two different meanings which we mark when necessary by a difference of emphasis, saying "better *for* it" when health is involved. And secondly an animal can be benefited by having its life saved. "Could you do anything for it?" can be answered by, "Yes, I managed to save its life." Sometimes we may understand this, just as we would for a plant, to mean that we had checked some disease. But we can also do something for an animal by scaring away its predator. If we do this, it is a good thing for the animal that we did, unless of course it immediately meets a more unpleasant end by some other means. Similarly, on the bad side, an animal may be worse off for our intervention, and this not because it pines or suffers but simply because it gets killed.

The problem that vexes us when we think about euthanasia comes on the scene at this point. For if we can do something for an animal— can benefit it—by relieving its suffering but also by saving its life, where does the greater benefit come when only death will end pain? It seemed that life was a good in its own right; yet pain seemed to be an evil with equal status and could therefore make life not a good after all. Is it only life without pain that is a good when animals are concerned? This does not seem a crazy suggestion when we are thinking of animals, since unlike human beings they do not have suffering as part of their normal life. But it is perhaps the idea of ordinary life that matters here. We would not say that we had done anything for an animal if we had merely kept it alive, either in an unconscious state or in a condition where, though conscious, it was unable to operate in an ordinary way; and the fact is that animals in severe and continuous pain simply do not operate normally. So we do not, on the whole, have the option of doing the animal good by saving its life though the life would be a life of pain. No doubt there are borderline cases, but that is no problem. We are not trying to make new judgements possible, but rather to find the principle of the ones we do make.

When we reach human life the problems seem even more troublesome. For now we must take quite new things into account, such as the subject's own view of his life. It is arguable that this places extra constraints on the solution: might it not be counted as a necessary condition of life's being a good to a man that he should see it as such? Is there not some difficulty about the idea that a benefit might be done to him by the saving or prolonging of his life even though he himself wished for death? Of course he might have a quite mistaken view of his own prospects, but let us ignore this and think only of cases where it is life as he knows it that is in question. Can we think that the prolonging of this life would be a benefit to him even though he would rather have it end than continue? It seems that this cannot be ruled out. That there is no simple incompatibility between life as a good and the wish for death is shown by the possibility that a man should wish himself dead, not for his own sake, but for the sake of someone else. And if we try to amend the thesis to say that life cannot be a good to one who wishes *for his own sake* that he should die, we find the crucial concept slipping through our fingers. As Bishop Butler pointed out long ago not all ends are either benevolent or self-interested. Does a man wish for death for his own sake in the relevant sense if, for instance, he wishes to revenge himself on another by his death? Or what if he is proud and refuses to stomach dependence or incapacity even though there are many good things left in life for him? The truth seems to be that the wish for death is sometimes compatible with life's being a good and sometimes not, which is possible because the description "wishing for death" is one covering diverse states of mind from that of the determined suicide, pathologically depressed, to that of one who is surprised to find that the thought of a fatal accident is viewed with relief. On the one hand, a man may see his life as a burden but go about his business in a more or less ordinary way; on the other hand, the wish for death may take the form of a rejection of everything that is in life, as it does in severe depression. It seems reasonable to say that life is not a good to one permanently in the latter state, and we must return to this topic later on.

When are we to say that life is a good or a benefit to a man? The dilemma that faces us is this. If we say that life as such is a good we find ourselves refuted by the examples given at the beginning of this discussion. We therefore incline to think that it is as bringing good things that life is a good, where it is a good. But if life is a good only because it is the condition of good things why is it not equally an evil when it brings bad things? And how can it be a good even when it brings more evil than good?

It should be noted that the problem has here been formulated in terms of the balance of good and evil, not that of happiness and unhappiness, and that it is not to be solved by the denial (which may be reasonable enough) that unhappiness is the only evil or happiness the only good. In this paper no view has been expressed about the nature of goods other than life itself. The point is that on any view of the goods and evils that life can contain, it seems that a life with more evil than good could still itself be a good.

It may be useful to review the judgements with which our theory must square. Do we think that life can be a good to one who suffers a lot of pain? Clearly we do. What about severely handicapped people; can life be a good to them? Clearly it can be, for even if someone is almost completely paralysed, perhaps living in an iron lung, perhaps able to move things only by means of a tube held between his lips, we do not rule him out of order if he says that some benefactor saved his life. Nor is it different with mental handicap. There are many fairly severely handicapped people—such as those with Down's Syndrome (Mongolism)—for whom a simple affectionate life is possible. What about senility? Does this break the normal connexion between life and good? Here we must surely distinguish between forms of senility. Some forms leave a life which we count someone as better off having than not having, so that a doctor who prolonged it would benefit the person concerned. With some kinds of senility this is however no longer true. There are some in geriatric wards who are barely conscious, though they can move a little and swallow food put into their mouths. To prolong such a state, whether in the old or in the very severely mentally handicapped is not to do them a service or confer a benefit. But of course it need not be the reverse: only if there is suffering would one wish for the sake of the patient that he should die.

It seems, therefore, that merely being alive even without suffering is not a good, and that we must make a distinction similar to that which we made when animals were our topic. But how is the line to be drawn in the case of men? What is to count as ordinary human life in the relevant sense? If it were only the very senile or very ill who were said not to have this life it might seem right to describe it in terms of *operation*. But it will be hard to find the sense in which the men described by Panin were not operating, given that they dragged themselves out to the forest to work. What is it about the life that the prisoners were living that makes us put it on the other side of the dividing line from that of most of the physically or mentally handicapped and of some severely ill or suffering patients? It is not that they were in captivity, for life in captivity can certainly be a good. Nor is it merely the unusual nature of their life. In some ways the prisoners were living more as other men do than the patient in the iron lung.

The idea we need seems to be that of life which is ordinary human life in the following respect—that it contains a minimum of basic human goods. What is ordinary in human life—even in very hard lives—is that a man is not driven to work far beyond his capacity; that he has the support of a family or community; that he can more or less satisfy his hunger; that he has hopes for the future; that he can lie down to rest at night. Such things were denied to the men in the Vyatlag camps described by Panin; not even rest at night was allowed them when they were tormented by bed-bugs, by noise and stench, and by routines such as body-searches and bath-parades—arranged for the night time so that work norms would not be reduced. Disease too can so take over a man's life that the normal human goods disappear. When a patient is so overwhelmed by pain or nausea that he cannot eat with pleasure, if he can eat at all, and is out of the reach of even the most loving voice, he no longer has ordinary human life in the sense in which the words are used here. And we may now pick up a thread from an earlier part of the discussion by remarking that crippling depression can destroy the enjoyment of ordinary goods as effectively as external circumstances can remove them.

The suggested solution to the problem is, then, that there is a certain conceptual connexion between *life* and *good* in the case of human beings as in that of animals and even plants. Here, as there, however, it is not the mere state of being alive that can determine, or itself count as, a good, but rather life coming up to some standard of normality. It was argued that it is as part of ordinary life that the elements of good that a man may have are relevant to the question of whether saving his life counts as benefiting him. Ordinary human lives, even very hard lives, contain a minimum of basic goods, but when these are absent the idea of life is no longer linked to that of good. And since it is in this way that the elements of good contained in a man's life are relevant to the question of whether he is benefited if his life is preserved, there is no reason why it should be the balance of good and evil that counts.

It should be added that evils are relevant in one way when, as in the examples discussed above, they destroy the possibility of ordinary goods, but in a different way when they invade a life from which the goods are already absent for a different reason. So, for instance, the connexion between *life* and *good* may be broken because consciousness has sunk to a very low level, as in extreme senility or severe brain damage. In itself this kind of life seems to be neither good nor evil, but if suffering sets in one would hope for a speedy end.

This, admittedly inadequate, discussion of the sense in which life is normally a good, and of the reasons why it may not be so in some particular case, completes the account of what euthanasia is here taken to be. An act of euthanasia, whether literally act or rather omission, is attributed to an agent who opts for the death of another because in his case life seems to be an evil rather than a good. The question now to be asked is whether acts of euthanasia are ever justifiable. But there are two topics here rather than one. For it is one thing to say that some acts of euthanasia considered only in themselves and their results are morally unobjectionable, and another to say that it would be all right to legalise them. Perhaps the practice of euthanasia would allow too many abuses, and perhaps there would be too many mistakes. Moreover the practice might have very important and highly undesirable side effects, because it is unlikely that we could change our principles about the treatment of the old and the ill without changing fundamental emotional attitudes and social relations. The topics must, therefore, be treated separately. In the next part of the discussion, nothing will be said about the social consequences and possible abuses of the practice of euthanasia, but only about acts of euthanasia considered in themselves.

What we want to know is whether acts of euthanasia, defined as we have defined them, are ever morally permissible. To be more accurate, we want to know whether it is ever sufficient justification of the choice of death for another that death can be counted a benefit rather than harm, and that this is why the choice is made.

It will be impossible to get a clear view of the area to which this topic belongs without first marking the distinct grounds on which objection may lie when one man opts for the death of another. There are two different virtues whose requirements are, in general, contrary to such actions. An unjustified act of killing, or allowing to die, is contrary to justice or to charity, or to both virtues, and the moral failings are distinct. Justice has to do with what men *owe* each other in the way of noninterference and positive service. When used in this wide sense, which has its history in the doctrine of the cardinal virtues, justice is not especially connected with, for instance, law courts but with the whole area of rights, and duties corresponding to rights. Thus murder is one form of injustice, dishonesty another, and wrongful failure to keep contracts a third; chicanery in a law court or defrauding someone of his inheritance are simply other cases of injustice. Justice as such is not directly linked to the good of another, and may require that something be rendered to him even where it will do him harm, as Hume pointed out when he remarked that a debt must be paid even to a profligate debauchee who "would rather receive harm than benefit from large possessions." [7] Charity, on the other

[7] David Hume, *Treatise*, book III, part II, section 1.

hand, is the virtue which attaches us to the good of others. An act of charity is in question only where something is not demanded by justice, but a lack of charity and of justice can be shown where a man is denied something which he both needs and has a right to; both charity and justice demand that widows and orphans are not defrauded, and the man who cheats them is neither charitable nor just.

It is easy to see that the two grounds of objection to inducing death are distinct. A murder is an act of injustice. A culpable failure to come to the aid of someone whose life is threatened is normally contrary, not to justice, but to charity. But where one man is under contract, explicit or implicit, to come to the aid of another injustice too will be shown. Thus injustice may be involved either in an act or an omission, and the same is true of a lack of charity; charity may demand that someone be aided, but also that an unkind word not be spoken.

The distinction between charity and justice will turn out to be of first importance when voluntary and nonvoluntary euthanasia are distinguished later on. This is because of the connexion between justice and rights, and something should now be said about this. I believe it is true to say that wherever a man acts unjustly he has infringed a right, since justice has to do with whatever a man is owed, and whatever he is owed is his as a matter of right. Something should therefore be said about the different kinds of rights. The distinction commonly made is between having a right in the sense of having a liberty, and having a "claim-right" or "right of recipience." [8] The best way to understand such a distinction seems to be as follows. To say that a man has a right in the sense of liberty is to say that no one can demand that he do not do the thing which he has the right to do. The fact that he has a right to do it consists in the fact that a certain kind of objection does not lie against his doing it. Thus a man has a right in this sense to walk down a public street or park his car in a public parking space. It does not follow that no one else may prevent him from doing so. If for some reason I want a certain man not to park in a certain place I may lawfully park there myself or get my friends to do so, thus preventing him from doing what he has a right (in the sense of a liberty) to do. It is different, however, with a claim-right. This is the kind of right which I have in addition to a liberty when, for example, I have a private parking space; now others have duties in the way of noninterference, as in this case, or of service, as in the case where my claim-right is to goods or services promised to me. Sometimes one of these rights gives other people the duty of securing to me that to which I have a right, but at other times their duty is merely to refrain from interference. If a fall of snow blocks my private parking space there is normally no obligation for anyone else to clear it away. Claim rights generate duties; sometimes these duties are duties of noninterference; sometimes they are duties of service. If your right gives me the duty not to interfere with you I have 'no right' to do it; similarly, if your right gives me the duty to provide something for you I have "no right" to refuse to

[8] See, for example, D. D. Raphael, "Human Rights Old and New," in D. D. Raphael, ed., *Political Theory and the Rights of Man* (London, 1967), and Joel Feinberg, "The Nature and Value of Rights," *The Journal of Value Inquiry* 4, no. 4 (Winter 1970): 243–57. Reprinted in Samuel Gorovitz, ed., *Moral Problems in Medicine* (Englewood Cliffs, New Jersey, 1976).

do it. What *I* lack is the right which is a liberty: I am not "at liberty" to interfere with you or to refuse the service.

Where in this picture does the right to life belong? No doubt people have the right to live in the sense of a liberty, but what is important is the cluster of claim-rights brought together under the title of the right to life. The chief of these is, of course, the right to be free from interferences that threaten life. If other people aim their guns at us or try to pour poison into our drink we can, to put it mildly, demand that they desist. And then there are the services we can claim from doctors, health officers, bodyguards, and firemen; the rights that depend on contract or public arrangement. Perhaps there is no particular point in saying that the duties these people owe us belong to the right to life; we might as well say that all the services owed to anyone by tailors, dressmakers, and couturiers belong to a right called the right to be elegant. But contracts such as those understood in the patient–doctor relationship come in in an important way when we are discussing the rights and wrongs of euthanasia, and are therefore mentioned here.

Do people have the right to what they need in order to survive, apart from the right conferred by special contracts into which other people have entered for the supplying of these necessities? Do people in the underdeveloped countries in which starvation is rife have the right to the food they so evidently lack? Joel Feinberg, discussing this question, suggests that they should be said to have "a claim," distinguishing this from a "valid claim," which gives a claim-right.

> The manifesto writers on the other side who seem to identify needs, or at least basic needs, with what they call "human rights," are more properly described, I think, as urging upon the world community the moral principle that *all* human needs ought to be recognized as *claims* (in the customary *prima facie* sense) worthy of sympathy and serious consideration right now, even though, in many cases, they cannot yet plausibly be treated as *valid* claims, that is, as grounds of any other people's duties. This way of talking avoids the anomaly of ascribing to all human beings now, even those in pre-industrial societies, such "economic and social rights" as "periodic holidays with pay." [9]

This seems reasonable, though we notice that there are some actual rights to service which are not based on anything like a contract, as for instance the right that children have to support from their parents and parents to support from their children in old age, though both sets of rights are to some extent dependent on existing social arrangements.

Let us now ask how the right to life affects the morality of acts of euthanasia. Are such acts sometimes or always ruled out by the right to life? This is certainly a possibility; for although an act of euthanasia is, by our definition, a matter of opting for death for the good of the one who is to die, there is, as we noted earlier, no simple connexion between that to which a man has a right and that which is for his good. It is true that men have the right only to the kind of thing that is, in general, a good: we do not think that people have the right to garbage or polluted

---

[9] Feinberg, "Human rights," Gorovitz, *Moral Problems in Medicine*, p. 465.

air. Nevertheless, a man may have the right to something which he himself would be better off without; where rights exist it is a man's will that counts not his or anyone else's estimate of benefit or harm. So the duties complementary to the right to life—the general duty of noninterference and the duty of service incurred by certain persons—are not affected by the quality of a man's life or by his prospects. Even if it is true that he would be, as we say, "better off dead," so long as he wants to live this does not justify us in killing him and may not justify us in deliberately allowing him to die. All of us have the duty of noninterference, and some of us may have the duty to sustain his life. Suppose, for example, that a retreating army has to leave behind wounded or exhausted soldiers in the wastes of an arid or snowbound land where the only prospect is death by starvation or at the hands of an enemy notoriously cruel. It has often been the practice to accord a merciful bullet to men in such desperate straits. But suppose one of them demands that he should be left alive? It seems clear that his comrades have no right to kill him, though it is a quite different question as to whether they should give him a life-prolonging drug. The right to life can sometimes give a duty of positive service, but does not do so here. What it does give is the right to be left alone.

Interestingly enough we have arrived by way of a consideration of the right to life at the distinction normally labelled "active" versus "passive" euthanasia, and often thought to be irrelevant to the moral issue.[10] Once it is seen that the right to life is a distinct ground of objection to certain acts of euthanasia, and that this right creates a duty of noninterference more widespread than the duties of care there can be no doubt about the relevance of the distinction between passive and active euthanasia. Where everyone may have the duty to leave someone alone, it may be that no one has the duty to maintain his life, or that only some people do.

Where then do the boundaries of the "active" and "passive" lie? In some ways the words are themselves misleading, because they suggest the difference between act and omission which is not quite what we want. Certainly the act of shooting someone is the kind of thing we were talking about under the heading of "interference," and omitting to give him a drug a case of refusing care. But the act of turning off a respirator should surely be thought of as no different from the decision not to start it; if doctors had decided that a patient should be allowed to die, either course of action might follow, and both should be counted as passive rather than active euthanasia if euthanasia were in question. The point seems to be that interference in a course of treatment is not the same as other interference in a man's life, and particularly if the same body of people are responsible for the treatment and for its discontinuance. In such a case we could speak of the disconnecting of the apparatus as killing the man, or of the hospital as allowing him to die. By and large, it is the act of killing that is ruled out under the heading of noninterference, but not in every case.

Doctors commonly recognise this distinction, and the grounds on which

---

10 See, for example, James Rachels, "Active and Passive Euthanasia," *New England Journal of Medicine* 292, no. 2 (9 Jan. 1975): 78–80.

some philosophers have denied it seem untenable. James Rachels, for instance, believes that if the difference between active and passive is relevant anywhere, it should be relevant everywhere, and he has pointed to an example in which it seems to make no difference which is done. If someone saw a child drowning in a bath it would seem just as bad to let it drown as to push its head under water.[11] If "it makes no difference" means that one act would be as iniquitous as the other this is true. It is not that killing is *worse* than allowing to die, but that the two are contrary to distinct virtues, which gives the possibility that in some circumstances one is impermissible and the other permissible. In the circumstances invented by Rachels, both are wicked: it is contrary to justice to push the child's head under the water—something one has no right to do. To leave it to drown is not contrary to justice, but is a particularly glaring example of lack of charity. Here it makes no practical difference because the requirements of justice and charity coincide; but in the case of the retreating army they did not: charity would have required that the wounded soldier be killed had not justice required that he be left alive.[12] In such a case it makes all the difference whether a man opts for the death of another in a positive action, or whether he allows him to die. An analogy with the right to property will make the point clear. If a man owns something he has the right to it even when its possession does him harm, and normally we have no right to take it from him. But if one day it should blow away, maybe nothing requires us to get it back for him; we could not deprive him of it, but we may allow it to go. This is not to deny that it will often be an unfriendly act or one based on an arrogant judgement when we refuse to do what he wants. Nevertheless, we would be within our rights, and it might be that no moral objection of any kind would lie against our refusal.

It is important to emphasise that a man's rights may stand between us and the action we would dearly like to take for his sake. They may, of course, also prevent action which we would like to take for the sake of others, as when it might be tempting to kill one man to save several. But it is interesting that the limits of allowable interference, however uncertain, seem stricter in the first case than the second. Perhaps there are no cases in which it would be all right to kill a man against his will *for his own sake* unless they could equally well be described as cases of allowing him to die, as in the example of turning off the respirator. However, there are circumstances, even if these are very rare, in which one man's life would justifiably be sacrificed to save others, and "killing" would be the only description of what was being done. For instance, a vehicle which had gone out of control might be steered from a path on which it would kill more than one man to a path on which it would kill one.[13] But it would not be permissible to steer a vehicle towards

[11] Ibid.
[12] It is not, however, that justice and charity conflict. A man does not lack charity because he refrains from an act of injustice which would have been for someone's good.
[13] For a discussion of such questions, see my article "The Problem of Abortion and the Doctrine of Double Effect," *Oxford Review*, no. 5 (1967); reprinted in Rachels, *Moral Problems*, and Gorovitz, *Moral Problems in Medicine*.

someone in order to kill him, against his will, for his own good. An analogy with property rights again illustrates the point. One may not destroy a man's property against his will on the grounds that he would be better off without it; there are however circumstances in which it could be destroyed for the sake of others. If his house is liable to fall and kill him that is his affair; it might, however, without injustice be destroyed to stop the spread of a fire.

We see then that the distinction between active and passive, important as it is elsewhere, has a special importance in the area of euthanasia. It should also be clear why James Rachels' other argument, that it is often "more humane" to kill than to allow to die, does not show that the distinction between active and passive euthanasia is morally irrelevant. It might be "more humane" in this sense to deprive a man of property that brings evil on him, or to refuse to pay what is owed to Hume's profligate debauchee; but if we say this we must admit that an act which is "more humane" than its alternative may be morally objectionable because it infringes rights.

So far we have said very little about the right to service as opposed to the right to noninterference, though it was agreed that both might be brought under the heading of "the right to life." What about the duty to preserve life that may belong to special classes of persons such as bodyguards, firemen, or doctors? Unlike the general public they are not within their rights if they merely refrain from interfering and do not try to sustain life. The subject's claim-rights are two-fold as far as they are concerned and passive as well as active euthanasia may be ruled out here if it is against his will. This is not to say that he has the right to any and every service needed to save or prolong his life; the rights of other people set limits to what may be demanded, both because they have the right not to be interfered with and because they may have a competing right to services. Furthermore one must enquire just what the contract or implicit agreement amounts to in each case. Firemen and bodyguards presumably have a duty which is simply to preserve life, within the limits of justice to others and of reasonableness to themselves. With doctors it may however be different, since their duty relates not only to preserving life but also to the relief of suffering. It is not clear what a doctor's duties are to his patient if life can be prolonged only at the cost of suffering or suffering relieved only by measures that shorten life. George Fletcher has argued that what the doctor is under contract to do depends on what is generally done, because this is what a patient will reasonably expect.[14] This seems right. If procedures are part of normal medical practice then it seems that the patient can demand them however much it may be against his interest to do so. Once again it is not a matter of what is "most humane."

That the patient's right to life may set limits to permissible acts of euthanasia seems undeniable. If he does not want to die no one has the right to practise active euthanasia on him, and passive euthanasia may also be ruled out where he has a right to the services of doctors or others.

[14] George Fletcher, "Legal Aspects of the Decision not to Prolong Life," *Journal of the American Medical Association* 203, no. 1 (1 Jan. 1968): 119–22. Reprinted in Gorovitz.

Perhaps few will deny what has so far been said about the impermissibility of acts of euthanasia, simply because we have so far spoken about the case of one who positively wants to live, and about his rights; whereas those who advocate euthanasia are usually thinking either about those who wish to die or about those whose wishes cannot be ascertained either because they cannot properly be said to have wishes or because, for one reason or another, we are unable to form a reliable estimate of what they are. The question that must now be asked is whether the latter type of case, where euthanasia though not *involuntary* would again be *non*voluntary, is different from the one discussed so far. Would we have the right to kill someone for his own good so long as we had no idea that he positively wished to live? And what about the life-prolonging duties of doctors in the same circumstances? This is a very difficult problem. On the one hand, it seems ridiculous to suppose that a man's right to life is something which generates duties only where he has signalled that he wants to live; as a borrower does indeed have a duty to return something lent on indefinite loan only if the lender indicates that he wants it back. On the other hand, it might be argued that there is something illogical about the idea that a right has been infringed if someone incapable of saying whether he wants it or not is deprived of something that is doing him harm rather than good. Yet on the analogy of property we would say that a right has been infringed. Only if someone had earlier told us that in such circumstances he would not want to keep the thing could we think that his right had been waived. Perhaps if we could make confident judgements about what anyone in such circumstances would wish, or what he would have wished beforehand had he considered the matter, we could agree to consider the right to life as "dormant," needing to be asserted if the normal duties were to remain. But as things are we cannot make any such assumption: we simply do not know what most people would want, or would have wanted, us to do unless they tell us. This is certainly the case so far as active measures to end life are concerned. Possibly it is different, or will become different, in the matter of being kept alive, so general is the feeling against using sophisticated procedures on moribund patients, and so much is this dreaded by people who are old or terminally ill. Once again the distinction between active and passive euthanasia has come on the scene, but this time because most people's attitudes to the two are so different. It is just possible that we might presume, in the absence of specific evidence, that someone would not wish, beyond a certain point to be kept alive; it is certainly not possible to assume that he would wish to be killed.

In the last paragraph we have begun to broach the topic of voluntary euthanasia, and this we must now discuss. What is to be said about the case in which there is no doubt about someone's wish to die? Either he has told us beforehand that he would wish it in circumstances such as he is now in, and has shown no sign of a change of mind, or else he tells us now, being in possession of his faculties and of a steady mind. We should surely say that the objections previously urged against acts of euthanasia, which it must be remembered were all on the ground of rights, had disappeared. It does not seem that one would infringe someone's right to life in killing him with his permission and in fact at his request. Why should someone not be able to waive his right to life, or rather, as would be more likely to happen, to cancel some of the duties of noninterference that this right entails? (He is more likely to say that he should be killed by this man at this time in this manner, than to say that anyone may kill him at any time and in any way.) Similarly someone may give permission for the destruction of his property, and request it. The important thing is that he gives a critical permission, and it seems that this is enough to cancel the duty normally associated with the right. If someone gives you permission to destroy his property it can no longer be said that you have no right to do so, and I do not see why it should not be the same with taking a man's life. An objection might be made on the ground that only God has the right to take life, but in this paper religious as opposed to moral arguments are being left aside. Religion apart, there seems to be no case to be made out for an infringement of rights if a man who wishes to die is allowed to die or even killed. But of course it does not follow that there is no moral objection to it. Even with property, which is after all a relatively small matter, one might be wrong to destroy what one had the right to destroy. For, apart from its value to other people, it might be valuable to the man who wanted it destroyed, and charity might require us to hold our hand where justice did not.

Let us review the conclusion of this part of the argument, which has been about nonvoluntary and involuntary euthanasia and the right to life. It has been argued that from this side come stringent restrictions on the acts of euthanasia that could be morally permissible. Active nonvoluntary euthanasia is ruled out by that part of the right to life which creates the duty of noninterference though passive nonvoluntary euthanasia is not ruled out, except where the right to life-preserving action has been created by some special condition such as a contract between a man and his doctor. Voluntary euthanasia is another matter: as the preceding paragraph suggested, no right is infringed if a man is allowed to die or even killed at his own request.

Turning now to the other objection that normally holds against inducing the death of another, that it is against charity, or benevolence, we must tell a very different story. Charity is the virtue that gives attachment to the good of others, and because life is normally a good, charity normally demands that it should be saved or prolonged. But as we so defined an act of euthanasia that it seeks a man's death for his own sake—for his good—charity will normally speak in favour of it. This is not, of course, to say that charity can require an act of euthanasia which justice forbids, but if an act of euthanasia is not contrary to justice—that is, it does not infringe rights—charity will rather be in its favour than against.

Once more the distinction between nonvoluntary and voluntary euthanasia must be considered. Could it ever be compatible with charity to seek a man's death although he wanted to live, or at least had not let us know that he wanted to die? I have argued that in such circumstances active euthanasia would infringe his right to life, but passive euthanasia would not do so, unless he had some special right to life-preserving service from the one who allowed him to die. What would charity dictate? Obviously when a man wants to live there is a presumption that he will be benefited if his life is prolonged, and if it is so the question of euthanasia does not arise. But it is, on the other hand, possible that he wants to live where it would be better for him to die: perhaps he does not realise the desperate situation he is in, or perhaps he is afraid of dying. So, in spite of a very proper resistance to refusing to go along with the man's own wishes in the matter of life and death, someone might justifiably refuse to prolong the life even of someone who asked him to prolong it, as in the case of refusing to give the wounded soldier a drug that would keep him alive to meet a terrible end. And it is even more obvious that charity does not always dictate that life should be prolonged where a man's own wishes, hypothetical or actual, are not known.

So much for the relation of charity to nonvoluntary passive euthanasia, which was not, like nonvoluntary active euthanasia, ruled out by the right to life. Let us now ask what charity has to say about voluntary euthanasia both active and passive. It was suggested in the discussion of justice that if of sound mind and steady desire a man might give others the *right* to allow him to die or even to kill him, where otherwise this would be ruled out. But it was pointed out that this would not settle the question of whether the act was morally permissible, and it is this that we must now consider. Could not charity speak against what justice allowed? Indeed it might do so. For while the fact that a man wants to die suggests that his life is wretched, and while his rejection of life may itself tend to take the good out of things he might have enjoyed, nevertheless his wish to die might here be opposed for his own sake just as it might be if suicide were in question. Perhaps there is hope that his mental condition will improve. Perhaps he is mistaken in thinking his disease is incurable. Perhaps he wants to die for the sake of someone else on whom he feels he is a burden, and we are not ready to accept this sacrifice whether for ourselves or others. In such cases, and there will surely be many of them, it could not be for his own sake that we kill him or allow him to die, and therefore euthanasia as defined in this paper would not be in question. But this is not to deny that there could be acts of voluntary euthanasia both passive and active against which neither justice nor charity would speak.

We have now considered the morality of euthanasia both voluntary and nonvoluntary, and active and passive. The conclusion has been that nonvoluntary active euthanasia (roughly, killing a man against his will or without his consent) is never justified; that is to say, that a man's being killed for his own good never justifies the act unless he himself has consented to it. A man's rights are infringed by such an action, and it is therefore contrary to justice. However, all the other combinations, nonvoluntary passive euthanasia, voluntary active euthanasia, and voluntary passive euthanasia are sometimes compatible with both justice and charity. But the strong condition carried in the definition of euthanasia adopted in this paper must not be forgotten; an act of euthanasia as here understood is one whose purpose is to benefit the one who dies.

In the light of this discussion let us look at our present practices. Are they good or are they bad? And what changes might be made, thinking now not only of the morality of particular acts of euthanasia but also of the indirect effects of instituting different practices, of the abuses to which they might be subject and of the changes that might come about if euthanasia became a recognised part of the social scene?

The first thing to notice is that it is wrong to ask whether we should introduce the practice of euthanasia as if it were not something we already had. In fact we do have it. For instance it is common, where the medical prognosis is very bad, for doctors to recommend against measures to prolong life, and particularly where a process of degeneration producing one medical emergency after another has already set in. If these doctors are not certainly within their legal rights this is something that is apt to come as a surprise to them as to the general public. It is also obvious that euthanasia is often practised where old people are concerned. If someone very old and soon to die is attacked by a disease that makes his life wretched, doctors do not always come in with life-prolonging drugs. Perhaps poor patients are more fortunate in this respect than rich patients, being more often left to die in peace, but it is in any case a well recognised piece of medical practice which is a form of euthanasia.

No doubt, the case of infants with mental or physical defects will be suggested as another example of the practice of euthanasia as we already have it, since such infants are sometimes deliberately allowed to die. That they are deliberately allowed to die is certain; children with severe spina bifida malformations are not always operated on even where it is thought that without the operation they will die; and even in the case of children with Down's Syndrome who have intestinal obstructions the relatively simple operation that would make it possible to feed them is sometimes not performed.[15] Whether this is euthanasia in our sense or only as the Nazis understood it is another matter. We must ask the crucial question, 'Is it for the sake of the child himself that the doctors and parents choose his death?' In some cases the answer may really be yes, and what is more important it may really be true that the kind of life which is a good is not possible or likely for this child, and that there is little but suffering and frustration in store for him.[16] But this must presuppose that the medical prognosis is wretchedly bad, as it may be for some spina bifida children. With children who are born with Down's Syndrome it is, however, quite different. Most of these are able to live on for quite a time in a reasonably contented way, remaining like children all their lives but capable of affectionate relationships and able to play games and perform simple tasks. The fact is, of course, that the doctors who recommend against life-saving procedures for handicapped infants are usually thinking not of them but rather of their parents and of other children in the family or of the "burden on society" if the children survive. So it is not for their sake but to avoid trouble to others that they

---

[15] I have been told this by a paediatrician in a well-known medical centre in the United States. It is confirmed by Anthony M. Shaw and Iris A. Shaw, "Dilemma of Informed Consent in Children," *The New England Journal of Medicine* 289, no. 17 (25 Oct. 1973): 885–90. Reprinted in Gorovitz.

[16] It must be remembered, however, that many of the social miseries of spina bifida children could be avoided. Professor R. B. Zachary is surely right to insist on this. See, for example, "Ethical and Social Aspects of Spina Bifida," *The Lancet*, 3 Aug. 1968, pp. 274–6. Reprinted in Gorovitz.

are allowed to die. When brought out into the open this seems unacceptable; at least we do not easily accept the principle that adults who need special care should be counted as too burdensome to be kept alive. It must in any case be insisted that if children with Down's Syndrome are deliberately allowed to die this is not a matter of euthanasia except in Hitler's sense. And for our children, since we scruple to gas them, not even the manner of their death is "quiet and easy"; when not treated for an intestinal obstruction a baby simply starves to death. Perhaps some will take this as an argument for allowing active euthanasia, in which case they will be in the company of an S.S. man stationed in the Warthgenau who sent Eichmann a memorandum telling him that "Jews in the coming winter could no longer be fed" and submitting for his consideration a proposal as to whether "it would not be the most humane solution to kill those Jews who were incapable of work through some quicker means." [17] If we say we are *unable* to look after children with handicaps we are no more telling the truth than was the S.S. man who said that the Jews could not be fed.

Nevertheless if it is ever right to allow deformed children to die because life will be a misery to them, or not to take measures to prolong for a little the life of a newborn baby whose life cannot extend beyond a few months of intense medical intervention, there is a genuine problem about active as opposed to passive euthanasia. There are well-known cases in which the medical staff has looked on wretchedly while an infant died slowly from starvation and dehydration because they did not feel able to give a lethal injection. According to the principles discussed in the earlier part of this paper they would indeed have had no right to give it, since an infant cannot ask that it should be done. The only possible solution—supposing that voluntary active euthanasia were to be legalised—would be to appoint guardians to act on the infant's behalf. In a different climate of opinion this might not be dangerous, but at present, when people so readily assume that the life of a handicapped baby is of no value, one would be loath to support it.

Finally, on the subject of handicapped children, another word should be said about those with severe mental defects. For them too it might sometimes be right to say that one would wish for death for their sake. But not even severe mental handicap automatically brings a child within the scope even of a possible act of euthanasia. If the level of consciousness is low enough it could not be said that life is a good to them, any more than in the case of those suffering from extreme senility. Nevertheless if they do not suffer it will not be an act of euthanasia by which someone opts for their death. Perhaps charity does not demand that strenuous measures are taken to keep people in this state alive, but euthanasia does not come into the matter, any more than it does when someone is, like Karen Ann Quinlan, in a state of permanent coma. Much could be said about this last case. It might even be suggested that in the case of unconsciousness this "life" is not the life to which "the right to life" refers. But that is not our topic here.

What we must consider, even if only briefly, is the possibility that

17 Quoted by Hannah Arendt, *Eichmann in Jerusalem* (London, 1963), p. 90.

euthanasia, genuine euthanasia, and not contrary to the requirements of justice or charity, should be legalised over a wider area. Here we are up against the really serious problem of abuse. Many people want, and want very badly, to be rid of their elderly relatives and even of their ailing husbands or wives. Would any safeguards ever be able to stop them describing as euthanasia what was really for their own benefit? And would it be possible to prevent the occurrence of acts which were genuinely acts of euthanasia but morally impermissible because infringing the rights of a patient who wished to live or whose wishes were unknown?

Perhaps the furthest we should go is to encourage patients to make their own contracts with a doctor by making it known whether they wish him to prolong their life in case of painful terminal illness or of incapacity. A document such as the Living Will seems eminently sensible, and should surely be allowed to give a doctor following the previously expressed wishes of the patient immunity from legal proceedings by relatives.[18] Legalising active euthanasia is, however, another matter. Apart from the special repugnance doctors feel towards the idea of a lethal injection, it may be of the very greatest importance to keep a psychological barrier up against killing. Moreover it is active euthanasia which is the most liable to abuse. Hitler would not have been able to kill 275,000 people in his "euthanasia" programme if he had had to wait for them to need life-saving treatment. But there are other objections to active euthanasia, even voluntary active euthanasia. In the first place it would be hard to devise procedures that would protect people from being persuaded into giving their consent. And secondly the possibility of active voluntary euthanasia might change the social scene in ways that would be very bad. As things are, people do, by and large, expect to be looked after if they are old or ill. This is one of the good things that we have, but we might lose it, and be much worse off without it. It might come to be expected that someone likely to need a lot of looking after should call for the doctor and demand his own death. Something comparable could be good in an extremely poverty-stricken community where the children genuinely suffered from lack of food; but in rich societies such as ours it would surely be a spiritual disaster. Such possibilities should make us very wary of supporting large measures of euthanasia, even where moral principle applied to the individual act does not rule it out.

[18] Details of this document are to be found in J. A. Behnke and Sissela Bok, eds., *The Dilemmas of Euthanasia* (New York, 1975), and in A. B. Downing, ed., *Euthanasia and the Right to Life: The Case for Voluntary Euthanasia* (London, 1969).

9 JOHN A. ROBERTSON

INVOLUNTARY EUTHANASIA OF DEFECTIVE NEWBORNS: A LEGAL ANALYSIS

[Professor Robertson's article begins with a thorough account of some of the major issues revolving around infanticide and the history of legal treatment of those issues. Among other things, he considers the liability of the parents, their duty to the defective infant, and the legal consequences of their failure to act when such failure results in the infant's death. He then turns to the liability of the physician and the hospital and the sources of their duties toward the infant. After discussing some of the defenses which may be raised against criminal or tort prosecution in such cases, he turns to an analysis of some of the arguments which have been advanced in favor of permitting involuntary euthanasia of defective newborns:]

1. DEFECTIVE INFANTS ARE NOT PERSONS

Children born with congenital malformations may lack human form and the possibility of ordinary, psychosocial development. In many cases mental retardation is or will be so profound, and physical incapacity so great, that the term "persons" or "humanly alive" [1] have odd or questionable meaning when applied to them. In these cases the infant's physical and mental defects are so severe that they will never know anything but a vegetative existence, with no discernible personality, sense of self, or capacity to interact with others. [2] Withholding ordinary medical

Reprinted by permission of the author and the publisher from *Stanford Law Review* 27 (1975): 246–261. Copyright 1975 by the Board of Trustees of the Leland Stanford Junior University. Some footnotes have been deleted or abbreviated, and the remainder have been renumbered.

[1] Commentary, *The Ethics of Surgery in Newborn Infants*, 8 CLINICAL PEDIATRICS 251 1969); *cf.* Grunberg, *Who Lives and Dies?*, N.Y. Times, Apr. 22, 1974, at 35, col. 2.
[2] *Id.* While the proposition appears to draw some support from Bracton's statement in a noncriminal context that a monster is not a human being, "Quia partus monstruosus est cum non nascatur ut homo," *cited* in G. Williams, THE SANCTITY OF LIFE AND THE CRIMINAL LAW 20–21 (1957), no case has ever held that a live human offspring is not a human being because of certain physical or mental deficits, and therefore may be killed. *See* G. Williams, *supra*, at 20–24. The state, in the exercise of its *parens patriae* power to protect persons incapacitated by infancy, neglect, or mental incompetence, recognizes that many "persons" incapable of leading an ordinary or normal life are nevertheless persons with rights and interests to be protected. *See, e.g.,* Herr, *Retarded Children and the Law: Enforcing the Constitutional Rights of the Mentally Retarded,* 23 Syr. L. Rev. 995 (1972). Even a slave was protected by the law of homicide even

care in such cases, one may argue, is justified on the ground that these infants are not persons or human beings in the ordinary or legal sense of the term, and therefore do not possess the right of care that persons possess.

Central to this argument is the idea that living products of the human uterus can be classified into offspring that are persons, and those that are not. Conception and birth by human parents does not automatically endow one with personhood and its accompanying rights. Some other characteristic or feature must be present in the organism for personhood to vest,[3] and this the defective infant arguably lacks. Lacking that property, an organism is not a person or deserving to be treated as such.

Before considering what "morally significant features" might distinguish persons from nonpersons, and examining the relevance of such features to the case of the defective infant, we must face an initial objection to this line of inquiry. The objection questions the need for any distinction among human offspring because of

> the monumental misuse of the concept of "humanity" in so many practices of discrimination and atrocity throughout history. Slavery, witchhunts and wars have all been justified by their perpetrators on the grounds that they held their victims to be less than fully human. The insane and the criminal have for long periods been deprived of the most basic necessities for similar reasons, and been excluded from society. . . .
>
> . . . Even when entered upon with the best of intentions, and in the most guarded manner, the enterprise of basing the protection of human life upon such criteria and definitions is dangerous. To question someone's humanity or personhood is a first step to mistreatment and killing.[4]

Hence, according to this view, human parentage is a necessary and sufficient condition for personhood, whatever the characteristics of the offspring, because qualifying criteria inevitably lead to abuse and untold suffering to beings who are unquestionably human. Moreover, the human species is sufficiently different from other sentient species that assigning its members greater rights on birth alone is not arbitrary.

This objection is indeed powerful. The treatment accorded slaves in the United States, the Nazi denial of personal status to non-Aryans, and countless other incidents, testify that man's inhumanity to man is indeed greatest when a putative nonperson is involved.[5] Arguably, however, a distinction based on gross physical form, profound mental incapacity, and the very existence of personality or selfhood, besides having an empirical basis in the monstrosities and mutations known to

---

though incapable of full social interaction. *See, e.g.,* Fields v. State, 1 Yager's Rep. 156 (Tenn. 1829). Thus, a judge in Maine recently had little difficulty in concluding that a deformed child with multiple anomalies and brain damage was "at the moment of live birth . . . a human being entitled to the fullest protection of the law." Maine Medical Center v. Houle, No. 74–145, at 4 (Super. Ct., Cumberland Cty., Feb. 14, 1974).

3 *See* Tooley, *Abortion and Infanticide,* 2 PHIL. & PUB. AFFAIRS 37, 51 (1972).

4 Bok, *Ethical Problems of Abortion,* 2 HASTINGS CENTER STUDIES, Jan. 1974, at 33, 41.

5 *See* Alexander, *Medical Science under Dictatorship,* 241 NEW ENG. J. MED. 39 (1949).

have been born to women [6] is a basic and fundamental one. Rather than distinguishing among the particular characteristics that persons might attain through the contingencies of race, culture, and class, it merely separates out those who lack the potential for assuming any personal characteristics beyond breathing and consciousness.

This reply narrows the issue: should such creatures be cared for, protected, or regarded as "ordinary" humans? If such treatment is not warranted, they may be treated as nonpersons. The arguments supporting care in all circumstances are based on the view that all living creatures are sacred,. contain a spark of the divine, and should be so regarded. Moreover, identifying those human offspring unworthy of care is a difficult task and will inevitably take a toll on those whose humanity cannot seriously be questioned. At this point the argument becomes metaphysical or religious and immune to resolution by empirical evidence, not unlike the controversy over whether a fetus is a person.[7] It should be noted, however, that recognizing all human offspring as persons, like recognizing the fetus to be a person,[8] does not conclude the treatment issue.

Although this debate can be resolved only by reference to religious or moral beliefs, a procedural solution may reasonably be considered. Since reasonable people can agree that we ordinarily regard human offspring as persons, and further, that defining categories of exclusion is likely to pose special dangers of abuse, a reasonable solution is to presume that all living human offspring are persons. This rule would be subject to exception only if it can be shown beyond a reasonable doubt that certain offspring will never possess the minimal properties that reasonable persons ordinarily associate with human personality. If this burden cannot be satisfied, then the presumption of personhood obtains.

For this purpose I will address only one of the many properties proposed as a necessary condition of personhood—the capacity for having a sense of self—and consider whether its advocates present a cogent account of the nonhuman. Since other accounts may be more convincingly articulated, this discussion will neither exhaust nor conclude the issue. But it will illuminate the strengths and weaknesses of the personhood argument and enable us to evaluate its application to defective infants.

Michael Tooley has recently argued that a human offspring lacking the capacity for a sense of self lacks the rights to life or equal treatment possessed by other persons.[9] In considering the morality of abortion and infanticide, Tooley considers "what properties a thing must possess in order to have a serious right to life," [10] and he concludes that:

> [h]aving a right to life presupposes that one is capable of desiring to
> continue existing as a subject of experiences and other mental states. This
> in turn presupposes both that one has the concept of such a continuing

[6] T. Beck & J. Beck, Elements of Medical Jurisprudence 422 (11th ed. 1960).
[7] See Tribe, Foreword—Toward a Model of Roles in the Due Process of Life and Law, Harv. L. Rev. 1, 18–20 (1973).
[8] See Thomson, A Defense of Abortion, 1 Phil. and Pub. Affairs 47 (1971).
[9] Tooley, supra note [3] at 49.
[10] Id. at 37.

entity and that one believes that one is oneself such an entity. So an entity that lacks such a consciousness of itself as a continuing subject of mental states does not have a right to life.[11]

However, this account is at first glance too narrow, for it appears to exclude all those who do not presently have a desire "to continue existing as a subject of experiences and other mental states." The sleeping or unconscious individual, the deranged, the conditioned, and the suicidal do not have such desires, though they might have had them or could have them in the future. Accordingly, Tooley emphasizes the capability of entertaining such desires, rather than their actual existence.[12] But it is difficult to distinguish the capability for such desires in an unconscious, conditioned, or emotionally disturbed person from the capability existing in a fetus or infant. In all cases the capability is a future one; it will arise only if certain events occur, such as normal growth and development in the case of the infant, and removal of the disability in the other cases. The infant, in fact, might realize its capability[13] long before disabled adults recover emotional balance or consciousness.

To meet this objection, Tooley argues that the significance of the capability in question is not solely its future realization (for fetuses and infants will ordinarily realize it), but also its previous existence and exercise.[14] He seems to say that once the conceptual capability has been realized, one's right to desire continued existence permanently vests, even though the present capability for desiring does not exist, and may be lost for substantial periods or permanently. Yet, what nonarbitrary reasons require that we protect the past realization of conceptual capability but not its potential realization in the future? As a reward for its past realization? To mark our reverence and honor for someone who has realized that state? Tooley is silent on this point.

Another difficulty is Tooley's ambiguity concerning the permanently deranged, comatose, or conditioned. Often he phrases his argument in terms of a temporary suspension of the capability of conceptual thought.[15] One wonders what he would say of someone permanently deranged, or with massive brain damage, or in a prolonged coma. If he seriously means that the past existence of a desire for life vests these cases with the right to life, then it is indeed difficult to distinguish the comatose or deranged from the infant profoundly retarded at birth. Neither will ever possess the conceptual capability to desire to be a continuing subject of experiences. A distinction based on reward or desert seems arbitrary, and protection of life applies equally well in both cases. Would Tooley avoid this problem by holding that the permanently comatose and deranged lose their rights after a certain point because conceptual capacity will never be regained? This would permit killing (or at least withholding of care) from the insane and comatose—doubtless an unappealing prospect. Moreover, we do not ordinarily think of

11 *Id.* at 49.
12 *Id.* at 50.
13 Tooley concedes that the infant attains this capacity in the first year of life, though further research is necessary to identify the exact time. *Id.* at 64.
14 *Correspondence,* 2 PHIL. & PUB. AFFAIRS 419 (1973).
15 *Id.* at 421–23.

the insane, and possibly the comatose, as losing personhood before their death. Although their personality or identity may be said to change, presumably for the worse, or become fragmented or minimal, we still regard them as specific persons. If a "self" in some minimal sense exists here then the profoundly retarded, who at least is conscious, also may be considered a self, albeit a minimal one. Thus, one may argue that Tooley fails to provide a convincing account of criteria distinguishing persons and nonpersons. He both excludes beings we ordinarily think of as persons—infants, deranged, conditioned, possibly the comatose—and fails to articulate criteria that convincingly distinguish the nonhuman. But, even if we were to accept Tooley's distinction that beings lacking the potential for desire and a sense of self are not persons who are owed the duty to be treated by ordinary medical means, this would not appear to be very helpful in deciding whether to treat the newborn with physical or mental defects. Few infants, it would seem, would fall into this class.[16] First, those suffering from malformations, however gross, that do not affect mental capabilities would not fit the class of nonpersons. Second, frequently even the most severe cases of mental retardation cannot be reliably determined until a much later period;[17] care thus could not justifiably be withheld in the neonatal period, although this principle would permit nontreatment at the time when nonpersonality is clearly established.[18] Finally, the only group of defective newborns who would clearly qualify as nonpersons is anencephalics, who altogether lack a brain, or those so severely brain-damaged that it is immediately clear that a sense of self or personality can never develop. Mongols, myelomeningoceles, and other defective infants from whom ordinary care is now routinely withheld would not qualify as nonpersons. Thus, even the most coherent and cogent criteria of humanity are only marginally helpful in the situation of the defective infant. We must therefore consider whether treatment can be withheld on grounds other than the claim that such infants are not persons.

2. NO OBLIGATION TO TREAT EXISTS WHEN THE COSTS OF MAINTAINING LIFE GREATLY OUTWEIGH THE BENEFITS

If we reject the argument that defective newborns are not persons, the question remains whether circumstances exist in which the consequences

[16] Warkany, for example, reports the incidence of anencephaly, the absence of all or most of an infant's brain, as approximately 1 in 1,000 for children born in hospital wards but notes that "remarkable variations have been reported from different areas." J. Warkany, *Congenital Malformations* (1971), at 189.
[17] *Id.* at 39.
[18] But other factors might lead to treatment at this later point in time. For example, if care and nurturing occur immediately after birth, a strong mother-child bond is built, which might prevent mothers from deciding to withhold care when a serious defect is discovered weeks later. Barnett, Leiderman, Globstein & Klaus, *Neonatal Separation: The Maternal Side of Interactional Deprivation*, 45 PEDIACTRICS 197, 197–99 (1970); Kennel & Klaus, *Care of the Mother of the High Risk Infant*, 14 CLIN. OBSTET. & GYNECOL., 926, 930–36 (1971).

of treatment as compared with nontreatment are so undesirable that the omission of care is justified. As we have seen, the doctrine of necessity permits one to violate the criminal law when essential to prevent the occurrence of a greater evil. The circumstances, however, when the death of a nonconsenting person is a lesser evil than his continuing life are narrowly circumscribed, and do not include withholding care from defective infants. Yet many parents and physicians deeply committed to the loving care of the newborn think that treating severely defective infants causes more harm than good, thereby justifying the withholding of ordinary care.[19] In their view the suffering and diminished quality of the child's life do not justify the social and economic costs of treatment. This claim has a growing commonsense appeal, but it assumes that the utility or quality of one's life can be measured and compared with other lives, and that health resources may legitimately be allocated to produce the greatest personal utility. This argument will now be analyzed from the perspective of the defective patient and others affected by his care.

a. The Quality of the Defective Infant's Life

Comparisons of relative worth among persons, or between persons and other interests, raise moral and methodological issues that make any argument that relies on such comparisons extremely vulnerable. Thus the strongest claim for not treating the defective newborn is that treatment seriously harms the infant's own interests, whatever may be the effects on others. When maintaining his life involves great physical and psychosocial suffering for the patient, a reasonable person might conclude that such a life is not worth living. Presumably the patient, if fully informed and able to communicate, would agree. One then would be morally justified in withholding lifesaving treatment if such action served to advance the best interests of the patient.

Congenital malformations impair development in several ways that lead to the judgment that deformed retarded infants are "a burden to themselves." [20] One is the severe physical pain, much of it resulting from repeated surgery that defective infants will suffer. Defective children also are likely to develop other pathological features, leading to repeated fractures, dislocations, surgery, malfunctions, and other sources of pain. The shunt, for example, inserted to relieve hydrocephalus, a common problem in defective children, often becomes clogged, necessitating frequent surgical interventions.[21]

Pain, however, may be intermittent and manageable with analgesics. Since many infants and adults experience great pain, and many defective infants do not, pain alone, if not totally unmanageable, does not sufficiently show that a life is so worthless that death is preferable. More im-

19 See Duff and Campbell, *Moral and Ethical Dilemmas in the Special-Care Nursery,* 289 NEW ENG. J. MED. 890 (1973).
20 Smith & Smith, *Selection for Treatment in Spina Bifida Cystica,* 4 BRIT. MED. J. 189, 195 (1973).
21 Ames & Schut, *Results of Treatment of 171 Consecutive Myelomeningoceles—1963 to 1968,* 52 PEDIATRICS 466, 469 (1972); Shurtleff & Foltz, *A Comparative Study of Meningomyelocele Repair or Cerebrospinal Fluid Shunt As Primary Treatment in Ninety Children,* MED. & CHILD NEURO. 57 (Supp. 13, 1967).

portant are the psychosocial deficits resulting from the child's handicaps. Many defective children never can walk even with prosthesis, never interact with normal children, never appreciate growth, adolescence, or the fulfillment of education and employment, and seldom are even able to care for themselves. In cases of severe retardation, they may be left with a vegetative existence in a crib, incapable of choice or the most minimal response to stimuli. Parents or others may reject them, and much of their time will be spent in hospitals, in surgery, or fighting the many illnesses that beset them. Can it be said that such a life is worth living?

There are two possible responses to the quality-of-life argument. One is to accept its premises but to question the degrees of suffering in particular cases, and thus restrict the justification for death to the most extreme cases. The absence of opportunities for schooling, career, and interaction may be the fault of social attitudes and the failings of healthy persons, rather than a necessary result of congenital malformations. Psychosocial suffering occurs because healthy, normal persons reject or refuse to relate to the defective, or hurry them to poorly funded institutions. Most nonambulatory, mentally retarded persons can be trained for satisfying roles. One cannot assume that a nonproductive existence is necessarily unhappy; even social rejection and nonacceptance can be mitigated. Moreover, the psychosocial ills of the handicapped often do not differ in kind from those experienced by many persons. With training and care, growth, development, and a full range of experiences are possible for most people with physical and mental handicaps. Thus, the claim that death is a far better fate than life cannot in most cases be sustained.

This response, however, avoids meeting the quality-of-life argument on its strongest grounds. Even if many defective infants can experience growth, interaction, and most human satisfactions if nurtured, treated, and trained, some infants are so severely retarded or grossly deformed that their response to love and care, in fact their capacity to be conscious, is always minimal. Although mongoloid and nonambulatory spina bifida children may experience an existence we would hesitate to adjudge worse than death, the profoundly retarded, nonambulatory, blind, deaf infant who will spend his few years in the back-ward cribs of a state institution is clearly a different matter.

To repudiate the quality-of-life argument, therefore, requires a defense of treatment in even these extreme cases. Such a defense would question the validity of any surrogate or proxy judgments of the worth or quality of life when the wishes of the person in question cannot be ascertained. The essence of the quality-of-life argument is a proxy's judgment that no reasonable person can prefer the pain, suffering, and loneliness of, for example, life in a crib at an IQ level of 20, to an immediate, painless death.

But in what sense can the proxy validly conclude that a person with different wants, needs, and interests, if able to speak, would agree that such a life were worse than death? At the start one must be skeptical of the proxy's claim to objective disinterestedness. If the proxy is also the parent or physician, as has been the case in pediatric euthanasia, the impact of treatment on the proxy's interests, rather than solely on those of the child, may influence his assessment. But even if the proxy were truly neutral and committed only to caring for the child, the problem of ego-centricity and knowing another's mind remains. Compared with the situation and life prospects of a "reasonable man," the child's potential quality of life indeed appears dim. Yet a standard based on healthy, ordinary development may be entirely inappropriate to this situation. One who has never known the pleasures of mental operation, ambulation, and social interaction surely does not suffer from their loss as much as one who has. While one who has known these capacities may prefer death to a life without them, we have no assurance that the handicapped person, with no point of comparison, would agree. Life, and life alone, whatever its limitations, might be of sufficient worth to him.[22]

One should also be hesitant to accept proxy assessments of quality-of-life because the margin of error in such predictions may be very great. For instance, while one expert argues that by a purely clinical assessment he can accurately forecast the minimum degree of future handicap an individual will experience, such forecasting is not infallible, and risks denying care to infants whose disability might otherwise permit a reasonably acceptable quality-of-life. Thus given the problems in ascertaining another's wishes, the proxy's bias to personal or culturally relative interests, and the unreliability of predictive criteria, the quality-of-life argument is open to serious question. Its strongest appeal arises in the case of a grossly deformed, retarded, institutionalized child, or one with incessant unmanageable pain, where continued life is itself torture. But these cases are few, and cast doubt on the utility of any such judgment. Even if the judgment occasionally may be defensible, the potential danger of quality-of-life assessments may be a compelling reason for rejecting this rationale for withholding treatment.

b. The Suffering of Others
In addition to the infant's own suffering, one who argues that the harm of treatment justifies violation of the defective infant's right to life usually relies on the psychological, social, and economic costs of maintaining his existence to family and society. In their view the minimal benefit of treatment to persons incapable of full social and physical development does not justify the burdens that care of the defective infant imposes on parents, siblings, health professionals, and other patients. Matson, a noted pediatric neurosurgeon, states:

> [I]t is the doctor's and the community's responsibility to provide [custodial] care and to minimize suffering; but, at the same time, it is also their responsibility not to prolong such individual, familial, and community suffering unnecessarily, and not to carry out multiple procedures and prolonged, expensive, acute hospitalization in an infant whose chance for acceptable growth and development is negligible.[23]

Such a frankly utilitarian argument raises problems. It assumes that because of the greatly curtailed orbit of his existence, the costs or suffer-

---

[22] Cf. *Gleitman v. Cosgrove*, 49 N.J. 22, 227 A.2d 689. . . .
[23] Matson, *Surgical Treatment of Myelomeningocele*, 42 PEDIATRICS 225, 226 (1968).

ing of others is greater than the benefit of life to the child. This judgment, however, requires a coherent way of measuring and comparing interpersonal utilities, a logical-practical problem that utilitarianism has never surmounted. But even if such comparisons could reliably show a net loss from treatment, the fact remains that the child must sacrifice his life to benefit others. If the life of one individual, however useless, may be sacrificed for the benefit of any person, however useful, or for the benefit of any number of persons, then we have acknowledged the principle that rational utility may justify any outcome. As many philosophers have demonstrated, utilitarianism can always permit the sacrifice of one life for other interests, given the appropriate arrangement of utilities on the balance sheet. In the absence of principled grounds for such a decision, the social equation involved in mandating direct, involuntary euthanasia becomes a difference of degree, not kind, and we reach the point where protection of life depends solely on social judgments of utility.

These objections may well be determinative. But if we temporarily bracket them and examine the extent to which care of the defective infant subjects others to suffering, the claim that inordinate suffering outweighs the infant's interest in life is rarely plausible. In this regard we must examine the impact of caring for defective infants on the family, health professions, and society-at-large.

The Family. The psychological impact and crisis created by birth of a defective infant is devastating. Not only is the mother denied the normal tension release from the stresses of pregnancy, but both parents feel a crushing blow to their dignity, self-esteem and self-confidence. In a very short time, they feel grief for the loss of the normal expected child, anger at fate, numbness, disgust, waves of helplessness, and disbelief. Most feel personal blame for the defect, or blame their spouse. Adding to the shock is fear that social position and mobility are permanently endangered. The transformation of a joyously awaited experience into one of catastrophe and profound psychological threat often will reactivate unresolved maturational conflicts. The chances for social pathology—divorce, somatic complaints, nervous and mental disorders—increase and hard-won adjustment patterns may be permanently damaged.

The initial reactions of guilt, grief, anger, and loss, however, cannot be the true measure of family suffering caused by care of a defective infant, because these costs are present whether or not the parents choose treatment. Rather, the question is to what degree treatment imposes psychic and other costs greater than would occur if the child were not treated. The claim that care is more costly rests largely on the view that parents and family suffer inordinately from nurturing such a child.

Indeed, if the child is treated and accepted at home, difficult and demanding adjustments must be made. Parents must learn how to care for a disabled child, confront financial and psychological uncertainty, meet the needs of other siblings, and work through their own conflicting feelings. Mothering demands are greater than with a normal child, particularly if medical care and hospitalization are frequently required. Counseling or professional support may be nonexistent or difficult to obtain. Younger siblings may react with hostility and guilt, older with shame and anger. Often the normal feedback of child growth that renders the turmoil of childrearing worthwhile develops more slowly or not at all. Family resources can be depleted (especially if medical care is needed), consumption patterns altered, or standards of living modified. Housing may have to be found closer to a hospital, and plans for further children changed. Finally, the anxieties, guilt, and grief present at birth may threaten to recur or become chronic.

Yet, although we must recognize the burdens and frustrations of raising a defective infant, it does not necessarily follow that these costs require nontreatment, or even institutionalization. Individual and group counseling can substantially alleviate anxiety, guilt, and frustration, and enable parents to cope with underlying conflicts triggered by the birth and the adaptations required. Counseling also can reduce psychological pressures on siblings, who can be taught to recognize and accept their own possibly hostile feelings and the difficult position of their parents. They may even be taught to help their parents care for the child.

The impact of increased financial costs also may vary. In families with high income or adequate health insurance, the financial costs are manageable. In others, state assistance may be available. If severe financial problems arise or pathological adjustments are likely, institutionalization, although undesirable for the child, remains an option. Finally, in many cases, the experience of living through a crisis is a deepening and enriching one, accelerating personality maturation, and giving one a new sensitivity to the needs of spouse, siblings, and others. As one parent of a defective child states: "In the last months I have come closer to people and can understand them more. I have met them more deeply. I did not know there were so many people with troubles in the world." [24]

Thus, while social attitudes regard the handicapped child as an unmitigated disaster, in reality the problem may not be insurmountable, and often may not differ from life's other vicissitudes. Suffering there is, but seldom is it so overwhelming or so imminent that the only alternative is death of the child.

Health Professionals. Physicians and nurses also suffer when parents give birth to a defective child, although, of course, not to the degree of the parents. To the obstetrician or general practitioner the defective birth may be a blow to his professional identity. He has the difficult task of informing the parents of the defects, explaining their causes, and dealing with the parents' resulting emotional shock. Often he feels guilty for failing to produce a normal baby. In addition, the parents may project anger or hostility on the physician, questioning his professional competence or seeking the services of other doctors. The physician also may feel that his expertise and training are misused when employed to maintain the life of an infant whose chances for a productive existence are so diminished. By neglecting other patients, he may feel that he is prolonging rather than alleviating suffering.

[24] Quoted in Johns, *Family Reactions to the Birth of a Child with a Congenital Abnormality*, 26 OBSTET. & GYNECOL. SURVEY 635, 637 (1971).

Nurses, too, suffer role strain from care of the defective newborn. Intensive-care-unit nurses may work with only one or two babies at a time. They face the daily ordeals of care—the progress and relapses—and often must deal with anxious parents who are themselves grieving or ambivalent toward the child. The situation may trigger a nurse's own ambivalence about death and mothering, in a context in which she is actively working to keep alive a child whose life prospects seem minimal.

Thus, the effects of care on physicians and nurses are not trivial, and must be intelligently confronted in medical education or in management of a pediatric unit. Yet to state them is to make clear that they can but weigh lightly in the decision of whether to treat a defective newborn. Compared with the situation of the parents, these burdens seem insignificant, are short term, and most likely do not evoke such profound emotions. In any case, these difficulties are hazards of the profession—caring for the sick and dying will always produce strain. Hence, on these grounds alone it is difficult to argue that a defective person may be denied the right to life.

Society. Care of the defective newborn also imposes societal costs, the utility of which is questioned when the infant's expected quality-of-life is so poor. Medical resources that can be used by infants with a better prognosis, or throughout the health-care system generally, are consumed in providing expensive surgical and intensive-care services to infants who may be severely retarded, never lead active lives, and die in a few months or years. Institutionalization imposes costs on taxpayers and reduces the resources available for those who might better benefit from it, while reducing further the quality of life experienced by the institutionalized defective.

One answer to these concerns is to question the impact of the costs of caring for defective newborns. Precise data showing the costs to taxpayers or the trade-offs with health and other expenditures do not exist. Nor would ceasing to care for the defective necessarily lead to a reallocation within the health budget that would produce net savings in suffering or life; in fact, the released resources might not be reallocated for health at all. In any case, the trade-offs within the health budget may well be small. With advances in prenatal diagnosis of genetic disorders, many deformed infants who would formerly require care will be aborted beforehand. Then, too, it is not clear that the most technical and expensive procedures always constitute the best treatment for certain malformations. When compared with the almost seven percent of the GNP now spent on health, the money in the defense budget, or tax revenues generally, the public resources required to keep defective newborns alive seem marginal, and arguably worth the commitment to life that such expenditures reinforce. Moreover, as the Supreme Court recently recognized,[25] conservation of the taxpayer's purse does not justify serious infringement of fundamental rights. Given legal and ethical norms against sacrificing the lives of nonconsenting others, and the imprecisions in diagnosis and prediction concerning the eventual outcomes of medical

---

[25] *Memorial Hosp.* v. *Maricopa County*, 415 U.S. 250 (1974).

care, the social-cost argument does not compel nontreatment of defective newborns.

---

1. Is the distinction drawn in some of these articles between active and passive euthanasia a genuine distinction? Is pulling the plug on an artificial respirator active or passive euthanasia? What criteria might one use to distinguish them?

2. There are indications that the court in *Saikewicz* employed utilitarian criteria in reaching its decision. Are such criteria appropriate for a court of law? Did the court reach the right decision? If Saikewicz's I.Q. had been 170, would it have made a difference? Should it?

3. Is the court's reluctance to permit doctors to make the life-and-death decision a matter of professional jealousy, or is there some more important principle behind it?

4. Do you agree with Kamisar's conclusions concerning the possibility of a person suffering intolerable pain making a rational decision to terminate his life, or to have it terminated?

5. If an individual has written a living will, asking his physician and his loved ones to terminate his life if he is in an irreversible coma or if he suffers from a terminal illness that also incapacitates him, should that will be honored? What safeguards can be erected to prevent unscrupulous relatives from taking advantage of such a living will in order to get rid of a wealthy but helpless old man?

6. Kamisar seems to conclude that there are *no* circumstances in which euthanasia should be permitted. Does this amount to a denial of a right to die? Is there such a right? How might one argue in its favor?

7. Do Kamisar and some of the other authors in this part make too much of the Nazi experience? How reasonable is it to employ the "wedge" argument in this context?

8. Virginia Braunsdorf was a spastic, crippled, "helpless parody of womanhood" who could not hold her head upright and who talked in gobbling sounds that only her father could understand. Her father held four jobs simultaneously because of the enormous expense entailed by her care. He finally resigned himself to putting her in a private sanitarium, but he worried about his health and her fate if he should die. He therefore took her from the sanitarium, placed a pillow behind her head, and shot her dead. He then attempted suicide by shooting himself twice in the chest and then, when he recovered consciousness, shot himself twice more. He recovered and was prosecuted for his daughter's murder by a district attorney who argued that she was human and had a right to live. If you had been on the jury, how would you have voted—and why?

9. In *People* v. *Roberts*, the defendant admitted that at the request of his terminally ill wife he mixed poison in her drink and placed it within her reach. He was found guilty of murder and sentenced to life

in prison. Was the law under which he was convicted just? If you had been in Roberts's position, would you have done what he did? Why or why not?

10. A noted religious philosopher has written, "Suffering for the Christian is not an absolute evil, but has redeeming features. It may be an occasion for spiritual growth and an opportunity to make amends for sin." What bearing, if any, does this have upon the euthanasia controversy?

11. How satisfactory are Robertson's suggestions that the family confronted with life with a defective child may seek counseling, state assistance, and other forms of relief instead of the death of the infant at birth?

12. Robertson says that the experience of living through a crisis "is a deepening and enriching one, accelerating personality maturation, and giving one a new sensitivity . . . ." Does this differ in any significant way from the comment made by the religious philosopher in point 10? Is it relevant to the euthanasia controversy?

13. Consider whether the following formulation of Robertson's position is fair: You (Robertson) are in effect saying that someone else, who has no real interest in the case at all, may dictate to the parents of defective children that they must live with such children, and all the personal, psychological, and economic burdens that they bring, for the rest of their lives.

IV
THE
RIGHTS
OF
DISTANT
PEOPLES

INTRODUCTION

The Stoics observed that people acquire rights and duties through their relations to one another: fathers and sons, husbands and wives, brothers and sisters, all have special rights and duties toward one another that they would not have toward other persons. But they also believed that the world was a single great city—a cosmopolis—and that all men and women are or ought to be its citizens and, therefore, brothers to one another. This concept, together with the ancient Jewish and Christian belief that all people are descended from a single couple created by God and are therefore members of the same family, led to the development of various theories of human rights—rights that pertain to every person, regardless of his or her ancestry, place of birth, or residence, strictly by virtue of the fact that every person is a human being. But it is not so obvious where that concept leaves us when we must come to grips with practical applications to people whom we cannot see, with whom we cannot converse, and whom we never meet face to face.

Hugo Adam Bedau analyzes the concept of a human right from a moral point of view and explores the morality of linking such rights to military assistance programs. He concludes, among other things, that there is a hierarchy of human rights and that a government's responsibility to feed its own people, for example, is less central than its responsibility not to torture anyone. He also concludes that any linkage between American foreign assistance programs and human rights ought to be confined to those human rights that have traditionally been recognized by the United States, thus excluding not only social and economic rights, but also political and civil rights, "as our history of racism and sexism shows."

Tom L. Beauchamp approaches the world hunger problem from a purely analytic point of view, devoting himself to the explication of such concepts as beneficence and distributive justice and applying them to world hunger. He too concludes that hundreds of millions of human beings may be left to starve, but he arrives at that conclusion through the principle of *triage,* under which one is justified in withholding aid from those whose cases are hopeless to provide more meaningful assistance to those who can benefit from it.

William Aiken warns against approaching such problems from a purely analytical point of view, arguing passionately against those who would countenance *triage* or a utilitarian approach to world hunger. Certain moral principles, he says, such as charity and the right of every human being to survive, take precedence over the long-term maximization of good for all.

Richard T. De George broadens the scope of the inquiry to include not only those who live in distant lands, but also those who will be born at some time in the distant future. Like the judges in the "wrongful life" cases who were perplexed by the logical difficulties of

ascribing rights to unconceived children who later happened to be
conceived and were born, De George asks whether unborn generations
have rights and whether we have obligations to them. He concludes that
the present generation has no legal or moral obligations toward future
generations and that "the primary values to be considered are those
of presently existing people, and not the projected or supposed values of
future generations."

HUGO ADAM BEDAU 10

HUMAN RIGHTS AND
FOREIGN ASSISTANCE PROGRAMS

INTRODUCTION

When a government attempts to link to its foreign policy a worldwide
concern for human rights, it faces a wide range of problems and challenges—conceptual, normative, administrative. Most of the interesting
and controversial philosophical issues that arise are best examined by
close study of a concrete case in which a government has forged such a
link in actual legislation. Thus, in 1976, Congress enacted Public Law
94-329, the International Security Assistance and Arms Export Control
Act. Section 502B of Title III constitutes the Human Rights provisions
of the Act, key portions of which include the following: "It is the policy
of the United States. . . to promote and encourage increased respect
for human rights and fundamental freedoms for all without distinction
as to race, sex, language, or religion . . . [and] to promote the increased
observance of internationally recognized human rights by all countries. . . . No security assistance may be provided to any country the
government of which engages in a consistent pattern of gross violations
of internationally recognized human rights. . . . The term 'gross violations of internationally recognized human rights' includes torture or
cruel, inhuman, or degrading treatment or punishment, prolonged detention without charges and trial, and other flagrant denial of the right to
life, liberty, or the security of person. . . ." [1]

My discussion of Section 502B falls into three parts. First, I shall

A revised version of an essay originally published in Peter G. Brown and Douglas
MacLean, eds., *Human Rights and U.S. Foreign Policy* (Lexington, Mass.: D. C. Heath,
1979). Copyright © 1979 by D. C. Heath and Company.
[1] See, for the full text, *Congressional Record*, 122:83 (June 2, 1976) at H5129–5130;
P.L. 94–329 (1976); and 90 Stat. 748–750.

sketch what it is for something to be a human right, quite apart from whether or not it is recognized in international law. This is a necessary step in the overall argument; it enables us to make explicit some of the important moral considerations that are at stake in the defense of human rights and in the protest of their violation. Next, I shall offer some arguments to show why the human rights cited in Section 502B are more important than others that might have been included, either by way of addition or as substitutes. Finally, I shall try to show the morality of linking these important human rights with our foreign policy and especially our military assistance programs.

THE CONCEPTION OF A HUMAN RIGHT

Section 502B alludes to the violation of "internationally recognized human rights" as the trigger to set in motion a review process that could culminate in termination of foreign assistance. The rights, violation of which are at issue, are "life, liberty, and security of person." One or more of these, it is implied, is always violated where "torture, cruel, inhumane, or degrading treatment or punishment, or prolonged detention without charges and trial" are permitted. There is no doubt that "life, liberty, and security of person" are "internationally recognized human rights," [2] and that "torture" and the rest violate them.[3] What is not so clear is precisely what it is for something to be a human *right,* as distinct from some other kind of right, and as distinct from universal human *needs.* When positive international law recognizes a human right, what is it that has been embodied in the law? An examination of these questions is essential if we are to understand what is at stake in the defense of human rights and in the protest of their violation.

History shows that human rights are as many and as diverse as the theory of human rights one defends. According to Hobbes, there is only one such right: "the right of nature" that each person has to do whatever is necessary to stay alive. Locke defends the familiar trio: "life, liberty, and property." Our own Declaration of Independence specifies a different trio: "life, liberty, and the pursuit of happiness." The French Declaration of Rights of Man cites four: "liberty, property, security, and resistance of oppression." After World War I, the Institute of International Law in its International Declaration of the Rights of Man declared "the equal right to life, liberty and property" to be the foremost among "the rights of man." After World War II, the U.N. Declaration of Human Rights listed more than three dozen human rights, headed by "life, liberty, and security of person." In his influential philosophical defense of "natural rights," H. L. A. Hart reduces them to one, "the equal right of all men to be free." [4] John Rawls, in his important philo-

---

[2] See Ian Browlie, ed., *Basic Documents on Human Rights* (Oxford: Clarendon Press, 1971).

[3] See Amnesty International, *Report on Torture* (New York: Farrar, Straus and Giroux, 1976).

[4] H.L.A. Hart, "Are There Any Natural Rights?" *The Philosophical Review*, 65:2 (April 1955), pp. 175–191, at p. 175.

sophical treatise, *A Theory of Justice,* proposes no list or set of human rights at all.[5] Yet it has been argued, rightly I think, that at the basis of his entire theory lies one such right, the right of all individuals "to equal concern and respect in the design and administration of the political institutions that govern them." [6] This sample from four philosophers and four manifestos spanning four centuries illustrates not only the diversity but also the continuity in substantive natural or human rights. Even apart from further argument, such a record is an adequate basis for claiming that there is considerable philosophical and political agreement on the human rights cited in Section 502B.

What is less clear is whether there is any common denominator for these different rights, something each theorist might grant to be true of all and only the substantive rights his theory contains. Is there a common logic of human rights more or less independent of the substantive content of the rights themselves? In recent years, it has been suggested that a right qualifies as a human right if and only if it has four general characteristics: (1) all and only human persons have such rights; (2) all persons have such rights equally; (3) the rights in question are not derived from any special status or relation of the person, and thus are not contingent for their possession upon any change or loss of such status or relation; and (4) the right can be asserted against or claimed from any and all other human persons and institutions.[7] Whatever else is true of the rights asserted in manifestos and by thinkers from Hobbes to Rawls, including the rights cited in Section 502B, there is no difficulty in holding that they all exhibit these four characteristics.

However, it is still obscure what it is about rights in general and human rights in particular that accounts for their relatively greater importance than many other moral considerations with which they are sometimes in competition. Traditionally, it has been thought that human rights are inalienable, or that they are absolute. Is either of these the feature in question?

To say that a right is *inalienable* is to say that a person who has it cannot voluntarily and irrevocably divest himself of it by gift, sale, or other transfer to another person. It does *not* mean that it is always wrong not to accord such a right, or that it cannot be voluntarily (and to that extent, quite properly) waived or neglected. In particular, the fact that a right is inalienable does not mean that it cannot be *forfeited.* The connection between inalienability and forfeiture is especially illuminating where the morality of slavery is in question. Equal liberty may safely be taken as the paradigm of an inalienable right. If it is inalienable then it becomes conceptually impossible for anyone to become voluntarily another's slave. Hence, either slavery is fundamentally immoral, depend-

5 John Rawls, *A Theory of Justice* (Cambridge, Mass.: Harvard University Press, 1971), mentions rights and uses them from one end of his argument to the other, including many central points—for example, in his statement of the principles of justice (pp. 60 ff., 302) .
6 Ronald Dworkin, "The Original Position," *University of Chicago Law Review,* 40:3 (Spring 1973), pp. 500–533, at p. 531.
7 Richard A. Wasserstrom, "Rights, Human Rights, and Racial Discrimination," *Journal of Philosophy,* 61:20 (October 29, 1964), pp. 628–640, at pp. 631–632.

ing as it does on alienating an inalienable right, or anyone who is rightfully the slave of another must have become so without alienating his liberty. Theorists such as Locke, who believed both in the inalienability of liberty and in the moral tolerability of slavery in some circumstances, resolved this seeming dilemma by introducing the idea of forfeiting a natural and inalienable right. (Forfeiture of rights is as much a part of the general logic of legal rights and special rights as is their waiver, neglect, or violation.) According to Locke, a person forfeits his natural right to life, for example, if he murders another person. Analogously, it could be argued that whenever a person commits a felony, he forfeits his natural rights to life, liberty, or property, depending upon the right violated. Thus, penal servitude need not involve the violation of a right to liberty, nor the denial that this right is inalienable.

Turning to the rights mentioned in Section 502B and the modes of their violation cited there, we can see the irrelevance of appeal to the inalienability of these rights as part of an argument to show the unjustifiability of their violation. Torturers, for example, need not challenge the inalienability of the right of each citizen to bodily security. All that the friends of torture need to insist is that their victims have forfeited the right to bodily security by virtue of the crimes they are believed to have committed. Torturers need not deny that there is a human right of bodily security, or that this right is inalienable. They certainly do not need to advance the bizarre argument that in torturing a person they do no wrong (violate no right of the victim) because that person gave, sold, or otherwise transferred a right to injure himself to his torturer. Consequently, the firm assurance that the right to bodily security is an inalienable human right does not suffice to show that torture violates anyone's rights and is to that extent morally wrong, any more than the alienability of the human right to property or to life suffices to show that fines and taxes (deprivation of property) or the death penalty (deprivation of life) are morally wrong because they violate an inalienable right.[8]

The problem with regarding human rights as *absolute* is quite different. To say that a right is absolute is to say that its scope and exercise are not relative to or contingent upon any other moral considerations in any circumstances. An absolute right, therefore, is something that no competing moral considerations could ever justifiably override or nullify. There are several problems with the idea that human rights are absolute rights. For one thing, it quickly becomes clear that the content of such a right—what it requires and what it forbids—is vague and without any prospect of clarification except arbitrarily. Suppose we assume that the right to life, for example, is an absolute right. Some who hold this view think that induced abortion violates the absolute right to life of a human fetus. Involuntary miscarriage, however, presumably does not. But what about the failure to try to keep persons alive as long as is medically possible, regardless of the costs and regardless of their own settled preferences and convictions? What about death from famine,

---

[8] I have discussed these matters in greater detail elsewhere; see H. A. Bedau, "The Right to Life," *Monist*, 52:4 (October 1968), pp. 550–572.

starvation, and fatal epidemic disease? Do these violate the absolute right to life if, or only if, they are owing to human mismanagement, or if, or only if, however caused, they could have been averted by effective human intervention? I doubt that it is possible to answer such questions except arbitrarily, so long as the right to life is regarded as an absolute right.

There is the further problem that the acknowledgment of even one absolute right tends to lead to the denial that it is an equal right for all persons, and it casts doubt on whether there can be a plurality of absolute rights. These consequences follow because of the way that actions taken by one person in exercise of an absolute right tend to encroach upon or violate what would otherwise be the equally absolute right of another. If free speech, for example, is an absolute right, then presumably those who have this right are within their rights to say what they please when and where they please. But this will surely lead not only to tolerating slander and libel but also to permitting persons to falsely shout "Fire!" in a crowded theater and to incite to riot. Because no society will allow such outrages, the doctrine of absolute rights is certain to encourage the view that there are no natural or human rights at all—as Jeremy Bentham's famous denunciation of the "absolute" Rights of Man of 1789 for its "anarchial fallacies" attests. It is hardly any wonder, therefore, that it is difficult to find a single clear case of a philosophical defense (as distinct from the assertion in a manifesto) of absolute human rights.

An exception can be made, it has been argued, in favor of the right not to be tortured.[9] It does seem that the right to bodily security that torture violates is a right that can be granted and protected without exception or contingency; to grant this right absolutely does not involve infringing upon or violating any right of anyone else. But even here many would not want to go so far. Suppose someone has constructed and cleverly hidden a "doomsday" machine, and set it to go off in a few hours—unless, say, we kill ten perfectly innocent persons whom the mad bomber hates. Would we refuse to torture him, if we could, for the sole purpose of extracting an account of where his infernal machine was located, so that we could try to destroy or disarm it? If we did torture him for this purpose, would we admit that we had violated an absolute right of his? Or would we argue that even though his right was absolute, he had forfeited it by his conduct, which threatened the no less absolute rights of countless others? Or would we argue that the immunity to torture conferred on him by his right to security was outweighed by the competing right to life of innocent persons?

The idea that human rights are inalienable and absolute obscures rather than illuminates the fundamental point vividly illustrated in the anecdote told by Maurice Cranston in his book *What Are Human Rights?* According to the story, several men in the Central African Republic had been convicted of theft and duly sentenced to imprisonment. Not content with this punishment, the President of the Republic personally ordered his soldiers to take these prisoners and beat them to death. He is reported to have declared with grim satisfaction, "There will be no more theft in the Central African Republic." Cranston comments,

---

9 Joel Feinberg, *Social Philosophy* (Englewood Cliffs, N.J.: Prentice-Hall, 1973), p. 87.

"Even if such methods *did* protect public order . . . the use of torture at the pleasure of a despot is precisely the kind of thing which declarations of the Rights of Man are meant to outlaw. . . ." [10] Modern thinkers who profess to take rights seriously stress that the essential and underlying feature of a theory of rights is to provide a veto for political action otherwise desirable and justified on the ground of collective preference or social advantage. If someone really has a *right* to something, then it is wrong to withhold it from him on no other ground than that it would be generally advantageous to do so.[11] This is as true whether it is a private individual or a government that does the withholding, and it is especially true where the right in question is a human right. Here we have the decisive and distinctive feature of rights, and it is the feature of paramount relevance to our concern in the present discussion.

What might be said for torture in the hypothetical case of the man with the "doomsday" machine cannot be said on behalf of the use of torture by the regimes that typically employ it. So, if it is granted that what torture violates is a human right to personal and bodily security, then excusing or justifying it on the grounds that it is useful to the preservation of "national security" collapses. It is precisely the point of the very concept of a human right to thwart such reasoning, to smother it in the crib. Once a government acknowledges that its citizens have basic human rights under law, then it can view subsequent charges of torture against these persons in only one of four ways. Either the government must disavow the torture and insist that it was inflicted through an excess of zeal or violence by officers who will be punished; or the government must argue that the torture was undertaken in protection of the conflicting but superior rights of others; or the government must confess that it did authorize the torture and the violation of rights involved, in which case some remedy to the victims is appropriately forthcoming and the highest responsible government officials should resign in disgrace; or the government must deny that the acts in question were acts of torture. What cannot be done with integrity and consistency is for the government to assert that its citizens have a human right of bodily integrity, that the government deliberately tortures some of its citizens, and that no one's rights are violated in such acts.

I have sketched an argument to the effect that although the substantive content of natural and human rights has varied over the centuries, as the writings of philosophers and the texts of manifestos prove, the conceptual nature of what it is to be a human or natural right shows a significant if often hidden continuity. It is true that domestic and international law may incorporate or assert rights quite independently of any moral or philosophical arguments for such rights and indifferent to any conceptual or logical features shared by these rights. Nevertheless, it is my view that the human rights identified in Section 502B are best understood as rights of which the foregoing account is true. To put this another

[10] Maurice Cranston, *What Are Human Rights?* (New York: Taplinger Publishing Co., 1973), pp. 70–71.
[11] See Ronald Dworkin, *Taking Rights Seriously* (Cambridge: Harvard University Press, 1978).

way, when we acknowledge that the rights mentioned by this law as relevant to the arms export policy of the United States are indeed human rights, part of what I mean and what I think others should mean as well is that these rights have the conceptual and normative features identified above. It is *because* they have these features that they are human rights and deserve to be recognized and protected as positive rights of international law.

PRIORITIES AMONG RIGHTS

Section 502B does not explicitly address itself to the violation of all human rights, and this poses a challenge. Even if it is agreed that linking human rights violations to terminating our foreign assistance programs is reasonable, it is still an open question whether the human rights appropriately so linked are all and only those actually incorporated into Section 502B. (The Jackson amendment to the Trade Act of 1973, for example, favored withdrawal of credits from nonmarket economies that denied their citizens the right to emigrate. Section 502B makes no mention of such a right, and in the hearings it was denied that the right to emigrate was included within the tacit scope of the rights cited in the section).[12] Instead, as we have seen, 502B cites torture as one of several incontestable examples of human rights violation, and it cites as the violated right(s) "the right to life, liberty, or security of person." But why should we choose these human rights as the ones whose violations are to set in motion restrictions on our foreign aid? In order to answer this question we need to look at the full array of basic human rights and determine whether there are priorities among them that Section 502B reflects.

It is possible to arrange human rights by reference to many different considerations, but for our purposes a basic tripartite division will suffice. With this taxonomy, we can sort rights according to whether their chief function is (1) to bar others from interfering with one's conduct, and thus to demark a certain sphere of privacy, liberty, or autonomy; or (2) to entitle the individual to participate in the institutions of self-government, and thus to affect the rules that arise from the rights in (1); or (3) to impose upon the government the responsibility to aid individuals by providing services and facilities beyond those that individuals can provide for themselves. These three categories are not meant to constitute an exclusive division, because there are unavoidable overlaps; but they are meant to be exhaustive.

Rights in the first category can be subdivided into (a) those that bar interference by other persons as such, and (b) those that bar interference by government, and thus by other persons acting in official capacities. The traditional rights of life, liberty, property, and security of person

---

[12] Remarks of Congressman Don Fraser, in "International Security Assistance Act of 1976," *Hearings of the Committee on International Relations, on H.P. 11963*, H.R., 94th Congress, 1976. Pages 497–522 are devoted to the Fraser-Solarz amendment, which ultimately became Section 502B of the current law.

fall mainly into subclass (a), and to protect them the criminal law is erected. Among the rights protected against invasions by government in subclass (b) there are (i) protected liberties, such as the rights of assembly, speech, and the press, and other activities that essentially involve social contact and relationships: and (ii) rights that limit the methods government may use in its presumed defense of the rights of its citizens, including especially the rights in subclass (1) (a) above. These are the rights that are violated by torture and prolonged detention without trial. Habeas corpus and most of the provisions of our Bill of Rights fall into one or the other of these two subcategories of (1) (b).

Rights in the second category include the right to vote and to run for political office, and the other rights specified in the Civil War amendments to our federal Constitution as well as such more recent amendments as the Twenty-fourth and Twenty-sixth. Insofar as the rights of free speech, press, and assembly can be seen as inseparable from the right to participate in the political processes of self-government, these rights, already located in category (1), also have a place in category (2).

The third category of rights can be subdivided into three subclasses. One of them, (a), contains the rights that are the source of the government's responsibility to create institutions to cope with persons who have interfered with the exercise by others of their rights in categories (1) and (2). The enforcement of the prohibitions of the criminal law through the design, financing, and administration of the police, the courts, and penal institutions can be viewed as a product of the rights in this subclass. A second subclass, (b), includes the jury trial, appellate courts, and other rights of criminal procedure, including habeas corpus. Even though these are rights to services and facilities and not merely rights to be let alone, no libertarian defender of the "minimal state" would object to the rights identified in these two subclasses.[13] Archliberals of this sort would object, however, to all or most of the rights in the third subclass, (c), the social and economic or welfare rights that bulk so large in Articles 22 through 30 of the U.N. Declaration of Human Rights but which were virtually unknown until quite recently in our own constitutional history.

In summary, then, we have the following structure of rights:

(1) Rights against interference
    (a) by other individuals (life, liberty, property, security of person)
    (b) by government in its protection of the rights of individuals or minorities
        (i) liberties (assembly, speech, press)
        (ii) limitations against abuse of police power
(2) Rights of participation in self-government (voting)
(3) Rights to services and facilities for the
    (a) prevention of interference with the exercise of individual rights (police, courts, prisons)
    (b) guarantee of due process
    (c) provision of the social minimum (schools, hospitals, and so on)

---

[13] See, for example, Robert Nozick, *Anarchy, State, and Utopia* (New York: Basic Books, 1974), especially Chapters 3 and 5.

Do any of these categories of rights have a preferred status with respect to the others? If choice must be made among violated rights to be protested, is there any basis for attempting to terminate some of these violations in precedence to others? I think it can be argued in several different ways that if the rights in category (1) (a) are our most important rights, then the violation by a government of rights in category (1) (b) (ii) must be the most important to protest and terminate.

There is, first, what we might call *the argument from indifference to economic contingencies.* It is not possible to implement social and economic rights unless a society enjoys a certain level of affluence. Poor societies cannot provide much in the way of criminal justice (police, courts), social security, public education, medical care, and so forth. But even the poorest society can require that its government leave its citizens and residents unmolested, free from torture, lengthy detention, cruel punishments, and other related harms. All that is required is governmental self-restraint. This suggests a criterion: roughly, the more fundamental a right is the less its provision and protection depend upon a society's resources and wealth. This has two important consequences. One is that there is little or no direct economic cost for a government to cease its human rights violations where some rights are concerned, whereas it will cost the government a good deal to cease violation of some other rights. The exercise of habeas corpus puts no strain on tax revenues, whereas it may cost a small fortune to build a new sewage treatment facility as a necessary step in the direction of providing for minimally decent health needs. The other consequence of importance is that by linking termination of foreign assistance to some human rights violations and not to others, as Section 502B does, the direct cost for the terminations is not borne by the poorest and least affluent members of society, as it would be if Section 502B were rewritten to terminate foreign assistance to a nation because its government violates the socioeconomic rights of its people.

A second line of consideration might be called *the argument from the functional interdependence among basic rights.* Persons cannot enjoy rights such as free speech or political participation unless certain of their other rights are relatively secure. So long as due process of law is denied, habeas corpus suspended, or self-incriminating testimony admissible at trial without reservation, the political climate is missing in which persons can take seriously the opportunity to govern themselves. In fact, the degree to which habeas corpus and related rights are denied can serve as a reliable index of the futility of democratic political processes. If persons thus oppressed nevertheless enjoy cradle-to-grave welfare rights, they do so as hostages to fortune and patronized victims of tyranny. It is an insult to one's dignity to have welfare rights at the same time one is subject to arbitrary detention without charge or trial, but the converse is not true. It might be objected that it is no less an insult to one's dignity to be guaranteed scrupulous police protection and an elaborate criminal justice system that incorporates every known safeguard to the rights of the accused when one is also left to starve. The reply is two-fold. A government may in fact be unable to do anything about the starvation of a good portion of its population; but a government is never unable to prohibit (and to that extent, end) the practice of torturing suspects.

Second, if the starvation is in fact a result of policy—for example, part of a program of genocide for a certain regional or ethnic minority—then it is of course a more massive violation of fundamental rights than even persistent torture is. In general, then, the government's responsibility to undertake to feed its own people remains less central than its responsibility not to torture. The people, after all, may be quite able to feed themselves, if only they are allowed to organize to do so. Only in a forcibly collectivized economy or in the face of (natural or man-made) catastrophe will government intervention be a necessary condition of avoiding starvation. What is true of starvation is hardly less true of unemployment and many other human needs at the present time.

The same conclusion can be reached by what might be called *the argument from primary goods*. A primary good is anything whatever that "a rational man wants whatever else he wants." [14] Among the primary social goods are "rights and liberties, opportunities and powers, income and wealth," as well as "a sense of one's own worth." [15] Although all human rights probably qualify as primary social goods, some meet this description more preeminently than others. Whatever else you want, if you are rational, you *don't* want to suffer the abuses of government power that torture and the like involve. You must want to be free of such violence to your body and your spirit. Perhaps you can even argue further that no rational man would trade his independence from governmental interference with his privacy, liberty, and personal security for publicly funded social services. At least, not if the interferences take the form cited in Section 502B: torture, prolonged detention without trial, and so forth. The reason is that every rational man has the prospect, in all but the most extreme circumstances, of being able to manage by his own efforts if simply left alone to do so. Confronted with the choice between governmental aid in the form of social services and governmental interference in the form of torture, a rational man would forego the aid in order to be free of the injury. Every act of torture, cruel and inhumane punishment, or detention without charge or trial directly inhibits freedom and self-respect in ways that failure to provide social services and institutions for self-government do not.

The same conclusion can be reached in yet another way, by what can be called *the argument from analogy to crime*. The violation by government of some human rights is strictly analogous to the commission by a private individual of heinous crimes. Thus, torture and the like have the same effects upon their victims as do the crimes of murder, aggravated assault and battery, and rape: disfigurement, mutilation, maiming, incapacitation, death. The failure to respect other human rights, however, is analogous only to a failure to confer (at worst, a withholding of) certain benefits. Government censorship, exclusion from the political process, or the lack of medical aid amount either to a relatively slight harm or to the failure to provide a service or benefit. Underlying this argument is the principle that, in general, causing someone a personal injury is much worse than failing to confer on someone a personal benefit. At

[14] Rawls, p. 92.
[15] Ibid.

the very worst, an individual incapable of fending for himself will suffer the natural consequences of his circumstances. No one will have undertaken to make him worse off. A person obviously has a more severe complaint against his government for subjecting him to torture than for the failure to undertake to make him better off. It is all the difference between an actively malignant despotism and a passively (or ineptly) benevolent despotism. If one had to choose, one would prefer to be the victim of the latter rather than of the former. John Stuart Mill expressed exactly the point at issue when he said, "A person may possibly not need the benefits of others, but he always needs that they should not do him harm." [16]

Finally, the history of our civilization during the past several centuries shows a progressive development of human rights under domestic law that gives us what we can call *the argument from cultural priority*. Traditional liberal doctrine makes it clear why such a development in the recognition of rights over time is coordinate with a reflective assessment of the relative importance of some rights over others. If a person has his rights of life, liberty, property, and security of person protected against invasion by his neighbors and free of tyrannical government violation as well, then given moderate industry on his part he can fend for himself to secure his other rights to the extent that they matter to him. Thus, in the time of Hobbes and Locke, public health care and old age security were deemed matters of public *charity*, not of individual *right*. As for such rights as voting, they were unequally distributed, being contingent upon property and sex qualifications. Only such rights as habeas corpus and jury trial were part of the law of the land and in theory available to all equally.

There is a lesson in this relevant to the provisions of Section 502B. If the United States is going to link human rights with its foreign policy, the rights in question must be rights that we have already undertaken to recognize in our domestic law. They ought not to be rights that our own government has ignored or violated with impunity until recently. They must not be rights about which there is still ideological or other controversy in our own country. They must be rights rooted in our constitutional history and practiced throughout the land. This is not true of any social or economic rights; it is not even true of political or civil rights, as our history of racism and sexism shows. But it is true of the rights singled out in Section 502B. If Justice Brandeis was correct when he wrote a half century ago that "the right to be let alone . . . [is] the right most valued by civilized men," [17] we can see why the rights singled out for special attention in Section 502B are not an arbitrary subset of all human rights, but deserve the priority this law would give them.

The overall argument so far gives us a sound basis for several of the steps required to justify the provisions of Section 502B: There are human rights that torture and related activities violate. These rights, asserted or implied by a long tradition of philosophical reflection, are now recognized under international law. Like all rights, these rights express the

---

[16] John Stuart Mill, *Utilitarianism*, part V, sixth paragraph from the end.
[17] *Olmstead* v. *United States*, 277 U.S. 438, 478 (1928).

principle that individual freedom, privacy, and autonomy shall not give way whenever they conflict with collective advantage or administrative convenience and efficiency. Finally, these rights have a preferred status even among human rights. What remains to be examined is the basis for undertaking to link their violations with our foreign policy.

RESPONDING TO VIOLATIONS OF RIGHTS

I have assumed from the start that it would be morally unacceptable to have a foreign policy, especially a foreign assistance program, that took no account of the violations of human rights by other countries. It is appropriate here to look more closely at why this is so, because it sheds light on the kind of responses to such violations that are feasible and appropriate. Consider for this purpose a largely hypothetical example. Suppose that in 1930 the government of nation A undertook to provide nonmilitary assistance to the government of nation B in the form of oil, gas, and other petrochemical products. Suppose further that within a couple of years the government of nation B was in the hands of a virulent anti-Semitic faction eager to embark on "the final solution to the Jewish problem." Let us suppose that this involved the construction of exter-mination camps in which lethal poisons would be used in large quan-tities, and that these poisons were to be manufactured from the raw materials being supplied by the government of nation A, a portion of which would be diverted to this new purpose. To make the argument simpler, let us assume that the government of nation B could not obtain these products elsewhere as cheaply, as promptly, and in such large supply as they could from the government of nation A. On the facts sup-posed, is it really conceivable that an adviser to the government of nation A, knowing all the facts, would think it morally permissible to recom-mend continuation of the foreign assistance? The only ground for such a view would have to be that the government of nation B intended to use these chemicals to violate the human rights only of *its own* nationals.

Under the operative assumptions in the example, there are both of two powerful reasons against continuing the export program. First, those in the government of nation A (and to that extent, its people as well) had become, or were on the verge of becoming, knowing accomplices in a monstrous crime against humanity. Thus, in favor of terminating the assistance there is *the argument from avoiding complicity in wrongdoing*. Second, by threatening to withdraw the aid, or actually terminating it, the government of nation A could exert leverage on the anti-Semitic government to cancel its extermination program, either by way of making it very difficult for them to continue or by making them give it up as the price they must pay in order to continue to receive our assistance (most of which, in the example, is being used for purposes wholly unrelated to their policy of genocide for Jews). This is *the argument from leverage to end wrongdoing*. No matter how politically inexpedient or futile it might turn out to be for our government to terminate its aid, it would be morally untenable for a government to be indifferent to human rights violations consequent to its foreign assistance program merely because the victims of these violations were foreign nationals on foreign territory.

To dispute this claim on moral grounds requires defense of the position that under *no* conditions do the human rights violations by one government, so long as they are perpetrated on its own soil and against its own nationals, establish the immorality of another government's refusal to reduce or terminate its aid and assistance to that country. On the contrary, though a nation's foreign policy by definition begins at the water's edge, it does not follow that its moral responsibilities stop there. So, if what might be called the doctrine of moral indifference in foreign policy matters cannot be seriously defended, then the question becomes one of deciding which human rights, when violated, where and in what ways, and by whom ought to be of concern in foreign policy, and what steps can and should be taken by a government to protest and, if possible, end these violations. The hypothetical example, in other words, suffices to establish the fundamental premise of morality on which any possible argument for Section 502B must ultimately rest.

Beyond both complicity and leverage, there is perhaps a third factor at work in Section 502B, more controversial than the other two. It would be incorrect to ascribe to this factor a large role, but it cannot be wholly neglected. Given that another government has systematically violated the most fundamental human rights of its population, it is extremely difficult for our government both to maintain its alliance (as embodied in the foreign assistance program) with that government, and to take no further notice of these violations beyond, say, an official protest to that nation's ambassador. In effect, Section 502B can be read as a demand that our government go further and inflict a quasi-punitive action—the withdrawal of a service or benefit—on those governments which are convicted by the Congress, as it were, after due investigation, of gross and sustained violations of the human rights of their own people. Of course, our government has no legal or political authority to "punish" another government in this or any other way. Nevertheless, there is a strong analogy at precisely this point between what Section 502B authorizes and the proper moral response to those individuals who violate the basic rights of others. As John Stuart Mill once noted, "To have a right . . . is . . . to have something which society ought to defend me in the possession of." [18] H.L.A. Hart has restated the same point: "There is . . . a special congruity in the use of force or the threat of force to secure . . . what is . . . someone's right. . . ." [19] It is in part in this spirit that we should understand the intended function of Section 502B.

A fully coherent social philosophy addressed to the existence of human rights, their incorporation into positive law, and the empirical fact of their actual or likely violation would also undertake to provide for preventive and remedial steps as well as for the punitive measures to which Mill and Hart alluded. Similarly, on the international scene, Section 502B can be seen as both a partially preventive and as a quasi-

[18] Mill, thirteenth paragraph from the end.
[19] Hart, p. 177.

punitive step for such violations. Withdrawal of continued arms exports, under the provisions of Section 502B, is not exactly punitive even if it is a negative sanction. Nor is application of the sanction provided by this section wholly preventive, as it might be if the availability of arms and training from the United States under its foreign assistance programs were the only way a government could set about to violate the human rights of its citizens. Nevertheless, Section 502B is a disincentive to such rights violations, and at worst a symbolic gesture expressing the judgment of Congress on the extent and significance of human rights violations in other countries.

Finally, making the criterion for our cutoff of foreign assistance "a consistent pattern of gross violations" of human rights, as Section 502B does, helps to exclude a response both premature and hypocritical. We know that violations of human rights occur in our own country at all levels of government (municipal, state, federal). We also know that it is a rare government official who is willing to acknowledge such acts and defend them for what they are. The very fact that they are concealed, denied, and explained away indicates the guilty conscience with which they are perpetrated in our society. However short we actually fall from the standard of impeccable observance of the rights to "life, liberty, and security of person," they are not subject to "a consistent pattern of gross violations" anywhere in the nation. Our proper embarrassment at their sporadic violations almost everywhere is not a reason for ignoring "a consistent pattern of gross violations" by other governments.

CONCLUSION

It has been said—properly, I think—that human rights are "the fundamental moral and social values which should be or should continue to be realized in any society fit for intelligent and responsible citizens," [20] "those minimal things without which it is impossible to develop one's capabilities and to live a life as a human being." [21] If so, then *all* law and policy, foreign no less than domestic, ought to be designed to foster the observance and to discourage the violations of human rights. It is a sobering fact, not to be forgotten, that it is governments rather than individuals that have the greatest capacity for violating human rights. Looked at from the moral point of view, it cannot be right for one nation to allow the people of another nation to become the hostages, captives, slaves, or victims of its own government. Restraints upon governments, or at least disincentives, to prevent and discourage violation of the rights of persons should be a concern of all governments and all peoples. It is on this understanding that Section 502B should be appraised.

[20] Margaret Macdonald, "Natural Rights," *Proceedings of the Aristotelian Society,* 47 (1946–1947), pp. 225–250, at p. 240.
[21] Wasserstrom, p. 636.

The fact of world hunger needs no introduction, but the proper role of moral and political philosophy in resolving this problem is less obvious. This paper is an essay in moral philosophy on the right to food, but its scope reaches beyond the issue of rights into related problems of allocation and distributive justice. The paper moves from a set of historical considerations regarding the origin of the idea of a right to food to progressively more complex and theoretical considerations of moral philosophy.

PRELIMINARY HISTORICAL CONSIDERATIONS

The idea of a right to food has uncertain origins, but its history is characterized far more by the rhetoric of political proposal than by careful analysis of the meaning and scope of proposed rights. Unlike rights such as the right to life, the right to liberty, and the right to property, assertions of a right to food are relatively recent phenomena. The recent origin as well as the uncertain legal and moral status of this right are shared with other recent proclamations of rights such as the right to health care, the right to die, and the right to a minimum wage. However, some of these rights have a longer and richer history than does the right to food. For example, the movement to proclaim a right to *health care* is a relatively recent phenomenon; but there is a long history in the United States and elsewhere of proclamations of a right to *health*—by which is meant a right to be protected against the health-threatening actions of others.

Serious modern discussions of a right to food, along with many discussions of other rights on an international level, can be traced at least to the December 10, 1948 Universal Declaration of Human Rights of the United Nations General Assembly. This document attempted to set forth "a common standard of achievement for all peoples." It specifically mentions a right to food, together with a very long list of postulated rights.[1] This declaration also illustrates the ambiguous history of proclamations of rights at the international level, for it does not appear to construe rights as entitlements. Its preamble gives the impression that the document is to be read as a blueprint for future actions and declara-

[1] "Universal Declaration of Human Rights," in *Human Rights: A Compilation of International Instruments of the United Nations* (New York: United Nations, 1973); see Articles 3 and 25.

tions of rights rather than as an assertion of rights that persons in their native states *now* possess. The declaration seems to function as a guide for progressive development, both of rights and of material security, rather than as an assertion of prevailing rights or so-called natural and human rights.

The U.N. document has proved difficult to interpret, due to its origins in political compromise. It includes rights taken from classic democratic sources, such as American and French declarations of independence, and rights adapted from statements by socialist states of programs for the establishment of minimum standards of living. The U.N. document is historically significant, nonetheless, for several reasons. Most of the important formal statements of human rights prior to 1948 were assertions of individual rights to independence and noninterference. That is, they were assertions of negative rights, the rights of individuals to be left alone or to be protected from the harmful actions of others. The U.N. document, perhaps more than any other source, broadens the scope of rights to include positive rights—the rights of individuals to be provided with goods and services. The document for the first time asserts rights to receive goods and services from collective entities, even on an international level.

The notion that rights are guiding ideals rather than existing entitlements has been given explicit recognition in many documents subsequent to the U.N. declaration. It might even be argued that this use of the term "rights" is the prevailing political use. Thus, in the report of the Symposium on Population and Human Rights at the World Population Conference in Bucharest (1974), also sponsored by the United Nations, it was formally recorded by some participants that "the right to an adequate standard of living, including food . . . would remain a *distant ideal* for many developing countries unless their economic growth was accelerated." [2] The word "right" is here clearly functioning to set forth a commendable or perhaps obligatory target, not to state an entitlement held by the citizens of developing countries. Indeed, it is probably safe to say that virtually all political statements about the right to food express guiding ideals rather than entitlements. In the writings of many religious organizations interested in the right to food, the use of the term "right" also fits this pattern. For example, the policy statement of Bread for the World, a self-described "Christian citizen's lobby on world hunger," proclaims that, "As Christians we affirm the right to food: the right of every man, woman, and child on earth to a nutritionally adequate diet. This right is grounded in the value God places on human life." [3] This statement bears only a superficial resemblance to eighteenth-century theological views about natural rights. When the authors of this policy statement explicate their immediate objectives, they state their views in the following language: "We need to think in terms of *long-range strategies* that deal with the causes of

[2] "Report of the Symposium on Population and Human Rights" of the World Population Conference, 19–30 August 1974 (New York: United Nations, 1974), pp. 16, 19 (italics added).
[3] "The Right to Food: A Statement of Policy." *Worldview* 18 (May 1975): 45.

hunger." [4] The document makes no pretense that rights are entitlements, enforceable or unenforceable.

Statements of the U.S. Congress invite a similar interpretation. The 1976 "Right-to-Food Resolution" in the House of Representatives fits this pattern. The lengthy testimony before the Subcommittee on International Resources, Food, and Energy finds its point of departure in a resolution passed by the House and Senate (and deriving from previous statements of the United Nations) to the effect that "every person in this country and throughout the world has the right to food—the right to a nutritionally adequate diet—and that this right is henceforth to be recognized as a cornerstone of United States policy." [5] As with the statement by a religious group, these hearings take on the sober atmosphere of tackling a job that must be done to reduce world hunger. There is no indication that individuals are now entitled to make claims for food but, rather, that U.S. policy should be directed toward "assisting" "the world's poorest people." This same pattern generally prevails in all political and religious statements on the right to food. Invariably these statements employ the language of "rights" to make a resolution or a policy statement without further analysis of what it means to be a right and without explicit assertion of entitlements.

In writings on moral philosophy, by contrast, the notion of a moral right to food is usually translated into the language of obligations to assist others or into language of the justice of fulfilling the basic needs of others. There are good reasons as to why such translations occur in both policy statements and writings on moral philosophy. These reasons all pertain to the logic of moral reasoning and the language of rights in particular, as we shall now see.

THE FOUNDATIONS OF RIGHTS IN ETHICAL THEORY

Because claims about human rights generally appear in political statements, they are seldom accompanied by argument regarding their basis and validity. I now turn specifically to the problem of analyzing the nature of rights—with special reference to the right to food.

Rights as Entitlements. Rights in moral philosophy and political theory have traditionally been understood not as ideals but rather as legal claims that entitle a person to some good, service, or liberty. Rights are entitlements as contrasted to privileges, personal ideals, group ideals, and acts of charity. Rights to food stamps or to Medicare are, as rights, no different from rights to receive an insurance benefit when required premiums have been paid: anyone *eligible* (under a legitimate description of eligibility) is entitled to receive all services and goods provided

---

4 *Ibid.* (italics added).

5 *The Right-to-Food Resolution.* Hearings before the Subcommittee on International Resources, Food, and Energy of the Committee on International Relations of the House of Representatives, Ninety-fourth Congress, 2d sess, on H. Cong. Res. 393, June 22–29, 1976 (Washington, D.C.: Government Printing Office, 1976), p. 2.

by the program. However, only someone with a *valid* claim has a right to something. The fact that one can argue in clever ways that one ought to receive a good or service is not sufficient grounds for a rights claim; for a good argument for something does not always amount to an entitlement. For example, even if there are good arguments favoring publicly funded food programs, such as free breakfasts and lunches in elementary schools, it does not follow that anyone has a right to food because of these arguments. It would not follow even if one demonstrated a pressing *need* for such programs. Thus, if there does not exist a valid claim to X, a person claiming entitlement to X may be demanding X or proposing a right to X, but nonetheless has no right to X. Such a demand or proposal posture seems the most accurate description of U.N. statements on universal rights, and it is perhaps for this reason that the sweeping claims in these documents have frequently come under attack.

Some writers have maintained that under conditions of scarcity there may exist "a right which is an entitlement *to* some good, but not a valid claim *against* any particular individual." [6] For example, one might say that a malnourished child in a country suffering from famine has a *right* to a nutritionally balanced diet but has no *valid claim* against any individual, group, or nation. This is a confusing use of the term "right"—in the U.N. tradition—and it provides one reason for distinguishing rights from mere claims, and mere claims from valid claims.

Legal and Moral Rights. Legal rights are entitlements supportable on legal grounds, whereas moral rights are entitlements supportable on moral grounds. Legal rights and moral rights are conceptually distinguishable even if in some social circumstance they might be coextensive. Moreover, moral rights can form a basis for justifying or criticizing legal rights, but the reverse relation does not hold. U.N. statements are assertions of moral rights ("human rights"), presumably ones aimed at reforming deficiencies in legal rights in certain countries. The U.S. Congress, by contrast, is concerned with legal rights, even if the arguments in congressional debates are often moral arguments.

Positive and Negative Rights. Rights claims are commonly distinguished into two types: negative and positive. This distinction is based on the difference between the right to be free from something (a liberty right) and the right to be provided with a particular good or service (a benefit right). It must not be thought, however, that negative, or liberty, rights do not require active interventions. The protection of a negative right commonly requires active protection against some possible harm. For example, to say that one has a right to health is, at least in some contexts, to claim that the state must intervene to protect citizens against dangerous chemicals, emissions, polluted waterways, and so on. The claim that there is a right to health, then, is plausibly construable as a negative right to active protection by the state. Rights to health care, by contrast, are positive rights that the state must provide health care goods and

---

[6] Joel Feinberg remarks on but does not endorse this position in "The Nature and Value of Rights," *Journal of Value Inquiry* 4 (Winter 1970): 255.

services. The right to food can also be regarded as a positive right in that it requires goods and services.

It is confusing to maintain, as does the Yale Task Force on Population Ethics, that in the "American rights tradition" (as, for example, the Bill of Rights) "rights are [merely] protections; they are procedures for applying and specifying the implementation of individual liberty; and there is *no specification of duties corresponding to rights.*" The Task Force goes on to argue that only when "rights make a claim on resources or requisite activity [do] they involve duties." The right to food is taken as a prime example of the latter kind of right by the Task Force, whereas negative, or "defensive," rights are said to be examples of the former.[7] The Task Force correctly maintains that assertions of a right to food are assertions of a positive right, but it wrongly concludes that not all rights entail duties or active interventions by others. Let us now see why all rights *do* entail duties.

The Correlativity Thesis. What does the general schema "X has a right to Y" mean? By using the positive–negative distinction, this schema can be analyzed as having two identifiable meanings: (1) Someone is obligated to provide Y to X, for example, the right to food can be analyzed as entailing that someone is obligated to provide food to X; (2) someone is obligated to abstain from or to prevent others from interfering with X's doing or obtaining Y, for example, the right to die, the right to privacy, and the right to a healthy environment should be treated as such liberty rights. Distinctions 1 and 2 can be integrated in abbreviated fashion into a single unit with the following meaning: "the moral system [or the legal system, where appropriate] imposes an obligation on someone Z to act so that X is enabled to have Y (if X wishes Y)." Common to all these analyses is the claim that the language of rights is translatable into the language of obligations.

It follows from this analysis that rights and obligations are correlative. One person's right entails an obligation on another's part, and all obligations similarly entail rights. For example, if a state promises or otherwise incurs an obligation to provide food to needy people, then a mechanism such as a food stamp system is adopted and the person can claim an entitlement to the food. Similarly, in the law it is often pointed out that a citizen's right to equal protection, to welfare, and so on entails an obligation of government to provide equal protection, welfare, and so on. This doctrine does not tell us whether rights are grounded in obligations or obligations in rights, and therefore the correlativity thesis is a *logical* thesis that does not in itself reveal the fundamental basis of moral claims.

It is widely maintained that not *all* obligations entail rights, because several classes of obligations do not seem to be correlated to rights claims. Joel Feinberg argues, for example, that duties of charity and conscience often function more on the order of gratuitous services than of debts to which one can make a claim. He contends that such words as "duty" and "obligation" have come to refer to any required action, whether the

---

[7] The Yale Task Force on Population Ethics, "Moral Claims, Human Rights, and Population Policies," *Theological Studies* 35 (March 1974): 91.

requirement derives from a right, a matter of conscience, a supererogatory ideal, or whatever. He therefore suggests that we distinguish between two senses of "required": (1) required by a moral duty and (2) required by some self-imposed stricture such as a rule of conscience or a commitment to charity.[8]

As I use the term "obligation," it means a duty that is morally binding on anyone in a position to perform an action of the appropriate description. Insofar as an obligation is universalizable on moral grounds— and not on charitable or other supererogatory grounds—the correlativity thesis holds. This argument rests on the position that we ought to distinguish sharply between moral obligations and self-imposed requirements based on "moral" ideals. Accordingly, if X must do something for Y on morally universalizable grounds, then Y has a right to claim it from X; but, if X "must" do it based on X's ideals (charitable, conscientious, etc.), then Y has no right to claim it from X. We shall turn momentarily to the principled moral basis for claims strong enough to generate rights to such commodities as food, especially at the international level.

The Prima Facie–Absolute Distinction. Must rights be understood as *absolute* claims? We earlier noted that rights can be insisted upon because they are entitlements to which one can lay valid claim. However, it is a far stronger thesis that rights are absolute in that they cannot be validly overridden. It is sometimes assumed, for example, that we have a right to life irrespective of competing claims or social conditions. If absolutistic, this thesis is implausible, as indicated by common moral judgments about capital punishment, international agreements about killing in war, and beliefs about the justifiability of killing in self-defense. At most, morality posits a right not to have one's life taken *without sufficient justification.* Rights, then, are contingent: They are entitlements, but they can be legitimately exercised and create actual duties on others only when circumstances indicate that the interests and claims of affected individuals can be satisfactorily served by permitting the right to have overriding status. For this reason rights claims should be classified as *prima facie* rather than as absolute. That is, they should be regarded as valid standing claims that may be overridden by more stringent competing claims.

When Henry Fribourg writes that we must choose whether "human rights" to food "should have priority over property rights," [9] he has landed on one of the more important moral and political problems in asserting a right to food. Because entitlements to food would inevitably require organized collective action, property owners' rights to land could in principle conflict with the rights of those who require the land for purposes of food production. Jan Narveson has pointed out that it is possible to view claims to a right to food in the current world situation as involving just this type of conflict:

8 Feinberg, *op. cit.,* pp. 244ff.
9 Henry A. Fribourg, "Food for Survival? Ethics, Food and People." *Phi Kappa Phi Journal* 56 (Spring 1976): 13.

If population policy is determined by rights, then whose rights are involved? And which of their rights are relevant? If . . . every human being has some fundamental rights, then it follows that every addition to the population of the world makes a certain additional, undeniable claim upon some of the world's resources, and therefore upon the rest of us who happen to control those resources. These claims must be balanced against our right to pursue the good life in whatever way we please.[10]

Fundamental and Derivative Rights. There are at least three senses in which rights might be said to be fundamental. First, it might be argued that they are morally fundamental because other rights may be derived from them, while they are not derived from other more basic rights. For example, it might be argued that the right to food is basic because it is not derived from rights such as the right to life, whereas nonfundamental rights such as those to have a nutritionally sound diet are derived from it. Second, it might be argued that certain rights are fundamental because they are preconditions or necessary conditions of *all* other rights. Life, liberty, and equality (of treatment and opportunity) have some claim to status as fundamental in this sense. The right to food may also have some claim to status as fundamental in this sense, for food may be as necessary to one's welfare as are life and liberty themselves. Samuel Gorovitz has argued that no right is more fundamental in this second sense than is the right to food, because "no right has meaning or value once starvation strikes." Starvation is the "ultimate deprivation," he argues, because "without food life ends, and rights are of value only to the living." [11]

Whatever the merits of Gorovitz's claim, it is perhaps most enlightening as a matter of moral theory to understand the right to food as a derivative rather than a fundamental right in the first sense mentioned. William Aiken has plausibly argued, for example, that the right to food is derivative from the right to be saved from starvation, which in turn is derivative from the right to be saved from preventible death due to deprivation.[12] All these rights, he argues, are based on obligations created by human need.

Natural Rights and Human Rights. As we have seen, it is held in such documents as the Universal Declaration of Human Rights of the United Nations that the right to food is a "natural" or "human" right. The idea of natural or human rights has a confusing history and probably reduces to an idealistic attempt to assert a list of rights that are universally believed in and that it is hoped political states would universally observe. Such assertions are best interpreted as statements of program-

---

10 Jan Narveson, "Moral Problems of Population," *The Monist* 57 (January 1973): 64.
11 Samuel Gorovitz, "Bigotry, Loyalty, and Malnutrition," in Peter G. Brown and Henry Shue, eds., *Food Policy: The Responsibility of the United States in the Life and Death Choices* (New York: Macmillan, 1977), pp. 131ff.
12 William Aiken, "The Right to Be Saved from Starvation," in William Aiken and Hugh LaFollette, eds., *World Hunger and Moral Obligation* (Englewood Cliffs, N.J.: Prentice-Hall, 1977) .

matic ideals to the effect that all basic human needs ought to be given status as individual claims by modern political states, even though conditions of scarcity may render it impossible that a *valid* claim be exercised. Certainly there is no reason to think that such alleged rights can always be validly claimed, especially on an international basis. It simply is not always possible to permit their exercise under prevailing economic conditions. Therefore, even political conferral of such rights would not mean that a valid claim or exercise of the "rights" would be possible. It also follows from previous considerations that such claims of human rights, and the obligations that support them, are merely *prima facie*. It is easy to interpret most international statements of rights and perhaps even statements of domestic rights to food in precisely this way.

MORAL OBLIGATIONS
AND THE PRINCIPLE OF BENEFICENCE

This analysis suggests that rights are grounded in obligations.[13] If so, a theory of rights, including the right to food, requires a theory of obligations for its justification. The existence of a right to food thus depends upon the existence of a moral obligation to provide food. The basis of such an obligation—if there is one—could be social utility, contractual agreement, or any number of other principles. It is crucial that a specifiable principle or set of principles be identified, for they will establish both the validity and scope of the right asserted.

The Principle of Beneficence. Our immediate problem is, "What principle or set of principles, if any, is sufficient to generate a right to food?" Although many different answers to this question have been offered, most have centered on the principle of beneficence as the most likely ground of a claim to this right. This principle asserts a duty to help others further their important and legitimate interests. But the application of this principle to the distribution of food raises many problems.

The term "beneficence" has quite a broad usage in English, including among its meanings the doing of good, active promotion of good, kindness, and charity. But beneficence is here understood as a *duty* and, thus, is distinct from mere kindness or charity.[14] In its most general meaning, it is the duty to help others further their important and legitimate interests when one can do so with minimal risk to himself or herself. The duty to confer benefits and actively to prevent and remove harms are all important, but of equal importance is the duty to balance

---

[13] The above analysis, of course, permits the interpretation that obligations are grounded in some higher reaches of ethical theory. This substantive matter cannot be explored here.

[14] This usage may be more fully explicated as follows: Sometimes in moral philosophy beneficence is used to refer to the *noninfliction* of harm on others, to the *prevention* of harm, and also to the *removal* of harmful conditions. However, because prevention nd removal generally require positive acts that assist others, I shall use the term "beneficence" to refer to actions involving prevention of harm, removal of harmful conditions, and positive benefiting, whereas a term such as "nonmaleficence" shall be reserved to refer to the noninfliction of harm.

the good it is possible to produce against the possible harms that might result from doing the good. It is thus appropriate to distinguish two functions served by the principle of beneficence: The first requires the provision of benefits, and the second requires a balancing of possible benefits and risks of harms when both might occur.

Firmly established in both the history of ethics and the history of U.S. international relations is the belief that the failure to increase the good of others when one is knowingly in a position to do so—and not simply failure to avoid harm—is morally wrong. Preventive medicine and active public health interventions provide many obvious examples: Once methods of treating yellow fever and smallpox were discovered in early modern medicine, for example, it was universally agreed that it would be immoral not to take positive steps to establish preventive programs. Food stamp programs in the United States presumably have a similar moral justification.

Still, there is a special problem about beneficence when applied to moral problems of food distribution. Because beneficence potentially demands extreme generosity in the moral life, some moral philosophers have argued that it is *virtuous,* but not a *duty,* to act beneficently. They have treated beneficent actions as akin to acts of charity or acts of conscience. From this perspective the positive benefiting of others by providing such goods as food is based on personal ideals beyond the call of duty and, thus, is supererogatory rather than obligatory. In this view, we are not *always* morally required to benefit persons, even if we are in a position to do so. For example, we are not morally required to perform all possible acts of charity, even for people who are starving. In what respects and within what limits, then, is beneficence a duty? And how does it apply to problems of food distribution?

Is Beneficence a Principle of Duty? Public support of agricultural research demonstrates that we do in fact think of some beneficent actions as demanded by social duties. The obligation to benefit members of society, including future generations, is generally cited as the primary justification of this and all publicly funded scientific research. There are many similar examples of actions justified on the basis of beneficence. Still, it is one thing to maintain that actions or programs are morally *justified* and quite another to maintain that they are morally *required.* Thus, it remains to be demonstrated that beneficent actions are *duties.* This demonstration is a matter of extreme importance because of the correlativity thesis. Rights, including the right to food, can be derived only from duty-based premises, not from mere demonstrations that actions are morally justifiable. That is, if we are to show that there is a right to food, we must show that there is a duty to provide the food— not merely that it is morally permitted to provide it. Moral philosophers have advanced several proposals designed to resolve this problem.

Of these the most significant for our purposes is one that maintains that obligatory beneficent actions can be grounded in a requirement to "prevent what is bad." In discussing the duty to provide food, Peter Singer relies heavily on a distinction between preventing evil and promoting good:

I begin with the assumption that suffering and death from lack of food, shelter, and medical care are bad. . . . I shall not argue for this view. People can hold all sorts of eccentric positions, and perhaps from some of them it would not follow that death by starvation is in itself bad. . . .

My next point it this: if it is in our power to prevent something bad from happening, without thereby sacrificing anything of comparable moral importance, we ought, morally, to do it. By "without sacrificing anything of comparable moral importance" I mean without causing anything else comparably bad to happen, or something that is wrong in itself, or failing to promote some moral good. . . . This principle seems almost as uncontroversial as the last one. It requires us only to prevent what is bad, and not to promote what is good.[15]

Singer's strategy is to argue that broad commitments of *positive* actions such as shipments of food can be grounded in the prevention of obviously bad outcomes such as starvation, without committing us to a still more broadly based promotion of what is good (e.g., in the form of government-sponsored food programs to improve nutrition in public schools).

This argument leaves the scope of the obligation to be beneficent in supplying food and the moral grounds of the obligation to be beneficent unresolved. Singer's conception of the scope of the obligation to be beneficent is captured by his contention that we must always act beneficently unless something of "comparable moral importance" must be given up by performing the action. In effect, he argues that we must always act positively to benefit others by acting to prevent harm, unless there is a stronger *prima facie* duty conflicting with and overriding an opportunity to provide such a benefit. But this demand is unrealistic and overly demanding, as Michael Slote has pointed out:

It also seems probable that there are limits to our obligations to help others by preventing harms and evils. To me at least it sometimes seems mistaken to suppose that one has an obligation to go and spend one's life helping sick and starving people in India or elsewhere. Part of the reason for this may be that it can at times seem perfectly understandable, from a moral standpoint, that one should want to lead one's own life and develop one's own plans and potentialities independently of what may be going on, for better or worse, with others outside one's own family. In other words, it can sometimes seem somewhat unfair or morally arbitrary that one's own special kind of fulfillment in life should be abrogated by the existence of states of affairs for which one was in no way responsible and which would tend not to enter into one's life plan. . . .

It is only when something like a basic life plan has to be sacrificed in order to prevent some evil that we feel any genuine hesitation to make such prevention obligatory. . . .

[15] "Famine, Affluence, and Morality," *Philosophy and Public Affairs* 1 (1972), as reprinted in T. Mappes and J. Zembaty, eds., *Social Ethics* (New York: McGraw-Hill, 1977), p. 317. This argument is updated in "Reconsidering the Famine Relief Argument," in Peter Brown and Henry Shue, eds., *Food Policy: The Responsibility of the United States in the Life and Death Choices* (New York: Macmillan, 1977).

[And to this argument I'would] add a *principle of positive* obligation to the effect that: "One has an obligation to prevent serious evil or harm when one can do so without seriously interfering with one's life plans or style and without doing any wrongs of commission." [16]

There may be unclarities and moral deficiencies in Slote's argument, but it is hard to imagine that morality, as we know it, is more demanding than his principles suggest. Of course, one might accept a personal moral *ideal* along the lines proposed by Singer. Society might even be more advantaged by attempting to make Singer's proposals an obligatory part of morality; but this outcome is far from obvious, given what we know about our ability to live up to such high ideals.

In general we would not say that the duty of benefience requires struggling, overworked, college students or parents of large middle-income families to work additional hours to provide food for starving nations. However, one who does nothing, when he or she could do something with little additional effort, is surely morally culpable. Such examples suggest that X has a duty of beneficence toward Y only if each of the following conditions is satisfied: [17] (1) Y is at risk of significant loss or damage, (2) X's action is directly relevant to the prevention of this loss or damage, (3) X's action would probably prevent it or help prevent it, and (4) the benefit that Y will gain outweighs any harms that X is likely to suffer and does not present more than minimal risk to X. To act more generously is morally praiseworthy but also is beyond the call of duty. In many instances where aid in the form of food could be provided, all four of these conditions would be satisfied and thus would seem to be morally required. But this sweeping generalization is subject to further constraints, because these four conditions are necessary but not (obviously) sufficient conditions of a *duty* of beneficence.

Despite the insufficiency of Singer's arguments, other important reasons can be offered for construing beneficence as a duty. Suppose that a person could be completely abstracted from society as an island unto himself or herself. That person's "right" to autonomous expression would be absolute, for society would have no claim on his or her actions or allegiance. Social claims on an individual seem only to arise in a social context. The duty to benefit others thus arises from complex social inter-actions. As David Hume pointed out in the eighteenth century,

All our obligations to do good to society seem to imply something reciprocal. I receive the benefits of society, and therefore ought to promote its interests.[18]

This view implies that we incur obligations to help others because we have willingly received, or at least willingly will receive, beneficial assistance from them. One who has not incurred such a reciprocal rela-

[16] Michael A. Slote, "The Morality of Wealth," in *World Hunger and Moral Obligation*, pp. 125–127.
[17] This formulation of these conditions is indebted to Eric D'Arcy, *Human Acts: An Essay in their Moral Evaluation* (Oxford: Clarendon Press, 1963), pp. 56–57.
[18] "On Suicide," as reprinted in S. Gorovitz et al., eds. *Moral Problems in Medicine* (Englewood Cliffs, N.J.: Prentice-Hall, 1976), p. 386.

tion of benefit would presumably have no duty to act beneficently. One justification, then, for the claim that beneficence is a duty resides in an implicit contract underlying the necessary give and take of social life. Unfortunately, this justification is of no use whatever as a ground for claims to the right to food unless one assumes that those who have a right to the food are contributing parties in an international social context. Because this contention seems *ad hoc* and highly questionable, it is unlikely that the reciprocity theory has any power to generate a right to food.

However, some of our duties to provide benefits to others derive not from general reciprocity relations but, rather, from special moral relationships with individuals. In particular, these duties stem from our previous wrongful acts and from explicit or implicit commitments (e.g., making promises and accepting positions involving requirements to benefit others). To focus on the most relevant categories, we often ought to act to benefit someone either because of our professional duties or because our promises require such acts. Thus, the lifeguard who has voluntarily accepted her position has a strong duty to try to rescue a drowning swimmer, even at considerable risk to herself. The claims that we make upon each other as parents, spouses, and friends similarly stem not only from interpersonal encounter but also from fixed rules, roles, and relations that constitute the matrix of obligations and duties.[19]

This ground for claims to the right to food is not promising, for it seems to beg the question. The heart of the question is whether one nation morally ought to commit itself to a relationship with other nations that creates the duty to provide food. For example, *should* the United States commit itself to provide massive aid in the first place? Human needs, actual or perceived, usually form the moral basis of such a benefiting relationship—not fixed rules, roles, and relations. These actual or felt needs are not enough in most circumstances to impose either a legal or a moral duty of service. The central question thus seems to be, "How much in the way of a moral obligation is created both by the needs of others and by the capacity of those who can satisfy those needs with only minimal risk to themselves?" Most serious discussions about the right to food in the end turn on this difficult and abstract question. This is recognized, for example, in Joseph Fletcher's 'argument that need is not a sound guideline for answering the question, "Under what conditions should we share our food?" Fletcher contends that need is not a sufficient criterion even for countries in which there is famine; for, he argues, any receiver country must exhibit responsibility on multiple levels to deserve the program of sharing. He maintains that the recipient country must exhibit not only responsible use of the food supplied but must also be willing to initiate a responsible domestic program to achieve "a balance between production and reproduction on some agreed time scale." [20] Fletcher's program is of course only one of many competing approaches to the allocation of food.

[19] Gorovitz, "Bigotry, Loyalty, and Malnutrition," p. 135.
[20] Joseph Fletcher, "Feeding the Hungry: An Ethical Appraisal," *Soundings* 59 (Spring 1976): 63.

However, resolution of these complex problems at a theoretical level is not possible apart from the resolution of a far deeper, more controversial, and more traditional problem in moral theory, one generally referred to as the problem of distributive justice. This complicated tangle of problems cannot be adequately treated here, but a general outline of relevant areas may indicate where controversies about the right to food have their roots.

DISTRIBUTIVE JUSTICE AND TRIAGE

The Nature of Distributive Justice. The single word most closely linked to the general meaning of "justice" is "desert." A person has been treated justly when she has been given what she deserves and can legitimately claim. The expression "distributive justice" refers more restrictively to the proper distribution of social benefits and burdens when some measure of scarcity exists. Recent literature on distributive justice has tended to focus on considerations of fair *economic* distribution, especially unjust distributions in the form of inequalities of income and wealth between different classes of persons and unfair tax burdens on certain classes. But clearly there are many problems of distributive justice, including ones of both the production and distribution of food.

The really difficult questions about justice arise when we try to specify the *relevant aspects* on the basis of which distributions are to be made. Any principles that so inform us are said to be material principles of justice, because they put material content into a theory. In the philosophy of distributive justice there are a few widely discussed, and almost as widely accepted, material principles. Each principle mentions the relevant property on the basis of which burdens and benefits should be distributed—normally, though not necessarily, a property or attribute that persons possess or fail to possess. What makes each principle a plausible candidate is the relevance of the property that it isolates. The following is a fairly standard list of major candidates for the position of valid principles of distributive justice:

1. To each person an equal share
2. To each person according to individual need
3. To each person according to individual effort
4. To each person according to societal contribution
5. To each person according to merit (individual ability)

There is no *a priori* barrier to acceptance of more than one of these principles, and some theories of justice accept all five as valid. Most societies use several of them, applying different principles of distribution in different contexts. In the United States, for example, unemployment and welfare payments are distributed on the basis of need (and to some extent on the basis of previous length of employment); jobs and promotions are in many sectors awarded (distributed) on the basis of demonstrated achievement and merit; the higher incomes of wealthy professionals are allowed (distributed) on the grounds of superior effort, merit, or social contribution (or perhaps all three); and, at least theoretically, the opportunity for elementary and secondary education is distributed equally to all citizens.

Theories of distributive justice are commonly developed by emphasizing and elaborating one or more of the material principles of distributive justice, perhaps in conjunction with other moral principles. Thus, *egalitarian* theories emphasize equality; *socialist* theories emphasize need; *capitalist* theories emphasize contribution and merit; and *utilitarian* theories emphasize a mixed use of such criteria so that public and private utility are maximized. The viability of any such theory of justice is determined by the quality of its moral argument to the conclusion that some one or more selected material principles ought to be given priority (or perhaps even exclusive consideration) over the others.

Consideration cannot here be given to the detailed nature either of principles or of theories of distributive justice. Nonetheless, it is important to see how, from such meager and abstract beginnings as "the principle of _____," both *relevant properties* and *public policies* based on justice can be developed. For example, consider the development of policies based on the principle of *need* as applied to the needs of starving peoples. First, how are we to understand the notion of a need? In general, the statement that a person needs something implies that *without it the person will be harmed*. Under the formal principle of justice, people of equal need should be treated equally in regard to the satisfaction of these needs, whereas those who have unequal needs should be treated unequally. However, this analysis of needs does not take us far, as we are not required to distribute equally for trivial needs. Presumably we are interested only in such *fundamental* needs as food, health care, and education, the lack of which leads to such fundamental harms as malnutrition or starvation, serious bodily injury, and ignorance of critical information. Satisfaction of these needs is necessary for survival in a state that is more desirable than nonsurvival.

Now, *if* one accepts a theory of distributive justice that permits appeal to the principle of need, then, as one refines the notion of needs, one moves closer to the properties necessary to the formulation of a position on such problems as the distribution of food. All public policies regarding the distribution of food based on distributive justice derive ultimately from the acceptance of one or more material principles of distributive justice and from some procedure for refining them. While this sort of theoretical refinement cannot be carried out here, it is of vital importance to notice the role of the first step in the argument—the acceptance of the principle of need as a valid principle of distributive justice. If one rejects rather than accepts the principle of need (while accepting, say, only contribution and merit), then one could judge such refinements inapplicable as a matter of justice and would be opposed in principle to the refinements and applications to public policy mentioned earlier. If one rejects all such principles—as libertarians, for example, are inclined to do—then one will almost surely hold in the end that the principle of distributive justice imposes no obligation to supply food and thus no right to obtain it.

Certainly it must be admitted—whatever one's theory of distributive justice—that on numerous occasions, especially those involving conflicting moral demands, moral principles do *not* in any decisive fashion determine relevant properties. In such cases a moral *decision* concerning the weight of competing moral claims is required, and this decision in turn fixes the acceptable relevant properties. A great many moral and public policy problems regarding the distribution of food involve dilemmas rooted in conflicting moral demands. There are powerful moral reasons in such cases for accepting two or more sets of different and competing bases of distribution as equally relevant (e.g., free market distributions versus utilitarian distributions), even though only one can be adopted and acted upon. Moral rules of distribution are not settled as the rules of tennis are, but they must be explicitly fixed by moral deliberation and decision making. In such cases it is neither unreasonable nor unfair if the final decision favors either of two or more competing positions.

The Problem of Triage. Problems of distributive justice and food have emerged most prominently through a controversy over whether *triage** ought to be used by wealthy nations in allocating scarce resources. Arguments paralleling those of Peter Singer, as well as assertions of rights by such bodies as the United Nations, fail to consider the possibility that food assistance *intended* to alleviate suffering and malnutrition may eventuate in the long run in greater suffering and harm than actual benefits for nations that are the recipients of the assistance. Garrett Hardin foresees precisely this disastrous possibility.[21] On the basis of predictions of long-term negative effects of assistance, he argues that no nation is morally required to assist any nation unwilling to adopt population policies that would align the size of the nation's population with available domestic food resources. The method of triage is applied to food assistance programs by a lexical system of allocation favoring, first, nations that are truly needy but would survive without the aid and, second, nations that have massive needs for food and population-control assistance but who can and will bring their population into line with food resources. The third set of nations are those with food problems that *cannot* be resolved over the long run because they will not or cannot bring their population into alignment with food resources. Assistance to these nations will ultimately increase rather than decrease their problems. According to hard-line exponents of a triage system, such as Hardin, the latter group of nations should receive no assistance.

---

* In field hospitals during wartime, *triage* meant dividing the wounded into three groups: those whose injuries were so severe that they were unlikely to benefit from medical aid; those whose injuries were so minor that they could get along without immediate attention; and those in between. Only the third group received immediate care. The first were allowed to die and the second waited. The application to hungry nations is obvious.   [ED.]

21 Garrett Hardin, "The Tragedy of the Commons," *Science* 162 (1968): 1243–1248; "Living on a Lifeboat," *BioScience* (October 1974): 561–568; and "Carrying Capacity as an Ethical Concept," in George R. Lucas, Jr., and Thomas W. Ogletree, eds., *Lifeboat Ethics: The Moral Dilemmas of World Hunger* (New York: Harper Forum Books, 1976).

Triage has been subjected to many impressive objections.[22] Both factual and moral problems have been discussed. There are factual problems about how to obtain evidence for the thesis that food assistance will only be an interim solution and over the long run will increase rather than decrease problems, thereby causing more suffering for the citizens of both the donor and recipient nations. Most moral objections are based on contentions, such as Singer's, that we are obliged to do all that we can, perhaps up to the point at which nothing of comparable moral importance must be sacrificed. Whatever the merits of such objections, two brief points in defense of triage deserve attention. First, triage is a proposed solution to problems of distributive justice that puts forward a general program, on a principled basis, for the distribution of food. Second, the program provides a way for distinguishing those who do from those who do not have a right to food. Citizens of nations eligible for food assistance have a right to food, because others have an obligation to provide it; but citizens in nations not eligible for food assistance do not have a right to food because others do not have obligations to provide it to them. Under this theory, too, rights depend upon obligations, which in turn derive from a general ethical theory about morally justified forms of distribution.

Rawls's Theory. Since 1971, John Rawls's book, *A Theory of Justice,* and his subsequent articles on the subject have dominated discussions of distributive justice. Not surprisingly, his revival of seventeenth- and eighteenth-century social contract theories has been seized upon by writers in many areas of applied ethics—for example, biomedical ethics and business ethics—with the intent of showing the implications of his theory for particular problems of just distribution. The attempt to apply Rawls's theory has also emerged in discussions of the right to food. In a recent article by Carlisle Ford Runge, it is argued that

> The demands for a new economic order directly reflect [Rawls's] view of justice, in which the developing countries, respected as "free and independent," reflecting their "integrity and equal sovereignty," demand that a choice be made to grant them distributive shares of the world's wealth and resources, as part of a new "global contract." . . . What the developing countries demand is . . . a redistribution very much along the lines of the principles of "justice as fairness" [as outlined by Rawls].[23]

This interpretation of Rawls rests on the assumption that international justice can be achieved if developing countries are conceived as parties

[22] For various replies, see Senator Mark Hatfield, "Rejecting 'Lifeboat Ethics': World Food and Population," *Congressional Record—Senate,* S-19198, (October 16, 1974); Peter Singer, "Survival and Self-interest: Hardin's Case against Altruism," *The Hastings Center Report* 8 (February 1978) : 37–39; Carl E. Taylor, "Economic Triage of the Poor and Population Control," *American Journal of Public Health* 67 (July 1977): 660–663; Nasir Islam, "New Ethics and Politics of World Food Scarcity," *International Perspectives* (November–December 1976): 18–22; and Daniel Callahan, "Doing Well by Doing Good," *The Hastings Center Report* 4 (December 1974), with replies in Vol. 5 (April 1975).
[23] Carlisle Ford Runge, "American Agricultural Assistance and the New International Economic Order," *World Development* 5 (1977) : 735.

to a "global contract" with other nations, where a fair contract is determined by principles of justice. That is, if we view the international situation of scarcity and distributive injustice much as we view similar domestic problems, we will have found a rationale rooted in justice itself for fundamental redistributions of food.

Unfortunately this interpretation of Rawls quite misses his point. Rawls says that his principles "define the appropriate distribution of the benefits and burdens of social cooperation," but an *allocative* conception is not Rawls's primary subject: "The conception of the [main principles of justice defended in the book] does not interpret the primary problem of distributive justice as one of allocative justice." [24] Though commentators commonly overlook the point, Rawls is not concerned with the actual burdens and benefits to be distributed to identifiable individuals or nations. Rather, he is concerned with the cooperative institutional arrangements within an organized political structure that *produce* the benefits and *create* the burdens that are to be distributed. His principles of justice do not, for example, mention properties possessed by individuals or nations on the basis of which their share of social resources is determined. Nor do his principles determine how wealth or other primary goods are to be distributed directly to individuals or nations.

Because Rawls sees organized society as a cooperative venture for mutual advantage, where entitlements are determinable only within the cooperative scheme, he is interested in the justice of productive social institutions. He sees the benefits deriving from individual contributions as a common product on which everyone has an equal claim. However, he is *not concerned with allotments when an already collected set of benefits and burdens is to be divided*—a point completely neglected by Runge. Without productive institutions there could be nothing to distribute, and the social structure defining a cooperative arrangement plainly can itself be either just or unjust. Rawls's problem is that of formulating principles of justice that will tightly govern organized social structures pertaining to the production and distribution of social and economic advantages. He argues, moreover, that "a distribution *cannot* be judged in isolation from the system of which it is the outcome." [25] Rawls thus is interested in social justice as embedded in the basic structure of society.

What, then, is "the basic structure of society" that determines distributions, if it is not some set of allocative rules or precepts? Rawls writes as follows in *A Theory of Justice:*

> For us the primary subject of justice is the basic structure of society, or more exactly, the way in which the major social institutions distribute fundamental rights and duties and determine the division of advantages from social cooperation. By major institutions I understand the political constitution and the principal economic and social arrangements. Thus the legal protection of freedom of thought and liberty of conscience,

[24] John Rawls, *A Theory of Justice* (Cambridge, Mass.: Harvard University Press, 1971), pp. 4, 88.
[25] *Ibid.*, pp. 61, 88.

competitive markets, private property in the means of production, and the monogamous family are examples of major social institutions. Taken together as one scheme, the major institutions define men's rights and duties and influence their life-prospects.[26]

"The basic structure is a public system of rules," [27] writes Rawls, a description that no doubt refers to the set of rules constituting the basic institutions. In his later article, "The Basic Structure as Subject," he argues that the basic structure is the "all-inclusive social system that determines background justice." [28] This system includes the set of rules governing legal institutions such as the Supreme Court, the set of rules establishing permissible marital and familial relationships (e.g., rules requiring monogamous families), rules establishing permissible property relationships, and rules establishing permissible social and economic inequalities.

With this brief background in mind, we may now discuss what Rawls does *not* attempt in his writings on justice. Rawls's emphasis on the basic structure leads him to work out a theory of justice at a "suitable level of generality." [29] Rawls refers to this level as "ideal theory"; it in no way encompasses the daily or even programmatic decisions that must be made, for example, about congressional allocation and bureaucratic regulation. His theory thus has no immediate application to everyday problems of government and international regulation. Any such "application" is indirectly mediated by the basic structure. Decisions in these matters are just if the basic structure is just. Decisions are unjust only if there is a relevant injustice in the basic structure.

Rawls correctly raised his theory to an appropriate level of generality. Philosophers have long had too grand an enterprise in mind in developing theories of justice. They often seem to have thought that cosmic theories of justice, public policy, and rights can be applied with consistency and rigor to the solution of many immediate social problems such as the appropriate distribution of food resources. But policies governing practical matters of great complexity cannot be deduced from highly abstract principles, whether of law or of moral philosophy. There also is no single consistent set of rights or material principles of justice that predictably applies when these problems of social justice arise. There are many such principles, and they sometimes apply and sometimes do not. Accordingly, those who would import an abstract theory of justice or a single principle of justice into the arena of food distribution policy, with the intention of decisively handling the issues, commit as serious an error as those who would totally exclude considerations of justice in favor of the politics of public policy. Principles of justice are certainly not irrelevant to the resolution of these matters; but they are only general guidelines, and often they simply cannot be brought to bear on the problems at all.

26 *Ibid.,* p. 7.
27 *Ibid.,* p. 84.
28 John Rawls, "The Basic Structure as Subject," *American Philosophical Quarterly* 14 (April 1977): Section IV.
29 *A Theory of Justice,* pp. 131, 304, 308.

CONCLUSION

The controlling argument in this paper turns upside down the commonly held conviction that a nation-state must supply resources because persons possess inalienable rights to the resources. It has been argued instead that, where there is a competition for scarce resources, persons often possess rights only because there exists a prior obligation requiring an allocational commitment. This obligation may be based on the principle of beneficence or on some account of distributive justice. Whatever the exact basis, allocational obligations and decisions have a moral priority over rights claims, and not vice versa.

Rights also are not absolute in conditions of scarcity, and they weaken as needs for food resources come into conflict with needs for other resources. The right to food weakens when the use of resources to make it available would endanger, reduce, or extinguish the supply of goods and services to which individuals can claim rights by virtue of some other, presumably equally justified, allocational commitments. Generally, rights such as the right to food must be exercised at the international level, not domestically within nation-states, for food transfers in pressing cases move across state boundaries through the actions of individual nation-states. Thus the moral justification of a right to food seems in the end to require a theory of beneficence or justice capable of transcending national concerns and boundaries.[30]

[30] Work on this paper was supported by funds from The Food and Climate Forum of The Aspen Institute for Humanistic Studies. The author gratefully acknowledges this source of support as well as critical comments on a former draft by Ruth Faden, R. Jay Wallace, Dorle Vawter, Sarah Finnerty, and the staff of Schnittker Associates.

WILLIAM AIKEN 12

WORLD HUNGER AND FOREIGN AID: THE MORALITY OF MASS STARVATION

I. THE PROBLEM

The world hunger crisis presents a peculiar problem for Americans: There is a world shortage of a vital resource, and we have (or are capable of producing) an abundance of that resource. So we have to decide what to do with our abundance, knowing full well that our decisions greatly affect conditions in other nations. Should we smile as we count among our many blessings the high profits to be made in the international food market? Should we try to limit production so as to ensure high prices and then sell to the highest bidder? (This would certainly help to eliminate our international trade deficit.) Or should we attempt to maximize the production of exportable food substances and impose a price ceiling so as to make this food available to impoverished nations that cannot compete with the wealthy nations in an open seller's market? Should the food we produce be used as a weapon to further our political interests abroad, as a bargaining point for military installations, trade benefits, or opportunities for business investments or as a means of buying friends and alliances? Or should we simply keep our abundance and thereby ensure lower domestic prices and security for ourselves and for future generations?

Our position is not unlike that in which the oil producing nations find themselves. They too have an abundance of a vital resource for which there is a world shortage. Should they limit production, refrain from price increases, apply political pressure (e.g., against supporters of Israel) with boycotts and embargoes? Where oil is concerned, the shoe is on the other foot, for the United States is one of the heaviest per capita users of petroleum products and is thus potentially one of the most helplessly dependent of nations with respect to petroleum. Fortunately, the oil producing nations have not imposed a "triage" policy and limited sales of oil to nations whose population exceeds their oil producing carrying capacity. Unlike the oil producing nations, we have occasionally responded to our "peculiar" situation by actually *giving away* our valuable resource in the form of direct emergency relief food aid, both through private charitable organizations and through governmental action. It is this aspect of our response to our situation that I shall discuss in greater detail.

Suppose that we put aside all the previous questions about selling for gain and bribing for influence and talk instead about giving away food. Of the many actions we can perform with our abundance, certainly this limited area looks straightforward, uncomplicated, less political, and, some would say, humanitarian. What could be less controversial than giving food to the hungry and "saving the children"? Yet even here extremely difficult decisions must be made. There is a greater demand for such aid than we can provide. Some policy must be established to enable us to decide which nations we should aid and which nations we cannot or will not assist. One approach might be to aid those nations that need the aid the most. Perhaps we ought to aid any nation in which there is massive malnourishment and death and disease due to starvation in preference to one in which there is only a minor problem of undernourishment.

But this approach is often viewed by policymakers as being simplistic rather than simple. They argue that it is "unrealistic," that it ignores other crucial factors. It is true, they say, that giving aid to the neediest appears to have beneficial consequences. But it blindly ignores the full range of consequences that flow from such actions. It is necessary, they argue, to pass beyond mere need to a consideration of the long-run consequences on recipient nations' population growth, economic stability, and development toward self-sufficiency. Is direct aid the most cost-effective means of alleviating the food shortage problem, or are there alternative forms of assistance that would be more efficient in eliminating the food shortage in that nation? What are the trade-offs between the present population's well-being and future generations' quality of life, between present suffering and possible future suffering, between encouraging dependency and overpopulation and promoting independence and reduced population growth? The realistic approach goes far beyond the simplistic criterion of "need." The realistic approach— derived from the familiar utilitarian methods of cost–benefit analysis with its language of objectives, means–ends considerations, alternative assessment, effectiveness and efficiency, long-range consequentialism, and quantification of value into discrete units—is a world of "trade-offs." As applied to the problem of world hunger, it leads to the conclusion that we ought not to give food aid to the neediest nations, because such action may not be the most effective means, in the long run, of maximizing total benefits derived from that aid, for it is likely to be inefficient, wasteful, minimally effective, detrimental, or even harmful to those it is intended to help.

But this entails some difficult moral trade-offs. First, great numbers of needy human beings will die of starvation. Yes, but—it will be claimed by the defenders of this approach—this will reduce the population growth rate and, in the long run, will most likely maximize total societal benefits such as goods distribution and national self-sufficiency. Second, the neediest nations will be paralyzed and become forever incapable of attaining modernization and development goals without some food assistance to relieve the burden of meeting immediate nutritional needs. Yes, but these needy nations have already gone too far, their populations have exceeded the carrying capacity of their territory, and the cost of restoring them to self-sufficiency, much less modernization, far exceeds the return to be gained. Third, the neediest have nowhere else to turn for help in feeding their population. Yes, but in time of scarcity we cannot afford to waste vital resources on stopgap measures; some tough trade-offs have to be made.

Lest we get caught up in the abstractions of our decision-making jargon, we must keep in mind that we are not discussing mere demographic statistics; we are discussing real people, mostly children, who are starving to death. As we juggle with our figures and balance our calculations, we are playing with the very lives of the world's least advantaged, most vulnerable and powerless peoples.

Justifications for this harsh approach may be divided into two major arguments: first, that we can maximize good consequences, in the long run, by not using resources to provide direct food aid to the neediest, and, second, that we can minimize harmful consequences, in the long run, by not providing direct food aid to the neediest. I shall call these arguments the "maximize good" and the "minimize harm" arguments and shall examine and criticize them separately.

II. THE "MAXIMIZE GOOD" ARGUMENTS

To be sure, cost-effectiveness criteria are helpful in laying out alternative courses of action when we must decide how to allocate scarce resources, for they allow us to compare the alternatives by a single set of standards. Naturally we want to be able to explore various possibilities for action and see how best to maximize the effectiveness of our actions so as to produce the greatest amount of good through our efforts. However, uncritical acceptance of a computer's determination of the maximally effective use of resources is morally irresponsible. Efficiency must sometimes be sacrificed for other ideals and principles whose utility cannot be quantified so easily. A just policy may not maximize good consequences; it may be inefficient or even wasteful. Moral actions are not investments and morality is not, and cannot be reduced to, economics.

We are urged to accept the proposition that giving aid to the neediest nations is wasteful, because they are so desperately impoverished that the problems of hunger, want, and suffering could not be substantially diminished by direct aid. It is tantamount to throwing money down a rathole. Moreover, by not wasting resources on the hopeless (the neediest), we will be able to use them on less needy (and less impoverished) nations to better effect. Our "seed capital" will generate, in the long run, a net increase in profitable returns.

Saving some people from death by starvation would be throwing money down the rathole if human beings are thought of as being morally equivalent to rats. Giving direct food aid to the neediest will not solve all their problems of suffering, misery, and want. At best, it may keep them alive a while longer. It is admittedly a stopgap measure since hunger, like other basic necessities, continues to demand satisfaction day by day. Direct aid cannot eliminate the causes of poverty and hunger. It is not the solution to want. But surely the relief of human suffering and the prevention of needless deaths is worthwhile. It is absurd to suppose that unless a problem can be solved in its entirety, it is a waste of effort to do anything at all about it, to assume that in all circumstances we find a total solution to a problem or do nothing at all about it. The police chiefs of our major cities realize that, even though a complete solution to the problem of crime may not be possible, it is worth the taxpayers' money to try, with "stopgap" measures if necessary, to do something to diminish its adverse effects.

When valuable resources are scarce, it is said, one must look to how one can do the most good with those resources. If an unlimited quantity of foodstuffs were available for direct aid, then diminishing any suffering, however temporary, would be good. But, when scarcity prevails, we must seek to do the most good with available supplies; and giving them to the neediest nations—to those that are so impoverished, overpopulated, and decimated by the effect of starvation that they are beyond all hope—is wasteful and unproductive. It is better to aid the less needy who, with some aid, will be capable of productive work and thus, eventually, of achieving self-sufficiency. Instead of stopgap measures for the hopeless, we can effect more permanent solutions to the problems of poverty for the not yet lost.

On the surface, this argument is convincing, but it is in fact fallacious. Although it appears to be urging maximum yield per pound of food donated, it has to do with the giving of assistance, which in a money economy means money, either in the form of developmental assistance or in the form of food aid. Those less than the neediest (the not-yet-lost) nations do not require food aid. They require developmental assistance (such as modernization, improved technology, increased employment opportunities, etc.) if they are to avoid seriously overrunning their ability to become self-sufficient and thus to feed their populations. The nations who lose in the triage are those whose immediate *need* is food in order to save lives. Of course developmental or any other kind of assistance would help to alleviate their growing problem of impoverishment. But food is needed now to sustain the population. Reduced to its essentials, the proponents of the trade-off argument urge us not to waste money on feeding people who are dying, but to save it to finance more permanent solutions to poverty for those who are not yet dying. It is assumed that the decision between spending money on direct assistance to provide for such necessities of life as food and spending money on such non-necessities as development programs is a morally neutral one. But surely there is a crucial moral difference between providing someone who could not otherwise obtain it the very means to live and providing someone else the means of improving his or her standard of living. Where such alternatives are before us, the relief of starvation should take precedence.

If applied to the domestic scene, the argument might go as follows: The bottom 2 percent of the impoverished in this country are beyond help: they are enfeebled with age, disabled, or retarded and are thus hopelessly beyond self-sufficiency. They must be ignored so that our scarce resources (welfare funds) can be used to benefit (by job training, education, supplemental income, etc.) those capable of work and thus of eventually becoming self-sufficient. Why waste precious resources on the hopelessly poor? In the long run greater good will result from ignoring them on behalf of those capable of maximizing the benefit from assistance expenditures by showing positive returns. Unfortunately, those who are lost in poverty must simply be abandoned. "Charity," under this new dispensation, is not helping the truly helpless with temporary relief, for this is a waste and at best serves only to make the giver feel magnanimous. Real charity is giving so as to maximize the good by carefully helping only those who can permanently benefit from your assistance. Dire need, to the point of death, gives no special claim against those who can render assistance. There is no special claim to assistance resulting simply because one is in desperate need of assistance for his or her very survival.

Domestically, we abandoned this view of "charity" long ago, for we have granted the severely impoverished and the needy a legal claim to assistance regardless of the potentially better uses we could find for our resources. The impoverished have a legal right to assistance just because they are in dire need, regardless of merit or any other considerations. Everyone has a right (entitlement) to survival and the goods and services necessary for it. But on the international scene we shift to the charity paradigm and see aid to others as a matter of pure benevolence.

However human beings, even those who live in other lands, have a moral right to survival, a right to be saved from preventable death due to deprivation, a right not to be allowed to die of want. The affluent have a duty to honor this right to be saved. Saving lives takes precedence, other things being equal, over the maximization of long-range good consequences when these two come into direct conflict and when we must make a choice between one or the other. When the trade-off is between saving lives in one country and promoting development and self-sufficiency in another, the saving of lives must be given the higher priority. Failure to do so is a violation of a fundamental human right.

It is sometimes argued that it is in the best interests of a nation that it not receive aid. In the long run, the consequences of not acting will be better than the consequences of acting, even though some good may result from acting. Our aid will only interfere with that nation's effecting a solution to its problems of poverty, hunger, and want. So, even though our action of assistance appears to be helpful, it leads to a less than optimal end result and, thus, delays a long-run solution to the problem. This paternalistic approach is like parents' refusal to give their children the answers to their homework problems so that they will learn how to solve problems themselves. So, too, it is argued, we should refuse to give aid to impoverished nations so that they might learn to solve their own problems. Aid will make them dependent, lazy, reluctant to work. It will rob them of incentive and the will to attack their problems. They will not act positively to curtail their population growth rate, reform land tenure, improve agricultural technology, or redistribute wealth. They will not act to nurture and conserve their own resources but, rather, will waste them and then seek to exploit the gift of aid to the maximum. Like foolish children, they will not heed the warnings of prudence, but, with selfish rising expectations, they will spend their resources recklessly, believing that Big Daddy will bail them out and continually give them more. They will foolishly overtax their environment and economy and will sacrifice the quality of life of future generations. Moreover, direct aid often breeds official corruption, theft, and black marketeering, and perpetuates the worst aspects of colonialism and foreign imperialism—for, once the dependency relation is set up, the social and economic reform that is necessary to clear up the causes of poverty will be suppressed by those who are in power. The masses' discontent will be pacified by gifts of food, and corrupt leaders will become entrenched.

This is reminiscent of the parent who evicts a child from his home at sixteen to sink or swim. If the child swims, he will have the satisfaction of being self-made, independent, capable. But what if the child sinks? So he suffers a bit. It will wake him up to the real world. If he goes hungry, it will teach him the value of a dollar and the virtue of hard work. If he ends up in serious trouble, he will learn that life is a struggle. It is better not to interfere, for he must solve his own problems. As applied to the people of impoverished nations, this view advocates letting starvation serve as a tool, for a little suffering and misery will wake them up. In effect, it is simply an application of some old adages: those who don't work (or reform or curtail population or conserve their environment, etc.) don't eat; the wages of sin (sloth, avarice, intemperance, lust) are death. But it fails to notice that the chief victims of such a policy are those most powerless of people within any nation—the starving children who must die to "wake" somebody up. It acquiesces in the sacrifice of innocent children for the long-range good of others. In the most impoverished nations, there are no easily enacted, quick solutions. No matter how just or diligent its leaders may be, they simply cannot feed the hungry population. It is not a matter of sink or swim, for the nation has already sunk and can only be resuscitated with assistance. By staying out of it, when we could save those presently starving, we are in effect approving the Malthusian solution—letting the human surplus die. Eventually, when enough people die off, the strain on their economy and resources will be eased.

Once again, however, this view has mistaken assistance for charity. Because there is nothing "wrong" with failing to be charitable, acquiescing in these deaths by neglect is not seen as wrong. Charity is optional. But those individuals whom we "allow to die" for the sake of society have a right to be saved. Failure to respond is death to the powerless. Where fundamental rights are involved, social utility calculations become irrelevant.

It is not permissible to exterminate 10 per cent of an impoverished country's population to conserve resources or to restore the population to a level that its productive capacity can support. So, too, letting people die when we could act to save them without unreasonable expense, risk, effort, or sacrifice to ourselves is to violate a right. But, unlike the right not to be killed, which is violated by actions, this right (the right to be saved from preventable death due to deprivation) is violated by omissions—failures to act.

It is mistakenly assumed that letting people die, though at times regrettable, is morally permissible if a good purpose is served and that dire need gives rise to no moral right of entitlement to the goods and services necessary to sustain life. On this view, because the value and dignity of persons resides in their liberty, not in their well-being, all claims to assistance are reduced to appeals for charity or benevolence. But the starving child, the drowning bather and the accident victim have a stronger claim against those in a position to render assistance than appeal to mere charity. They have a morally justified claim of right against others. So, even though it may appear to be morally permissible not to "interfere" and thus to let the powerless die, it is not. Such failure to render assistance is, *prima facie*, morally reprehensible. Only if we cannot render assistance are we automatically excused from the duty to save lives. But we can assist. There is, at present, no scarcity of food. Rather, there is a severe maldistribution of food, an enormous waste of vegetable protein being fed to animals, and a waste of land used for luxury crops. There is no real shortage. The impoverished can be aided with little expense or sacrifice by us.

Because people have a right to be saved from preventable death due to deprivation, the argument, that in the long run a better solution will result by noninterference, breaks down. The price of injustice is too high to pay for obtaining optimal conditions for problem solving.[1]

[1] For a more detailed account and defense of this "right to be saved," see my "The Right to Be Saved from Starvation," in William Aiken and Hugh LaFollette, eds., *World Hunger and Moral Obligation* (Englewood Cliffs, N.J.: Prentice-Hall, 1977), pp.

III. THE "MINIMIZE HARM" ARGUMENTS

There are some who argue that giving aid to the neediest actually causes harm, in the long run, to the recipients. Feeding starving people worsens the problem, resulting in a net increase in suffering. So we should not give aid to the neediest to avoid harming them. "Causing harm" can be interpreted in three distinct ways. First, it can mean interference with obtaining optimal conditions for problem solving. I have discussed this claim in the previous section and do not regard it as harm. Second, it can mean not merely interfering with obtaining better consequences, but causing bad ones. Third, it can mean that the act violates rights or is harmful in the strict sense. I shall refer to the last two as the weak and the strong senses of "harm," respectively.

With the acknowledgement of the right to be saved, I believe the need criterion can be upheld even when giving according to this criterion may cause bad consequences, so that, even when the trade-off is between saving present lives and potentially harming (in the weak sense) others, the former must prevail. However, it is the strong sense of harm (when rights are violated) that raises the toughest problems—when the trade-off is the honoring of one right at the expense of another. Here is where the debate on the need criterion's applicability should be waged—in the arena of conflict of rights.

But, first, the weak sense of harm. Suppose that you have good reason to believe that a given act will cause undesirable effects. *Prima facie,* you should refrain from that act as one should avoid causing bad consequences to occur. You should not distract your roommate while he or she is cramming for an important exam. You should refuse the alcoholic's pleas for a drink, because assisting will in fact have very bad consequences for him or her. So, too, it is argued, we must refuse the cries for aid from certain impoverished nations (the neediest) for they too are suffering from a chronic illness, the population disease.

A generous offer of aid will temporarily relieve the craving, as it does for the alcoholic. But the consequences are just as bad, as it worsens the problem and promotes the disease. Every child saved from starvation will grow up to produce more children who will starve because the nation's limit of people is already surpassed. Saving people now causes a worse situation in the future. The population disease is not cured by saving people from starvation; as Garrett Hardin often expresses it, you cannot cure a cancer by feeding it.[2] Kind or generous actions that lower the death rate (giving food, medical supplies and vaccines, water purification technology, etc.) will cause, in the long run, bad consequences for the recipient nation by increasing the net amount of misery and suffering. But the bad consequences extend far beyond this. Saving people now will reduce the quality of life for future generations, for the greater the quantity of people, the lesser the quality of life. There will

---

85–102. Also see my "Starvation, Morality, and the Right to Be Saved" (Ph.D. diss., Vanderbilt University, 1977).

[2] For example, see Hardin's "Lifeboat Ethics: The Case against Helping the Poor," in Aiken and LaFollette, *op. cit.,* p. 18.

be less liberty, less opportunity, and less room for individual initiative. There will be fewer goods to go around and less potential to produce goods because the environment will be overexploited and damaged (due to farming marginal lands, denuding forests, and polluting rivers). It could also lead to the suffering that results from political and economic upheaval and violence spawned by overcrowding and scarcity. All these bad consequences may follow from giving direct food aid to the neediest. So, for the good of the recipient nation, it is best to ignore its cries for help. Like alcoholism, you cannot cure the population disease by giving what is craved. Giving food will only cause harm.

What is wrong with this argument? On pure cost–benefit grounds it appears convincing enough. But the disease analogy is deceptive. In the case of the sick alcoholic, withholding liquor is designed to prevent evil consequences from occurring to him or her. We refuse to aid X to avoid harm to X. But, in the case of aiding nations, we would be withholding aid to some (those starving now) to prevent bad consequences to others (future generations). Treating a whole population as one moral entity is not uncommon, but it is deceptive, for what is really being called for is the sacrifice of some individuals for others. This puts us squarely in the utilitarian world of moral decision making, and, as we said earlier, moral rights are constraints on social utility calculations. They set the boundaries of justifiable acts. Rights control the circumstances under which some may be sacrificed for others—either to maximize good consequences for others or to minimize bad consequences for others. Sometimes bad consequences must be accepted as the price we pay for respecting human rights and for protecting the interests of individuals.

But human rights are not absolute. They are defeasible, and there will be circumstances in which they can be justifiably overridden. The more stringent a right is, the more difficult it is to override it. Although some rights may be easily overridden to prevent evil consequences from occurring to others, the right to life cannot be. If a terrorist threatens to blow up the bridges leading to Manhattan unless you kill your neighbor, you ought not to kill your neighbor. A sheriff cannot justifiably surrender a prisoner to a bloodthirsty lynch mob to prevent a riot. Severely retarded infants are not killed to avoid the expense that their lifelong institutionalization will cost others.

Individuals must not be sacrificed for the group. So too, the right to be saved from preventible death due to deprivation protects individuals from being sacrificed for others. One protects human life from unwarrantable abuse, the other from unwarrantable neglect. If it is wrong to kill a defective newborn, it is also wrong to "let it die" by withholding food from it. If it is wrong to kill 10 per cent of a population to save the environment, to defuse revolution, to preserve the standard of living, to perpetuate economic patterns, then it is also wrong to "let die" for these reasons. Evil consequences should be avoided, but not at the price of ignoring the two rights that fundamentally protect human life: the right to life and the right to be saved.

But even these two important rights that protect human life may, on occasion, be defeated. I suggest that they cannot justifiably be overridden simply on cost–benefit grounds unless two conditions are met: (1) the evil consequences that would result from honoring the right would be disastrous, far surpassing in harm that done by violating the right, and (2) honoring the right would directly and unavoidably cause these bad consequences for others.

Very few circumstances would meet these strict conditions. However, imaginative examples might be created; for instance, hypnotized managers of reservoirs who threaten to pollute a major city's water supply or deranged missile operators who threaten to trigger a nuclear war. There are times when the cost is great enough and the consequences certain enough that we should fail to honor the protective rights of individuals (by letting die or even killing).

But are these two conditions met in the case of aiding the neediest of countries? Would giving food to the neediest unavoidably cause great harm to the recipient population?

The effects of severe worldwide overpopulation could be so catastrophic as to warrant overriding certain rights. But great harm need not follow from feeding the neediest. The alleged evil consequences follow only if increased populations inevitably result from saving the starving. But the disastrous consequences of overpopulation can be forestalled or prevented, for they are not inevitable. There are at least three other ways to alleviate the effects of the "population disease": decrease the birth rate, redistribute wealth and power, and increase efficiency of resource use.

The first of these, birth control, is the most sensible answer. The population explosion can be reversed by having fewer children. Voluntary use of birth control devices is preferable to mandatory population control, but the latter is also an effective alternative. If overpopulation is the problem, then it makes far more sense to cut back on the creation of more people than to sacrifice those persons presently living so that more can be created.

So too for the second method of preventing the bad consequences from following, the redistribution of wealth and power. It is often assumed that the presence of starving people in a nation is the result of overpopulation and that any aid will push it beyond its environmental limit and eventually make matters worse.[3] But the mere presence of poverty and starvation is not an automatic sign of overpopulation with its future disastrous consequences. Quite often the problem is not the amount of resources available to support the population, but the *distribution* of those resources. Repressive, exploitative, unjust, neocolonial socioeconomic structures (often backed by Western economic and military interests) prevent any increase in population from being absorbed into the economy and thus gaining productive self-sufficiency.

Overpopulation then is relative to real resources available for use to the entire population. It is a disease only if there are no alternative socioeconomic arrangements that would alleviate the extreme scarcity of

---

[3] I have shown in "The Carrying Capacity Equivocation," in *Social Theory and Practice* 6 (Spring 1980), that this type of argument is fallacious as it equivocates between a biological and an economic sense of "carrying capacity."

resources among the more impoverished. This becomes clear from an examination of the ratios of persons per cultivatable acre in the neediest countries. By this standard, some of the poorest nations are actually un-derpopulated. However, because their wealth is being skimmed off and is grossly maldistributed, it appears that there are too many persons for the available resources. If 10 per cent of the population controls 90 per cent of the resources, and, as a result, masses of impoverished people are dying, the country is not suffering from the "population disease" but from injustice. The solution is not to accept the status quo and to collaborate in its perpetuation by withholding food aid, thus violating one of the few rights of the powerless that we can honor, but to en-courage change in the pattern of distribution, thus increasing the stan-dard of living for each individual and helping to ensure economic security for the destitute. This in turn will help reduce the need for very large families and thus will contribute to a decline in the birthrate.

The third method is to increase productive efficiency. Increased efficiency in productivity can be accomplished by development of labor-intensive, low-technology agricultural and industrial methods that seek to maximize use of local talent and resources for indigenous (rather than for foreign) interests. Because many of the neediest nations are previous colonies of the affluent world, they need to adapt their resource use from a colonial, capital-intensive, export-oriented production model to a more self-serving and self-sufficient model.[4] Reorganization of resource use and productive power will help to absorb the increasing population and so reduce the extreme misery and suffering of the poor. This will allow time for the evolution of a policy to implement lower fertility rates that is compatible with local customs and traditions.

The last and perhaps most compelling argument against food aid is the claim that feeding the neediest results in the violation of others' rights. By helping some now, we harm (in the strict sense) others. Here the focus on the balance of good and bad consequences is exchanged for one on the trade-off between claims of right. The dilemma is between violating X's right or Y's right. There is a conflict of rights, and one must be overridden by the other. We must decide on the stringency of the claims and assign a priority. This is not an easy task even in cases of conflicts between claims of legal rights in which there is a clear de-cision procedure and a mechanism for adjudication. It is far more difficult to adjudicate conflicting claims of moral rights.

The most common appeal to the conflict of rights in this debate is to contrast the rights of future generations with those of present living people. Future generations are entitled to a habitable environment and a reasonably comfortable existence. By feeding the starving now, we will be depriving future generations of their rights. It may be better to over-ride the rights of a few to honor the rights of future generations.

Although there are some conceptual difficulties in speaking of the moral rights of such nonexistent entities as future generations, let us suppose that such a claim is sensible and that future people do have

---

[4] For a detailed account of this alternative, see F. M. Lappé and J. Collins, *Food First, Beyond the Myth of Scarcity* (Boston: Houghton Mifflin, 1977).

rights (contingent upon being born). We may also assume that they have rights that are to be considered equal in kind and strength to those of living persons. Neo-Malthusians could accept my position that humans have a right to be saved from preventible death due to deprivation and still advocate that the neediest should not be saved. The argument would be that to honor the right of n starving persons now, which we can do, will lead to n^2 starving persons in the future (due to population increase) whose rights we *cannot* honor (we will not have the means to do it). So by honoring the rights of n persons now, we must fail to honor the rights of n^2 persons later. However, if we override the right of n persons now, we will not have to override the rights of n^2 persons later, as these future persons will not exist. In the long run fewer claims of right to be saved must be denied.

Technically the reply could be that the duty is owed to save persons as long as it is possible to do so (that is, until the right simply cannot be honored). But rhetorically, I think this argument has great power, for it makes the trade-off extremely clear—let children starve today or there will be even more starving children tomorrow. The humanitarian thing to do seems to be to let the few (10,000 to 12,000 a day) die today, pitting the few wide-eyed children of today against the many more bloated-belly children of tomorrow. We must, to prevent inevitable future suffering, let some die today. It would be cruel to trade off the rights of the children of tomorrow.

But the lines of conflict need not be drawn this way. The argument is very persuasive, but it is a camouflage to hide the real trade-off that must be faced in the debate over giving food aid to the neediest. To pit present people against future people hides the intense conflict of rights that pervades this issue, the conflict between the rights of presently living, contemporary people. The real trade-off here has nothing to do with future peoples' suffering because such suffering can be prevented by lowering the birth rate and by redistributing wealth and productive power within and between nations. The real trade-off of rights pits the right of present starving people to be saved against (1) the right to un-limited procreation among those incapable of supporting additional births and (2) the rights of property of those controlling and benefiting from present social and economic distribution and production arrangements. We are really trading off the lives of the powerless for procreative freedom and property rights.

The starving are being used by both the poor and the rich in a propaganda battle. The rich, assuming that property rights override the right to be saved (since they obviously benefit from current property arrangements), want to see the trade-off between procreative freedom and saving the starving. Don't give any food aid, they say, without erecting effective population control measures. We won't save even one starving child unless you curtail your birth rate. Your "liberty to procreate" must be overridden or we will ignore your children's right to be saved. You cannot have both, the choice is yours. You are the cause of the children's starving. "No food without birth control."

The poor, on the other hand, claim that the problem arises, not because there are too many people, but because too many *rich* people waste energy and squander resources. A whole family can live on the resources wasted by an American on his or her pets. It is the unjust distribution of wealth, the wasteful and exploitative productive and trade practices that cause the problem. Without the rich draining the earth's resources, there would be no starving children. The world cannot tolerate any more of the wasteful rich who cause the suffering of children.

Two of our most sacred institutions, family and property, are being challenged. The conflict is between these two institutions and the well-being and the very lives of the impoverished. The cost of large families is death to the children. The cost of affluent life-styles is the lives of the world's most helpless. These are the real trade-offs on which moral deliberation should concentrate. How much is our affluent standard of living worth? What is the cost in lives of our overconsumption, our waste, and our riches? And how many babies will the poorest let starve as they exercise their procreative freedom? How many dead babies does it take to prove virility, to abide ancient customs of high fertility?

Both property rights and procreative freedom must be reevaluated. Priorities must be reassessed in light of the right of the most powerless to life. Both the rich and the poor must relinquish some of their respective "rights" in favor of the right of the starving to be saved. Population control is essential but no more so than redistribution of wealth and the means of production. Population control can be encouraged in impoverished nations through the incentive of substantial and effective developmental assistance. In this way, both goals can be met with each side making a reasonable compromise.

Starving children need not suffer and die. Food aid need not be used as a club to force population control. Nor is it necessary to flaunt the misery of the poor as a symbol of international economic injustice. A bargain can be struck between population control and redistribution. Property rights can be exchanged for procreative liberty. An ecologically sensible and just international policy that will solve problems equitably while being responsible to future generations can be developed. Children should not be required to pay for the sins of their parents, especially when the price for them is life itself.[5]

5 I am grateful to Burton Leiser for helpful editorial suggestions and modifications.

13 RICHARD T. DE GEORGE
DO WE OWE THE FUTURE ANYTHING?

The desire to avoid pollution—however defined—involves concern for the duration and quality of human life. Problems dealing with the quality of human life inevitably involve value judgments. And value judgments are notorious candidates for debate and disagreement. Yet in discussions on pollution the desirability of the continuance of the human race is generally taken for granted; most people feel that a continuous rise in the standard of living would be a good thing; and many express a feeling of obligation towards future generations. How well founded are these judgments? The purpose of this paper is to examine the validity and some of the implications of three statements of principles which have a direct bearing on this question and so on the debate concerning pollution and its control. The three principles are the following:

1. Only existing entities have rights.
2. Continuance of the human race is good.
3. Continuous increase in man's standard of living is good.

I

The argument in favor of the principle that only existing entities have rights is straightforward and simple: Non-existent entities by definition do not exist. What does not exist cannot be the subject or bearer of anything. Hence it cannot be the subject or bearer of rights.

Just as non-existent entities have no rights, so it makes no sense to speak about anyone's correlative duty towards non-existent entities. Towards that which does not exist we can have no legal or moral obligation, since there is no subject or term which can be the object of that obligation. Now it is clear that unconceived possible future human beings do not exist, though we can think, e.g., of the class of human beings which will exist two hundred years from now. It follows that since this class does not (yet) exist, we cannot have any obligations to it, nor to any of its possible members. It is a presently empty class.

More generally, then, presently existing human beings have no obligation to any future-and-not-yet existing set or class of human beings. We owe them nothing and they have no legitimate claim on us for the simple reason that they do not exist. No one can legitimately defend

Reprinted from Eugene E. Dais, ed., *Law and the Ecological Challenge* (AMINTA-PHIL II) (Buffalo: William S. Hein & Co., 1978), pp. 180–190, by permission of the author and the publisher. Copyright 1978 by William S. Hein & Co. All rights reserved.

their interests or represent their case in court or law or government, because they are not, and so have no interests or rights.

It follows from this that a great deal of contemporary talk about obligations to the future, where this means to some distant future portion of mankind, is simply confused. In dealing with questions of pollution and clean air—as well as with similar issues such as the use of irreplaceable resources—there can be no legitimate question of the *rights* of unconceived future human beings or of any supposedly correlative *obligation* of present-day human beings *to* them.

Some people may find this to be counterintuitive. That it is not so may perhaps become clearer if we consider what I take to be the feelings of many—if not most—people with respect to the past.

Consider the general attitude towards the ancient Greeks and Romans. Did they owe us anything? Did they have any duties or obligations to us? It is clear there are no sanctions we can impose on them and no way we can enforce any obligations we may claim they had towards us. But surely even to raise the question of their obligation to us is odd. We may rejoice in what has been saved of the past and handed down to us, and we may regret that some of Plato's dialogues have been lost or that the Library at Alexandria was burned, or that Rome was sacked. But though we may regret such events and though we may judge that they were in some sense ills for mankind or the result of immoral actions, they were not immoral because of any obligation past generations had to us.

The situation is little changed if we come up to more recent—though not too recent—times. The American Founding Fathers had no obligation to us. They could scarcely have envisaged our times or have been expected to calculate the effects of their actions on us. Or consider the unrestrained slaughter of American buffalo for sport. Such action may have been immoral and a waste of a natural resource; but if it was immoral it was not because present-day Americans have any right to have inherited more buffalo than we did.

Since it is not possible to impose sanctions on past generations it makes no sense to speak of legal obligations or even of moral obligations of those generations to us. At best, as some minority groups have been arguing, we might claim that present-day beneficiaries of past injustices are obliged to make restitution to the present descendents of those who in the past suffered injustice. This is a plausible claim, and might serve as a model in the future for some portion of mankind claiming that it has a legal or moral claim against another portion for exploitation or oppression by their forefathers. Whatever the obligation to make restoration for past injustices, however, the injustice was an injustice not primarily against present generations but against those past generations whose rights were violated or whose property or lives were unjustly taken, or who were otherwise oppressed or exploited.

The situation is basically similar today vis-à-vis future generations. Our primary obligation with respect to the control of pollution or to the use of resources is to presently existing human beings rather than to possible future human beings. The best way to protect the interests of future generations—if we choose to use this language—may be to conserve the environment for ourselves. But my present point is that in dealing with questions of public policy or legislation, the primary values to be considered are those of presently existing people, and not the projected or supposed values of future generations. To argue or act as if we could know the wants or needs of generations hundreds or more years hence is to deceive ourselves, perhaps so as to have an excuse to ignore present-day wants and needs. Hence questions about the amount and kind of pollution to be tolerated, the resources to be rationed or preserved, should not be decided in terms of far distant future needs or requirements but in terms of present and near-future needs and requirements.

It is correct that for the first time in the history of mankind presently living human beings have it within their power to annihilate mankind or to use up irreplaceable resources. But these new capacities do not change the status of our responsibilities or obligations, despite the fact that they are increased. If we do annihilate mankind, it will be no injustice to those who never were and never will be. If we were foolishly to use up vital, irreplaceable resources or disrupt the ecosystem, the reason it would be wrong or bad, unjust or immoral—and so the reason why it might now be something requiring legislation to prevent—is not its effects on those who do not yet exist, but its effects on those who do.

The thrust of the principle we are considering is that present generations or individuals must be considered primary in any calculation of value with respect to either pollution control or the distribution and use of the limited resources of the earth. The rights of presently existing people carry with them the obligation to respect their rights, e.g., to enjoy at least minimal levels of food, shelter, and the like. No one and no generation is required to sacrifice itself for imaginary, non-existent generations of the future. What does have to be considered is the future of presently existing persons—infants as well as adults.

We undoubtedly feel closer to our as yet unconceived descendents—those once removed from the present generation of children—than we do to many people living in places far distant from us, with different customs and values; and if we were to choose between raising the standard of living of these to-us foreign people and preserving our wealth to be shared by our descendents, we might well opt for the latter. To do so is to aggregate to ourselves the right to conserve present resources for those to whom we choose to pass them on at the expense of those presently existing who do not share them. Since, however, presently existing people have rights to the goods of the earth, there seems to be a *prima facie* obligation to attempt to raise the level of living and comfort of presently existing people, wherever they may be, rather than ignoring them and worrying only about our own future heirs. Underfed and impoverished areas of the world may require greater attention and impose greater obligations than non-existent future generations.

Insofar as modern technology is world-significant, so too are some aspects of pollution. Mercury poured into streams finds its way into the ocean and into fish caught in international waters and shipped around the world; fall-out from nuclear blasts circles the globe. If present-day legislative principles in the United States are sufficient to handle the problems posed by pollution in our own country, it is certainly not the case that there are effective means of controlling the problem internationally. The cost of pollution' control prevents poorer countries from simultaneously developing their technology in order to raise their living standards and spend the money and resources necessary to curb pollution. It is in cases such as these that it becomes especially important to be conscious of the principle discussed here which emphasizes the overbearing right of existing persons as opposed to the putative rights of nonexistent persons.

The argument that only existing entities have rights, however, must be correctly understood. For though we cannot have obligations to nonexistent entities, we do have an obligation for those whom we bring into the world. Before a couple conceives a child they have the obligation to make sure that they can raise him properly, that he will have enough to eat, and so on. He seems to have the right to these things once he is born and his parents have the obligation to keep him alive—at least under ordinary circumstances—once he is born. If he has no rights before he is conceived, and if his parents have no obligations to him because he is then not yet, what sort of obligation do they have at that time and to whom?

When we say that potential parents should not bring children into the world unless they are able to care for them and raise them free from the perpetual threat of starvation and misery, we are envisaging a choice between bringing them into the world or not. In effect we admit that the potential parents have no obligation to or for offspring who will never be conceived. They will have an obligation *to* the child only when he does exist, and they will have an obligation *for* the child to society. So their obligations are contingent, and they in part involve a contingent obligation to a contingent entity. One should assume the responsibility for one's actions. If one's actions produce children, then one should assume the responsibility of caring for them; and if individual parents cannot, then others should, because of the right of the then existing child to continued life. But unless there is a specific or a general obligation to have children, the contingent obligation to or for these contingent beings can be legitimately escaped simply by not conceiving them.

Secondly, although we may admit that non-existent entities do not now have any rights and so we now have no *obligations* to them, yet as soon as they are conceived or born or attain self-consciousness (the arguments involved in settling the issue of when they become human persons are beside the point here) they *will* have rights and we *will* have obligations to them. Consequently we must consider the obligations we will have to them when they do exist and the rights they will have when they do exist, even though neither of these is now present.

Although there is no full fledged obligation to provide, e.g., clean air, for countless future generations, we will have an obligation to provide something for at least those future persons or generations for whom or for which we are rather closely responsible. Generations overlap considerably; but any group in the position to influence and change things, though it cannot be expected to be responsible for generations hundreds, much less thousands of years hence, can be expected to take into account those persons who will be alive within the next fifty or a hundred years.

A large number of these people already exist; and if future generations are produced—as barring some global catastrophe they will be—they *will* have rights and these rights must be considered at least as potential rights. The amount of consideration should be proportional to the probability that they will exist, and should be considered especially by those responsible for bringing them into the world.

Furthermore, if starting from the premise that non-existent entities can have no rights it follows that presently existing persons have no correlative obligations towards them, and so no such obligations to unborn generations, this does not mean that people may not want to consider future possible generations from some point of view other than one of such obligation and take them into account in other ways and for other reasons.

Obviously men are concerned about their own futures and those of their presently existing children and of the presently acknowledged right of their children to have children; it is a claim which must be weighed. Though we cannot assume that the children of present-day children will have exactly the same desires and values as we, there is good reason to believe they will be sufficiently similar to us so that they will need fresh air, that they will not be able to tolerate excessive amounts of mercury or DDT in their food, and that they will probably share a good many of our desires. To speak of the *right* of non-existing future persons to have children in their turn is to treat them as actual. It amounts to saying that if conditions remain more or less the same and if the presently possible entities become actual, then, when they do, they will have the rights we presently attribute to actually existing persons. Our present interest in their happiness, however, is already an actual interest which must be considered and it might impel—though not strictly require—us to leave as many options open to those who will come after us as possible, consistent with taking care of our own needs and wants.

Since most people living now would consider it possible to be living twenty years hence, the conditions of life which the next as yet unborn generation will face is a condition of life which we who presently exist will also face. So with respect to at least one, two, three or perhaps four generations hence, or for roughly fifty to a hundred years hence, it can plausibly be argued that we plan not only for unborn generations but also for ourselves. Our concern for them is equally concern for ourselves. And we do have rights. If this is the case, we can legitimately think and plan and act for the future on the basis of our own concerns, which include *our* hopes and desires for our real or anticipated offspring. But we should be clear about what we are arguing, and not confuse our rights and desires with the supposed rights of non-existent entities.

II

The second principle was: Continuance of the human race is good.

What does this mean and what does it imply?

We have already seen that if we bring children into the world then we assume certain responsibilities and that these children have certain rights. One alternative was to decide not to have children if they could not be properly cared for or supported. On an individual level this right is generally acknowledged. On a broader scale some people have generalized the argument that collectively we should not bring into the world more children than the earth as a whole can satisfactorily maintain and provide for. Hence there are campaigns for birth control, zero population growth, and so on.

Advocates of population limitation are at one with others who worry about man annihilating himself by pollution in that they both consider the indefinite continuance of the human race as something worthwhile and worth planning for.

Yet can we give any sense to the question: how long should the human race survive? We know that some species have had their span of years on earth and have given way to other species. To ask how long the dinosaur should have survived would be an odd question; for to say that it should have survived for a shorter or longer time than it did would be to speak as if the laws of nature should have been different, or as if the dinosaur's continued existence was a good which it could have done something to prolong beyond the time that it did. It is precisely in this sense—that the survival of the human species is a good in itself and that we should do what we can to keep it going—that we say that the human race should continue to survive. To utter this is to make a value judgment and to express our feelings about the race, despite the fact that we as individuals will die. Some people speak blithely about its being better for the human species to continue for another thousand years than for another five hundred; or for 500,000 rather than 100,000, and so on. But the content which we can give to such statements—other than expressing the judgment that human life is a good in itself, at least under certain circumstances—seems minimal. For we cannot imagine what human life would be like in the far distant future, nor what we can or should do to help make it the case that one of those figures rather than the other is the one that actually becomes the case.

If tomorrow some sort of radiation from the sun were to render all human beings sterile, we could anticipate the demise of the human race as more and more of the present population died off. We could anticipate the difficulties of those who were the relatively last to die. And we could take some solace in the fact that the radiation would have been an act of God and not the result of the acts of men. The demise of the human race would in this case be similar to the extinction of the dinosaur. If a similar occurrence was the result of the acts of men, though the result would be the same, it would make more sense in the latter case than in the former to say that man should have continued longer as a species. Just as we consider murder and suicide wrong, so we consider wrong the fouling of the air or water to such an extent that it kills others or ourselves or the whole human race.

Thus, though no injustice is done to those who will never exist because of our actions, and though we do not violate any of their rights—since they have none—we can in some sense say that with the extinction of the human race there would be less value in the world than if it had continued to exist. If we have an obligation to attempt to create and preserve as much value in the world as possible, then we have an obligation to continue the human race, where this does not necessarily mean an obligation to procreate as many people as possible but to achieve as much value as possible, taking into consideration the quality of life of those who will be alive. The basis for the obligation comes not from a consideration of rights, but from a consideration of value.

Such a calculation, obviously, is something which each generation can perform only with respect to the time it is alive and able to act. It can help assure that when it dies those who are still living are in such a condition as to preserve human life and to pass it on at as high a qualitative level as possible. And if that happened consistently each year, each decade, each century, then until there was some act of God presumably man would continue indefinitely—which is a thought we may take some pleasure in contemplating, despite the fact that beyond a rather small number of years we will not be affected by whether the race continues or not.

Thus far, then, though we do not have any obligation *to* non-existent entities, we can legitimately anticipate the future needs and requirements of ourselves and of those who will probably come soon after us; furthermore, since we can make out the case that it would be good for the human race to continue, we have the obligation to do what we can to forestall its demise. This leads us to the third principle.

III

The last of the three principles I proposed at the start of this paper was: Continuous increase in man's standard of living is good. It is a principle which a large number of people seem to subscribe to, one underlying much of our industrial and technological growth and a good deal of the concern for a constantly expanding GNP. As a principle, however, it is both ambiguous and dubious.

There are at least four basic interpretations which can be given to the principle: (1) it can be taken to refer to advancement up the economic ladder by people on an individual basis; (2) it might be understood as a statement about the hopes and aims of each generation for the succeeding generation; (3) it might mean that the standard of living of at least some men should continue to rise, pushing forward the heights to which men can rise; and (4) it can be interpreted to mean that all men in a given society, or throughout the world, should be brought up to a certain constantly rising level of life.

The differences in interpretation are extremely important and both stem from and give rise to different sets of value judgments concerning production, distribution, development of resources, and expenditure of resources on pollution control.

1. The individualistic interpretation puts its emphasis on an individual's ability through work, savings, ingenuity, or other means to advance himself economically. The Horatio Alger ideal, the rise from poverty to wealth, is the model. Increasing one's standard of living became the goal of workers as expressed in the labor union movements,

and its results are clearly visible in the high standard of living enjoyed by many large segments of the population in the United States and other industrialized countries. Together with this rise has come the pollution from automobiles and factories and the birth of a small counter-culture which has called into question the necessity, the wisdom, and the value of a constantly rising standard of living.

The hope of a better life expresses an undeniable value when one's life is barely tolerable. It makes less sense as one's needs are more and more taken care of; and the principle becomes dubious once one has achieved a certain standard of living somewhere considerably well above the minimal necessary for survival. There is a point of diminishing returns beyond which the price one has to pay in terms of energy, time, money, and resources expended does not produce correspondingly significant benefits. And if enough people reach that state, then the society's energy and efforts become counter-productive. The result we are seeing is that the attempt to achieve a constantly higher standard of living has resulted in a lower quality of life for all, partially through pollution. This fact, admittedly, is little comfort to those who have not yet arrived at a tolerable level of life and for whom the aspiration to raise their standard of living is a real good; the present point, however, is that at least beyond a certain level the principle cannot be achieved and if acted on may serve to produce more harm than good. (The related problem of inequity in a society will be considered further under the fourth interpretation.)

2. The interpretation of the principle which expresses the hope of parents that their children will have a better life than they suffers the same fate as the preceding interpretation. Where the level of life is already good, the desire that their children's be even better may well be questionable for the reasons we have already seen. Children, of course, have no right to be better off than their parents, although those who are badly off might well wish those they love to enjoy more of the goods of life than they themselves have.

If some generation is to enjoy a higher standard of living than others, however, it is not necessary that it always be some future generation. The desire that some future generation of human beings should be better off than present generations may be the desire of some members of present generations. But it is nothing owed to future generations. Some parents sacrifice themselves and deny themselves for the benefit of their children; some carefully save their wealth only to have their children squander it. In some cases such self-sacrifice is noble and evokes our praise; in others, it is foolish. But any such case of self-sacrifice is above the demands of duty, as is obvious when we see children attempting to demand such sacrifice from their parents as if it were their right. Nor does any parent or group have the right through legislation to demand such sacrifice from others for his own or for other people's children.

3. The view that at least some men should live at constantly higher levels so as to push mankind constantly forward seems hardly defensible for a number of reasons. The first is that it is difficult to describe what a constantly higher standard of living could mean for only a few since their lives are so closely connected to other men and to the energy, pollution,

and population problems they all face. Secondly, standard of living is not the same as quality of life. Simple increase in the standard of living, if measured by the goods one has, simply does not make much sense beyond a certain point. For one's needs beyond that point are artificial, and it is not at all clear that satisfying them makes one happier or more comfortable or any of the other things that an increase in the standard of living is supposed to do, and for which reasons it is desired as a good. Thirdly, it can well be argued that it is unlikely that the constantly higher standard advocated for the few—if sense can be made of it—will help do anything but increase the difference between the level of life of the haves and the have-nots. If taken to mean not that a few men in an advanced industrial society should push mankind forward but that the advanced industrial societies should continue to advance at the expense of the non-industrial societies, then this seems to go clearly against the rights of the latter, and so not be a worthy end at all.

4. The fourth interpretation is the most plausible and has the most vocal defenders today. It maintains that all men in a given society (and ideally throughout the world) should be brought up to a certain constantly rising minimal level of life—at least constantly rising for the foreseeable future, given the wide distance between the level of life of the haves and the have-nots. This is the impetus behind minimum income legislation on the American domestic scene. Globally, it affects the relations between have and have-not countries, between the industrially developed and the underdeveloped countries, and is one of the bases for advocating foreign aid programs of various sorts.

The right of all men to a minimal standard of living is one that I would argue in favor of. But my present concern is to note that the right to a constantly rising minimum is contingent upon the ability of the earth and of society to provide it. If world resources are able to adequately sustain only a limited number of people, and if more than that number are born, the distribution of goods cannot extend sufficiently far; and those societies which contributed most to the overpopulation of their land and of the earth in general may well have to bear the brunt of the evil consequences.

A continuously rising standard of living therefore is never a right, not always a good, and most often simply one good to be measured against other goods and available resources.

IV

What then, if anything, do we owe future generations? We do not owe them a better life than we enjoy, nor do we owe them resources which we need for ourselves.

When dealing with renewable resources a sound principle might be that, other things being equal, they should not be used up at a faster rate than that at which they can be replaced. But when they are needed at a greater rate than that at which they can be replaced, rationing is insufficient and they raise a problem similar to that raised by non-renewable resources. One can argue that the latter should be used up sufficiently slowly so that there are always reserves; but this may mean using less and less each year or decade, despite increasing demand. An alternative is simply to use what we need, attempting to keep our needs rational, and to face crucially diminished supplies when we are forced to face them, hoping in the meantime that some substitutes will be discovered or developed.

Frequently problems of this type have been approached from a utilitarian point of view, and such an approach is instructive. Let each man count for one, the argument goes, whether he be a present man or a future man. The happiness of each is on a par as far as importance and intrinsic goodness are concerned. But increasing the sum of total happiness is better than its opposite. If by increased growth or unlimited use now of limited resources we increase our happiness by a small amount, but doom those who come after us to struggling along without some important natural resources; and if by conserving our natural resources now our happiness or at least that part which is made up of comfort is somewhat less than it could be, but the happiness of many million or billions who come after us is greater than it would otherwise be, then the moral thing to do is to conserve our resources now and share them with future generations.

This argument presupposes first that there will be the future generations it hypothesizes, that these future generations will want pretty much the same things that we do in order to be happy, that they will not overuse the goods of the earth, and that they will not be able to find any suitable substitutes. If we saved only to have them squander, then no more good might be achieved than if we had spent liberally and they had proportionally less; or if they find, e.g., alternate energy sources, then our penury resulted in less good than there might have been.

In earlier times the ploy of this kind of argument was to trade on the happiness of countless generations in the future as a result of some sacrifice of our happiness now. But there are now a sufficient number of doubts about there being future generations, about their not finding alternative resources, and about our present sacrifices leading to their happiness (since there might be so many of them anyway) as to render the argument less convincing than it might formerly have been.

In any calculus of pleasure or good there is no necessity for future generations to enjoy a higher standard of living at the expense of present generations. If there will be a peak in the standard somewhere along the line, followed by a decline, it might just as well be the present generation which enjoys the peak through the utilization of resources, which, since limited, will be used up sooner or later. There is no greater good served by future generations being the peak since obviously when it comes to their turn, if it is improper for us to enjoy more than our successors, and if this is the proper way to feel, they should feel so also.

Both because of these considerations and because of the large number of unknowables concerning the future, short range considerations are surer and more pertinent than long range considerations. The threshold of pollution has been recently crossed so that it is now obvious that something must be done; legislation consequently is being passed. The amount and kind of pollution to be tolerated, the resources to be rationed or preserved should not be decided in terms of far distant needs or requirements but in terms of present and near-future needs and requirements.

Production involves wastes which have now reached the pollution stage. Its control is costly. The cost must be borne either by the producer (who will pass it on to the consumer) or by society at large through the taxes required, e.g., to purify water. The principle that whoever causes the pollution must pay for cleaning it up, or that no production should be allowed without the mechanism provided to prevent pollution, will make some kinds of production unprofitable. In this case, if such production is considered necessary or desirable, it will have to be subsidized. If society cannot pay for total cleanup it might have to settle for less than it would like; or it might have to give up some of its production or some of the goods to which it had become accustomed; or it might have to forego some of the products it might otherwise produce. Such choices should not be made a priori or by the fiat of government, but by the members of society at large or by as many of them interested and aware and informed enough to help in the decision making process.

There are presently available the means nationally for allocating resources and for controlling use and production through automatic market and natural mechanisms as well as through legislation. Where legislation poses the greatest difficulty is not on the national level but on the international level. For technology has brought us into one closely interdependent world faster than the social and legal mechanisms for solving the world-wide problems of resources, population, and pollution have been able to develop.

The problems posed by the ecological challenge are many and complex. But in dealing with them it should be clear that we owe nothing *to* those who do not yet and may never exist; that nonetheless we do have an obligation to promote the continuance of the human race, and so have an obligation *for* those whom we produce; that though at least minimum standards of living for all are desirable, if some generation is to enjoy the peak it need not be other generations; and that the choice of how to use our resources and continue or control our pollution depends on the price all those concerned wish to pay and the values we wish to espouse and promote.

POINTS TO PONDER

1. How sound are Bedau's arguments concerning the linkage that he believes ought to be established (or eliminated) between foreign assistance programs and those human rights that have traditionally been recognized in the United States?

2. In Bedau's hypothetical example of nation A and the anti-Semitic nation B, suppose that A had in the past compiled a racist record of its own. What would the results be, according to Bedau's analysis? Would other considerations, based on the arguments from avoiding complicity

in wrongdoing and from leverage to end wrongdoing, be sufficient to overcome the problem? How?

3. Is there a human right not to starve? If so, does it imply that others have a duty to come to the aid of starving people? Which others? Do those others have the right to demand that the starving adopt policies that they (the food suppliers) feel are in their own, as well as others', best interests? Defend the principle(s) upon which you base your answer.

4. Beauchamp does not flatly reject the conclusion that a nation might turn its back upon a starving population without suffering from serious pangs of guilt. *Triage* would seem to permit one to do so. Indeed, it might well *require* that one do so. Is this an acceptable moral position?

5. Analyze Aiken's words very carefully. He makes no bones about his feelings. Do the other authors in this section use value-laden terms that disguise their intention to persuade? (Aiken certainly does not disguise his.)

6. What premises or principles does Aiken appeal to, either explicitly or by implication, in his argument? Are they plausible or reasonable? Ask the same questions to yourself about Bedau, Beauchamp, and De George.

7. Does the mere fact that people are so remote from us that we cannot immediately touch them absolve us of all responsibility for them and their welfare? If the detonation of a nuclear bomb would severely injure people in a far-off land, surely the mere fact that they are far away is not sufficient to remove all responsibility from those who caused harm to them. But it would appear from De George's article that if such a detonation severely injured some future generation, or some of its members, those who caused the injury would bear no moral responsibility toward them. To be sure, the injured parties could not press their claims against the persons whose actions brought about their injuries because they would not be accessible. But is accessibility relevant in assessing moral responsibility?

8. Go over De George's article once again, substituting spatial nouns and adjectives for temporal ones. Does the argument hold up once that change has been made? Is there some unique quality about time that renders De George's conclusions plausible? Or is he simply mistaken?

9. A parable tells of a king who visits an aged man and finds him planting a tiny seedling in his garden. The king asked him why he was planting the tree when it was so unlikely that he would enjoy any of its fruit. The old man replied, "My grandfather planted such a tree before I was born, and I enjoyed its fruits all the days of my life. I am doing the same now for my grandchildren." Is this mere sentimentality, or is some sound moral point being made by the author of the parable?

10. Comment on each of the following statements:

   a. President Roosevelt should have ordered the bombing of the Nazi death camps, for he could have saved thousands of innocent victims from the gas chambers if he had done so.

   b. If the United States had not been attacked by the Japanese at Pearl Harbor, America would have been perfectly justified in staying out of World War II.

c. The United States should not have denied most favored nation treatment to the Soviet Union to secure more humane treatment and greater respect for the human rights of Soviet Jews and other minorities. What the Russians do within their own borders is an internal affair of theirs and is no business of ours.

d. The Hooker Chemical Company should not be held responsible for the injuries caused to residents who have been poisoned by seeping chemicals along its old dump at the Love Canal in Niagara Falls, for it owes nothing to the future generations. It harmed no one at the time it was dumping the chemicals and employed the most advanced safeguards then known to science.

e. The Alaskan wilderness should be preserved for future generations, just as Yellowstone Park was preserved for us. Our present need for oil and minerals and timber should not be permitted to outweigh the future interests of our descendants.

f. We have a moral obligation to assist victims of famine in foreign lands, for some day we may need their help in return.

V

FREE
SPEECH
AND
FREEDOM
OF
THE
PRESS

INTRODUCTION

In 1927, Justice Brandeis wrote about the values of free speech, arguing that it is a fundamental principle of American government that public discussion is a public duty, and that without free speech, such discussion is futile. The founding fathers recognized the risks to which all human institutions are subject, he said, but they also believed that "the path of safety lies in the opportunity to discuss freely supposed grievances and proposed remedies; and that the fitting remedy for evil counsels is good ones." Some years before, Justice Holmes argued that "we should be eternally vigilant against attempts to check expression of opinions that we loathe and believe to be fraught with death, unless they so imminently threaten immediate interference with the lawful and pressing purposes of the law that an immediate check is required to save the country."

Nevertheless, the courts have (somewhat inconsistently) recognized some exceptions to the free speech rule: Fighting words and obscenity have often been held to be forms of unprotected speech. Some forms of expression that are on the borderline between action and speech have been particularly troublesome. Should it be permissible to wear a black armband in a public school as a sign of political protest? If burning things in general is prohibited in public places, should people be permitted to burn their draft cards or flags as forms of symbolic speech?

In the *Skokie* case, members of the American Nazi Party, who advocate the abolition of First Amendment freedoms for those who are the objects of their racist policies, invoked the First Amendment in defense of their right to display their symbols and denounce Jews in a predominantly Jewish suburb of Chicago. Many of the residents of the village had personally suffered at the hands of the Nazis in Europe and had lost their families in the extermination camps. The difficult question posed here is whether persons advocating the destruction of the democratic system itself should be permitted to employ its protections to further their cause. In addition, there is a question as to the right of a municipality to control public marches and demonstrations that threaten to provoke a violent response and that in any case are deliberately designed to give deep offense to many of its residents.

Frederick Schauer argues that if unlimited rein is given to those who advocate the destruction of democratic institutions, they just might persuade enough people to adopt their platform, thus destroying the very freedoms they exploit.

Joel Feinberg and Ann Garry bring fresh perspectives to the problem of pornography. Feinberg, not content to accept on faith the proposition that there is no such thing as pornography, draws upon a number of fields, including the law, to provide criteria by which pornography may be meaningfully distinguished from art. Garry, concerned about possible moral objections to pornography, asks whether it necessarily degrades people and suggests a scenario for producing "nonsexist and morally acceptable" pornographic films.

14

VILLAGE OF SKOKIE V. NATIONAL SOCIALIST PARTY OF AMERICA, I

Illinois Court of Appeals, 51 Ill. App. 3d 279,
9 Ill. Dec. 90, 366 N.E.2d 347 (1977)

PER CURIAM:

Plaintiff, village of Skokie, filed a complaint in the circuit court of Cook County on April 28, 1977, praying for the issuance of an injunction prohibiting defendants, the National Socialist Party of America and certain individual officers and members of the Party, from engaging in various activities in the village on May 1. . . . The issue in this appeal is generally, whether plaintiff met its burden of proof for the issuance of a prior restraint on defendants' first amendment rights, and specifically whether the swastika is protected speech under the circumstances of this case. . . .

The complaint alleged the following pertinent facts. The village of Skokie contains a population of approximately 70,000 persons, of whom approximately 40,500 are of the Jewish religion, Jewish ancestry, or both. Included within the Jewish population are hundreds of persons who are survivors of Nazi concentration camps and many thousands whose families and close relatives were murdered by the Nazis. A large percentage of the Jewish population of Skokie is organized into groups and organizations. At the hearing, the above allegations were stipulated to by both parties. The complaint further alleged the nature of defendant Party's purpose, and stated that the "uniform of the National Socialist Party of America consists of the storm trooper uniform of the German Nazi Party embellished with the Nazi swastika." It is alleged that on March 20, the village police chief was informed by defendant Collin of defendants' intention to march on the village's sidewalks on May 1. As a result of publicity from the news media and early morning phone calls purportedly made by members of the defendant Party to Skokie residents whose names indicated the probability of their Jewish faith or ancestry it was common knowledge in the village, particularly among the Jewish population, that the defendant Party intended to march in Skokie on May Day. The complaint further alleged:

> . . . The threatened march of the defendants on May 1st has aroused the passions of thousands of individuals of Jewish faith or ancestry within the Village and more particularly has aroused the passions of the survivors of the Nazi concentration camps who are taking measures unknown to the plaintiff to thwart the threatened march.
>
> 10. The march of the defendants on May 1, 1977 is a deliberate and

wilful attempt to exacerbate the sensitivities of the Jewish population in Skokie and to incite racial and religious hatred. Such march, if not restrained by Order of this Court, constitutes a grave and serious threat to the peace of the citizens of the Village of Skokie.

11. By reason of the ethnic and religious composition of the Village of Skokie and the circumstances alleged above, the public display of the swastika in connection with the proposed activities of the defendant, National Socialist Party of America, constitutes a symbolic assault against large numbers of the residents of the Plaintiff village and an incitation to violence and retaliation.

The complaint prayed for the issuance of an injunction enjoining defendants from various activities in the village of Skokie on May 1.

Defendants filed a motion to dismiss stating that the complaint fails to state a cause of action upon which relief can be granted; seeks relief barred by the first and fourteenth amendments to the United States Constitution and alleges facts which are untrue. The motion to dismiss referred to an affidavit of one of the individual defendants appended thereto.

The affidavit stated that the affiant has been a leader of the defendant Party for seven years and has propounded the Party's platform by peaceable public assemblies, parades and speechmaking in the Chicago area. . . . [He had] stated that the assembly would take place in early afternoon without obstruction of traffic and that demonstrators would obey all laws and would march on the sidewalk in single file.

The affidavit also stated that the assembly would consist of 30 to 50 demonstrators who would conduct a picket line, marching in single file in front of the Skokie Village Hall and that demonstrators would wear their uniforms including a swastika armband. Demonstrators would carry placards and banners containing slogans such as "Free Speech For The White Man." The affiant had no plans to distribute handbills at this assembly. . . .

. . . A resident of Skokie, an officer in several Jewish organizations, testified that he learned of the planned demonstration from the newspapers. As a result, meetings of some 15 to 18 Jewish organizations, within Skokie and surrounding areas, were called, and a counterdemonstration was scheduled for the same day as the demonstration planned by defendants. The witness estimated that some 12,000 to 15,000 people were expected to participate. In the opinion of the witness, this counterdemonstration would be peaceful if defendants did not appear. However, if they did appear, the outrage of the participants might not be controllable. The witness testified that other counterdemonstrations were planned by other groups.

Skokie introduced other opinion evidence that bloodshed would occur if the defendants demonstrated as planned. The mayor of the village of Skokie testified regarding his opinion, formed after discussion with leaders of community and religious groups, that if the march or demonstration by defendants took place, an uncontrollably violent situation would develop.

Plaintiff also called as a witness a Jewish resident who was a survivor of Nazi concentration camps. He testified as to the effect the swastika has on him and other survivors. According to his testimony, the swastika is a symbol that his closest family was killed by the Nazis, and that the lives of him and his children are not presently safe. He further stated that he does not presently intend to use violence against defendants should they appear in Skokie, but that when he sees the swastika, he does not know if he can control himself. He further testified that between 5000 and 7000 survivors of the Nazi holocaust reside in the village of Skokie. . . .

After hearing arguments of counsel, the trial court entered an order enjoining defendants

> from engaging in any of the following acts on May 1, 1977, within the Village of Skokie: Marching, walking or parading in the uniform of the National Socialist Party of America; Marching, walking or parading or otherwise displaying the swastika on or off their person; Distributing pamphlets or displaying any materials which incite or promote hatred against persons of Jewish faith or ancestry or hatred against persons of any faith or ancestry, race or religion.

. . .

The question before the court is whether plaintiff, village of Skokie, has met its heavy burden of showing justification for the imposition of the circuit court's prior restraint upon defendants' rights to freedom of speech and public assembly. . . .

. . . The first issue is whether plaintiff has overcome the presumptive invalidity of the prior restraint on defendants' planned demonstration to be held in front of the Skokie Village Hall if defendants would not wear their uniforms. The evidence presented to the trial court showed that defendants would not obstruct traffic, would obey all laws, would march in single file on the sidewalk and would carry placards and banners containing slogans such as "Free Speech For The White Man," "White Free Speech," and "Free Speech For White America." Defendants planned to distribute no written material, and would not make any derogatory public statements, written or oral, directed at any ethnic or religious group. In short, the evidence pertaining to the defendants' conduct showed nothing other than a peaceful assembly of 30–50 persons demonstrating for 20–30 minutes against what they believed was an unfair Park District ordinance requiring the posting of a high bond prior to the issuance of a park permit for demonstrations. Looking only at defendants' expected conduct, no conclusion may be drawn from the record other than a planned exercise of "basic constitutional rights in their most pristine and classic form." Yet, the other evidence presented to the trial court showed that if the defendants ever appear in Skokie to demonstrate, there was and is a virtual certainty that thousands of irate Jewish citizens would physically attack the defendants. The trial court entered the order enjoining the demonstration, stating that he thought defendants "intended to incite riot, to cause bodily harm, and to do all those things that the Constitution does not give a defendant a right to do."

The law of our nation is clear as to the question of whether the presence of hostile spectators or bystanders may justify the restraint of otherwise legal first amendment activities. "As to the possibility of there being hostile audience members causing violence, the law is quite clear that such considerations are impermissible . . . ." the rule has been that if the communications expressed do not fit into an exception stripping them of first amendment protections, then under our Constitution, the public expression of ideas may not be prohibited merely because the ideas themselves are offensive to the hearers. "The threat of a hostile audience cannot be considered in determining whether a permit shall be granted or in ruling on a request for an injunction against a demonstration. . . . Thus, our laws bespeak what should be; for were it otherwise, enjoyment of constitutional rights by the peaceable and law-abiding would depend on the dictates of those willing to resort to violence." Since the plaintiff has failed to meet its burden of proof, in so far as the injunction order purports to enjoin defendants from marching, walking or parading in the village of Skokie without reference to the uniform of the National Socialist Party of America, it is reversed.

The second issue, therefore, is whether plaintiff has overcome the presumptive invalidity of the prior restraint on defendants' demonstrating while wearing the uniform of the National Socialist Party of America in the village of Skokie. The complaint states, *inter alia:*

> The members of the National Socialist Party of America have patterned their conduct, their uniform, their slogan and their tactics along the pattern of the German Nazi Party, including the adoption of the hated swastika. The uniform of the National Socialist Party of America consists of the storm trooper uniform of the German Nazi Party embellished with the Nazi swastika.

As we view both the plaintiff's definition and the evidence, the uniform of the defendant Party consists of two separate and distinct elements, the storm trooper uniform and the swastika. Each element shall be considered separately, for it is in the interest of law and justice that an injunction should not be broader than is necessary. The wearing of the swastika will be discussed in conjunction with Part B of the injunction order.

The testimony disclosed that the storm trooper uniform of the German Nazi Party consists of a brown shirt and is worn with a swastika. . . . The defendants' wearing of such a uniform is admittedly an expression that their goals are similar to those of the German Nazi Party. The thorny issue arising is whether the wearing of the storm trooper uniform *sans* swastika is protected speech under the first amendment. If so, it may not generally be prohibited.

The wearing of distinctive clothing to express a thought or idea is generally the type of a symbolic act which is considered protected speech within the first amendment. For example, a black armband worn by schoolchildren to protest the Vietnam War was held protected speech in *Tinker* v. *Des Moines Independent Community School District* (1969),

393 U.S. 503, 89 S.Ct. 733, 21 L.Ed.2d 731. Similarly, a jacket bearing the words "Fuck the Draft" was held protected speech in *Cohen* v. *California* (1971), 403 U.S. 15, 91 S.Ct. 1780, 29 L.Ed.2d 284. . . . In both cases, in the absence of other circumstances the wearing of distinctive clothing was considered only the communication of ideas and therefore protected speech. There are, of course, circumstances which could remove speech from the sphere of protection. The advocacy of abstract force or violence is generally protected speech "except where such advocacy is directed to inciting or producing imminent lawless action and is likely to incite or produce such action." . . . In the instant case, plaintiff argues that the Nazi uniform is the symbolic equivalent of a public call to kill all Jews and is a direct incitation to immediate mass murder, which is not entitled to first amendment protection. The record does not support this conclusion. There is not one bit of evidence in the record that the uniform without the swastika would have such an effect. There has been no showing that there are persons who would be directly and immediately incited to commit mass murder as a result of seeing defendants' storm trooper uniforms.

. . .

We do . . . need to carefully consider the exception of fighting words. According to the rule in *Chaplinsky* v. *New Hampshire* (1942),

> it is well understood that the right of free speech is not absolute at all times and under all circumstances. There are certain well-defined and narrowly limited classes of speech, the prevention and punishment of which have never been thought to raise any Constitutional problem. These include the lewd and obscene, the profane, the libelous, and the insulting or "fighting" words—those which by their very utterance inflict injury or tend to incite an immediate breach of the peace. It has been well observed that such utterances are no essential part of any exposition of ideas, and are of such slight social value as a step to truth that any benefit that may be derived from them is clearly outweighed by the social interest in order and morality. (315 U.S. at 571–72, 62 S.Ct. at 769.)

Such "fighting" words are those personally abusive epithets which, when addressed to an ordinary citizen, as a matter of common knowledge, are inherently likely to provoke violent reaction. The evidence of record does not support a conclusion that the uniform *sans* swastika constitutes fighting words. There is no testimony that anyone in the village of Skokie would consider the uniform itself as an abusive epithet which would provoke him to violent reaction. Nor can this court say as a matter of law and common knowledge that the brown-shirt uniform stripped of all other symbols is inherently likely to provoke violent reaction. Rather, the wearing of such a uniform must be considered, in the context of the instant case, as symbolic speech protected by the first amendment. Above all, "the First Amendment means that government has no power to restrict expression because of its message, its ideas, its subject matter, or its content." Any shock effect caused by such a uniform must be attributed to the content of the ideas expressed or to the onlookers' dislike of demonstrations by defendants. "But '[i]t is firmly settled that under our Constitution the public expression of ideas may not be prohibited merely because the ideas are themselves offensive to some of their hearers,' [citations] or simply because bystanders object to peaceful and orderly demonstrations." Since plaintiff has failed to meet its burden of proof, that portion of the injunction order which purports to enjoin defendants from wearing the uniform of the National Socialist Party of America without other symbols such as the swastika, while marching, walking or parading in the village of Skokie is reversed as being an unconstitutional prior restraint of defendants' first amendment rights.

The third issue on appeal is whether the plaintiff has overcome the presumptive invalidity of the prior restraint on defendants' "marching, walking or parading or otherwise displaying the swastika on or off their person," which is Part B of the injunction order. Since the display of the swastika is an expression of defendants' ideas, however odious and repulsive to most members of our society, it will generally be considered protected speech unless it falls within the exceptions discussed in connection with the wearing of the uniform. There is no showing that the display or wearing of the swastika will incite anyone to immediately commit mass murder in furtherance of the aims of the German Nazi Party, or to commit any unlawful act in furtherance of the goals of the defendant Party.

The original complaint filed in this cause alleges that by reason of the ethnic and religious composition of the village and the particular circumstances of this case, the public display of the swastika by defendants will incite large numbers of Skokie residents to violence and retaliation. We understand this portion of the complaint, although inartfully drafted in haste, to allege under the circumstances of this case that the display of the swastika constitutes fighting words and is therefore not protected by the first amendment. The evidence taken at the hearing which relates to this allegation is illuminating.

One Skokie resident who was a survivor of German concentration camps testified that to him, the swastika is a symbol that his closest family was killed by the Nazis and that he presently fears his death and the death of his children at the hands of those displaying the swastika. He feels strongly about the defendants and their swastika and does not know if he can control himself should he see a swastika in the village where he lives. By implication, a great many of the other 5000 to 7000 survivors of the holocaust who reside in Skokie may not be able to control themselves under similar circumstances. The mayor of the plaintiff village (who testified that he is a Roman Catholic) stated at the hearing that there was a "terrible feeling of unrest regarding the parading of the swastika in the Village of Skokie, a terrible feeling expressed by people in words that they should not have to tolerate this type of demonstration, in view of their history as a people." The legal question, therefore, is whether the display of the swastika in the village of Skokie, under the circumstances of this case, would constitute "fighting words."

Since *Chaplinsky v. New Hampshire* the fighting words exception has been well established in our law and is a viable rule, but it has been noted that *Chaplinsky* has been significantly limited by cases which hold protected the peaceful expression of views which stirs people to anger because of the content of the expression, or perhaps of the manner in which it is conveyed, and that breach of the peace and disorderly conduct statutes may not be used to curb such expression. . . .

The evidence conclusively shows that at least one resident of Skokie considered the swastika to be a personally abusive epithet which was, in light of his personal history, inherently likely to provoke a violent reaction in him if the swastika were intentionally displayed by defendants in the village of Skokie. Other evidence shows by implication that similar or identical feelings were shared by thousands of other residents of the village of Skokie. . . . The evidence shows precisely that substantial numbers of citizens are standing ready to strike out physically at whoever may assault their sensibilities with the display of the swastika. We feel that the subjective portion of the fighting words test has been satisfied.

The objective portion of the fighting words test follows. Would the ordinary citizen be provoked to violent reaction? We cannot say more than the evidence shows that the average Jewish resident of the village of Skokie would be provoked. . . . If the swastika would naturally offend thousands of Jewish persons in Skokie, then it must be said that it would offend all those who respect the honestly held faith of their fellows, including the ordinary citizen.

The remaining portion of the objective test is whether the swastika, as a matter of common knowledge, is inherently likely to provoke violent reactions among those of the Jewish persuasion or ancestry if brought in close proximity to their homes or places of worship. As stated in dissent to an unrelated issue in *Anderson* v. *Vaughn* (D.Conn.1971), 327 F. Supp. 101, 106:

> By way of illustration, if one were to parade a Ku Klux Klan flag or other such emblem into an NAACP meeting it would quite likely provoke a riotous reaction; or to publicly carry a Nazi flag into a synagogue would certainly be calculated to incite disorder; or to display a Viet Cong flag at a political gathering of loyal Americans might well be calculated to provoke an incitement to violence. Contrary conclusions would be both unreal and naive. . . .

. . .

The swastika is a symbol which, as demonstrated by the record in this case and as a matter of common knowledge, is inherently likely to provoke violent reaction among those of the Jewish persuasion or ancestry when intentionally brought in close proximity to their homes and places of worship. The swastika is a personal affront to every member of the Jewish faith, in remembering the nearly consummated genocide of their people committed within memory by those who used the swastika as their symbol. This is especially true for the thousands of Skokie residents who personally survived the holocaust of the Third Reich. They remember all too well the brutal destruction of their families and communities by those then wearing the swastika. So too, the tens of thousands of Skokie's Jewish residents must feel gross revulsion for the swastika and would immediately respond to the personally abusive epithets slung their way in the form of the defendants' chosen symbol, the swastika. The epithets of racial and religious hatred are not protected speech, and we find that the village of Skokie has met its heavy burden of justifying the prior restraint imposed upon the defendants' planned wearing and display of the swastika. So that there should be no confusion, Part B of the injunction order, dealing with the swastika, is modified to read: "Intentionally displaying the swastika on or off their persons, in the course of a demonstration, march, or parade within the Village of Skokie." As thus modified, the order is affirmed. . . .

15 VILLAGE OF SKOKIE V. NATIONAL SOCIALIST PARTY OF AMERICA, II

Supreme Court of Illinois, 69 Ill.2d 605, 14 Ill. Dec. 890, 373 N.E.2d 21 (1978)

PER CURIAM:
Plaintiff, the village of Skokie, filed a complaint in the circuit court of Cook County seeking to enjoin defendants, the National Socialist Party of America (the American Nazi Party) and 10 individuals as "officers and members" of the party, from engaging in certain activities while conducting a demonstration within the village. The circuit court issued an order enjoining certain conduct during the planned demonstration. The appellate court modified the injunction order, and, as modified, defendants are enjoined from "[i]ntentionally displaying the swastika on or off their persons, in the course of a demonstration, march, or parade." . . .

It is alleged in plaintiff's complaint that the "uniform of the National Socialist Party of America consists of the storm trooper uniform of the German Nazi Party embellished with the Nazi swastika"; that the plaintiff village has a population of about 70,000 persons of which approximately 40,500 persons are of "Jewish religion or Jewish ancestry" and of this latter number 5,000 to 7,000 are survivors of German concentration camps; that the defendant organization is "dedicated to the incitation of racial and religious hatred directed principally against individuals of Jewish faith or ancestry and non-Caucasians"; and that its members "have patterned their conduct, their uniform, their slogan and their tactics along the pattern of the German Nazi Party. . . ."

Defendants moved to dismiss the complaint. In an affidavit attached to defendants' motion to dismiss, defendant Frank Collin, who testified that he was "party leader," stated that on or about March 20, 1977, he sent officials of the plaintiff village a letter stating that the party members and supporters would hold a peaceable, public assembly in the village on May 1, 1977, to protest the Skokie Park District's requirement that the party procure $350,000 of insurance prior to the party's use of the Skokie public parks for public assemblies. The demonstration was to begin at 3 P.M., last 20 to 30 minutes, and consist of 30 to 50 demonstrators marching in single file, back and forth, in front of the village hall. The marchers were to wear uniforms which include a swastika emblem or armband. They were to carry a party banner containing a swastika emblem and signs containing such statements as "White Free Speech," "Free Speech for the White Man," and "Free Speech for White America." The demonstrators would not distribute handbills, make any derogatory statements directed to any ethnic or religious group, or obstruct traffic. They would cooperate with any reasonable police instructions or requests.

At the hearing on plaintiff's motion for an "emergency injunction" a resident of Skokie testified that he was a survivor of the Nazi holocaust. He further testified that the Jewish community in and around Skokie feels the purpose of the march in the "heart of the Jewish population" is to remind the two million survivors "that we are not through with you" and to show "that the Nazi threat is not over, it can happen again." Another resident of Skokie testified that as the result of defendants' announced intention to march in Skokie, 15 to 18 Jewish organizations, within the village and surrounding area, were called and a counterdemonstration of an estimated 12,000 to 15,000 people was scheduled for the same day. There was opinion evidence that defendants' planned demonstration in Skokie would result in violence. . . .

The only issue remaining before this court is whether the circuit court order enjoining defendants from displaying the swastika violates the first amendment rights of those defendants. . . .

"It is firmly settled that under our Constitution the public expression of ideas may not be prohibited merely because the ideas are themselves offensive to some of their hearers," and it is entirely clear that the wearing of distinctive clothing can be symbolic expression of a thought or philosophy. The symbolic expression of thought falls within the free speech clause of the first amendment, and the plaintiff village has the heavy burden of justifying the imposition of a prior restraint upon defendants' right to freedom of speech.

The village of Skokie seeks to meet this burden by application of the "fighting words" doctrine first enunciated in Chaplinsky v. New Hampshire (1942), 315 U.S. 568. That doctrine was designed to permit punishment of extremely hostile personal communication likely to cause immediate physical response, "no words being 'forbidden except such as have a direct tendency to cause acts of violence by the persons to whom, individually, the remark is addressed.'" In Cohen the Supreme Court restated the description of fighting words as "those personally abusive epithets which, when addressed to the ordinary citizen, are, as a matter of common knowledge, inherently likely to provoke violent reaction."

Plaintiff urges, and the appellate court has held, that the exhibition of the Nazi symbol, the swastika, addresses to ordinary citizens a message which is tantamount to fighting words. Plaintiff further asks this court to extend *Chaplinsky*, which upheld a statute punishing the use of such words, and hold that the fighting-words doctrine permits a prior restraint on defendants' symbolic speech. In our judgment we are precluded from doing so.

In *Cohen*, defendant's conviction stemmed from wearing a jacket bearing the words "Fuck the Draft" in a Los Angeles County courthouse corridor. The Supreme Court for reasons we believe applicable here refused to find that the jacket inscription constituted fighting words. That court stated:

> The constitutional right of free expression is powerful medicine in a society as diverse and populous as ours. It is designed and intended to remove governmental restraints from the arena of public discussion, putting the decision as to what views shall be voiced largely into the hands of each of us, in the hope that use of such freedom will ultimately produce a more capable citizenry and more perfect polity and in the belief that no other approach would comport with the premise of individual dignity and choice upon which our political system rests.
>
> To many, the immediate consequence of this freedom may often appear to be only verbal tumult, discord, and even offensive utterance. These are, however, within established limits, in truth necessary side effects of the broader enduring values which the process of open debate permits us to achieve. That the air may at times seem filled with verbal cacophony is, in this sense not a sign of weakness but of strength. We cannot lose sight of the fact that, in what otherwise might seem a trifling and annoying instance of individual distasteful abuse of a privilege, these fundamental societal values are truly implicated. . . . "[S]o long as the means are peaceful, the communication need not meet standards of acceptability."
>
> Against this perception of the constitutional policies involved, we discern certain more particularized considerations that peculiarly call for reversal of this conviction. First, the principle contended for by the State seems inherently boundless. How is one to distinguish this from any other offensive word [emblem]? Surely the State has no right to cleanse public debate to the point where it is grammatically palatable to the most squeamish among us. Yet no readily ascertainable general principle exists for stopping short of that result were we to affirm the judgment below. For, while the particular four-letter word [emblem] being litigated here is perhaps· more distasteful than most others of its genre, it is nevertheless often true that one man's vulgarity is another's lyric. Indeed, we think it is largely because governmental officials cannot make principled distinctions in this area that the Constitution leaves matters of taste and style so largely to the individual.
>
> Finally, and in the same vein, we cannot indulge the facile assumption that one can forbid particular words without also running a substantial risk of suppressing ideas in the process. Indeed, governments might soon seize upon the censorship of particular words [emblems] as a convenient guise for banning the expression of unpopular views. We

have been able, as noted above, to discern little social benefit that might result from running the risk of opening the door to such grave results.

The display of the swastika, as offensive to the principles of a free nation as the memories it recalls may be, is symbolic political speech intended to convey to the public the beliefs of those who display it. It does not, in our opinion, fall within the definition of "fighting words," and that doctrine cannot be used here to overcome the heavy presumption against the constitutional validity of a prior restraint.

Nor can we find that the swastika, while not representing fighting words, is nevertheless so offensive and peace threatening to the public that its display can be enjoined. We do not doubt that the sight of this symbol is abhorrent to the Jewish citizens of Skokie, and that the survivors of the Nazi persecutions, tormented by their recollections, may have strong feelings regarding its display. Yet it is entirely clear that this factor does not justify enjoining defendants' speech. . . .

In summary, as we read the controlling Supreme Court opinions, use of the swastika is a symbolic form of free speech entitled to first amendment protections. Its display on uniforms or banners by those engaged in peaceful demonstrations cannot be totally precluded solely because that display may provoke a violent reaction by those who view it. Particularly is this true where, as here, there has been advance notice by the demonstrators of their plans so that they have become, as the complaint alleges, "common knowledge" and those to whom sight of the swastika banner or uniforms would be offense are forewarned and need not view them. A speaker who gives prior notice of his message has not compelled a confrontation with those who voluntarily listen.

As to those who happen to be in a position to be involuntarily confronted with the swastika, the following observations from *Erznoznik* v. *City of Jacksonville* (1975), 422 U.S. 205, are appropriate:

> The plain, if at all times disquieting, truth is that in our pluralistic society, constantly proliferating new and ingenious forms of expression, "we are inescapably captive audiences for many purposes." Much that we encounter offends our esthetic, if not our political and moral, sensibilities. Nevertheless, the Constitution does not permit government to decide which types of otherwise protected speech are sufficiently offensive to require protection for the unwilling listener or viewer. Rather, absent the narrow circumstances decribed above [home intrusion or captive audience], the burden normally falls upon the viewer to "avoid further bombardment of [his] sensibilities simply by averting [his] eyes."

Thus by placing the burden upon the viewer to avoid further bombardment, the Supreme Court has permitted speakers to justify the initial intrusion into the citizen's sensibilities.

We accordingly, albeit reluctantly, conclude that the display of the swastika cannot be enjoined under the fighting-words exception to free speech, nor can anticipation of a hostile audience justify the prior restraint. Furthermore, *Cohen* and *Erznoznik* direct the citizens of Skokie that it is their burden to avoid the offensive symbol if they can do so without unreasonable inconvenience. Accordingly, we are constrained to reverse that part of the appellate court judgment enjoining the display of the swastika. That judgment is in all other respects affirmed.

16 FREDERICK SCHAUER

FREE SPEECH AND THE PARADOX OF TOLERANCE

In an important footnote in *The Open Society and Its Enemies,* Karl Popper poses what he calls "the paradox of tolerance."[1] If the political and legal doctrine of freedom of speech is intended to permit the continuing reexamination of received opinions to identify and to expose error, then it may be paradoxical to allow such freedom to those who would use it to eliminate the very process that justifies free speech as a distinct principle. There exist individuals or groups who believe that freedom of speech, or freedom in a more general sense, should be eliminated or greatly curtailed. Allowing freedom of speech to such people, it is argued, is allowing freedom of speech to be used for its own destruction. By permitting such individuals or groups to speak, we increase the probability of their gaining power (or so the paradox presumes), thereby undermining the epistemological process that generates the free speech principle. The purpose of this paper is to subject this seeming paradox to critical examination. The goal is to determine whether or not freedom of speech, where it obtains as a distinct legal doctrine, should be available to those who would, were they in power, eliminate or significantly restrict the liberty of speech upon which they now rely.

The problem presented by the paradox is more than hypothetical. The argument from the paradox has been used in England by those who seek statutes, regulations, judicial decisions, or enforcement practices restricting the activities of the National Front. In the United States the same argument was relied upon by those who sought (unsuccessfully)[2] to ban the march of the American Nazi Party in Skokie, Illinois. It is an argument that has been and is to some extent still employed in opposing free speech for Communists and others of the political left. And, perhaps

Copyright 1981, Frederick Schauer. This is the first publication of this article.
    This essay was originally presented at a conference of the Royal Institute of Philosophy in Lancaster, England, September 14, 1979. The author is indebted to Mary Jane Morrison for helpful comments on an earlier draft.
[1] K. Popper, *The Open Society and Its Enemies,* 5th ed. (London: Routledge & Kegan Paul, 1966), vol. 1, p. 265.
[2] *National Socialist Party* v. *Skokie,* 432 U.S. 43 (1977); *Smith* v. *Collin,* 437 U.S. 98 S.Ct. 3085 (1978).

most importantly, it is a principle that has been specifically embodied in Article 30 of the Universal Declaration of Human Rights of 1948 and Article 17 of the European Convention on Human Rights, the latter providing that "Nothing in this Convention may be interpreted as implying for any State, group, or person any right to engage in any activity or perform any act aimed at the destruction of any of the rights and freedoms set forth herein or at their limitation to a greater extent than is provided for in the Convention." In 1957 this article formed the basis of a decision of the European Commission of Human Rights upholding the outlawing of the German Communist Party in the face of an objection based on Articles 10 and 11, which guarantees freedom of expression and association.[3] The Bonn Constitution of 1949 contains a provision similar to Article 17, and this was used in 1951 to support the outlawing of the Sozialistische Reichspartei, a neo-Nazi party.[4]

Suppose that there is a group whose members believe that society will best be served if national unity and cooperation are treated as preeminent values, that one of the group's central policies is that this goal is fostered by the forcible elimination of dissent from officially prevailing views in politics, philosophy, morals, and science, that this policy is inseparable from the group's overall political aims, and that this is a policy advocated by all members of the group in public discourse. Let us call this hypothetical group the National Unity League. The question is whether or not, where free speech is recognized as both a legal principle and a positive political value, it is a freedom that should include the speech here described.

The paradox thus presented points up the ambiguity surrounding most references to the principle of free speech. Where freedom of speech has specific grounding in a written constitution, as in the United States, the legal and political uses of the term merge, and the scope and force of the free speech principle are recurrent issues in adjudication. Because in Great Britain freedom of speech is not part of a written constitution, and because free speech principles do not therefore act as a legal restriction on legislative power, freedom of speech has been described as "residual" or "extra-legal." [5] Such descriptions are misleading, however, for they imply that freedom of speech does not have the force or effect ascribed to other legal doctrines and that free speech is thus more the concern of political theorists than of lawyers. But, in some areas of law, development of common law principles has and continues to be controlled or at least influenced by the principles of freedom of speech. Sedition, blasphemy, contempt, and defamation, particularly the defense of fair comment, are examples. In other areas, free speech principles are incorporated in statutes or are essential in application of those statutes. In either case interpretation of the doctrine of free speech is necessary. Examples would be obscenity, incitement to racial hatred,

---

[3] Case No. 250/57, 20 July 1957, Yearbook 1, p. 222.
[4] See F. Castberg, Freedom of Speech in the West (New York: Oceana Pubs., 1960), pp. 378, 387–390.
[5] See G. Williams, "The Concept of Legal Liberty," in R. Summers, ed., Essays in Legal Philosophy (Oxford: Basil Blackwell, 1970), pp. 121–123; O. H. Phillips, Constitutional and Administrative Law (London: Sweet & Maxwell, 1973), p. 415.

and (perhaps) official secrets. Finally, freedom of speech is *perceived* by Parliament as a limitation'on legislative power and is thus a significant factor in the drafting of legislation. Yet, as long as the ambiguity in the concept of free speech remains unresolved, there is little hope that this doctrine can be applied rationally and consistently to concrete issues. The paradox of tolerance presents this very problem.

In saying that freedom of speech is ambiguous, I mean that that term can be taken to refer to any one of several rather different concepts. The problem is not merely that there can be numerous different conceptions or applications of the same concept but, rather, that the underlying concepts themselves may be quite similar. Because both the meaning and the application of a doctrine turn on the philosophical underpinnings of that doctrine, it is impossible to apply the doctrine of free speech to difficult problems unless we have some idea of its deeper purpose. Where several different possibilities are available, the selection among those possibilities determines the scope of the liberty, in the issue under discussion as well as for most other potential applications of the free speech principle.

Popper generates his paradox by presuming that the deep theory, to use Ronald Dworkin's expression, of the free speech principle is that freedom of speech is essential to the advancement of human knowledge. Whether this occurs by the identification of objective truth, as for example under the traditional theories of Milton and Locke, or instead by the identification of error, as Mill and Popper argue, is not germane to the point under discussion. Either formulation of the theory adopts the proposition that unimpeded discussion is most likely to lead to an increase in knowledge, to some more desirable epistemic state. For the sake of simplicity I will refer to this argument as the argument from truth. It may be that truth is a good in itself, as J. M. Finnis has recently argued.[6] On the other hand, knowledge or truth may be merely instrumental to utility or some other social goal. But this dispute is not particularly relevant here. We may take the advancement of knowledge as desirable, without further discussion. The argument from truth is based on the relationship of freedom of speech to the attainment of this goal. But it does not hold that open discussion is a sufficient condition for the identification of truth. Such a view is epistemologically untenable. Nor does it follow that free speech is even a necessary condition for the advance of knowledge. As Geoffrey Marshall has said, "We have at the moment rational assurance that the earth is roundish in shape from photographs produced by astronauts, and we should still have it if the Flat Earth Society were an illegal organization."[7] What *is* contended is that freedom of opinion and contradiction are *in general* extremely valuable in assisting the growth of knowledge and should be protected for that reason alone.

Under this view freedom of speech is not so much an individual interest as it is a societal interest. Society as a whole benefits when

---

[6] J. M. Finnis, "Scepticism, Self-refutation, and the Good of Truth," in P. M. S. Hacker and J. Raz, eds., *Law, Morality, and Society* (Oxford: Clarendon Press, 1977), pp. 247–267.
[7] G. Marshall, *Constitutional Theory* (Oxford: Clarendon Press, 1971), p. 158.

knowledge advances. Under this theory we recognize free speech as an individual legal liberty only instrumentally, because by so doing we most effectively encourage the diversity of opinion that benefits society and upon which the argument from truth arises. Additionally, the argument relies upon a rather profound scepticism. Following both Mill and Popper, we are encouraged to allow the expression of any opinion, regardless of its apparent error, because there is always a possibility that such opinion is correct and the received opinion is wrong. Only by allowing the expression of all views do we account for the possibility that knowledge may advance by the identification of error in received views, resulting in the replacement of falsehood by something that, if not certainly true, is at least more likely true.

There are both strong and weak versions of the argument from truth, but under either version the speech of our hypothetical National Unity League would properly be excluded from the application of the free speech principle. The weak version recognizes that, although we may never achieve certainty, we can still have more confidence in the truth of some views than we have in others. It is at bottom a probabilist epistemology. Thus we allow the expression of the dissenting view because of the *possibility* that it might be correct and the received view erroneous. But we must recognize that, in most cases where there is a *possibility* that the dissenting view is correct, there is a *probability* that it is incorrect. To take our example, the fact that there may be a remote possibility that the precepts of the National Unity League represent correct doctrine still means that there is a probability that such doctrine is incorrect. Therefore we must balance the advantages to society flowing from the possibility of its truth (gaining and acting on new knowledge) against the social disadvantages of the free expression of an incorrect view (the likelihood being that this incorrect view will in fact influence people to act in accordance with it). In statistical terms, we are looking at the expected value of tolerance and comparing it with the expected value of suppression. If we assume that truth is immediately evident to everyone, then there is no risk, because there is no possibility that the incorrect view will influence anyone. But such naïveté needs no further discussion. It is much more reasonable to say that some propositions are more likely true than others and that false ideas may have harmful effects. If this is so, then on this weak version of the argument from truth certain views will be so likely false *and* harmful that the balance will be against allowing their expression.

Under the strong version of the argument from truth, we elevate the goal of increased knowledge to a position of lexical priority (in the Rawlsian sense) over all other values. Here even the remotest possibility that the rejected doctrine is in fact correct requires that we not suppress it, because no harm flowing from the expression of the opinion can be great enough to outweigh the possibility of losing even the smallest bit of knowledge. Superficially then, the strong version of the argument from truth would suggest that we tolerate the National Unity League despite the likelihood that its opinions are of no value and despite the fact that its position is a position against freedom. But we must look deeper. This strong version holds that *no* view is immune from error. And if no opinion is immune from error, then the process of reexamining received opinion must remain open if knowledge is to advance. If we allow the propagation of the view that dissent must be suppressed, and if this tolerance may in fact lead to acceptance of intolerance as prevailing doctrine, then we are undermining our long-run goal, as the process of continuing reexamination of accepted doctrine is essential for the progress of knowledge. Upholding this process and establishing the advance of knowledge as our preeminent goal means that we must take the process *a priori*. The one infallible opinion is the belief in our fallibility. Hence, any speech inconsistent with this *a priori* proposition would be outside the scope of the free speech principle and ought to be suppressed.

Therefore, either version of the argument from truth would permit the suppression of the views of those who would argue against the continuance of a system of free speech. It is not that members of the National Unity League have no title to claim rights under a principle in which they do not believe, although Rawls and others have persuasively argued this position.[8] It is rather that the argument from truth is parasitic upon an epistemic process. Speech that is inconsistent with the process cannot with consistency be allowed protection by the legal rights that are derived from the process.

But the argument from truth is not the only concept to which the locution "freedom of speech" may refer. Rather than using the words "free speech" to refer to a system of epistemic advancement, we may mean instead a system in which governmental decisions are directly or indirectly based on the will of the people expressed through some form of free elections. Many different systems would fit this broad definition. At the risk of suggesting problems not relevant here, I will call this system "democracy" and the free speech principle derived from it the "argument from democracy." Under the argument from democracy, free speech is a necessary condition to the effective operation of the democratic process, serving to inform the electorate of facts and opinions relevant to choices that are to be made *by* the electorate. The argument from democracy incorporates a consensus epistemology, holding that *political* truth is defined as that which commands the support of the body politic. Under such a theory, speech relating to public issues must be free, because it is the people and not their servants, the public officials, who decide among disputed issues of political doctrine or the qualifications of public officials. This concept of free speech explains the deference we pay to freedom of speech in developing the law of defamation, especially the defense of fair comment. In the United States, the argument from democracy has generated the much broader *privilege* to attack public policy and public officials, a privilege first established in the leading case of *The New York Times Co.* v. *Sullivan*.[9] Under the argument from democracy, speech in the public domain is protected, not because it may or may not lead to truth, but because it is relevant to decision making by the public. As Denis Lloyd has expressed it, free

[8] See J. Rawls, *A Theory of Justice* (Cambridge, Mass.: Harvard University Press, 1971), pp. 216—221.
[9] 376 U.S. 254 (1964).

speech gives us the "possibility of developing and crystallizing public opinion, and allowing it to be brought to bear upon the governmental organs of the state." [10]

The argument from democracy would again seem at first glance to require the tolerance of expression even by those who would oppress others, or who would eliminate free speech, such as the National Unity League. This view of democracy may leave to the electorate the decision of which political theory to adopt, be it democracy, fascism, nazism, communism, or whatever. Under this theory, which recognizes equal rights of political participation, the political views of members of the National Unity League, for example, could not be denied expression any more than they could be denied the right to vote.

But again it is necessary to go back to the *a priori* assumptions of the argument from democracy. If government by the people is the basis of this argument, then this is the deep theory that occupies the same position here that scepticism or fallibilism occupied in the argument from truth. It would be illogical under the argument from democracy to allow the expression of views inconsistent with the democratic process, as only the value of ensuring the optimal operation of the democratic process mandates the heightened protection of the expression of opinion. If the protection of speech is instrumental to the protection of democracy, then speech that would undermine democracy has no title to protection.

Both the argument from truth and the argument from democracy are, as I have said, based on societal rather than on individual interests. They are not theories of "rights" or "liberties" in any strong sense, because they are not based on any underlying moral or political notion of an *individual* right against the state. In *application,* both the argument from truth and the argument from democracy generate rights against the state, but only because the creation of such rights serves the long-run interest of society as a whole. These are individual rights theories only indirectly. They do not hold that an individual right is superior to the public interest. Individual rights are here created only so that we are not led to sacrifice the long-run public interest to ephemeral views of the short-run public interest. Under the argument from truth and the argument from democracy, free speech is a right only in a positivist and rather weak sense.

A *stronger* version of free speech as a right is seen in the writings of Professor Dworkin. Dworkin and others, such as David Richards,[11] view freedom of speech as an individual moral right that emerges as a legal right because of the individual's moral right to speak, not because of society's overall interest in the product of that speech. Under this view, free speech is protected, not because it is instrumental to any societal good, but because it inheres in people solely by virtue of their being people.

This view of freedom of speech best supports the alternative terminology, "freedom of expression." This is the term that is used, for ex-

---

10 D. Lloyd, *The Idea of Law* (London: Penguin Books, 1964), p. 152.
11 D. A. Richards, "Free Speech and Obscenity Law: Toward a Moral Theory of the First Amendment," *University of Pennsylvania Law Review* 123 (1974): 45.

ample, in Article 10 of the European Convention on Human Rights. This terminology adds an additional ambiguity, however, because there are two quite different senses of the word "expression." If I purchase a color television set that produces a picture only in black and white, I may *express* my dissatisfaction to the merchant who sold me the television set. In this sense "expression" is virtually synonymous with "communication." But I may also *express* my anger by throwing a paperweight through the television screen. Used in this sense, "expression" is not communicative. Here we are talking about *self-expression*, the external manifestation of some inner feeling or emotion. The confusion is compounded because expression in the first sense—communication—is one form of expression in the second sense—self-expression. Because both the argument from truth and the argument from democracy find their roots in the value of communicating ideas and information, freedom of speech is the more precise term to refer to either of these theories. Freedom of communication, or liberty of communication, would be even better, because we are actually talking about a liberty in the strict sense and because it is possible to communicate nonlinguistically, as with pictures, flags, or black armbands. But the individual rights theory of free speech is a *free expression* theory, in the second sense of "expression," because it is based on a person's right of expression, regardless of whether there is a listener, regardless of the value of what is expressed, and regardless of whether the particular expression adds to the store of human knowledge. Under this individual exprssion theory, free speech or free communication is but one component of a broader conception of liberty, and it is not surprising, therefore, that many who adopt such a view find free speech in the same philosophical base in which they find many other forms of individuality, such as the right to engage in private homosexual conduct or the right to be free of state interference with personal appearance.[12]

Under this individual liberty interpretation of the concept of free speech, it would seem more likely that we would want to protect the speech of our hypothetical totalitarian organization, the National Unity League. Because it is the personal rights of the members that form the basis of the free speech claim, denying that right is denying them the right to equal respect for their views that is at the heart of this libertarian concept of freedom of speech. But, although Professor Dworkin and other individualist theorists take this very position,[13] it is possible to argue that here again speech that is or may be inconsistent with liberty has no claim on libertarian theory. If liberty in the broad sense is the given, then speech that jeopardizes that liberty is subject to restriction for the very same reasons that both the argument from truth and the argument from democracy may use to prohibit speech that jeopardizes the process of searching for truth or the process of democratic government. Moreover, if the basis of the individual rights theory is a Rawlsian conception of maximum liberty consistent with an equal liberty for all,

[12] See R. Dworkin, *Taking Rights Seriously* (London: Duckworth, 1977), 184–205, 240–278.
[13] See R. Dworkin, *The New York Review of Books*, 7 December 1978, p. 41.

then speech that does in fact have a tendency to reduce liberty for others, or speech that denies others equal respect, may have no claim to protection under the theory.[14]

Here, as before, a closer look at the theory underlying "free speech" leads to a more precise definition of the right. And in many instances, as with that under discussion, the more precise definition of the right excludes the problem case and dissolves the paradox.

There is another concept of freedom of speech, however, that leads to the contrary conclusion. This interpretation denies that speech has any particular value, at least not such great value as to justify the heightened protection that we normally associate with the free speech principle. This concept does hold, however, that governing authorities ought to have less power to regulate speech than they have to regulate other forms of human conduct. The reasons for this are varied and are often more intuitive than strictly empirical. But part of this rationale is a seeming human inclination *against* dissent and criticism, as well as the related observation that slippery-slope arguments appear to have more validity when we are talking about regulating speech than when other objects of regulation are at issue. If these observations are true, then speech should be given greater protection than is given to other forms of conduct merely to ensure against the dangers of overregulation. Under this theory, free speech emerges by negative implication—speech is protected not so much because speech is good but because its regulation is bad.

If this is indeed the justification for freedom of speech, then we have quite a different concept, and we must reformulate the paradox of tolerance. The issue now is not whether the intolerant should be allowed to speak in support of their intolerance, but whether and under what circumstances society can allow some officials to decide who shall speak and who shall not. It is a question of allocation of power. The question is *who* should decide issues of political truth and *who* should decide when some one or some group has forfeited the protection of the free speech principle. As a question of allocation of power, free speech is most conspicuously a question of constitutional law.

Under this view, the resolution of the paradox differs from the resolution reached under other concepts of free speech. For here the regulation of the speech in question is the very evil at which the principle of free speech is addressed. The issue is not whether totalitarian groups should be allowed to speak, but whether anyone should have the power to decide which groups are totalitarian and which are not—whether we can with confidence entrust to a licensing authority, to a county council, or to a court the power to withhold privileges from groups because they are *perceived* as being totalitarian, antidemocratic, or fascist. It is an argument based on experience, history, psychology, and strategy as much as it is a philosophical argument. It is grounded, ultimately, on the idea that we must overprotect speech to make sure that we are not underprotecting it. It recognizes that much speech, such as that at issue here, is not in fact worth protecting. But it also recognizes that, even if

[14] See Richards, *op. cit.*

we can say in some instances that some speech can be identified as harmful or worthless, we cannot have any confidence in any institution we might establish to make that determination on a regular basis. Although referring only to the issue of truth, Joel Feinberg has put it well: "There are serious risks involved in granting any mere man or group of men the power to draw the line between those opinions that are known infallibly to be true and those not so known, in order to bar expression of the former. Surely, if there is one thing that is *not* infallibly known, it is how to draw that line." [15] It is obvious that we must draw lines in all areas of law. But the instant argument is based on the presumption that drawing lines is more difficult here than in other areas. If this is indeed the case, then our inability to discriminate between valuable and worthless utterances leads us to grant a measure of strategic protection we would not grant if we were as confident of our ability to determine unprotected speech as we are of our ability to determine whether other types of conduct should be unprotected.

One important point needs to be mentioned. In each scenario I have described, it is assumed that the expression of the totalitarian views at issue *will* substantially increase the likelihood of those views predominating. I have in each case assumed a substantial risk to whatever underlying goal is taken to support the right to freedom of speech. But these assumptions as to cause and effect conceal a major issue. If any concept of free speech is to be meaningful, our use of that concept must imply that a legislature or court is less free to regulate speech than it is to regulate any other activity, at least activity not protected by a right of equivalent strength. That is, free speech means that government is to some extent precluded from dealing with harms or effects caused by speech even though it could, as a matter of that government's general political theory, deal with the same or commensurate harms caused by other means. Thomas Scanlon has previously noted this essential feature of free speech doctrine,[16] and it underlies the clear and present danger principle in American free speech doctrine.[17] This is consistent with the view of free speech rights as *immunities* in the Hohfeldian sense. An immunity need not be absolute. But at the very least it does mean that the legislature or a court is *less free* to restrict certain forms of activity. The corollary is that the individual is *more free* to engage in that activity. Awkward as it may sound to ears accustomed to ordinary usage, it is possible here to be more or less immune. A right in the sense that I use it here means that a citizen is more immune from state control when he or she engages in speech, for example, than when he or she engages in other forms of conduct, because the state has a greater burden of justification. It must have a better reason. Reasons that are normally good enough will not be good enough if it is speech that is being restricted. Without this concept free speech is merely a platitude.

Thus, even if under some concept of free speech the expression of

[15] J. Feinberg, "Limits to the Free Expression of Opinion," in J. Feinberg and H. Gross, eds., *Philosophy of Law* (Encino, Calif.: Dickenson, 1975), p. 136.
[16] T. Scanlon, "A Theory of Freedom of Expression," *Philosophy & Public Affairs* 1 (1972): 204.
[17] *Schenck* v. *United States*, 249 U.S. 47 (1919), per Holmes, J.

antifreedom views is basis enough for suppression, the burden of proof concerning the likelihood of the effect that justifies the restriction is greater than would otherwise be required. It is not enough to hypothesize that expression of antifreedom views might have the effect of lessening freedom. It must be quite clearly established that this is the case. To require less is to fail to recognize the deeper meaning of the concept of an immunity right. *Any* view of free speech allows its restriction if certain harms can be shown to flow from the speech in question. The paradox of tolerance does not show that under some theories this standard of proof may be relaxed. It shows only that a particular effect is entitled to be counted among the harms that justify restrictions on freedom of speech.

I have presented the paradox of tolerance from the perspective of four concepts of free speech. The resolution of the paradox of tolerance is but an example of the way in which the application of the principle varies with the concept of that principle that is perceived as its base. To assume that free speech has one and only one meaning is a significant mistake. And, if I may conclude on a word of practical warning, it is therefore a mistake to borrow or use the words of a doctrine without understanding the underlying concept. To suggest, for example, that free speech protection may conveniently be transposed from the European Convention on Human Rights to English law is to make this very mistake. To borrow the words without having a deeper theory of why those words are being used is to stumble in the dark.

JOEL FEINBERG 17

OBSCENITY, PORNOGRAPHY, AND THE ARTS: SORTING THINGS OUT

Should pornography be forbidden? Many say "no," if only for fear that prohibition would lead to censorship of genuine works of art. Others say "yes," at least partly on the ground that pornography is "obscene." A careful examination of the arguments on both sides often reveals a lamentable failure to communicate at all because of different and clashing understandings of what obscenity, pornography, and works of art are. Often, too, the arguments are unconvincing because of subtle equivocations in the slippery terms "obscene," "pornography," and "art." The essay that follows is primarily an exercise in definition, or "conceptual analysis," an effort to obviate at least those confusions in the debate that are avoidable by carefully sorting out the key concepts involved.[1]

1. IS PORNOGRAPHY OBSCENE?

There is no more unfortunate mistake in the discussion of obscenity than simply to identify that concept, either in meaning or in scope of designation, with pornography.[2] To call something obscene, in the standard use of the term, is to condemn that thing as shockingly vulgar or blatantly disgusting. So understood, the term is used either to state that the object is apt to cause widespread offense, or to endorse offense as an appropriate reaction to it, or both. The corresponding term "pornographic," on the other hand, is a purely descriptive word referring to sexually explicit writing and pictures designed entirely and plausibly to induce sexual excitement in the reader or observer. To use the terms "obscene" and "pornographic" interchangeably, then, as if they referred to precisely the same things, is to beg the essentially controversial question of whether any or all (or only) pornographic materials really are obscene. Surely, to those thousands or millions of persons who delight in pornographic books, pictures, and films, the objects of their attachment do not seem disgusting or obscene. If these materials are nevertheless "truly obscene," they are not so merely by virtue of the definitions of the terms "obscene" and "pornography" but rather by virtue of their blatant violation of some relevant standards, and to establish their obscenity requires serious argument and persuasion. In short, whether any given acknowledged bit of pornography is *really* obscene is a logically open question to be settled by argument, not by definitional fiat.

Oddly enough the U.S. Supreme Court has committed itself to a different usage. In searching for definitions and tests of what it calls "obscenity," it has clearly had on its collective mind only verbal, pictorial, and dramatic materials and exhibitions designed effectively to be instruments of erotic arousal. "Obscene" has thus come to *mean* "pornographic" in the court's parlance. Justice Harlan quite explicitly

[1] The two paragraphs that follow are drawn with only minor changes from my article "Pornography and the Criminal Law," *University of Pittsburgh Law Review* 40 (1979) : 567ff.

[2] High on the honor roll of those who have *not* made this pernicious error is the late Paul Goodman, who wrote in his article "Pornography, Art, and Censorship" [reprinted in D. A. Hughes, ed., *Perspectives on Pornography*, (New York: St. Martin's Press, 1970), pp. 42–60] that "The pornographic is not *ipso facto* the obscene" but, rather, simply that which is designed and used for the purpose of arousing sexual desires. But "if the stirring of desire is *defined* [emphasis added], and therefore treated, as obscene, how can a normal person's interest in sex be anything *but* shameful? This is what shame is, the blush at finding one's impulse to be unacceptable. . . . So the court [by treating pornography as *ipso facto* obscene] corrupts. It is a miserable social policy." The honor roll also includes Stanley Edgar Hyman, whose essay "In Defense of Pornography" also is reprinted in the Hughes collection; David A. J. Richards, *The Moral Criticism of Law* (Belmont, Cailf.: Wadsworth, 1977); and Frederick F. Schauer, *The Law of Obscenity* (Washington, D.C.: Bureau of National Affairs, 1976).

underwrote this usage in *Cohen* v. *California* in 1971.[3] Robert Paul
Cohen had been convicted in a county court of disturbing the peace by
wearing a jacket emblazoned on its back with the words "Fuck the
Draft." When the U.S. Supreme Court considered his appeal, Harlan
wrote:

> This is not . . . an obscenity case. Whatever else may be necessary to give
> rise to the State's broader power to prohibit obscene expression, such
> expression must be, in some way, erotic. It cannot plausibly be maintained
> that this vulgar allusion to the Selective Service System would conjure
> up such psychic stimulation in anyone likely to be confronted with Cohen's
> crudely defaced jacket.[4]

If only erotic uses of language can be "obscene," then the most typical
uses of the tabooed vocabulary of "dirty words" (for example, in angry
insults) are not in the slightest degree obscene—an absurd consequence
that the Court is apparently prepared to live with.

An even more bizarre instance of this distorted usage comes from a
lower court that was committed to follow the Supreme Court's example.
In the 1977 case, *Connecticut* v. *Anonymous*,[5] a high school student appealed his conviction under a statute that declares it to be criminal to
make an "obscene gesture." The youth in this case had rashly insulted
the occupants of a police cruiser. The gesture in question, in which one
extends the middle finger, is an ancient form of insult called "giving
the finger." The appellate court decreed that the gesture was not
obscene (not even in the sense intended in the statute) because "to be
obscene, the expression must be in a significant way erotic . . . . It can
hardly be said that the finger gesture is likely to arouse sexual desire.
The more likely response is anger." The reason why this opinion fills the
ordinary reader with amazement is that, given the ordinary associations
of the term "obscene" with offensiveness (disgust, shock to sensibility,
etc.), the court seems to be saying that only sexy things can be offensive,
a judgment that is either plainly false (if it is an empirical description of
what things in fact offend people) or morally perverse (if it is a judgment about what kinds of things are appropriate objects of offense).

2. PORNOGRAPHIC WRITING VERSUS
LITERARY AND DRAMATIC ART

A more difficult definitional tangle confronts writers who attempt to
state (in a non-question-begging way) the relation between pornography,
on the one hand, and the arts of literature and drama, on the other.
Works of literature do have one thing in common, at least, with works
of pornography: they both are found in books. But that is hardly sufficient to establish their identity, or even to relate them closely as
species of some common, and theoretically interesting, genus. Books,

[3] 91 S.Ct. 1780 (1971).
[4] *Ibid.*
[5] 377 A.2d 1342.

after all, are an enormously heterogenous lot. Cookbooks contain recipes for preparing meals; telephone books enable one to discover the telephone numbers of friends or business firms; dictionaries explain meanings of words and prescribe standard spellings; pornographic books induce sexual desire; novels, plays, and short stories . . . . Well, works of literature are something else again. The question that has divided literary citics into disputing factions is, "To what extent may pornography be judged as legitimate literature rather than merely ersatz eroticism?" [6] But this question, which has also interested the courts, presupposes an inquiry into the characteristic, and hence defining, functions of pornographic and literary works, whether books, plays, or films. [7]

The three leading answers to the question whether pornography can be literature are (1) that pornography and literature are as different from one another as novels are from telephone books, but that pornography (like telephone books) can be useful, for all that, provided only that it not be confused with literature; (2) that pornography is a corruption or perversion of genuine literature, properly judged by literary standards, and always found wanting; (3) that pornography is, or can be, a form of literature properly judged by literary standards, and sometimes properly assigned high literary merit by those standards. The debate is easily confused by the fact that there can be within the same work a criss-cross or overlap of "characteristic functions." An undoubted work of literature can incidentally excite sexual longing in the reader just as it can arouse anger, pity, or any other passion. And an undoubted work of pornography—pure hard-core pornography—may here and there contain a line of poetic elegance and be "well written" throughout. Moreover, books of one kind can be put to the "characteristic use" of books of another kind: one could masturbate to passages in Joyce, Lawrence, or the Old Testament, for example. [8] But then one can also use a novel as a guide to correct spelling (though that does not make novels into cryptodictionaries), or, for that matter, to sit on, or to prop doors open. Despite these unavoidable overlaps of properties and uses, one can hope, in principle, to describe accurately the characteristic functions of works of different kinds. Novels can be used as dictionaries and works of pornography as door props, but that is not what each is primarily *for*.

The most persuasive advocate of the first view of the relation between pornography and literature (and a writer who has in fact persuaded me) is Anthony Burgess. He is well worth quoting at length.

A pornographic work represents social acts of sex, frequently of a perverse or wholly fantastic nature, often without consulting the limits

[6] Douglas A. Hughes, ed., *Introduction to Perspectives on Pornography* (New York: St. Martin's Press, 1970), p. xiv.
[7] Precisely parallel questions can be raised, of course, about the characteristic features of pictorial art (painting and sculpture) and pornographic pictures.
[8] There are no doubt some strange souls, somewhere or other, at some time or other, who have found even dictionaries, cookbooks, and telephone books useful aids to masturbation. See Earl Finbar Murphy, "The Value of Pornography," *Wayne Law Review* 10 (1964): 655ff. for some amazing examples. There is hardly any limit to human differences, especially sexual differences. But that fact should not hinder efforts at definitions and classification.

of physical possibility. Such works encourage solitary fantasy, which is then usually quite harmlessly discharged in masturbation. A pornographic book is, then, an instrument for procuring a sexual catharsis, but it rarely promotes the desire to achieve this through a social mode, an act of erotic congress: the book is, in a sense, a substitute for a sexual partner.[9]

Burgess, of course, is talking about what other writers[10] have called "hard-core pornography" as opposed to "erotiç realism." The former is the name of a category of materials (books, pamphlets, pictures, and films), now amounting to a flood, that make no claim, however indirect, to serious literary or artistic purpose and simply portray very graphically, and with unrestrained explicitness and enthusiasm, sexual acts and objects for all tastes. Erotic realism, on the other hand, is a category of literature in which sexual events, desires, longings, and so on are portrayed, often vividly and often at length, but always as part of a serious literary effort to be true to life. Sexual thoughts and activities are, of course, a vitally important part of the lives of most people. They often determine who we are, whom we encounter, what happens to us, and in which direction our lives develop. Hence, they are naturally important, often supremely important, elements in the characterizations and plots of novels that are concerned to render truly the human condition, comment critically upon it, and evoke appropriate emotions in response to it. Works of hard-core pornography are not intended to do any of these things. Their aim is to excite sexually, and that is an end of the matter.

Hard-core pornography, Burgess reminds us, has something in common with what he calls "didactic works" of other kinds, for example, political propaganda in the form of fiction, stories whose whole purpose is to arouse anger at a tyrant, or revolutionary ardor, or charitable assistance.

A pornographic work and a didactic work (like Smile's *Self-help*) have this in common: they stimulate, and expect the discharge of the stimulation to be effected in real-life acts—acts of masturbation or acts of social import. They differ from a work of literature in that the purpose of literary art is to arouse emotions and discharge those emotions as part of the artistic experience. This is what Aristotle meant by his implied doctrine of catharsis . . . . If we read a book or see a play or film and are then driven to discharge the aroused emotion in some solitary or social act, then we have experienced good pornography or good didacticism but very bad art.[11]

In fact (to be more generous), we have not experienced (literary) art at all, just as when we find the number we want in a phone book we have

[9] Anthony Burgess, "What Is Pornography?" in Hughes, *op. cit.*, p. 5.
[10] Following E. and B. Kronhausen, *Pornography and the Law* (New York: Ballantine Books, 1959).
[11] Burgess, *op. cit.*, p. 6.

had a good "reference experience" but not a literary one. No one would think of confusing a telephone book with a novel; but the confusion of pornography with (erotic) literature is both common and pernicious. "Pornography," Burgess concludes, "is harmless so long as we do not corrupt our taste by mistaking it for literature." [12]

George Steiner, the leading spokesman for the second view, is less tolerant of pornography, perhaps because of his understandable impatience with the pretentious variety that mistakes itself for literature. To anyone who has surveyed the primary literature of hard-core pornography in any "adult" bookstore, Steiner's description of its standardly recurring features will seem right on target. He cites the limited number of basic themes and shrewdly notes how they correspond to the biological limitations on actual lovemaking, there being a severely limited number of "amorous orifices" in the human body, and "the mechanics of orgasm imply[ing] fairly rapid exhaustion and frequent intermission." [13] In any case, "dirty books are maddeningly the same." [14] Despite variations in trappings, race or class of the characters, or background settings, hard-core pornography always follows "highly conventionalized formulas of low-grade sadism [where one partner rejoices in his or her abject humiliation], excremental drollery, and banal fantasies of phallic prowess or feminine responsiveness. In its own way the stuff is as predictable as a Scout manual." [15] Or, we might add, as a dictionary or a telephone book.

High-grade pornography by well-known writers with literary pretentions, insofar as it too is pure pornography, does no better. Steiner's verdict here too will seem to hit the target to anyone who has struggled through the more egregious works of Henry Miller, Jean Genet, or William Burroughs. Speaking of an all-star collection of "high porn" called the *Olympia Reader,* Steiner's patience collapses: "After fifty pages of 'hardening nipples,' 'softly opening thighs,' and 'hot rivers' flowing in and out of the ecstatic anatomy, the spirit cries out, not in hypocritical outrage, not because I am a poor Square throttling my libido, but in pure, nauseous boredom. Even fornication cannot be as dull, as hopelessly predictable, as all that." [16] Fornication, of course, is by no means dull, unless one tries to make a full-time job out of it.

That "high porn" is still pure porn, no matter how you slice it, is a point well worth making in reply to all the pretentious critical hogwash that would find some mysterious literary merit in the same old stuff when served up by fashionable names. No one has made the point better than Steiner. And no one has documented more convincingly the harm to imagination, to taste, to language itself that can come from mistaking pornography for literature. But, for all that, Steiner's essay is no answer to Burgess. Literature is one thing, and pornography is another. If, nevertheless, pornography is judged by literary standards, it must always

---

[12] *Loc. cit.*
[13] George Steiner, "Night Words: High Pornography and Human Privacy," reprinted in Hughes, *op. cit.,* p. 97.
[14] *Ibid.,* p. 98.
[15] *Loc. cit.*
[16] *Ibid.,* p. 103.

get low marks, and if one persists in reading it and using it in the manner appropriate only to literature, then one converts it into hideously bad literature, and the results will be corrupting in a way common to *all* bad literature—slick westerns, soap operas, tear-jerkers, mass-produced mysteries, and Gothic romances. But there is no necessity that pornography by misconstrued in this way, and little evidence that it commonly is.

An able defender of the third view, Kenneth Tynan, defines pornography in the same way Burgess does, so that there is an apparent contrast between pornography and literature. Yet Tynan insists that when pornography is done well, that is to say, artfully, there is no reason to deny it the laudatory label of art. Pornography, he says, "is orgasmic in intent and untouched by the ulterior motives of traditional art. It has a simple and localized purpose: to induce an erection [or, presumably, the corresponding effect in women, a substantial consumers' group oddly forgotten by Tynan]. And the more skillfully the better."[17] So far, so good. There will be no objection yet from Burgess. Moreover, quite apart from the question of whether pornography can aspire to be literature without ceasing to be pornography, it can be quite valuable, and not merely "harmless," just for being what it is. Not everybody has a use for it, of course, any more than everybody needs a dictionary or a phone book, but it can be extremely useful for various well-defined classes of the population. Unlike some other writers,[18] Tynan fails to mention geriatric depressives and couples whose appetites lag to their own distress, but he does mention four other classes: First, those with minority tastes who cannot find like-minded mates; second, those who are "villainously ugly" of face or body and "unable to pay for the services of call girls";[19] third, "men on long journies, geographically cut off from wives and mistresses," for whom pornography can be "a portable memory, a welcome shortcut to remembered bliss, relieving tension without involving disloyalty";[20] and finally "uncommitted bachelors, arriving alone and short of cash in foreign cities where they don't speak the language."[21] This too is an important point, well made.

The next step in Tynan's argument is the one that makes a sharp break with both Burgess and Steiner:

> Because hard-core performs an obvious physical function, literary critics have traditionally refused to consider it a form of art. By their standards, art is something that appeals to such intangibles as the soul and the imagination; anything that appeals to the genitals belongs in the category of massage. What they forget is that language can be used in many delicate and complex ways to enliven the penis. It isn't just a matter of bombarding the reader with four letter words.[22]

[17] Kenneth Tynan, "Dirty Books Can Stay," in Hughes, *op. cit.*, p. 111.
[18] For example, Vivian Mercier, "Master Percy and/or Lady Chatterly," in Hughes, *op., cit.*, p. 24.
[19] Tynan, *op. cit.*, p. 112.
[20] *Loc. cit.*
[21] *Loc. cit.*
[22] *Ibid.*, p. 113.

It is a pity that Tynan neither quotes nor cites examples. The standard porn of the hard-core shops follows the patterns disclosed by Steiner so unswervingly that one suspects they were all composed by the same salacious computer. Readers are not simply bombarded with four-letter words; they are also assaulted by the same clichés—the trembling lips and cherry pink nipples, the open thighs and warm rivers of semen—in book after book. But what if hard-core pornography *were* done artfully? Would it be literature then in that (largely) hypothetical event?

There is a linguistic confusion underlying the question that is not easily sorted out. Almost *any* form of purposeful or creative human activity can be done either crudely or artfully. One can compose or perform music crudely or artfully; one can design or erect buildings crudely or artfully; one can write poems crudely or artfully. Music, architecture, and poetry are art forms. When they are done artfully, they are good music, architecture, or poetry; when done crudely, the result is (usually) bad music, architecture, or poetry. Bad art, however, is still art. A badly written novel is still a novel, and a badly composed photograph is still a photograph. On the other hand, one can make a phone book or dictionary crudely or artfully; one can mend a blouse or repair a carburetor crudely or artfully; one can throw a baseball or shoot a basket crudely or artfully. But it does not follow that reference compilation, repair work, and sports are art forms. Surely they are not among the fine arts.

Still it is possible, I suppose, for one to *think* of dictionary making, auto mechanics, and baseball as art forms. Professional practitioners may well think of their work as simply an occasion for artful enterprise and achievement. But, even if we grant that (with some reluctance), it does not follow that the artful construction of telephone books is *literature*, or that the artful repair of eroded buildings is *architecture*, or that the artful fielding of the second-base position is *ballet*. Nor does it follow that the artful "enlivening of the penis" with language is literature. "A thing is what it is, and not another thing."

3. ARTFUL PORNOGRAPHY: THE FILM *EMMANUELLE*

The recent films of the French director Just Jaeckin are perhaps as good examples of artful pornography as one can find. His 1973 film *Emmanuelle* became within a year the most profitable film in the history of the French movie industry, and his 1975 sequel, *The Story of O,* employing a similar formula, seems designed to break the record. Both films are produced with an artfulness that sets them off from almost all other essentially pornographic films. *Emmanuelle* is in many ways actually beautiful: It is set in exotic Bangkok whose picturesque streets and gorgeous gardens, and nearby jungles and mountains, are photographed with a wizardry that would win it awards if it were a travel documentary film. And, as one reviewer said of *The Story of O,* "It is filmed through delicate soft focuses and is so prettily presented that it might have been served up by Chanel." [23] The background music in *Emmanuelle* is sophisticated and erotic—perhaps the most suggestive music since Ravel's *Bolero*—and played sensitively by a full symphony orchestra. There are highly effective dance scenes, originally choreographed but in traditional Oriental patterns. For all its artfulness, however, *Emmanuelle* is no more a work of dramatic or literary art than a well-decorated and tastefully produced cookbook is a novel. Its sole theme or "plot" is the story of how the wife of an overworked French diplomat overcomes her boredom by abandoning herself to the sensual life with partners of all ages, genders, and races. Insofar as progression is suggested in the "story," it consists in her dawning appreciation at the end of the film of the attractions of group sex. Apart from that, the "story" is simply a hook on which to hang twelve or fifteen sexual adventures of the same stereotyped genres that are repeated monotonously in the literature of hard-core porn: coitus (as always punctuated with gasps and squeals) with a stranger in the darkness of a commercial airliner; coitus with another stranger in the locked restroom of the same plane; a sexual affair with another woman; a casual masturbation in a boring interval; a rough coitus act granted as a prize to the victor in a Siamese boxing match (here a touch of sadomasochism), a simultaneous sexual encounter with several men, and so on. The film clearly satisfies Steiner's criteria of pornography and equally clearly fails to satisfy the Burgess–Aristotle criterion of dramatic art. Not that it tries and fails; it fully succeeds in achieving what it sets out to do.

Pornographic as it is, however, *Emmanuelle* is in no obvious way obscene. Artfulness and obscenity do not sit easily together. Sex acts are filmed in shadowy pantomime; the details are simulated or merely suggested. There is no close-up camera work focusing on sex organs or the contact that stimulates them. Male sex organs are not shown at all. (This omission is typical of the double standard that generally prevails in works of pornography meant to sell to large general audiences. The commercial assumption is that the audiences are primarily *men* who will be titillated by scenes of female homosexuality but repelled or threatened by parallel episodes with men, or even by the unveiling of the masculine sex organ.) There is, in short, very little that is gross or obtrusive in the film, or likely to diminish its aphrodisiac effectiveness.

4. PORNOGRAPHIC PICTORIAL ART, POETRY, AND PROGRAM MUSIC

Although pornographic films and books, insofar as they are purely pornographic, can never aspire to the status of dramatic and literary art no matter how artfully they are produced, a quite different verdict seems to be required for pornographic pictorial art. That surprising result is no real paradox, however. Rather, it is explained by the em-

[23] Bernard Drew's review in Westchester-Rockland Newspapers (the Gannett chain), November 17, 1975.

pirical fact that the characteristic purposes of pictorial art and pornography can be jointly satisfied by one and the same picture. A painting
of a copulating couple that satisfied the relevant standards for good
painting would *ipso facto* be a work of pictorial art; it might be done in
exquisitely harmonizing color, with properly balanced composition,
subtlety of line, successful lighting effects, and depicted figures of
memorably graceful posture and facial expressiveness. Such a painting
might also be designed primarily to stimulate the genitals of the observer. Insofar as it also achieved that goal, it would be a work of pornography. The defining features of literature and pornography, however,
mutually exclude one another for the reasons given by Burgess. To be
sure, a long and complex literary work might contain whole sections
that are purely pornographic, or contain art and pornography in various
complex combinations and alternations. Such a work could be called both
literary and pornographic, just as a dictionary that contained chapters
of a novel between each alphabetical section would be both a dictionary
and a novel. But the literary and pornographic parts would be separate
and distinguishable, unlike the painting, which can be both pictorial
art and pure pornography at the same time and as a whole. The point
applies even more forcibly, I should think, to that rarer genre, pornographic program music. It is possible, I think, for a composer deliberately to set out to create a musical aphrodisiac and succeed in that aim,
and also in the same work to create a genuine piece of music, even a
work of high musical merit.

It is difficult to find any reason why a poem cannot in principle
satisfy high literary standards and also achieve the deliberate aim of
pornography, to arouse the reader. Very likely then lyric poetry should
be classified with pictorial art and program music in this respect rather
than with other species of literature. Still it is surpassingly difficult to find
clear and noncontroversial examples of works that are at once good or at
least serious poems and also effective pornographs; and that difficulty
may reside in the nature of the two objectives and natural impediments
to their successful cross-breeding. (Love poems, of course, are an altogether different matter.) [24] What *clearly* cannot be both literary art
and pornography, if the argument thus far is sound, are works that tell
stories and have subtly structured *plots*—short stories, novels, plays,
dramatic films. Tragedies cannot be erotically arousing on balance and
still achieve their essential goals, for the reasons given by Aristotle and
Burgess. Pathos can be gripping, edifying, and saddening, but it is not
possible for it to achieve its characteristic ends while also evoking
erotic feelings in the reader or observer. Comedy is especially incapable
of being pornography (though it may work its own purposes on erotic
materials), because a laugh is a "discharge within the work," not a cause

---

[24] No doubt a genuine love poem of high literary merit like the biblical "Song of
Songs" can be used pornographically, as any kind of thing can be used for a purpose
other than that for which it is made and which defines the kind of thing it is. On
this see E. F. Murphy, *op. cit.* It is more natural and less dogmatic, however, to
classify artful love poems that celebrate the joy of sexual love with pornographic
pictorial art that achieves genuine aesthetic merit and to attribute the relative scarcity
of the former to the greater difficulty of the genre.

of further tensions to be discharged in "real life acts." The funny bone is not a sex organ.

5. CAN PORNOGRAPHY BE ART?
THE MINIMAL RELEVANCE OF THE QUESTION

Interesting as the question may be for aestheticians and critics, why does it matter to a social philosopher whether pornography is art or something *sui generis*? Of course, insofar as American courts acknowledge a special social value, or "redeeming social importance" to works of art, even poor works of art, to that extent the relation between art and pornography is a question of vital practical importance. But interesting as the question is in its own right, and crucial as it may be for the application of American constitutional law, it has very little importance for the philosopher or social critic whose concern is to discover what restrictive legislation could be passed by an ideal legislature as determined by the morally correct principles for limiting individual liberty. One such principle is that severely offensive (disgusting, shocking, revolting) public behavior that is not reasonably avoidable may be prohibited as a kind of public nuisance. A legislature is generally thought to have the right to control offensive behavior, *within carefully circumscribed circumstances,* by means of the criminal law, even when that behavior (or depicted behavior) is not directly injurious to health or wealth. But what relevance to this right and its limits is there in the fact that the offensiveness in question is, or is not, attached inextricably to a work of art? After all, offensiveness is offensiveness whatever its source, and, if it is unavoidable offensiveness that confers the right of prohibition on the legislature, what relevance can the other characteristics of the offending object have?

There is surely *some* relevance in the fact that the offense stems from a work of art. Both the civil and the criminal law of nuisance empowers courts to weigh the degree (intensity and extent) of the offense caused by a given activity against the "reasonableness" of the offending conduct. One of the standards, in turn, for judging the reasonableness of offending or inconveniencing behavior is its general social utility, that is, "the social value which the law attaches to its ultimate purpose." [25] Just as in nuisance law offensive noises and smells are not prohibited when they are the unavoidable concomitants of the operations of a socially useful industry, but are enjoined when they are the products of merely private diversions of little social value,[26] so the criminal law might prohibit offensive materials and actions when they

[25] William Prosser, *Handbook of the Law of Torts,* 2nd ed. (St. Paul, Mo.: West Publishing Co., 1955), p. 411.

[26] As Prosser puts it, "The world must have factories, smelters, oil refineries, noisy machinery, and blasting, even at the expense of some inconvenience to those in the vicinity, and the plaintiff [in a civil suit] may be required to accept and tolerate some not unreasonable discomfort for the general good. . . . On the other hand, a foul pond, or a vicious or noisy dog will have little if any social value, and relatively slight annoyance from it may justify relief." *Ibid.,* p. 412.

have no further "redeeming" social function, but permit them when the offense is the side effect of a socially useful purpose. The fact that publicly offensive, sexually explicit materials happen also to be serious works of literature is relevant to the social utility of the offending conduct (the creating and exhibiting of the offensive work) insofar as serious literary and artistic endeavors have social value and deserve to be encouraged in the public interest. The offense can be a price worth paying for the generally useful public practice of producing literary works, just as noise, smoke, and stench might be a price worth paying for the existence of boiler factories, power plants, and slaughterhouses. Where the offensiveness of pornography is not linked to a serious artistic intention, however, there may be no redeeming social value to counterbalance it (certainly none of an artistic kind), and in that case the offense principle, assuming that its other conditions are satisfied, would permit its prohibition.

But even pure hard-core pornography with no literary or dramatic pretensions, as Kenneth Tynan pointed out, can have a certain social utility, so there is no "open and shut case" derived from the offense principle for banning it. The balancing of values in its case may be a close matter. The case for banning pornography that *is* art, on the other hand, insofar as it is derived from a carefully formulated offense principle, would be very weak. However much social value we ascribe to pure pornography on Tynan-like grounds, we must concede that works of literature, drama, pictorial art, and music have a much higher social value as a class (including both successful and unsuccessful specimens) than works of pure pornography, so that *their* legal prohibition would be a much greater loss. And so long as pornographic intent in a work of music or pictorial art does not have a *negative* social value, the value of these objects as works of art is undiminished by their aphrodisiac content or function. To make criminal the production or exhibition of any subclass of art objects would be to produce a "chilling effect" on the entire artistic enterprise and threaten to diminish its contributions to our civilization.[27]

The relevance of these considerations about the "reasonableness" or "social value" of offensive materials and actions is severely restricted, however, to those untypical situations in which the standards for determining the seriousness of the offense itself have not been fulfilled. The "seriousness" of the offense is a function of (1) how widespread the susceptibility to it is,[28] (2) how severe it will be in the typical case, (3) how much inconvenience would be involved in the effort to avoid it, and (4) whether or not the offended states of mind in question were voluntarily incurred, or the risk of offense voluntarily assumed. Surely, in most controversial instances of pornographic exhibition, either the offending materials do not offend intensely, or durably, or universally, and hence are not properly judged "obscene" in the first place (or at

[27] In addition, attempts to create art objects, insofar as they are forms of personal expression, have a "special position" on that ground too.
[28] In particular, offended states that occur only because of the offended party's abnormal susceptibility to offense are not to count as "very serious" offenses, although they surely are genuine.

least not obscene *enough*); *or* they are reasonably avoidable, and hence not a serious inconvenience to anyone; *or* the risk of offense is voluntarily assumed by those who witness them, and hence no captive audience exists; *or* only those with abnormal susceptibilities to offense could have reasonably been expected to be offended in the first place. Moreover, some of these standards for determining the existence or degree of offense are often preemptive. In particular, if the only observers are willing observers, then it is wholly pointless to consider whether a film or book with explicitly sexual themes has social value or not, and the question of whether it is a genuine work of art becomes otiose. It is unfair to prohibit on pain of criminal punishment any object or behavior that is both harmless and in the circumstances inoffensive, whether it is a genuine work of art or not.

6. HOW CAN SEX (OF ALL THINGS) BE OBSCENE?

The final question to consider about the relation between obscenity and pornography is one whose perplexity is no less keen for being raised typically as a kind of afterthought. The question is not whether explicit depictions of sexual behavior as such are in fact obscene, but rather, how could sex, a department of life so highly valued by almost all of us, *possibly* be obscene? How is an extremely offended reaction to explicit sexual depictions even possible? In particular, how could sex, of all things, induce something like the "yuk reaction," an extreme form of disgust and repugnance? Even more puzzling at first sight, since the word "obscene" in its standard use endorses such disgust, how could the yuk reaction be the *appropriate* response to the unrestrained depiction of sexuality? These questions are profound and difficult and belong ultimately to the psychologist rather than to the philosopher, but the shadowy outline of their answers, at least, is visible to all. What is clear is that the answers must be of at least two kinds: (1) Sexual explicitness (to use a vague generic term) violates a certain type of moral sensibility, and (2) sexual explicitness when extremely coarse and obtrusive can shock by reducing "psychic distance," even when moral sensibility is not involved. I shall consider these distinct factors in turn.

The word "obscene" is commonly applied to behavior thought to be immoral. When we use the word in this way, we do not reserve it necessarily for what we consider the most immoral behavior; secret, devious, or subtle private immoralities, no matter how seriously wrong they may seem to be, are not called "obscene" at all.[29] Rather, we think of those immoralities that are absolutely open and shameless, and therefore "shocking" or "disgusting," as the typically obscene ones. The word "obscene" emphasizes how shocking they are to behold, not how flagrant they are as departures from a moral norm. Thus utterly cynical, obvious, or brazen falsehoods told with amazing aplomb before observ-

---

[29] For a detailed analysis of the concept of the obscene and its relation to the concept of immorality, see my "The Idea of the Obscene," The Lindley Lecture (Lawrence: University of Kansas Press, 1979).

ers who know that they are intentional are "obscene lies"; bloated profits, made by exploiting public disasters and then openly bragged about, are "obscene profits." Similarly, blatant exhibitions of tabooed conduct, lewd revelings in the death or suffering of others, naked corruption, and stark depersonalizations are all proper subjects for the predicate "obscene." It is the grossly obtrusive offense to sensibility that elicits judgments of obscenity, whether the sensibility in question be moral, religious, patriotic, or merely gustatory (disgusting foods seem obscene) or sensory (disgusting smells seem obscene).

Naturally enough, persons who hold certain moral convictions about sexual conduct will find blatantly obtrusive exhibitions or depictions of tabooed sexuality obscene, not *simply* because they violate moral standards but because they do so openly and blatantly. Given that such is the case, the sensibilities of these persons would command the respect, and, if only other things were equal, the protection, of the law.

This account, however, is still too vague to allay the puzzlement that generated this psychological inquiry. Hardly anyone holds the conviction that *all* sexual behavior as such is wrong, whatever the circumstances and whoever the actors. At most, people find illicit or unlicensed sex, sex out of marriage, solitary sex, or sex at inappropriate times and places to be immoral. Yet many people find the *depiction* or explicit *description* of any sexual conduct at all, licit or illicit, to be obscene. How then could the obscenity stem from the perceived violation of moral principle?

The answer, I suspect, must employ the distinction between *what is depicted,* which is not thought to be obscene, at least not on moral grounds, and *the act of depicting it,* which may under the circumstances be a blatantly offensive violation of moral norms. What is immoral (by the standards of some offended parties) in vivid depictions or unvarnished descriptions of the sex acts of real or fictitious persons, even when those acts in the depicted circumstances are entirely licit, are the "impure thoughts" in the minds of the beholders, which are in large part "desires in the imagination" for what would be immoral if realized. When the beholder finds the depiction obscene (on this account), he finds his own spontaneous concupiscence disgusting, and it quickly curdles into shame and revulsion; or, if the beholder is part of a group, he or she may think of the inevitably impure ideas in the minds of the others as disgusting, or may take the act of showing or describing sex as itself blatantly immoral insofar as it is meant to exploit the weakness of the audience and induce impure thoughts in receptive minds. So it is not that what is depicted is thought to be immoral, but rather that the act of depicting it in those circumstances, and the spectacle of its common perception, with those motives, intentions, and likely effects, is thought to be immoral and—because the immorality is unsubtly shameless and open—obscene.

The second explanation of how sex can come to seem obscene has nothing to do with anyone's conception of morality. Even persons who utterly reject the prevailing sexual taboos may find some sexual depictions offensive to the point of obscenity. The reactions of such persons are to be sharply contrasted with those of people with prudish moral sensibilities who get trapped between their own salacity and shame. The disgust of this second group is not moral disgust. Rather, it is the spontaneous revulsion to what is overpoweringly close that is commonly produced not only by crude pornography but by other kinds of experiences as well. George P. Elliott has diagnosed the phenomenon well:

> Psychologically, the trouble with [artless] pornography is that, in our culture at least, it offends the sense of separateness, of individuality, of privacy . . . . We have a certain sense of specialness about those voluntary bodily functions each must perform for himself—bathing, eating, defecating, urinating, copulating . . . . Take eating, for example. There are few strong taboos around the act of eating; yet most people feel uneasy about being the only one at table who is or who is not, eating, and there is an absolute difference between eating a rare steak washed down by plenty of red wine and watching a close-up movie of someone doing so. One wishes to draw back when one is actually or imaginatively too close to the mouth of a man enjoying his dinner; in exactly the same way one wishes to remove oneself from the presence of man and woman enjoying sexual intercourse.[30]

"Not to withdraw," Elliott adds, "is to peep, to pervert looking so that it becomes a sexual end in itself." [31] Here he makes a different point and a less tenable one. The point is (or should be) that if we are going to look without being disgusted, we had better look from a proper distance, not that looking at all is a "perversion." Not only erotically realistic art but also artful pornography *can* satisfy the criterion of distance, and when it does we identify imaginatively with one of the parties whom we watch rather than thinking of ourselves as intrusive third parties or embarrassed "peepers."

Pornographers whose aim is aphrodisiac rather than emetic might well consult Elliott for good tips. He tells us, with convincing examples, how the problem of distance is solved in pictorial art, while implying that the same solutions must be forever unavailable to the pornographer, but that is because he identifies pornography quite arbitrarily with the gross and artless kind. Distance is preserved in erotic pictorial art through the use of artificial stylized images, as in the throngs of erotic statues on Indian temples, by making the erotic image small, or by sketching it in with only a few details:

> One does not want to be close to a man while he is defecating nor to have a close-up picture of him in that natural, innocent act—not at all because defecating is reprehensible, only because it is displeasing to intrude upon. One would much rather have a detailed picture of a thief stealing the last loaf of bread from a starving widow with three children than one of Albert Schweitzer at stool. However, Brueghel's painting "The Netherlandish Proverbs" represents two bare rear ends sticking out of a

30 George P. Elliott, "Against Pornography" in Hughes, *op. cit.,* pp. 75–76.
31 *Ibid.,* p. 76.

window, presumably of people defecating into the river below, and one quite enjoys the sight—because it is a small part of a large and pleasant picture of the world and because the two figures are tiny, sketched in, far away.[32]

What should we say—or, more to the point, what should the law say—about those persons whose psyches are not accurately described by Elliott, persons with special kinky tastes who prefer their psychic distances short and their sexual perceptions large and detailed? Tiny Gulliver (as Elliott reminds us) is "revolted by every blemish on the breast of the Brobdingnagian wet nurse suckling the baby." [33] Even though the breast was pleasingly shaped and would have been delightful to behold had its proportions been suited to persons of Gulliver's size, it extended six feet from the nurse's body and its nipple was "half the size of a man's head." Swift makes his point well, and most readers are appalled in their imaginations, but what are we to say of the special reader who is sexually excited by the very thought of this normally emetic object? The law, of course, should say nothing at all, provided that satisfaction of the quirky taste is not achieved at the cost of direct offense to unwilling observers.

The more interesting point, however, is that the overwhelming majority of people do *not* enjoy being spatially or psychologically close to the physiological organs and processes deemed "private" in our culture. To revel in these objects is about as common a pastime, I should think, as reveling in the slinky, slimy, smelly things that most of us find immediately repellant to the senses and thus in an analogous way obscene.

7. SUMMARY

Obscenity and pornography are entirely distinct concepts that overlap in their applications to the world but by no means coincide. Obscene things are those that are apt to offend people by eliciting such reactions as disgust, shock, and repugnance. Moreover, when we call something obscene we usually wish to endorse some form of offense as the appropriate reaction to it. Pornography, on the other hand, simply consists of all those pictures, plays, books, and films whose *raison d'être* is that they are erotically arousing. Some obscene things (e.g., dirty words and insulting gestures) are not pornographic. Indeed some obscene things have nothing whatever to do with sex. Human wastes and other disgusting objects fall into that subcategory of the obscene, as do acts of rejoicing in the misfortunes of others, racial slurs, shameless lies, and other blatant but nonsexual immoralities. Some pornographic things, for example, artful paintings, are not obscene. Others, such as close-up, highly magnified photographs of sexual couplings are obscene, though their very obscenity tends to defeat their pornographic purpose.

[32] *Ibid.,* p. 77.
[33] *Loc. cit.*

Pornography ought to be prohibited by law only when it is obscene and then precisely because it is obscene. But obscenity (extreme offensiveness) is only a necessary condition, not a sufficient condition, for rightful prohibition. In addition, the offending conduct must not be reasonably avoidable, and the risk of offense must not have been voluntarily assumed by the beholders. (No doubt additional conditions might also be added such as, for example, that reasonable efforts have been made to exclude children.)

The defining purposes of plotted fiction and dramatic literature cannot be satisfied by a work that is also properly denominated pornographic. On the other hand, there is no contradiction in the idea of a pornographic painting, musical composition, or (perhaps) poem. But the question whether or not art can be pornographic, while obviously important for American constitutional law, which places limits on what legislatures *may* do, is of less interest to critical social philosophy, which asks what legislatures *ought* to do from among the alternative courses permitted them. The Supreme Court has interpreted the First Amendment as permitting legislatures to prohibit all obscenity that is not also art.[34] Reasonable liberty-limiting principles also give special importance to works of art but prevent legislatures from prohibiting even obscene *nonart,* provided that it is not imposed on unwilling audiences. It is quite unnecessary to determine whether (or to what degree) a given book or film is also art, when the only people who experience it are either unoffended or have voluntarily assumed the risk of offense in advance.

Finally, we considered how sexual conduct could possibly seem obscene to anyone given the universal human propensity to derive extreme pleasure from it. Those who find pornography obscene, we concluded, do so either when it is done in circumstances that render it both immoral and blatantly and shamelessly obtrusive (and thus shocking to moral sensibility) or else when it has reduced psychic distance to the threshhold of repugnance or disgust, even when no moral considerations are involved.

[34] See Justice Brennan's opinion in *Roth* v. *United States,* 354 U.S. 476 (1957) and subsequent cases, such as *Manual Enterprises* v. *Day,* 370 U.S. 478 (1962); *Ginzburg* v. *United States,* 370 U.S. 403 (1963); *Mishkin* v. *New York,* 383 U.S. 502 (1963); *Memoirs* v. *Massachusetts,* 383 U.S. 413 (1963); *Miller* v. *California,* 413 U.S. 15 (1973); and *Paris Adult Theater I* v. *Slaton,* 413 U.S. 49 (1973). Of course expressions of opinion, scientific findings, and the like are also "absolutely protected" by the First Amendment. In the Court's verbal usage, genuine works of art, expressions of opinion, and the like are not called "obscene" in the first place. It might have been more natural to say that we have a constitutional right to attempt to create and exhibit works of art, *even obscene ones,* to express political opinions, *even obscene ones,* and so on. When the court says that the First Amendment does not protect obscenity, it means that it does not protect obscene nonart, obscene nonexpression, and the like. In short, it does not protect mere erotic stimulants or symbolic aphrodisiacs.

18 ANN GARRY

PORNOGRAPHY AND RESPECT FOR WOMEN

Pornography, like rape, is a male invention, designed to dehumanize women, to reduce the female to an object of sexual access, not to free sensuality from moralistic or parental inhibition. . . . Pornography is the undiluted essence of anti-female propaganda.

Susan Brownmiller, *Against Our Will: Men, Women and Rape* [1]

It is often asserted that a distinguishing characteristic of sexually explicit material is the degrading and demeaning portrayal of the role and status of the human female. It has been argued that erotic materials describe the female as a mere sexual object to be exploited and manipulated sexually. . . . A recent survey shows that 41 percent of American males and 46 percent of the females believe that "sexual materials lead people to lose respect for women." . . . Recent experiments suggest that such fears are probably unwarranted.

Presidential Commission on Obscenity and Pornography [2]

The kind of apparent conflict illustrated in these passages is easy to find in one's own thinking as well. For example, I have been inclined to think that pornography is innocuous and to dismiss "moral" arguments for censoring it because many such arguments rest on an assumption I do not share—that sex is an evil to be controlled. At the same time I believe that it is wrong to exploit or degrade human beings, particularly women and others who are especially susceptible. So if pornography degrades human beings, then even if I would oppose its censorship I surely cannot find it morally innocuous.

In an attempt to resolve this apparent conflict I discuss three questions: Does pornography degrade (or exploit or dehumanize) human

Social Theory and Practice 4 (Spring 1978): 395–421. As reprinted in Sharon Bishop and Marjorie Weinzweig, eds., *Philosophy and Women* (New York: Wadsworth, 1979), pp. 128–139. Reprinted by permission of Ann Garry.
[1] (New York: Simon & Schuster, 1975), p. 394.
[2] *The Report of the Commission on Obscenity and Pornography* (Washington, D.C., 1970), p. 201. Hereinafter, *Report*.

beings? If so, does it degrade women in ways or to an extent that it does not degrade men? If so, must pornography degrade women, as Brownmiller thinks, or could genuinely innocuous, nonsexist pornography exist? Although much current pornography does degrade women, I will argue that it is possible to have nondegrading, nonsexist pornography. However, this possibility rests on our making certain fundamental changes in our conceptions of sex and sex roles.

I

First, some preliminary remarks: Many people now avoid using "pornography" as a descriptive term and reserve "obscenity" for use in legal contexts. Because "pornography" is thought to be a judgmental word, it is replaced by "explicit sexual material," "sexually oriented materials," "erotica," and so on.[3] I use "pornography" to label those explicit sexual materials intended to arouse the reader or viewer sexually. I seriously doubt whether there is a clearly defined class of cases that fits my characterization of pornography. This does not bother me, for I am interested here in obvious cases that would be uncontroversially pornographic—the worst, least artistic kind. The pornography I discuss is that which, taken as a whole, lacks "serious literary, artistic, political, or scientific merit."[4] I often use pornographic films as examples because they generate more concern today than do books or magazines.

What interests me is not whether pornography should be censored but whether one can object to it on moral grounds. The only moral ground I consider is whether pornography degrades people; obviously, other possible grounds exist, but I find this one to be the most plausible.[5] Of the many kinds of degradation and exploitation possible in the production of pornography, I focus only on the content of the pornographic work. I exclude from the discussion (i) the ways in which pornographic film makers might exploit people in making a film, distributing it, and charging too much to see it; (ii) the likelihood that actors, actresses, or technicians will be exploited, underpaid, or made to lose self-respect or self-esteem; and (iii) the exploitation and degradation surrounding the prostitution and crime that often accompany urban centers of pornography.[6] I want to determine whether pornography shows (ex-

3 Report, p. 3, n. 4; and p. 149.
4 Roth v. United States, 354 U.S. 476, 489 (1957).
5 To degrade someone in this situation is to lower her/his rank or status in humanity. This is morally objectionable because it is incompatible with showing respect for a person. Some of the other moral grounds for objecting to pornography have been considered by the Supreme Court: Pornography invades our privacy and hurts the moral tone of the community. See Paris Adult Theatre I v. Slaton, 413 U.S. 49 (1973). Even less plausible than the Court's position is to say that pornography is immoral because it depicts sex, depicts an immoral kind of sex, or caters to voyeuristic tendencies. I believe that even if moral objections to pornography exist, one must preclude any simple inference from "pornography is immoral" to "pornography should be censored" because of other important values and principles such as freedom of expression and self-determination.
6 See Gail Sheehy, Hustling (New York: Dell, 1971) for a good discussion of prostitution, crime, and pornography.

presses) and commends behavior or attitudes that exploit or degrade people. For example, if a pornographic film conveys that raping a woman is acceptable, then the content is degrading to women and might be called morally objectionable. Morally objectionable content is not peculiar to pornography; it can also be found in nonpornographic books, films, advertisements, and so on. The question is whether morally objectionable content is necessary to pornography.

II

At the beginning of this paper, I quoted part of a passage in which the Presidential Commission on Obscenity and Pornography tried to allay our fears that pornography will lead people to lose respect for women. Here is the full passage:

> It is often asserted that a distinguishing characteristic of sexually explicit material is the degrading and demeaning portrayal of the role and status of the human female. It has been argued that erotic materials describe the female as a mere sexual object to be exploited and manipulated sexually.
>
> One presumed consequence of such portrayals is that erotica transmits an inaccurate and uninformed conception of sexuality, and that the viewer or user will (a) develop a calloused and manipulative orientation toward women and (b) engage in behavior in which affection and sexuality are not well integrated. A recent survey shows that 41% of American males and 46% of the females believe that "sexual materials lead people to lose respect for women" (Abelson et al. 1970). Recent experiments (Mosher 1970a, b; Mosher and Katz 1970) suggest that such fears are probably unwarranted.[7]

The argument to which the Commission addresses itself begins with the assumption that pornography presents a degrading portrayal of women as sex objects. If users of pornography adopt the view that women are sex objects (or already believe it and allow pornography to reinforce their beliefs), they will develop an attitude of callousness and lack of respect for women and will be more likely to treat women as sex objects to be manipulated and exploited. In this argument the moral objection to be brought against pornography lies in the objectionable character of the acquired attitudes and the increased likelihood of objectionable behavior—treating women as mere sex objects to be exploited rather than as persons to be respected.

A second moral argument, which does not interest the Commission, is that pornography is morally objectionable because it exemplifies and recommends behavior that violates the moral principle to respect persons. This argument contains no reference to immoral consequences: there need be no increased likelihood of behavior degrading to women. Pornography itself treats women not as whole persons but as mere sex

[7] *Report*, p. 201. References cited can be found in notes 12, 13, 14, and 22, below.

objects "to be exploited and manipulated sexually." Such treatment is a "degrading and demeaning portrayal of the role and status" (and humanity) of women.

I will explain and discuss the first argument here and the second argument in Part III of this paper. The first argument depends on an empirical premise—that viewing pornography leads to an increase in "sex calloused" attitudes and behavior.[8] My discussion of this premise consists of four parts: (1) examples of some who accept the premise (Susan Brownmiller and the Supreme Court); (2) evidence presented for its denial by Donald Mosher for the Presidential Commission; (3) a critical examination of Mosher's studies; and (4) a concluding argument that, regardless of who (Mosher or Brownmiller) is correct, moral grounds exist for objecting to pornography.

1

Although I know of no social scientist whose data support the position that pornography leads to an increase in sex calloused behavior and attitudes, this view has popular support. For example, the Presidential Commission survey cited above finds it supported by 41 percent of American males and 46 percent of the females. In addition, passages from both Susan Brownmiller and the United States Supreme Court illustrate a similar but more inclusive view: that use of pornography leads to sex callousness or lack of respect for women (or something worse) and that we do not need social scientists to confirm or deny it.

The following passage from Brownmiller forms part of her support for the position that liberals should rethink their position on pornography because pornography is anti-female propaganda:

> The majority report of the President's Commission on Obscenity and Pornography tried to pooh-pooh the opinion of law enforcement agencies around the country that claimed their own concrete experience with offenders who were caught with the stuff led them to conclude that pornographic material is a causative factor in crimes of sexual violence. The commission maintained that it was not possible at this time to scientifically prove or disprove such a connection.
>
> But does one need scientific methodology in order to conclude that the anti-female propaganda that permeates our nation's cultural output promotes a climate in which acts of sexual hostility directed against women are not only tolerated but ideologically encouraged?[9]

In at least two 1973 opinions, the Supreme Court tried to speak to the relevance of empirical data. They considered antisocial acts in general, without any thought that "sex calloused" behavior would be particularly antisocial. In *Kaplan* v. *California,* the Court said:

[8] Sex callousness is a term used by Donald Mosher in the studies to be discussed here. See notes 12 and 13 below. Although the concept of sex callousness will be explained later, the core of the meaning is obvious: To be a sex calloused male is to have attitudes toward women (e.g., lack of respect) conducive to exploiting them sexually.
[9] Brownmiller, *Against Our Will,* p. 395

A state could reasonably regard the "hard-core" conduct described by Suite 69 as capable of encouraging or causing anti-social behavior, especially in its impact on young people. States need not wait until behavioral experts or educators can provide empirical data before enacting controls of commerce in obscene materials unprotected by the First Amendment or by a constitutional right to privacy. We have noted the power of a legislative body to enact such regulatory law on the basis of unprovable assumptions.[10]

From *Paris Adult Theatre* v. *Slaton:*

But, it is argued, there is no scientific data which conclusively demonstrates that exposure to obscene materials adversely affects men and women or their society. It is urged on behalf of the petitioner that, absent such a demonstration, any kind of state regulation is "impermissible." We reject this argument. . . . Although there is no conclusive proof of a connection between antisocial behavior and obscene material, the legislature of Georgia could quite reasonably determine that such a connection does or might exist.[11]

The disturbing feature of these passages is not the truth of the view that pornography leads to sex callousness but that the Court and Brownmiller seem to have succumbed to the temptation to disregard empirical data when the data fail to meet the authors' expectations. My intention in citing these passages is not to examine them but to remind the reader of how influential this kind of viewpoint is. For convenience I call it "Brownmiller's view"—the position that pornography provides a model for male sex calloused behavior and has a numbing effect on the rest of us so that we tolerate sex calloused behavior more readily.

2

Donald L. Mosher has put forward evidence to deny that use of pornography leads to sex callousness or lack of respect for women.[12] In a study for the Presidential Commission, Mosher found that "sexually arousing pornographic films did not trigger sexual behavior even in the [sex calloused] college males whose attitudes toward women were more conducive to sexual exploitation" (p. 306), and that sex calloused attitudes toward women decreased after the viewers saw pornographic films.

Mosher developed the operative concept of "sex callousness" in one study for the Commission,[13] then used the concept as part of a more comprehensive study of the effects of pornography.[14] In the second study

10 413 U.S. 115, 120 (1973).
11 413 U.S. 49, 60–61.
12 "Psychological Reactions to Pornographic Films," *Technical Report of the Commission on Obscenity and Pornography,* vol. 8 (Washington, D.C., 1970), pp. 255–312. Hereinafter, *Tech. Report,* often cited by page number only in body of text.
13 "Sex Callousness toward Women," *Tech. Report,* vol. 8, pp. 313–25.
14 "Psychological Reactions to Pornographic Films," See note 12. Both of Mosher's experiments used the same questions to test "sex callousness"; I treat the experiments together, citing only page numbers in the body of the text. As far as I know, no other social scientists are working on the relationship between pornography and sex

Mosher rated his 194 unmarried undergraduate male subjects for "sex callousness." Men who have sex calloused attitudes approve of and engage in "the use of physical aggression and exploitative tactics such as falsely professing love, getting their dates drunk, or showing pornography to their dates as a means of gaining coitus" (pp. 305–6). Men rated high in sex callousness believe that sex is for fun, believe that love and sex are separate (p. 306), and agree to statements such as "Promise a woman anything, but give her your _____." When a woman gets uppity, it's time to _____ her," and "_____ teasers should be raped" (p. 314, expletives deleted in report). Mosher suggests that this attitude is part of the "Macho syndrome" (p. 323).

The highly sex calloused men rated the two pornographic films they saw as more enjoyable and arousing, and less offensive or disgusting than did other subjects; but, like all of the subjects, these men did not increase their sexual activity. Mosher found no increase in "frequencies of masturbation, heterosexual petting, oral-genital sex, or coitus" in the twenty-four hours after the subjects saw the two films.[15] He did not indicate whether a change occurred in the proportion of exploitative sexual behavior to nonexploitative sexual behavior.

In addition, the data from all the male subjects indicated a *decrease* in their sex calloused attitudes. The sharpest decrease occurred in the twenty-four hours after they saw the films. Two weeks later, their level of sex callousness was still lower than before they viewed the films. Although Mosher used several "equivalent" tests to measure callousness and did not explain the differences among them, the test I saw *(Form B)* was presumably typical: It measured the extent to which the subjects agreed or disagreed with statements such as "_____ teasers should be raped."

Mosher's explanation for the decrease in sex calloused attitudes is, in his own words, "speculative." Sex callousness is an expression of "exaggerated masculine style" that occurs during a period of male development ("ideally followed by an integration of love with exploitative sex" [pp. 322–23]). During this period, men, especially young men without occupational success, use the "macho" conquest mentality to reassure themselves of their masculinity. Mosher thinks that seeing a pornographic film in the company of only men satisfies the need for macho behavior—the same need that is satisfied by exploiting women, endorsing calloused attitudes, telling "dirty" jokes, or boasting about one's sexual prowess. Thus the immediate need to affirm the sex calloused statements

---

callousness toward women. Mosher made another study with Harvey Katz that is on even less secure ground. They asked undergraduate males to "aggress verbally" at female student assistants before and after seeing a pornographic film. No increase in verbal aggression occurred after they saw the film. The authors seem to be aware of many limitations of this study; particularly relevant here are the facts that only verbal aggression was tested and that the film did not show violent or aggressive behavior. "Pornographic Films, Male Verbal Aggression Against Women, and Guilt." *Tech. Report,* vol. 8. pp. 357–77.

15 *Tech. Report,* vol. 8, p. 255. In his "Conclusions" section, Mosher qualifies the claim that no increase occurred in sexual behavior for sex calloused males. He says that they "reported no increased heterosexual behavior" (p. 310).

about women decreases once the men have seen the pornographic films (pp. 322–23, 306–7).

3

For Mosher pornography is an outlet for the expression of calloused attitudes—not, as for Brownmiller, a model for calloused behavior. Some of the limitations of Mosher's study are clear to him; others apparently are not. My comments on his study fall into three categories: the limitations of his design and method, difficulties with his conclusions about sexual behavior, and difficulties with his conclusions about calloused attitudes. I am not raising general methodological issues; for example, I do not ask what measures were used to prevent a subject's (or experimenter's) civil libertarian beliefs from influencing a subject's tendency to show less calloused attitudes after seeing the films.

Limitations of Design and Method. (i) Mosher's was a very short-term study: His last questions were asked of subjects two weeks after they saw the pornographic films. But since pornography is supposed to provide only a temporary outlet, this limitation may not be crucial. (ii) Mosher believes that, given the standard of commercial pornography, the films he showed displayed more than the usual amount of affection and less than the usual amount of exploitative, "kinky," or exclusively male-oriented appeal. (iii) His test was designed only to measure the most readily testable, gross ways of talking callously about, and acting callously toward women. Women, especially recently, have become aware of many more and less subtle ways in which men can express hostility and contempt for them. An obvious example is a man who would deny that "most women are cunts at heart" but would gladly talk about women as "chicks" or "foxes" to be captured, conquered, and toyed with. In short, many more men than Mosher thinks might well fall into the "sex calloused" class; and the questions asked of all the men should have included tests for more subtle forms of callousness.

Conclusions About Sexual Behavior. One of the most problematic parts of Mosher's study is that he did not test whether exploitative sexual behavior increased after the films were viewed; he tested only whether *any* sexual behavior increased and whether the endorsement of statements expressing calloused attitudes increased. One learns only that no increase occurred in the sexual behavior of the subjects (both calloused and not so calloused). One wants to know how the sex calloused men treated their partners after they saw the films; the frequency of sex, increased or not, implies nothing about the quality of their treatment of their female partners. It is not enough for Mosher to tell us that a decrease occurred in endorsing statements expressing calloused attitudes. Mosher himself points out the gap between verbal behavior in the laboratory and behavior in real-life situations with one's chosen partners.[16]

[16] "Pornographic Films, Male Verbal Aggression Against Women, and Guilt," *Tech. Report*, vol. 8, pp. 372–73.

Conclusions About Calloused Attitudes. (i) The most serious diffculty is one that Mosher recognizes. There was no control for the possibility that the men's level of sex callousness was unusually high in the beginning as a result of their anticipation of seeing pornographic films. (ii) Nor was there a control for the declining "shock value" of the statements expressing calloused attitudes. (iii) No precise indication of the relative decreases in sex calloused attitudes for the high- and low-callousness groups was given. Mosher states the differences for high- and low-guilt groups and has told us that highly calloused men tend to feel less guilt than other men; [17] however, one wants to know more precisely what the different effects were, particularly on the high-callousness group. (iv) Mosher realizes that his explanation for the decrease in calloused attitudes is still speculative. If seeing pornography with a group of men provides an outlet for callousness, there should be a control group of subjects seeing pornography while isolated from others. There should also be a control group experience not involving pornography at all. For example, subjects in such a group could watch a film about a Nazi concentration camp or about the first American presidents.

4

Although I am obviously critical of Mosher's work, let us suspend for a moment our critical judgment about his data and their interpretation. Even if the experience of seeing pornographic movies with other undergraduate men provides an opportunity to let out a small amount of male contempt and hostility toward women, very little follows from this for social policy or moral judgments. No sensible person would maintain that a temporary outlet is an adequate substitute for getting to the root of a problem. Given the existence of a large reservoir of male contempt and hostility toward women, and given that our society is still filled with pressures to "affirm one's manhood" at the expense of women, there is little reason to suppose a "cathartic" effect to be very significant here. Much of the research on the effects of pornography indicates that *any* effect it has—positive or negative—is short lived. At best pornography might divert or delay a man from expressing his callousness in an even more blatantly objectionable manner.

One could make the point in moral terms as follows: Sex calloused attitudes and behavior are morally objectionable; if expressing one's sex calloused attitudes lessens them temporarily, they are still morally objectionable if they persevere at some level. The most that one could say for pornography is that expressing callousness by enjoying pornography in a male group is a lesser evil than, for example, rape or obnoxiously "putting down" a woman in person. This is saying very little on behalf of pornography; it is still morally objectionable.

If pornography is morally objectionable even if Mosher is correct, then given the two alternatives posed, it is surely morally objectionable. For Brownmiller's alternative, remember, was that pornography provides

---

[17] *Tech. Report,* vol. 8, p. 274. The low-guilt subjects showed a rebound in sex callousness two weeks after seeing the films; however, the level of callousness still did not reach the prefilm level.

a model for sex calloused behavior and has a numbing effect on many of us so that we more readily tolerate this behavior. This view, much more obviously than Mosher's, implies that pornography is morally objectionable.[18]

Before leaving Mosher and Brownmiller, let me point out that their views are not wholly incompatible. They disagree about pornography's function as an outlet or a model, of course, but Mosher's data (as he interprets their significance) are compatible with the numbing effect of pornography. Pornography may have numbed all of us (previously sex calloused or not) to the objectionable character of exploitative sex: the fact that the sex calloused men were numbed does not imply that they will feel the need to endorse calloused attitudes just after expressing their callousness in other ways. Further, Mosher's data have no bearing at all on the numbing influence on women; certainly Brownmiller means for her claim to apply to women too.

One final point remains to be considered. The Presidential Commission assumes a connection between sex callousness and the lack (or loss) of respect for women; for it appealed to Mosher's data about sex callousness to show that pornography probably will not lead people to lose respect for women.[19] But look at the results of replacing Mosher's talk about sex calloused attitudes with talk about respect for women: One would conclude that seeing pornography (with a group of men) leads to an increase in respect for women. The explanation would be that men who tend toward low respect for women can use pornography as a way of expressing their low respect. They then feel no need to endorse statements exemplifying their low respect because they have just expressed it. "Therefore" pornography provides the opportunity for their respect for women to increase. The last idea is bothersome: To think of viewing and enjoying pornography as a way of expressing lack of respect, and at the same time as a way of expressing or increasing respect, seems very strange. This is not to say that such a feat is impossible. Given our complex psychological make-up, we might be able to express both respect and lack of respect at the same time in different ways; it might also be possible to express disrespect that leads to respect (e.g., if shame at feeling disrespect leads to a temporary increase in respect). But one would need far more information about what actually happens before agreeing that any of these possibilities seems very plausible. It is necessary to spell out both the possible connections and suitable explanations for each. Without much more information, one would not want to base either favorable moral judgments about pornography or social policy on the possibility that pornography can lead to more respect for women.

Although much more remains to be said about the connection between pornography and respect for women. I will defer discussion of it to Part III of this paper. For now, let us note that even if the Presidential Commission appropriately allayed our fears about being molested on

---

[18] Of course, pornography might have no effect at all. If this were true, some other basis must be found before calling it morally objectionable.
[19] *Report,* p. 201.

street corners by users of pornography, it would not have been warranted in placating us with the view that pornography is morally acceptable. It is fortunate that it did not try.

III

The second argument I will consider is that pornography is morally objectionable, not because it leads people to show disrespect for women, but because pornography itself exemplifies and recommends behavior that violates the moral principle to respect persons. The content of pornography is what one objects to. It treats women as mere sex objects "to be exploited and manipulated" and degrades the role and status of women. In order to evaluate this argument, I will first clarify what it would mean for pornography itself to treat someone as a sex object in a degrading manner. I will then deal with three issues central to the discussion of pornography and respect for women: how "losing respect" for a woman is connected with treating her as a sex object: what is wrong with treating someone as a sex object: and why it is worse to treat women rather than men as sex objects. I will argue that the current content of pornography sometimes violates the moral principle to respect persons. Then, in Part IV of this paper, I will suggest that pornography need not violate this principle if certain fundamental changes were to occur in attitudes about sex.

To many people, including Brownmiller and some other feminists, it appears to be an obvious truth that pornography treats people, especially women, as sex objects in a degrading manner. And if we omit "in a degrading manner," the statement seems hard to dispute. How could pornography *not* treat people as sex objects?

First, is it permissible to say that either the content of pornography or pornography itself degrades people or treats people as sex objects? It is not difficult to find examples of degrading content in which women are treated as sex objects. Some pornographic films convey the message that all women really want to be raped, that their resisting struggle is not to be believed. By portraying women in this manner, the content of the movie degrades women. Degrading women is morally objectionable. While seeing the movie need not cause anyone to imitate the behavior shown, we can call the content degrading to women because of the character of the behavior and attitudes it recommends. The same kind of point can be made about films (or books or TV commercials) with other kinds of degrading, thus morally objectionable, content—for example, racist messages.[20]

20 Two further points need to be mentioned here. Sharon Bishop pointed out to me one reason why we might object to either a racist or rapist mentality in film: it might be difficult for a Black or a woman not to identify with the degraded person. A second point concerns different uses of the phrase "treats women as sex objects." A film treats a subject—the meaninglessness of contemporary life, women as sex objects, and so on—and this use of "treats" is unproblematic. But one should not suppose that this is the same use of "treats women as sex objects" that is found in the sentence "David treats women as sex objects"; David is not treating the *subject* of women as sex objects.

The next step in the argument is to infer that, because the content or message of pornography is morally objectionable, we can call pornography itself morally objectionable. Support for this step can be found in an analogy. If a person takes every opportunity to recommend that men rape women, we would think not only that his recommendation is immoral but that he is immoral too. In the case of pornography, the objection to making an inference from recommended behavior to the person who recommends is that we ascribe predicates such as 'immoral' differently to people than to films or books. A film vehicle for an objectionable message is still an object independent of its message, its director, its producer, those who act in it, and those who respond to it. Hence one cannot make an unsupported inference from "the content of the film is morally objectionable" to "the film is morally objectionable." Because the central points in this paper do not depend on whether pornography itself (in addition to its content) is morally objectionable. I will not try to support this inference. (The question about the relation of content to the work itself is, of course, extremely interesting: but in part because I cannot decide which side of the argument is more persuasive. I will pass.[21]) Certainly one appropriate way to evaluate pornography is in terms of the moral features of its content. If a pornographic film exemplifies and recommends morally objectionable attitudes or behavior, then its content is morally objectionable.

Let us now turn to the first of our three questions about respect and sex objects: What is the connection between losing respect for a woman and treating her as a sex object? Some people who have lived through the era in which women were taught to worry about men "losing respect" for them if they engaged in sex in inappropriate circumstances find it troublesome (or at least amusing) that feminists—supposedly "liberated" women—are outraged at being treated as sex objects, either by pornography or in any other way. The apparent alignment between feminists and traditionally "proper" women need not surprise us when we look at it more closely.

The "respect" that men have traditionally believed they have for women—hence a respect they can lose—is not a general respect for persons as autonomous beings; nor is it respect that is earned because of one's personal merits or achievements. It is respect that is an outgrowth of the "double standard." Women are to be respected because they are more pure, delicate, and fragile than men, have more refined sensibilities, and so on. Because some women clearly do not have these qualities, thus do not deserve respect, women must be divided into two groups—the good ones on the pedestal and the bad ones who have fallen from it. One's mother, grandmother, Sunday School teacher, and usually one's wife are "good" women. The appropriate behavior by which to express respect for good women would be, for example, not swearing or telling

[21] In order to help one determine which position one feels inclined to take, consider the following statement: It is morally objectionable to write, make, sell, act in, use, and enjoy pornography; in addition, the content of pornography is immoral; however, pornography itself is not morally objectionable. If this statement seems extremely problematic, then one might well be satisfied with the claim that pornography is degrading because its content is.

dirty jokes in front of them, giving them seats on buses, and other "chivalrous" acts. This kind of "respect" for good women is the same sort that adolescent boys in the back seats of cars used to "promise" not to lose. Note that men define, display, and lose this kind of respect. If women lose respect for women, it is not typically a loss of respect for (other) women as a class but a loss of self-respect.

It has now become commonplace to acknowledge that, although a place on the pedestal might have advantages over a place in the "gutter" beneath it, a place on the pedestal is not at all equal to the place occupied by other people (i.e., men). "Respect" for those on the pedestal was not respect for whole, full-fledged people but for a special class of inferior beings.

If a person makes two traditional assumptions—that (at least some) sex is dirty and that women fall into two classes, good and bad—it is easy to see how that person might think that pornography could lead people to lose respect for women or that pornography is itself disrespectful to women.[22] Pornography describes or shows women engaging in activities inappropriate for good women to engage in—or at least inappropriate for them to be seen by strangers engaging in. If one sees these women as symbolic representatives of all women, then all women fall from grace with these women. This fall is possible, I believe, because the traditional "respect" that men have had for women is not genuine, wholehearted respect for full-fledged human beings but half-hearted respect for lesser beings, some of whom they feel the need to glorify and purify.[23] It is easy to fall from a pedestal. Can we imagine 41 percent of men and 46 percent of women answering "yes" to the question, "Do movies showing men engaging in violent acts lead people to lose respect for men?"?

Two interesting asymmetries appear. The first is that losing respect for men as a class (men with power, typically Anglo men) is more difficult than losing respect for women or ethnic minorities as a class. Anglo men whose behavior warrants disrespect are more likely to be seen as exceptional cases than are women or minorities (whose "transgressions" may be far less serious). Think of the following: women are temptresses: Blacks cheat the welfare system: Italians are gangsters: but the men of the Nixon administration are exceptions—Anglo men as a class did not lose respect because of Watergate and related scandals.

The second asymmetry concerns the active and passive roles of the sexes. Men are seen in the active role. If men lose respect for women because of something "evil" done by women (such as appearing in pornography), the fear is that men will then do harm to women—not that women will do harm to men. Whereas if women lose respect for

---

[22] The traditional meaning of "lose respect for women" was evidently the one assumed in the Abelson survey cited by the Presidential Commission. No explanation of its meaning is given in the report of the study. See H. Abelson et al., "National Survey of Public Attitudes Toward and Experience With Erotic Materials," *Tech. Report*, vol. 6, pp. 1–137.

[23] Many feminists point this out. One of the most accessible references is Shulamith Firestone, *The Dialectic of Sex: The Case for the Feminist Revolution* (New York: Bantam, 1970), especially pp. 128–32.

male politicians because of Watergate, the fear is still that male politicians will do harm, not that women will do harm to male politicians. This asymmetry might be a result of one way in which our society thinks of sex as bad—as harm that men do to women (or to the person playing a female role, as in a homosexual rape). Robert Baker calls attention to this point in " 'Pricks' and 'Chicks': A Plea for 'Persons.' " [24] Our slang words for sexual intercourse—"fuck," "screw," or older words such as "take" or "have"—not only can mean harm but have traditionally taken a male subject and a female object. The active male screws (harms) the passive female. A "bad" woman only tempts men to hurt her further.

It is easy to understand why one's proper grandmother would not want men to see pornography or lose respect for women. But feminists reject these "proper" assumptions: good and bad classes of women do not exist: and sex is not dirty (though many people believe it is). Why then are feminists angry at the treatment of women as sex objects, and why are some feminists opposed to pornography?

The answer is that feminists as well as proper grandparents are concerned with respect. However, there are differences. A feminist's distinction between treating a woman as a full-fledged person and treating her as merely a sex object does not correspond to the good-bad woman distinction. In the latter distinction, "good" and "bad" are properties applicable to groups of women. In the feminist view, all women are full-fledged people—some, however, are treated as sex objects and perhaps think of themselves as sex objects. A further difference is that, although "bad" women correspond to those thought to deserve treatment as sex objects, good women have not corresponded to full-fledged people; only men have been full-fledged people. Given the feminist's distinction, she has no difficulty whatever in saying that pornography treats women as sex objects, not as full-fledged people. She can morally object to pornography or anything else that treats women as sex objects.

One might wonder whether any objection to treatment as a sex object implies that the person objecting still believes, deep down, that sex is dirty. I don't think so. Several other possibilities emerge. First, even if I believe intellectually and emotionally that sex is healthy, I might object to being treated *only* as a sex object. In the same spirit, I would object to being treated *only* as a maker of chocolate chip cookies or *only* as a tennis partner, because only one of my talents is being valued. Second, perhaps I feel that sex is healthy, but it is apparent to me that you think sex is dirty; so I don't want you to treat me as a sex object. Third, being treated as any kind of object, not just as a sex object, is unappealing. I would rather be a partner (sexual or otherwise) than an object. Fourth, and more plausible than the first three possibilities, is Robert Baker's view mentioned above. Both (i) our traditional double standard of sexual behavior for men and women and (ii) the linguistic evidence that we connect the concept of sex with the concept of harm point to what is wrong with treating women as sex objects. As I

[24] In Richard Wasserstrom, ed., *Today's Moral Problems* (New York: Macmillan, 1975), pp. 152–71; see pp. 167–71. Also in Robert Baker and Frederick Elliston, eds., *Philosophy and Sex* (Buffalo, N.Y.: Prometheus Books, 1975).

said earlier, 'fuck' and 'screw', in their traditional uses, have taken a male subject, a female object, and have had at least two meanings: harm and have sexual intercourse with. (In addition, a prick is a man who harms people ruthlessly; and a motherfucker is so low that he would do something very harmful to his own dear mother.) [25] Because in our culture we connect sex with harm that men do to women, and because we think of the female role in sex as that of harmed object, we can see that to treat a woman as a sex object is automatically to treat her as less than fully human. To say this does not imply that no healthy sexual relationships exist; nor does it say anything about individual men's conscious intentions to degrade women by desiring them sexually (though no doubt some men have these intentions). It is merely to make a point about the concepts embodied in our language.

Psychoanalytic support for the connection between sex and harm comes from Robert J. Stoller. Stoller thinks that sexual excitement is linked with a wish to harm someone (and with at least a whisper of hostility). The key process of sexual excitement can be seen as dehumanization (fetishization) in fantasy of the desired person. He speculates that this is true in some degree of everyone, both men and women, with "normal" or "perverted" activities and fantasies.[26]

Thinking of sex objects as harmed objects enables us to explain some of the first three reasons why one wouldn't want to be treated as a sex object: (1) I may object to being treated only as a tennis partner, but being a tennis partner is not connected in our culture with being a harmed object; and (2) I may not think that sex is dirty and that I would be a harmed object; I may not know what your view is; but what bothers me is that this is the view embodied in our language and culture.

Awareness of the connection between sex and harm helps explain other interesting points. Women are angry about being treated as sex objects in situations or roles in which they do not intend to be regarded in that manner—for example, while serving on a committee or attending a discussion. It is not merely that a sexual role is inappropriate for the circumstances; it is thought to be a less fully human role than the one in which they intended to function.

Finally, the sex-harm connection makes clear why it is worse to treat women as sex objects than to treat men as sex objects, and why some men have had difficulty understanding women's anger about the matter. It is more difficult for heterosexual men than for women to assume the role of "harmed object" in sex: for men have the self-concept of sexual agents, not of passive objects. This is also related to my earlier point concerning

[25] Baker, in Wasserstrom, *Today's Moral Problems*, pp. 168–169.
[26] "Sexual Excitement," *Archives of General Psychiatry* 33 (1976): 899–909, especially p. 903. The extent to which Stoller sees men and women in different positions with respect to harm and hostility is not clear. He often treats men and women alike, but in *Perversion: The Erotic Form of Hatred* (New York: Pantheon, 1975), pp. 89–91, he calls attention to differences between men and women especially regarding their responses to pornography and lack of understanding by men of women's sexuality. Given that Stoller finds hostility to be an essential element in male-oriented pornography, and given that women have not responded readily to such pornography, one can speculate about the possibilities for women's sexuality; their hostility might follow a different scenario; they might not be as hostile, and so on.

the difference in the solidity of respect for men and for women; respect for women is more fragile. Despite exceptions, it is generally harder for people to degrade men, either sexually or nonsexually, than to degrade women. Men and women have grown up with different patterns of self-respect and expectations regarding the extent to which they deserve and will receive respect or degradation. The man who doesn't understand why women do not want to be treated as sex objects (because he'd sure like to be) would not think of himself as being harmed by that treatment; a woman might.[27] Pornography, probably more than any other contemporary institution, succeeds in treating men as sex objects.

Having seen that the connection between sex and harm helps explain both what is wrong with treating someone as a sex object and why it is worse to treat a woman in this way, I want to use the sex-harm connection to try to resolve a dispute about pornography and women. Brownmiller's view, remember, was that pornography is "the undiluted essence of anti-female propaganda" whose purpose is to degrade women.[28] Some people object to Brownmiller's view by saying that, since pornography treats both men and women as sex objects for the purpose of arousing the viewer, it is neither sexist, antifemale, nor designed to degrade women; it just happens that degrading of women arouses some men. How can this dispute be resolved?

Suppose we were to rate the content of all pornography from most morally objectionable to least morally objectionable. Among the most objectionable would be the most degrading—for example, "snuff" films and movies which recommend that men rape women, molest children and puppies, and treat nonmasochists very sadistically.

Next we would find a large amount of material (probably most pornography) not quite so blatantly offensive. With this material it is relevant to use the analysis of sex objects given above. As long as sex is connected with harm done to women, it will be very difficult not to see pornography as degrading to women. We can agree with Brownmiller's opponent that pornography treats men as sex objects, too, but we maintain that this is only pseudoequality; such treatment is still more degrading to women.[29]

In addition, pornography often exemplifies the active/passive, harmer/harmed object roles in a very obvious way. Because pornography today is male-oriented and is supposed to make a profit, the content is designed to appeal to male fantasies. Judging from the content of the

[27] Men seem to be developing more sensitivity to being treated as sex objects. Many homosexual men have long understood the problem. As women become more sexually aggressive, some heterosexual men I know are beginning to feel treated as sex objects. A man can feel that he is not being taken seriously if a woman looks lustfully at him while he is holding forth about the French judicial system or the failure of liberal politics. Some of his most important talents are not being properly valued.
[28] Brownmiller, *Against Our Will*, p. 394.
[29] I don't agree with Brownmiller that the purpose of pornography is to dehumanize women; rather it is to arouse the audience. The differences between our views can be explained, in part, by the points from which we begin. She is writing about rape; her views about pornography grow out of her views about rape. I begin by thinking of pornography as merely depicted sexual activity, though I am well aware of the male hostility and contempt for women that it often expresses. That pornography degrades women and excites men is an illustration of this contempt.

most popular legally available pornography, male fantasies still run along the lines of stereotypical sex roles—and, if Stoller is right, include elements of hostility. In much pornography the woman's purpose is to cater to male desires, to service the man or men. Her own pleasure is rarely emphasized for its own sake; she is merely allowed a little heavy breathing, perhaps in order to show her dependence on the great male "lover" who produces her pleasure. In addition, women are clearly made into passive objects in still photographs showing only close-ups of their genitals. Even in movies marketed to appeal to heterosexual couples, such as *Behind the Green Door*, the woman is passive and undemanding (and in this case kidnapped and hypnotized as well). Although many kinds of specialty magazines and films are gauged for different sexual tastes, very little contemporary pornography goes against traditional sex roles. There is certainly no significant attempt to replace the harmer/harmed distinction with anything more positive and healthy. In some stag movies, of course, men are treated sadistically by women; but this is an attempt to turn the tables on degradation, not a positive improvement.

What would cases toward the least objectionable end of the spectrum be like? They would be increasingly less degrading and sexist. The genuinely nonobjectional cases would be nonsexist and nondegrading; but commercial examples do not readily spring to mind.[30] The question is: Does or could any pornography have nonsexist, nondegrading content?

IV

I want to start with the easier question: Is it possible for pornography to have nonsexist, morally acceptable content? Then I will consider whether any pornography of this sort currently exists.

Imagine the following situation, which exists only rarely today: Two fairly conventional people who love each other enjoy playing tennis and bridge together, cooking good food together, and having sex together. In all these activities they are free from hang-ups, guilt, and tendencies to dominate or objectify each other. These two people like to watch tennis matches and old romantic movies on TV, like to watch Julia Child cook, like to read the bridge column in the newspaper, and like to watch pornographic movies. Imagine further that this couple is not at all uncommon in society and that nonsexist pornography is as common as this kind of nonsexist sexual relationship. The situation sounds fine and healthy to me. I see no reason to think that an interest in pornography

[30] Virginia Wright Wexman uses the film *Group Marriage* (Stephanie Rothman, 1973) as an example of "more enlightened erotica." Wexman also asks the following questions in an attempt to point out sexism in pornographic films:
Does it [the film] portray rape as pleasurable to women? Does it consistently show females nude but present men fully clothed? Does it present women as childlike creatures whose sexual interests must be guided by knowing experienced men? Does it show sexually aggressive women as castrating viragos? Does it pretend that sex is exclusively the prerogative of women under twenty-five? Does it focus on the physical aspects of lovemaking rather than the emotional ones? Does it portray women as purely sexual beings? ("Sexism of X-rated Films," *Chicago Sun-Times*, 28 March 1976.)

would disappear in these circumstances.[31] People seem to enjoy watching others experience or do (especially do well) what they enjoy experiencing, doing, or wish they could do themselves. We do not morally object to people watching tennis on TV: why would we object to these hypothetical people watching pornography?

Can we go from the situation today to the situation just imagined? In much current pornography, people are treated in morally objectionable ways. In the scene just imagined, however, pornography would be nonsexist, nondegrading, morally acceptable. The key to making the change is to break the connection between sex and harm. If Stoller is right, this task may be impossible without changing the scenarios of our sexual lives—scenarios that we have been writing since early childhood. (Stoller does not indicate whether he thinks it possible for adults to re-write their scenarios or for social change to bring about the possibility of new scenarios in future generations.) But even if we believe that people can change their sexual scenarios, the sex-harm connection is deeply entrenched and has widespread implications. What is needed is a thorough change in people's deepseated attitudes and feelings about sex roles in general, as well as about sex and roles in sex (sexual roles). Although I cannot even sketch a general outline of such changes here, changes in pornography should be part of a comprehensive program. Television, children's educational material, and nonpornographic movies and novels may be far better avenues for attempting to change attitudes: but one does not want to take the chance that pornography is working against one.

What can be done about pornography in particular? If one wanted to work within the current institutions, one's attempt to use pornography as a tool for the education of male pornography audiences would have to be fairly subtle at first; nonsexist pornography must become familiar enough to sell and be watched. One should realize too that any positive educational value that nonsexist pornography might have may well be as short-lived as most of the effects of pornography. But given these limitations, what could one do?

Two kinds of films must be considered. First is the short film with no plot or character development, just depicted sexual activity in which nonsexist pornography would treat men and women as equal sex partners.[32] The man would not control the circumstances in which the partners had sex or the choice of positions or acts; the woman's preference would be counted equally. There would be no suggestion of a power

31 One might think, as does Stoller, that since pornography today depends on hostility, voyeurism, and sado-masochism (*Perversion*, p. 87) that sexually healthy people would not enjoy it. Two points should be noticed here, however: (1) Stoller need not think that pornography will disappear because hostility is an element of sexual excitement generally; and (2) voyeurism, when it invades no one's privacy, need not be seen as immoral; so although enjoyment of pornography might not be an expression of sexual health, it need not be immoral either.
32 If it is a lesbian or male homosexual film, no one would play a caricatured male or female role. The reader has probably noticed that I have limited my discussion to heterosexual pornography, but there are many interesting analogues to be drawn with male homosexual pornography. Very little lesbian pornography exists, though lesbian scenes are commonly found in male-oriented pornography.

play or conquest on the man's part, no suggestion that "she likes it when I hurt her." Sexual intercourse would not be portrayed as primarily for the purpose of male ejaculation—his orgasm is not "the best part" of the movie. In addition, both the man and woman would express their enjoyment; the man need not be cool and detached.

The film with a plot provides even more opportunity for nonsexist education. Today's pornography often portrays the female characters as playthings even when not engaging in sexual activity. Nonsexist pornography could show women and men in roles equally valued by society, and sex equality would amount to more than possession of equally functional genitalia. Characters would customarily treat each other with respect and consideration, with no attempt to treat men or women brutally or thoughtlessly. The local Pussycat Theater showed a film written and directed by a woman *(The Passions of Carol),* which exhibited a few of the features just mentioned. The main female character in it was the editor of a magazine parody of *Viva.* The fact that some of the characters treated each other very nicely, warmly, and tenderly did not detract from the pornographic features of the movie. This should not surprise us, for even in traditional male-oriented films, lesbian scenes usually exhibit tenderness and kindness.

Plots for nonsexist films could include women in traditionally male jobs (e.g., long-distance truckdriver) or in positions usually held in respect by pornography audiences. For example, a high-ranking female Army officer, treated with respect by men and women alike, could be shown not only in various sexual encounters with other people but also carrying out her job in a humane manner.[33] Or perhaps the main character could be a female urologist. She could interact with nurses and other medical personnel, diagnose illnesses brilliantly, and treat patients with great sympathy as well as have sex with them. When the Army officer or the urologist engage in sexual activities, they will treat their partners and be treated by them in some of the considerate ways described above.

In the circumstances we imagined at the beginning of Part IV of this paper, our nonsexist films could be appreciated in the proper spirit. Under these conditions the content of our new pornography would clearly be nonsexist and morally acceptable. But would the content of such a film be morally acceptable if shown to a typical pornography audience today? It might seem strange for us to change our moral evaluation of the content on the basis of a different audience, but an audience today is likely to see the "respected" urologist and Army officer as playthings or unusual prostitutes—even if our intention in showing the film is to counteract this view. The effect is that, although the content of the film seems morally acceptable and our intention in showing it is morally flawless, women are still degraded.[34] The fact that audience attitude is

[33] One should note that behavior of this kind is still considered unacceptable by the military. A female officer resigned from the U.S. Navy recently rather than be court-martialed for having sex with several enlisted men whom she met in a class on interpersonal relations.

[34] The content may seem morally acceptable only if one disregards such questions as, "Should a doctor have sex with her patients during office hours?" More important is

so important makes one wary of giving wholehearted approval to any pornography seen today.

The fact that good intentions and content are insufficient does not imply that one's efforts toward change would be entirely in vain. Of course, I could not deny that anyone who tries to change an institution from within faces serious difficulties. This is particularly evident when one is trying to change both pornography and a whole set of related attitudes, feelings, and institutions concerning sex and sex roles. But in conjunction with other attempts to change this set of attitudes, it seems preferable to try to change pornography instead of closing one's eyes in the hope that it will go away. For I suspect that pornography is here to stay.[35]

POINTS TO PONDER

1. In the first *Skokie* case, the court cites the *Chaplinsky* rule on fighting words, "those which by their very utterance inflict injury or tend to incite an immediate breach of the peace." Such words, it said, "are no essential part of any exposition of ideas, and are of such slight social value as a step to truth that any benefit from them is clearly outweighed by the social interest in order and morality." Is this a reasonable test? Is it objective, or does it depend upon the sensitivities of the person to whom the words are directed? Should one person's freedom of speech be diminished by another's extra sensitivity? On the other hand, should

---

the propriety of evaluating content wholly apart from the attitudes and reactions of the audience; one might not find it strange to say that one film has morally unacceptable content when shown tonight at the Pussycat Theater but acceptable content when shown tomorrow at a feminist conference.

[35] Three "final" points must be made:

1. I have not seriously considered censorship as an alternative course of action. Both Brownmiller and Sheehy are not averse to it. But as I suggested in note 5, other principles seem too valuable to sacrifice when options are available. In addition, before justifying censorship on moral grounds one would want to compare pornography to other possibly offensive material: advertising using sex and racial stereotypes, violence in TV and films, and so.
2. If my nonsexist pornography succeeded in having much "educational value," it might no longer be pornography according to my definition. This possibility seems too remote to worry me, however.
3. In discussing the audience for nonsexist pornography, I have focused on the male audience. But there is no reason why pornography could not educate and appeal to women as well.

Earlier versions of this paper have been discussed at a meeting of the Society for Women in Philosophy at Stanford University, California State University, Los Angeles, Claremont Graduate School, Western Area Meeting of Women in Psychology, UCLA Political Philosophy Discussion Group, and California State University, Fullerton Annual Philosophy Symposium. Among the many people who made helpful comments were Alan Garfinkel, Jackie Thomason, and Fred Berger. This paper grew out of "Pornography, Sex Roles, and Morality," presented as a responding paper to Fred Berger's "Strictly Peeking: Some Views on Pornography, Sex, and Censorship" in a Philosophy and Public Affairs Symposium at the American Philosophical Association, Pacific Division Meeting, March, 1975.

people be subject to abusive epithets and be expected to stand idly by without reacting to them?

2. In the second case, the court cited the Supreme Court's opinion in the *Cohen* ("Fuck the Draft") case: "While the particular four-letter word [emblem] being litigated here is perhaps more distasteful than most others of its genre, it is nevertheless often true that one man's vulgarity is another's lyric." What is your reaction to this argument? Is it sound?

3. Do you agree that the burden ought to be upon the viewer to "avoid further bombardment of [his or her] sensibilities simply by averting [his or her] eyes"?

4. Would the Skokie Village Council have been justified in banning a Nazi demonstration that was planned for 3:00 in the morning and was to include a mass march past the homes of prominent Jews, with loudspeakers blaring Nazi marches and denunciations of the Jewish people? Would such a ban violate any important constitutional rights?

5. Suppose that the Ku Klux Klan rented space on municipal buses and subways to advertise messages alleging the inferiority of blacks and advocating their deportation to Africa. Should the bus company be permitted to reject such advertising cards? Would such a rejection constitute an infringement of First Amendment rights?

6. After reading Schauer's article, what reasonable conclusions can one draw as to the justification for the principle of free speech? Is any one of the theories he mentions adequate?

7. Schauer seems to be convinced that it is impossible to discriminate between valuable and worthless utterances. Is he correct in this?

8. Taking into account Feinberg's careful distinction between obscenity and pornography, is his conclusion that obscene pornography may be prohibited by law under the conditions he describes (that it is not reasonably avoidable and that it offends beholders who have not voluntarily assumed the risk) consistent with First Amendment freedoms? Does Feinberg go *too* far in permitting pornographic materials that do *not* meet all those criteria to be displayed, distributed, or enjoyed? On what principle ought they to be permitted (or banned)?

9. In some cities, it is possible to visit theaters in which fellatio and sexual intercourse take place on the stage in full view of the audience. Assuming that the "performers" participate voluntarily and that the audience knows exactly what it will be seeing before it enters the theater, should such performances be banned on Feinberg's principles? Explain; also, make your own judgment about the matter, on whatever principles you think ought to apply to such cases.

10. Consider whether any of the following ought to be prohibited by law:

    a. an obscene billboard in a busy downtown area

    b. a pornographic book or magazine

    c. a triple-X movie on television

    d. a man and his wife copulating in a public park at noon on a summer day

11. Ann Garry's thesis revolves around the concept of degradation. What are the salient characteristics of degradation? What does an act of degradation consist of?

12. Is the mere depicting of degradation morally objectionable, or must the depiction itself somehow *be* degrading? Compare, for example, the depiction of the capture, the transportation. and the enslavement of black Africans in the first episode of the television series *Roots* (which surely depicts the degradation of human beings) with a film in which blacks are portrayed as subhuman, ignorant, and incapable of refinement or civilized virtues. Would either of these be immoral? Why?

13. Is it logically possible to produce a nonsexist, morally acceptable pornographic film? Compare the analyses of Garry and Feinberg before answering the question.

14. Garry compares watching tennis on TV with watching pornographic films—i.e., films that lack serious literary, artistic, political, or scientific merit and yet graphically depict sex acts (cf. her definition on page 255 above). Is the analogy appropriate? Are there significant differences between watching people play tennis and watching them copulate which render the one immoral while the other is morally neutral, or does it simply depend upon whether someone is being exploited? Is it sufficient for a film graphically depicting sex acts to be nonsexist and non-exploitative for it to be "morally acceptable"? If the acts depicted were extreme closeups of defecation, would they—or could they—be morally acceptable? Consider once again the analysis set forth in Feinberg's article. And compare Garry's views with the theory of privacy enunciated by Parker in Selection 19 below. Does privacy have anything to do with the morality of pornographic literature, films, or other art works?

VI

THE
RIGHT
OF
PRIVACY
AND
INDIVIDUAL
AUTONOMY

INTRODUCTION

The right of privacy has traditionally been understood as referring principally to the right not to be intruded upon in one's home, to have one's personal papers or business affairs meddled with by persons who have not been invited to do so, to be free of eavesdropping and spying of various sorts. But since the late nineteenth century, the concept of privacy has expanded to embrace almost anything that might be included under the very broad "right to be let alone" that is mentioned in several of the selections that follow.

This constantly broadening right now appears to encompass not only the right not to be spied upon, but also the individual's right to *do* what he or she pleases (within certain still-undefined limits) without state interference. So the right to use contraceptives, the right to have an abortion, and the right to purchase and read sexually titillating materials have all been included under the right of privacy. More recently, homosexuals and other persons whose life-styles are different from that of the majority, and are also regarded with some degree of suspicion, contempt, or hatred by others, have claimed that they have a right to their way of life and that their actions should not be subject to interference by state authority so long as what they do is private and confined to consenting adults. Here, too, the argument is based upon the concept of privacy

Richard B. Parker introduces us to this form of privacy in his astute analysis of the concept. He advances a rather novel definition of "privacy" that ought to be exceedingly helpful in analyzing and passing judgment upon the various cases and issues that arise and are defended under the claim that they are or ought to be protected as part of the right to privacy.

One of the most controversial areas in which similar arguments are being advanced is the rights of homosexuals. Some homosexuals have demanded that they be accorded all the rights that are given to heterosexuals, including the right of marriage to one another. In *Baker* v. *Nelson,* a clerk refused to issue a marriage license to a homosexual couple, who sued on the ground that such refusal was irrational and invidiously discriminatory, denying them the fundamental right to marry. In *Doe* v. *Commonwealth's Attorney,* the plaintiffs attempted to establish that a statute outlawing consensual homosexual relations between adults in private violated their constitutional rights of due process, freedom of expression, and privacy and imposed a cruel and unusual punishment upon them. What is most noteworthy about the selection is the opinion of the dissenting judge, who took up the cudgels in favor of extending the right of privacy to such relationships.

Samuel McCracken argues that homosexual behavior is, in some sense, unnatural. According to McCracken, homosexuals and others whose actions tend to restrict population growth are renouncing responsibility for the continuance of the human species. He finds that the lives of gays are not particularly gay and that they are in fact self-destructive and wretched.

David A. J. Richards criticizes the majority in *Doe*, arguing that the principle of autonomy incorporated in the right of privacy ought to guarantee a fundamental moral equality to all, including homosexuals, and that a denial of their right to express their sexual preferences amounts to a deprivation of a fundamental human right. He subjects the concept of "unnaturalness" to a searching analysis and concludes that it is vague and in any case improperly applied to homosexual behavior.

RICHARD B. PARKER 19

A DEFINITION OF PRIVACY

I. INTRODUCTION

The Supreme Court handed down a six-to-three decision in *United States v. White* [1] on April 19, 1971. In the case, government agents testified at trial to incriminating conversations between a government informant and defendant White which the agents overheard by monitoring the frequency of a radio transmitter concealed on the informant. The agents acted without a warrant. The Supreme Court, reversing the court of appeals,[2] held that the defendant's fourth amendment rights had not been invaded because his constitutionally justifiable expectations of privacy had not been violated.[3] It would probably surprise most people to learn that the Supreme Court has said that constitutionally justifiable expectations of privacy do not include the expectation that our conversations are not being simultaneously transmitted to an unknown audience by the person to whom we are speaking. The decision raises the larger questions: What is privacy? and Why should "privacy" be the key term for interpretation of the fourth amendment?

From *Rutgers Law Review* 27 (1974): 275–296. Reprinted by permission of the author and the editors of *Rutgers Law Review*.

I am indebted to David A. J. Richards, Peter Williams, Kenneth I. Winston, and especially John B. Moore, for their careful criticisms of earlier versions of this article. My debt is no less to Jeffrey Blustein, Donald DeSalvo, Joshua Rabinowitz and John Stevens, as well as to my faculty colleagues at Rutgers Law School, Julius Cohen, Thomas Cowan and David Haber. The article also benefited from a reading to the Tuesday Evening Club at Rockefeller University on April 3, 1973.
[1] 401 U.S. 745 (1971).
[2] 405 F.2d 838 (7th Cir. 1969), *rev'd*, 401 U.S. 745 (1971).
[3] 401 U.S. at 752–54.

The aims of this article are (1) to present and defend a definition of privacy which explains the close connection privacy has with the fourth amendment, and with some of the other amendments in the Bill of Rights; (2) to use the definition to clarify what privacy means in other legal and non-legal contexts; and, (3) to apply the definition to *United States v. White* to illustrate how an abstract definition of privacy can affect the analysis of a case.

II. DEFINITION

Currently, there is no consensus in the legal and philosophical literature on a definition of privacy. For some, privacy is a psychological state, a condition of "being-apart-from-others" closely related to alienation.[4] For others, privacy is a form of power, "the control we have over information about ourselves," [5] or "the condition under which there is *control* over acquaintance with one's personal affairs by the one enjoying it," [6] or "the individual's ability to control the circulation of information relating to him." [7] Another noted author on privacy defines it as "the *claim* of individuals, groups, or institutions to determine for themselves when, how, and to what extent information about them is communicated to others." [8] For still others, an important aspect of privacy is the freedom not to participate in the activities of others, a freedom which is lost when we are forced to hear the roar of automobile traffic or breathe polluted air.[9] Given such a diversity of definitions, indicating uncertainty whether privacy is a psychological state, a form of power, a right or claim, or a freedom not to participate, to say that what the fourth amendment protects are constitutionally justifiable expectations of privacy is to be unclear about the purpose of the fourth amendment.

Ideally, a definition of privacy should meet the following three criteria. First, it should fit the data. Data, for purposes of this article, means our shared intuitions of when privacy is or is not gained or lost. A suggested definition of privacy might be overbroad or too narrow or both. For instance, to define privacy as being left alone [10] is clearly overbroad. Although every loss of privacy may be a case of our not being left alone, there are many cases of not being left alone which are not losses of privacy; one example is having income tax withheld from a paycheck. To define privacy as control over who sees us performing sexual intercourse is to make our definition too narrow. Although all

---

[4] Weinstein, *The Uses of Privacy in the Good Life*, in PRIVACY, NOMOS XIII 94 (Pennock & Chapman, eds. 1971) [hereinafter cited as PRIVACY].
[5] FRIED, AN ANATOMY OF VALUES 140 (1970) [hereinafter cited as FRIED].
[6] Gross, *Privacy and Autonomy*, in PRIVACY, *supra* note 4, at 169.
[7] MILLER, THE ASSAULT ON PRIVACY 25 (1971) [hereinafter cited as MILLER]. Professor Miller does think that his definition is the one which most lawyers and social scientists would agree contains "the basic attribute of an effective right of privacy." *Id.*
[8] WESTIN, PRIVACY AND FREEDOM 7 (1968) (emphasis added) [hereinafter cited as WESTIN].
[9] *See* Van Den Haag, *On Privacy*, in PRIVACY, *supra* note 4, at 161.
[10] COOLEY, TORTS 29 (2d. ed. 1888), *cited in* Warren & Brandeis, *The Right to Privacy*, 4 HARV. L. REV. 193, 195 (1980), a seminal article in the legal literature on privacy.

loss of such control may be a lóss of privacy, privacy includes many other matters.

A second criterion by which to judge a definition of privacy is that of simplicity. It may be that our shared concept of privacy is a grabbag of several different personal interests with no common characteristics. Thus the simplest definition may have to include a list. For example, privacy may be the ability of the individual to lead his life without anyone

(a) interfering with his family and home life;
(b) interfering with his physical or mental integrity or his moral and intellectual freedom;
(c) attacking his honor and reputation;
(d) placing him in a false light;
(e) disclosing irrelevant embarrassing facts about him;
(f) using his name, identity or likeness;
(g) spying or prying on, watching and besetting him;
(h) interfering with his correspondence;
(i) misusing his private communications, written or oral; or
(j) disclosing information given or received by him in circumstances of professional confidence.[11]

Perhaps gains or losses of privacy are gains or losses of freedom from this list of evils. The standard of simplicity dictates that if some characteristics common to all or some of these evils could be found and the length of the list reduced, so much the better.

A third criterion which a definition of privacy should meet is applicability by lawyers and courts. The legal process places limits on the subtlety and sophistication of the definitions it uses. Our definition of privacy must be able to appear in instructions to jurors, in complaints, and in court opinions. The standard of applicability requires us to prefer a useful approximation of the truth over a less useful but closer approximation of the truth.

The latter two criteria of simplicity and applicability can be distinguished from each other by the purposes for which each criterion is included. The point of the criterion of simplicity is theoretical elegance. The point of the criterion of applicability is usefulness in the legal process. The two criteria can conflict, and either will conflict with the first criterion which requires that the definition fit the data. Our definition of privacy should be as true (fit the data), as beautiful (simple), and as useful (applicable) as possible. These three ideals will be compromised by one another in any definition of privacy, but the more adequate the definition, the less the necessary compromise.

Philosophers have suggested to me that an attempt to find a single short definition of privacy is misguided. If truth were the only criterion for a definition, I would agree. There is no single definition of privacy which fits all the data. A reason for ignoring some difficult counter-

---

11 *Conclusions of the Nordic Conference on the Right of Privacy,* in PRIVACY AND THE LAW, A REPORT BY THE BRITISH SECTION OF THE INTERNATIONAL COMMISSION OF JUSTICE 45 (Littman & Carter-Rusk eds. 1970).

examples and proposing a definition of privacy which must be to some extent prescriptive is that the law needs some short, commonly agreed upon definition of privacy. I seek in this article a definition which will capture not only what is at stake in many fourth amendment cases, but will make sense of the Court's recent appeal to privacy to justify a right to abortion,[12] as well as clear up the theoretical disarray in the tort of invasion of privacy.[13] In a wide variety of factual settings, the law defends or regretfully sacrifices privacy. The use of the same word suggests that the same thing is at stake whether the problem is bugged informers, abortion, or the use of one's picture in advertising. Yet phrases like "human dignity and and individuality,"[14] or "being let alone,"[15] cover situations which have little connection with privacy.

The criteria to fit to the data and applicability by courts and lawyers both dictate that an adequate definition of privacy allow us to discuss separately these five questions: (1) whether a person *has* lost or gained privacy, (2) whether he *should* lose or gain privacy, (3) whether he *knows* that he has lost or gained privacy, (4) whether he *approves or disapproves* of the loss or gain, and (5) how he *experiences* that loss or gain.

Of the various definitions of privacy in the literature, those which speak of privacy as a form of power, of control over something,[16] do allow us to discuss the above five questions separately. For instance, if privacy is defined as "the control we have over information about ourselves,"[17] the question of whether a person has lost or gained such control in a given situation can be discussed separately from the question of whether he should have lost or gained that control, and both questions are independent of the questions of whether he knows he has lost or gained that control, how the loss or gain feels to him, and whether he approves or disapproves.

If privacy is defined as a psychological state, it becomes impossible to describe a person who has had his privacy temporarily invaded without his knowledge, since his psychological state is not affected at all by the loss of privacy. It is interesting and important to study what it is like to experience various gains and losses of privacy. One of the reasons the law protects privacy in certain situations is to protect us as individuals from suffering mental distress. But privacy should not be defined as, for example, freedom from various sorts of mental distress, or as the experience of being apart from others.[18] Such definitions of privacy will be unable to cover those situations where we lose or gain privacy with no corresponding change in our mental state.

By the same token, an adequate definition of privacy should not beg questions of whether we *should* lose or gain privacy in a given situation.

---

12 Roe v. Wade, 401 U.S. 113 (1973); Doe v. Bolton, 401 U.S. 179 (1973).
13 See text accompanying notes 47–57 *infra*.
14Bloustein, *Privacy as an Aspect of Human Dignity: An Answer to Dean Prosser*, 39 N.Y.U.L. Rev. 962, 1001–07 (1964) [hereinafter cited as Bloustein].
15 Warren & Brandeis, *supra note* 10, at 195.
16 See notes 5–7 *supra* and accompanying text.
17 Fried, *supra* note 5, at 140.
18 Weinstein, Privacy, *supra* note 4, at 94.

The problem of defining what is gained or lost when privacy is gained or lost should be distinct from the problems of (1) when people should gain or lose privacy, or (2) whether they have moral or legal rights to privacy in any given situation. Courts, which must weigh claims to privacy against other important interests, would benefit if the definition of privacy being used could be agreed to by all parties without prejudice to any side. Definitions of privacy as control over something (for instance, over information about ourselves) meet this test. One can distinguish the question of whether a person has lost or gained such control from the question of whether he should lose or gain it or whether he has a right to such control in his particular situation.

These considerations lead to the conclusion that Fried, Miller, Gross, and others were correct to define privacy as a form of power or control over something.[19] But definitions of privacy as "control over information about ourselves,"[20] or "the individual's ability to control the circulation of information relating to him"[21] are clearly overbroad. Consider the student whose examination unexpectedly reveals that he has not studied, or imagine the person who is snubbed at a party by the guest of honor, revealing to all present his low standing with that guest. In both cases, and in others like them, information about these people becomes known to others without their consent. They lose control of it; yet we would not say that they have suffered a loss of privacy.

Not every loss or gain of control over information about ourselves is a loss or gain of privacy. It is tempting to try and limit the definition of privacy to control over certain items of information. But this approach is a mistake. Although there is some information which seems peculiarly related to privacy (for example, the color of our pubic hair), a loss of control over most items of information about ourselves is sometimes related to privacy and sometimes not. Thus, in some contexts, loss of control over who knows our names is felt to be a loss of privacy, but not in other contexts. Also, to define privacy in terms of control over certain specific items of information has the disadvantage of making that definition of privacy relative to a particular culture or sub-culture. This is undesirable for two reasons. First, it is logically possible to make cross-cultural comparisons of the importance which a given culture places on privacy. If privacy is defined relative to each culture, these comparisons could not be made. Thus, the proposed criterion of fitting the definition to the data requires that an adequate definition of privacy allow for the logical possibility of such comparisons. Second, the criteria of simplicity and applicability require a definition applicable to all human cultures: simplicity clearly requires one rather than many definitions; and in a country as heterogeneous as the United States, applicability requires that a definition of privacy usable by the law not be tied to certain items of information.

In addition to being overbroad, the definition of privacy as control over information about ourselves seems also to be too narrow. There

19 See notes 5–7 *supra* and accompanying text.
20 FRIED, *supra* note 5, at 140.
21 MILLER, *supra* note 7, at 25.

seem to be many losses or gains of privacy which are only marginally related to information about ourselves. One example is the loss of privacy involved in being forced to bear an unwanted child; another example is the loss of privacy when someone sits next to us in a deserted public place. Consider also the case of a woman's lover who, just after he has left her side, peers in through the window in order to see her once more in the nude. She has suffered a loss of privacy, yet it seems inaccurate to describe her loss of privacy as a loss of control of information about herself. It is true that she has lost some control over information about herself. Her lover knows that her body has not changed, that she has not put on her clothes. Yet the essence of her loss of privacy is not a loss of control over information. It is a loss of control over who, at that moment, can see her body.

Using an extended sense of "information," we might say that loss of control over who can see us is a loss of control over information about ourselves. If this sort of case were atypical, we might be justified in squeezing it in under the rubric "information," in order to have a simple, applicable definition. But far from being atypical, control over who can see us, hear us, touch us, smell us, and taste us, in sum, control over who can sense us, is the core of the concept of privacy. It is control over the sort of information found in dossiers and data banks which is marginal to the concept of privacy.

The thesis defended in this article is that privacy is control over who can sense us. What is gained by those who sense a person, and not by those who read the most detailed description of him, could be called "information," but it would be misleading to use that word. Moreover, whatever is gained is hard to define. But the ways by which it is gained are clear. They are the five senses. Therefore, the proposed definition is expressed as "control over who can sense us."

Consider one more situation which may clarify the distinction between controlling who can sense us and controlling the circulation of information about ourselves. Imagine an astronaut in a space capsule with all his bodily functions being monitored by electrodes attached to his body. Ground control knows more about the position and state of the astronaut's body than the astronaut does himself. One can still imagine the astronaut switching off the television camera photographing the interior of the capsule when he evacuates feces in order to have "a little privacy." But what does the astronaut gain by being able to switch off the camera? He does gain some control over some information, if only the information that the monitoring system is working correctly. He does have the power to deny to ground control the ability to corroborate the information they receive from the electrodes. But beyond that, the astronaut's ability to shut off the television camera has no effect on his control over information about himself. Yet if he lost the ability to shut off the camera, he would suffer a severe loss of privacy. What he would lose is the ability to control who can *see* him evacuating which is more essential to privacy than control over who can *know* that he is evacuating. Privacy is often used to control the circulation of information about ourselves, but privacy itself is control over who can sense us.

The definition of privacy defended in this article is that *privacy is control over when and by whom the various parts of us can be sensed by others.* By "sensed," is meant simply seen, heard, touched, smelled, or tasted. By "parts of us," is meant the parts of our bodies, our voices, and the products of our bodies. "Parts of us" also includes objects very closely associated with us. By "closely associated" is meant primarily what is spatially associated. The objects which are "parts of us" are objects we usually keep with us or locked up in a place accessible only to us. In our culture, these objects might be the contents of our purse, pocket, or safe deposit box, or the pages of our diaries. For some other culture these objects might be eating utensils or the inside of a personal shrine. What these objects happen to be in any given culture is not part of my definition of privacy.[22]

"Parts of us" tends very strongly to mean the physical parts. Control over who "senses" elements of our personal character, our desires, or our psychological states, is not generally part of privacy itself, although we often use control over who can sense us physically to control who sees how we feel. The man who was humiliated by being snubbed at the party suffered no loss of privacy because he did not lose control over who could sense a physical part of him.[23] If he had been humiliated by having his shirt or toupee torn off, or by having his conversation recorded and played back to the merriment of all, or by having a candid photograph taken and shown around, he would have suffered a loss of privacy. He would have lost control over who could see or hear parts of him. Similarly, the student whose ignorance is revealed by the examination has not lost any privacy,[24] although he may choose not to let the examiner see his paper, an exercise of his privacy, in order not to have his ignorance revealed. All of us use our control over who can sense the physical parts of us, our privacy, to conceal our character, desires, or temporary mental states. We may refuse to meet someone, an exercise of our privacy, in order not to reveal our attitude toward him. But if our attitude, character, desires, or temporary mental states become known, that fact does not constitute a loss of privacy.

It may be objected that, in some contexts, our desires and psychological states are private information; and surely, to lose control of private information is to lose privacy. But I do not think this is the case. Private information is information which we can usually employ our privacy to protect. Similarly, a loss of control over private information is usually the result of a loss of privacy. (What that information is varies from culture to culture.) But there is no necessary connection between a loss of control over private information and a loss of privacy. If we tell someone that we are homosexual, we lose control over private information, but we do not necessarily lose privacy.

When privacy is defined as control over when and by whom the parts of us are sensed by others, "sense" is used as a summary for the verbs: "see," "hear," "touch," "smell," and "taste," as those words are ordinarily used. When we say that X saw Y's diary, we might mean, depending on the context, that X read the diary, or that X simply saw

---

[22] See text following note 21 *supra* on the necessity of keeping the basic definition of privacy applicable to all cultures.
[23] *Id.*
[24] *Id.*

that it existed. Either could be a loss of privacy by this definition, which simply incorporates normal usage of the verb, "to see," with all its ambiguities. Also, this definition does imply that if X read Y's diary, Y's loss of privacy would be the same regardless of the contents of the diary. The offense against Y's privacy is that the diary was seen, meaning in this case, read. Y may value his privacy, his control over who can see the diary, much more if the diary contains revealing information. But the loss of privacy would be the same no matter what the contents of the diary, for in either case, Y lost the same degree of control over who saw his diary.

The loss of privacy would, however, be much less if X did not identify the diary he saw as Y's diary. To the extent that the informational content of what is sensed by others identifies it as part of a particular person, the informational content makes a difference in the degree of privacy lost. Thus a single line in a diary might identify to the onlooker the identity of the author of the diary and greatly increase his loss of control over who could sense part of *him*.[25] If he remains anonymous, he retains control over who can sense him as a distinct individual. Some privacy is lost even if the diary goes unidentified, but much less. In sum, apart from information which identifies who is being sensed, the information revealed when we are sensed does not affect the degree of the loss in privacy, *i.e.,* the loss of control over when and by whom we are sensed. Some losses of privacy may matter much more to us than others, usually because of the information revealed. But when the degree of loss of control is the same, the loss of privacy is the same.[26] This fact allows us to keep separate the questions of how much privacy has been lost, and why we disapprove of that loss.

, In the situation involving a person who has his conversation recorded at the party,[27] loss of privacy is primarily loss of control over who can hear his voice; what is actually said affects the degree of loss of privacy only if it identifies the person as the speaker.[28] What happens to the tape recording, however, greatly affects the degree of his loss of privacy. If the tape is not erased, but instead is carried away by someone who can play it elsewhere, the man suffers an additional loss of privacy. Whether the recording is ever replayed has no effect on the degree of loss of privacy, for the loss consists not in being listened to, but in losing control over when and by whom one is listened to.[29]

25 Another example is a wart in a photograph of a nude body which identifies to the onlooker whose body it is.

26 Thus the loss of privacy is the same whether the photograph in note 25 shows one as healthy or as the victim of a loathsome disease.

Gross, PRIVACY, *supra* note 6, at 170, noted the fact that if, in applying for a job, "I submit a detailed account of my life while my friend presents only the barest resume of his, I am not giving up more of privacy than he."

27 See text accompanying note 23 *supra.*

28 What is said will of course affect how the person feels about the loss of privacy. But one of the proposed criteria for an adequate definition of privacy is that the degree of loss or gain of privacy is logically independent of how the person losing or gaining privacy happens to feel about it.

29 This is true of any definition of privacy as control over something. If privacy is a control over the circulation of information about oneself, privacy is lost as control is lost, even if the person taking the control never uses it to circulate the information.

To sum up, privacy is control over when and by whom the (physical) parts of us (as identifiable persons) can be seen or heard (in person or by use of photographs, recordings, TV, etc.), touched, smelled, or tasted by others.

There are at least two major objections to this definition of privacy. First, the definition proposed here may be far too narrow. It does not include the government agent who questions all one's neighbors about one's affairs discovering information one did not want disclosed, or the case of a national data bank which gathers information from various sources to construct a detailed personal profile revealing facts that one would never have disclosed voluntarily. These seem to be instances of loss of privacy where there has been no loss of control over when and by whom one is sensed.

The second major objection is that the sort of control that has been defined as privacy is too humble and instrumental to account for the high reputation which privacy enjoys. I shall return to this second objection. The burden of the argument shall be that privacy is indeed much more important as a means than as an end, and that much of the confusion surrounding privacy results from incorrectly identifying it with the ends it enables us to achieve. However, it deserves its reputation because it is crucial to the exercise of almost every important right and freedom.

To consider the first objection, that the definition ignores the loss of privacy which results when information about individuals is gathered, collated, and stored, I believe that what seems a loss of privacy here is actually a loss of the value of our privacy due to three different factors.

First, one's privacy loses value when information about oneself is gathered, because one of the important uses made of privacy is to control the flow of information about oneself. One reason why people wish to sense others is to gain information about them. Normally, a person can exercise his privacy and deny others the information they seek. But if those others, possess it already, they do not need to sense the person. One may still have his privacy, his control over when and by whom he can be sensed by others, but to the degree he cannot use it to control the flow of information about himself, that privacy is less valuable to him.

Second, the gathering of information about an individual lessens the value of his privacy by making it less secure. A person or government possessed of that information can more easily take an individual's privacy away. If X knows where Y lives, Y's name, occupation, and personal and financial resources, then should X wish to put Y under surveillance or imprison Y, or otherwise deprive Y of control over who may sense him, it is much easier for X to do so. To some extent X's power is a loss of control by Y over who senses Y, *i.e.*, a loss of privacy per se. To that extent, data banks and the like do not represent a counter-example to this definition of privacy. But generally, the collection of data by government and other institutions, as described by Westin [30]

---

[30] WESTIN, *supra* note 8, especially Part II. But see WESTIN & BAKER, DATABANKS IN A FREE SOCIETY (1972), where Westin takes a more sanguine view.

and Miller,[31] is not a loss of privacy per se, but rather a threat to one's privacy.

Third, the existence of this threat devalues one's privacy by making one constantly uncertain of whether one still has it. Like any form of power, privacy can only be fully enjoyed and exercised if one is sure he actually has it. Privacy can be lost or gained unintentionally. A person can be pleased or unaware that he has lost privacy. But the value of privacy to him is in part a function of whether he knows he has it. If one is in doubt about whether he has privacy in a given situation, whether he has control over when and by whom he is sensed, a large part of the value of what privacy he does have is destroyed. People will often not use their privacy if they are not sure they have it. A government which in fact cannot listen to or look at its citizens at will does not destroy their privacy. But whatever the facts, if citizens believe that the government can and might sense them at will, a large part of the value of privacy is destroyed. Citizens may in fact have privacy, but they will not enjoy or make full use of that privacy. A government which collects extensive information is generally a government which citizens believe has the ability and will to look or listen without permission. The existence of such a government thus devalues privacy, even when it does not actually cause a loss of privacy per se.

Having discussed how the collection of information about people can devalue their privacy, let us examine further the positive value of privacy as defined here. Charles Fried, working from a definition of privacy as the individual's control over information about himself, described the instrumental nature of privacy and explained why privacy is valuable:

> There is a puzzle here, since we do not feel comfortable about asserting that privacy is intrinsically valuable, an end in itself—privacy is always for or in relation to something or someone. On the other hand, to view privacy as simply instrumental, as one way of getting other goods, seems unsatisfactory too. For we feel that there is a necessary quality, after all, to the importance we ascribe to privacy. This perplexity is displayed when we ask how privacy might be traded off against other values. We wish to ascribe to privacy more than an ordinary priority. My analysis attempts to show why we value privacy highly and why also we do not treat it as an end in itself.
>
> Briefly, my argument is that privacy provides the rational context for a number of our most significant ends, such as love, trust and friendship, respect and self-respect. Since it is a necessary element of those ends, it draws its significance from them. And yet since privacy is only an element of those ends, not the whole, we have not felt inclined to attribute to privacy ultimate significance.[32]
>
> . . . It is my thesis that privacy is not just one possible means among others to insure some other value, but that it is necessarily related to ends and relations of the most fundamental sort: respect, love, friendship,

31 MILLER, *supra* note 7, especially Chapter II.
32 FRIED, *supra* note 5, at 137–38.

and trust. Privacy is not merely a good technique for furthering these fundamental relations; rather without privacy they are simply inconceivable. They require a context of privacy or the possibility of privacy for their existence. To make clear the necessity of privacy as a context for respect, love, friendship, and trust is to bring out also why a threat to privacy seems to threaten our very integrity as persons. To respect, love, trust, or feel affection for others and to regard ourselves as the objects of love, trust, and affection is at the heart of our notion of ourselves as persons among persons, and privacy is the necessary atmosphere for these attitudes and actions, as oxygen is for combustion.[33]

Most of what Fried says seems even more true if my more physical definition of privacy is substituted for his. For instance, Fried noted, correctly, that the creation of intimacy is a use made of privacy. Using his definition of privacy as the individual's control over information about himself, he said:

> Intimacy is the sharing of information about one's actions, beliefs, or emotions which one does not share with all, and which one has the .right not to share with anyone. By conferring this right, privacy creates the moral capital which we spend in friendship and love.[34]

One objection to this statement is that we often share a great deal of personal information with those with whom we are not intimate. And although the sharing of information is part of intimacy, it is not the major part. A husband may *know* less about his wife than does her best woman friend. But because husband and wife choose to constantly sense one another, husband and wife will be much more intimate. This choice is an exercise of privacy. The same is true of intimate friends. What makes them intimate is not just what they choose to reveal to each other, but that they constantly choose to be in one another's presence, usually without passing on much new information, and with no further purpose than the pleasure of one another's company.[35]

The connection of privacy with trust, love, friendship, respect, and

---

[33] *Id.* at 140.
[34] *Id.* at 142.
[35] What lovers love most is to see one another, and they prefer sight to all the other senses, because love exists and is generated by sight more than any other sense. Is it, similarly, true of friends that the most desirable thing for them is to live together? [Apparently, yes;] for friendship is an association or community, and a person has the same attitude toward his friend as he has toward himself. Now, since a man's perception that he exists is desirable, his perception of his friend's existence is desirable, too. But only by living together can the perception of a friend's existence be activated, so that it stands to reason that friends aim at living together. And whatever his existence means to each partner individually or whatever is the purpose that makes his life desirable, he wishes to pursue it together with his friends. That is why some friends drink together or play dice together, while others go in for sports together and hunt together, or join in the study of philosophy: whatever each group of people loves most in life, in that activity they spend their days together. For since they wish to live together with their friends, they follow and share in those pursuits which, they think, constitute their life together. ARISTOTLE, NICOMACHEAN ETHICS, 1171B29–1172A8 at 271 (Ostwald trans. 1962).

self-respect is generally much closer using this article's definition of privacy than using a definition centering on information. Even so, these values are not "inconceivable" without privacy or the possibility of privacy. One can realize these values in a concentration camp or shipwrecked and adrift in an open boat.[36] But clearly, as an empirical matter, the possibility of their realization is greatly enhanced by privacy. Any importance which privacy, by this definition, loses by not being necessarily related to trust, love, friendship, respect, and self-respect, it regains by being a practical necessity for a greater number of basic human rights and freedoms than does privacy defined as control of information about oneself. The reason that privacy is so prized is that its loss is a prerequisite for a violation of most of one's other basic rights and freedoms.

One example of this is the right to freedom of movement, the right not to be confined against one's will. Confinement is almost always accompanied by a loss of privacy as it has been defined here; conversely, exercise of the right of freedom of movement generally requires such privacy—control over when and by whom one will be sensed by others. Control of information about oneself is not so clearly a prerequisite to freedom of movement. An individual may have freedom of movement even though everything about him is known; and he may lose freedom of movement even though he keeps control over information about himself. Refugees being taken to a concentration camp serve as an example. If their captors care little about them as individuals, and give them numbers instead of taking their names, they may have lost little privacy if privacy is defined as control over information about oneself—even though many of their basic rights have been denied.

Privacy is a humble sort of power. We feel it to be important because its loss is, as an empirical matter, a condition of the loss of most of what we value personally and politically. But it is not identical to or logically necessary to those things we value. It is like good soil, which, although empirically necessary for many majestic trees and beautiful flowers and extremely valuable as a condition of their existence and growth, is not identical with or logically related to any of them.

III. APPLICATION

Because privacy is empirically necessary to virtually all of our basic political rights, it is indirectly protected by most of the provisions of the Bill of Rights. For instance, the fifth amendment protection against self-incrimination also protects against imprisonment and the resulting loss of privacy generally necessary to force a confession.[37] The sixth

---

36 Fried's treatment of privacy in AN ANATOMY OF VALUES is part of a larger discussion of rational ends and actions to which this comment does not do justice.

37 Beginning from Fried's definition of privacy as control over information about oneself, FRIED, *supra* note 5, at 140, Gerstein, *Privacy and Self-Incrimination*, 80 ETHICS 87–101 (1970), quite naturally interpreted the fifth amendment as a direct protection of privacy. However, he said it was a protection not so much of the flow of incriminating information as a protection against being forced to make public a private judgment of self-condemnation. Quite apart from the question of whether this is an

amendment guarantee of a speedy and fair trial and the eighth amendment prohibition of excessive bail also protect indirectly our control over who can sense us. But some constitutional provisions are peculiarly related to privacy as I have defined it. Three in particular are: the first amendment protection of free association; the third amendment protection against the quartering of soldiers in private homes; and the fourth amendment protection against unreasonable searches and seizures of persons, houses, papers, and effects.[38]

Justice Black objected vociferously to the extension of the fourth amendment to cover eavesdropping. He argued that the fourth amendment was "aimed directly at the abhorred practice of breaking in, ransacking and searching homes and other buildings and seizing people's personal belongings without warrants issued by magistrates." [39] For him, the amendment did not create a "general right . . . so as to give this Court the unlimited power to hold unconstitutional everything which affects privacy." [40] He also expressed fear that the vagueness and ambiguity of the term "privacy" would later be used to whittle down our basic rights against the Government.[41]

This article's definition of privacy attempts to correct some of the overbreadth and vagueness of other definitions of privacy. Also, it specifies that power or control which the authors of the fourth amendment were trying to preserve for each citizen in protecting his person, house, papers, and effects. When the fourth amendment was written, protection from the breaking into homes and other buildings and the seizure of persons and their personal belongings without warrants was sufficient to protect privacy as defined here. No additional prohibition on eavesdropping or a reference to privacy was necessary. But given modern life styles, and the technology of the telescopic lens and parabolic microphone, the protection of privacy now requires more than protection against physical trespass and seizure. The change in the legal means of protection is seen in the progression of cases from *Olmstead v. United States* [42] to *Katz v. United States*.[43] However, the basic value protected

---

adequate account of the fifth amendment, both it and Fried's definition of privacy are illustrations of privacy itself being confused with the ends privacy is used to serve.

[38] The first, third and fourth amendments are also the provisions which Justice Stewart singled out in *Katz* v. *United States,* 389 U.S. 347, 350 (1967), as particularly protecting privacy.

[39] Katz v. United States, 389 U.S. 347, 367 (1967) (Black, J., dissenting).

[40] *Id.* at 374 (dissenting opinion).

[41] Griswold v. Connecticut, 381 U.S. 479, 509 (1965) (Black, J., dissenting).

[42] 277 U.S. 438 (1928).

[43] 389 U.S. 347 (1967). Not until 1928 in *Olmstead* v. *United States* did the Court deal with the fourth amendment problems generated by the development of machines—the telephone and radio—which made it possible both to carry on and to eavesdrop on oral conversations at a distance. In a five-to-four decision, the Supreme Court, per Chief Justice Taft, held that messages passing over telephone lines outside a person's home or office are not protected by the fourth amendment because (1) such messages are not things which can be "seized," and (2) they can be intercepted without entry into the defendant's premises and hence there is no "search" of a constitutionally protected place. 277 U.S. at 463–66.

Justice Brandeis, in an eloquent dissent, argued that precedent required a broader construction of the fourth amendment. *Id.* at 471–85. He noted that the Government had made no attempt to defend the methods employed by its agents and had conceded that, if their behavior constituted a "search" or "seizure," then that behavior was indeed unreasonable and constitutionally proscribed. By narrowly construing the words "search" and "seizure," the Court, he thought, had lost sight of the purpose of the fourth amendment:

> The makers of our Constitution undertook to secure conditions favorable to the pursuit of happiness. They recognized the significance of man's spiritual nature, of his feelings and of his intellect. They knew that only a part of the pain, pleasure and satisfactions of life are to be found in material things. They sought to protect Americans in their beliefs, their thoughts, their emotions and their sensations. They conferred, as against the Government, the right to be let alone—the most comprehensive of rights and the right most valued by civilized men. To protect that right, every unjustifiable intrusion by the Government upon the privacy of the individual, whatever the means employed, must be deemed a violation of the Fourth Amendment.

Id. at 478. In *Nardone* v. *United States*, 302 U.S. 379 (1937), the Court undercut its decision in *Olmstead* when it interpreted section 605 of the Federal Communications Act of 1934 to be a prohibition against the interception and divulgence of telephone and telegraph communications, including divulgence in a trial court. The Court's decision in *Nardone* framed the issue of the protection of citizens against wire tapping by federal agents as a problem of interpreting and applying an act of Congress rather than the fourth amendment. With the 1934 Act available as justification for curbing the practice of wiretapping by federal agents, only cases in which there was no tapping of telephone or telegraph lines could force the Court to make use of the fourth amendment to check abuse of the new technology by federal agents. The first such case to reach the Court was *Goldman* v. *United States*, 316 U.S. 129 (1942).

In *Goldman,* federal agents entered defendant's offiice without a search warrant. They planted a dictaphone with a wire leading to an office next door which was not owned or leased by the defendant. When they returned the following day to the next door office, the dictaphone had broken. The agents, however, were able to make use of a detectaphone, a device which, when placed against a wall, picks up sounds on the other side of the wall, to overhear an incriminating conversation. The Court decided, five-to-three, that the evidence was admissible because the use of the detectaphone did not constitute an actual physical trespass into the office of the defendant, and therefore the case could not be distinguished from *Olmstead.* *Goldman* makes clear that if the evidence of the conversation had come from the dictaphone, rather than the detectaphone, it would have been inadmissible on fourth amendment grounds because gathered by trespass without a warrant.

It was not, however, until *Silverman* v. *United States,* 365 U.S. 505 (1961), that the Court actually excluded a defendant's conversation on fourth amendment grounds. In *Silverman,* federal agents (members of the District of Columbia police), acting without a warrant, used a spike mike to penetrate a wall and overhear an incriminating conversation. That conversation was held inadmissible under the fourth amendment on the ground that it was the penetration of the wall which distinguished the case from *Goldman.* It was "the reality of an actual intrusion in a constitutionally protected area" which made the significant difference. *Id.* at 512. The Court distinguished "intrusion in a constitutionally protected area" from "technical trespass," indicating uneasiness with *Goldman's* emphasis on trespass; but Justice Stewart concluded the Court's opinion by saying: "We find no occasion to re-examine Goldman here [and protect conversation absent intrusion into a "constitutionally protected area"], but we decline to go beyond it, by even a fraction of an inch." *Id.*

By expressly bringing conversation under the warrant protection of the fourth amendment, but limiting that protection to cases where there was intrusion into a constitutionally protected area, the Court placed itself partially within the tradition of the fourth amendment as protection for those aspects of privacy attaching to property (protection against intrusion into certain areas) and partially within the tradition well represented by Justice Brandeis in his dissent in *Olmstead*, of the fourth amendment as protection for a broader right of privacy attaching to persons (protection of conversation).

In *Katz* v. *United States*, 389 U.S. 347 (1967), the Court opted for the personal interpretation. In *Katz,* federal agents, acting without a warrant, attached an elec-

by the fourth amendment (and also protected by other provisions of the Bill of Rights, particularly the first and third amendments) remains the same. It is privacy defined as control over who can sense us, valuable both for itself and as an empirically necessary condition for the exercise of most other rights and freedoms.

The application of this definition of privacy to the recent abortion decisions of the Supreme Court [44] is fairly straightforward. If privacy is a loss of control over by whom one can be sensed, then to be forced to go through pregnancy, childbirth, and especially raising a child is a severe loss of privacy which can last many years. On the other hand, if privacy is control over information about oneself, then Justice Rehnquist may be correct in stating that privacy has little to do with abortion.[45] This article's definition of privacy provides an answer to those puzzled about the specific relation of privacy to control over one's body.[46]

At this point another area of the law in need of a unifying definition of privacy, the tort of invasion of privacy, warrants some discussion. It is possible in most of the states in this country for one citizen to sue another citizen for "invasion of privacy." It is only in the last 100 years or so that the courts have recognized such a cause of action, stimulated in large part in this country by Warren and Brandeis' famous article, "The Right to Privacy," which appeared in the *Harvard Law Review* [47] in 1890. Since then, the "right to privacy" has been successfully invoked in a wide range of tort cases. In 1960, William Prosser examined more than three hundred such cases in an attempt to discover exactly what interest was being protected.[48] He concluded that there

---

tronic listening device similar to a detectaphone to the outside of a glass public telephone booth where the defendant was making incriminating calls. (There was no tapping of the telephone line itself). On the basis of the earlier cases, counsel for both sides argued the questions of whether the booth was a constitutionally protected area and whether physical penetration of the booth was necessary to violate the defendant's fourth amendment rights. The Court, per Justice Stewart, rejected this formulation of the problem and held that "the Fourth Amendment protects people, not places." *Id.* at 351. He went on to say:

> The Government's activities in electronically listening to and recording the petitioner's words violated the privacy upon which he justifiably relied while using the telephone booth and thus constituted a "search and seizure" within the meaning of the Fourth Amendment. The fact that the electronic device employed to achieve the end did not happen to penetrate the wall of the booth can have no constitutional significance.

Id. at 353.
[44] Roe v. Wade, 410 U.S. 113 (1973); Doe v. Bolton, 410 U.S. 179 (1973).
[45] Roe v. Wade, 410 U.S. 113, 172 (1973) (Rehnquist, J., dissenting). Also, Justice Stewart, in his concurring opinion, conspicuously failed to invoke the concept of privacy. *See id.* at 167–71.
[46] Both Justice Blackmun writing for the Court in *Wade,* and Justice Douglas in a concurring opinion in that case were puzzled by this problem. *See id.* at 152–56, 211–15.
  See Cantor, *A Patient's Decisions to Decline Life-Saving Medical Treatment: Bodily Integrity Versus the Preservation of Life,* 26 RUTGERS L. REV. 228, 236–42 (1973), where the author argues that bodily integrity is the most basic aspect of personal privacy and both has and should receive significant constitutional protection.
[47] Warren & Brandeis, *supra* note 10.
[48] Prosser, *Privacy,* 48 CALIF. L. REV. 383 (1960).

was no single characteristic common to every putative loss of privacy. But he did note four characteristics, at least one of which was present in each case. They were:

(1) An intrusion upon the plaintiff's seclusion or solitude, or into his private affairs;
(2) Public disclosure of embarrassing private facts about the plaintiff;
(3) Publicity which placed the plaintiff in a false light in the public eye;
(4) Appropriation for the defendant's advantage, of the plaintiff's name or likeness.[49]

Four years after Prosser's article appeared, Edward Bloustein wrote an answer which concluded that there was some characteristic common to all of Prosser's cases, namely that what was protected when privacy was protected was the dignity of the individual.[50] Bloustein also concluded that what "distinguishes the invasion of privacy as a tort from other torts which involve insults to human dignity and individuality is merely the means used to perpetrate the wrong." [51] Although "human dignity and individuality" will not do as a definition of privacy, Bloustein was correct in concluding that what is protected by the tort of invasion of privacy is also protected by many other torts, such as assault and battery, false imprisonment, infliction of mental distress, trespass, and various sorts of negligence.[52]

In light of this situation, some commentators have questioned the wisdom of having a separate cause of action for "invasion of privacy." [53] The justification for allowing it is that it affords legal protection of privacy in those situations not covered by more traditional torts. Also, having a separate tort of invasion of privacy may stimulate judicial imagination and provide a flexible category for courts to invoke in responding to new threats to privacy.[54]

In support of the definition of privacy presented here, many of the leading cases in the development of the tort of invasion of privacy involve a loss of control over when the plaintiff can be sensed by others.[55]

---

[49] *Id.* at 389.

[50] Bloustein, *supra* note 14, at 1000–07.

[51] *Id.* at 1003.

[52] For a history of the tort of invasion of privacy which incorporates Prosser's 1960 article, and a description of these other torts see the classic treatise on this subject, PROSSER, TORTS (4th ed. 1971).

[53] *See, e.g.,* Kalven, *Privacy in Tort Law—Were Warren and Brandeis Wrong,* 31 LAW CONTEMP. PROB. 326 (1966). This article is one of several on privacy in the same issue of the journal.

[54] *See* Freund, *Privacy: One Concept or Many,* in PRIVACY, *supra* note 4, at 182. This flexibility is also an attractive aspect of the use of the concept of privacy to interpret the Bill of Rights.

[55] *See* Prince Albert v. Strange, 2 DeGex & Sm. 652 (1849) (injunction against publication of drawings made by Prince Albert and Queen Victoria for private use); Roberson v. Rochester Folding-Box Co., 171 N.Y. 538, 64 N.E. 442 (1902) (use of plaintiff's picture to advertise flour); Pavesich v. New England Life Ins. Co., 122 Ga. 190, 50 S.E. 68 (1905) (use of plaintiff's picture to advertise insurance) ; Haelan Laboratories v. Topps Chewing Gum, 202 F.2d 866 (2d Cir. 1953) (right of a baseball player to sell exclusive license for the use of his picture on bubblegum cards upheld); DeMay v. Roberts, 46 Mich. 160, 165, 9 N.W. 146, 149 (1881) (plaintiff's right to control who could watch her give birth was upheld as part of her right to privacy).

Many that do not [56] can be explained as a loss of the value of privacy as defined above in much the same way that the collection by others of information about an individual devalues his privacy.[57]

A full examination of the cases collected by Prosser, and a reorganization of them in light of this new definition of privacy, would be far beyond the scope of this paper. A complete defense of this definition or any other would have to take account of the data represented by the cases which Prosser has collected. Leaving that task unfinished, this discussion will turn back to the application of the new definition of privacy to *United States v. White*.[58]

Justice White set forth the problem in *United States v. White* as follows:

> If the conduct and revelations of an agent operating without electronic equipment do not invade the defendant's constitutionally justifiable expectations of privacy, neither does a simultaneous recording of the same conversation made by the agent or by others from transmissions received from the agent to whom the defendant is talking and whose trustworthiness the defendant necessarily risks.[59]

Justice White's argument challenges us to discover some basis for drawing a constitutional distinction between the old-fashioned unbugged informer and the electronically bugged informer. He was clear and correct in stating that actual expectations of privacy by the defendant cannot account for that distinction:

> Our problem is not what the privacy expectations of particular defendants in particular situations may be or the extent to which they may in fact have relied on the discretion of their companions. Very probably, individual defendants neither know nor suspect that their colleagues have gone or will go to the police or are carrying recorders or transmitters. Otherwise, conversation would cease and our problem with these encounters would be nonexistent or far different from those now before us. Our problem, in terms of the principles announced in *Katz*, is what expectations of privacy are constitutionally "justifiable"—what expectations the fourth amendment will protect in the absence of a warrant. So far, the law permits the frustration of actual expectations of privacy by permitting authorities to use the testimony of those associates who for one reason or another have determined to turn to the police, as well as by authorizing the use of informants in the manner exemplified by *Hoffa* and *Lewis*.[60]

[56] *See, e.g.*, Melvin v. Reid, 112 Cal. App. 285, 297 P. 91 (1931) (reformed prostitute who had been the defendant in a notorious murder trial had her hidden past revealed to all by a motion picture, *The Red Kimono*, based on her life story and released without her consent); Sidis v. F-R Publishing Corp., 113 F.2d 806 (2d Cir. 1940) (the *New Yorker* magazine published an account of the current reclusive life of a former mathematical child prodigy).
[57] See text accompanying notes 30–31 *supra*.
[58] 401 U.S. 745 (1971).
[59] *Id.* at 751.
[60] *Id.* at 751–52. *Hoffa* v. *United States*, 385 U.S. 293 (1966), holds that a defendant cannot make use of the fourth amendment to prevent an informer from testifying to

Thus the unexpected or novel nature of surveillance by radio transmission or tape recorder cannot be the basis for fourth amendment protection from the bugged informer; nor can the betrayal itself be that basis, for the fourth amendment gives no protection against betrayal by an old-fashioned unbugged informer; nor can the dissemination of information by the informer, for it is disseminated both by the bugged and unbugged informer. The only possible peg on which to hang a constitutional difference between the two sorts of informers seems to be the effectiveness of their dissemination of information. The bugged informer obtains an exact and unimpeachable record of what transpired. But since the difference in effectiveness can harm only the guilty and might protect the innocent from being framed by an informer, it cannot be the requisite difference.[61]

Justice White's argument rests on the unarticulated assumption that expectations of privacy are expectations of control over information about oneself. If privacy is conceived as control over information, then it is voluntarily surrendered to both the old-fashioned and the bugged informer. Since the old-fashioned informer needs no warrant to take advantage of one's surrender of privacy, neither does the bugged informer, who differs only in effectiveness from the old-fashioned informer. For Justice White, the important constitutional line is drawn between speaking to an informer and losing control of incriminating vital information, and speaking to a trustworthy non-informer and not losing control of that information. The Government needs a warrant to eavesdrop on the latter sort of conversation because the Government is unilaterally causing a loss of privacy—a loss of control over information. But it needs no warrant where the individual speaks to an informer, for in that case his loss of privacy is due to his own voluntary action, and the Government needs no warrant to take advantage of that loss any more than it needs a warrant to use whatever evidence a defendant exposes to the public. The fourth amendment cannot, after all, protect voluntarily relinquished privacy.

Given this article's definition of privacy, however, privacy is not surrendered by speaking to anyone, informer or friend. We choose to let him hear us, and retain the power to stop speaking to him. The old-fashioned unbugged informer does not cause us to lose privacy itself; he only diminishes the value of privacy by passing on information we wished to use privacy to protect.[62] But the bugged informer usurps control over the number of people actually listening. He unilaterally causes

<hr>

a conversation he had with the defendant, even though the informer was a long-term associate of the defendant who was recruited and paid by the government to betray him.

In *Lewis v. United States*, 385 U.S. 206 (1966), decided the same day, the informer was not a long-term associate of the defendant. The difference was decisive for Chief Justice Warren who dissented in *Hoffa* and wrote the opinion in *Lewis*.

[61] For a full discussion of these points see Greenawalt, *The Consent Problem in Wiretapping and Eavesdropping: Surreptitious Monitoring With the Consent of a Participant in a Conversation,* 68 COLUM. L. REV. 189 (1968).

[62] He may also diminish the value of privacy if it is suspected that he is a bugged informer; and he diminishes the value of privacy because he could easily take away privacy by donning a transmitter.

a loss of privacy in the same way that eavesdropping by the Government on a conversation with a non-informer causes a loss of privacy conceived as control over information. Under this article's definition of privacy, the important constitutional line should be drawn between speaking to a bugged informer and losing control over who can hear us, and speaking to anyone else—trustworthy friend or old-fashioned informer. The Government's use of the bugged informer is a unilateral taking of privacy itself. The Government's use of an old-fashioned informer is, like a dossier or a data bank, an attack on the value of privacy but not on privacy itself. If the fourth amendment is said to protect privacy, then a warrant should be required for a bugged informer. Perhaps it should also be required for an old-fashioned informer. The point is that the nature of privacy itself provides a sound foundation for making a constitutional distinction between an old-fashioned unbugged informer and a bugged informer.

This article's definition of privacy does not dictate a decision one way or the other on the facts of *United States v. White.* The Supreme Court in the future may still decide that the interest in law enforcement outweighs the costs of the loss of privacy incurred by allowing bugged informers to operate without warrants. But the distinction does allow a clear line to be drawn between the old-fashioned unbugged informer of *Hoffa* [63] on the one hand (which did not involve a loss of privacy per se) and the bugged informer of *On Lee v. United States* [64] and *Lopez v. United States* [65] and *White,* [66] on the other hand (involving

---

[63] 385 U.S. 293 (1966).

[64] In *On Lee* v. *United States,* 343 U.S. 747 (1952), Chin Poy, an old acquaintance and former employee of the defendant, entered the defendant's laundry and engaged him in incriminating conversation. Chin Poy was secretly transmitting the conversation to a federal agent outside the laundry. In a five-to-four decision, the Supreme Court found no error in allowing the federal agent to testify at trial concerning that which he had heard. The basis of the decision was that Chin Poy had not trespassed, but had been in the laundry with the consent of the defendant; nor had the federal agent violated the defendant's fourth amendment rights, for he had never entered the laundry. His overhearing of the conversation on his radio receiver was analogized to the use of binoculars from outside a defendant's premises without trespassing.

[65] In *Lopez* v. *United States,* 373 U.S. 427 (1963) decided eleven years after *On Lee,* a federal agent recorded his conversation with the defendant. The recording was introduced at trial along with the agent's testimony. The Court voted six-to-three to sustain the admissibility of the recording on the theory that it only corroborated the informer's testimony, thus implying that the recordings could not have been introduced by themselves. This question, however, was explicitly reserved by the Court. Justice Brennan dissented in *Lopez,* equating the use of a recorder with the transmission of the conversation to a third party. He reasoned that each allows independent evidence of the content of a conversation to be introduced in court. *Id.* at 447, 450 (Brennan, J., dissenting). Because of this equivalence, he criticized the majority for failing to come to grips with *On Lee,* a case which in 1963, the date of *Lopez,* they probably would not have reaffirmed, since the interpretation of the fourth amendment as protecting personal privacy rather than privacy attaching to property had gained considerable ground since *On Lee* was decided.

[66] Only Justices Stewart, Blackmun and Chief Justice Burger concurred in Justice White's opinion in *White.* 401 U.S. at 746. Justice Black voted with the majority on the basis of his dissent in *Katz* that the fourth amendment does not protect against eavesdropping. *Id.* at 754. Justice Brennan also voted with the majority because the Court had held in *Desist* v. *United States,* 394 U.S. 244 (1969), that *Katz* applied

a direct loss of privacy). We can more clearly express just why electronic surveillance is different from old-fashioned informing.

A new definition of privacy settles no questions of what protection the law should give to privacy or to the economic, social, and political value of that privacy in any given situation.[67] But where lines can naturally and easily be drawn, they often will be drawn. And where lines are drawn often has an influence on what decisions are made. The clearer the understanding of what privacy is, the wiser judgments will be concerning when to protect it and when to sacrifice it. *United States v. White* seems an unwise decision. By attempting to define more clearly the concept of privacy, I hope to have made more apparent what the Court has sacrificed.

20
DOE V. COMMONWEALTH'S ATTORNEY FOR CITY OF RICHMOND
403 F. Supp. 1199 (E.D. Va. 1975)

BRYAN, Senior Circuit Judge:
Virginia's statute making sodomy a crime is unconstitutional, each of the male plaintiffs aver, when it is applied to his active and regular homosexual relations with another *adult male, consensually* and *in private*. They assert that local State officers threaten them with prosecution for violation of this law, that such enforcement would deny them their Fifth and Fourteenth Amendments' assurance of due process, the First

---

prospectively only. *Id.* at 755–56. Since the facts of *White* occurred before *Katz* was decided, he felt bound by *Desist* to vote to reverse the Court of Appeals in *White*. He referred, however, to his dissent in *Lopez*, which stated that *Lopez* and *On Lee* are indistinguishable, and reaffirmed his belief that neither result was justified, and that *Lopez, On Lee* and therefore *White* should have been decided in favor of the defendant. Justices Harlan, Douglas, and Marshall were of the opinion that *On Lee* was no longer good law and all three dissented in *White*. *Id.* at 756 (Douglas, J., dissenting), *id.* at 768 (Harlan, J., dissenting), *id.* at 795 (Marshall, J., dissenting). Justice Harlan argued at length, in order to avoid the prospectivity of *Katz* as announced in *Desist,* that *On Lee* was dead law well before *Katz* was decided.

[67] Anyone interested in these questions might begin with the writings of Hannah Arendt, a contemporary political philosopher who has done important theoretical work on the place of privacy in our lives. See especially ARENDT, THE HUMAN CONDITION (1958). For an explanation of why privacy has been neglected by many other political philosophers see McCloskey, *The Political Ideal of Privacy,* 21 PHILOSOPHICAL Q. 303, 304 (October, 1971).

Amendment's protection of their rights of freedom of expression, the First and Ninth Amendments' guarantee of privacy, and the Eighth Amendment's forbiddance of cruel and unusual punishments. A declaration of the statute's invalidity in the circumstances is prayed as well as an injunction against its enforcement. Defendants are State prosecuting officials and they take issue with the plaintiffs' conclusions. With no conflict of fact present, the validity of this enactment becomes a question of law.

So far as relevant, the Code of Virginia, 1950, as amended, provides:

§ 18.1–212. Crimes against nature.—If any person shall carnally know in any manner any brute animal, or carnally know any male or female person by the anus or by or with the mouth, or voluntarily submit to such carnal knowledge, he or she shall be guilty of a felony and shall be confined in the penitentiary not less than one year nor more than three years.

Our decision is that on its face and in the circumstances here it is not unconstitutional. No judgment is made upon the wisdom or policy of the statute. It is simply that we cannot say that the statute offends the Bill of Rights or any other of the Amendments and the wisdom or policy is a matter for the State's resolve.

I. Precedents cited to us as *contra* rest exclusively on the precept that the Constitution condemns State legislation that trespasses upon the privacy of the incidents of marriage, upon the sanctity of the home, or upon the nurture of family life. This and only this concern has been the justification for nullification of State regulation in this area. Review of plaintiffs' authorities will reveal these as the principles underlying the referenced decisions.

In *Griswold v. Connecticut*, 381 U.S. 479, (1965), plaintiffs' chief reliance, the Court has most recently announced its views on the question here. Striking down a State statute forbidding the use of contraceptives, the ruling was put on the right of marital privacy—held to be one of the specific guarantees of the Bill of Rights—and was also put on the sanctity of the home and family. Its thesis is epitomized by the author of the opinion, Mr. Justice Douglas, in his conclusion:

We deal with a right of privacy older than the Bill of Rights—older than our political parties, older than our school system. Marriage is a coming together for better or for worse, hopefully enduring and intimate to the degree of being sacred. It is an association that promotes a way of life, not causes; a harmony in living, not political faiths; a bilateral loyalty, not commercial or social projects. Yet it is an association for as noble a purpose as any involved in our prior decisions.

That *Griswold* is premised on the right of privacy and that homosexual intimacy is denunciable by the State is unequivocally demonstrated by Mr. Justice Goldberg in his concurrence, . . . [citing Justice Harlan]:

Adultery, *homosexuality* and the like are sexual intimacies *which the State forbids* . . . but the intimacy of husband and wife is necessarily an essential and accepted feature of the institution of marriage, an institution which the State not only must allow, but which always and in every age it has fostered and protected. *It is one thing when the State exerts its power either to forbid extramarital sexuality* . . . or to say who may marry, but it is quite another when, having acknowledged a marriage and the intimacies inherent in it, it undertakes to regulate by means of the criminal law the details of that intimacy. (Emphasis added.)

Equally forceful is the succeeding paragraph of Justice Harlan:

In sum, even though the State has determined that the use of contraceptives is as iniquitous as any act of extra-marital sexual immorality, the intrusion of the whole machinery of the criminal law into the very heart of marital privacy, requiring husband and wife to render account before a criminal tribunal of their uses of that intimacy is surely *a very different thing indeed from punishing those who establish intimacies which the law has always forbidden and which can have no claim to social protection.* (Emphasis added.)

. . .

II. With no authoritative judicial bar to the proscription of homosexuality—since it is obviously no portion of marriage, home or family life—the next question is whether there is any ground for barring Virginia from branding it as criminal. If a State determines that punishment therefor, even when committed in the home, is appropriate in the promotion of morality and decency, it is not for the courts to say that the State is not free to do so. In short, it is an inquiry addressable only to the State's Legislature.

Moreover, to sustain its action, the State is not required to show that moral delinquency actually results from homosexuality. It is enough for upholding the legislation to establish that the conduct is likely to end in a contribution to moral delinquency. Plainly, it would indeed be impracticable to prove the actuality of such a consequence, and the law is not so exacting.

If such a prospect or expectation was in the mind of the General Assembly of Virginia, the prophecy proved only too true in the occurrences narrated in *Lovisi v. Slayton,* 363 F.Supp. 620 (E.D.Va. 1973, now on appeal in the Fourth Circuit). The graphic outline by the District Judge there describes just such a sexual orgy as the statute was evidently intended to punish. The Lovisis, a married couple, advertised their wish "to meet people" and in response a man came to Virginia to meet the Lovisis on several occasions. In one instance the three of them participated in acts of fellatio. Photographs of the conduct were taken by a set camera and the acts were witnessed by the wife's daughters, aged 11 and 13. The pictures were carried by them to school.

Although a questionable law is not removed from question by the lapse of any prescriptive period, the longevity of the Virginia statute does testify to the State's interest and its legitimacy. It is not an upstart notion; it has ancestry going back to Judaic and Christian law.[1] . . . The immediate parentage may be readily traced to the Code of Virginia of 1792. All the while the law has been kept alive, as evidenced by periodic amendments, the last in the 1968 Acts of the General Assembly of Virginia, c. 427.

In sum, we believe that the sodomy statute, so long in force in Virginia, has a rational basis of State interest demonstrably legitimate and mirrored in the cited decisional law of the Supreme Court. . . .

The prayers for a declaratory judgment and an injunction invalidating the sodomy statute will be denied.

MERHIGE, District Judge (dissenting).

. . . In my view, in the absence of any legitimate interest or rational basis to support the statute's application we must, without regard to our own proclivities and reluctance to judicially bar the state proscription of homosexuality, hold the statute as it applies to the plaintiffs to be violative of their rights under the Due Process Clause of the Fourteenth Amendment to the Constitution of the United States. The Supreme Court decision in *Griswold v. Connecticut* is, as the majority points out, premised on the right of privacy, but I fear my brothers have misapplied its precedential value through an apparent over-adherence to its factual circumstances.

The Supreme Court has consistently held that the Due Process Clause of the Fourteenth Amendment protects the right of individuals to make personal choices, unfettered by arbitrary and purposeless restraints, in the private matters of marriage and procreation. I view those cases as standing for the principle that every individual has a right to be free from unwarranted governmental intrusion into one's decisions on private matters of intimate concern. A mature individual's choice of an adult sexual partner, in the privacy of his or her own home, would appear to me to be a decision of the utmost private and intimate concern. Private consensual sex acts between adults are matters, absent evidence that they are harmful, in which the state has no legitimate interest.

To say, as the majority does, that the right of privacy, which every citizen has, is limited to matters of marital, home or family life is unwarranted under the law. Such a contention places a distinction in marital-nonmarital matters which is inconsistent with current Supreme Court opinions and is unsupportable.

In my view, the reliance of the majority on Mr. Justice Harlan's dissenting statement in *Poe v. Ullman*, 367 U.S. 497, (1961), is misplaced. After *Griswold*, by virtue of *Eisenstadt v. Baird*, 405 U.S. 430, (1972), the legal viability of a marital-nonmarital distinction in private sexual acts if not eliminated, was at the very least seriously impaired. In *Eisenstadt*, the Court declined to restrict the right of privacy in sexual matters to married couples:

[1] Leviticus 18:22: "Thou shalt not lie with mankind, as with womankind: it is abomination." Again, 20:13: "If a man also lie with mankind, as he lieth with a woman, both of them have committed an abomination: they shall surely be put to death; their blood shall be upon them." "Sodomy" was used in the earlier laws interchangeably with buggery and other "unnatural sex acts". Davis, *Criminal Law.* (1838) p. 133.

Yet the marital couple is not an independent entity with a mind and heart of its own, but an association of two individuals each with a separate intellectual and emotional makeup. If the right of privacy means anything, it is the right of the *individual,* married or single, to be free from unwarranted governmental intrusion into matters so fundamentally affecting a person as the decision whether to bear or beget a child.

. . .

Griswold, in its context, applied the right of privacy in sexual matters to the marital relationship. *Eisenstadt,* however, clearly demonstrates that the right to privacy in sexual relationships is not limited to the marital relationship. Both *Roe* and *Eisenstadt* cogently demonstrate that intimate personal decisions or private matters of substantial importance to the well-being of the individuals involved are protected by the Due Process Clause. The right to select consenting adult sexual partners must be considered within this category. The exercise of that right, whether heterosexual or homosexual, should not be proscribed by state regulation absent compelling justification.

This approach does not unqualifiedly sanction personal whim. If the activity in question involves more than one participant, as in the instant case, each must be capable of consenting, and each must in fact consent to the conduct for the right of privacy to attach. For example, if one of the participants in homosexual contact is a minor, or force is used to coerce one of the participants to yield, the right will not attach. Similarly, the right of privacy cannot be extended to protect conduct that takes place in publicly frequented areas. However, if the right of privacy does apply to specific courses of conduct, legitimate state restriction on personal autonomy may be justified only under the compelling state interest test.

Plaintiffs are adults seeking protection from the effects of the statute under attack in order to engage in homosexual relations in private. Viewing the issue as we are bound to, as Mr. Justice Blackmun stated in *Roe v. Wade,* "by constitutional measurement, free of emotion and predilection," it is my view that they are entitled to be protected in their right to privacy by the Due Process Clause.

The defendants, represented by the highest legal officer of the state, made no tender of any evidence which even impliedly demonstrated that homosexuality causes society any significant harm. No effort was made by the defendants to establish either a rational basis or a compelling state interest so as to justify the proscription of § 8.1–212 of the Code of Virginia, presently under attack. To suggest, as defendants do, that the prohibition of homosexual conduct will in some manner encourage new heterosexual marriages and prevent the dissolution of existing ones is unworthy of judicial response. In any event, what we know as men is not forgotten as judges—it is difficult to envision any substantial number of heterosexual marriages being in danger of dissolution because of the private sexual activities of homosexuals.

On the basis of this record one can only conclude that the sole basis of the proscription of homosexuality was what the majority refers to as the promotion of morality and decency. As salutary a legislative goal as this may be, I can find no authority for intrusion by the state into the private dwelling of a citizen. . . . Socially condemned activity, except- ing that of demonstrable external effect, is and was intended by the Constitution to be beyond the scope of state regulation when conducted within the privacy of the home. "The Constitution extends special safe- guards to the privacy of the home. . . . ." Whether the guarantee of personal privacy springs from the First, Fourth, Fifth, Ninth, the penum- bra of the Bill of Rights, or, as I believe, in the concept of liberty guaranteed by the first section of the Fourteenth Amendment, the Su- preme Court has made it clear that fundamental rights of such an inti- mate facet of an individual's life as sex, absent circumstances warranting intrusion by the state, are to be respected. My brothers, I respectfully suggest, have by today's ruling misinterpreted the issue—the issue centers not around morality or decency, but the constitutional right of privacy.

I respectfully note my dissent.

SAMUEL McCRACKEN 21

ARE HOMOSEXUALS GAY?

. . . The so-called "gay-rights" question cannot be understood without reference to the history of the rights question in general. The past two decades have witnessed a subtle change in our understanding of the concept of rights. The movement that crested with the passage of the 1964 Civil Rights Act was waged in the interest of blacks. But the rights that movement sought to secure were never defined as black (or Negro) rights. They were civil rights believed to belong at law to all groups, and the movement sought to assure them to a group that was signally denied them.

The principal rights guaranteed were the right to vote, the right to use public accommodations, and the right to be free from discrimination in employment. The groups protected were racial and religious minori- ties. Protection was not explicitly accorded minorities as such, but it was assumed that for preponderant groups such protection would be re- dundant. Allan Bakke had not yet been heard from. Even though women were in the numerical majority, it was soon proposed to add them to the protected groups.

Several facts were common to all these cases: there was a widespread denial of the rights in question. Because women got in so far ahead of blacks on the right to vote, this did not figure for them in the past decades. And although the denial of their right to public accommoda-

These excerpts are reprinted from *Commentary* 67 (January 1979): 23–28 by permission. Copyright 1979 by the American Jewish Committee.

tions was limited to fairly specialized institutions such as men's bars, they were and are the subject of discrimination in employment. For good or for worse, the movement to extend these rights to women has been characterized as a fight for "women's rights." Such a phrase must be used with greater precision if it is not gradually to suggest special rights common only to women—e.g., the "right" to tax-supported abortions or child care—instead of rights belonging to all but denied in practice to women.

The other commonality was that the groups in question were involuntary and regarded by society as morally neutral. (Religious belief may be thought voluntary by the irreligious, or the other-religious, but the same principle that distinguishes religious from ethical conscientious objectors holds good here: if one has, as it were, a meta-belief that all one's beliefs are ordained by God, one may well assume that one has no choice in holding them. For the state to classify such a belief as voluntary is in fact to deny freedom of religion to all its holders. Further, although religious views are certainly not morally neutral, the First Amendment compels us to treat them as so.)

The notion of "gay rights" can be seen to be in sharp contrast to the original concept of civil rights, and indeed to have advanced the degeneracy of the concept even further than the latter-day notion of "women's rights." It is obviously a vexed question as to whether the condition of homosexuality itself is involuntary or voluntary; all those who hold it to be voluntary obviously place it in a very different category from being born black or a woman. Moreover, even if one considers the state of homosexuality as involuntary, its practice is clearly not. The concept of "being in the closet" recognizes an option clearly not open to members of racial minorities or women.

Even more striking is the fact that homosexuals are not in reality the object of widespread denial of rights. They have never been denied the right to vote, and their access to public accommodations has been essentially unlimited. (Of course a homosexual male transvestite, if recognized as such, may well be denied entrance to a restaurant: but so may a heterosexual male transvestite, if recognized as such. This is very different from the case of a black denied entrance to a restaurant simply because he is black, no matter what his dress or demeanor.)

Nor is there pervasive discrimination against homosexuals in employment. This is not to say that there is none, but in this connection it should be noted that some of the homosexual magazines which support laws to protect homosexuals from job discrimination also run solicitations for advertising claiming that homosexuals have a substantially higher income than the average.

It seems likely, then, that the force behind the "gay-rights" movement springs less from a desire to prevent potential discrimination and more from a hope that, declared a protected status, homosexuality will gain widespread legitimacy. If this is true, then "gay-rights" ordinances are obviously being misused. And, indeed, in ways possibly deleterious to homosexuals, for when homosexuality is ringingly declared by popular vote *not* to be a protected status—as, e.g., in Dade County, Florida, and

Eugene, Oregon—homosexuals may be considerably worse off than when the people had not spoken to the issue one way or the other.

There is, however, a special case in which homosexuals are the object not only of actual *de facto* discrimination but of proposals to enact *de jure* discrimination. This is the case of schoolteachers.

A number of the recent "gay-rights" campaigns, notably the one in Dade County, have centered on the issue of whether homosexuals can be barred from teaching in the public schools. Moreover, in California the defeated Proposition 6 explicitly dealt with the question. This is a highly emotional issue; much discussion pro and con has taken a simplistic view of the matter, but a little thought will show it to be as complicated an issue as any that bedevils the debate on homosexuality.

The argument against the employment of homosexuals as schoolteachers takes two forms. The cruder of these maintains that homosexuals will seduce or otherwise molest their young charges. The subtler maintains that homosexuals are an inappropriate role model for the young. The typical response to the first charge is that the great majority of all child molesters are heterosexual males, who ought therefore, on this logic, to be banned from the schoolroom as a group. The typical response to the second is that one's sexual orientation is already formed by the time one enters school, and that if teachers were role models in such matters, more students in the parochial schools would grow up to be nuns.

On first blush the child-molestation argument seems easily disposed of: the evidence is that homosexuals are, at worst, no more disposed to molest children than heterosexuals. And one knows many homosexuals who are clearly decent and law-abiding people, no more likely to molest children than to mug adults. Why, then, should this fear be so perdurable? One possible answer is that it is entirely irrational and has no basis, any more than the fear that Jews poison wells. But that is too glib, for the male homosexual culture has in it tendencies which suggest, rightly or wrongly, that homosexuals are more likely than heterosexuals to engage in statutory rape, if not child molestation.

Last year near Boston, a number of men were indicted for alleged sexual relations with adolescent boys. The cases have not yet come to trial, and I am not going to anticipate their outcomes and use them as evidence. But the cases gained unusual publicity as a result of an only slightly related controversy that followed the arrest. This was very suggestive. Something called the Boston-Boise Committee was established to support the defendants. (There had been similar prosecutions in Boise two decades ago.) This group sponsored a lecture by Gore Vidal, and the then Chief Justice of the Massachusetts Superior Court, already under judicial investigation on charges of financial irregularity, chose to attend the lecture. In the event, his attendance at a meeting dealing with cases that might come under his judicial notice was made the basis of additional charges of impropriety. Censured by the state Supreme Court, he finally resigned.

In the debate that arose over his attendance, an official of the Boston-

Boise Committee wrote letters to the newspapers, containing, among other statements, the claim that the youths alleged to be involved were not children, being often as old as fourteen or fifteen, and suggesting strongly that there was nothing particularly wrong in voluntary sexual relations involving boys of such an age. That is, the so-called Wolfenden standard, tolerating any sexual conduct between consenting adults, and only beginning to be written into law, was too restrictive: the law should condone sexual conduct among consenting people, or at least among pairs of consenting adults and minors.

Articles also appeared in the local "alternative press" dealing with the lives of teenage male prostitutes, intimating that such youths were certainly better off living in concubinage with older men than hustling on the streets, and extolling the virtues of something called "boylove," a term apparently freely adapted from a somewhat more traditional one, "pederasty."

To these straws in the wind might be added the fact that there has recently been formed in England an organization to secure sexual liberty for the young—composed, so it seems, entirely of adult and no doubt disinterested male homosexuals.

Now, it is unlikely, had a large number of professional men in Boston been charged with sexual conduct with fourteen-year-old girls, that people would have rallied to their support waving the banner of "girllove." In discussing heterosexual relations, there is still a general comprehension of the doctrine of informed consent. It is not often argued that merely because an adult can persuade a fourteen-year-old girl to go to bed with him, she is in any philosophical sense capable of consenting to do so. And indeed, if the notion of informed consent be valid for heterosexual relationships, it is *a fortiori* so for homosexual relationships, which are, as is admitted by all but the most fanatical and uncritical admirers of homosexuality, more problematical than heterosexual ones.

The existence of homosexual men who not only traffic in child prostitution but defend the practice as desirable certainly must feed the widespread belief that homosexuals, teachers included, are likely to molest children. And the belief is fed whether or not it is true, as I believe it is not. (I am speaking now of the primary and secondary schools. Most of the students in college are legally adults, and if homosexual teachers in college are no more involved with their students than heterosexual teachers are, that should be enough.)

As to the second argument: if it were true that all children in school arrive there with their sexual preferences already fixed, that would not in itself dispose of the question of homosexual teachers, merely of whether or not they could, if they desired, make homosexuals out of children who would not otherwise be so.

It is certainly a very fashionable idea that sexual identity is shaped early in life. This is perhaps understandable simply in that it is a convenient position for those who wish to advocate greater legitimacy for homosexuality. Moreover, it is implicit in Freud's explanation of how homosexuals come to be, and although this explanation—that the child fails in his attempt to identify with his father and becomes fixated on his mother—has been replaced among Freudians by the view (currently also under attack) that the homosexual in childhood suffered from a dominating mother and an ineffectual father, it retains some plausibility in the absence of a clear superior.

And so it is often maintained that while almost all males go through a stage of homosexuality in adolescence, those predestined to be heterosexuals grow out of it as adults and those predestined to be homosexuals do not, and remain homosexuals all their lives. It is no use trying to "cure" such people, even if one agrees that they ought to be cured, because they are what they are, no more to be transformed into heterosexuals than adult heterosexuals are into homosexuals.

Although laundered of any moral judgments, this view has a slightly Calvinist ring to it. But the real trouble with it is that it does not entirely accord with experience. For literature and experience do not lack for examples of males who go through an intense and active homosexual stage as adults and later settle down to adjusted and undeviating lives of heterosexuality, marriage, and parenthood. The late Evelyn Waugh is a typical example, and most people with substantial homosexual acquaintance know of less eminent cases. Moreover, the claim that no one is made homosexual by early homosexual contact has still to be proved. In addition, boys of fourteen may find homosexuality, if it is offered them, an attractive choice, especially now that the traditional disapproval is fading away and no longer operates as a deterrent. Homosexuality holds out the possibility of avoiding an adjustment to adult life that is always difficult, and has become more so with the rise of Women's Lib. Many, perhaps most, boys at this age find girls rather forbidding. The establishment of a homosexual relationship delays the coming to grips with these formidable creatures and may call it off altogether. It is an age, if one is to make a satisfactory adjustment, when the temptation to homosexual behavior is perhaps best avoided altogether.

Yet if it is possible that some students who would grow up as heterosexuals might be thwarted in this development by the rare homosexual teacher, that does not seem to me to be, in and of itself, a good argument for banning homosexuals from teaching. So strict a calculation of the odds would infallibly ban everyone else as well.

A rational law in this area would, first of all, bring down the heavens on any teacher, of whatever sex, who engaged in sexual conduct, of whatever sort, with any student, of either sex. And while protecting the private sexual behavior of teachers—as the law ought to protect the private sexual behavior of all consenting adults—it might well require them to keep it private. This requirement might lie more heavily on homosexuals as a group than on heterosexuals, for it is evident that a number of homosexuals carry their sex lives into the public arena in a way that heterosexuals generally do not, e.g., in public toilets or parks. In a situation in which it was not illegal to be a homosexual, and in which being a homosexual was not in itself grounds for dismissal as a teacher, school boards might well doubt the stability of those who insisted on publicity.

The controversy over homosexual teachers is a classic case of the malign consequences of treating homosexuals as an oppressed group needing the sort of explicit mention in civil-rights law established, say, for blacks. The passage of superfluous ordinances establishing "gay rights" led first to a string of repeals, with the necessary implication that homosexuals had fewer rights than others, and then to explicitly discriminatory legislation like California's Proposition 6. It is beyond understanding why that proposal's sponsors, having written into the first part of the bill language adequate to deal with homosexuals and trample on the Constitution into the bargain, insisted on adding, in the second part, language calculated to enlist in the opposite camp every heterosexual in California not animated by violent anti-homosexualism. This turn of affairs is owing almost entirely to the insistence of homosexual activists on attaining the status of an officially registered and protected endangered species.

IV

A rational view of homosexuality has always been very difficult to hold and to propagate. It has been the subject of a great deal of ignorant and often vicious prejudice, e.g., the popular view that most or all male homosexuals are slavering to seduce the young, that all male homosexuals are repellently effeminate, that all female homosexuals are repellently mannish, that all homosexuals are desperately unhappy. Homosexuals themselves have been the objects only of limited discrimination, but some of it—e.g., police entrapment, harassment of gay bars and brutality toward their customers—has been serious and indefensible.

Under such conditions, it has been customary, among the sorts of enlightened people who care about civil rights generally and worry about persecuted minorities in particular, to lump homosexuals together with other minorities who can be accurately said to have no problems that do not stem ultimately from the prejudice of others. This tendency, in recent years, has increasingly kept many people from facing some obvious facts about homosexuality.

First, it is, in a certain sense, unnatural. The categories "natural" and "unnatural" are so thoroughly abused in our time that I hesitate to use them. One is tempted to annihilate the distinction by declaring that whatever is, is natural. Theorists and analysts of homosexuality naturally make much of the universal distribution of homosexuality throughout humanity, and indeed of a sort of homosexuality in the animal world. C. A. Tripp, writing in *The Homosexual Matrix*,[1] provides an exhaustive review of the varieties of homosexual experience in savage cultures, including one in which it is essentially compulsory.

I use the term "natural" here to mean "appropriate to the nature

[1] McGraw-Hill, 1975. This work, which comes to many of the same conclusions as *Homosexualities*, is an engagingly iconoclastic psychoanalytic treatment of the topic. Tripp gives the impression of vast erudition in the lore of homosexuality, e.g., the facts that while surgeons are about as heterosexual as most people, some surgical specialties are largely filled by homosexuals, and that violinists are on the whole heterosexual, pianists much less so. But a good deal of his analysis of the causes of homosexuality boils down to "because they prefer it that way."

of man," for I am at a loss to know what other term to use in dealing with the obvious fact that human bodies seem more obviously designed for heterosexual intercourse than for homosexual, both as to technique and as to purpose. This is not to suggest that homosexual sex cannot be pleasurable, a suggestion that could be sincerely refuted by millions. But it is to note that there are in fact "natural" equivalents for the lubricants and dildoes that figure prominently in the do-it-yourself literature in this area, and to the extent that techniques of homosexual love-making evade the necessity of these, they are adaptations of parts and not the whole of heterosexual equivalents.

And it seems to me that one cannot honestly ignore the relation of sex to reproduction; although we have successfully made the heterosexual act independent of procreation, and bid fair to make procreation independent of the heterosexual act, we cannot forget their original entanglement. It is not surprising that an age which has, in other contexts, developed a considerable animus against the family and the production of children, should look more complacently upon homosexuality, the sterile practice of which is now in less clear contrast with marriage than it once was. It should not be forgotten that some homosexuals get married and have children whom they raise in homosexual milieus, or that some lesbian theorists offer proposals for lesbian motherhood through artificial insemination. But we are dealing here with minorities: the modal homosexual existence is a childless one.

The advocates of depopulation have made it less easy to realize the obvious fact that our existence is largely dependent upon children. By "our existence" I do not mean only the metaphysical continuation of the human race through generations yet unborn. I mean also the well-being of a couple of generations already born and still alive and well. Anyone who doubts this should consider what further sharp declines in the birth rate are likely to mean to the Social Security fund, to our footloose use of the federal deficit, or to the provision of medical care and social services to the old.

The fact is that homosexuality generally entails a renunciation of responsibility for the continuance of the human race and of a voice in the dialogue of the generations. This is a renunciation made also by some heterosexuals and indeed by some married heterosexuals. There is, however, a still greater renunciation made by homosexuals, and that is of the intricate, complicated, and challenging process of adjusting one's life to someone so different from oneself as to be in a different sex entirely.

Running through the homosexual literature is a recognition of renunciation, usually seen as a positive good. One of those interviewed in *Word Is Out* points out the lesser demands of life as a homosexual:

> . . . gay people have more fun than your average married guy in a home with two or three kids. You have more time and money. You don't have the responsibilities. . . . I can lavish . . . presents . . . on my nephews and take them to the zoo and have a great old time. When they get tired and cranky I take them back to mommy and dad—you know, dad has just finished paying two hundred bucks for their teeth.

And another pursues a similar thought:

> It's so hard to be a straight man, harder than to be a faggot, because the rewards are so stupid—the rewards that you are told you can have. Whereas if you're a faggot, I guess you can make up your own rewards. . . . It's more fun to be a faggot because nobody expects anything of us.

This last comment is astute: it is harder to live a complete life than a partial one, and easier to live in fantasy than in reality. Both of the *Joy* books are shot through with the pleasures of fantasy, presented as the quintessentially homosexual sensibility. This should be expected, for homosexuality is often, although not universally, allied to a striking form of fantasy known as inversion.

It is important to distinguish between homosexuality and inversion. The former term implies no more than a sexual or affectional preference for the same sex. Interviewed recently on the BBC, a young male homosexual activist offered a minimalist definition that would be hard to beat: "I fancy men." Inversion implies something more and indeed something different: the aping of the sex to which one does not belong. This can run from the mild—say, a manner in a man that some might call feminine—to the extreme—say, the full-bodied imposture of transvestitism. Indeed, inversion is most perfectly exemplified in the practice of transsexualism, where the imposture becomes as physically persuasive as an elaborate and expensive medical technology can make it.

It should be seen that inversion represents, in varying degrees, a violent rejection of things as they are. Let us pass over men whose attitudes are subtly "feminine," because such categories are just now in disrepute, and consider the mildest generally recognized level of inversion. A man who refers to the men around him as "she" and accepts the same from them rejects a simple biological fact that irresistibly conflicts with his desire for sexual relationships with other men.

To such rejections many male homosexuals add gross effeminancy of manner and a few add cross-dressing. Whatever one feels about the propriety of such behavior, it is hard to think of it as anything other than maladjustment. Men who, not being Napoleon or Teddy Roosevelt, dress and act like these historic gentlemen, are a byword not merely for maladjustment but for madness. This rejection is perhaps less striking in heterosexual transvestites, who are more likely to cross-dress in private, as an incident of sexual relations. But it still represents an astonishing defiance of the real world. It misses the point of such phenomena entirely to dismiss them on the grounds that mannerisms and dress are in any event not natural but societal constructs. That society identifies them as female is precisely why they are aped. Because contemporary Western society no longer defines suits as an exclusively male garment, it becomes increasingly difficult for transvestitism even to exist among females.

Transsexualism—both of role only, in which the homosexual remains physically intact, and of physical identity, in which surgery and hormones intervene to counterfeit the structure of the other gender—represents an ultimate rejection of reality through an attempt to change it. It is noteworthy how often surgically created transsexuals are actually treated by the rest of the world as if they really had changed their sex. The philosopher John Silber has pointed out the strangeness of this: as if a woman were in fact no more than a mutilated man with a severe hormone imbalance. One would expect that feminists, even those who do not play tennis, would find such an implication more offensive than they have.

It is not necessary to view all rejections of reality as deleterious to see that a group in which rejections of this sort are very much more common than is usual must be different in some regard. The high rate of attempted suicide reported in *Homosexualities* is strong evidence that this difference is not an unmixed blessing. But what of possible advantages? A. L. Rowse attempts to show in *Homosexuals in History* [2] that almost everyone of interest in history has been homosexual and that most virtues are symptomatic of homosexuality, and Tripp notes the oft-remarked fact that homosexuals seem to predominate in certain of the arts.

And indeed much homosexual advocacy battens on the alleged creativity of homosexuals—male homosexuals, from the examples, although this is never specified as a theoretical point. To confirm or disprove such claims with real precision would require massive research into the homo/hetero balance in, say Seicento Florence or late 19th-century St. Petersburg. But let us concede the point: although the balance varies from art to art, the arts do seem to have a much higher male homosexual population than life at large. This is a phenomenon which is more often remarked on than analyzed. Tripp regards the evidence that might be used to explain the phenomenon as so contradictory that it almost defines analysis, as when the sexual orientation of violinists seems to differ from that of the pianists.

The school of psychological theory most obviously prepared to pronounce on this subject is 100-proof Freudianism, which, as we remember, has a notable opinion about the relations of sex and art—that the latter is a "sublimation" of the former. Considering that most male homosexuals, on the evidence of *Homosexualities* and other less scientific sources, are as sexually active as rabbits, one might expect them to be rather dull sorts artistically. This is not, of course, the view of the homosexual culture itself: the view there, as neatly expressed in Mart Crowley's play, *The Boys in the Band,* is that "it takes a fairy to make something really pretty."

In light of the doctrine of sublimation, one is led to wonder whether all that activity really adds up to a real sex life of the sort Freud was talking about. One is also led into further and controversial speculations about the fact that there is almost no cult of the creative among female homosexuals. Female homosexuals, as I remarked earlier, seem a world apart from the males, and to be as a group less distinguishable from their

---

[2] Macmillan, 1977. Like so much of Rowse's work, a rollicking good read for reasons certainly unintended by the author.

heterosexual counterparts. Is it possible that female homosexuality is a more adequate counterfeit of female heterosexuality than male homosexuality is of male heterosexuality? Or is it possible that the sublimation mechanism itself is peculiar to males?

These are questions of the sort that cry out for answers, but which rarely get asked any more, apparently in deference to more pressing ideological and political agendas. . . .

If we face things as they are, we recognize that homosexuals as a group are as gifted and intelligent as anyone else. In my own experience, I recognize that some of the most stable, responsible, and decent people I know are homosexuals. But I must also recognize that the most self-destructive and wretched of my friends have been exclusively homosexual and that "gay" is the very last term to describe them.

We must face things as they are. Much of the new sensibility regarding homosexuality fails to do so, and from such a failure no one, heterosexual or homosexual, can in the long run gain.

22 DAVID A. J. RICHARDS

SEXUAL AUTONOMY AND THE CONSTITUTIONAL RIGHT TO PRIVACY: A CASE STUDY IN HUMAN RIGHTS AND THE UNWRITTEN CONSTITUTION

[Professor Richard's article takes the form of a critique of *Doe* v. *Commonwealth's Attorney for Richmond*. In the first portion of the article, omitted here, Richards asks how the Supreme Court can legitimately appeal to an unwritten constitution when the purpose of the Founding Fathers was to limit governmental power by providing a written text. He is particularly interested in exploring the rationale behind the decision in *Doe*, which excluded homosexual acts between consenting adults from the scope of the constitutional right of privacy, versus the court's decision to uphold the right of married and unmarried persons to use contraceptives, to have abortions, and to use pornographic materials in their homes. The Bill of Rights, he says, was part of and gave expression to a developing moral theory regarding individual

Reprinted by permission of the author and the publisher from *Hastings Law Journal* 30 (1979): 957ff. Portions of the article and many footnotes were deleted, and footnotes are renumbered. Copyright 1979 Hastings College of Law.

rights that had been stated by Milton, Locke, Rousseau, and Kant. This theory, he says, rests upon two crucial assumptions: "that persons have the capacity to be autonomous in living their lives; second, that persons are entitled, as persons, to equal concern and respect in exercising their capacities for living autonomously." This leads to what he calls the rights thesis: "that rights trump utilitarian considerations, that rights may be weighed only against rights, and that rights justify, *in extremis,* forms of ultimate disobedience."

[The central developmental task of becoming a person, Richards argues, is the development of one's capacities for separation and individuation, of making independent decisions as to what one's life shall be like, deciding for oneself which desires will be developed and which disowned, which capacities cultivated and which left barren, with whom one will or will not identify. Underlying recognition of this aspect of autonomy is the principle of "fundamental moral equality," a guarantee to each person that he or she will receive equal concern and respect as that person exercises his or her autonomy. A denial of human rights amounts, in the end, to expression of disrespect or contempt for the individual's capacity for autonomy. Apologists for the enslavement of blacks and the subjection of women often argued that blacks and .women were permanently children or childlike and thus needed paternalistic interference in their attempts to express themselves or develop their own personalities. "The advance of the rights thesis has rested on the repudiation of these arguments, which we now perceive as resting on an unjustified contempt that prevented the realization of the capacity of those suppressed."

[The rights thesis also denies the propriety of allowing utilitarian calculations to override the range of significant life choices and requires that considerations of rights be weighed only against other rights of comparable weight.

[Richards proceeds now to consider the development of the constitutional right of privacy, quoting from Justice Brandeis's dissent in *Olmstead* v. *United States* (277 U.S. 438, 478 (1928)).]

The makers of our Constitution undertook to secure conditions favorable to the pursuit of happiness. They recognized the significance of man's spiritual nature, of his feelings and of his intellect. They knew that only a part of the pain, pleasure and satisfactions of life are to be found in material things. They sought to protect Americans in their beliefs, their thoughts, their emotions and their sensations.

When Brandeis summarized this foundational right as "the most comprehensive of rights and the right most valued by civilized men," he was, I believe, invoking the general conception of human rights, founded on autonomy and equal concern and respect. Certain of the principles of constitutional justice upon which Brandeis relied are concerned with issues having deep connection with personal dignity and the right to control highly personal information about oneself. Such information control is one of the primary ways in which persons autonomously establish their self-conception and their varying relations to other persons through selective information disclosure. Without some legally guaranteed right to control such information, personal autonomy is degraded at its core. From *personal* self-definition and self-mastery it is debased into the impersonal and fungible conventionalism that uncontrolled publicity inevitably facilitates. Accordingly, arguments, premised on the foundational values of equal concern and respect for autonomy, justify the protection of conventional privacy interests under tort law, as well as under various constitutional guarantees.

Actions protected by principles enunciated in *Griswold* and subsequent cases are denominated "private" not because they rest on information control but because substantive constitutional principles define conclusive reasons why they may not properly be the subject of encroachment by the state or by private individuals. Such rights are sensibly called "rights to privacy" in the sense that constitutional principles debar forms of state and private regulatory or prohibitory intrusion into the relevant areas of people's lives: on the basis of these principles, interference in these areas is unwarranted.

What is at stake here is nothing less than the basic moral vision of persons as having human rights: that is, as autonomous and entitled to equal concern and respect. This vision, correctly invoked by Warren and Brandeis in developing rights to information control, similarly underlies the constitutional right to privacy. In order to explain with care how this is so, I now turn to a deeper examination of the content of the moral principles involved in this latter right, and how they express the underlying values of autonomy and equal concern and respect to which Brandeis appeals. This examination will show why the constitutional right to privacy is a natural and defensible development rooted in the unwritten constitution which gives sense to the constitutional design.

THE CONCEPT OF MORALITY
AND THE TRANSVALUATION OF VALUES

The constitutional right of privacy cases typically arise in areas where there is a strong conventional wisdom that certain conduct is morally wrong and where the justice of that wisdom is under fundamental attack. It is no accident that the right of privacy is conceived by its proponents not merely as an advisable or charitable or even wise thing to concede, but as a *right*.[1] Proponents conceive matters involving rights, not as human weaknesses or excusable defects that others should benevolently overlook, but as positive moral goods that one may demand and enforce as one's due. Accordingly, the constitutional right to privacy is, in part, to be understood in terms of a transvaluation of values: certain areas of conduct, traditionally conceived as morally wrong and thus the proper object of public regulation and prohibition, are now perceived as affirmative goods the pursuit of which does not raise serious moral questions and thus is no longer a proper object of public critical concern.

[1] *See generally* Wasserstrom, *Rights, Human Rights, and Racial Discrimination*, 61 J. PHILOSOPHY 628 (1964).

How, philosophically, are we to interpret and understand such changes? First, as used here to explain the constitutional right to privacy, transvaluation of values refers to changes in the lower-order rules and conventions, namely, in the light of contemporary evidence and conditions, certain lower-order conventions are no longer justified by ultimate moral considerations. For example, according to one influential model, sex is only proper for the purpose of procreation. Many would argue, however, that the distinctive force of human, as opposed to animal, sexuality is that it is *not* rigidly procreational. To the extent that the traditional model of sexuality is discarded in favor of a non-procreational model, rigid moral rules prohibiting forms of non-procreational sex are no longer perceived as justified by ultimate moral considerations.

In order to provide reasonable criteria to assess the justifiability of such shifts, we must return to our discussion of the foundations of constitutional morality. As we saw, autonomy and equal concern and respect justify the constitutional immunity of human rights from political bargaining. Since one crucial ground for political bargaining is public morality, constitutional values require that the content of the public morality must be squared with the underlying values of constitutional morality. The primacy of the free exercise and establishment of religion clauses shows that at the core of constitutional values is religious toleration, understood as neutrality between those visions of the good life that are fundamental to autonomous capacities. Conceptually, contractarians give expression to this moral value by the ignorance assumption which deprives the contractors of any basis for keying the choice of ultimate principles to their possibly parochial vision of the good life. These values of constitutional morality ineluctably put determinate constaints on the content of the public morality which is the foundation of the criminal law and the enforcement of which pervades the entire legal system.

What is the constitutionally permissible content of the legal enforcement of morals? Regarding this question, recent moral philosophy has been increasingly occupied with the clarification of the conceptual structure of ordinary moral reasoning. The concept of morality or ethics is not an openly flexible one; there are certain determinate constraints on the kind of beliefs that can be counted as ethical in nature. Some examples of these constraints are the principles of mutual respect—treating others as you would like to be treated in comparable circumstances, universalization—judging the morality of principles by the consequences of their universal application; and minimization of fortuitous human differences (like clan, caste, ethnicity, gender, and color) as a basis for differential treatment. It follows from this conception that a view is not a moral one merely because it is passionately and sincerely held, or because it has a certain emotional depth, or because it is the view of one's father or mother or clan, or because it is conventional. On the contrary, the moral point of view affords an impartial way of assessing whether any of these beliefs, which may often press one to action, is in fact worthy of ethical commitment.

In similar ways and for similar reasons, not everything invoked by democratic majorities as justified by "public morality" is, in fact, morally justified. From the moral point of view, we must always assess such claims by whether they can be sustained by the underlying structure of moral reasoning—by principles of mutual respect, universalization, and minimization of fortuity. In this regard, constitutional morality is at one with the moral point of view. The values of equal concern and respect for personal autonomy, that we have unearthed at the foundations of American constitutionalism, are the same values that recent moral theory, following Kant, has identified as the fundamental values of the moral point of view. This kind of moral analysis affords definite constraints on what may permissibly or justifiably be regarded as an ethical belief. In an area where public attitudes about public morality are, in fact, demonstrably not justified by underlying moral constitutional principles, laws resting on such attitudes are constitutionally dubious. There being no defensible moral principle to sustain state interference, the matter is not a proper object of state concern. In this soil, the constitutional right to privacy took root in *Griswold*.

The understanding of *Griswold* and its progeny begins with repudiation of the procreational model of sexual love which was given its classic formulation by St. Augustine.[2] For Augustine, sexuality was a natural object of continuing shame because it involved loss of control. Accordingly, the only proper form of sex was that which was done with the controlled intention to procreate; sexuality without procreation or independent of such intentions was, for Augustine, intrinsically degrading. It follows from this view that certain rigidly defined kinds of intercourse in conventional marriage, always with the intention to procreate, are alone moral; contraception, whether within or outside marriage, extramarital and, of course, homosexual intercourse are forbidden since these do not involve intent to procreate.

Augustine's argument rests on a rather remarkable fallacy. Augustine starts with two anthropological points about human sexual experience: first, humans universally insist on having sex alone and unobserved by others, and second, humans universally cover their genitals in public. Augustine argues that the only plausible explanation for these two empirical facts about human sexuality is that humans experience sex as intrinsically degrading because it involves the loss of control: this perception of shame, in turn, must rest on the fact that the only proper form of sex is having it with the controlled intention to procreate; sexuality is intrinsically degrading because we tend to experience it without or independent of the one intention that alone can validate it. Assuming, *arguendo*, the truth of Augustine's anthropological assumptions, it does not follow that humans must find sex intrinsically shameful. These facts are equally well explained by the fact that people experience embarrassment in certain forms of publicity of

---

2 *See* AUGUSTINE, THE CITY OF GOD 577–94 (H. Bettenson trans. 1972). St. Thomas is in accord with Augustine's view. Of the emission of semen apart from procreation in marriage, he wrote: "[A]fter the sin of homicide whereby a human nature already in existence is destroyed, this type of sin appears to take next place, for by it the generation of human nature is precluded." T. AQUINAS, ON THE TRUTH OF THE CATHOLIC FAITH: SUMMA CONTRA GENTILES, pt. 2, ch. 122(9), at 146 (V. Bourke trans. 1946).

their sexuality, not shame in the experience of sex itself. Shame is conceptually distinguishable from embarrassment in that its natural object is a failure of personally esteemed competent self-control, whether the failure is public or private; embarrassment, in contrast, is experienced when a matter is made public that properly is regarded as private. The twin facts adduced by Augustine are, indeed, better explained by the hypothesis of embarrassment, not shame. Surely many people experience no negative self-evaluations when they engage in sex in private which is what the hypothesis of embarrassment, not shame, would lead us to expect. For example, people may experience pride in knowing that other people know or believe that they are having sex (the recently married young couple). There is no shame here, but there would be severe embarrassment if the sex act were actually observed. That people would experience such embarrassment reveals something important about human sexual experience, but it is not Augustine's contempt for the loss of control of sexual passion. Sexual experience is, for human beings, a profoundly personal, spontaneous, and absorbing experience in which they express intimate fantasies and vulnerabilities which typically cannot brook the sense of an external, critical observer. That humans require privacy for sex relates to the nature of the experience; there is no suggestion that the experience is, *pace* Augustine, intrinsically degrading.

The consequence of Augustine's fallacy is to misdescribe and misidentify natural features of healthy sexual experience, namely, the privacy required to express intimate sensual vulnerabilities, in terms of putatively degraded properties of sexual experience per se. In fact, this latter conception of sexuality relies on and expresses an overdeveloped wilfullness that fears passion itself as a form of loss of control, as though humans cannot with self-esteem indulge emotional spontaneity outside the rule of the iron procreational will. Such a conception both underestimates the distinctly human capacity for self-control and overestimates the force of sexuality as a dark, unreasoning, Bacchic possession whose demands inexorably undermine the rational will. It also fails to fit the empirical facts, indeed contradicts them. Human, as opposed to animal, sexuality is crucially marked by its control by higher cortical functions and thus its involvement with the human symbolic imagination, so that sexual propensities and experience are largely independent of the reproductive cycle. Consequently, humans use sexuality for diverse purposes—to express love, for recreation, or for procreation. No one purpose necessarily dominates; rather, human self-control chooses among the purposes depending on context and person.

The constitutional right to privacy was developed in *Griswold* and its progeny because the procreational model of sexuality could no longer be sustained by sound empirical or conceptual argument. Lacking such support, the procreational model could no longer be legally enforced on the grounds of the "public morality," for it failed to satisfy the postulate of constitutional morality that legally enforceable moral ideas be grounded on equal concern and respect for autonomy and demonstrated by facts capable of empirical validation. Accordingly, since anticontraceptive laws are based on the concept that nonprocreational sex is unnatural, the *Griswold* court properly invoked the right of privacy to invalidate the Connecticut statute. For similar reasons, laws prohibiting the use of pornography in the home were invalidated. Subsequently, abortion laws were also struck down because the traditional objection to them rested, in large part, on the procreational model and the residuum of moral condemnation that was not clearly sustained by sound argument.

If the right to privacy extends to sex among unmarried couples or even to autoeroticism in the home, it is difficult to understand how in a principled way the Court could decline to consider fully the application of this right to privacy, consensual, deviant sex acts. The Court might distinguish between heterosexual and homosexual forms of sexual activity; but could this distinction be defended rationally? At bottom, such a view must rest on the belief that homosexual or deviant sex is unnatural. Under this view, such practices would have to be excluded altogether from the scope of the constitutional right to privacy just as obscenity is excluded from first amendment protection. However, an analysis of the application of the notion of the "unnatural" to deviant sexual acts and an examination of the moral force of the constitutional right to privacy seems to compel the clear and decisive rejection of such a view.

The use of so imprecise a notion as "unnatural" to distinguish between those acts not protected by the constitutional right to privacy and those which are so protected is clearly unacceptable. The case where the constitutional right to privacy had its origin was one involving contraception—a practice which the Augustinian view would deem unnatural. Yet, the Court has apparently concluded that the "unnaturalness" of contraception or abortion is constitutionally inadmissible and cannot limit the scope of the right to privacy. In considering the constitutional permissibility of allowing majoritarian notions of the unnatural to justify limitations on the right to privacy, the Court must take into account two crucial factors: (1) the absence of empirical evidence or sound philosophical argument that these practices are unnatural; and (2) the lack of any sound moral argument, premised on equal concern and respect, that these practices are in any sense immoral. In particular, as we saw in the contraception and abortion decisions, the Court impliedly rejected the legitimacy of both the classic Augustinian view of human sexuality and the associated judgments about the exclusive morality of marital procreational sex. The enforcement of majoritarian prejudices, without any plausible empirical basis could be independently unconstitutional as a violation of due process rationality in legislation. To enforce such personal tastes in matters touching basic autonomous life choices violates basic human rights. The moral theory of the Constitution, built as a bulwark against "serious oppressions of the minor party in the community," requires that such human rights be upheld and protected against majoritarian prejudices.

For the same reasons that notions of the unnatural are constitutionally impermissible in decisions involving contraception, abortion, and the use of pornography in the home, these ideas are also impermissible in the constitutional assessment of laws prohibiting private forms of sexual deviance between consenting adults. No empirical evidence compels a finding that homosexuality is unnatural. Indeed, there have been cultures that possessed normative assumptions of what is natural that nevertheless did not regard homosexuality as unnatural. Indeed, societies (including ancient Greece) have included or include homosexuality among legitimate sexual conduct, and some prescribe it in the form of institutional pederasty. Individuals within our own culture have assailed the view that homosexuality is unnatural by adducing various facts which traditionalists either did not know or did not understand. For example, it is now known that homosexual behavior takes place in the animal world, suggesting that homosexuality is part of our mammalian heritage of sexual responsiveness.

Some have attempted to distinguish between individuals who are exclusively homosexual and the general population based on symptoms of mental illness or measures of self-esteem and self-acceptance. In general, however, apart from their sexual preference, exclusive homosexuals are psychologically indistinguishable from the general population.

The view sometimes expressed that male homosexuality necessarily involves the loss of desirable character traits probably rests on the idea that sexual relations between males involve the degradation of one or both parties to the status of a woman. This view, however, rests on intellectual confusion and unacceptable moral premises since it confuses sexual preference with gender identity, whereas, in fact, no such correlation exists. Male homosexuals or lesbians may be quite insistent about their respective gender identities and have quite typical "masculine" or "feminine" personalities. Their homosexuality is defined only by their erotic preference for members of the same gender. The notion that the status of woman is a degradation is morally repugnant to contemporary jurisprudence and morality. If such crude and unjust sexual stereotypes lie at the bottom of antihomosexuality laws, they should be uprooted, as is being done elsewhere in modern life.

Finally, homosexual preference appears to be an adaptation of natural human propensities to very early social circumstances of certain kinds, so that the preference is settled, largely irreversibly, at a quite early age.

The cumulative impact of such facts is clear. The notion of "unnatural acts," interpreted in terms of a fixed procreational model of sexual functioning, deviations from which result in inexorable damage or degradation, is not properly applied to homosexual acts performed in private between consenting adults. Such activity is clearly a natural expression of human sexual competences and sensitivities, and does not reflect any form of damage, decline or injury. To deny the acceptability of such acts is itself a human evil, a denial of the distinctive human capacities for loving and sensual experience without ulterior procreative motives—in a plausible sense, itself unnatural.

There is consequently no logically consistent explanation for the Court's refusal to enforce concepts of the "unnatural" in the case of contraception while permitting statutes based on similar concepts to prohibit sexual deviance. Indeed, the moral arguments in the latter case are more compelling. For one thing, at the time *Griswold* was decided, statutes condemning and prohibiting forms of contraception probably no longer reflected a majoritarian understanding of the unnaturalness of this form of birth control. Accordingly, the need for constitutional protection, while proper, was not exigent. In the case of homosexuality, however, there is good reason to believe that, as a group, homosexuals are subject to exactly the kind of unjust social hatred that constitutional guarantees were designed to combat.

A second way by which the Court might justify its restricted application of the right of privacy would be to focus on the morality of the acts in question. Presumably, the naturalness of homosexual experience would not in itself legitimize such experience, if homosexuality were shown to be immoral. There is, however, no sound moral argument to sustain any longer the idea that homosexuality is intrinsically immoral.

The concept of morality, proposed herein, puts certain constraints— mutual respect, universalization, minimization of fortuity—on the kinds of beliefs and arguments that can properly be regarded as ethical in nature. Certainly, such constraints would dictate certain prohibitions and regulations of sexual conduct. For example, respect for the development of capacities of autonomous rational choice would require that various liberties, guaranteed to mature adults, might not extend to persons presumably lacking rational capacities, such as children. Nor is there any objection to the reasonable regulation of obtrusive sexual solicitations or, of course, to forcible forms of intercourse of any kind. Such regulations or prohibitions would secure a more equal expression of autonomy compatible with a like liberty for all, thus advancing underlying values of equal concern and respect. In addition, forms of sexual expression would be limited by other moral principles that would be universalized compatibly with equal concern and respect, for example: principles of not killing, harming or inflicting gratuitous cruelty; principles of paternalism in narrowly defined circumstances; and principles of fidelity. Thus, as formulated, the relevant limiting moral and constitutional principles permit some reasonable, legitimate restrictions on complete individual freedom.

Statutes that absolutely prohibit deviant sexual acts such as that considered in *Doe* cannot be justified consistently with the principles just discussed. Such statutes are not limited to forcible or public forms of sexual intercourse, or to sexual intercourse by or with children but extend to private, consensual acts between adults as well. To say that such laws are justified by their indirect effect of stopping homosexual intercourse by or with the underaged would be as absurd as to claim that absolute prohibitions on heterosexual intercourse could be similarly justified. There is no reason to believe that homosexuals as a class are any more involved in offenses with the young than heterosexuals. Nor is there any reliable evidence that such laws inhibit children from being naturally homosexual who would otherwise be naturally heterosexual. Sexual preference is settled, largely irreversibly, in very early childhood well before laws of this kind could have any effect. If the state has any legitimate interest in determining the sexual preference of its citizens, which is doubtful, that interest cannot constitutionally be secured by overbroad statutes, that tread upon the rights of exclusive homosexuals of all ages and that, in any event, irrationally pursue the claimed interest.

Other moral principles also fail to justify absolute prohibitions on consensual sexual deviance. Homosexual relations, for example, are not generally violent. Thus, prohibitory statutes could not be justified by moral principles of nonmaleficence. There is no convincing evidence that homosexuality is either harmful to the homosexual or correlated with any form of mental or physical disease or defect. To the contrary, there is evidence that antihomosexuality laws, which either force homosexuals into heterosexual marriage unnatural for them or otherwise distort and disfigure the reasonable pursuit of natural emotional fulfillment, harm homosexuals and others in deep and permanent ways. Accordingly, principles of legitimate state paternalism do not here come into play.

One quite relevant set of facts that would justify prohibitions of homosexuality would be empirical support for the view that homosexuality is a kind of degenerative social poison that leads directly to disease, social disorder and disintegration. Principles of constitutional justice must be compatible with the stability of institutions of social cooperation. Thus, if the above allegation were true, prohibition of homosexuality might be justified on the ground that such prohibition would preserve the constitutional order, so that justice on balance would be secured. These beliefs are quite untenable today, however. Many nations, including several in Western Europe, have long allowed homosexual acts between consenting adults, with no consequent social disorder or disease.

One final moral argument has been used to justify a general prohibition upon homosexuality—the argument invoked by the district court in *Doe* as "the promotion of morality and decency." That court believed this to be the ultimate ground for the legitimacy of the Virginia sodomy statute. The argument takes three forms: (1) a general jurisprudential thesis about the relation of law and morals; (2) an interpretation of the moral principles discussed previously; and (3) the point of view of a certain form of theological ethics. None of these views can be sustained.

The classic modern statement of the jurisprudential thesis was made by Devlin [3] against Hart,[4] repeating many of the arguments earlier made by Stephen [5] against Mill.[6] The Devlin-Hart debate centered on the jurisprudential interpretation of the Wolfenden Report, which recommended, *inter alia,* the abolition of the imposition of criminal penalties for homosexual acts between consenting adults. Devlin, in questioning the Report, focused on the proposition that certain private immoral acts are not the law's business. The criminal law, Devlin argued, is completely unintelligible without reference to moral-

[3] *See generally* P. DEVLIN, THE ENFORCEMENT OF MORALS 9–13 (1965).
[4] *See* H. L. A. HART, LAW, LIBERTY, AND MORALITY (1963).
[5] J. STEPHEN, LIBERTY. EQUALITY, FRATERNITY 135–78 (1967).
[6] J. S. MILL, *On Liberty,* in THE PHILOSOPHY OF JOHN STUART MILL 271–93 (M. Cohen ed. 1961) [hereinafter cited as *On Liberty*].

ity, which it enforces. The fact that two parties agree to kill one another, for example, does not relieve the killer of criminal liability, for the act in question is immoral. The privacy of the act (between consenting adults perhaps in the privacy of the home) is irrelevant. Similarly, the criminal law in general arises from morality. Morality, Devlin maintains, is the necessary condition of the existence of society. Thus, to change the law in such a way as to violate that morality is to threaten the stability of the social order. Morality, in this connection, is to be understood in terms of the ordinary man's intuitive sense of right and wrong, as determined, Devlin suggests, by taking a man at random. Just as we prove the standards of negligence for purposes of civil or criminal liability by appealing to the judgment of ordinary men acting as jurors, so may we prove applicable standards of morality. Ordinary men morally loathe homosexuality; accordingly, homosexuality is immoral and must be legally forbidden.

Superficially, Devlin's argument appears to be constitutionally acceptable. There should be no constitutional objection to prohibiting clearly immoral acts that threaten the existence of society. Further, it is surely plausible that law and morals have a deep and systematic connection of the kind Devlin suggests. Nevertheless, such abstractly plausible propositions will not support the specific argument which Devlin propounds. Although Devlin is probably correct in asserting that the criminal law arises from the morality that it enforces, he nevertheless falsely identifies morality with conventional social views in a way that renders unthinkable, if not unintelligible, the whole idea of moral criticism and reform of social convention. Adoption of this view would effectively turn the measure of legally enforceable moral ideas into an interim victory of one set of contending ideological forces over another. Moreover, there is no good reason to make this identification of morality and social convention, since it is based on an indefensible and naive moral philosophy as well as an unexamined and unsound sociology.

The attraction of Devlin's theory for judges is its apparent objectivity; it affords a definite criterion for the morality that the law enforces without appeal to subjective considerations. But the empirical objectivity of existing custom has nothing to do with the notions of moral impartiality and objectivity that are, or should be, of judicial concern in determining the public morality on which the law rests. The idea that the pursuit of the latter must collapse into the former is a confusion of inquiries, arising from an untenable and indefensible distinction between subjective moral belief and the public morality of the law. There is no such distinction. Views, to be moral, require a certain kind of justification. Judges, in interpreting legally enforceable moral ideas, must appeal to the kind of reasoning that is moral. They do not as judges abdicate their responsibility for moral reasoning as persons. On the contrary, competence and clarity in such reasoning comprise the virtue that we denominate judicial.

Devlin's theory is for such reasons theoretically and practically unacceptable. Even if it could be defended on such grounds, however, it must be rejected as it is incompatible with the moral theory of human rights implicit in the constitutional order. The Constitution rests on the idea that moral rights of individuals cannot be violated, notwithstanding majoritarian sentiments to the contrary. Accordingly, the Supreme Court has rightly upheld constitutional rights against popular racial and sexual prejudices. Prejudices against the vulnerable, largely powerless homosexual minority must be similarly circumscribed.

That this popular argument for preserving moral standards is objectionable in moral and constitutional principle is then apparent. The district court in *Doe,* however, employed another form of argument, not similarly objectionable, as it rests on an interpretation of the moral principles which do relevantly regulate sexual conduct. It suggested that the moral issue before it was not that homosexuality is objectionable per se, but rather that in the present state of society homosexuality tends to evade certain moral principles, for example, principles of fidelity intrinsic in heterosexual marriage and family obligations.[7] The court's use of this argument is, however, fundamentally fallacious. In support of its proposition, the court cited a case that involved fellatio among a married couple and a third adult and distribution of pictures of the said acts in school by the couple's daughters (aged 11 and 13). The latter fact was alleged to show that conduct not immoral in itself may be condemned because "the conduct is likely to end in a contribution to moral delinquency." The citation of a case of apparently heterosexual sodomy, involving clear elements of a waiver of privacy rights as evidence for the propriety of proscribing clearly private homosexual sex is a remarkable nonsequitur, illustrating the kind of shabby reasoning to which courts are driven in order to lend a shred of moral plausibility to these prohibitions.

Aside from this specific argumentative fallacy, there remains the general intuition that homosexuality, if allowed, would violate moral principles implicit in the institution of the heterosexual family. While this line of thought has the general form of an acceptable moral and constitutional argument, its factual assumptions are utterly unsupported by evidence. For example, the argument makes the unsupported assumption that prohibiting homosexuality would encourage heterosexual marriage. But, as Judge Merhige indicated in his dissent in *Doe,* such a claim is so empirically flimsy as to be "unworthy of judicial response." For one thing, historical and contemporary data show that homosexual connections are compatible with heterosexual marriage. The many countries which have legalized homosexual relations show no decline in the incidence of heterosexual marriage. It thus appears that prohibitions of homosexual relations have no effect on heterosexual marriage.[8]

---

[7] Doe v. Commonwealth's Attorney for Richmond, 403 F. Supp. 1199, 1202 (E.D. Va. 1975). The Court, thus, focused on the analysis of Lovisi v. Slayton, 363 F. Supp, 620 (E.D. Va. 1973), aff'd, 539 F.2d 349 (4th Cir.) (en banc), cert. denied, 429 U.S. 977 (1976). This case involved both a breach of the traditional marital bond (a threesome, two of whom are a married couple, engaging in fellatio) and elements of degradation of the young (the children, aged 11 and 13, who distributed pictures of their parents' activities in school).

[8] Some homosexuals do marry and have children. P. WILSON, THE SEXUAL DILEMMA 52–53 (1971). In general, those whose sexuality is entirely homosexual can function heterosexually for periods of time. D. WEST, HOMOSEXUALITY 233–34 (1968); Knight, *Overt Male Homosexuality,* in SEXUAL BEHAVIOR AND THE LAW 442–43 R. Slovenko ed.

The intuition regarding homosexuality and the decline of the hetero-sexual family is ancient. According to this view, consensual homosexual acts in private are not of social concern, but the way of life that such sex acts exemplify is. To legitimate these sex acts is to legitimate an undesirable way of life; thus these sex acts, even in private between consenting adults, may justly be prohibited.

The substance of this intuitive allegation should be examined with care, for a form of it bears the imprimatur of the Supreme Court it-self.[9] The suggestion is this: public knowledge of the legitimacy of homosexual acts would undermine the capacity of heterosexuals to sus-tain the way of life required for the monogamous nuclear family and the personal sacrifices that such a way of life requires. But no one in the Western cultural tradition could reasonably claim that the existence of legitimate alternative ways of life outside heterosexual marriage un-dermine social stability. The legitimacy of remaining unmarried has not undermined the heterosexual family. Indeed, one form of the un-married state, religious celibacy, has long been regarded by influential Western religions as sanctified; this fact has not, however, made the heterosexual family less stable.

Why, then, should the recognition of homosexuality as a legitimate way of life be treated in a radically different way? The suggestion must be that homosexual preference is so strong and universal and hetero-sexual preference so weak (and conventional family life so unattrac-tive) that people would on a massive scale tend not to undertake hetero-sexual marriage if homosexuality as a way of life were legitimate. But, as we have seen, there is not even a shred of empirical support for these views. While a small minority of the population naturally experiences erotic pleasure exclusively with people of the same gender, the great majority is exclusively heterosexual.

Aside from the facts of natural eroticism, the attractions of hetero-sexual marriage are deep-seated and permanent features of the human condition. Human beings, generally raised in the nuclear heterosexual family, naturally regard the cooperation and creative sharing that typi-fies the heterosexual family as the answer, or part of the answer, to the recurrent human problem of loneliness and isolation. For most people, conventional marriage is and will long remain the standard—supplying

---

1965). By employing sexual fantasies of a person for whom they experience erotic feeling, people can thus have intercourse with people in whom they experience nothing erotic. Note Kinsey's description of how people have intercourse with prosti-tutes they find unattractive: "As far as his psychologic responses are concerned, the male in many instances may not be having coitus with the immediate sexual partner, but with all of the other girls with whom he has ever had coitus, and with the entire genus Female with which he would like to have coitus." A. KINSEY, W. POMEROY, C. MARTIN & P. GEBHARD, SEXUAL BEHAVIOR IN THE HUMAN FEMALE 684 (1953). In the case of exclusive homosexuals, the effect of thus frustrating natural feeling to conform to conventional models of conduct is probably to starve and waste resources of spontaneous and individual human feeling.

[9] See the development of this argument in the obscenity context in Paris Adult Thea-tre I v. Slaton, 413 U.S. 49 (1973); for critical commentary thereon, see Richards, *Free Speech and Obscenity Law: Toward a Moral Theory of the First Amendment*, 123 U. PA. L. REV. 45, 83–90 (1974).

a natural response to human needs for sexual release, intimacy, and the desire for tangible immortality (child-rearing). It is a bizarre failure of imagination and perspective so to underestimate the attractions of family life as to suppose that the legitimacy of homosexuality as a way of life would have any significant effect on it at all. Even in this era of growing sexual freedom and rising divorce rates, there is no sign that heterosexual marriage as an institution is in general less attractive. The rising divorce rates show, not a distaste for marriage, but only less willingness to stick with the original partners in marriage. The important and striking feature of this phenomenon is that divorced people typically remarry; they reject their previous partner, not the institution of marriage itself.

Certainly, the crude argument that if everyone were homosexual there would, disastrously, be an end of the human species universalizes absurdly a principle not seriously debated, namely, that everyone should or must be homosexual. Rather, the principle under discussion is whether, given the overwhelming naturally heterosexual majority and the small naturally homosexual minority, the state should, at a minimum, be tolerantly neutral between sexual preferences.

The "way of life" argument cannot be sustained as an empirical proposition, even though it can be understood as the psychological residue of fear and loathing unmistakably left by the long tradition that condemned homosexuality and nonprocreative sex in general as unnatural. The existence and nature of these prejudices, which take the form of homophobia, are interesting and important psychological questions. They are probably significantly connected to a standard masculine fear of passivity and feminine rejection of aggressive activity, of which male or female homosexuality, respectively, is mistakenly supposed the ultimate symbol. Homophobia thus appears as a form of intrapsychic defense against any suggestion of "unmasculine" passivity or "unfeminine" aggressiveness. Such underlying stereotypes are under widespread attack today: many men and women, heterosexual and homosexual, justly refuse any longer to dichotomize and disfigure their natures along poles of conventional masculine-feminine stereotypes that are unjust in principle, no longer socially sensible, and inhumanely unfulfilling to individuals. Clearly, as a matter of law, the prejudices based on such stereotypes should have no force independent of the empirical assumptions on which they rest. Undoubtedly, residues of guilt and fear remain long after we reject on rational grounds the beliefs on which those guilts and fears rest. But, this psychological truth does not validate such regressive emotions as a legitimate basis for law. If the life of reason requires us to circumscribe such negative emotions as a basis for ethical conduct, the morality of law can require no less.

In any event, it is difficult to understand how the state has the right, on moral grounds, to protect heterosexual love at the expense of homosexual love. Equal concern and respect for autonomous choice seem precisely to forbid the kind of calculation that this sort of sacrifice contemplates. In principle, these values, as we have seen, forbid the sacrifice of the fundamental interests of one group in order to secure the greater happiness of other groups or of the whole. These values prescribe moral and constitutional benchmarks of human decency, resting on respect for the interest of all persons equally in general goods, and thereby the power of majority rule to plough under the interests of minorities is limited.

Finally, there is reason to believe that the argument for protecting marriage and the family is hypocritically proposed. If the argument were meant seriously, state laws against fornication and adultery would be vigorously pressed in addition to the anti-homosexuality laws. But, in many states, such laws either do not exist or penalize homosexuality much more severely than heterosexual offenses. This suggests what should by now be reasonably clear: antihomosexuality laws rest not on reasonable moral argument consistently pursued, but on ancient prejudice and the last remaining vestige of ideas, elsewhere eschewed, of unnatural sexual witchcraft and demonology.

The last available form of moral argument in support of absolute prohibitions of consensual adult homosexual relations, certainly implicit in Devlin's argument, is that of theological ethics—the moral principles enforceable at law are dictated by the Judeao-Christian God. Since traditional Judaeo-Christian thought appears to condemn nonprocreative sex in general and homosexuality in particular, these condemnations, being by definition moral, may be enforced at law. There are two conclusive objections to this argument: one moral, the other constitutional.

Morally, invoking theological ethics in support of the moral condemnation of homosexuality runs afoul of a philosophical argument of metaethical principle and a normative argument of casuistry. Metaethically, there are powerful objections to a theological analysis of morality without appeal to the constraints of mutual respect, universalization, and minimization of fortuity previously discussed. Certainly, the traditional view of Christian theology has been that moral concepts have a natural authority antecedent to divine revelation; accordingly, moral concepts even for theologians must be explicable without a circular appeal to divine revelation. Metaethically, moral reasoning is logically independent of religious reasoning. Accordingly, it is fallacious to invoke purely theological reasoning to rebut the independent force of a valid moral argument. Psychological studies of moral development suggest that ethical reasoning is, in fact, unrelated to religious training or affiliation. Normatively, the tradition of theological casuistry, on which Devlin rests his case, is now under critical scrutiny from within theology. There is growing controversy within religious groups as to the proper interpretation of Biblical prohibitions conventionally believed to condemn homosexuality,[10] and indeed invoked to this end by the lower

---

[10] Thus, the Sodom and Gomorrah episode, *Genesis* 19, traditionally taken to show that homosexuality is contrary to God's will in that He punished those cities by fire and brimstone, is apparently not about homosexuality at all. *See* D. BAILEY, HOMOSEXUALITY AND THE WESTERN CHRISTIAN TRADITION 1–28 (1955); J. McNEILL, THE CHURCH AND THE HOMOSEXUAL 42–50 (1976). Even the seemingly clear *Leviticus* prohibitions have been analyzed by Biblical scholars as not being about homosexuality per se. *See, e.g.,* S. DRIVER, DEUTERONOMY 264 (1896); McNEILL at 56–60; N. SNAITH, THE CENTURY BIBLE: LEVITICUS AND NUMBERS 126 n.22 (New ed. 1967). Other scholars, however, disagree about this latter prohibition. *See* BAILEY at 30. Even Catholic theologians have

court in *Doe*.[11] This tradition of rational theology, including attacks by Catholic theologians on the procreational model of sexuality,[12] indicates that even the religious foundations on which these laws were constructed are now seen to be jerry-built.

Finally, whatever the constitutional permissibility of the frank invocation of theological ethics in Devlin's England where Church and State are not constitutionally separate, in the United States the free exercise and establishment of religion clauses of the first amendment stand as an absolute bar to the enforcement of theological ethics of the form implicit in Devlin's argument.[13] Our earlier analysis of the structure of constitutional morality clarifies why this is so. The primary postulate of the American Constitution is the moral principle of religious tolerance, the idea of fundamental constitutionally mandated neutrality between the disparate visions of the good life at the profound level of personal self-definition occupied by religious and philosophical beliefs. Accordingly, constitutional principles require that only those principles may be legally enforced which express the values of equal concern and respect for autonomous self-definition in terms of the many permissible visions of the good life compatible with these values. These principles require, *inter alia*, that any legally enforceable standards of conduct must rest on generally acceptable empirical standards and must not contravene the underlying values of equal concern and respect.

SEXUAL AUTONOMY, THE RATIONAL CHOICE OF ONE'S SELF, AND HUMAN RIGHTS

. . . Contemporary understanding of the strategic importance to self-respect and personhood of sexual autonomy requires that we similarly guarantee full liberty to enjoy and express love. At the core of this understanding lies Freud's central idea, independently confirmed by comparative ethology and anthropology, that human sexuality, rooted

---

argued that these prohibitions do not attack or condemn exclusive homosexuals: "[The Scriptures'] aim is not to pillory the fact that some people experience this perversion inculpably. They denounce a homosexuality which had become the prevalent fashion and had spread to many who were really quite capable of normal sexual sentiments . . . . Lack of frank discussion has allowed a number of opinions to be formed about [homosexuals] which are unjust when applied generally, because those who have such inclinations in fact are often hard-working and honourable people." A NEW CATECHISM 384–85 (K. Smith trans. 1967), *cited in In re* Labady, 326 F. Supp. 924, 930 (S.D.N.Y. 1971); *cf.* BAILEY at x–xii (similar distinction between the invert and pervert).
[11] 403 F. Supp. at 1202 n.2. Such citation of Old Testament texts in support of the intrinsic evil of homosexuality is common in American judicial opinions. *See, e.g.,* DAWSON v. VANCE, 329 F. Supp. 1329 (S.D. Tex. 1971), which cites the Sodom and Gomorrah episode at *Genesis* 19:1-29 in support of the proposition that the "practice is inherently inimical to the general integrity of the human person." *Id.* at 1322.
[12] *See, e.g.,* M. VALENTE, SEX: THE RADICAL VIEW OF A CATHOLIC THEOLOGIAN (1970); J. McNEILL, S.J., THE CHURCH AND THE HOMOSEXUAL 89–107 (1976).
[13] *See* Epperson v. Arkansas, 393 U.S. 97 (1968); W. BARNETT, SEXUAL FREEDOM AND THE CONSTITUTION 74–93 (1973); Henkin, *Morals and the Constitution: The Sin of Obscenity,* 63 COLUM. L. REV. 391 (1963).

in the high degree of cortical control of sexuality, serves complex imaginative and symbolic purposes, and thus is extraordinarily plastic and malleable.[14] Freud thus introduced into scientific psychology what artists have always known and expressed: that for humans to experience sex is never, even in solitary masturbation, a purely physical act, but is embued with complex evaluational interpretations of its real or fantasied object, often rooted in the whole history of the person from early childhood on. Freud's theory of the defenses clarifies some of the imaginative manipulations of sexual feelings that are sometimes destructive, but are also sometimes adaptive. For the latter, consider Freud's own celebration of the eroticism of work that he called sublimation.[15]

Understanding of unconscious imaginative processes was, for Freud, not a concessive plea for irrationalism but a deepening of our understanding of the concept of autonomy and of the person; for knowledge of the unconscious mind and its processes deepens the range and strength of the ego or self in controlling id and superego impulses: "Where id was, there shall ego be." [16] Through our self-conscious retrieval and investigation of the fantasy data of the unconscious (dreams, free associations, slips, and the like), we may achieve a remarkable capacity to deepen our control and understanding of mental processes that are otherwise inexplicable, and often stupidly, rigidly, and self-destructively repetitive. Through our knowledge of the unconscious defenses and their form in our own lives, we are able to assess consciously the work of the unconscious, deciding whether desires disowned by the unconscious should be reclaimed (repression) or desires promoted by the unconscious should be cut back (sublimation and projection). We may, in addition, render ourselves self-conscious and independent of our earliest most intense emotional identifications, achieving an understanding of our life history so that we may see our lives and what we want from them individually as our own and not as the unconscious derivative of the wishes of significant others; with this kind of understanding, we deepen our autonomy to decide with what or with whom in our life history we will or will not identify or continue to identify.

To see human autonomy in this deeper way and to understand the powerful role of sexuality as an independent force in the imaginative life and general development of the person is to acknowledge the cen-

[14] "The sexual instinct . . . is probably more strongly developed in man than in most of the higher animals; it is certainly more constant, since it has almost entirely overcome the periodicity to which it is tied in animals. It places extraordinarily large amounts of force at the disposal of civilized activity, and it does this in virtue of its especially marked characteristic of being able to displace its aim without materially diminishing in intensity. This capacity to exchange its original sexual aim for another one, which is no longer sexual but which is psychically related to the first aim, is called the capacity for *sublimation*." S. FREUD, *"Civilized" Sexual Morality and Modern Nervous Illness*, in 9 THE COMPLETE PSYCHOLOGICAL WORKS OF SIGMUND FREUD 181, 187 (Standard ed. 1908).

[15] See generally, S. FREUD, *Civilization and its Discontents*, in 21 THE COMPLETE PSYCHOLOGICAL WORKS OF SIGMUND FREUD (Standard ed. 1930).

[16] See S. FREUD, *New Introductory Lectures on Psycho-Analysis*, in 22 THE COMPLETE PSYCHOLOGICAL WORKS OF SIGMUND FREUD 80 (Standard ed. 1933).

tral role of sexual autonomy in the idea of a free person. This view of autonomy has necessary implications for the widening application of human rights to sexuality. Sexuality, in this view, is not a spiritually empty experience that the state may compulsorily legitimize only in the form of rigid, marital procreational sex, but one of the fundamental experiences through which, as an end in itself, people define the meaning of their lives. Consider the following specific ways in which this is so.

First, sexual love is profoundly misdescribed by the sorrowing Catholic dismissal of sexuality as an unfortunate and nonspiritual concomitant of propagation, for sexuality has for humans the independent status of a profound ecstasy that makes available to a modern person experiences increasingly inaccessible in public life: self-transcendence, expression of private fantasy, release of inner tensions, and meaningful and acceptable expression of regressive desires to be again the free child—unafraid to lose control, playful, vulnerable, spontaneous, sensually loved. While people may choose to forego this experience, any coercive prohibition of it amounts to the deprivation of an experience central in human significance.

Second, sexual love is sometimes a crucial ingredient in forming lasting personal relationships and thus can facilitate the good that these relationships afford in human life. Such durable relationships founded on sexual intimacy are happily denominated a form of knowledge, in Biblical locution, for they afford to people the capacity for a secure disclosure of self, not only through exposure of sexual vulnerabilities, but also through the sharing of recesses of the self otherwise remote and inaccessible. Accordingly, choices involving these relationships are among the most important strategic decisions in one's life plan. The choice of one's lover, whether in or outside marriage, involves one's entire self-conception. As one major recent study of the human life cycle clarifies, the choice of one's lover is one with one's life "dream"; as the "dream" changes, so must the relationship.[17] The disclosure of self that love involves, the mutual shaping of expectations and life styles, the sharing of common aspirations and hopes—all these, and others, suggest the extraordinary significance of decisions about matters of love in the design of a human life.

Third, the force of sexual love in human life expresses itself in the desire to participate with the beloved in the development of and care for common projects created by the relationship. Some of these projects take on a durable character in terms of objects or activities or even persons who survive the relationship. In so doing they embody the lasting value of the relationship and perhaps thus satisfy, in some measure, the longing of human self-consciousness for evidence of the immortal and imperishable self.

In summary, one may appeal to the plausible thought that love is part of what is commonly meant by the meaning of life. Surely, such love may not necessarily take sexual forms; it may, for example, take the form of a diffuse benevolence toward larger or smaller groups of

17 *See* D. LEVINSON, THE SEASONS OF A MAN'S LIFE 91–111, 237, 245–251 (1978).

people, or even devotion to an abstract entity. But, the absence of love in any form from a human life renders a life plan incoherently empty at its core and the life of the spirit deformed and miserably twisted. . . .

[Richards proceeds to apply the contractarian position described by John Rawls, reverting to the theory of the "original position" in which rational persons determine collectively what rights they will retain in a state to which they all agree to owe allegiance. Sexual autonomy, he says, is a crucial ingredient of self-respect. Hence, the original con-tractors would not agree to any principle that would permit restrictions upon themselves in this regard. This leads him to conclude that "the principle of love [is] a civil liberty," under which "every person is guaranteed the greatest equal liberty, opportunity and capacity to love, compatible with a like liberty, opportunity and capacity for all." They cannot "smuggle in" covert premises or prejudices based upon religious duties or distaste for certain kinds of love, for "the concept of love says nothing about the form of its physical expression other than, for ex-ample, that it involves forms of intimate closeness expressing the evi-dent intention of good to another. . . . A large and indeterminate class of forms of sexual intercourse is compatible with the aims of love."]

This principle explains and justifies the sense in which the consti-tutional right to privacy is a *right*. The constitutional concept expresses an underlying moral principle resting on the enhancement of sexual autonomy, the self-determination of the role of sexuality in one's life which protects the values foundational to the concept of human rights, equal concern and respect for autonomy. Accordingly, in the absence of countervailing moral argument, laws which determine how one will have sex and with what consequences are constitutionally invalid. Such considerations explain the unconstitutionality of laws proscribing con-traception, abortion, and the use of pornography in the home. They also explain why antihomosexuality laws violate a constitutional right.

Freedom to love means that a mature individual must have autonomy to decide how or whether to love another. Restrictions on the form of love imposed in the name of the distorting rigidities of convention that bear no relation to individual emotional capacities and needs would be condemned. Individual autonomy, in matters of love, would ensure the development of people who could call their emotional natute their own, secure in the development of attachments that bear the mark of spontaneous human feeling and that touch one's original impulses. In contrast, restrictions on this individual autonomy would starve one's emotional capacities, withering individual feeling into conventional gesture and strong native pleasures into vicarious fantasies.

Antihomosexuality laws egregiously violate these considerations. First, laws prohibiting homosexual conduct inhibit persons inclined to-ward this form of sexual activity from obtaining sexual satisfaction in the only way they find natural. Second, these laws probably encourage blackmail by providing a means by which homosexuals can be threatened with exposure and prosecution. Such vulnerability to blackmail may discourage employers from hiring homosexuals, on the ground that they are security risks. Third, laws prohibiting consensual adult homosexual activity provide a ground for discrimination against people of homosexual preference in employment, housing, and public accommodation.

Consider the effects of such laws on exclusive homosexuals who alone find homosexual relations naturally satisfying. Traditionally, these individuals do one of three things. First, they may utterly disown sexuality and the sexual aspect of their selves, dedicating themselves, perhaps, to an impersonal benevolence. Second, they may heterosexually marry, using homosexual fantasies when engaging in sex with their spouse. Third, they may be practicing covert homosexuals either exclusively or in some combination with the second alternative. Each of these options, compelled by the state of the law, outrageously violates human rights.

First, the legal compulsion of celibacy, in the absence of any good reason, unfairly compels homosexuals to personal sacrifices which would be regarded as unthinkable if demanded of heterosexuals. Of course, celibacy may be, for some people, a rational life choice. But, to compel people to disown their most basic emotional propensities is to demand that life be only gesturally lived behind impersonal masks, that expression be always artfully choreographed and never naturally spontaneous, and that the body be experienced as an empty sepulchre.

Second, the experience of heterosexual marriage without natural eroticism is hollow, frequently leading to marital instability and divorce, both of which may be damaging to the children. In the place of the kinds of relationships found natural, homosexuals fail to experience forms of deep personal release, pointlessly and sometimes dishonestly inflict harms on others, as they inflict on themselves unnecessary burdens of self-sacrifice.

Third, the cumulative effect of antihomosexuality laws is to deprive practicing homosexuals of the experience of a secure self-respect in their competence in building personal relationships. The degree of emotional sacrifice thus exacted for no defensible reason seems among the most unjust deprivations that law can compel. Persons are deprived of a realistic basis for confidence and security in their most basic emotional propensities. Criminal penalty, employment risks, and social prejudice converge to render dubious a person's most spontaneous native urges, dividing emotions, physical expression and self-image in a cruelly gratuitous way. The deepest damage is to the spiritual and imaginative dimension that gives human sexual love its significance. Persons surrounded by false social conceptions that are supported by law find it difficult to esteem their own emotional propensities and natural expression. Without such self-esteem love finds no meaningful or enduring object. Instead of being assured a fair opportunity to develop loving capacities and fair access to love, the homosexual's capacity to express such feelings is driven into a secretive and concealed world of shallow and often anonymous physical encounters. The achievement of emotional relationships of any depth or permanence is made a matter of heroic individual effort when it could, like heterosexual relations, be part of the warp and woof of the ordinary social possibility.

In thus forbidding exclusive homosexuals to express sexual love in the only way they find natural, the law deprives them of the good in life that love affords.

INAPPROPRIATE PATERNALISTIC ARGUMENTS

. . . . No good argument can be made that paternalistic considerations would justify interferences in basic choices such as whether to marry, bear children or be heterosexual. Indeed, in many cases such choices seem clearly rational. There is widespread consensus that it is rational for many people to limit family size by contraceptives; in such ways, people satisfy their desires for having children and have additional resources better to advance their ends in general. It is no more irrational, I believe, to suppose that for some people not having children would better advance their ends; whatever ends having children advances can be secured in alternative ways (for example, being in a profession that cares for the young, investing one's immortal longings in other forms of enduring projects, etc.) and not having children may free people to advance their own and others' good in ways otherwise improbable. Finally, the idea that it is per se irrational to engage in homosexual relations is no more defensible. Suppose one is an exclusive homosexual, who from early age has experienced natural eroticism either in fact or in fantasy, only with people of the same gender. Such an individual experiences spontaneous self-expression and fulfillment and meaningful relations only in homosexual relations. Since love is such a fundamental good in human life, it would surely be rational to develop a personal life in which one's natural sexual self can find meaningful expression. The idea of change of sexual preference is unacceptable not merely because it is painful and probably doomed to failure but because, given the depth of sexuality, it would transmogrify the self in which one has self-esteem. The appeal to social opprobrium rests on a circular appeal to the still extant force of invalid and unjust moral judgments. It is simply not irrational to refuse to sacrifice the foundations of one's personal happiness to vicious social prejudices, for such sacrifices degrade the foundations of autonomous self-respect and thus reduce freedom to cowardly, servile, and fear-ridden conventionalism. For many, such a life is simply not worth living. How, then, are we even to *understand* the invocation of paternalistic arguments of irrationality in this context? The answer, I believe, is that in making such judgments people do not take seriously or responsibly what it is to be the agent, in this case, an exclusive homosexual. They suppose that these people are somehow real heterosexuals who must be prodded to realize their latent desires. This fantasy cannot be sustained as an empirical proposition; it is simply a make-weight psychiatric correlate to already accepted moral judgments. This substitution of personal values for the ends of the agent is, of course, improper paternalism. The development of the constitutional right to privacy is, in part, to be understood as a bar to such arguments, allowing the agent the scope of personal autonomy in these matters that is their moral and human right.

It is fair to regard the judgments of conventional family life as "the meaning of life" as a kind of metaphysical familism. It is, however, important to see the limited force that such normative judgments should be accorded. Certainly, such normative judgments are important and deeply significant; indeed, nothing can be more important to individuals than basic life choices. But it is crucial to see that such judgments are not properly regarded as ethical or moral judgments, in the sense of expressing moral requirements applicable at large on the basis of mutual concern and respect, universalization, and minimization of fortuity. Undoubtedly, in making basic life choices, we assume moral principles of such kinds as background conditions; we assume, typically, that none of the available life choices violates moral requirements. But the substance of such life choices is not dictated by such ethical boundary conditions. Rather, typically, we are morally *at liberty* to adopt any of a number of life plans. In an important sense, then, metaphysical familism is an expression of a nonethical judgment, a view of the more satisfying, and thus more rational, basic life plan. Accordingly, such judgments are entitled to no more legal or constitutional force than any other ideological vision of the good life not dictated by ethical principles. In particular, it is *deeply* mistaken to confuse the moral depth of the constitutional right to privacy, as a right to autonomy, with the ideology of metaphysical familism.

Such confusions are, of course, familiar to many moral traditions. One thinks, for example, of the many religious codes of detailed casuistry that regulate, in the name of "morality," the most detailed features of people's quite personal lives. In an earlier discussion, I discussed a philosophical form of this confusion, namely, Plato's idea that there are no limits to legitimate state paternalism. Against such views stands the radical vision of autonomy and mutual concern and respect, which accords to persons *as such* the right to create their own lives on terms fair to all. To see people in this way is to affirm basic intrinsic limits on the degree to which, even benevolently, one person may control the life of another. Within ethical constraints, people are free to adopt a number of disparate and irreconcilable visions of the good life. Indeed, the adoption of different kinds of life plans, within these constraints, affords the moral good of different experiments in living by which people can more rationally assess such basic life choices. Since rigid moral prescriptions in many of these areas are no longer appropriate, people *should* make these choices in as imaginative, creative, exploratory, and inventive a way as human wit can devise, consulting one's personal desires, wants, needs, competences and how one most harmoniously wishes them concurrently and complementarily to develop and be satisfied over a life time. Perhaps, people fear freedom in this sense, preferring conventional solutions. That is their right. But, such choices deserve no special moral approbation; they do not help us more rationally and courageously to choose our lives. In this sense, the constitutional right to privacy protects not only the autonomy rights of individuals, but facilitates the social and moral good that experiments in living afford to society at large—refreshing and deepening the social imagination about the role of children in human life, about the improper force of "masculine" and "feminine" stereotypes in human love and work, and about the varieties of humane sexual arrangements. . . .

In conclusion, the critics of the constitutional right to privacy are wrong. It is they, not the Court, who have lost touch with the moral vision underlying the constitutional design. The institutional protection of moral personality requires that this right be recognized. A case like *Doe* shows not that the constitutional right to privacy is incoherent, but that the Court has failed consistently to apply or articulately to understand its underlying principles. *Doe* is deeply, morally wrong. Sexual autonomy is a human right in terms of which people define the meaning of their lives. In particular, the persecution of homosexuals, for that is the name we may now properly give it, deserves not constitutional validation, but systematic and unremitting attack. To appeal to popular attitudes, in the way in which *Doe* implicitly does, is precisely to withhold human rights when, as a shield against majoritarian oppression, they are most exigently needed. Homosexuals have the right to reclaim the aspects of the self that society has traditionally compelled them to deny; they, like other persons, have the right to center work and love in a life they can authentically call their own.

POINTS TO PONDER

1. The right to privacy is nowhere mentioned in the Constitution. The Supreme Court has found it in the "penumbras" and "emanations" of various provisions in the Bill of Rights (see the various opinions in *Griswold* v. *Connecticut,* 381 U.S. 479 (1965)). Is this language merely another way of saying that the Court has found it desirable for such a right to be protected and has thus read it into the Constitution? Is this constitutional amendment by judicial fiat? See Justice Black's dissenting opinion in *Griswold.*

2. How satisfactory is Parker's definition of privacy as "control over when and by whom the various parts of us can be sensed by others"? Does it apply as straightforwardly as Parker says it does to the right of a woman to have an abortion? More particularly, is it necessary to distinguish conceptually between those privacy rights that entitle people not to be perceived (sensed, spied upon) or to have their images, their acts, and their affairs opened up to the world, on the one hand, and those rights of *autonomy* that entitle people to *do* what they please without interference by others, on the other?

3. In *Doe,* the court concludes that the sodomy statute has "a rational basis" and therefore upholds it. What is, or might be, the rational basis upon which such a statute would stand?

4. Judge Merhige argues that there must be a "compelling state interest" to justify such a statute. The courts often use this phrase to indicate that they will subject statutes that appear to infringe fundamental rights to very close and strict scrutiny. The "rational basis" test is

applied to statutes that do not infringe fundamental rights and tends to be quite deferential to the legislature. Did the Virginia statute infringe anyone's fundamental rights?

5. McCracken claims that homosexuality is unnatural, defining that term as "inappropriate to the nature of man." Does this statement provide enlightenment as to what public policy on homosexuality ought to be?

6. McCracken condemns those (including both homosexuals and heterosexuals) who renounce childbearing. Among the grounds for that condemnation he cites the effects of the falling birth rate upon the Social Security fund, the federal deficit, and the provision of medical care and social services to the elderly. How might defenders of the renunciation principle respond to this challenge?

7. Richards responds, in a sense, to the question asked in point 1 by arguing that there is an "unwritten Constitution" as well as a written one. Is this a satisfactory solution to the problem? If there is such an unwritten Constitution, how can one discover what is in it?

8. How would Richards' conception of privacy square with Parker's?

9. Does Richards' discussion of "natural" and "unnatural" satisfactorily resolve the controversy? Consider the various senses in which these terms can be used, paying particularly close attention to distinctions between prescriptive or normative uses of the term and descriptive uses.

10. How might Richards respond to McCracken's concerns about marriage and childbearing?

11. Certain religious groups have long advocated and practiced sexual abstinence and celibacy. Persons who have accepted the celibate life have been praised for the sacrifices they have made and for their devotion to religious ideals. In view of the positions advocated by the various articles included in this part, how might one assess the morality of those who support or participate in the life of the monastery or the convent?

VII

AFFIRMATIVE ACTION AND REVERSE DISCRIMINATION

INTRODUCTION

Affirmative action programs arose out of a desire on the part of many persons, both in government and in the private sector, to hasten the demise of racism in the schools, in employment, and elsewhere. The Supreme Court's order to proceed with the integration of public schools "with all deliberate speed," issued in its 1954 desegregation case (*Brown* v. *Board of Education*), was implemented with more deliberation than speed. Disappointment and frustration with the pace of school integration led to programs designed to eliminate racism and all of its manifestations in every segment of society, not with all deliberate speed, but immediately, so that no more generations of blacks and members of other minority groups would pass through the system, waiting for their turn to enter on a basis of genuine equality.

But as officials implemented the laws that Congress passed, some felt that what had previously been thought to be a move toward the elimination of racism was in fact (or at least in their judgment) becoming a new form of racism—what some called "reverse discrimination." The claim was that instead of eliminating considerations of race, sex, or religion in education, hiring, and other areas, such considerations became paramount. Instead of eliminating questions about race and ethnic background on application forms, such questions came to be looked upon as essential; for without such information, *preferential treatment* could not be extended to those who belonged to previously deprived groups. In two early cases, *DeFunis* v. *Odegaard* and *Bakke* v. *Regents,* white male students were prevented from entering law school and medical school because of preferential treatment that was accorded applicants whose racial or ethnic backgrounds entitled them to preferential treatment—that is, to admission with test scores and grade point averages that were significantly lower than those that white male applicants had to have achieved even to be considered as serious contenders. Bakke and DeFunis both had scores and averages higher than those of minority applicants who were admitted—but they were excluded because of their racial background.

More recently, the focus of attention has moved to the business sector, and the *Weber* case, included here, is the first significant pronouncement that the Supreme Court has made on the issue of affirmative action in employment. The Court was sharply divided—and two of its nine members did not participate in consideration of the case. In addition to the decision of the Court and excerpts from the dissenting opinions, an article on the case by Carl Cohen, published shortly before the Court rendered its verdict, is included, for it explores with great thoroughness both the background of the case and some important moral principles that are at stake in the *Weber* decision.

These materials do not begin to provide the broad range of points of view or the many philosophical arguments that have been propounded in defense of and in opposition to affirmative action programs. Such a task would require a volume in itself. But the *Weber* case, Professor Cohen's comments on it, and the articles by Mary Anne Warren and Diana Axelsen (which consider other important aspects of the problem) give a reasonably good sampling of some of the principal approaches to this exceedingly complex and controversial issue.

MARY ANNE WARREN 23

SECONDARY SEXISM
AND QUOTA HIRING

I want to call attention to a pervasive form of discrimination against women, one which helps to explain the continuing male monopoly of desirable jobs in the universities, as elsewhere. Discrimination of this sort is difficult to eliminate or even, in some cases, to recognize, because (1) it is not explicitly based on sex, and (2) it typically *appears* to be justified on the basis of plausible moral or practical considerations. The recognition of this form of discrimination gives rise to a new argument for the use of numerical goals or quotas in the hiring of women for college and university teaching and administrative positions.

I shall argue that because of these de facto discriminatory hiring practices, minimum numerical quotas for the hiring and promotion of women are necessary, not (just) to compensate women for past discrimination or its results, or to provide women with role models, but to counteract this *ongoing* discrimination and thus make the competition for such jobs more nearly fair. Indeed, given the problems inherent in the compensatory justice and role-model arguments for reverse discrimination, this may well be the soundest argument for the use of such quotas.

I. PRIMARY AND SECONDARY SEXISM

Most of us try not to be sexists; that is, we try not to discriminate unfairly in our actions or attitudes toward either women or men. But it is not a simple matter to determine just which actions or attitudes discriminate unfairly, and a sincere effort to avoid unfair discrimination

From *Philosophy & Public Affairs* 6 (Spring 1977). Copyright 1977 by Princeton University Press. Reprinted by permission.

is often not enough. This is true of both of the forms of sexism that I wish to distinguish.

In its primary sense, "sexism" means *unfair discrimination on the basis of sex*. The unfairness may be unintentional; but the cause or reason for the discrimination must be the sex of the victim, not merely some factor such as size or strength that happens to be correlated with sex. Primary sexism may be due to dislike, distrust, or contempt for women, or, in less typical cases, for men or hermaphrodites. Or it may be due to sincerely held but objectively unjustified beliefs about women's properties or capacities. It may also be due to beliefs about the properties women *tend* to have, which are objectively justified but inappropriately applied to a particular case, in which the woman discriminated against does not have those properties.

For instance, if members of a philosophy department vote against hiring or promoting a woman logician because they dislike women (logicians), or because they think that women cannot excel in logic, or because they know that most women do not so excel and wrongly conclude that this one does not, then they are guilty of primary sexism. This much, I think, is noncontroversial.

But what should we say if they vote to hire or promote a man rather than a woman because he has a wife and children to support, while she has a husband who is (capable of) supporting her? Or because they believe that the woman has childcare responsibilities which will limit the time she can spend on the job? What if they hire a woman at a lower rank and salary than is standard for a man with comparable qualifications, for one of the above reasons? These actions are not sexist in the primary sense because there is no discrimination on the basis of sex itself. The criteria used *can* at least be applied in a sex-neutral manner. For instance, it might be asserted that if the woman candidate had had a spouse and children who depended upon her for support, this would have counted in her favor just as much as it would in the case of a man.

Of course, appeals to such intrinsically sex-neutral criteria may, in some cases, be mere rationalizations of what is actually done from primary sexist motives. In reality, the criteria cited may not be applied in a sex-neutral manner. But let us assume for the sake of argument that the application of these criteria *is* sex-neutral, not merely a smoke screen for primary sexism. On this assumption, the use of such criteria discriminates against women only because of certain contingent features of this society, such as the persistence of the traditional division of labor in marriage and childrearing.[1]

Many people see nothing morally objectionable in the use of such intrinsically sex-neutral yet de facto discriminatory criteria. For not only may employers who use such criteria be free of primary sexism, but their actions may appear to be justified on both moral and pragmatic grounds. It might, for instance, be quite clear that a department will really do more to alleviate economic hardship by hiring or promoting a man with dependents rather than a woman with none, or that a particular woman's

---

[1] I mean, of course, the tradition that the proper husband earns (most of) the family's income, while the proper wife does (most of) the housekeeping and childrearing.

domestic responsibilities will indeed limit the time she can spend on the job. And it might seem perfectly appropriate for employers to take account of such factors.

Nevertheless, I shall argue that the use of such considerations is unfair. It is an example of secondary sexism, which I define as comprising all those actions, attitudes and policies which, while not using sex itself as a reason for discrimination, do involve sex-correlated factors or criteria and do result in an unfair impact upon (certain) women. In the case of university hiring policies, secondary sexism consists in the use of sex-correlated selection criteria which are not valid measures of academic merit, with the result that women tend to be passed over in favor of men who are not, in fact, better qualified. I call sexism of this sort *secondary*, not because it is any less widespread or harmful than primary sexism, but because (1) it is, in this way, indirect or covert, and (2) it is typically parasitic upon primary sexism, in that the injustices it perpetuates—for example, those apparent from the male monopoly of desirable jobs in the universities—are usually due in the first instance to primary sexism.

Two points need to be made with respect to this definition. First, it is worth noting that, although in the cases we will be considering the correlations between sex and the apparently independent but de facto discriminatory criteria are largely due to past and present injustices against women, this need not always be the case. The discriminatory impact of excluding pregnancy-related disabilities from coverage by employee health insurance policies, for example, probably makes this an instance of secondary sexism. Yet it is certainly not (human) injustice which is responsible for the fact that it is only women who become pregnant. The fact that the correlation is due to biology rather than prior injustice does not show that the exclusion is not sexist. Neither does the fact that pregnancy is often undertaken voluntarily. If such insurance programs fail to serve the needs of women employees as well as they serve those of men, then they can escape the charge of sexism only if—as seems unlikely—it can be shown that they cannot possibly be altered to include disabilities related to pregnancy without ceasing to serve their mutually agreed upon purposes, and/or producing an even greater injustice.

This brings us to the second point. It must be stressed that on the above definition the use of valid criteria of merit in hiring to university positions is not an instance of secondary sexism. Some might argue that merit criteria discriminate unfairly against women, because it is harder for women to earn the advanced degrees, to write the publications, and to obtain the professional experience that are the major traditional measures of academic merit. But it would be a mistake to suppose that merit criteria as such are therefore sexist. They are sexist only to the extent that they understate women's actual capacity to perform well in university positions; and to that extent, they are invalid as criteria of merit. To the extent that they are valid, that is, the most reliable available measurements of capacities which are indeed crucial for the performance of the job, they are not unjust, even though they may result in more men than women being hired.

If this seems less than obvious, the following analogy may help. It is surely not unjust to award first prize in a discus throwing contest to the contestant who actually makes the best throw (provided, of course, that none of the contestants have been unfairly prevented from performing up to their capacity on this particular occasion), even if some of the contestants have in the past been wrongly prevented from developing their skill to the fullest, say by sexist discrimination in school athletic programs. Such contestants may be entitled to other relevant forms of compensation, for example, special free training programs to help them make up for lost time, but they are not entitled to win this particular contest. For the very *raison d'être* of an athletic contest dictates that prizes go to the best performers, not those who perhaps *could* have been the best, had past conditions been ideally fair.

So too, a university's central reasons for being dictate that positions within it be filled by candidates who are as well qualified as can be found. Choosing less qualified candidates deprives students of the best available instruction, colleagues of a more intellectually productive environment, and—in the case of state-funded universities—the public of the most efficient use of its resources.[2] To appoint inferior candidates defeats the primary purposes of the university, and is therefore wrong-headed, however laudable its motivations. It is also, as we shall see, a weapon of social change which is apt to backfire against those in whose interest it is advocated.

II. SECONDARY RACISM

Secondary sexism has parallels in secondary racism, as well as secondary antihomosexual bias, and the like.[3] Irving Thalberg has explored some of the arguments used by white liberals to rationalize their refusal to change practices which oppress blacks, without appealing to old-fashioned doctrines of white superiority.[4] Some of the strategies of resistance which he analyzes—for example, the charge of reverse discrimination and the appeal to standards—are frequently used in opposition to special hiring programs not only for blacks but also for women, and will be dealt with in that context later. Conversely, some of the secondary sexist policies

[2] It might be argued that the hiring process ought not to be based on merit alone, because there are cases in which being a woman, or being black, might itself be a crucial job qualification. As Michael Martin points out, this might well be the case in hiring for, say, a job teaching history in a previously all white-male department which badly needs to provide its students with a more balanced perspective. See "Pedagogical Arguments for Preferential Hiring and Tenuring of Women Teachers in the University," *The Philosophical Forum* 5, no. 2: 325–333. I think it is preferable, however, to describe such cases, not as instances requiring a departure from the merit principle, but as instances in which sex or race itself, or rather certain interests and abilities that are correlated with sex or race, constitutes a legitimate qualification for a certain job, and hence a measure of merit, vis-à-vis that job.
[3] My thanks to Michael Scriven, who discussed this and related points with me, and whose comments have been most helpful.
[4] Irving Thalberg, "Justifications of Institutional Racism," *The Philosophical Forum* 3, no. 2 (Winter 1971–1972): 243–263.

which we shall consider may function at times to exclude racial minorities.

Thalberg, however, denies the legitimacy of the analogy between racism and sexism. He finds it ludicrous for a middle-class white woman to compare her oppression with that of blacks:

> She is annoyed because she can't get a baby-sitter when she likes. They can barely feed their children . . . She is indignant because a male co-worker gets promoted before she does, or receives more salary for less work. They will never get into the same league with their oppressors.[5]

Such invidious comparisons are not uncommon. George Sher has recently argued that reverse discrimination is justified in the hiring of blacks but not in the hiring of women, since women have not, to the same degree as blacks, been denied the opportunity to obtain the qualifications necessary to compete on an equal basis with white men.[6] I shall have more to say about this argument later. Although I concentrate here on secondary sexism in academic hiring, it is not because I consider secondary racism any less important but because it comprises a somewhat separate set of phenomena.

III. SECONDARY SEXISM IN UNVERSITY HIRING

Consider the following policies, which not infrequently influence hiring, retention, and promotion decisions in American colleges and universities:

1. Antinepotism rules, proscribing the employment of spouses of current employees.
2. Giving preference to candidates who (are thought to) have the greater financial need, where the latter is estimated by whether someone has, on the one hand, financial ·dependents, or, on the other hand, a spouse capable of providing financial support.
3. The "last hired–first fired" principle, used in determining who shall be fired or not rehired as a result of staffing cutbacks.
4. Refusing promotions, tenure, retention seniority, or pro-rata pay to persons employed less than full time, where some are so employed on a relatively long-term basis and where there is no evidence that such persons are (all) less well qualified than full time employees.
5. Hiring at a rank and salary determined primarily by previous rank and salary rather than by more direct evidence of a candidate's competence, for example, degrees, publications, and student and peer evaluations.
6. Counting as a negative factor the fact that a candidate has or is thought to have, or to be more likely to have, childcare or other

---

[5] Thalberg, p. 247.
[6] George Sher, "Justifying Reverse Discrimination in Employment," *Philosophy & Public Affairs* 4, no. 2 (Winter 1975): 168–169.

domestic responsibilities which may limit the time s/he can spend on the job.

7. Giving preference to candidates with more or less uninterrupted work records over those whose working careers have been interrupted (for example, by raising children) in the absence of more direct evidence of a present difference in competence.

8. Not hiring, especially to administrative or supervisory positions, persons thought apt to encounter disrespect or lack of cooperation from peers or subordinates, without regard for whether this presumed lack of respect may be itself unjustified, for example, as the result of primary sexism.

9. Discriminating against candidates on the grounds of probable mobility due to the mobility of a spouse, present or possible.

Each of these practices is an example of secondary sexism, in that while the criterion applied does not mention sex, its use nevertheless tends to result in the hiring and promotion of men in preference to women who are not otherwise demonstrably less well qualified. I suggest that in seeking to explain the continuing underrepresentation of women in desirable jobs in the universities, we need to look not only toward primary sexist attitudes within those institutions, and certainly not toward any intrinsic lack of merit on the part of women candidates,[7] but toward covertly, and often unintentionally, discriminatory practices such as these.

Of course, none of these practices operates to the detriment of women in every case; but each operates against women much more often than against men, and the cumulative effect is enormous. No doubt some of them are more widespread than others and some (for example, the use of antinepotism rules) are already declining in response to pressures to remove barriers to the employment of women. Others, such as policies 3 and 4, are still fairly standard and have barely begun to be seriously challenged in most places. Some are publicly acknowledged and may have been written into law or administrative policy, for example, policies 1, 3, 4, and 5. Others are more apt to be private policies on the part of individual employers, to which they may not readily admit or of which they may not even be fully aware, for example, policies 2, 6, 7, and 8. It is obviously much more difficult to demonstrate the prevalence of practices of the latter sort. Nevertheless, I am certain that all of these practices occur, and I strongly suspect that none is uncommon, even now.

This list almost certainly does not include all of the secondary sexist practices which influence university hiring. But these examples are typical, and an examination of certain of their features will shed light on the way in which secondary sexism operates in the academic world and on the reasons why it is morally objectionable.

In each of these examples, a principle is used in choosing between

---

[7] With respect to one such measure, books and articles published, married women Ph.D.'s published as much or slightly more than men, and unmarried women only slightly less. See "The Woman Ph.D.: A Recent Profile," by R. J. Simon, S. M. Clark, and K. Galway, in *Social Problems* 15, no. 2 (Fall 1967): 231.

candidates that in practice acts to discriminate against women who may even be better qualified intrinsically than their successful rivals, on any reliable and acceptable measure of merit.[8] Nevertheless, the practice may *seem* to be justified. Nepotism rules, for instance, act to exclude women far more often than men, since women are more apt to seek employment in academic and/or geographical areas in which their husbands are already employed than vice versa. Yet nepotism rules may appear to be necessary to ensure fairness to those candidates and appointees, both male and female, who are *not* spouses of current employees and who, it could be argued, would otherwise be unfairly disadvantaged. Similarly, giving jobs or promotions to those judged to have the greatest financial need may seem to be simple humanitarianism, and the seniority system may seem to be the only practical way of providing job security to *any* portion of the faculty. For policies 5 through 9, it could be argued that, although the criteria used are not entirely reliable, they may still have *some* use in predicting job performance.

Thus each practice, though discriminatory in its results, may be defended by reference to principles which are not intrinsically sex-biased. In the context of an otherwise sexually egalitarian society, these practices would probably not result in de facto discrimination against either sex. In such a society, for instance, men would not hold a huge majority of desirable jobs, and women would be under no more social or financial pressure than men to live where their spouses work rather than where they themselves work; thus they would not be hurt by nepotism rules any more often, on the average, than men.[9] The average earning power of men and women would be roughly equal, and no one could assume that women, any more than men, ought to be supported by their spouses, if possible. Thus the fact that a woman has an employed spouse would not be thought to reduce her need for a job any more—or any less—than in the case of a man. We could proceed down the list; in a genuinely nonsexist society, few or none of the conditions would exist which cause these practices to have a discriminatory impact upon women.

Of course, there may be other reasons for rejecting these practices,

[8] I am assuming that whether a candidate is married to a current employee, or has dependents, or a spouse capable of supporting her, whether she is employed on a part-time or a full-time basis, her previous rank and salary, the continuity of her work record, and so on, are not in themselves reliable and acceptable measures of merit. As noted in example 5, more direct and pertinent measures of merit can be obtained. Such measures as degrees, publications, and peer and student evaluations have the moral as well as pragmatic advantage of being based on the candidate's actual past performance, rather than on unreliable and often biased conjectures of various sorts. Furthermore, even if there is or were *some* correlation (it would surely not be a *reliable* one) between certain secondary sexist criteria and job performance, it could still be argued that employers are not morally entitled to use such criteria, because of the unfair consequences of doing so. As Mary Vetterling has observed, there might well be some correlation between having "a healthy and active sex life" and "the patience and good humor required of a good teacher"; yet employers are surely not entitled to take into account the quality of a person's sex life in making hiring and promotion decisions. "Some Common Sense Notes on Preferential Hiring," *The Philosophical Forum* 5, no. 2: 321.
[9] Unless, perhaps, a significant average age difference between wives and husbands continued to exist.

besides their discriminatory impact upon women. Nepotism rules might be unfair to married persons of both sexes, even in a context in which they were not *especially* unfair to women. My point is simply that these practices would not be instances of sexism in a society which was otherwise free of sexism and its results. Hence, those who believe that the test of the justice of a practice is whether or not it would unfairly disadvantage any group or individual *in the context of an otherwise just society* will see no sexual injustice whatever in these practices.

But surely the moral status of a practice, as it operates in a certain context, must be determined at least in part by its actual consequences, in that context. The fact is that each of these practices acts to help preserve the male monopoly of desirable jobs, in spite of the availability of women who are just as well qualified on any defensible measure of merit. This may or may not suffice to show that these practices are morally objectionable. It certainly shows that they are inconsistent with the "straight merit" principle, that is, that jobs should go to those best qualified for them on the more reliable measures of merit. Hence, it is ironic that attempts to counteract such de facto discriminatory practices are often interpreted as attacks on the "straight merit" principle.

IV. WHY SECONDARY SEXISM IS UNFAIR

Two additional points need to be stressed in order to show just why these practices are unfair. In the first place, the contingent social circumstances which explain the discriminatory impact of these practices are themselves morally objectionable, and/or due to morally objectionable practices. It is largely because men *are* more able to make good salaries, and because married women are still expected to remain financially dependent upon their husbands, if possible, that the fact that a woman has an employed husband can be seen as evidence that she doesn't "need" a job. It is because a disproportionate number of women must, because of family obligations and the geographical limitations these impose, accept part-time employment even when they would prefer full time, that the denial of tenure, promotion and pro-rata pay to part-time faculty has a discriminatory impact upon women. That women accept such obligations and limitations may seem to be their own free choice; but, of course, that choice is heavily conditioned by financial pressures—for example, the fact that the husband can usually make more money—and by sexually stereotyped social expectations.

Thus, the effect of these policies is to compound and magnify prior social injustices against women. When a woman is passed over on such grounds, it is rather as if an athlete who had without her knowledge been administered a drug to hamper her performance were to be disqualified from the competition for failing the blood-sample test. In such circumstances, the very least that justice demands is that the unfairly imposed handicap not be used as a rationale for the imposition of further handicaps. If the unfair handicaps that society imposes upon women cause them to be passed over by employers because of a lack of straight merit, that is one thing, and it is unfortunate, but it is not obvious that it involves unfairness on the part of the employers. But if those handicaps are used as an excuse for excluding them from the competition regardless of their merit, as all too often happens, this is quite another thing, and it is patently unfair.

In the second place, practices such as these often tend to perpetuate the very (unjust) circumstances which underlie their discriminatory impact, thus creating a vicious circle. Consider the case of a woman who is passed over for a job or promotion because of her childcare responsibilities. Given a (better) job, she might be able to afford day care, or to hire someone to help her at home, or even to persuade her husband to assume more of the responsibilities. Denying her a job because of her domestic responsibilities may make it almost impossible for her to do anything to lessen those responsibilities. Similarly, denying her a job because she has a husband who supports her may force him to continue supporting her and her to continue to accept that support.

Both of these points may be illustrated by turning to a somewhat different sort of example. J. R. Lucas has argued that there are cases in which women may justifiably be discriminated against on grounds irrelevant to their merit. He claims, for example, that it is "not so evidently wrong to frustrate Miss Amazon's hopes of a military career in the Grenadier Guards on the grounds not that she would make a bad soldier, but that she would be a disturbing influence in the mess room." [10]

But this is a paradigm case of secondary, and perhaps also primary, sexism; it is also quite analogous to practice 8. To exclude women from certain jobs or certain branches of the military on the grounds that certain third parties are not apt to accept them, when that nonacceptance is itself unreasonable and perhaps based on sexual bigotry, is to compound the injustice of that bigotry. If it is inappropriate for soldiers to be disturbed or to make a disturbance because there are women in the mess room, then it is wrong to appeal to those soldiers' attitudes as grounds for denying women the opportunities available to comparably qualified men. It is also to help ensure the perpetuation of those attitudes, by preventing male soldiers from having an opportunity to make the sorts of observations which might lead to their eventually accepting women as comrades.

Thus, these practices are morally objectionable because they compound and perpetuate prior injustices against women, penalizing them for socially imposed disadvantages which cannot be reliably shown to detract from their actual present capacities. We may conclude that the hiring process will never be fair to women, nor will it be based on merit alone, so long as such practices persist on a wide scale. But it remains to be seen whether numerical hiring quotas for women are a morally acceptable means of counteracting the effects of sexist hiring practices.

V. WEAK QUOTAS

I shall discuss the case for mandatory hiring quotas of a certain very minimal sort: those based on the proportion of women, not in the population as a whole, but among qualified and available candidates in each

[10] J. R. Lucas, "Because You are a Woman," *Moral Problems*, ed. James Rachels (New York: Harper & Row, 1975), p. 139.

academic field. Such a "weak" quota system would require that in each institution, and ideally within each department and each faculty and administrative rank and salary, women be hired and promoted at least in accordance with this proportion. If, for instance, a tenured or tenure-track position became available in a given department on an average of every other year, and if women were twenty percent of the qualified and available candidates in that field, then such a quota system would require that the department hire a woman to such a position at least once in ten years.[11]

Needless to say, this is not a formula for rapid change in the sexual composition of the universities. Suppose that the above department has twenty members, all male and all or almost all tenured, that it does not grow, and that it perhaps shrinks somewhat. Under these not atypical circumstances, it could easily take over forty years for the number of women in the department to become proportional to the number of qualified women available, even if the quota is strictly adhered to, and the proportion of qualified women does not increase in the meantime. Consequently, some would argue that such a quota system would be inadequate.[12]

Furthermore, it *could* be argued that if the job competition were actually based on merit, women would be hired and promoted at a *higher* rate than such a weak quota system would require, since the greater obstacles still encountered by women on the way to obtaining qualifications ensure that only very able women make it.[13] Or, it might be argued that women should be hired and promoted in more than such proportional numbers, in order to compensate for past discrimination or to provide other women with role models. Indeed, some existing affirmative action plans, so I am told, already require that women be hired in more than proportional numbers. Nevertheless, I will not defend quotas higher than these minimal ones. For, as will be argued in Section IX, higher quotas at least give the appearance of being unfair to male candidates, and it is not clear that either the compensatory justice or the role-model argument is sufficient to dispel that appearance.

VI. QUOTAS OR GOALS?

Before turning to the case for such minimal hiring quotas, we need to comment on the "quotas vs. goals" controversy. Those who oppose the

[11] In practice problems of statistical significance will probably require that quotas be enforced on an institution-wide basis rather than an inflexible department-by-department basis. Individual departments, especially if they are small and if the proportion of qualified women in the field is low, may fail to meet hiring quotas, not because of primary or secondary sexism, but because the best qualified candidates happen in fact to be men. But if no real discrimination against women is occurring, then such statistical deviations should be canceled out on the institutional level, by deviations in the opposite direction.

[12] See Virginia Held, "Reasonable Progress and Self-Respect," *The Monist* 57, no. 1: 19.

[13] Gertrude Ezorsky cites in support of this point a study by L. R. Harmon of over 20,000 Ph.D.'s, which showed that "Women . . . Ph.D.'s are superior to their male counterparts on all measures derived from high school records, in all . . . specializations." *High School Ability Patterns: A Backward Look from the Doctorate*, Scientific Manpower [sic] Report No. 6, 1965, pp. 27–28; cited by Ezorsky in "The Fight Over University Women," *The New York Review of Books* 21, no. 8 (16 May 1974): 32.

use of numerical guidelines in the hiring of women or racial minorities usually refer to such guidelines as *quotas,* while their defenders usually insist that they are not quotas but *goals.* What is at issue here? Those who use the term "quotas" pejoratively tend to assume that the numerical standards will be set so high or enforced so rigidly that strong reverse discrimination—that is, the deliberate hiring of demonstrably less well qualified candidates—will be necessary to implement them.[14] The term "goal," on the other hand, suggests that this will not be the case, and that good faith efforts to comply with the standards by means short of strong reverse discrimination will be acceptable.[15]

But whatever one calls such minimum numerical standards, and whether or not one suspects that strong reverse discrimination has in fact occurred in the name of affirmative action, it should be clear that it is not *necessary* for the implementation of a quota system such as I have described. Neither, for that matter, is weak reverse discrimination— that is, the deliberate hiring of women in preference to equally but not better qualified men.[16] For if hiring decisions were solely based on reliable measures of merit and wholly uncorrupted by primary or secondary sexist policies, then qualified women would *automatically* be hired and promoted at least in proportion to their numbers, except, of course, in statistically abnormal cases.[17] Consequently, reverse discrimination will *appear* to be necessary to meet proportional quotas only where the hiring process continues to be influenced by sexist practices—primary or secondary, public or private.

In effect, the implementation of a minimum quota system would place a price upon the continued use of sexist practices. Employers would be forced to choose between eliminating sexist practices, thus making it possible for quotas to be met without discriminating for or against anyone on the basis of sex, and practicing reverse discrimination on an ad hoc basis in order to meet quotas without eliminating sexist practices. Ideally, perhaps, they would all choose the first course, in which case the quota system would serve only to promote an ongoing check upon, and demonstration of, the nonsexist nature of the hiring process.

In reality, however, not all secondary sexist practices can be immedi-

---

14 See, for instance, Paul Seaburg, "HEW and the Universities," *Commentary* 53, no. 2 (February 1972): 38–44.

15 In practice, strong reverse discrimination is specifically prohibited by HEW affirmative action guidelines, and good faith efforts to implement affirmative action programs without resorting to strong reverse discrimination have been accepted as adequate. Nevertheless, though I would not wish to see *these* features of affirmative action policies changed, I prefer the term "quota" for what I am proposing, because this term suggests a standard which will be enforced, in one way or another, while the term "goal" suggests—and affirmative action is in great danger of becoming—a mere expression of good intentions, compliance with which is virtually unenforceable.

16 The distinction between strong and weak reverse discrimination is explored by Michael Bayles in "Compensatory Reverse Discrimination in Hiring," *Social Theory and Practice* 2, no. 3: 303–304, and by Vetterling, "Common Sense Notes," pp. 320–323.

17 This conclusion can be avoided only by assuming either that qualified women would not want better jobs if these were available, or that they are somehow less meritorious than comparably qualified men. The first assumption is absurd, since women who do not want desirable jobs are not apt to take the trouble to become qualified for them; and the second assumption is amply refuted by empirical data. See, for instance, the studies cited in fnn. 6 and 13.

ately eliminated. Some forms of secondary sexism have probably not yet been recognized, and given the nature of the interests involved it is likely that new forms will tend to spring up to replace those which have been discredited. More seriously, perhaps, some secondary sexist policies, such as the seniority system, cannot be eliminated without an apparent breach of contract (or of faith) with present employees. Others—for example, hiring on the basis of need—may survive because they are judged, rightly or wrongly, to be on the whole the lesser evil. A quota system, however, would require that the impact of such secondary sexist practices be counterbalanced by preferential treatment of women in other instances. Furthermore, it would hasten the elimination of all sexist policies by making it in the interest of all employees, men as well as women, that this be done, since until it is done both will run the risk of suffering from (sexist or reverse) discrimination. Certainly their elimination would be more probable than it is at present, when it is primarily women who have a reason based on self-interest for opposing them, yet primarily men who hold the power to eliminate or preserve them.

The most crucial point, however, is that under such a quota system, even if (some) employers do use weak discrimination in favor of women to meet their quota, this will not render the job competition especially unfair to men. For, as I will argue, unfairness would result only if the average male candidate's chances of success were reduced to below what they would be in an ongoing, just society, one in which men and women had complete equality of opportunity and the competition was based on merit alone; and I will argue that the use of weak reverse discrimination to meet proportional hiring quotas will not have this effect.

VII. QUOTAS AND FAIRNESS

Now one way to support this claim would be to argue that in an ongoing, just society women would constitute a far higher proportion of the qualified candidates in most academic fields and that therefore the average male candidate's chances would, other things being equal, automatically be reduced considerably from what they are now. Unfortunately, however, the premise of this argument is overly speculative. It is possible that in a fully egalitarian society women would still tend to avoid certain academic fields and to prefer others, much as they do now, or even that they would fail to (attempt to) enter the academic profession as a whole in much greater numbers than at present.

But whatever the proportion of male and female candidates may be, it must at least be the case that in a just society the chances of success enjoyed by male candidates must be no greater, on the average, and no less than those enjoyed by comparably qualified women. Individual differences in achievement, due to luck or to differences in ability, are probably inevitable; but overall differences in the opportunities accorded to comparably qualified men and women, due to discrimination, would not be tolerated.

The question, then, is: Would the use of weak discrimination in favor of women, to a degree just sufficient to offset continuing sexist discrimination against women and thus to meet minimum quotas, result in lowering the average chances of male candidates to below those of comparably qualified women? The answer, surely, is that it would not, since by hypothesis men would be passed over, in order to fill a quota, in favor of women no better qualified only as often as women continue to be passed over, because of primary or secondary sexism, in favor of men no better qualified.

In this situation, individual departures from the "straight merit" principle might be no less frequent than at present; indeed, their frequency might even be doubled. But since it would no longer be predominantly women who were repeatedly disadvantaged by those departures, the overall fairness of the competition would be improved. The average long-term chances of success of *both* men and women candidates would more closely approximate those they would enjoy in an ongoing just society. If individual men's careers are temporarily set back because of weak reverse discrimination, the odds are good that these same men will have benefited in the past and/or will benefit in the future—not necessarily in the job competition, but in *some* ways—from sexist discrimination against women. Conversely, if individual women receive apparently unearned bonuses, it is highly likely that these same women will have suffered in the past and/or will suffer in the future from primary or secondary sexist attitudes. Yet, the primary purpose of a minimum quota system would not be to compensate the victims of discrimination or to penalize its beneficiaries, but rather to increase the overall fairness of the situation—to make it possible for the first time for women to enjoy the same opportunity to obtain desirable jobs in the universities as enjoyed by men with comparable qualifications.

It is obvious that a quota system implemented by weak reverse discrimination is not the ideal long-term solution to the problem of sexist discrimination in academic hiring. But it would be a great improvement over the present situation, in which the rate of unemployment among women Ph.D.'s who are actively seeking employment is still far higher than among men with Ph.D.'s, and in which women's starting salaries and chances of promotion are still considerably lower than those of men.[18] Strong reverse discrimination is clearly the least desirable method of implementing quotas. Not only is it unfair to the men who are passed over, and to their potential students and colleagues, to hire demonstrably less well qualified women, but it is very apt to reinforce primary sexist attitudes on the part of all concerned, since it appears to presuppose that women cannot measure up on their merits. But to presume that proportional hiring quotas could not be met without strong reverse discrimination is also to make that discredited assumption. If, as all available evidence indicates, women in the academic world are on the average just as hard-working, productive, and meritorious as their male colleagues, then there can be no objection to hiring and promoting them at

---

[18] Elizabeth Scott tells me that her survey of 1974–1976 figures reveals that, in spite of affirmative action policies, unemployment among women Ph.D.'s who are actively seeking work is about twice as high as among men Ph.D.'s and that the starting salaries of women Ph.D.'s average $1,200 to $1,500 lower than those of men.

least in accordance with their numbers, and doing so will increase rather than decrease the extent to which success is based upon merit.

VIII. ARE QUOTAS NECESSARY?

I have argued that minimum proportional quotas such as I have described would not make the job competition (especially) unfair to men. But it might still be doubted that quotas are necessary to make the competition fair to women. Why not simply attack sexist practices wherever they exist and then let the chips fall as they may? Alan Goldman argues that quotas are not necessary, since, he says, other measures—for example, "active recruitment of minority candidates, the advertisement and application of nondiscriminatory hiring criteria . . . and the enforcement of these provisions by a neutral government agency" [19] would suffice to guarantee equal treatment for women. Goldman claims that if women candidates are as well qualified as men then, given these other measures, they will automatically be hired at least in proportion to their numbers. Indeed, he suggests that the only basis for doubting this claim is "an invidious suspicion of the real inferiority of women . . . even those with Ph.D.'s." [20] That discrimination against women might continue to occur in spite of such affirmative measures short of quotas, he regards as "an untested empirical hypothesis without much prima facie plausibility." [21]

In a similar vein, George Sher has argued that blacks, but not women, are entitled to reverse discrimination in hiring, since the former but not the latter have suffered from a poverty syndrome which has denied them the opportunity to obtain the qualifications necessary to compete on an equal basis with white men.[22] He views reverse discrimination —and presumably hiring quotas—as primarily a way of compensating those who suffer from present competitive disadvantages due to past discrimination, and claims that since women are not disadvantaged with respect to (the opportunity to obtain) qualifications, they are not entitled to reverse discrimination.

What both Goldman and Sher overlook, of course, is that women suffer from competitive disadvantages quite apart from any lack of qualifications. Even if primary sexism were to vanish utterly from the minds of all employers, secondary sexist practices such as those we have considered would in all likelihood suffice to perpetuate the male monopoly of desirable jobs well beyond our lifetimes. Such practices cannot be expected to vanish quickly or spontaneously; to insist that affirmative action measures stop short of the use of quotas is to invite their continuation and proliferation.

[19] Alan H. Goldman, "Affirmative Action," *Philosophy & Public Affairs* 5, no. 2 (Winter 1976): 185.
[20] Goldman, p. 186.
[21] Goldman, p. 185.
[22] Sher, p. 168.

IX. THE COMPENSATORY JUSTICE
AND ROLE-MODEL ARGUMENTS

Most of the philosophers who have recently defended the use of goals
or quotas in the hiring of women and/or minority group members have
assumed that this will necessarily involve at least weak and perhaps
strong reverse discrimination, but have argued that it is nevertheless
justified as a way of compensating individuals or groups for past injustices or for present disadvantages stemming from past injustices.[23] Others
have argued that reverse discrimination is justified not (just) as a form
of compensatory justice, but as a means of bringing about certain future
goods—for example, raising the status of downtrodden groups,[24] or providing young women and blacks with role models and thus breaking
the grip of self-fulfilling expectations which cause them to fail.[25]

If one is intent upon arguing for a policy which would give blacks
or women "advantages in employment . . . greater than these same
blacks or women would receive in an ongoing just society," [26] then perhaps it is necessary to appeal to compensatory justice or to the role
model or to other utilitarian arguments to justify the prima facie unfairness to white males which such a policy involves. But there is no need
to use these arguments in justifying a weak quota system such as the one
described here, and indeed, it is somewhat misleading to do so. For, as we
have seen, such a system would not lower the average male candidate's
overall chances of success to below what they would be if the selection
were based on merit alone. It would simply raise women's chances, and
lower men's, to a closer approximation of what they would be in an
ongoing just society, in which the "straight merit" principle prevailed.
This being the case, the fact that quotas may serve to compensate some
women for past or present wrongs, or to provide others with role models,
must be seen as a fortuitous side effect of their use and not their primary
reasons for being. The primary reason for weak quotas is simply to increase the present fairness of the competition.

Furthermore, there are problems with the compensatory justice and
role-model arguments which make their use hazardous. It is not clear
that either suffices to justify any use of reverse discrimination beyond
what may in practice (appear to) be necessary to implement weak quotas.
For, granted that society as a whole has some obligation to provide
compensation to the victims of past discrimination, and assuming that
at least some women candidates for university positions are suitable
beneficiaries of such compensation, it is by no means clear that male
candidates should be forced to bear most of the burden for providing
that compensation. It would be plausible to argue on the basis of compensatory justice for, say, tax-supported *extra* positions for women, since

---

23 See Bayles and Sher, respectively.
24 Irving Thalberg, "Reverse Discrimination and the Future," *The Philosophical Forum*
5, no. 2: 307.
25 See Marlene Gerber Fried, "In Defense of Preferential Hiring," *The Philosophical
Forum* 5, no. 2: 316.
26 Charles King, "A Problem Concerning Discrimination," *Reason Papers*, no. 2 (Fall
1975), p. 92.

then the burden would be distributed relatively equitably. But compensatory justice provides no case for placing an extra, and seemingly punitive, burden on male candidates, who are no more responsible for past and present discrimination against women than the rest of us.

Similarly, however badly women may need role models, it is not clear that male candidates should be disproportionately penalized in order to provide them. It can be argued on the basis of simple fairness that male candidates' chances should not be allowed to remain *above* what they would be in a just society; but to justify reducing them to *below* that point requires a stronger argument than simply appealing to compensatory justice or the need for role models.

Nor does it help to argue that the real source of the injustice to male candidates, if and when preferential hiring of women results in lowering the former's chances to below what they would be in a just society, is not the preferential hiring policy itself, but something else. Thomas Nagel, for instance, argues that reverse discrimination is not seriously unjust, even if it means that it is harder for white men to get certain sorts of jobs than it is for women and blacks who are no better qualified, since, he suggests, the real source of the injustice is the entire system of providing differential rewards on the basis of differential abilities.[27] And Marlene Fried argues that the root of the injustice is not preferential hiring, but the failure of those with the power to do so to expand job opportunities so that blacks and women could be hired in increasing numbers without hiring fewer men.[28]

Unfortunately, we cannot, on the one hand, reject secondary sexist practices because of their contingent and perhaps unintended discriminatory effects, and, on the other hand, accept extenuations such as these for a policy which would, in practice, discriminate unfairly against (white) men. These other sources of injustice are real enough; but this does not alter the fact that if reverse discrimination were practiced to the extent that certain men's chances of success were reduced to below those enjoyed, on the average, by comparably qualified women, then it would at least give every appearance of being unfair to those men. After all, the primary insight necessary for recognizing the injustice of secondary sexist policies is that a policy must be judged, at least in part, by its consequences in practice, regardless of whether or not these consequences are a stated or intended part of the policy. If a given policy results in serious and extensive injustice, then it is no excuse that this injustice has its roots in deeper social injustices which are not themselves easily amenable to change, at least not if there is any feasible way of altering the policy so as to lessen the resulting injustice.

I think we may conclude that while proportional quotas for the hiring of women are justified both on the basis of the merit principle and as a way of improving the overall fairness of the competition, it is considerably more difficult to justify the use of higher quotas. The distinction between such weak quotas and higher quotas is crucial, since al-

[27] Thomas Nagel, "Equal Treatment and Compensatory Justice," *Philosophy & Public Affairs* 2, no. 4 (Summer 1973): 348–363, especially p. 353.
[28] Fried, p. 318.

though higher quotas have, in practice rarely been implemented, the apparent injustice implied by what are typically *assumed* to be higher quotas has generated a backlash which threatens to undermine affirmative action entirely. If quotas are abandoned, or if they are nominally adopted but never enforced, then employers will be free to continue using secondary and even primary sexist hiring criteria, and it is probable that none of us will see the day when women enjoy job opportunities commensurate with their abilities and qualifications.

DIANA AXELSEN

24

WITH ALL DELIBERATE DELAY: ON JUSTIFYING PREFERENTIAL POLICIES IN EDUCATION AND EMPLOYMENT

I. INTRODUCTION

One of the issues which has most blatantly revealed the racist and sexist nature of American institutions is the implementation of affirmative action programs and stronger preferential policies in education and employment. The most striking characteristic of many discussions of such policies is the absence of any serious historical perspective on the role that genocide and cultural imperialism have played in the development of this country, and, in particular, in the evolution of its patterns of distribution of economic, political, and social power.[1] In this article I shall

Copyright 1978 by Philosophical Forum. First published in *Philosophical Forum* 9 (1978): 264–268.

This article is based on two earlier papers presented in symposia on reverse discrimination and preferential policies, one at the meetings of the American Philosophical Association, Eastern Division, in December, 1972, and the other at a conference of the Society for Women in Philosophy, in Chapel Hill, North Carolina, in May, 1973. I wish to thank Hugo Bedau, Lois B. Moreland, Howard Richards, and Richard Wasserstrom for many useful suggestions. I am especially indebted to Helen Williams and Quincy Tillman for help in preparing various versions of this manuscript.

[1] Some notable exceptions include Irving Thalberg, "Visceral Racism," *The Monist,* Vol. 56, No. 4, Oct., 1972; Irving Thalberg, "Justification of Institutional Racism," *Philosophical Forum,* III, Winter, 1972; Hugo Bedau, "Compensatory Justice and the Black Manifesto," *The Monist,* LVI, January, 1972; Virginia Held, "Reasonable Progress and Self-Respect," *The Monist,* Vol. 57, No. 1, 1973; "The Justification of Reverse Discrimination," Tom L. Beauchamp, mimeographed; and Boris I. Bittker, *The Case for Black Reparations* (New York: Random House, 1973). Others could be mentioned, but they remain exceptions in the discussion of "reverse discrimination," or what I prefer to call "preferential policies." It should also be noted that Title VII of the Civil Rights

summarize some of the main values relevant to the issue of preferential policies; examine some of the criticisms raised against such policies; consider some of the arguments which support them; and, finally, argue that an important justification for preferential policies can be based on the rights of individuals and groups to reparations for past and present injustices. Though various individuals and groups have legitimate claims to reparations, I shall focus on those of Black persons in the United States today.

Let us begin by looking at two quotations which reflect the radically different perspectives from which the question of preferential policies for Blacks can be viewed. The first is a remark by W.E.B. DuBois, in *The Souls of Black Folk*. Though he was acutely aware of the problems confronting Black people, and though in 1903 he identified the problem of the twentieth century as the problem of the color line, he could also affirm:

> We darker ones come even now not altogether empty-handed; there are to-day no truer exponents of the pure human spirit of the Declaration of Independence than the American Negroes; there is no true American music but the wild sweet melodies of the Negro slave; the American fairy tales and folk-lore are Indian and African; and all in all, we black men seem the sole oasis of simple faith and reverence in a dusty desert of dollars and smartness.[2]

More than 70 years later, the United States is still confronted with the problem of the color line, though an international analysis might suggest a revision of the claim to say that the problem is the coincidence of the color line and the poverty line. The inequities confronted in the 1970's cannot be divorced from the historical context out of which they arose, nor can they be understood and corrected without the guidance of those who suffer from them.

In his article, "Reparations for Blacks?," Graham Hughes is sensitive to the legitimacy of Black demands for reparations. Yet Hughes apparently sees the problem as primarily a need to re-distribute economic and political power. The underlying problem of accepting cultural pluralism is largely ignored. Hughes uses the Rawls-Runciman contractual model of social justice to define the problem. According to this model, we decide whether a method for distributing social benefits is just by asking a rational and self-interested person whether he or she would be willing to take part in such a social distribution procedure, if he or she

---

Act of 1964 does not require that employers abandon non-discriminatory criteria of merit. Affirmative action programs initiated by employers to comply with Title VII, or by educational institutions to comply with HEW guidelines, are simply required to ensure that applicants are chosen on the basis of legitimate qualifications. Only when an employer or educational admissions committee moves beyond such an "affirmative action policy" to favor minority members or women whom it regards as less qualified or no more qualified than white males, shall I speak of preferential policies. I shall assume that no argument is needed to defend the weaker policies of non-discrimination.
[2] W. E. B. DuBois, "The Souls of Black Folk," in *Three Negro Classics* (New York: Avon, 1965), p. 220.

did not know his or her particular life situation at the beginning. The assumption is that the rational person would be willing to take part in practices which offer essentially equal opportunities and minimal risks of catastrophe. The use of this culture-bound model of rationality to identify claims for reparations in the U.S. leads Hughes to the following statement:

> The contractual model provides a firm foundation for a partial redistribution of wealth when gross inequalities exist. . . . it is a way of presenting a judgment of injustice that should have an immediate appeal to the ordinary man for it entails a question to which we can all respond without sophisticated argument: "Would you be willing to enter a lottery in which you had a random chance of being a black person in the United States?" We may guess that the majority reply is going to be negative. It would also be negative, of course, if the chance in the lottery were to be healthy or sick, assuming that the person we invite to enter the lottery is presently healthy. But the point is that being sick is for the most part a natural accident while the miseries that surround the business of being black in America are the product of past and present institutions and social practices. If these institutions and practices have resulted in a position where a person would not be willing to take a fair chance of being black then they must be condemned as unjust and a corresponding duty to rectify arises.[3]

The two quotations above, expressing very different attitudes toward Blackness, are illustrative of the problems underlying current preferential policies programs. One is reminded of Nikki Giovanni's lines, ". . . I really hope no white person ever has cause to write about me/because they never understand Black love is Black wealth and they'll/probably talk about my hard childhood and never understand that/all the while I was quite happy."[4] Essentially, programs to eliminate social injustice have been designed by white males; and these policy-makers have too frequently ignored the cultural dimensions of the problem. The aim of the policies has been to bring the outsiders in, on the terms of the insiders. This, in effect, means a continuation of the same cultural imperialism that helped to create the initial injustices. An example here is the use of HEW guidelines to undermine Black control of predominantly Black institutions, just as the 1954 Brown decision, and present desegregation programs fail to provide Blacks the means for creating educational structures to meet needs as Blacks define them. With these considerations in mind, I shall argue not only that a reparations approach is essential in our thinking about preferential policies, but also that the methods of implementing such policies should be defined by those whom they are intended to benefit.

In discussion of preferential policies, women and minority groups

---

[3] Graham Hughes, "Reparations for Blacks?", *The New York University Law Review*, Vol. 43, Dec., 1968. Reprinted in Tom L. Beauchamp, ed., *Ethics and Public Policy* (Englewood Cliffs, New Jersey: Prentice-Hall, 1975). Quote is from Beauchamp, pp. 24–25.
[4] Nikki Giovanni, in the poem "Nikki Rosa."

are often considered together. The arguments below can in principle be offered to support both the claims of ethnic groups and those of women, regarded as a group whose interests and history cut across ethnic lines. Whether such arguments are sound will depend on empirical facts concerning the group in question. In general, however, I think that the case of white women in the United States differs in essential respects from that of certain ethnic minorities, and that significant distinctions must be drawn among the various ethnic groups as well. I shall comment on this issue in the latter sections of the paper.

II. AN OUTLINE OF RELEVANT VALUES

The first step in understanding the problem is to identify the relevant ethical values. There seem to be at least three:

1. The obligation to pursue policies that meet the criteria of distributive justice, and, in particular, the obligation not to discriminate on morally irrelevant grounds in distributing social benefits such as jobs and educational places. We shall assume that distributive justice requires us to provide equality of opportunity, and thus in some cases to provide compensation for handicaps which prevent persons from competing on an equal basis for social benefits. Thus, for example, providing special training for blind persons could be seen as a form of compensation falling within the range of distributive justice. The ways in which such needs arise may be quite varied, and an adequate system of distributive justice will presumably provide for the contingencies identified by rational persons.

2. The obligation to promote social welfare, e.g., by ensuring a distribution of skills that is relatively efficient yet preserves other values the society may stress, such as some degree of freedom of choice in work roles.

3. The obligations of compensatory justice, to compensate victims of injustice. Here we are using the concept of compensatory justice to refer to one's right to remedy for some injury he or she has suffered in violation of his or her rights. In this sense, one is entitled to such benefits only when a prior injustice has occurred. Thus, this usage corresponds to Bernard Boxill's notion of reparations.[5]

The kinds of compensation Boxill considers which do not involve prior injustice will be subsumed in this essay under the notion of distributive justice. Compensatory justices in our sense will be concerned with compensation for wrongs arising because of actions, practices, or policies which have failed to conform to the requirements of distributive justice.

Having surveyed three values relevant to the issue of preferential

[5] Bernard Boxill, "The Morality of Reparation," *Social Theory and Practice*, Vol. 2, No. 1, 1972. Reprinted in Richard Wasserstrom, ed., *Today's Moral Problems* (New York: Macmillan, 1975). See especially Wasserstrom, pp. 210–212.

policies, we turn now to their specific implications for admissions and employment.

III. THE OBLIGATIONS OF DISTRIBUTIVE JUSTICE

The concepts of equality and non-discrimination are central in our discussion. A discriminatory practice or policy is typically taken to be one which makes unjust distinctions among persons. Thus, definition of a discriminatory policy in employment or education presupposes a general concept of distributive justice as applied to social policy. The definition I shall apply here is drawn essentially from the one formulated by John Rawls in *A Theory of Justice,* though it is also related to analyses proposed by William Frankena and Gregory Vlastos,[6] and it has been expanded by W. G. Runciman and Graham Hughes.

A hiring or admissions policy shall be taken to satisfy the criteria of distributive justice, provided that:

1. It provides equal treatment to all persons, with respect to ensuring freedoms, recognizing human worth and dignity, providing for human welfare, and providing opportunities to develop fundamental capacities; or,

2. It provides for inequalities according to merit, work, and agreements made, which are justified on the grounds that they will benefit all who participate in the practices. More precisely, "Social and economic inequalities [for example, those embodied in hiring and admission practices] are to be arranged so that they are both (a) to the greatest benefit of the least advantaged and (b) attached to offices and positions open to all under conditions of fair equality of opportunity."[7]

The demands of distributive justice, as we shall see, provide prominent arguments for opposing preferential policies or "reverse discrimination." Inequalities based simply on race or sex do not typically benefit all who participate in the practice, although they may do so in specific cases to be discussed below. Often, in the course of righting earlier wrongs, injustice may be done to others, specifically, to white males. We see this concern expressed in an opinion by Justice C. J. Hale, of the Washington State Supreme Court, in the well-known Marco DeFunis

6 John Rawls, *A Theory of Justice* (Cambridge: Harvard University Press, 1971); William K. Frankena, "The Concept of Social Justice," in *Social Justice,* ed. Richard B. Brandt (Englewood Cliffs, New Jersey: Prentice-Hall, 1962); pp. 1–29; and Gregory Vlastos, "Justice and Equality," *ibid.,* pp. 21–72. See also Hughes, in Beauchamp.

7 Rawls, p. 84. A problem may arise, however, when one must choose between satisfying (1) and (2). Rawls has suggested that we ought to prefer the latter whenever this allows us to increase the total benefit. He justifies this claim by arguing that we should concern ourselves with benefit as perceived and experienced by rational persons; and, he says, "A rational individual is not subject to envy, at least when the differences between himself and others are not thought to be the result of injustice and do not exceed certain limits." Rawls, p. 530. He holds that the inequities allowed by a just society will not foster envy. See pp. 530–541 of *A Theory of Justice* for a fuller discussion of this point.

case.[8] This opinion was a dissent from the Court's reversal of an order admitting DeFunis to the University of Washington Law School. Justice Hale wrote that racial inequalities cannot be adequately dealt with by "shifting inequalities from one man to his neighbor."[9] We encounter the fear that preferential policies will establish a kind of quota system which will simply compound existing injustices. Thus, for example, Judge Joseph Halpern of the Appellate Division of the Superior Court of New Jersey argued that hiring quotas are illegal, because the quota method "fashions a remedy on a class quota basis . . . and leads to insoluble problems and piles discrimination on top of discrimination."[10] A philosophical justification for such legal opinions has been provided by Lisa Newton and Carl Cohen, who argue that preferential policies do such violence to distributive justice that they *can* serve only to undermine social values which presumably we all wish to preserve.[11] Similar concerns are being voiced in connection with the Alan Bakke case in California.

IV. THE ROLE OF UTILITARIAN CONSIDERATIONS

John Rawls says at the beginning of *A Theory of Justice:*

> Justice is the first virtue of social institutions, as truth is of systems of thought. A theory however elegant and economical must be rejected or revised if it is untrue; likewise laws and institutions no matter how efficient and well-arranged must be reformed or abolished if they are unjust. Each person possesses an inviolability founded on justice that even the welfare of society as a whole cannot override.[12]

The utilitarian may disagree with this claim, arguing that the highest good is the general welfare. In a society where extreme misery exists, the utilitarian might argue that a practice which will help a large number of people is desirable even though unjust according to Rawls' criteria. However, one of the assumptions on which we shall proceed is that considerations of justice take precedence over utilitarian ones.

Another conflict between values may arise when we ask whether the claims of distributive justice always take precedence over those of compensatory justice. As Rawls acknowledges, principles of distributive justice do not tell us how to proceed in our less-than-ideal world, where it appears impossible to create conditions of equal opportunity without committing acts which violate the principles of distributive justice. While he does argue against utilitarianism, Rawls does not attempt to analyze

[8] DeFunis v. Odegaard, 82 Wash. 2d 11, 507 P. 2d 1169 (1974); cert. denied 94 S. Ct. 1704 (1974).
[9] *Atlanta Journal,* May 2, 1973. See also Albert Shanker, "Preferential Treatment vs. Constitutional Rights," *The New York Times,* May 13, 1973; and David L. Kirp and Mark G. Yudof, "DeFunis and Beyond," *Change,* Nov. 1974.
[10] *Atlanta Journal,* May 15, 1975.
[11] Carl Cohen, "The DeFunis Case; Race and the Constitution," *The Nation,* Feb. 8, 1975; and Lisa Newton, "Reverse Discrimination as Unjustified," *Ethics,* Vol. 83, No. 4, 1973.
[12] Rawls, p. 3.

systematically the conflict between compensatory and distributive justice. Rather, he focuses on constructing a non-utilitarian theory of distributive justice. However, the issue of preferential policies forces us to confront conflicts between the two forms of justice. Utilitarian considerations are relevant here for those who do not regard the utilitarian principle as fundamental.

One need not adopt utilitarianism to hold that social welfare is relevant to the moral evaluation of preferential policies. Indeed, the criteria of distributive justice themselves require that we examine the social costs and benefits of such policies. One who feels that the claims of distributive justice should not be overridden by utilitarian considerations may still find that utilitarian arguments strengthen the case for or against preferential policies.

At this point, we should distinguish four possibilities: the minority or female candidate may be the most qualified; the minority or female candidate may be equally as qualified as the white male; he or she may be minimally qualified but not the most qualified; or he or she may lack even minimal qualifications. Opponents of preferential policies have emphasized the dangers of lowering standards of admissions and performance. As we shall discuss in detail later, however, candidates may often fail to meet existing standards not because they are unqualified for the task, but because of inadequate and biased criteria. Moreover, introducing new criteria for qualification is not equivalent to a lowering of standards. We shall consider this issue when we examine the concept of merit.

Still, it is important to realize that preferential policies may fail to benefit even those who are favored. For example, if students cannot benefit from existing academic programs, and if no provision is made for adapting programs to meet their needs, the results may be detrimental to all involved. Of course, it may often be the case that such adaptation will come most quickly when students are admitted so that they can bring pressure to bear for themselves.

We must decide whether our aim is to maintain, reform, or destroy existing practices and the larger social institutions surrounding them. A revolutionary might see favoring minorities and women as morally unjustifiable because it fosters acceptance of the economic and social systems within which unjust practices exist. In this connection, we can note the viewpoints of several Black students at the University of California in Berkeley. Asked what they thought about the demands being made to increase the number of Black students on campus, Black students described as "militants" or "radical activists" said that all colleges and universities should be open free to any Black applicant; but a student described as "revolutionary" replied:

> I have mixed feelings about the mess. I've seen too many potentially political Brothers and Sisters come to Cal and get sucked into the damn system. They forget about the problems faced by Black people and start going for themselves. If the school has the right political atmosphere, yes, there should be more Blacks. But, if it hasn't, I'd just as soon see Black people stay on the "block," because out there they are not going

to be sucked in by intellectual bull. The truth about Black people's position in America is "everyday" out there.[13]

The Marxist may argue that preferential policies do not address the need to re-structure the economic system in a much more radical way, and may in fact lessen the pressure to do so by providing minor benefits and by creating divisiveness among members of the working class. However, this objection seems to overlook the realities of racism in the U.S. today, as it is expressed in the economic and legal systems. Using 1970 statistics from the U.S. Census Bureau, Victor Perlo has documented the radical economic inequalities in the U.S. and shown that the most striking correlations are between poverty and race. Although committed to the establishment of a socialist society in the United States, Perlo argues that an attack on such economic inequalities is a pre-condition for creating working class solidarity in the United States; thus, he views preferential policies as enhancing the possibilities for socialism. He argues,

> When we speak of programs meeting the special requirements of Black people we mean those which specify priority of benefit to Blacks, with quantitative and time targets for achieving equality in the given sector. Not that these and programs for all the people are mutually exclusive. Usually the special priorities for Blacks (and other minorities) will be parts of programs directly beneficial to all working people. But some will not, although it is our contention that all programs moving toward equality are objectively beneficial to all working people . . . . the ending of discrimination requires concretely defined preferential treatment of Blacks in admission, employment, etc. Minimum numbers and percentages of Blacks and maximum time limits must be specified. Machinery for systematic checkup and penalties must be provided, sufficiently severe to deter noncompliance.[14]

Perlo also points out the relatively minor effect of such measures on whites:

> . . . an increase in Black admissions to law school from 5% to 15%—using hypothetical figures—represents an increase of 200%, while the corresponding reduction in the admission of whites, from 95% to 85% of the total, represents a decline of only a little more than 10% . . . . the decline in percentage of admissions accruing to whites will not be in any sense discrimination against whites, but merely the correction of historical discrimination in favor of whites.[15]

Perlo concludes that preferential policies should be supported by anyone committed to eradicating gross economic injustice, whether one favors the continuance of capitalism or regards socialism as necessary for the achievement of full human equality.

[13] Harry Edwards, *Black Students* (New York: International Publishers, 1975), p. 109.
[14] Victor Perlo, *Economics of Racism* (New York: International Publishers, 1975), pp. 240–241.
[15] Perlo, p. 243.

V. THE OBLIGATIONS ,OF COMPENSATORY JUSTICE

One of the most powerful arguments for preferential policies rests on the moral claims of ethnic minorities and women for compensation. In this section, we shall examine two types of compensation that might be claimed, and outline the "ideal" case of compensation. Then, we shall consider some criteria which might be used to identify individuals and groups who can legitimately claim compensation. Next, we shall examine some objections to preferential policies as a method of rendering compensation. Lastly, we shall note some factors which tend to support such policies.

A. Grounds for Compensation

The first form of compensation which seems appropriate is compensation to persons now living, for injuries they themselves have received as a result of individualized or institutionalized racism and sexism. One could include here the psychological effects of sexual and racial stereotypes in the mass media, as well as the effects of more clearly defined institutions such as the Federal government, the public schools, and the judicial system. Note that we refer here to injuries to the persons who shall receive compensation, not to injuries received by their ancestors. Neither this form of compensation nor the following one requires an appeal to the principle that persons now living are entitled to compensation simply in virtue of their blood relationships to persons injured at an earlier time.

The second form of compensation which seems appropriate is compensation to persons now living, for present inequities resulting from earlier injustices. The claim here is that many people in the United States—primarily whites—have privileges which are unjust because they derive from prior exploitation of ethnic minorities. Arnold Kaufman formulated this principle as it applies to Blacks and whites in the U.S., as follows:

> The sons of privilege are being asked to compensate the sons of slaves whether or not the former are responsible for the disabilities of the latter. . . . It is not claimed that the sons of slavemasters are sinners because their fathers sinned. Rather, the demand that the sons of slavemasters make restitution to the sons of slaves rests on the claim that the former enjoy great and undeserved advantages, as a result of accidents of social inheritance directly connected to the existence of slavery.[16]

Thus, demands for compensation from living whites are based on their possession of undeserved benefits, not on the basis of specific actions. The principle could be extended to claims by other groups suffering similar inequities deriving from exploitation. The existence of rights of inheritance in the U.S. is one basis for these claims, though formal inheritance is by no means the only way by which economic and political powers have been transmitted.

[16] Arnold Kaufman, "Black Reparations—Two Views," *Dissent*, 1969, pp. 319–320.

In discussing the compensation due as a result of such claims, we presuppose a model of just compensation. Such a model would require an analysis of the notion of injury, and would distinguish between the actions of individuals and the effects of institutions. While I am not prepared to offer such a model, some intuitions about it may be relevant, and may indicate some useful areas for further research. Ideally, compensation would be made to injured individuals, on the basis of an examination of each case. In the least problematic case, compensation would be made "in kind," though this notion needs more analysis than we can give it here.

Another factor concerns who will pay the compensation. We need to distinguish two senses of "paying compensation." In one sense, the hiring official or admissions officer may be said to pay compensation, since he or she administers it. In another sense, however, the person who pays compensation is the person required to sacrifice a job or place in school under the policy of preferring minorities and women. Ideally, the sacrifice required of a person would be proportional to the injury inflicted by that person or the unjust benefits possessed by him or her.

B. Criteria for Identifying Legitimate Claims To Compensation

While many ethnic groups in the United States have been victims of discrimination, past and present genocidal actions have been directed toward some groups on a scale so massive that it is difficult to imagine any adequate reparation. The extermination or near-extermination of various Native American peoples; the experience of slavery and the racism which continues today; and the annexation of portions of Mexico and the subsequent policies towards Mexicans and Mexican-Americans are examples of the sort of oppression which makes compensation a moral imperative. In identifying groups entitled to compensation, it is important to be sensitive to disrespect for life, economic exploitation, and political disenfranchisement. The existence of cultural imperialism is also an important part of the record. Current statistics on social welfare are also relevant, since they help to identify groups which benefit least from American wealth. Among the most significant statistics are those relating to life expectancy, infant mortality rates, family income, unemployment rates, job status, and levels of educational attainment. Examination of such statistics, and their underlying causes, bears out the claim that discriminatory practices of the past continue to have concrete manifestations today.[17]

In analyzing claims to compensation, the situation of women must also be considered. Sexism has operated from the beginnings of this nation, and statistical evidence can be amassed here to show its continuing

---

[17] See Perlo, *ibid.*: Robert S. Browne, "The Economic Basis for Reparations to Black America," Journal of *Black Political Economy*, 2, (1972), No. 2, p. 70; and Lois B. Moreland, *White Racism and the Law* (Columbus, Ohio: Charles E. Merrill, 1970). The latter analyzes in detail the ways in which the U.S. Supreme Court has contributed to the maintenance of racism by refusing to extend the prohibitions of the Fourteenth Amendment to cover all forms of racial discrimination. A useful analysis of women's economic situation can be found in Gloria Steinem's "If We're So Smart, Why Aren't We Rich," in *Ms.*, Vol. L., No. 12, June, 1973, pp. 37–39 and 125–127.

effects. Robert Baker has also analyzed the linguistic evidence for sexism,[18] and a history of denigrating language similar to that used for many ethnic minorities is present. However, the position of women from minority groups such as those mentioned above should be distinguished from the situation of white women. Thus, for example, in looking at statistical data on income, it is true that we find Black males with a higher income than white females; but when we consider the higher percentage of non-white women who are heads of households, the interpretation of this statistic will be different from the one frequently given to support the claim of women to compensation.

C. Objections to Preferential Policies as a Method of Compensation

In this paper I shall not argue extensively for what I take to be the obvious fact that certain ethnic minorities, and women generally, have suffered injuries and inequities of the sorts described under (A) above. We shall examine objections raised by persons who acknowledge that some compensation is due, but who feel that preferential policies are not morally justifiable forms of reparations.

A variety of objections to preferential policies are frequently raised. We shall examine four of these.

1. Failure to fit the ideal model of compensation

In following preferential policies in employment and education, it seems highly impractical to consider each person's case individually. Thus, if reparations are directed toward groups, it is possible that they may sometimes be made to individuals who do not deserve compensation, or at least to those who are not as deserving as a white male who has suffered discrimination. For example, a white male may have a history of brutal discrimination because he is an ex-convict, a political radical, a homosexual, because he is poor, or simply for some purely personal reason. Such possibilities indicate that preferential policies can give rise to injustice in particular cases, and do not fit the ideal model of compensation described above.

Moreover, the persons who are required to sacrifice jobs or school places will not always have committed actions injuring minorities or women; and they may not have the greatest amount of undue privilege. The persons who have benefitted most from previous discrimination will not typically be those who lose out under a preferential policy, for they are likely to be in the most secure and powerful positions. This outcome again does not fit the ideal model of compensation.

2. The dangers of the quota system

Another objection to preferential policies, when accompanied by specific time tables and quota systems, is that such procedures will threaten the maintenance of distributive justice. We have already alluded to these concerns in (III) above.

3. The problem of "where to stop"

A similar concern is voiced by persons who feel that demands for reparations cannot be given in appropriate quantitative terms. This

---

[18] Robert Baker, " 'Pricks' and 'Chicks': A Plea for Persons," in Wasserstrom, pp. 152–171.

problem is seen as raising the danger of giving too much in the way of reparations, and thus of creating a new injustice.

4. The irrelevance of historical analysis

Finally, there are those who would resist the appeal to historical analysis as a basis for distinguishing among ethnic groups. The western response, reflecting a patriarchal white male interpretation of experience, tends to see such historical perspectives as appeals to a principle of vengeance. While acknowledging that current discrimination should be abolished, and that injuries done to those now living deserve compensation, the notion of reparations due as a result of psychological alliance with one's foreparents is seen as indefensible.

D. Reasons for Preferential Policies as a Method of Compensation

1. Transition to a just state

There are several ways of responding to these criticisms. First, one can argue that preferential policies will hasten progress toward distributive justice in relatively straightforward ways. Such policies can be expected to produce desirable psychological changes among ethnic minorities and women. For example, members of these groups are likely to develop new aspirations as a result of having role models in positions where there are now few such persons. Second, favoring minorities and women in jobs and education will lead to a more nearly just distribution of economic and legal representation. Such a redistribution is not only desirable in itself but also will make possible further re-distribution in the directions of social justice.

2. The issue of merit

Secondly, preferential policies force us to take a serious look at the entire concept of merit. The question of merit raises at least three different issues:

a. Deciding what constitutes appropriate criteria of merit;

b. Deciding whether a given applicant meets these criteria, and perhaps to what degree he or she does so, and,

c. Ensuring that the chosen criteria are in fact used as a basis for selection.

Minority members and women have charged that none of these tasks is presently adequately carried out in all areas of employment and education. Criticism on this point has come from diverse sources. For example, economist Milton Friedman has emphasized the difficulty of setting and enforcing meaningful standards for employment. While his aim is to argue against governmental intervention in employment, his criticism of licensing procedures is relevant to the problem of merit. Though such procedures are supposed to impose standards of performance in various areas, he claims that:

> . . . any relationship between the requirements imposed and the qualities which the licensure is intended to assure is rather far-fetched. The extent to which such requirements go is sometimes little short of ludicrous.[19]

[19] Milton Friedman, *Capitalism and Freedom* (Chicago: University of Chicago Press, 1962), pp. 141–142.

The areas of licensing and testing for merit really point to the under-lying problem of interest groups which use these supposed criteria of merit to maintain their own power.

A somewhat different problem is the pervasive assumption that the white male interpretation of experience is the only correct one. Although in general we would not expect race and sex to constitute criteria of merit in themselves, Richard Wasserstrom has given a powerful argument to show that they may do so in the context of university admissions and employment.[20] His argument rests essentially on the claim that since race and sex shape our experience in radical ways—at least in society as we know it—persons of differing races and sexes have different perspec-tives and will give different interpretations of the same physical events. In order to avoid accepting uncritically the assumption that the white male viewpoint is the right one, representatives of other viewpoints must be included in the university, simply in order for it to carry out its mis-sion to pursue truth. The point becomes even more convincing if we accept DuBois' claim that the function of the university "is, above all, to be the organ of that fine adjustment which forms the secret of civiliza-tion."[21] Using a wider variety of examples, one might extend the argu-ment to apply beyond the university setting; surely almost any task lends itself to discussion concerning the most desirable approach, at least when the task is viewed in its social context. (Compare, for instance, discussing a single surgical procedure in isolation, to discussing that procedure as a part of a whole institution of health care delivery.) Thus, the issue of merit forces us to re-examine traditional criteria. There are at least two advantages to such a procedure. First, new perspectives may result in new and more justifiable criteria not only for judging what solutions are appropriate to the problems, but also for identifying the significant prob-lems confronting us as citizens of the world today. Second, when rational criteria cannot be agreed upon, adding minority members and women to the decision-making process should produce a fairer compromise than present decision-makers can achieve.

However, an important issue about merit is raised by Thomas Nagel in his article, "Equal Treatment and Compensatory Discrimination."[22] Nagel suggests that in a just society, economic and social rewards would not be based on the ability to succeed in the professional competition of a technologically advanced society with a market economy. Rather, he argues, such rewards would be distributed in a more egalitarian fashion, perhaps with some allowances made for factors such as willingness to work. Merit, he suggests, may be relevant in deciding what kinds of opportunities to offer persons, but it ought not be relevant to the dis-tribution of other rewards, at least to the degree that it presently is. Thus, when we use performance-related criteria to assign jobs and school places, we are in fact perpetuating an injustice, because implicitly we are also awarding undeserved economic and other rewards which accompany

[20] Richard Wasserstrom, "The University and the Case for Preferential Treatment," mimeographed.
[21] DuBois, p. 268.
[22] Thomas Nagel, "Equal Treatment and Compensatory Discrimination," *Philosophy and Public Affairs*, Summer, 1973, Vol. 2, No. 4.

these opportunities. So, Nagel suggests, to depart from performance-related criteria decreases this injustice, at least when the departure involves compensatory justice. Thus, one could argue that in the present situation, distributive justice requires a departure from present reliance on performance-related criteria, even apart from the issue of compensation for racial and sexual discrimination. Nagel's argument, too, suggests that if neither strict adherence to performance criteria nor preferential policies provide distributive justice, and if distributive justice cannot be achieved without radical changes in society, then at present we may opt for preferential policies on the basis of social utility.

Minorities and women may also succeed in attacking an insidious assumption which Nagel makes throughout his article: that human beings fall naturally into such categories as intelligent and unintelligent, talented and untalented, beautiful and ugly. He remarks, "When racial and sexual injustice have been reduced, we shall still be left with the great injustice of the smart and the dumb." [23] Nagel's view is that society ought to ignore this regrettable inequality in distributing many of its benefits. But when racial and sexual injustices have been eliminated, we may cease to see such clear distinctions among persons.

But surely, one may reply, one can distinguish between efficient, productive institutions (presumably chosen by smart people), and inefficient, unproductive ones (presumably the kind that would exist if power were accorded to the dumb). No doubt the just society will have to make some assessment of skills, in distributing tasks; but since the criteria for judging institutions to be efficient and productive will be rather different from the current ones, there is no reason to think that the kind of "smartness" that has produced current institutions will continue to be valued or will continue even to exist. A different society may greatly decrease the degrees and types of differences that we now take for granted.

3. Overlap of groups victimized by discrimination

One other consideration should be noted before we move in more detail to the reparations issue. There is a notable overlap of certain ethnic minorities with other groups which have been discriminated against: e.g., disproportionately large numbers of Blacks, Chicanos, and Native Americans are poor and have arrest records. The case of Gregory v. Litton Systems illustrates the practice of using an applicant's arrest record in a racially discriminatory fashion. The discriminatory operation of such a criterion can be seen in the following figures. If a person is arrested at least once, he is likely to be arrested seven times in his lifetime if he is white; a Black arrested at least once is likely to be arrested a total of 12.5 times. Moreover, Blacks account for 45 per cent of all "suspicion" arrests, and a larger percentage of Blacks than whites are arrested but never convicted. Blacks are also arrested more than whites for crimes that are frequently reported. The Ninth Circuit Court of Appeals, in a decision handed down in December, 1972, upheld a July 1970 decision that exclusion of job applicants with arrest records is a violation of the 1964 Civil Rights Act.[24] However, though there has been some voluntary

---

[23] Nagel, p. 362.
[24] *Civil Liberties,* May, 1973, No. 296, p. 5.

compliance with this ruling, violations continue and greater enforcement will be needed. Indeed, as long as arrest records remain on file even in the absence of a conviction, the possibility for abuse of such information exists.[25] Discrimination against rehabilitated drug addicts is another way in which ethnic minorities have been penalized. And while our discussion here is confined to discrimination within the area of employment, the correlation between being non-white and having an arrest record or a history of drug usage points to much broader issues of social justice. To explore these would reinforce the legitimacy of minority claims for reparations.

4. Magnitude of reparations due and improbability of adequate reparation

Even if one acknowledges that some inequities will result if such policies are followed, one can still argue that still greater inequities will result if such policies are not followed. As Virginia Held and others have pointed out, without strong measures, the transition to a just society can be expected to be unjustifiably slow.[26] Two empirical questions are relevant here. First, we need to discuss the magnitude of compensation due women and minorities for injuries and inequities of the sorts mentioned. Second, we must consider the probability that compensation will be made through methods other than preferential policies. Some persons may balk at the demand that the issue be discussed in quantitative and probabilistic terms; but we must attempt such comparisons if the decision for or against preferential policies is to be made in a rational way. But such comparisons do not commit us to a utilitarian view of justice, nor do they imply that all the injustices of racism and sexism can be measured.

To answer these empirical questions is not a task for philosophical inquiry as such. The answers would involve, first, a detailed examination of the effects of social institutions on various ethnic minorities and on men and women. Then, we would need to assess the probability of compensation through methods other than preferential policies. While much research remains to be done, it seems obvious that the magnitude of compensation due is almost incalculably great and likelihood of adequate compensation by any other means rather small. It would seem to me that one of the most important obligations of American citizens is to examine the existing evidence on these points and weigh the reparations argument accordingly. It will be of particular importance to examine the ways in which discriminatory criteria have operated in the area of employment and education, since the compensation provided by preferential policies operates in these areas. Much attention has been focused on discrimination in school admissions and on employment in academia and the professional fields generally. However, discrimination [in employment] has been particularly vicious in other areas of employment, and its existence strengthens the case for preferential policies. To illustrate the kind of evidence appropriate to the issue in question, I want to examine briefly three legal cases which illuminate this point.

[25] This possibility has led some persons to recommend the automatic expungement of arrest records. For a discussion of this point, and of Gregory v. Litton, see Harriet Katz Berman, "Breaking the Bars," *Civil Liberties*, May, 1963, No. 296, pp. 5–6.
[26] Held, *ibid.*

One of the landmark cases in this area is that of Griggs v. Duke Power, which eventually led to a U.S. Supreme Court decision on March 8, 1971. This proceeding was brought by 13 of the 14 Black employees at the Dan River Steam Station of Duke Power, in Draper, North Carolina. The District Court found that prior to July 2, 1965, the Company had openly discriminated on the basis of race in the hiring and assigning of employees at the Dan River plant. The plant was organized into five operating departments: (1) Labor; (2) Coal Handling; (3) Operations; (4) Maintenance; and (5) Laboratory and Test. Blacks were employed only in the Labor Department, where the highest paying jobs paid less than the lowest paying jobs in the other four "operating" departments in which only whites were employed.

In 1955 the Company began requiring a high school education for initial assignment to any department except Labor, and for transfer from Coal Handling to any of the other three departments. In 1965 completion of high school was made a requirement for transferring from Labor to any other department. However, white employees without a high school diploma who were hired before 1955 continued to perform satisfactorily and achieve promotions at the same rate as high school graduates. Their performance indicates that a high school education was irrelevant to job performance. The requirement operated in a discriminatory fashion since a significantly smaller percentage of Blacks completed high school in North Carolina at that time.[27]

The Company added a further requirement for new employees on July 2, 1965, the date on which Title VII became effective. To qualify for placement in any but the Labor Department, an applicant had to register satisfactory scores on two professional aptitude tests, as well as having a high school education. In September, 1965, the Company began to permit incumbent employees who lacked a high school education to qualify for transfer from Labor or Coal Handling to a job in one of the other departments by passing two tests, the Wonderlic Personnel Test, which purports to measure general intelligence, and the Bennett Mechanical Aptitude Test. Neither was intended to measure the ability to learn to perform a particular job or category of jobs. Since the requisite scores for hiring and transfer approximated the national median for high school students, they were more stringent than the high school requirement, since approximately half of all high school graduates would thus be screened out.

The District Court had found that while the Company previously followed a policy of overt racial discrimination, such discrimination had ceased, and that Title VII was not intended to provide corrective action for prior inequities. The case then went to the Court of Appeals, which held that since there was no showing of a discriminatory intent on the part of the employer, there was no violation of the Civil Rights Act. However, when the case finally went to the U.S. Supreme Court, the Court held that, under the Civil Rights Act, practices, procedures or tests cannot be used if they maintain the effects of prior discriminatory

[27] According to 1960 census data, 34 per cent of white males in North Carolina had completed high school, compared to 12 percent of Black males.

practices, even if they are neutral in terms of intent. It held that the employer bears the responsibility for showing that any given requirement is directly related to job performance. The evidence showed that white employees who had not completed high school or met the test criteria continued to perform satisfactorily and make progress in the departments for which these requirements were imposed. The Supreme Court thus reversed the Court of Appeals decision and ordered that these requirements be abandoned.[28]

There are two important lessons to be drawn from this case. First, in assessing the magnitude of compensation due minorities and women, we must consider not only direct discrimination but also this sort of covert discrimination operating in the area of job requirements. Second, the challenge to such requirements will be a lengthy one. Despite Griggs v. Duke Power, the use of discriminatory criteria is continuing to create just claims for compensation. It was not until September, 1972, that U.S. District Court Judge Gordon Thompson, Jr., prohibited the Imperial Irrigation District of California from using any further employment tests except in simple typing tests, until other exams were validated according to the Equal Employment Opportunity Commission's guidelines on employee selection procedures. This action was the result of a suit filed by the California Rural Legal Assistance on behalf of the Imperial Valley chapters of the NAACP and the Mexican-American Political Association, along with three individuals. The judge also ordered that the defendants

> shall take all actions necessary to ensure that as soon as possible the proportion of Chicanos and Blacks in the IID work force generally, and in each job classification (including supervisory and management positions), shall equal the proportion of Chicanos and Blacks in the general population of Imperial County, as shown by the latest United States Bureau of the Census figures. Similarly, defendants shall take all actions necessary to insure that as soon as possible the proportion of all other racial and ethnic groups employed at the IID shall be equal to their proportion in the general population of Imperial County, as shown by the latest United States Bureau of the Census figures.[29]

According to the 1970 census, the minority population of Imperial County is 53.6 per cent. Hiring figures from September through December, 1972 showed 63.8 per cent of the new employees hired by the IID were minority group members. While Attorney Derek Weston of the California Rural Legal Assistance noted in February, 1973, that the IID "has made impressive progress in fulfilling its affirmative action plan," [30] it is important to emphasize the circumstances that led up to this progress. Judge Thompson's decision did not come until seven years after the passage of Title VII—and it was the result of an 18-day trial. Though

[28] Willie S. Griggs et. al., Petitioners, v. Duke Power Company, U.S. Supreme Court No. 124, October Term, 1970.
[29] National Association for the Advancement of Colored People, et. al., v. Imperial Irrigation District, et. al., U.S. District Court for the Southern District of California, No. 70-302-GT, Consent Decree.
[30] San Diego Union, Feb. 12, 1973.

the IID had adopted an Affirmative Action Program on June 29, 1971, even this did not come until nine months after the suit was filed. Moreover, lengthy and expensive court challenges continue across the United States, and we cannot assume that compliance with court orders will always be prompt. One other case may be mentioned to emphasize this point. On December 3, 1973, the NAACP, Western Region, found it necessary to file with the United States Attorney General a "Pattern and Practice" Civil Rights Complaint against all nine campuses of the University of California. The complaint documented the massive exclusion of Blacks from employment opportunities at the academic and non-academic levels. The complaint noted that a similar "pattern and practice" of exclusion existed with respect to the Mexican-American community. Attorney General Robert H. Bork and the University of California system have yet to deal with the inequities documented in the complaint.[31]

5. The psychological relevance of historical events

Finally, a comment should be made concerning the relevance of historical analysis to the issue of reparations. I believe that until adequate reparations are made to ethnic minorities and women, there will continue to be justifiable resentment on the part of those members of these groups who see themselves as psychologically allied to their foreparents. To claim that such resentment—hardly a pleasant state—constitutes a basis for reparations is not simply to appeal to a principle of vengeance. It is to appeal to a violation of one of the rights guaranteed by distributive justice, namely, the right to recognition of one's worth and dignity as a person. The sense of identification involved in such a violation cannot be adequately understood within an individualistic world-view. If one's concept of self-identity includes the being of one's ancestors, then one does not suffer simply on behalf of one's ancestors; rather, the suffering is one's own. Moreover, the identification does not arise only out of anger. It reflects, too, the positive sense of community which many of us feel with some who have died, and the concern we feel for children in future generations. The interpretation of this attitude as an individualistic desire for revenge is a distortion of the love and communal interpretation of experience which motivates many of us to continue to struggle toward a just society.

VI. METHODS OF IMPLEMENTATION

Finally, what are the implications of the arguments for and against preferential policies, for the choice among ethnic minority candidates and

[31] NAACP, Western Division, on behalf of 1.8 Million California Black Citizens, Complainants, v. University of California, Office of the President, Berkeley, Davis, Irvine, Los Angeles, Riverside, San Diego, San Francisco, Santa Barbara, and Santa Cruz Campuses, and Charles Hitch in his Official Capacity as President of the University of California, Defendant. Class Action, Civil Rights, Three Judge Federal Court Complaint, filed before the United States Attorney General, United States Department of Justice. Among the data cited were: only 37 (00.8%) of the 4,274 tenured faculty at the nine University campuses are Black; only 10 (2%) of the 545 librarians employed at the nine campuses are Black; at every occupational level whites earn substantially more than their Black counterparts.

white women who may be competing for the same position? Ideally, such choices might not be necessary, but in fact, since those who ought to make the largest sacrifices will likely make the least, such choices will arise. On this issue, those who justify preferential policies primarily in terms of reparations may come to a different conclusion from those who defend them primarily as a method of moving from an unjust to a just state. For, if distributive justice requires that selection in employment and education not be based on race or sex, and if race and sex do not in general affect merit, then one may well adopt the view that a just distribution will reflect the proportion of women and ethnic minorities in the population. Thus, one could formulate a decision procedure as follows: Other things being equal, choose that candidate whose group is furthest from proportional representation.[32] Since women constitute so much larger a proportion of the population than does any minority group, this principle may often lead to preferring women of any race over male candidates, even if we discount from the proportion to be represented those women who choose not to compete for jobs or academic places.

In contrast, the reparation defense suggests that the magnitude of the compensation due should be the deciding factor. Although we have not looked at the evidence here, it is hard to imagine that the reparations due white women as a class could possibly approach that due such groups as Blacks and other oppressed minorities. Note, for example, that the use of general intelligence tests, the high school graduation requirement, and arrest records operate primarily to discriminate against certain ethnic minorities. Moreover, now that the relevance of the doctorate as a credential for college teaching is being questioned, another pertinent statistic may be noted: One per cent of the doctorates in the U.S. are held by Blacks, while 19 per cent are held by women, the overwhelming majority of whom are white.[33]

It is imperative to note the comments of a Black woman, Linda LaRue, in an article, "The Black Movement and Women's Liberation." She asks,

Can we really expect that white women, when put in direct competition for employment, will be any more open-minded than their male counterparts when it comes to the hiring of black males and females in the same positions for which they are competing? From the standpoint of previous American social interaction, it does not seem logical that white females will not be tempted to take advantage of the fact that they are white, in an economy that favors whites.[34]

[32] This principle requires further clarification, since it does not specify what group should be examined in determining representation. Administrative and economic divisions suggest the most likely definitions of the relevant groups; but still, one would need to decide whether the appropriate group is, for example, an entire state university system, a single institution within it, or a single department within that institution. To take another example, the group might be the construction industry in the U.S. or in a single city; or it might be a specific construction project.
[33] *Atlanta Journal*, December 19, 1972.
[34] Linda LaRue, "The Black Movement and Women's Liberation," *The Black Scholar*, May, 1970, pp. 35–42.

Nathan and Julia Hare note, too, that

> Many black women are convinced that, before giving up his own, the white man would take the black man's jobs and give them to white women, pushing the black man still farther down. To this extent, the goals of Women's Liberation and Black Liberation are viewed as contradictory.[35]

We have noted earlier the misleading use of statistics concerning the income of white women as compared to that of Black males. Another instructive example concerns the implementation of HEW guidelines with respect to implementation of the 1964 Civil Rights Act, Titles VII and VIII of the Public Health Service Act, Title IX of the Education Amendments of 1972, and Executive Order 11246. While HEW has been criticized by both minority and women's groups for a lack of zeal in enforcement, women have been able to marshall far greater legal and financial resources to force implementation of the various directives. Moreover, their viewpoints have been given much more attention in shaping the direction that implementation will take. Let us consider a single example. Many Blacks have vehemently opposed the effect of HEW guidelines on predominantly Black colleges, since in certain cases the guidelines are seen as an attempt to destroy the unique heritage of these schools and to prevent them from maintaining their identity as Black institutions. In contrast, note the vast amount of time, thought, and resources that has gone into the implementation of equal rights for women. For example, in sports, the various alternatives have been extensively explored, and attention has been given to women's own perspectives.

White women, then, should be particularly sensitive to the considerations which prompt the comments of LaRue and the Hares. This sensitivity should lead to an insistence on special attention to the needs of ethnic minorities who have been victimized by America's systematic and prolonged racism.

Autonomy in Policy Formation and Implementation

Emphasis must also be given to allowing victimized groups themselves to determine what form compensation should take. Preferential policies surely are an acceptable interim measure to many; but consideration should be given to allowing the ethnic groups in question to determine the form in which they desire to receive reparations. As various persons have pointed out, proposals for land re-allotment raise almost insuper-

[35] Nathan and Julia Hare, "Black Woman 1970," *Transaction*, November–December, 1970, Vol. 8, No. 12, pp. 65–90. A broader perspective is taken by Maureen Kempton, in "All We Want for Christmas Is Our Jobs Back," in *Ms.*, Vol. IV, No. 6, December, 1975, pp. 69–72 and 114. She suggests, ". . . since both the senior white males and the junior female or minority employees are all innocent victims of the employers' discriminatory practices, should any of the workers lose their jobs? Instead, why not put the onus on the responsible party: let the employers pay for their past evils." p. 70. But while morally correct, Ms. Kempton's proposal is hardly likely to be implemented on any massive scale. Thus, seniority disputes in this period of high unemployment will only heighten the conflict which concerns LaRue and the Hares.

able problems, given the composition of the current American population. Direct financial reparations raise other difficulties. However, only when we move beyond the process of justifying minor measures such as preferential policies, and begin to confront realistically a massive restructuring of the social order, can we claim to be moving with any deliberate speed toward a genuinely just state. We must give those deserving reparations the tools to deal with these problems, rather than avoiding the moral issues by further debate about the moral or legal acceptability of reparations to the victims of American exploitation.

CARL COHEN 25

WHY RACIAL PREFERENCE IS ILLEGAL AND IMMORAL

The role of race in assuring social justice is again squarely before the Supreme Court in a case whose full and revealing name is: *Kaiser Aluminum & Chemical Corporation and United Steelworkers of America, AFL-CIO v. Brian F. Weber, individually and on behalf of all other persons similarly situated.*

Weber, a white unskilled steelworker, is Bakke's analogue. The Steelworkers Union and Kaiser Aluminum are not the only forces against him. The United Auto Workers and the United Mine Workers, the National Education Association, the Coalition of Black Trade Unionists, and assorted other unions are against him. The American Civil Liberties Union is against him. Even the United States government is formally aligned against him. On Weber's side is the Anti-Defamation League of B'nai B'rith (with some associated non-Jewish ethnic groups) and, according to repeated surveys, an overwhelming majority of the American population, including a majority of the black population.

But the issues at stake here, touching the most fundamental rights of individual persons, are not to be decided by counting noses. The chief things going for Weber are the Fourteenth Amendment of the U.S. Constitution, the Civil Rights Act of 1964 as amended, and sound moral principles. Thrice is he armed who hath his quarrel just.

Weber has thus far been victorious, both in the Federal District Court, and in the Federal Court of Appeals (5th Circuit, New Orleans). His formidable opponents find it difficult to overcome the plain words of the law applied straightforwardly to the established facts of his case. The law (Title VII of the Civil Rights Act, Sec. 703) forbids flatly all

Reprinted from *Commentary,* by permission; copyright 1979 by the American Jewish Committee.

discrimination in employment because of race.[1] Beyond any possible doubt (as we shall see) Weber was discriminated against by his employer, and classified by his employer, and had his status as an employee adversely affected because of his race. That the employment practice through which this was done is a violation of this federal law is an ineluctable conclusion of any rational mind.

Is it not remarkable, then, that unions, industry, and government should now join in the effort to persuade the Supreme Court to evade this conclusion? Weber's opponents are neither foolish nor evil. They seek, somehow, to surmount the barriers to racially discriminatory treatment in order to achieve objectives they think good. Reflection upon this case will oblige the Supreme Court—and all citizens who would reach thoughtful judgment on these issues—to reconsider those objectives, and to appraise the means by which they have been pursued.

The *Bakke* case, and the *DeFunis* case before it, dealt with racially discriminatory practices in professional-school admissions—a matter for which the middle classes have, rightly, a tender concern. *Weber* deals with racial discrimination in blue-collar employment. The injury done Brian Weber was at least as great as that done Allan Bakke, and the class Weber formally represents is very much larger, if less articulate, than that directly affected by racially preferential school admissions. It is disturbing, therefore, that the voices raised in behalf of Weber's rights, and the rights of literally millions of individual citizens in like circumstances, are so painfully few. Silence now from quarters that were outspoken in opposition to racial preference in higher education may lead some to infer that self-interest, more than justice, was what motivated that earlier concern.

In both spheres—school admissions and industrial employment—the same issues arise: in the allocation of scarce goods, may one's race count in one's favor? If ever, when? In *Bakke* a racially preferential admission system at the University of California Medical School at Davis was struck down, but attention to race in the admissions process was there held permissible within certain very narrow limits: to advance the diversity of an entering class, or to remedy the condition of specific persons who had been discriminated against by the school using the racial instrument. *Weber* is in many important respects different. Here the factor of diversity does not enter; here matters pertaining to intellectual qualifications are replaced by matters pertaining to seniority. Here the stakes are greater and the underlying moral issues are presented more cleanly.

[1] Subsection (a) of Sec. 703 reads:
"It shall be an unlawful employment practice for an employer—
(1) to fail or refuse to hire or discharge any individual, or otherwise to discriminate against any individual with respect to his compensation, terms, conditions, or privileges of employment, because of such individual's race, color, religion, sex, or national origin; or
(2) to limit, segregate, or classify his employees or applicants for employment in any way which would deprive any individual of employment opportunities or otherwise adversely affect his status as an employee, because of such individual's race, color, religion, sex, or national origin" 42 U.S. Codes 2000e—2(a) (1970).

I

This is what happened. Kaiser (Kaiser Aluminum & Chemical Corporation) and the union (United Steelworkers of America, AFL-CIO) sought to increase the number of minority workers in the skilled crafts at Kaiser's Gramercy, Louisiana, plant. To this end, in a 1974 collective-bargaining agreement, they changed the system whereby employees would enter on-the-job training for craft positions. Prior craft experience was eliminated as a requirement, and entrance ratios, by race, were established for acceptance in the job-training program. For each white worker admitted one minority worker would be admitted, until the percentage of minority craft workers in the Gramercy plant roughly approximated the percentage of the minority population in the surrounding area, then about 40 per cent. Dual seniority lists were established, one black and one white, and each two vacancies filled with the persons at the top of the two racially distinct lists.

It was an inevitable result of this system that some employees would be favored because of their race, and some would be injured because of theirs. Brian Weber was refused admission to the job-training program although his seniority was higher than some employees from the other racial list who were admitted. Weber sued on his own behalf and on behalf of all non-minority employees who applied for on-the-job training at the Gramercy plant after that labor agreement was signed. A racially preferential scheme for allocating on-the-job training opportunities, he argues, is a clear violation of the Federal Civil Rights Act.

One portion of Title VII of that Act deals explicitly with on-the-job training programs. That portion (subsection (d) of Sec. 703) reads as follows:

> It shall be an unlawful employment practice for any employer, labor organization, or joint labor-management committee controlling apprenticeship or other training or retraining, *including on-the-job training programs*, to discriminate against any individual because of his race, color, religion, sex, or national origin in admission to, or employment in, any program established to provide apprenticeship or other training [42 U.S. Codes 2000e–2 (d) (1970); emphasis added].

Was it prescience that caused the Congress to formulate this ban with language so precisely and indubitably covering the case at hand? Not at all. Title VII had as its purpose the elimination of all ethnic favoritism in employment; there had been, at the time of its adoption, plenty of experience of the ways in which racial prejudice can be given effect—one of the commonest being in job-training programs. In that form as in all forms, said the Congress in effect, racial discrimination in employment is no longer permissible.

How can Kaiser and the union (and the U.S. Department of Justice) reasonably argue that such a scheme is indeed lawful or fair? They contend that the law, properly interpreted, does not forbid this variety of racial preference, which they think justified by our history of discrimination. They contend that if the pursuit of pressing social objectives now imposes incidental costs on individuals, Weber and his like are the right persons to bear those costs. They contend that they were ordered, by the U.S. government, to introduce racial preference of precisely this kind. And they contend that Weber wasn't really injured by this program at all. I examine these arguments in turn.

II

"Kaiser and the union [the first argument begins] reached an agreement that was fully in accord with the spirit of Title VII. Theirs was a voluntary effort to bring a greater number of minority workers into the skilled crafts. Congress never intended to forbid such voluntary efforts. If now the product of such agreements, reached through collective bargaining, is struck down, the cause of racial justice will have been dealt a devastating blow.

"We must [this argument continues] permit management and labor to join, as in this case, to correct a racially unbalanced situation flowing from the historical and social realities of American life. Blacks have been discriminated against, cruelly and consistently, by industry and by unions. Now an effort is being made to give redress. It is an ironic inversion of the Civil Rights Act to use that Act to forbid the only instruments that may effectively achieve its own intended result.

"It is true [the argument proceeds] that Title VII specifies that preferential treatment of racial minorities is not required [Section 703 (j)]. But that is not to say it is forbidden. When its aim is precisely that of the Act itself, it must not be forbidden. Weber relies upon the narrowest construction of the words and misses—inadvertently or deliberately—the remedial spirit of the law and of the Kaiser program here in question."

The main pillar of Weber's opposition comes to this: "If the Court agrees that racial quotas such as this one are discriminatory, we will be kept from doing what many of us think it is necessary to do, and do quickly, in the interest of long-term justice. Let it be understood, therefore [the argument concludes], that this quota, although it does of course distinguish by race, and does, admittedly, give favor by race, does not 'discriminate' by race in the bad sense that the law condemns. When we come to realize that some plans for racial balance, while they may have adverse effects upon some white workers, are nevertheless justified by pressing societal needs, we will also see what interpretation of the law is required by justice."

To put the argument plainly is to see both its earnestness and its frailty. The requirements of the Civil Rights Act, which in turn were intended to give concrete meaning to the constitutional demand that no citizen be denied the equal protection of the laws, were aimed at bringing to a final halt all formal discrimination on the basis of race—and color, religion, sex, and national origin. It certainly was not intended, and it obviously was not formulated, to forbid only such racial discrimination as employers and unions thought objectionable, while permitting any racially discriminatory schemes that employers and unions might by agreement find worthy or convenient. What the employer and union happen to prefer, whether their motives be honorable or crass, has absolutely no weight, says the law in effect, against the *right* of each individual citizen to be dealt with, in matters pertaining to employment, without regard to race, religion, or national origin.

III

"But that cannot be the correct interpretation of the law," answer Kaiser and the union in chorus, "because the Supreme Court has several times, in the years since, recognized the lawfulness and wisdom of racially preferential employment schemes. Indeed, our federal courts have *ordered* the imposition of such racial preference in some cases! So it is clearly false that *all* racial preference has been forbidden. If that is so, then it is not obviously true that *this* scheme for racial preference has been forbidden."

This rejoinder brings us to the core, legal and moral, of the controversy in *Weber*. What kind of attention to race does the Civil Rights Act (and, indirectly, the Constitution) permit? And what should it permit? In the *Bakke* case, this question was complicated by the entry of First Amendment considerations pertaining to the robust exchange of ideas in the classroom; the holding in *Bakke* was tangled by the fact that Justice Powell's pivotal opinion, although condemning racial favoritism, permits attention to race to advance diversity among an entering school class. Here, in *Weber,* such First Amendment considerations are totally absent. What, if anything, remains to justify race-conscious employment practices?

There is a clear and honorable answer to this question, given forcefully by federal courts at every level. Title VII of the Civil Rights Act forbids all deliberate discrimination by race, save only in cases where racial classification is absolutely essential to give redress to *identifiable persons* injured by racial discrimination *and where the injury done them was done by the same party upon whom the numerical program is imposed.* One purpose only may justify numerical schemes using racial categories: the *making whole* of those to whom redress for racial injury is specifically owed, by those who owe it.

For example: the known victims of racial discrimination by a trucking company have been held entitled, as a remedy, to a place in the seniority lists of that company that would have been theirs if they had not been so victimized. To put them now in as good a place as they would have been in but for the discriminatory employment practice from which they can be shown to have suffered, it may be necessary to attend to race. Only in that way can the victims be made whole; they would otherwise remain subordinate to persons who, had it not been for racial discrimination in that company, would now be their subordinates. (See *Franks* v. *Bowman Transportation Co.* 424 U.S. 747 [1976].) In such cases, the racially oriented remedy cannot be refused on the ground that the effect on other employees is adverse because, although the employees who suffer from the imposition of the plan are very possibly innocent themselves, they have clearly benefited, in seniority, from the specific discriminatory practice for which remedy is being given. Race-conscious remedies for the victims of illegal discrimination are lawful, consistent with Title VII, only in such circumstances.

Weber and Kaiser Aluminum are in no such circumstances. Upon examining the facts, the Federal District Court found that Kaiser had not been guilty of any discriminatory hiring or promotion at its Gramercy plant. Kaiser's industrial-relations superintendent at that plant testified that, prior to 1974, Kaiser had vigorously sought trained black craftsmen from the general community. Advertising in periodicals and newspapers that were published primarily for black subscribers, Kaiser found it very difficult to attract black craftsmen. The evidence established two key facts:

1. Kaiser had a serious, operational, no-discrimination hiring policy at its Gramercy plant from the day of that plant's opening in 1958.

2. Not one of the black employees who were offered on-the-job training opportunities over more senior white employees (pursuant to the 1974 Labor Agreement) had been subject to any prior employment discrimination by Kaiser.

From these facts it is an inescapable conclusion that the quota system at Kaiser's Gramercy plant was not an instrument for the specific redress of persons injured by racial discrimination there; it was unabashed racial preference aimed at numerical proportions having nothing to do with past conduct in that plant. Such preference Title VII outlaws. The distinction, between impermissible racial preference and permissible remedy for past discrimination, is put eloquently by the Circuit Court of Appeals in affirming Weber's rights:

> If employees who have been arbitrarily favored are deprived of benefits capriciously conferred on them in order that those who were arbitrarily deprived may receive what they should, in fairness, have had to begin with, no law is violated. This is so even if both the class whose rights are restored and the class required to "move over" are defined by race—if the original arbitrariness was defined in that manner. And the reason is that no one is being favored or disfavored, advantaged or injured, under these circumstances *because* of race; rather, those who have been unjustly deprived receive their due and those who have been arbitrarily favored surrender some of the largesse capriciously conferred on them. That these consequences end by race is a mere incident of the fact that they began that way.[2]

---

[2] 653 F. 2d 216, 225 (1977); page references below refer to this decision. The Supreme Court has agreed. In a case arising from a plan devised to give remedy to school employees within a previously discriminatory system, the Supreme Court declined review of a decision that, in view of the source and nature of that earlier injury, a minority worker may there be entitled to preferential treatment "not because he is black, but because, and only to the extent that, he has been discriminated against" *Chance* v. *Board of Examiners,* 534 F. 2d 993, 999 (1976); cert. denied 431 U.S. 965 (1977).

But those who were favored by race at Weber's expense were admittedly not the victims of such original arbitrariness. The Circuit Court's support of Weber is therefore categorical: "[U]nless a preference is enacted to restore employees to their rightful places within a particular employment scheme it is strictly forbidden by Title VII" (p. 225).

IV

Since it is clear that the beneficiaries of this racial program were not victims of Kaiser's previous discrimination, and equally clear that the use of dual seniority lists is an explicit effort to favor blacks over whites, the defenders of this program are compelled to resort to a different justification—past "societal discrimination."

"We cannot deny [say the defenders in effect] that the two-list system deliberately favors one race over another. But we do deny that favoring this race at this time in this country is unfair. We contend that, in view of the historical discrimination against blacks (and other minorities), the racially preferential device now before us is entirely justifiable. It is justifiable not only because blacks have been so long oppressed, but because, as a corollary, whites have been unfairly *advantaged* by race prejudice. The white employees of Kaiser who are passed over by this plan may indeed be innocent of any racial discrimination themselves, but they have been and are the beneficiaries of racial discrimination by others. This is the heart of our justification. Favor to blacks now is just because of the favor whites have enjoyed until now."

This is the principled argument by which many without selfish interests in these programs are persuaded that they are fair. One might have expected the American Civil Liberties Union, for example, to spring to the defense of the rights of an almost defenseless individual. Instead it joins the forces against Weber because the ACLU has convinced itself that his rights have not really been infringed on, even though he suffers from deliberate disadvantage because of race. How can that be?

"Racial preference in employment is justified [the argument proceeds] when it is a response to the morally legitimate demand that the *lingering effects* of past racial discrimination be remedied. The lingering effects of historical oppression include the continuing losses of decent employment, together with the money and status that it brings. But the same historical race prejudice that has systematically blocked minorities from access to decent jobs has conferred an involuntary benefit upon whites because, while the number of desirable jobs remains roughly constant, the elimination of competition by minority workers results in the availability of desirable jobs for whites in generous disproportion to their numbers. This benefit is conferred even upon those whites who may, in fact, deplore the prejudice from which they gain. Yet they did gain. Now, with racial quotas favoring blacks, they lose. Their present loss is morally justified by their earlier gain. The primary target of racially preferential programs should be those guilty of past unlawful discrimination, of course. But where those guilty parties simply cannot be identified or are no longer available to make restitution, a secondary but legitimate target is the unjust enrichment attributable to that racial discrimination. Quota plans, like the one devised by Kaiser and the union, seek to redistribute that unjust enrichment. Seen in this light, their fairness—the moral rightness of racial preference for societal re-balancing—cannot be denied." So reasons the ACLU explicitly, and many other honest citizens implicitly, in giving pained approval to race quotas.

The argument fails utterly upon inspection. It relies upon a premise that is clearly and admittedly false in the *Weber* case and like cases. And were all its premises true, they could still not justify the racial preference here in question.

Consider the premises first. The adverse impact on Weber is held justifiable by his unjust enrichment resulting from the bad conduct of others. But if Weber were in any way the beneficiary of past discrimina-tion, he certainly was not unjustly enriched by employment discrimination in the Gramercy plant. In that plant, it is agreed by advocates of the quota and by the courts, there had been no refusal to hire or promote blacks or other minorities, no racial discrimination from which Weber benefited. But the injustice done to Weber is manifested in the loss of entitlements he earned by ten years of work *in that plant*—not in the Kaiser Corporation or in the workforce at large. His entitlements in this matter cannot have been acquired as the result of the historical miscon-duct of others. Long before Weber came to work at that plant, blacks and whites received equal employment treatment there—so the claim that simply by virtue of his having the seniority that he did in the Gram-ercy plant Weber was enjoying an unjust enrichment is simply false. That false premise cannot justify "redistribution." The Circuit Court put the matter crisply: "Whatever other effects societal discrimination may have, it has had—by the specific finding of the court below—*no effect* on the seniority of any party here. It is therefore inappropriate to meddle with any party's seniority or with any perquisites attendant upon it, since none has obtained any unfair seniority advantage at the expense of any other" (p. 226).

But suppose *arguendo* (what is not true) that Weber had been un-fairly enriched by past racial discrimination. What would follow? The enrichment thus identified might then be a target for redistribution. Among whom? To take from Weber and give to another because Weber got his seniority "unjustly" could conceivably be justified (if ever) *only* if those to whom the redistribution were made were the same persons from whom the spoils had been taken in the first instance. The appealing argument by which so many are persuaded makes the faulty supposition that if X has gained fortuitously but undeservedly from some uniden-tifiable Y, we are morally justified in taking from him and giving to a wholly different Z who suffered no loss to X's benefit, but who happens to be of the same *race* as that injured but unidentifiable Y. Buried in this reasoning process is the mistaken premise that the distribution of goods or opportunities is rightly made by racial categories. Z, the person now given preference over X because of race, has a right to get from him (this premise supposes) because Z is black, and blacks have been so long oppressed. But rights do not and cannot inhere in skin-color groups. Individuals have rights, not races. It is true, of course, that many persons have been cruelly deprived of rights simply because of their blackness. Whatever the remedy all such persons deserve, it is deserved by those injured and because of their injury; nothing is deserved because of the color of one's skin. This is the philosophical nub of the *Weber* case.

V

So long-lasting and self-perpetuating have been the damages done to many blacks and others by discrimination that some corrective steps must be undertaken. The moral anxiety created by this need for affirmative action accounts, in part, for the willingness of some to tolerate outright racial quotas. In the passion to make social restitution, sensitive and otherwise fair-minded people have gotten the moral claims of living persons badly confused. The head of the Office of Federal Contract Compliance (by whom, as we shall see, Kaiser was threatened) epitomizes this confusion: "Society is trying to correct an age-old problem, and Weber is a victim of that process. There is nothing I can say to him. This is something that has to happen. The question is whether you give priority to a group that's been systematically deprived of opportunity while Brian Weber's parents and grandparents were not discriminated against. If someone has to bear the sins of the fathers, surely it has to be their children" (New York *Times Magazine,* February 25, 1979).

But deliberately visiting the sins of the fathers upon their innocent sons and grandsons, to the special advantage of persons not connected with the original sinning, is conduct neither lawful nor morally right. To suppose that both the beneficiaries of redress and those who are made to carry its burden are properly identified by race is, to be plain, racism. It is ethical racism because supposed with good will. It is simplistic because, on this view, race by itself—without consideration of the nature or degrees of past injuries, present advantages, or future pains—is sufficient to trigger the preferential device. The mistaken view in question is therefore properly entitled *simplistic ethical racism.*

Injuries are suffered in fact, claims made and burdens carried, by individual persons. Civil society is constituted to protect the rights of individuals; the sacrifice of fundamental individual rights cannot be justified by the desire to advance the well-being of any ethnic group. Precisely such justification is precluded by the Fourteenth Amendment of our Constitution, whose words—no state "shall deny to any person within its jurisdiction the equal protection of the laws"—express no mere legalism but a philosophical principle of the deepest importance. Explicating that clause, in a now famous passage, the Supreme Court wrote: "The rights created by the first section of the Fourteenth Amendment are, by its terms, guaranteed to the individual. The rights established are personal rights. . . . Equal protection of the laws is not advanced through indiscriminate imposition of inequalities (*Shelly* v. *Kraemer* 334 U.S. 1, 22 [1948]).

The nature and degree of the injury done to many Americans because they were black or brown or yellow varies greatly from case to case. Some such injuries may justify compensatory advantage now to those injured. But the calculation of who is due what from whom is a very sticky business; compensatory instruments are likely to compound injustice unless the individual circumstances of all involved—those who were originally hurt, those who benefit now, and those who will bear the cost—are carefully considered. Whatever compensatory advantage may be given—in employment or elsewhere—it must be given to all and only those who have suffered like injury, without regard to their race. What we may not do, constitutionally or morally, is announce in effect: "No matter that you, X, were innocent and gained no advantage; you are white and therefore lose points. No matter whether you, Z, were damaged or not; you are black and therefore gain points." If the moral ground for compensatory affirmative action is the redress of injury, the uninjured have no claim to it, and all those individuals of whatever ethnic group who have suffered the injury in question have an equal claim to it.

Racially based numerical instruments have this grave and unavoidable defect: they cannot make the morally crucial distinctions between the blameworthy and the blameless, between the deserving and the undeserving. As compensatory devices they are under-inclusive in failing to remedy the same damage when it has been done to persons of the non-favored races; they are over-inclusive in benefiting some in the favored categories who are without claims, often at substantial cost to innocent persons. Except in those cases where the discriminatory policy of the employer is established, and the identity of injured applicants or employees determinable, racial preference in employment is intolerably blunt, incapable of respecting the rights of individuals.

VI

This unsuitability of the racial means to the compensatory end partly explains the queasiness of language with which the advocates of "numerical instruments" defend their schemes. Although they believe their aims are good, there is yet widespread shame among them that they resort to racial preference to advance them. Hence the use of euphemisms like "disadvantaged" in identifying the beneficiaries of racial programs, when what is really meant is "black" or "minority." Not all minorities are disadvantaged, and not all those disadvantaged are minorities, obviously. But it is tempting to hide the racial character of a program which, if exposed, would be legally and morally intolerable.[3]

"Affirmative action"—a phrase that now pervades our language—has commonly been used in the same duplicitous way. Affirmative steps to eliminate racially discriminatory practices rightly win the assent of all. Affirmative efforts to recruit fairly (whether for on-the-job training pro-

[3] In the original trial of the *Bakke* case, the University of California defended the racial quotas at the Davis medical school as being for all "disadvantaged" students. When the court noted that not a single disadvantaged person who was not of an ethnic minority had been admitted in all the years of that program's operation, the university in effect conceded the misdescription. Not a pretty business.

grams or for professional schools), affirmative inquiry to determine whether testing is job-related and to insure that evaluation of performance is not racially infected—in such forms affirmative action is of unquestionable merit. But when, in the name of affirmative action for racial equality, the deliberately unequal treatment of the races is introduced, we suffer a national epidemic of double-speak. Employment advertisements everywhere exhibit this duplicity with an almost ritualized motto: "An equal opportunity/affirmative action employer." The very term "affirmative action" has lost its honor and has become, for most, a euphemism for racial preference.

The unsavory character of their means is recognized by the advocates of racial instruments; that recognition is revealed by an inclination to be covert in conduct and to equivocate in language. Unsavoriness is tolerated here, however, even by organizations whose normal pride it is to expose immoral expedience in the body politic. Nothing is more indicative of the true spirit of a community than the character of the instruments it permits, and of those it precludes, in advancing public policy. Police surveillance to root out spies, the suppression of speech (radical or conservative) to protect the peace—all such instruments are rejected in a decent society. Civil libertarians wisely insist that we forswear instruments that invade the rights of individuals, even when forswearing proves inconvenient. The use of such instruments is precluded, forbidden not just to evil people but to all people. Preference by race is one of these forbidden instruments. The very high priority given to this exclusionary principle, and its applicability to all including the state itself, marks it as *constitutional* in the most profound sense.

Efforts to cut constitutional corners—however well-intentioned—corrupt a civil society. The means we use penetrate the ends we achieve; when the instrument is unjust, the outcome will be infected by that injustice. This lesson even civil libertarians have always to be relearning.

VII

The inconsistency between racially preferential means and the end of honestly equal treatment is exquisitely exhibited in one aspect of the *Weber* case upon which Kaiser and the union place much emphasis. "We are caught [say they] in a monstrous double bind. What will you have us do? Desegregate, you say. Integrate your workforce; show us that you mean to undo, affirmatively, the wrongs earlier done. We do it, making serious efforts to increase the number of minorities in craft jobs through advertisement, recruitment, encouragement. We get some results, but they are not dramatic. Then you—the nation speaking through your regulatory agencies—tell us that what we have done is not enough. You threaten us! Of course we take action in response to your threat—and having done so, we are threatened at law on the other side! Such inconsistency is unbearable. You, the body politic, must speak with one tongue!"

What is that first threat of which Kaiser complains? It came from the Office of Federal Contract Compliance whose regulations mandate "affirmative action" by all government contractors. The withdrawal of all federal contracts was the price Kaiser might have had to pay if, to avoid being found in "non-compliance," racial preference for minorities had not been introduced. Whence does the OFCC get the authority to make such threats? From an order of the President of the United States, say they, Executive Order 11246. This order requires federal contractors to take affirmative action to prevent low employment of women and minorities in their workforces, on the assumption that most disproportionately low employment is the result of discrimination. Since the racial instrument agreed upon was a direct response to federal authority exercised under that valid order, it is outrageous now, say Kaiser and the union, to attack us for violation of the Civil Rights Act.

This response to official inconsistency cannot help but evoke some sympathy. But as a defense of racial quotas it is worthless. The argument fails on two levels. First, Executive Order 11246 does not require and cannot justify racial quotas in cases like this one, in which the conduct of the employer has not been unlawfully discriminatory. The Order says nothing about numerical ratios. Indeed, its plain words *forbid* all racial preference. The relevant passage of that Order reads: "The contractor will take affirmative action to insure that applicants are employed, and that employees are treated during employment, without regard to their race, color, religion, sex, or national origin" (30 Fed. Reg. 12319 [1965]).

Some numerical plans to protect employment for minorities have been upheld by the courts as valid executive actions—but they have been so upheld as responses to specifically identified violations by those upon whom the remedy was imposed. The so-called Philadelphia Plan was held permissible under Title VII, but that holding was explicitly tied to prior exclusionary practices by the six trade unions controlling the workforce in the construction industry in Philadelphia. Whatever tools the Office of Federal Contract Compliance may think itself entitled to employ, it has no authority in law, and certainly none in morals, to press for a racial quota in cases where, as here, those getting preference under the scheme had not been injured by that employer, and those injured by the scheme had not benefited from any misconduct of that employer.

The argument fails at a second level as well. If Executive Order 11246 be interpreted so as to authorize the OFCC to require racial quotas in cases like this one, the Executive Order itself is plainly unlawful, an illegitimate exercise of administrative authority in conflict with federal statute. The Civil Rights Act specifically prohibits racial classification in admission to on-the-job training programs (Sect. 703(d); cited above, p. 41). The quota plan devised by Kaiser and the union is, as we have seen, patently in violation of this section. When the law and an executive order clash, there can be no doubt of the outcome. Writes the Circuit Court: "If Executive Order 11246 mandates a racial quota for admission to on-the-job training by Kaiser, *in the absence of any prior hiring or promotion discrimination,* the executive order must fall before this direct congressional prohibition" (p. 227).

Only by resolutely enforcing the rights of citizens can the insolence of office be restrained. Individual workers, without power or money, need to be protected against civil servants who take it upon themselves to threaten in order to be able to report numerical ratios they think desirable, claiming only to be following the orders of their superiors.

VIII

Defenses of racial preference—by efforts to reinterpret the law, by confused arguments based on "societal discrimination," by claim of executive order—all collapse. It is important to see why they *should* collapse. The defenders, conscious of their own righteous pursuit of racial justice, little doubt that the tools they wish to employ would have the good consequences they hope for. To question the merit of those tools is for them almost a betrayal of the oppressed in whose behalf they claim to battle. In their eyes the conflict is only over whether they are to be permitted to do a good deed—i.e., give preference to racial minorities— not whether it is a good deed, or whether its consequences will be good.

Decency of motivation, however, does not insure the goodness of the immediate object, or the goodness of its consequences. Racial justice is an aim that all share; it is distorted when transformed into formulas for ethnic proportionality in workforces and professions based (as in this case) upon ethnic populations in the surrounding area. What accounts for this transformation? Motives honorable in their general statement are blended with a vision of cultural homogeneity that is profoundly unhealthy. The objectives then sought in making that blend operational often prove inconsistent with the original aim. It is this inchoate vision of homogeneity—made concrete in numerical proportions—that lies behind racial instruments like the one at issue in *Weber*. Federal Appellate Courts have not been oblivious to the evils that ensue:

> There are good reasons why the use of racial criteria should be strictly scrutinized and given legal sanction only where a compelling need for remedial action can be shown. . . . Government recognition and sanction of racial classifications may be inherently divisive, reinforcing prejudices, confirming perceived differences between the races, and weakening the government's educative role on behalf of equality and neutrality. It may also have unexpected results, such as the development of indicia for placing individuals into different racial categories. Once racial classifications are imbedded in the law, their purpose may become perverted: a benign preference under certain conditions may shade into malignant preference at other times. Moreover, a racial preference for members of one minority might result in discrimination against another minority, a higher proportion of whose members had previously enjoyed access to a certain opportunity [*Associated General Contractors of Massachusetts Inc.* v. *Altshuler* 490 F. 2d 9, 17-18 (1973)].

In this spirit three Federal Circuit Courts have repeatedly refused to approve racial quotas in the absence of proved past discriminatory practice dictating that specific remedy.

Racial classifications have insidious long-term results: anger and envy flowing from rewards or penalties based on race; solidification of racial barriers and the encouragement of racial separatism; inappropriate entry of race into unrelated intellectual or economic matters; the indirect support of condescension and invidious judgments among ethnic groups—in sum, the promotion of all the conditions that produce racial *dis*harmony and racial *dis*integration. What Kaiser and the union defend is very far from an innocuous good deed. It is a plan having very damaging consequences to very many people.

Some of the damage, direct and substantial, is done to those, like Weber and Bakke, who bear the immediately resulting burden. "Society" does not pay; the "white majority" does not pay; individual citizens pay. The penalty to them is great and undeserved. One notable feature of the *Bakke* decision, almost entirely overlooked by commentators and the press, is the fact that all nine Supreme Court Justices there agreed that, as a result of the quota system used by the medical school at Davis, Allan Bakke was done a constitutional injury—that is, an injury he should not have to suffer unless it can be well justified. Even the four Justices who thought the injury could be justified took the hurt done to him very seriously. One of those four (that is, one of the group who did *not* side with Bakke), Justice Blackmun, refers to the injury done to Bakke as an "ugly" one. The other five Justices struck down that racially preferential program; Powell among them condemns the damage such programs do. The Washington Supreme Court, too, in deciding against Marco DeFunis in an analogous case, did not deny that he had been seriously hurt, and candidly rejected the claim that such quotas are "benign." A program giving special favor to racial minorities, say they, "is certainly not benign with respect to nonminority students replaced by it" (*DeFunis* v. *Odegaard* 507 P. 2d 1182). *Reverse discrimination* is not an invention or a hypothesis yet to be confirmed; it is a sociological and legal fact.

IX

The reality of the evils flowing from racial instruments introduces one of the most intriguing aspects of the *Weber* case. A dispute arises between the District and the Circuit Court beneath which lies a momentous philosophical issue. Numerical remedies based on race do damage, the two courts agree; they further agree that this is a case in which the imposition of such a numerical remedy cannot be justified because there has been, in fact, no previous unlawful discrimination by the employer here. However, in those cases in which such remedy might prove justifiable (previous discriminatory practice in that setting being alleged), the following question arises: may that numerical instrument of redress be devised and executed on the authority of the employer and union acting jointly? Or is a racial quota permissible as remedy only on the express authority of the judiciary? The District Court not only found the remedy unjustifiable, but held in addition that such painful remedies would in no case be in the province of unions and management to impose. The Circuit Court, agreeing on the first point, did not agree on the second. Voluntary remedial action (said they) is preferable to court action; therefore, to insist upon judicial imposition of remedies would interfere unduly with reasonable private amelioration. The underlying issue here is the locus of authority in resolving questions of justice. Which court is the wiser?

In permitting numerical remedies to be imposed (if at all) only by the judiciary, the District Court, I submit, is deeply right. The reasons for this are several and complicated.

First, the question of whether the circumstances are such as to justify the imposition of a numerical remedy (a question that must be answered affirmatively if any such remedy is to be lawful) is precisely the kind of question that cannot be answered fairly by employers and unions acting in their joint interests. Individuals will bear the burden; if the case were of a kind to justify the imposition of that burden on Weber and his like, past discrimination by that employer in that context must be proved or admitted. No employer is likely to make that admission. To do so would invite a host of very expensive lawsuits in behalf of those injured. Employers will therefore enter such agreements only with the understanding that no past discrimination has been proved or admitted. That very understanding (however arguable it may be) on which an employer might be willing to enter an agreement with a union to give racial preference to minorities is precisely the understanding which, if reflecting the facts truly, shows that racial preference unjustly injurious and unlawful.

This peculiar feature of "voluntary" racial instruments is admitted—even emphasized, ironically—by the UAW, the NEA, and other assorted unions. If (they argue) voluntary racial preference is permissible only when the employer's past conduct would be found in violation of Title VII, there will be no voluntary race-conscious action. For, as they agree: "[I]t is usually difficult to predict whether or not [previous] discrimination would be found" (associated unions, brief amici, p. 13). Indeed! For this reason precisely it is a question of such a kind that no answer to it reached as part of a labor-management agreement could be trusted.

The aggregated unions continue: "Moreover, the employer would, by taking voluntary action, put itself in a no-win situation in a suit such as this. Either its past conduct will be determined to be unlawful, thereby inviting litigation by discriminatees, or the remedial action will be found unlawful, and liability to white employees will exist" (ibid.). Just so! But the authors of this candid statement apparently do not see where their argument leads. They would like the courts to conclude that, since the present standard (that "voluntary" racial quotas suppose the same finding of unlawful discrimination which alone might justify court-imposed remedies) effectively precludes "voluntary" quotas altogether, we should permit the introduction of a new standard, one that would allow "voluntary" quotas under some factual circumstances that—as they admit—would not justify a court in imposing them! What could serve as such a standard? The lone dissenting judge of the Circuit Court, pursuing the same line, is driven to propose an astounding answer: A "voluntary" quota plan should be upheld, he suggests, if it is "a *reasonable remedy* for an *arguable violation* of Title VII" (p. 230, emphasis added).

This standard is neither feasible in practice, nor morally acceptable if it were. As a practical matter, such notions as "reasonable remedy" and "arguable violation" have virtually no objective content. Only the courts could resolve, on a case-by-case basis, disputed claims about "arguable violations" and about the reasonableness of remedy. Endless litigation could not be avoided—but it is the elimination of time-consuming litigation that is alleged to be the great merit of "voluntary" racial instruments. The increase in court involvement that would result undercuts any proposed justification of "voluntary" quotas on grounds of efficiency.

More important than its inefficiency, however, is the fact that the proposed standard (that a voluntary quota plan should be upheld if it is "a reasonable remedy for an arguable violation of Title VII") is morally unacceptable. Just remedies presuppose some determinable wrongs for which they give redress and by which they are justified. It is confusion of mind to propose a *remedy* for an *arguable* violation; one cannot put right what might prove on more judicious examination to have been no wrong at all.

All "voluntary" quotas (i.e., those introduced without court imposition) presuppose reliance upon some standard that must encounter essentially the same problem. The philosophical dimensions of the dispute between the two courts here emerge. The Circuit Court's position exhibits irremedial moral defect: by permitting racially preferential programs without the backing of judicial authority, it permits the delegation of questions of justice to private hands that are neither equipped, nor disposed, nor authorized to resolve them fairly.

To resolve a matter of individual right the bargaining process between labor and management is almost the worst imaginable tool. The impartial determination of facts without regard to interest, and the honest application of principles without regard to advantage, are essential in adjudicating questions of right—but the elimination of regard for self-interest and advantage is precisely what is impossible at the bargaining table.

Even if the needed impartiality were possible there, it would be inappropriate, uncommon, and surely could not be relied upon. Union and management bargainers are duty-bound to press for the advantage of the units they represent. The process is designed to deal with issues of pay and working conditions, not with the protection of individual rights. Justice entails giving to each his due—whether or not he or others can negotiate for it successfully.

Most important, the authority to resolve questions of justice cannot lie in a labor-management bargain. Individual rights *may not*—as a matter of law or morals—be bargained away. As a matter of constitutional principle, the Supreme Court has spoken definitively on this issue. A union, they agree, may waive some of its rights to *collective* activity, such as the right to strike, in a bargaining agreement made with the aim of economic advantage for its members. The Court continues:

Title VII, on the other hand, stands on plainly different ground; *it concerns not majoritarian processes, but an individual's right to equal employment opportunities.* Title VII's strictures are absolute and represent a congressional command that *each* employee be free from discriminatory practices. Of necessity, *the rights conferred can form no part of the collective bargaining process* since waiver of these rights would defeat the paramount congressional purpose behind Title VII. In these circumstances, an employee's rights under Title VII are not susceptible of prospective waiver [*Alexander v. Gardner-Denver Co.* 415 U.S. 36, 51–52 (1974), emphasis added].

Contracts reached through collective bargaining may, of course, introduce different terms of employment for different groups of employees in the light of the relevant conditions of those groups. Race, however, is never relevant in that sense. Because racial discrimination invariably touches the non-bargainable rights of all individuals adversely affected, race itself has been identified as an inappropriate criterion for the classification of employees.[4]

In sum: the courts have repeatedly held that, in compromising with an employer, a union may not take race into account. Programs like the one at issue in *Weber* explicitly take race into account. The conclusion of this syllogism is inescapable.

The unions take another tack. "You fail to note [they rejoin in effect] that this is a *voluntary* program. Weber and his fellows may be said to have relinquished their rights in this matter because, when the plan was devised, they were adequately represented by their union. The union has a duty to represent all of its members; its bargainers are selected democratically; and since white workers constitute a majority of the bargaining unit, the union process may be relied upon to reach no agreement that will violate the rights of individual white members."

It is hard to take this argument seriously. Union process is often genuinely democratic; negotiators for unions generally do seek to represent the interests of all the members of the bargaining unit. But the most sympathetic review of union process could not rationally conclude that the fairness of unions to their members over the long term has been such as to justify the delegation, to bargainers, of matters of fundamental individual right. The current flow of complaints about reverse discrimination in employment contracts in itself provides substantial evidence that the bargaining process, notwithstanding its general fairness, cannot be depended upon in this sphere. "Voluntary" is an appealing word. But its use here suggests what is not true—that those who were injured by the racial instruments devised in the contract did themselves volunteer to carry the burden. To call Weber's sacrifice "voluntary" is most inappropriate.

---

[4] The Supreme Court has written: "[T]he statutory power to represent a craft and to make contracts as to wages, hours, and working conditions does not include the authority to make among members of the craft discriminations not based on such relevant differences. Here the discriminations based on race alone are obviously irrelevant and invidious. Congress plainly did not undertake to authorize the bargaining representative to make such discriminations" *Steele* v. *Louisville & Nashville R.R. Co.,* 323 U.S. 192, 203 (1944).

This defense of "voluntary" racial instruments (even if unions were invariably sensitive to matters of individual right) avoids the key question of legitimate authority. At stake here are the rights of individuals to the most fundamental of democratic conditions—equal treatment under the law—and, moreover, their rights to that equal treatment as it bears upon the most suspect of all categorical distinctions, race. Even legislators, it may be argued, however powerful their assembly, honorable their election, and dutiful their conduct, may not take from individual citizens certain fundamental rights. With the noblest of intentions, it is not within their authority to pursue public policy at the cost of compromising the individual citizen's right not to be discriminated against because of his race or religion. Philosophers will differ about the grounds of legislative authority, but few will seriously deny that upon such authority there must be some hard limits. Unequal treatment because of race is as clear an example as there is of the violation of those limits.

If the principle here expressed were somehow mistaken, if it were sometimes just, in the cause of racial redress, to sacrifice the rights of some blameless non-beneficiaries to advantage others who had not been injured, even so it would at least be certain that no such decision could be properly made by any save the legislature of highest authority, subject to the review of the court of highest jurisdiction. The notion that, to encourage "voluntary affirmative-action plans," we may bypass the body politic, investing unions and management with the authority to bargain with fundamental human rights, makes the prospect of a reversal in the *Weber* case very distressing. Not substantive entitlements alone are at issue here, but also the procedural rights of working people to have questions of justice decided by legislatures and courts.

X

Weber and *Bakke* are closely analogous in this procedural regard. Weber's right to equal treatment was infringed on by a union-management agreement, Bakke's by a medical-school admissions committee. Legitimate authority was exceeded in both cases. When it was asked, in *Bakke,* for what purposes a university might consider race in admissions, Justice Powell replied, in his decisive opinion, that it may be considered for the sake of student diversity (to support the exchange of ideas in accord with First Amendment concerns), or, conceivably, as redress for the specific victims of specific injustices. "Societal discrimination" as a ground for racial preference he explicitly considered and rejected. Powell wrote:

> We [i.e., the Supreme Court] have never approved a classification that aids persons perceived as members of relatively victimized groups at the expense of other innocent individuals, in the absence of judicial, legislative, or administrative findings of constitutional or statutory violations [references omitted]. After such findings have been made, the governmental interest in preferring members of the injured groups at the expense of others is substantial, since the legal rights of the victims must

be vindicated. In such a case the extent of the injury and the consequent remedy will have been judicially, legislatively, or administratively defined. Also, the remedial action usually remains subject to continuing oversight to assure that it will work the least harm possible to other innocent persons competing for the benefit. Without such findings of constitutional or statutory violations it cannot be said that the government has any greater interest in helping one individual than in refraining from harming another. Thus the government has no compelling justification for inflicting such harm [*University of California Regents* v. *Bakke* 57 L. Ed. 2d 750, 782-83 (1978)].

But findings of constitutional or statutory violations it is not the business of private bodies—unions, or managements, or medical-school committees—to make. Powell continued:

Petitioner [the Regents of the University] does not purport to have made, *and is in no position to make,* such findings. . . . [Even] isolated segments of our vast governmental structures are not competent to make those decisions, at least in the absence of legislative mandates and legislatively determined criteria [references omitted]. Before relying upon these sorts of findings in establishing a racial classification, a governmental body must have the authority and capability to establish, in the record, that the classification is responsive to identified discrimination (p. 783; emphasis added).

Powell's point is that a medical-school admissions committee (even though indirectly an agent of the state) is entirely without the requisite authority. Kaiser and the union have a far weaker claim to the needed authority than did they. An admissions committee is not competent to make the findings that might justify racial preference, granted. But if the admissions committee had sought to present such findings of identified discrimination at the Davis medical school (discrimination that, in fact, the university specifically denies), they might conceivably contend that as one agent of one arm of one element of the state, it was within their province to do so—and thus might conceivably seek to justify their racial program as remedy. That claim must fail, the mission of the medical school and all its subsidiary elements being educative, not judicial. Any analogous claim made by Kaiser and the union—that they are authorized to make findings of "societal discrimination" that will justify inflicting harm on Weber and other blameless parties—is totally without warrant.

XI

In the absence of any showing or admission of previous illegal discrimination at the Gramercy plant, every defense of racially preferential remedy must prove unsatisfactory. Sensitive to this point, the American Civil Liberties Union argues at length that the factual circumstances of this case have been misunderstood, that Kaiser Aluminum *did* discriminate against minorities. The pattern of employment by Kaiser at other

plants in earlier years is reviewed, and much is made of the racially disproportionate impact, at the Gramercy plant, of a "purportedly neutral
criterion." Using the percentage of the minority population in the surrounding parishes of Louisiana as benchmark,[5] the argument concludes
that Kaiser's workforce at the Gramercy plant in skilled-craft positions
was "severely underrepresentative." Putting aside the question of how
"representativeness" might rationally be established, or, if it had been
established, what bearing that would have upon the lawfulness of Kaiser's
previous conduct, it is important to note that the entire thrust of this
argument is misdirected. The *Weber* case presents an appeal to our highest court on a matter of fundamental principle. That principle must be
argued on the basis of a factual record properly established at trial in a
responsible Federal District Court. Appellate Courts, and the Supreme
Court, face the question of principle *given that record*. Even the District
Court could analyze only the facts brought before it by the parties.
Kaiser testified to its non-discriminatory practices at the Gramercy
plant from its opening, and of its efforts to recruit black craftsmen from
the general community. They would not and could not report otherwise. If (as some now claim) the record should have shown hidden unlawful
conduct by Kaiser, such findings could only have entered the record at
the trial level. At this point the issue is, supposing the record complete
and accurate, whether, *without* such previous violations established, this
racial quota is permissible.

To contend that the facts of the matter *could* be viewed differently
is to blind oneself to the essence of the controversy. Had the courts found,
after examining all testimony, that Kaiser had previously discriminated
against minorities in its Gramercy plant, the issue now to be decided
here would not even have arisen.[6]

XII

All arguments thus far explored incorporate the realization that individuals are indeed injured when disadvantaged solely because of their
race. Brian Weber did not get the job-training opportunity he was entitled to. Most ordinary people, and most judges, have no difficulty in
seeing that. So zealous are some of the advocates of racial preference,
however, that they claim not to see it. Weber was never really hurt, say
they. He has a legitimate complaint only if he was discriminated against
unfairly. But he wasn't discriminated against at all! Hence he has no
case.

[5] ACLU and Society of American Law Teachers, brief *amici*, p. 11. The inappropriate-
ness of such figures in estimating fairness with respect to employment in the skilled
crafts is so obvious, and has been so often remarked, that one is embarrassed for the
ACLU to find such an argument here pursued. See Thomas Sowell, "Are Quotas Good
for Blacks?," COMMENTARY, June 1978.

[6] Might an appellate court not reverse an inferior court because of its mistaken interpretation of the facts as appearing in the record? Only in those rare circumstances
in which the treatment of the facts by the inferior court was "clearly erroneous." That
claim would be untenable in this case.

Puzzling though this claim appears on its face, it is honestly defended, in two ways. First, it is argued, Weber has lost nothing more than seniority entitlements. But seniority systems may be altered by labor-management agreement, and in any event, seniority rights are not vested in the individual employee but in the collective-bargaining unit. Therefore, when a voluntary quota plan results in Weber's getting less than he expected in view of his greater seniority, he loses nothing that belonged to him in the first place. The injury done to him (it is contended) is apparent, not real.

This argument is twice faulty. It underplays the importance of individual seniority entitlements in the industrial context; and it does not face up to the discriminatory nature of the seniority deprivation in this case.

In allocating scarce opportunities and goods in the industrial world, seniority is critically important. For very many workers a host of matters—job security, opportunities for advanced training, vacation and retirement benefits—depend chiefly upon the number of years of service they have given. Nothing remains to them after years of service but their seniority claims. To deny that harm is done to an unskilled worker on an hourly wage when he is deprived of entitlements flowing normally from ten years' seniority shows gross moral insensitivity. Seniority does not insure qualification for positions demanding special talents, of course; but where qualifications are roughly equal, or not distinguishable, seniority above all other considerations will be relied upon in the interests of fairness.

Seniority entitlements are tied to individuals, not just to the bargaining unit. In matters of job assignment, transfer, layoff and recall, and job training, opportunities must be distributed among competing employees. Competitive-status seniority is therefore of great moral as well as practical importance, and directly affects individuals more importantly than it does the bargaining collective. Non-competitive benefits also—pensions, sick leave, paid vacations—are commonly determined in part by length of service and therefore must be tied to individuals. Seniority, the Supreme Court writes, "has become of overriding importance, and one of its major functions is to determine who gets or who keeps an available job" (*Humphrey* v. *Moore* 375 U.S. 335, 346–47 [1964]). The "who" in this passage refers to individual persons, not to groups.

Seniority systems are bargainable, true. It does not follow, however, that all seniority rights are bargainable. It is essential not to confuse the *system* of seniority with individual *entitlements* under a given system in force. Once a seniority system has become a reality in rule and practice, a worker's rights and expectations under that system are his and very precious to him. It is callous to minimize the injury done when such rights are not respected.

When the ground of that disrespect is race, the injury is particularly offensive. Entitlements in themselves minor (which an opportunity for on-the-job training is not) become matters of grave concern when manipulated for racial reasons. Where one must sit on a bus or go to the toilet understandably becomes a source of rage and an issue of constitutional proportions when the determination is made by race. Protests over segregated lunch counters had as their target not the culinary opportunities denied, but the immoral character of the ground of their denial. Even if Weber's seniority expectations be thought trivial, the racial ground of the unequal treatment he received is very far from trivial.

Some who understand very clearly why Allan Bakke was injured when excluded from medical school in a racially discriminatory way fail to see that the injury done to Brian Weber is equally unjust. Applicants to a competitive program, they appreciate, have a right to evaluation on some set of relevant criteria—past performance, intellectual promise, character, or whatever—and if deserving on the basis of those criteria, ought not be deprived of place because of race. But if the performance qualifications of all applicants are roughly equal (as were those of Weber and the minority workers chosen in his place), where, they ask, is the injustice?

The injustice lies in the deprivation, on improper grounds, of what one is otherwise entitled to. The basis for the entitlement will be different in different contexts. Scarce places in medical or law schools are rightly allocated to persons best exhibiting the characteristics that have been determined relevant to the studies or profession to be pursued. Scarce on-the-job training opportunities are rightly allocated to those having certain seniority entitlements. The bases of Weber's and Bakke's claims to that of which they were deprived are very different; but both were wrongly denied what they would have received if the scarce available goods had been distributed in accord with established criteria in a morally just way. Both were the plain victims of racial discrimination, losing out because of the color of their skin.

Persons concerned about such injustice when done in the academic world ought seriously to consider the wisdom of remaining silent when essentially the same injustice (although with respect to different entitlements) is done in the industrial world. If preference by race should be found, in the *Weber* case, to justify the deprivation of what is fairly earned by a laborer, the security of what is fairly earned by anyone in any sphere is similarly threatened.

XIII

If the damage to Weber cannot reasonably be minimized, can it be wholly denied? This is the second line of defense to which Kaiser and the union fall back in the effort to show that Weber was not discriminated against at all. Weber's rights were not infringed on, they say, because he never had any seniority rights to job training here. The argument goes like this: "Where admission to a training program is properly a function of seniority, and seniority, like Weber's, is untainted by the employer's previous discrimination, he would be damaged if race were allowed to supervene. But Weber errs in thinking that seniority gives him any claim under *this* quota program, which was initiated in 1974, by Kaiser and the union, specifically to increase minority representation in the craft employments. New rights were then created, Kaiser and the union agreeing to use seniority only for the distribution of available slots *within* the two racial lists, black and white. If, in the new plan, they had agreed to use the lottery method—two separate lotteries, one for whites and one for blacks—it would be obvious that seniority was not the real issue here. They could have done just that. Weber's claim that he was deprived of seniority rights is a red herring, because the mode of selecting from each racial pool is irrelevant. So the Kaiser plan, as the dissenting judge wrote, 'stands or falls on its separation of workers into two racial pools for assignment to job training' (p. 235)."

This argument is a compound of perceptivity and blindness. Seniority was the system deliberately adopted by Kaiser and the union—but they did not make that choice at random. Years of past work in the very plant where those training opportunities were to arise was thought the fairest consideration in allocating scarce places to otherwise equally qualified workers. Seniority was adopted as a relevant and rational principle. To create two seniority lists, black and white, and then choose the top person from each list, even if he has less seniority than the fourth or twentieth person on the other list, is to override the seniority principle with race. If the basis chosen for the fair distribution of scarce opportunities had not been seniority, but (say) a lottery, then the just application of the lottery principle would require that *it* not be overridden by race. It is therefore perceptive to note that the real issue here goes beyond seniority—that the plan fails simply because it separates the workers into two *racial* pools—every such separation being necessarily invidious. Any system used to distribute opportunities among the members of each racial pool, even if of itself fair, must be distorted by that antecedent racial classification. Whatever besides seniority might prove just as a ground for the distribution of goods, skin color isn't it.

Is it correct to say, then, that Weber had no seniority rights at all? No. When it is agreed by union and employer that, for allocating these job-training opportunities, length of service is the appropriate basis, employees acquire entitlements on that basis. The injustice of racial favoritism manifests itself, in this case, in the deprivation of those entitlements. Were a worker's entitlements based on some other feature of his circumstances—his experience or his performance on a competitive examination—then the injustice of racial favoritism might be manifested in the deprivation of entitlements flowing from those. Weber has a right to non-discriminatory treatment. To contend that he never had any rights in this matter because the respect in which he was discriminated against isn't the only respect in which he might have been discriminated against is a last-ditch effort to obscure the wrong that was done him.

XIV

The villain of the piece—here, in *Bakke,* wherever it raises its head—is preference by race. The *Weber* case provides an opportunity to reaffirm the moral and constitutional commitment to govern ourselves without preference to any by reason of color, or religion, or national origin. If we undermine that commitment—even though it be in an honest effort to do good—we will reap the whirlwind.

26 U.S. SUPREME COURT

UNITED STEELWORKERS OF AMERICA V. WEBER

443 U.S. 193 (1979)

[The facts of the case are summarized in Carl Cohen's article just preceding.]

MR. JUSTICE BRENNAN delivered the opinion of the Court.

. . .

II

We emphasize at the outset the narrowness of our inquiry. Since the Kaiser-USWA plan does not involve state action, this case does not present an alleged violation of the Equal Protection Clause of the Constitution. Further, since the Kaiser-USWA plan was adopted voluntarily, we are not concerned with what Title VII requires or with what a court might order to remedy a past proven violation of the Act. The only question before us is the narrow statutory issue of whether Title VII *forbids* private employers and unions from voluntarily agreeing upon bona fide affirmative action plans that accord racial preferences in the manner and for the purpose provided in the Kaiser-USWA plan. That question was expressly left open in *McDonald* v. *Santa Fe Trail Trans. Co.*, 427 U.S. 273, 281 n. 8 (1976) which held, in a case not involving affirmative action, that Title VII protects whites as well as blacks from certain forms of racial discrimination.

Respondent argues that Congress intended in Title VII to prohibit all race-conscious affirmative action plans. Respondent's argument rests upon a literal interpretation of §§ 703 (a) and (d) of the Act. Those sections make it unlawful to "discriminate . . . because of . . . race" in hiring and in the selection of apprentices for training programs. Since, the argument runs, *McDonald* v. *Santa Fe Trans. Co., supra,* settled that Title VII forbids discrimination against whites as well as blacks, and since the Kaiser-USWA affirmative action plan operates to discriminate against white employees solely because they are white, it follows that the Kaiser-USWA plan violates Title VII.

Respondent's argument is not without force. But it overlooks the significance of the fact that the Kaiser-USWA plan is an affirmative action plan voluntarily adopted by private parties to eliminate traditional patterns of racial segregation. In this context respondent's reliance upon a literal construction of § 703 (a) and (d) and upon *McDonald* is misplaced. It is a "familiar rule, that a thing may be within the letter of the statute and yet not within the statute, because not within its spirit, nor within the intention of its makers." The prohibition against racial discrimination in §§ 703 (a) and (d) of Title VII must therefore be read against the background of the legislative history of Title VII and the historical context from which the Act arose. Examination of those sources makes clear that an interpretation of the sections that forbade all race-conscious affirmative action would "bring about an end completely at variance with the purpose of the statute" and must be rejected.

Congress' primary concern in enacting the prohibition against racial discrimination in Title VII of the Civil Rights Act of 1964 was with "the plight of the Negro in our economy." 110 Cong. Rec. 6548 (remarks of Sen. Humphrey). Before 1964, blacks were largely relegated to "unskilled and semi-skilled jobs." Because of automation the number of such jobs was rapidly decreasing. As a consequence "the relative position of the Negro worker [was] steadily worsening. In 1947 the non-white unemployment rate was only 64 percent higher than the white rate; in 1962 it was 124 percent higher." Congress considered this a serious social problem. As Senator Clark told the Senate:

> The rate of Negro unemployment has gone up consistently as compared with white unemployment for the past 15 years. This is a social malaise and a social situation which we should not tolerate. That is one of the principal reasons why this bill should pass.

Congress feared that the goals of the Civil Rights Act— the integration of blacks into the mainstream of American society—could not be achieved unless this trend were reversed. And Congress recognized that that would not be possible unless blacks were able to secure jobs "which have a future." As Senator Humphrey explained to the Senate:

> What good does it do a Negro to be able to eat in a fine restaurant if he cannot afford to pay the bill? What good does it do him to be accepted in a hotel that is too expensive for his modest income? How can a Negro child be motivated to take full advantage of integrated educational facilities if he has no hope of getting a job where he can use that education?
>
> . . .
>
> Without a job, one cannot afford public convenience and accommodations. Income from employment may be necessary to further a man's education, or that of his children. If his children have no hope of getting a good job, what will motivate them to take advantage of educational opportunities.

These remarks echoed President Kennedy's original message to Congress upon the introduction of the Civil Rights Act in 1963.

> There is little value in a Negro's obtaining the right to be admitted to hotels and restaurants if he has no cash in his pocket and no job.

Accordingly, it was clear to Congress that "the crux of the problem [was] to open employment opportunities for Negroes in occupations which have been traditionally closed to them," and it was to this problem that Title VII's prohibition against racial discrimination in employment was primarily addressed.

It plainly appears from the House Report accompanying the Civil Rights Act that Congress did not intend wholly to prohibit private and voluntary affirmative action efforts as one method of solving this problem. The Report provides:

> No bill can or should lay claim to eliminating all of the causes and consequences of racial and other types of discrimination against minorities. There is reason to believe, however, that national leadership provided by the enactment of Federal legislation dealing with the most troublesome problems *will create an atmosphere conducive to voluntary or local resolution of other forms of discrimination.* (Emphasis supplied.)

Given this legislative history, we cannot agree with respondent that Congress intended to prohibit the private sector from taking effective steps to accomplish the goal that Congress designed Title VII to achieve. The very statutory words intended as a spur or catalyst to cause "employers and unions to self-examine and to self-evaluate their employment practices and to endeavor to eliminate, so far as possible, the last vestiges of an unfortunate and ignominious page in this country's history," cannot be interpreted as an absolute prohibition against all private, voluntary, race-conscious affirmative action efforts to hasten the elimination of such vestiges. It would be ironic indeed if a law triggered by a Nation's concern over centuries of racial injustice and intended to improve the lot of those who had "been excluded from the American dream for so long," constituted the first legislative prohibition of all voluntary, private, race-conscious efforts to abolish traditional patterns of racial segregation and hierarchy.

Our conclusion is further reinforced by examination of the language and legislative history of § 703 (j) of Title VII. Opponents of Title VII raised two related arguments against the bill. First, they argued that the Act would be interpreted to *require* employers with racially imbalanced work forces to grant preferential treatment to racial minorities in order to integrate. Second, they argued that employers with racially imbalanced work forces would grant preferential treatment to racial minorities, even if not required to do so by the Act. Had Congress meant to prohibit all race-conscious affirmative action, as respondent urges, it easily could have answered both objections by providing that Title VII would not require or *permit* racially preferential integration efforts. But Congress did not choose such a course. Rather Congress added § 703 (j) which addresses only the first objection. The section provides that nothing contained in Title VII "shall be interpreted to *require* any employer . . . to grant preferential treatment . . . to any group because of the race . . . of such . . . group on account of" a de facto racial imbalance in the employer's work force. The section does *not* state that "nothing in Title VII shall be interpreted to *permit*" voluntary affirmative efforts to correct racial imbalances. The natural inference is that Congress chose not to forbid all voluntary race-conscious affirmative action.

The reasons for this choice are evident from the legislative record. Title VII could not have been enacted into law without substantial support from legislators in both Houses who traditionally resisted federal regulation of private business. Those legislators demanded as a price for their support that "management prerogatives and union freedoms . . . be left undisturbed to the greatest extent possible." Section 703 (j) was proposed by Senator Dirksen to allay any fears that the Act might be interpreted in such a way as to upset this compromise. The section was designed to prevent § 703 of Title VII from being interpreted in such a way as to lead to undue "Federal Government interference with private businesses because of some Federal employee's ideas about racial balance or imbalance." Clearly, a prohibition against all voluntary, race-conscious, affirmative action efforts would disserve these ends. Such a prohibition would augment the powers of the Federal Government and diminish traditional management prerogatives while at the same time impeding attainment of the ultimate statutory goals. In view of this legislative history and in view of Congress' desire to avoid undue federal regulation of private businesses, use of the word "require" rather than the phrase "require or permit" in § 703 (j) fortifies the conclusion that Congress did not intend to limit traditional business freedom to such a degree as to prohibit all voluntary, race-conscious affirmative action.

We therefore hold that Title VII's prohibition in §§ 703 (a) and (d) against racial discrimination does not condemn all private, voluntary, race-conscious affirmative action plans.

III

We need not today define in detail the line of demarcation between permissible and impermissible affirmative action plans. It suffices to hold that the challenged Kaiser-USWA affirmative action plan falls on the permissible side of the line. The purposes of the plan mirror those of the statute. Both were designed to break down old patterns of racial segregation and hierarchy. Both were structured to "open employment opportunities closed to them."

At the same time the plan does not unnecessarily trammel the interests of the white employees. The plan does not require the discharge of white workers and their replacement with new black hires. Nor does the plan create an absolute bar to the advancement of white employees; half of those trained in the program will be white. Moreover, the plan is a temporary measure; it is not intended to maintain racial balance, but simply to eliminate a manifest racial imbalance. Preferential selection of craft trainees at the Gramercy plant will end as soon as the percentage of black skilled craft workers in the Gramercy plant approximates the percentage of blacks in the local labor force.

We conclude, therefore, that the adoption of the Kaiser-USWA plan for the Gramercy plant falls within the area of discretion left by Title VII to the private sector voluntarily to adopt affirmative action plans designed to eliminate conspicuous racial imbalance in traditionally segregated job categories. Accordingly, the judgment of the Court of Appeals for the Fifth Circuit is

Reversed.

. . .

MR. CHIEF JUSTICE BURGER, dissenting.

The Court reaches a result I would be inclined to vote for were I a Member of Congress considering a proposed amendment of Title VII. I cannot join the Court's judgment, however, because it is contrary to the explicit language of the statute and arrived at by means wholly incompatible with long-established principles of separation of powers. Under the guise of statutory "construction," the Court effectively rewrites Title VII to achieve what it regards as a desirable result. It "amends" the statute to do precisely what both its sponsors and its opponents agreed the statute was *not* intended to do.

When Congress enacted Title VII after long study and searching debate, it produced a statute of extraordinary clarity, which speaks directly to the issue we consider in this case. In § 703 (d) Congress provided:

> It shall be an unlawful employment practice for any employer, labor organization, or joint labor-management committee controlling apprenticeship or other training or retraining, including on-the-job training programs to discriminate against any individual because of his race, color, religion, sex, or national origin in admission to, or employment in, any program established to provide apprenticeship or other training.

Often we have difficulty interpreting statutes either because of imprecise drafting or because legislative compromises have produced genuine ambiguities. But here there is no lack of clarity, no ambiguity. The quota embodied in the collective-bargaining agreement between Kaiser and the Steelworkers unquestionably discriminates on the basis of race against individual employees seeking admission to on-the-job training programs. And, under the plain language of § 703 (d), that is "an *unlawful* employment practice."

Oddly, the Court seizes upon the very clarity of the statute almost as a justification for evading the unavoidable impact of its language. The Court blandly tells us that Congress could not really have meant what it said, for a "literal construction" would defeat the "purpose" of the statute—at least the congressional "purpose" as five Justices divine it today. But how are judges supposed to ascertain the *purpose* of a statute except through the words Congress used and the legislative history of the statute's evolution? One need not even resort to the legislative history to recognize what is apparent from the face of Title VII—that it is specious to suggest that § 703 (j) contains a negative pregnant that permits employers to do what §§ 703 (a) and (d) unambiguously and unequivocally *forbid* employers from doing. Moreover, as MR. JUSTICE REHNQUIST's opinion—which I join—conclusively demonstrates, the legislative history makes equally clear that the supporters and opponents of Title VII reached an agreement about the statute's intended effect. That agreement, expressed so clearly in the language of the statute that no one should doubt its meaning, forecloses the reading which the Court gives the statute today.

Arguably, Congress may not have gone far enough in correcting the effects of past discrimination when it enacted Title VII. The gross discrimination against minorities to which the Court adverts—particularly against Negroes in the building trades and craft unions—is one of the dark chapters in the otherwise great history of the American labor movement. And, I do not question the importance of encouraging voluntary compliance with the purposes and policies of Title VII. But that statute was conceived and enacted to make discrimination against *any* individual illegal, and I fail to see how "voluntary compliance" with the no-discrimination principle that is the heart and soul of Title VII as currently written will be achieved by permitting employers to discriminate against some individuals to give preferential treatment to others.

Until today, I had thought the Court was of the unanimous view that "discriminatory preference for any group, minority or majority, is precisely and only what Congress has proscribed" in Title VII. Had Congress intended otherwise, it very easily could have drafted language allowing what the Court permits today. Far from doing so, Congress expressly *prohibited* in §§ 703 (a) and (d) the discrimination against Brian Weber the Court approves now. If "affirmative action" programs such as the one presented in this case are to be permitted, it is for Congress, not this Court, to so direct. . . .

MR. JUSTICE REHNQUIST, with whom THE CHIEF JUSTICE joins, dissenting.

In a very real sense, the Court's opinion is ahead of its time: it could more appropriately have been handed down five years from now, in 1984, a year coinciding with the title of a book from which the Court's opinion borrows, perhaps subconsciously, at least one idea. Orwell describes in his book a governmental official of Oceania, one of the three great world powers, denouncing the current enemy, Eurasia, to an assembled crowd:

> It was almost impossible to listen to him without being first convinced and then maddened. . . . The speech had been proceeding for perhaps twenty minutes when a messenger hurried onto the platform and a scrap of paper was slipped into the speaker's hand. He unrolled and read it without pausing in his speech. Nothing altered in his voice or manner, or in the content of what he was saying, but suddenly the names were different. Without words said, a wave of understanding rippled through the crowd. Oceania was at war with Eastasia! . . . The banners and posters with which the square was decorated were all wrong! . . .
>
> [T]he speaker had switched from one line to the other actually in mid-sentence, not only without a pause, but without even breaking the syntax.

Today's decision represents an equally dramatic and equally unremarked switch in this Court's interpretation of Title VII.

The operative sections of Title VII prohibit racial discrimination in employment *simpliciter*. Taken in its normal meaning, and as understood by all Members of Congress who spoke to the issue during the legislative debates, this language prohibits a covered employer from considering race when making an employment decision, whether the race be black or white. Several years ago, however, a United States District Court held that "the dismissal of white employees charged with misappropriating company property while not dismissing a similarly charged Negro employee does not raise a claim upon which Title VII relief may be granted." This Court unanimously reversed, concluding from the "uncontradicted legislative history" that "Title VII prohibits racial discrimination against the white petitioners in this case upon the same standards as would be applicable were they Negroes. . . ."

We have never waivered in our understanding that Title VII "prohibits *all* racial discrimination in employment, without exception for any particular employees." In *Griggs* v. *Duke Power Co.*, 401 U.S. 424, (1971), our first occasion to interpret Title VII, a unanimous court observed that "[d]iscriminatory preference, for any group, minority or majority, is precisely and only what Congress has proscribed." And in our most recent discussion of the issue, we uttered words seemingly dispositive of this case: "It is clear beyond cavil that the obligation imposed by Title VII is to provide an equal opportunity for *each* applicant regardless of race, without regard to whether members of the applicant's race are already proportionately represented in the work force."

Today, however, the Court behaves much like the Orwellian speaker earlier described, as if it had been handed a note indicating that Title VII would lead to a result unacceptable to the Court if interpreted here as it was in our prior decisions. Accordingly, without even a break in syntax, the Court rejects "a literal construction of § 703 (a)" in favor of newly discovered "legislative history," which leads it to a conclusion directly contrary to that compelled by the "uncontradicted legislative history" unearthed in *McDonald* and our other prior decisions. Now we are told that the legislative history of Title VII shows that employers are free to discriminate on the basis of race: an employer may, in the Court's words, "trammel the interests of white employees" in favor of black employees in order to eliminate "racial imbalance." Our earlier interpretations of Title VII, like the banners and posters decorating the square in Oceania, were all wrong.

As if this were not enough to make a reasonable observer question this Court's adherence to the oft-stated principle that our duty is to construe rather than rewrite legislation, the Court also seizes upon § 703 (j) of Title VII as an independent, or at least partially independent, basis for its holding. Totally ignoring the wording of that section, which is obviously addressed to those charged with the responsibility of interpreting the law rather than those who are subject to its proscriptions, and totally ignoring the months of legislative debates preceding the section's introduction and passage, which demonstrate clearly that it was enacted to prevent precisely what occurred in this case, the Court infers from § 703 (j) that "Congress chose not to forbid all voluntary race-conscious affirmative action."

Thus, by a *tour de force* reminiscent not of jurists such as Hale, Holmes, and Hughes, but of escape artists such as Houdini, the Court eludes clear statutory language, "uncontradicted" legislative history, and uniform precedent in concluding that employers are, after all, permitted to consider race in making employment decisions. It may be that one or more of the principal sponsors of Title VII would have preferred to see a provision allowing preferential treatment of minorities written into the bill. Such a provision, however, would have to have been expressly or impliedly excepted from Title VII's explicit prohibition on all racial discrimination in employment. There is no such exception in the Act. And a reading of the legislative debates concerning Title VII, in which proponents and opponents alike uniformly denounced discrimination in favor of, as well as discrimination against, Negroes, demonstrates clearly that any legislator harboring an unspoken desire for such a provision could not possibly have succeeded in enacting it into law.

I

Kaiser opened its Gramercy, La., plant in 1958. Because the Gramercy facility had no apprenticeship or in-plant craft training program, Kaiser hired as craft workers only persons with prior craft experience. Despite Kaiser's efforts to locate and hire trained black craftsmen, few were available in the Gramercy area, and as a consequence, Kaiser's craft positions were manned almost exclusively by whites. In February 1974, under pressure from the Office of Federal Contract Compliance to increase minority representation in craft positions at its various plants, and hoping to deter the filing of employment discrimination claims by minorities, Kaiser entered into a collective-bargaining agreement with the United Steelworkers of America (Steelworkers) which created a new on-the-job craft training program at 15 Kaiser facilities, including the Gramercy plant. The agreement required that no less than one minority applicant be admitted to the training program for every nonminority applicant until the percentage of blacks in craft positions equaled the percentage of blacks in the local work force. Eligibility for the craft training programs was to be determined on the basis of plant seniority, with black and white applicants to be selected on the basis of their relative seniority within their racial group.

Brian Weber is white. He was hired at Kaiser's Gramercy plant in 1969. In April 1974 Kaiser announced that it was offering a total of nine positions in three on-the-job training programs for skilled craft jobs. Weber applied for all three programs, but was not selected. The successful candidates—five black and four white applicants—were chosen in accordance with the 50% minority admission quota mandated under the 1974 collective-bargaining agreement. Two of the successful black applicants had less seniority than Weber. Weber brought the instant class action in the United States District Court for the Eastern District of Louisiana, alleging the use of the 50% minority admission quota to fill vacancies in Kaiser's craft training programs violated Title VII's prohibition on racial discrimination in employment. The District Court and the Court of Appeals for the Fifth Circuit agreed, enjoining further use of race as a criterion in admitting applicants to the craft training programs.

II

Were Congress to act today specifically to prohibit the type of racial discrimination suffered by Weber, it would be hard pressed to draft language better tailored to the task than that found in § 703 (d) of Title VII:

> It shall be an unlawful employment practice for any employer, labor organization, or joint-management committee controlling apprenticeship or other training or retraining, including on-the-job training programs to discriminate against any individual because of his race, color, religion, sex, or national origin in admission to, or employment in, any program established to provide apprenticeship or other training.

Equally suited to the task would be § 703 (a) (2), which makes it unlawful for an employer to classify his employees "in any way which would deprive or tend to deprive any individual of employment opportunities or otherwise adversely affect his status as an employee, because of such individual's race, color, religion, sex, or national origin."

Entirely consistent with these two express prohibitions is the language of § 703 (j) of Title VII, which provides that the Act is not to be interpreted "to require any employer . . . to grant preferential treatment to any individual or to any group because of the race . . . of such individual or group" to correct a racial imbalance in the employer's work force. Seizing on the word "require," the Court infers that Congress must have intended to "permit" this type of racial discrimination. Not only is this reading of § 703 (j) outlandish in the light of the flat prohibitions of §§ 703 (a) and (d), but, as explained Part III, it is totally belied by the Act's legislative history.

Quite simply, Kaiser's racially discriminatory admission quota is flatly prohibited by the plain language of Title VII. This normally dispositive fact, however, gives the Court only momentary pause. An "interpretation" of the statute upholding Weber's claim would, according to the Court, " 'bring about an end completely at variance with the purpose of the statute.' " To support this conclusion, the Court calls upon the "spirit" of the Act, which it divines from passages in Title VII's legislative history indicating that enactment of the statute was prompted by Congress' desire "to open employment opportunities for Negroes in occupations which [had] been traditionally closed to them." But the legislative history invoked by the Court to avoid the plain language of §§ 703 (a) and (d) simply misses the point. To be sure, the reality of employment discrimination against Negroes provided the primary impetus for passage of Title VII. But this fact by no means supports the proposition that Congress intended to leave employers free to discriminate against white persons. In most cases, "[l]egislative history . . . is more vague than the statute we are called upon to interpret." Here, however, the legislative history of Title VII is as clear as the language of §§ 703 (a) and (d), and it irrefutably demonstrates that Congress meant precisely what it said in §§ 703 (a) and (d)—that *no* racial discrimination in employment is permissible under Title VII, not even preferential treatment of minorities to correct racial imbalance.

[Justice Rehnquist proceeded to review the legislative history— essentially, the congressional debates—of the sections to which the Court referred in justifying its decision. For example, he cited Representative Celler's defense of the bill against its critics. Celler denied that the Equal Employment Opportunity Commission would have the power to prevent a business from employing and promoting the people it wished or that a federal official would be able to order the hiring and promotion of employees of certain racial or religious groups. Celler continued,

> The Bill would do no more than prevent . . . employers from discriminating against or in favor of workers because of their race, religion, or national origin.

The EEOC would not have the power to rectify existing racial or religious imbalance in employment by requiring the hiring of certain people simply because they were members of a particular racial or religious group.

[Senator Humphrey, the bill's primary moving force in the Senate, repeatedly emphasized that Title VII "does not limit the employer's freedom to hire, fire, promote, or demote for any reasons—or for no reasons—so long as his action is not based on race" and that the bill did not authorize "any official or court to require any employer or labor union to give preferential treatment to any minority group." He reiterated this theme over and over again: "Race, religion, and national origin are not to be used as the basis for hiring and firing. Title VII is designed to encourage hiring on the basis of ability and qualifications, not race or religion."

[Two other supporters of the bill, Senators Clark and Case, said that "any deliberate attempt to maintain a racial balance, whatever such a balance may be, would involve a violation of Title VII because maintaining such a balance would require an employer to hire or to refuse to hire on the basis of race." Justice Rehnquist went on to quote Clark and Case, observing that it was as if they were directing their remarks at Brian Weber:

> If a business has been discriminating in the past and as a result has an all-white working force, when the title comes into effect the employer's obligation would be simply to fill future vacancies on a nondiscriminatory basis. He would not be obliged—*or indeed permitted*—to fire whites in order to hire Negroes, *or to prefer Negroes for future vacancies, or, once*

Negroes are hired, to give them special seniority rights at the expense of the white workers hired earlier. (Emphasis added.)

[And Senator Williams added that "to hire a Negro solely because he is a Negro is racial discrimination, just as much as a 'white only' employment policy. Both forms of discrimination are prohibited by Title VII of this bill." He went on to say that the bill "would prohibit preferential treatment for any particular group."

[Justice Rehnquist concluded his dissenting opinion as follows:]

Our task in this case, like any other case involving the construction of a statute, is to give effect to the intent of Congress. To divine that intent, we traditionally look first to the words of the statute and, if they are unclear, then to the statute's legislative history. Finding the desired result hopelessly foreclosed by these conventional sources, the Court turns to a third source—the "spirit" of the Act. But close examination of what the Court proffers as the spirit of the Act reveals it as the spirit animating the present majority, not the Eighty-eighth Congress. For if the spirit of the Act eludes the cold words of the statute itself, it rings out with unmistakable clarity in the words of the elected representatives who made the Act law. It is *equality*. Senator Dirksen, I think, captured that spirit in a speech delivered on the floor of the Senate just moments before the bill was passed:

[T]oday we come to grips finally with a bill that advances the enjoyment of living; but, more than that, it advances the equality of opportunity.

I do not emphasize the word 'equality' standing by itself. It means equality of opportunity in the field of education. It means equality of opportunity in the field of employment. It means equality of opportunity in the field of participation in the affairs of government . . . .

That is it.

Equality of opportunity, if we are going to talk about conscience, is the mass conscience of mankind that speaks in every generation, and it will continue to speak long after we are dead and gone.

There is perhaps no device more destructive to the notion of equality than the *numerus clausus*—the quota. Whether described as "benign discrimination" or "affirmative action," the racial quota is nonetheless a creator of castes, a two-edged sword that must demean one in order to prefer another. In passing Title VII Congress outlawed *all* racial discrimination, recognizing that no discrimination based on race is benign, that no action disadvantaging a person because of his color is affirmative. With today's holding, the Court introduces into Title VII a tolerance for the very evil that the law was intended to eradicate, without offering even a clue as to what the limits on that tolerance may be. We are told simply that Kaiser's racially discriminatory admission quota "falls on the permissible side of the line." By going not merely *beyond,* but directly *against* Title VII's language and legislative history, the Court has sown the wind. Later courts will face the impossible task of reaping the whirlwind.

1. Can you offer any justifications for hiring or promoting a person who has a spouse and children to support over one who does not that would meet Mary Anne Warren's objections to such practices? Would it make a difference if the principle were applied without discriminating against women (or men) as such?

2. Insurance actuaries seem to have established the fact that women tend to outlive men, that their chances of living beyond a given age, particularly at the upper age of the average life span, are significantly greater than those of men. Consequently, most insurance and pension plans have distinguished between the premiums paid and the benefits offered to men and women. The Teachers Insurance and Annuity Association (TIAA), for example, which insures a very large proportion of college instructors, has offered retiring female professors smaller payments per month for a given investment than it has offered to retiring males who began to collect on their pension plans at the same age and with the same investment. The assumption was that on the average, at the time of the retiree's death, he or she would have collected the same amount because the female retiree would have collected more payments (having lived longer) than the male. Because of a number of court decisions prompted by cases brought by feminist groups, TIAA is in the process of changing this policy. Premiums and annuity payments will be equalized for males and females. If mortality tables are correct, women will, on the average, collect more from their annuity policies than will men, although both will have contributed equal numbers of dollars to the plan. Is this a form of secondary sexism?

3. Mary Anne Warren lists a number of policies that are frequently used in employment decisions at American universities and elsewhere— policies such as the antinepotism rule, the last hired–first fired principle, differential treatment of full-time and part-time employees, and so on. Although she admits that such rules may have independent justifications, she seems to rule out their use because they tend, on the whole, to discriminate against women. Is her position on this issue justified? What would it take for a policy to be acceptable to Professor Warren?

4. Is Professor Warren's system of weak quotas more or less satisfactory than a strong quota system? Or are all quota systems ipso facto unsatisfactory?

5. Is Professor Warren correct in arguing that "compensatory justice provides no case for placing an extra . . . burden on male candidates, who are no more responsible for past and present discrimination against women than the rest of us"?

6. Diana Axelsen refers to a "culture-bound model of rationality." Is there such a thing? Is there black rationality, white rationality, male rationality, female rationality, Hispanic rationality? What is rationality?

7. In Section V–B of her paper, Professor Axelsen notes that certain ethnic groups in the United States have been victims of "past and present genocidal actions . . . on a scale so massive that it is difficult to imagine any adequate reparation." What evidence is there that anyone is presently a victim of genocidal actions within the United States, or by the United States?

8. Professor Axelsen also refers to the experience of slavery and racism that certain racial and ethnic groups have undergone, and suggests that these facts, as well as such others as "cultural imperialism," account for high infant mortality rates, low family income, and other phenomena among those groups. She also notes that there are linguistic symptoms of sexism, just as there are of racism. What are her criteria for legitimate claims to compensation—such horrifying crimes as slavery or genocide in the past? The use of denigrating language? Present hardships? Of these (or any others you can identify), which, if any, constitutes an acceptable criterion—and how would you apply it (or them)?

9. Professor Axelsen claims that the "western response" reflects a "patriarchal white male interpretation of experience," which "tends to see [certain] historical perspectives as appeals to a principle of vengeance." What does this mean—and what evidence is there in its favor? Or is there any?

10. List the assumptions that Professor Axelsen makes but does not make explicit in her article, and consider whether they are reasonable. Do the same with the other articles in Part VII.

11. Carl Cohen alleges that "beyond any possible doubt Weber was discriminated against by his employer . . . because of his race." Is Professor Cohen correct? Explain. If Weber *was* discriminated against, is such discrimination wrong? Why?

12. Cohen distinguishes between those situations in which racial classifications are "absolutely essential" and those in which such classifications are not at all justifiable. How can such distinctions be maintained, if at all?

13. Cohen claims that the "philosophical nub" of the *Weber* case is the principle that "the remedy all such persons [i.e., those persons who have been cruelly deprived of rights simply because of race] deserve . . . is deserved by those injured and because of their injury; nothing is deserved because of the color of one's skin." Is this truly the philosophical nub of the case? Even if it is, should it be permitted to rule in the courts while the injustices of the past still weigh upon us?

14. Cohen may be accused of undue attention to and emphasis upon mere legalisms, the explication of constitutional provisions and statutes and regulations, without paying enough attention to the just claims of oppressed people. Would such an accusation be appropriate?

15. Are Cohen's forebodings, as expressed in the last paragraph of his article, justified?

16. In *Weber* both the Court majority and Justice Rehnquist (in his dissenting opinion) appeal to the legislative history of the statute in support of their views. Should the legislative history make any difference? Should the Court merely appeal to principles of justice, rather than engage in such voluminous research into the comments of legislators during debate on a bill?

17. The Court majority concludes that the statute's prohibition against racial discrimination "does not condemn all private, voluntary race-conscious affirmative action plans." If it does not, should a statute clearly condemning all such plans be passed? Why or why not?

18. Is Justice Rehnquist's characterization of the Court as being like the Orwellian speaker accurate, or is it merely a rhetorical flourish?

19. Justice Rehnquist concludes his argument with some remarks on equality. Are those remarks to the point? What is meant by "equality"? Does meaningful equality exist in the United States? Does your answer to these questions make any difference as to the policies the government ought to follow?

20. On July 2, 1980, the Supreme Court of the United States decided *Fullilove* v. *Klutznick,* another important affirmative action case. The case concerned a provision of the Public Works Employment Act of 1977, known as the "minority business enterprise" (MBE) provision, which provided that at least ten per cent of federal funds granted for local public works projects must be used by the state or local grantee to procure services or supplies from businesses owned by minority group members, defined as United States citizens "who are Negroes, Spanish-speaking, Orientals, Indians, Eskimos, and Aleuts," unless there was an administrative waiver. Under the regulations issued by the federal government, it was recognized that contracts would be awarded to bona fide MBE's even though they were not the lowest bidders, and provided for various other advantages to minority firms, such as waiver of bonding requirements. The suit was brought by several construction contractors and subcontractors, who alleged that they had sustained economic injury due to the MBE requirement, arguing that it was unconstitutional on its face and that it violated their right of Equal Protection of the Laws. In upholding its constitutionality, Chief Justice Burger invoked Sec. 5 of the Fourteenth Amendment, which provides that Congress may "enforce by appropriate legislation" the equal protection guarantees of that Amendment. He concluded that it is up to Congress to decide what legislation is appropriate, and that the Court must defer to the judgment of Congress in that regard. Do you agree?

21. Chief Justice Burger also invoked an earlier decision of the Supreme Court (*Swann* v. *Charlotte-Mecklenberg Board of Education,* 402 U.S. 1[1971]), which had held that the courts, in formulating remedies for school segregation, unavoidably had to examine the racial composition of the student bodies of the schools involved, and that it was therefore not possible for Congress or the courts to act in a wholly "color-blind" fashion. Does the analogy hold? Do you agree with the principle?

22. Burger rejected the plaintiffs' complaint that they were subject to economic hardship as a result of the program. The failure of nonminority firms to receive certain contracts was an incidental consequence of the program and not its objective. Hence, it was not impermissible to expect innocent parties to share the burden. Is this argument persuasive?

23. In a concurring opinion, Justice Powell noted that it had been estimated that only .25% of all the funds expended yearly on construction work in the United States would be set aside under this program for

approximately four percent of the nation's contractors (namely, those who are members of minority groups). It would have no effect on the ability of the remaining 96% of contractors to compete for 99.75% of construction funds. He therefore concluded that "any marginal unfairness to innocent nonminority contractors is not sufficiently significant—or sufficiently identifiable—to outweigh the governmental interest" served by the program. What is your reaction to this argument?

24. Justice Powell noted that the Court was dedicated to the proposition "that the Constitution envisions a Nation where race is irrelevant. The time cannot come too soon when no governmental decision will be based upon immutable characteristics of pigmentation or origin. But in our quest to achieve a society free from racial classification, we cannot ignore the claims of those who still suffer from the effects of identifiable discrimination." Do you agree? Do you believe that race-conscious university admissions, hiring, and contracting will further the goal of achieving a nation where race is irrelevant? If so, how? If not, why not?

25. Much the same point had been made by Justice Blackmun in the *Bakke* case: "In order to get beyond racism, we must first take account of race." In that case, Justice Marshall had said, "It is because of a legacy of unequal treatment that we now must permit the institutions of this society to give consideration to race in making decisions about who will hold the positions of influence, affluence, and prestige in America. For far too long, the doors to those positions have been shut to Negroes. If we are ever to become a fully integrated society, one in which the color of a person's skin will not determine the opportunities available to him or her, we must be willing to take steps to open those doors." Are these alternative formulations helpful in resolving the issue raised in point 24?

26. In his dissenting opinion in the *Fullilove* case, Justice Stewart recalled the history of the Supreme Court's decisions in cases involving racial discrimination, and concluded that "one clear lesson" emerged from it: "Under our Constitution, the government may never act to the detriment of a person solely because of that person's race. The color of a person's skin and the country of his origin are immutable facts that bear no relation to ability, disadvantage, moral culpability, or any other characteristics of constitutionally permissible interest to government. 'Distinctions between citizens solely because of their ancestry are by their very nature odious to a free people whose institutions are founded upon the doctrine of equality.' In short, racial discrimination is by definition invidious discrimination." On the ground that the guarantee of equal protection is of universal application, extending to all persons and not just to those who are members of a racial minority, he concluded that the law under attack in this case was unconstitutional and that the good intentions of Congress were not sufficient to remove its "arbitrariness and unfairness," at least from the perspective of one who was detrimentally affected by its "racial discriminatory" provisions. Even Congress, he said (in opposition to the Chief Justice's argument, cited above in point 20), must obey the

Constitution. Is this a sufficient response to the opinions expressed by members of the majority?

27. Justice Stewart also objected to one of the inevitable consequences of affirmative action laws: that they require "the odious practice of delineating the qualities that make one person a Negro and make another white." He was also concerned that such preferential programs would reinforce stereotypes under which certain groups are held to be unable to achieve success without special protection. And he objected to a lesson he feared the public would learn from such legislation: that the apportionment of rewards and penalties can legitimately be made according to race, rather than merit or ability, and that people can or should view themselves and others in terms of their racial characteristics. Are Justice Stewart's fears groundless, are they misplaced, or do they have some merit?

28. In his dissenting opinion, Justice Stevens objected to the fact that the program would confer special benefits ("monopoly privileges," he called them) upon a relatively small "entrepreneurial subclass," namely, those who either possessed or were able to borrow working capital. He called this "a somewhat perverse form of reparation," since "those who are the most disadvantaged within each class are the least likely to receive any benefit from the special privilege even though they are the persons most likely still to be suffering the consequences of the past wrong." Do you agree? If so, what remedy would you suggest?

29. Justice Stevens asked why these six racial classifications ("Negroes, Spanish-speaking, Orientals, Indians, Eskimos, and Aleuts") and no others were given special preference. "Why are aliens excluded from the preference although they are not otherwise ineligible for public contracts? What percentage of Oriental blood or what degree of Spanish-speaking skill is required for membership in the preferred class? How does the legacy of slavery and the history of discrimination against the descendants of its victims support a preference for Spanish-speaking citizens who may be directly competing with black citizens in some overpopulated communities? Why is a preference given only to owners of business enterprises and why is that preference unaccompanied by any requirement concerning the employment of disadvantaged persons?" Are these questions legitimate, or are they merely rhetorical? How would you answer them? How do you think Congress and the courts ought to answer them? On what grounds do you base your answers?

VIII
ESPIONAGE

INTRODUCTION

Espionage is an area that has received relatively little attention from professional philosophers. Consequently, these selections have been written by persons in other fields. The contributions in this part were chosen because they are particularly instructive, because the individuals who wrote them are especially well qualified to speak and write authoritatively about an exceedingly difficult area, and because it is an area that ought to be called to the attention of philosophers and philosophy students, one that is rich with problems of the sort that philosophers might be able to analyze with some degree of success and to which they might make an important contribution. For too long, questions raised by some of the more notorious activities of the CIA have been left to emotionally charged debaters and politically motivated investigators. It is time, perhaps, for cooler heads to consider some of the fundamental questions raised by the entire range of activities of intelligence services.

Ray S. Cline argues that national intelligence agencies are a moral imperative and that they are not inconsistent with a free and open society. In addition to some important historical background, Cline appeals to the "just war" concept to defend covert activities. He says that covert activities by the CIA can be morally justified if they are duly authorized by appropriate political bodies and are directed toward the achievement of certain essential national objectives.

In his rejoinder to Cline, Francis M. Wilhoit calls into question the assumptions made by Cline in setting up his argument—assumptions that Wilhoit says Cline made without (in many instances) explicitly saying so. Wilhoit focuses upon the moral as well as the legal problems raised by the CIA's activities and asks how some of them can possibly be justified. Wilhoit does not pretend to have answered all of the questions raised by the CIA's activities, or even to have asked them. Indeed, it is precisely our failure to ask them that seems to disturb him most and gives rise to his most disturbing normative judgments.

RAY S. CLINE 27
NATIONAL INTELLIGENCE: A MORAL IMPERATIVE

In all the world today the overlapping and often conflicting moral standards of right and wrong prescribed by community cultural norms or individual conviction are subsumed in the larger fabric of the political and judicial processes of the sovereign nation state. Since there are about 160 independent nations now and the national processes vary drastically from country to country, morality in its practical influence on the behavior of men and women in society reflects a great diversity of regional and situational ethics. In fact these differences in cultural and political concepts of what is good and what is bad lie at the root of a great deal of the international tension and conflict that are endemic to this century.

An open, pluralistic society like that of the United States guarantees representative government, civil rights for individuals, and political protection for minority cultural, religious, and ethnic groups. Its normal legal and community processes eschew secrecy in the interests of public accountability of government and the governed alike. The American system of moral values is based on and tends to idealize openness and general conformity with publicly established patterns of civic behavior within the limits of constitutionally guaranteed human rights.

Many observers of the development of a central intelligence system in the United States in the past forty years have seriously questioned whether an intelligence bureaucracy working for the most part in secret is able to carry on its work in a way compatible with the moral standards of American society. Some of the critics argue that secrecy is in itself immoral and that it is wrong for our government to accumulate secret information about international affairs and about American citizens who may be involved with foreigners and foreign situations.

In the second half of the twentieth century, all nations in the world have had to play a serious game in international relations against the backdrop of the enormous destructiveness of modern military weapons. Their survival is at stake in a fierce competition for economic resources. To protect their security, safeguard their social and economic welfare, and avoid damaging conflicts in this volatile era, the indispensable requirement for national leaders who have to make critical foreign policy decisions is accurate intelligence about the surrounding world.

In his pioneer historical analysis of *Strategic Intelligence for American World Policy,* written soon after World War II, veteran OSS and CIA officer Sherman Kent rightly placed intelligence in this crucial role, stating, "If foreign policy is the shield of the republic, as Walter Lippmann has called it, then strategic intelligence is the thing that gets the shield to the right place at the right time. It is also the thing that stands ready to guide the sword."[1] Since the beginning of World War II, the United States has been trying to build up a central, coordinated national intelligence system capable of playing its part efficiently in strategic decision making at the level of national government.

As the United States approaches the 1980s, it faces so many hostile forces on several fronts that the imperative of creating a sound foreign policy and military defense posture is higher than ever before. With economic, political, and—not infrequently—military pressures unfriendly to the United States mounting, the intelligence role must be played properly and well by trained actors in the intelligence community, especially in the central, coordinating element in the community, the Central Intelligence Agency. Knowledge of foreign situations, which data collection and analysis produce, is vital to our national survival. Our statesmen must know in advance of shifts in power, especially among the closed societies, if they are to plot a course of action that will not fail in preserving our own free, open society in a dangerous world. Despotism, tyranny, arbitrary rule without law—these forms of totalitarian government have swept across Central Eurasia, communist Asia, and into parts of Africa, where approximately 40 percent of the world's population live in states whose hostility toward the United States is a matter of principle. Only in the United States are voices raised demanding that we face these dangers without the protection that can be provided by effective intelligence work probing the capabilities and purposes of hostile governments. To be effective, of course, intelligence agencies must operate in secret because they are trying to find out things that foreign leaders are hiding.

During the Revolutionary War George Washington appreciated the value of intelligence and without hesitation sought reliable information about the British army that was operating in what Great Britain considered its colonial territory. His instructions to one of his trusted colonels read, "The necessity of procuring good Intelligence is apparent and need not be further urged. All that remains for me to add is, that you keep the whole matter as secret as possible."[2] Ten years later the Founding Fathers, having won their independence, wrote in the Constitution a variety of positive provisions and processes designed, as the Preamble says, to "establish Justice, insure domestic Tranquility, provide for the common defence, promote the general Welfare, and secure the Blessings of Liberty to ourselves and our Posterity."

Having first organized a secret intelligence network in wartime and then, in peacetime, written a sophisticated political document setting forth the constitutional objective of a free society, the U.S. leaders demonstrated to their own satisfaction that this nation had a moral

---

[1] Sherman Kent, *Strategic Intelligence for American World Policy* (Princeton, N.J.: Princeton University Press, 1951), p. viii.
[2] John C. Fitzpatrick, ed., *The Writings of George Washington from the Original Manuscript Sources, 1745–1799* (Washington, D.C.: Government Printing Office, 1933), Vol. 8, p. 479.

right to exist and consequently, in addition, a right to defend itself. It would be turning morality inside out to claim that the victory they set out to win in 1776 and the law of the land they framed in 1787 portended any lessening of the priority of these two basic rights. Preoccupied with creating a new nation in North America, they did not want to lose the right of self-defense and self-determination of national identity, although they also were intent on establishing representative government and human rights as part of the national legacy.

Their standard of moral propriety allowed them, in all conscience, to reject actions designed to thwart the national interest and to adopt measures to promote it. They fought, killed, spied, and deceived their enemies in the larger purpose of establishing a constitutional government to protect life, liberty, and the pursuit of happiness.

Yet for 150 years, American citizens fired by these efforts neglected to set up an official coordinated central intelligence system in peacetime that would provide information warning of impending disasters and helping, whenever possible, to avert wars. The American people felt secure on a continent flanked by two oceans, and they let intelligence operations lie fallow whenever there was no immediate military menace to them.

Not until Europe began to crumble under the onslaught of Hitler's armies did Americans realize that an intelligence system to support national decision making was a necessity. In July 1941, shortly before Pearl Harbor showed that he should have acted earlier, President Franklin D. Roosevelt, in his capacity of commander-in-chief of the army and navy, issued a directive setting up the office of Coordinator of Information (COI). The COI's mission was (1) "to collect and analyze all information and data, which may bear upon national security" and (2) "to make such information and data available to the President and to such departments and officials of the Government as the President may determine." [3]

This was the nation's first effort in the field of modern intelligence. Before it had gotten beyond the preliminary organizing stages, the nation was hit by the surprise attack on Pearl Harbor, marking the entry of U.S. forces into World War II. Soon the task of collecting and analyzing data was passed on to a wartime agency, the Office of Strategic Services (OSS), formally designated to replace COI in June 1942.

OSS carried out its mission with distinction at home and in every theater of war, but it was abolished when the Axis powers capitulated in 1945. Two years elapsed after the close of World War II before a permanent U.S. intelligence structure received a legislative base. It was then that the Congress passed the National Security Act of 1947. The operative language of the act called for the establishment of the CIA and charged it "to correlate and evaluate intelligence relating to the national security, and provide for the appropriate dissemination of such intelligence." [4] CIA was clearly intended to engage in clandestine intel-

[3] Ray S. Cline, *Secrets, Spies and Scholars* (Washington, D.C.: Acropolis Books, 1976), p. 35. This presidential directive was printed in the *Federal Register*.
[4] *Ibid.*, p. 96.

ligence collection—espionage—as a "service of common concern . . . more efficiently accomplished centrally." [5]

In proposing the national security legislation to the Congress, President Harry Truman, who had succeeded President Roosevelt at his death in 1945, explained: "I wanted one top-level permanent setup in the government to concern itself with advising the President on high policy decisions. . . . This new organization gave us a running balance and a perpetual inventory of where we stood and where we were going on all strategic questions affecting the national security." [6] The information base for these presidential policy deliberations was to be provided by CIA, created at the same time as the National Security Council and made responsible through the council to the president.

The CIA was a latecomer. Germany, Japan, Great Britain, and Russia entered World War II with well-established national intelligence systems. In England the art of intelligence had been refined for more than 300 years; British spies were recruited from Oxford and Cambridge clerics as well as from what Queen Bess's secretary of state called "low fellows" in the streets. The Germans, under Nazi rule, had built very large intelligence organizations conducting clandestine operations throughout Europe and in both North and South America. The all-powerful Russian service, now called the KGB, was founded by Lenin after the Bolshevik triumph in 1917 to "defend the revolution" by secret penetrations both within the Soviet Union and abroad.

In the era of so-called peace that followed World War II, the CIA developed with urgency in what the Soviets themselves called a "stern world." It is almost a miracle that this country could have survived the disaster and humiliation of the Pearl Harbor surprise attack and then by the 1950s and 1960s have developed under CIA's leadership the best intelligence system in the world. The agency concentrated on assembling a well-qualified staff, many with experience in OSS. About 90 percent of the intelligence effort was spent on collecting information and on analytical research—finding out about and explaining trends and patterns in an increasingly turbulent world.

The Communists took over the Chinese mainland in 1949; North Korea began to make menacing preparations for war, which was launched in 1950; Stalin, having consolidated his position in control of Poland, Hungary, and Rumania, seized political power in Czechoslovakia and started his campaign to destroy Tito; and the USSR exploded its first atomic bomb some years ahead of military intelligence predictions. Sources included all that CIA could lay its hands on: newspapers, radio broadcasts, signal intercepts, reports of diplomatic and military officers stationed abroad, foreign agents, and liaison counterparts in friendly countries. Analysts concentrated on publishing a current intelligence "daily" for the president, a scholarly summary of events—quick and authoritative—with the best evidentially based answers to the strategic questions that could be hammered out by CIA experts.

5 Ibid.
6 Harry S. Truman, Memoirs (Garden City, N.Y.: Doubleday, 1956), Vol. II, pp. 58–59.

The units involved in this analytical research by January 1952 included an economic and geographical office, a scientific office, and a large current reporting office. They were supported by a reference and library unit, which later became a computerized file of classified intelligence materials, including a biographic register of foreign, nonmilitary personalities. The patterns of international thrust and parry were complex but were all related to strategic containment of the Soviet Union and the People's Republic of China while building and strengthening alliances with friendly nations.

In this period the United States and its allies considered a major threat to be the Soviet practice of sending into Western Europe and the Mideast secret political agents to work with local communist parties and other discontented elements in society to create economic and political chaos, to buy off or intimidate noncommunist political leaders, and to dominate electoral processes by infusions of money, propaganda, and technical advice for favored candidates. To discover the exact dimensions of communist activity in all the countries of the world and to counter and negate communist political gains were two main tasks entrusted to CIA.

. It was under pressure of U.S. officials of the day that CIA expanded its duties beyond collection of information and analytical research into covert political and paramilitary action. One of the first acts of the new National Security Council at the end of 1947 was to assign a special group associated with CIA the task of preventing the Communists from winning the Italian elections of April 1948. The CIA covert action in support of the moderate parliamentary center in Italy was successful, and the tasks passed to CIA multiplied. After the outbreak of the Korean conflict, covert action was viewed as a valuable asset for strengthening friendly societies without employing the armed forces.

The sense of the charges placed upon CIA by the White House and the Department of State in these years was summed up by the Hoover Commission in 1954, when it reported to the Congress: "We must develop effective espionage and counterespionage services. We must learn to subvert, sabotage, and destroy our enemies. . . . It is now clear that we are facing an implacable enemy whose avowed objective is world domination by whatever means and at whatever cost. There are no rules in such a game. If the U.S. is to survive, long-standing American concepts of 'fair play' must be reconsidered." [7] At that time no one questioned the morality of using CIA to conduct this covert part of the strategic contest—a contest in which U.S. basic national security, actual survival, was believed to be at risk by such sober and patriotic men as Harry Truman, Dwight Eisenhower, Dean Acheson, George Kennan, and John Foster Dulles.

Responding to the instructions issued by the Congress and the White House, CIA developed institutional resources to collect clandestine in-

[7] U.S. Congress, Senate, *Final Report of the Select Committee to Study Governmental Operations with Respect to Intelligence Activities*, 94th Cong., 2d sess., Report No. 94–755, April 26, 1976, p. 9.

formation from espionage and counterespionage, and, in selected cases and areas, to neutralize communist political thrusts with political action schemes. In a sense these covert action operations were extensions of diplomacy designed to prevent resort to war. In assessing the morality of such actions, the responsible citizen has help from a large body of philosophical literature on the doctrine of "just war" as part of the western Christian tradition.

The theory of "just war" contends that political authority must be judged by whether an act of war (1) is directed toward a morally justifiable end, such as self-defense, (2) employs means appropriate to the end and not excessive or destructive to the ultimate goal, and (3) has a reasonable chance of success. If covert action is "just" and its objectives ethically sound, then—in the light of international dangers that might impinge on our constitutional rights of national tranquility, defense, and general welfare—conducting secret operations in support of security of an open and free society is *prima facie* moral. The task is to ensure, as in the case of war, that intelligence activities are indeed aimed at ends contributing to our security, that the means employed are defensible, and that the chances of success are reasonably good. In fact, these are the judgments that the president, his executive staff, and the Congress made in the past and repeatedly must make in establishing policy governing intelligence programs and approving specific plans for action.

CIA's covert action personnel peaked at about 3,000, or about one sixth of the 18,000 employees that eventually constituted the work force of the entire agency at its top strength. Because many of these were engaged in clerical, secretarial, and routine administrative duties, they never did anything that was immoral or unethical. Only a few hundred professional covert action officers became involved in real cloak-and-dagger action programs. The bulk of the agency employees had no firsthand contact with this kind of work. As a result imagination and exaggeration of CIA's exploits abroad ran rampant, both inside the agency and in Washington's cocktail circuit. The James Bond enthusiasts in analytical and administrative jobs in CIA, as well as journalists and politicians who observed from the outside, were stimulated by the occasional CIA headline to visualize extraordinary escapades in a fantasy world of spy fiction. They conjured up a vast mythology of experimentation with mind-altering drugs on hosts of unwitting subjects, frequent firefights, assassinations, and long chases in search of communist agents with female spies who looked like Ursula Andress.

In fact, most covert action merely involved passing counterintelligence identifications and other information on foreign situations to friendly political leaders and publicists in radio or press circles abroad. Money was often transferred to support the organization of groups whose journalistic or political goals coincided with U.S. foreign policy. But the ambitious political interventions such as in Iran in 1953 and such highly publicized paramilitary operations as the Laos secret army a few years later were actually few. They gave a distorted view of the scale of activity, which even CIA employees with no firsthand knowledge of covert action operations—for example, Victor Marchetti and E. Drexel Godfrey, Jr.—tended to substantiate as true in their postretirement writing.* Most of the experienced covert action personnel kept their silence, thus allowing the myth of the ubiquitous and iniquitous CIA to spread widely by the credulous as well as by hostile critics or gleeful foreign intelligence agents.

Covert operations supported thousands of foreign policy programs. They reached an all-time high in 1964, dropped by 50 percent by 1968, and are virtually nonexistent today. In the beginning they consisted of propaganda and political action carried out in forty-eight countries, principally in the Far East, Western Europe, and the Middle East. Later, the Bay of Pigs disaster prompted counterinsurgency activities in Latin America, Africa, and the Far East; and the war in Vietnam demanded a small paramilitary program that expanded into Laos until 1971. Most were low-risk, low-cost projects, and many were remarkably successful. CIA got a lot of credit, which it only partly deserved, and for which much later it was to get most of the blame—blame that largely belonged to the policymakers who reviewed all plans, issued directives, and examined the results.

Covert operations went awry when U.S. officials from the president on down imposed upon the agency virtually impossible tasks, often too large, often impractical. In the late 1960s in Vietnam and Laos, President Lyndon Johnson plunged the CIA into covert action on a massive scale—too massive to remain covert long. Then, after 1970, President Richard Nixon and his national security assistant, Dr. Henry Kissinger, inexpertly set out to win their strategic battles by waging them covertly. They pumped money into Chile and hastily and clumsily invested in Italian politics, where communist electoral gains had continued. These actions mostly came to grief, and the second round of intervention in Italy never got off the ground. In these operations the CIA followed orders, often unwillingly and reluctantly. All the errors and failures—though, of course, few of the successes—of CIA surfaced in the wake of the Watergate investigations that led President Nixon to resign under threat of impeachment.

Criticisms of the CIA multiplied as the facts of its history became known to many for the first time. Although the CIA has never come close to being an American Gestapo, the moral tone of much of the public criticism suggests this was a real danger. It is interesting to note that in the fall of 1977 when Richard Helms, CIA veteran and director from June 1966 to February 1973, was sentenced for two misdemeanors in a Washington court, the Soviets were celebrating in Moscow's Bolshoi Theater the one-hundredth anniversary of the birth of Felix Dzerzhinsky, known in the West as the ruthless and bloodthirsty founder of the Russian intelligence service. Yuriy Andropov, a member of the Politburo, spared no words of praise for "Iron Felix, Knight of the Revolution, a Proletarian Jacobin . . . a soldier true to his duty and to his oath." [8]

* Victor Marchetti wrote his book with John D. Marks. It is entitled *The CIA and the Cult of Intelligence* (New York: Alfred A. Knopf, 1974). E. Drexel Godfrey, Jr., published his article, "Ethics and Intelligence," in *Foreign Affairs*, April 1978.

[8] Foreign Broadcast Information Service, *Soviet Union, Daily Report* (Washington, D.C.: U.S. Department of Commerce, National Technical Information Service), Vol. III, No. 176, September 12, 1977, p. R2.

For the dedicated Soviet intelligence officers, 500,000 strong and honored for being revolutionary activists, the United States is an easy target. American society is open, individual rights are cherished, and the press is free. The nation stands for orderly change and restraint of violence, particularly undiscriminating terror, totalitarian revolution, and war. This kind of politically pluralist society is in a minority; only 20 percent of the 4.25 billion people in the world enjoy such rights as the U.S. Constitution provides.

The Soviet Union and all other communist nations conceal within their borders as prime state secrets nearly every aspect of national policy and behavior. Policymakers in the United States cannot afford to face this kind of international environment without knowing what developments may be encroaching upon our national security.

What then can the United States do to protect the American people and their way of life? Are bribery, deception, or blackmail justified in these circumstances despite their departure from the norms of American moral propriety? Should a U.S. citizen live abroad under an assumed name or under cover of some protective organization that conceals his intelligence identity if it is necessary to provide our political leaders with information they need to make wise defense and foreign policy decisions? Should operators open the mail of Americans having suspicious contacts with foreigners in the quest for hard evidence of espionage or treason? Are the activities of American students worth watching at home and abroad if they are encouraged and sponsored by communist rabble-rousers? When is it the task of the U.S. intelligence service to counter, combat, and disrupt the efforts of those who are trying to penetrate and, if possible, destroy our social and political structure? What intelligence operations are illegal and immoral when the danger to U.S. security is so great? Are secret intelligence activities in this time of deadly international political conflict any different from the actions of soldiers at war who are obliged to shoot to kill?

All these questions when answered in the negative by critics of the CIA's secret operations ignore the traditional philosophic endorsement of the right of self-determination and self-defense. The CIA's covert actions can be morally justified if they are duly authorized by duly constituted political authority and are plainly aimed at and not excessive to the needs of the nation to "insure domestic Tranquility, provide for the common defence, promote the general Welfare, and secure the Blessings of Liberty to ourselves and our Posterity." In fact, if American security and liberty require it, most citizens in this country could probably agree that maintaining an effective national intelligence system is a moral imperative.

FRANCIS M. WILHOIT

28

THE MORALITY OF NATIONAL INTELLIGENCE: A REJOINDER

As a distinguished and articulate participant-observer in the field of intelligence, Ray Cline has few equals. Like Spinoza in another context, he has made "a ceaseless effort to ridicule, not to bewail, nor to scorn human actions, but to understand them." That is all highly admirable, but more important from the perspective of moral philosophy is the fact that he is attuned to the difficult ethical dilemmas that confront all serious practitioners and students of the intelligence art. One may disagree with some of his moral conclusions, as I do, and yet concede that he has thought deeply about this most controversial peacetime function of the democratic nation state. With a subtle sense of history, Mr. Cline eschews bland generalities and in his richly textured, multi-level analysis goes far beyond simplistic notions to spell out some of the key issues that moral philosophy must come to grips with in this field.

Basically, Mr. Cline is wrestling with the inevitable dilemma that results from the need for a supersecret, "realistic" intelligence agency in an open, moral, democratic society. Indeed, ever since the founding of the CIA, thoughtful Americans have been torn between their Judeo-Christian ethical values and their strong desire to exercise world power and influence by whatever means necessary.[1] His essay is a valuable contribution to the ongoing debate about how best to adapt the American polity and its intelligence agencies to the vastly changed circumstances of world affairs. If he does not ultimately settle the question of how to reconcile Machiavelli and Calvin in the American setting, he makes a respectable stab at doing so.

The strengths of Mr. Cline's argumentation are worth noting at the outset of this rejoinder. His summary account of the founding of the CIA is felicitously succinct and factual. His depiction of the modern state's vital need for intelligence information is compelling. His stress

[1] Among the numerous post-World War II works dealing with intelligence in general and the CIA in particular, the following are particularly recommended: Miles Copeland, *Without Cloak or Dagger* (New York: Simon & Schuster, 1974); A. Dulles, *The Craft of Intelligence* (New York: Harper & Row, 1963); Y. H. Kim, ed., *The Central Intelligence Agency: Problems of Secrecy in a Democracy* (Lexington, Mass.: D. C. Heath, 1968); Philip Agee, *Inside the Company: CIA Diary* (Baltimore: Penguin Books, 1975); L. Kirkpatrick, *The Real CIA* (New York: Macmillan, 1968); P. J. McGarvey, *CIA: The Myth and the Madness* (Baltimore: Penguin Books, 1972); H. H. Ransom, *The Intelligence Establishment* (Cambridge, Mass.: Harvard University Press, 1970); and D. Wise and T. Ross, *The Invisible Government* (New York: Random House, 1964).

on the relativity of ethics in the contemporary world is controversial but relevant. His emphasis on intelligence as a crucial component in strategic decision making is particularly well taken. His pointing out that about 90 percent of the CIA's work is not cloak-and-dagger espionage but the more or less routine collection and analysis of strategic information will surprise some but is on the mark. And, finally, his description of the legal and political restraints on democratic intelligence agencies can never be overstressed.

The flaws in the essay, on which I shall focus, are both logical and moral and involve a number of omissions, unexamined premises, ethical ambiguities, and an unwillingness to face certain unpleasant facts.

Mr. Cline sets up something of a straw man near the beginning of his essay when he maintains that there are critics abroad who believe that all secrecy is immoral and hence condemn every kind of governmental secrecy. There doubtless are left-wing perfectionists, including anarchists, who take that extreme view, but surely most of the people who write and speak about the moral problems of intelligence are not to be placed in that category. Responsible critics of intelligence, in and out of government, do not question the necessity of conducting secret intelligence activities. Rather what they object to is surrounding intelligence secrecy with a plea of absolute "CIA privilege" such as Nixon's ill-fated claim of total executive privilege.

More fundamentally, Mr. Cline takes for granted the private–public dichotomy in the field of ethics, without, however, expressly mentioning that fact or philosophically justifying it. Although the postulation of such a moral dichotomy has been commonplace in political theory and political science since the Renaissance, such moral philosophers as Plato, Aristotle, and St. Thomas never took it for granted, and thus it can hardly be called self-warranting. It may well be that, whereas private deceit, violence, and murder are clearly immoral, similar actions committed by or in the name of the state are at worst amoral; yet one surely has an obligation, in espousing that position, to acknowledge openly that one is doing so.

Mr. Cline does not, of course, praise CIA "immorality" for its own sake, nor is his basic attitude in any sense to be equated with ethical nihilism. He in fact quite obviously embraces the whole range of democratic values; but his apparent abdication of moral judgment in regard to CIA actions seems to affirm that, in the specific situation of the modern nation-state, the tactical and strategic rules of power have priority over the canons of Judeo-Christian morality. The CIA certainly did not invent treachery, fraud, or political murder. But at least before the advent of the amoralism of modern intelligence, such acts—whether public or private—were deemed to be regrettable exceptions to the standard rules of moral behavior, regardless of how common they were. However, since the time of Machiavelli, such actions, committed in the name of national security, have been integrated into a moral order of their own and are now deemed to be positive goods so long as they serve to acquire, retain, or expand state power.

Once launched on this road of argumentation, one ultimately has to face the question, where do you draw the line? Or, more simply, where do you stop? In other words, are all means—including tyrannicide and nuclear war—justified if the end is national security? And, even more to the point, is it impossible to commit a moral wrong when your sole motivation is advancing the national interest?

Mr. Cline and other apologists for the CIA, by boldly rationalizing the need of what would otherwise be immoral actions, have brought us face to face once again with the old post-Renaissance doctrine of *raison d'état,* which was resurrected in the nineteenth century as *Realpolitik* and recently given new prominence by ex-President Nixon and Henry Kissinger. According to this CIA-approved principle of political ethics, every act of the state or its agencies is permissible, especially in the field of foreign relations, if it proves advantageous to one's country. It follows, therefore, that the basic moral imperative of this doctrine is that secret intelligence agencies are not only absolutely crucial to a nation's survival, but also that they are fully justified in putting the security and well-being of the state above all other considerations. Centuries ago, Machiavelli went to the heart of the matter when he wrote that "where the very safety of the country depends upon the resolution to be taken, no considerations of justice or injustice, humanity or cruelty, nor of glory or of shame, should be allowed to prevail." [2] The rule of international life, in other words, is dominate or be dominated: take it or leave it, but do not moralize about it.

Although the concept of national interest remains hazy and subjective, the CIA and its supporters have always operated on the assumption that "putting all other considerations aside, the only question should be, what course will save the life and liberty of the country." [3] Presumably such an attitude precludes utopian expectations as well as the kind of sentimental diplomacy that would expose a nation to subversion from more unscrupulous powers. But what such a commitment does to traditional ideas of morality and to other people's perceptions of our ethical principles is quite another matter.

Mr. Cline's implicit embrace of *raison d'état* thinking comes down in the end to a kind of "naïve instrumentalism" that exaggerates the effectiveness of peacetime intelligence while neglecting the social, ethical, and international consequences of giving intelligence agencies a virtual blank check in certain key areas of public policy. Carried far enough, the issue of the morality or immorality of agencies such as the CIA would bring us right back to the medieval confrontation between realism and nominalism. Clearly those who take a strong pro-CIA position seek to convert the autonomy of national intelligence into a kind of moral universal that already is in the process of being congealed and reified. Once all the overt and covert aspects of the CIA's work come to be viewed as essential components of our national experience, the CIA will be well on its way to the status of a political universal like the Constitution and the American Dream. In this regard we must all be nominalists, as we insist that the CIA is simply an acronym for a particular governmental agency

---

[2] Quoted in Lee Cameron McDonald, *Western Political Theory: From Its Origins to the Present* (New York: Harcourt, Brace & World, 1962), p. 211.
[3] *Ibid.*

that has no universal, autonomous existence but operates solely at the sufferance of the people and their laws.

CIA apologists not only blithely accept the inevitable relativity of ethics in world affairs, thus weakening their right to condemn other governments. They go further and posit the unarticulated major premise that decisions of intelligence agencies should be made and evaluated almost entirely on the basis of utilitarian considerations. That, of course, raises a host of moral and practical policy problems and is a position that one should not embrace without serious reservations. It may not be quite accurate to state, as Napoleon once wrote, that "in the long run, the sword will always be conquered by the spirit." But surely the sword of our democratic power, along with its CIA shield, will be a more efficacious freedom promoter, even in the strict utilitarian sense, if it is constantly subjected to the restraints of a national moral spirit and tempered by a recognition of the limits of pragmatic amoral thinking. It is well to recall here that, even though Pope John Paul II has neither troops nor CIA and is not a card-carrying utilitarian, he has become one of the most influential factors in the equation of global politics—almost entirely because of the moral authority that his person and office command. My argument is not that in evaluating the CIA's performance we should eschew utilitarian considerations and judge only in terms of ideological or moral absolutes. Far from it. I would argue, rather, that we should never let our utilitarian values totally divorce us from the basic moral matrix of American democracy. Neither utility nor the pursuit of utility is a substitute for justice. Nor is the Augustinian concept of a "just war," about which Mr. Cline makes a good deal, an acceptable surrogate.

A few comments are now in order about the general relationship between law, morality, and the CIA. In his brief excursus into history, Mr. Cline quite accurately noted that the Founding Fathers included among the preambular goals of the Constitution of 1787 the objectives of ensuring domestic tranquility and providing for the common defense. He inferred from this, without quite saying so, that Madison, Washington, and Hamilton were thereby indirectly legitimating the kinds of extralegal activities the CIA has frequently been accused of engaging in. All well and good.

But an interesting omission in Mr. Cline's historical comments is his total failure to mention, let alone discuss, the "Statement and Account" clause of the Constitution, which provides that "No Money shall be drawn from the Treasury, but in consequence of Appropriations made by Law; *and a regular Statement and Account of the Receipts and Expenditures of all public Money shall be published from time to time.*" [4] (Italics added.) Now, as Mr. Cline well knows, the CIA's receipts and expenditures are not made public, as are those of other federal agencies, even though the Constitution clearly commands that. Various critics of the CIA have brought this omission to the attention of the courts in the form of lawsuits, but so far the courts have refused to make the agency literally follow this provision of the nation's basic law. Technically the

[4] U.S. Constitution, Art. I, Sect. 9, Cl. 7.

clause would seem to assure popular control over such secret agencies as the CIA; but, because the courts have held that enforcement of this section is entirely a congressional responsibility, that has not turned out to be the case. The Supreme Court recently denied a taxpayer the right of standing to challenge in court the constitutionality of a federal law that allows the CIA to account for its expenditures "solely on the certificate of the Director." Although this decision may well satisfy the imperatives of utility and possibly be in accord with the intentions of the Framers, in the words of Justice Douglas writing in dissent, it "effectively reduces that clause to a nullity, giving it no purpose at all." [5]

More important from the legal and moral perspective than the CIA's failure to publicize its finances is its well-known record of "dirty tricks" carried out more or less covertly in foreign countries. Now, of course, law and morality are not identical. Yet democratic theory has always assumed the intersection of these concepts; and thus, when the CIA transgresses national and international law to overthrow an anti-U.S. government or to prop up a pro-U.S. dictator, it would appear to be acting simultaneously both illegally and immorally—at least by the old ethics.

But forgetting for the moment such abstractions as law and morality and returning to the practical world of national security, can the vaunted "triumphs" of the CIA since World War II really be justified even in the narrow utilitarian calculus of success and failure? To be sure, the overthrow of Mosaddeq in Iran (1953), of Arbenz in Guatemala (1954), and of Allende in Chile (1973) [6] seemed to be in the short-run national interest of the United States. But, in the long perspective of history, can utilitarian rationalizers of the CIA's dirty tricks say apodictically that these actions maximized the *long-run* national interests of the United States, let alone the interests of the Iranian, Guatemalan, and Chilean peoples? I think not. The Manichaean thinking that has sparked the CIA's most spectacular "successes" holds that the political right is always good and the left always bad—a premise that is neither rational nor truly conducive to long-term utility.

Few today would perhaps agree with the statement of the early Irish Republican leader, Daniel O'Connell, that "what is morally wrong can never be politically right"; but, unless we are willing totally to abdicate moral judgment where national interests are at issue and embrace the Hegelian dictum that *"die Weltgeschichte ist das Weltgericht,"* we should not dismiss O'Connell's ethical imperative out of hand, especially not where human freedom is involved.

[5] *United States* v. *Richardson,* 418 U.S. 166 (1974). Justices Stewart, Marshall, and Brennan also dissented in this case.
[6] For an excellent scholarly appraisal of the CIA's role in "destabilizing" the Allende government, see Paul E. Sigmund, *The Overthrow of Allende and the Politics of Chile, 1964–1976* (Pittsburgh, Pa.: University of Pittsburgh Press, 1977), pp. 112–122, 259–260, and 285–286. See also U.S. Congress, House, Foreign Affairs Committee, Subcommittee on Interamerican Affairs, *United States and Chile During the Allende Years, 1970–73,* 94th Cong., 1st sess., 1975, pp. 255–371. Near the end of 1974 Congress voted to prohibit CIA secret operations for other than intelligence-gathering purposes "unless and until the President finds that each such operation is important to the national security of the United States and reports, in a timely fashion, a description and scope of such operations to the appropriate committees of the Congress."

Even if one grants the occasional necessity of destabilizing foreign governments and assassinating foreign leaders, one would surely be hard put to justify the *domestic* dirty tricks of the CIA on legal, moral, or pragmatic grounds. Almost certainly the agency has frequently gone beyond the limits set by the National Security Act of 1947, since that act clearly proscribed CIA involvement on the U.S. domestic scene. And though Mr. Cline is inclined to make light of these domestic shenanigans, we now know from the Rockefeller Report of 1975 and from other sources that the CIA engaged in illegally wiretapping U.S. citizens in this country, kept illegal files on U.S. citizens, and supervised massive surveillance of the mails. In the late 1970s, former CIA Director Richard Helms was indicted for lying to a congressional committee about the CIA's covert activities, while an unidentified agent was charged with snooping into the supersensitive files of the House committee that investigated the assassination of President Kennedy. It now appears that, in the domestic as in the foreign field, government officials who deal in secrets have learned little from recent history and can be trusted about as far as we can throw them left-handed. It is true, as Mr. Cline suggests, that the CIA operates only at the sufferance of the president, but it is also true that both Presidents Nixon and Ford attempted to limit some of the agency's clandestine activities without much success. Nor has congressional oversight been any more efficacious.

Quite aside from the so-called victories of the CIA's foreign and domestic underground work, what can possibly be said to justify the moral, legal, and political fiasco that the CIA-sponsored Bay of Pigs operation turned out to be? It is hardly surprising that Mr. Cline barely alluded to this darkest blot on the CIA's escutcheon, for there is almost nothing good to be said about it—except that it made us all a little more conscious of the unrestrained nature of CIA's Big Brother power. According to a recent study of that incredible project of our "invisible government," the scenario was largely plotted and developed by Richard Bissell, Jr., then chief of CIA's covert operations. To his credit, President Kennedy was unenthusiastic but finally reluctantly went along with the agency's bizarre preparations.[7] In reading the history of those cruel days in April—days that might well have ignited World War III—one is struck less by the utter immorality of the venture than by its unbelievable ineptness. Later, when the CIA tried to assassinate Castro by using the Mafia and other devious means, its record was equally futile and inept. The end result was that, far from strengthening this country's national security, the abortive assaults on Castro and his island fortress significantly weakened the United States—morally, politically, and diplomatically. Even Machiavelli, faced with such ineptitude, would have been forced to the conclusion that governmental inefficiency of that magnitude merits the pejorative label of sin.

Mr. Cline and the thousands of nameless CIA operatives who have served their nation in fair and foul weather deserve the gratitude of all Americans for their efforts to advance the cause of security and human freedom. But they have failed—and signally failed—in not adequately

[7] See Peter Wyden, *Bay of Pigs: The Untold Story* (New York: Simon & Schuster, 1979).

dealing with the dialectical tension between pragmatic realism and moral idealism that lies at the very heart of our intelligence dilemma. They should take the lead in developing an ethic and a jurisprudence of secret intelligence that would go beyond Bernard Mandeville's simplistic "private vices, public virtues" concept. Of course, we must all be pragmatists in our understanding of the imperatives of power politics in an increasingly competitive world; yet we must also recognize that there must be a clear moral purpose to American actions in all areas of intelligence. Without such a purpose and vision, our national ideals will ultimately disappear.

CIA apologists doubtless feel, with some justification, that critics of the agency dress up moral problems in utopian clothes and fantasy and thereby evade the cruel difficulties of being merely human in a Darwinian world. Some, reacting to our alleged "openness excesses," would even go so far as Great Britain, where there is no Freedom of Information Act and where a restrictive Official Secrets Act shields the government bureaucracy from awkward scrutiny. But we should all be grateful that the United States has chosen a different path. If that path of open government has its "excesses," they are the kinds of excesses that generally promote, not hinder, the cause of human freedom. In this regard, let it be noted that G. Gordon Liddy and E. Howard Hunt were not figments of the media's collective image-making: They were flesh-and-blood spooks who acted as though they were Nietzschean supermen beyond both moral and statutory law. Other examples of such intelligence *hubris* could readily be adduced, but, heeding William of Occam, one should not needlessly multiply them to make the point that the excesses of openness are nothing compared with the CIA's record of operational excesses.

Mr. Cline is to be commended for being more willing than most CIA defenders to face up to the hard moral choices that intelligence agencies pose for democratic societies. Still, in the final analysis, his essay is not the argument of a moral philosopher writing for other philosophers but an activist's call for patriotic commitment and untrammeled clandestine action. What we must never lose sight of in this regard is that, when action occurs without adequate moral restraints or considerations, it may in the long run be self-defeating. Bearing that in mind, I should like to conclude this rejoinder with the suggestion that the really hard, critical, moral questions about the CIA's nether side remain unanswered, and indeed unasked. For that omission, we are all culpable.

POINTS TO PONDER

1. Cline quotes the Hoover Commission's report with seeming approval: "We must learn to subvert, sabotage, and destroy our enemies. . . . There are no rules in such a game." Is it true that there are no rules? Ought there to be some? In the dangerous game of international politics, are there no limits to what a nation that prides itself on its adherence to the principles of democracy and liberty and justice can do? If such

limits *do* exist, what might they be, and how—realistically—can they be implemented without seriously compromising the nation's security?

2. How would you answer the questions posed by Cline in the last two paragraphs of his article? To what moral or philosophical principles would you appeal?

3. Wilhoit distinguishes "left-wing perfectionists" from "responsible critics of intelligence," but he offers no criteria for making the distinction. When does a critic of the CIA become irresponsible?

4. Is Wilhoit's charge that Cline has abdicated moral judgment in regard to CIA actions justified?

5. Wilhoit asks whether tyrannicide is justified if the end is national security. He appears to be assuming that tyrannicide is generally immoral. Suppose that the tyrant is an Adolf Hitler or an Ayatollah Khomeini. Would it be immoral to assassinate him?

6. Wilhoit concludes his paper with the suggestion that the really hard, critical, moral questions remain "unanswered, and indeed unasked." What might such questions be?

7. In *A Man Called Intrepid,* William Stevenson gives an account of intelligence operations prior to and during World War II. Among other things, he describes the breaking of German and Japanese codes; the discovery of the microdot, which had been developed by German intelligence and had worked extremely effectively; and the operations that prevented the atomic bomb from being developed by the Nazis before their defeat by the Allies. Two of the many incidents described in this remarkable book are worthy of some evaluation, from a moral point of view:

    a. The British had cracked the German code. It was absolutely essential that this fact be kept hidden from the Germans, for its usefulness would immediately have been compromised away. Knowledge of the code gave the British vital information on Nazi troop movements and plans. In November 1940, British intelligence learned that the Germans planned to destroy Coventry. Hitler planned to annihilate civilian targets to crush British morale. If Churchill evacuated the city, the enemy would know that the British had cracked their code. If he did not, thousands of civilians would die or be seriously wounded. What was the prime minister's moral duty? (Coventry was subjected to such a devastating raid on November 14 that the Germans boasted that every town in England would be "Coventryized.")

    b. In 1945, the Germans captured some Danish agents whose knowledge of the importance of Niels Bohr's work on nuclear fission might have had dangerous consequences. It was assumed that under torture some of them would eventually talk. They were imprisoned in Gestapo headquarters in the heart of Copenhagen. Sven Truelsen, a Danish military intelligence expert, urged the British to bomb the building at its foundations, destroying Gestapo files that were kept in the lower floors, and giving the prisoners, who were kept in the upper floors, a chance to escape. Such a raid was particularly dangerous as the dive bombers would be stretched to the outer limits of their range. They would have to fly at wave-top level to duck under German radar, weaving below the rooftops to get one-shot strikes. To make the dilemma even worse, a convent school adjoining the building would be crowded with children during the raid. It was almost inevitable that some civilian lives would be lost, however accurately the bombs struck. The papers that the Gestapo had not yet had a chance to analyze contained enough information to enable them to destroy the Danish underground movement. Should the Air Force commander have ordered the raid? (He did, and the Gestapo's incriminating files were destroyed. In the raid, thirty Danish agents managed to escape. One of the RAF pilots, confused by the fires, struck a pole. His aircraft plunged into the Catholic school, his bombs blowing up on impact. Ten airmen, twenty-seven teachers, and eighty-seven children were killed, and many other civilians were badly mutilated. One of the navigators returned to the site after the war and was astonished when parents of the dead children tried to comfort him. "They wanted me to know," he said, "that the raid was necessary.")

IX
TERRORISM

INTRODUCTION

The use of terroristic tactics for political ends is not new. But it has assumed unprecedented proportions during the past two decades, affecting virtually all the western democracies in one way or another, disrupting international air travel, and costing thousands of lives in many countries. The terrorists themselves frequently attempt to justify their actions on the ground that they are necessary for the ultimate achievement of what they usually believe to be worthy revolutionary goals. They view their victims—usually unarmed civilians—as unfortunate souls who happen to get in the way, unless they are labeled as collaborators with the enemy or as the enemy itself. (The Puerto Rican Christian pilgrims who were gunned down in the Tel Aviv airport were labeled collaborators, because they had chosen to visit Israel; and the bankers and other businessmen who have been murdered or "knee-capped" in Italy are considered to be the enemy himself.) Those who are sympathetic to the aspirations of the terrorists are hard put to defend their tactics, but numerous efforts have been made to do so, often by suggesting that one person's terrorist is another's freedom fighter.

Kai Nielsen argues that when a state exceeds its legitimate authority, any force that it may exercise against its people is a form of violence. Conscientious citizens committed to democracy, he says, may legitimately resort to counterviolence under certain circumstances. Terrorism is justified when its ultimate aim is the realization of a socialist revolution, according to Nielsen, its justification being the fact that it works.

Abraham Edel, on the other hand, concludes that there are insuperable obstacles to the acceptance of terrorism, one of which is Kant's principle that people ought always to be treated as ends in themselves and never as means only. Terrorists necessarily treat human beings as means to the achievement of their political, economic, or social goals.

Responding directly to Nielsen's arguments, Nicholas Fotion concludes that terrorism is *prima facie* wrong, although he is prepared to grant that under certain carefully defined circumstances, some forms of terrorism may be morally justifiable. Fotion insists that the burden of proof is upon the terrorists: They must demonstrate that they are morally justified in committing their acts against the victims who have fallen under their power, and they must bear a heavy burden of guilt if they fail to do so.

KAI NIELSEN
VIOLENCE AND TERRORISM: ITS USES AND ABUSES

29

I

Mass-media talk of the role of terrorism and violence generally tends to be emotional with a high level of ideological distortion. I shall try to clear the air and establish that we cannot, unless we can make the case for pacifism, categorically rule out in all circumstances its justifiable use even in what are formally and procedurally speaking democracies. Yet terrorism is a minor tactical weapon for revolutionary socialists, which *sometimes* may rightly be employed to achieve the humane ends of socialism but typically is counterproductive and often very harmful to a revolutionary movement. When and where it should be employed is a tactical question that must be decided—though not without some general guidelines—on a case-by-case basis. It should be viewed like the choice of weapons in a war. It cannot reasonably be ruled out as something to which only morally insane beasts or fanatical madmen would resort. In the cruel and oppressive world in which we find ourselves, it, like other forms of violence, can be morally justifiable, though typically, but not always, its use is a sign of weakness and desperation in a revolutionary movement and thus, in most contexts, but not all, is to be rejected, at least on prudential grounds.

A humane person who understands what it is to take the moral point of view will deplore violence, but—unless that person thinks that pacifism can be successfully defended—he or she will recognize that sometimes the use of violence is a *necessary* means to a morally worthwhile end and that moral persons, while hating violence in itself, must, under these circumstances, steel themselves to its employment. Such moral persons will, of course, differ as to when those occasions will occur and will differ over what constitutes a morally worthwhile end.

I shall *assume* here that pacifism is not a rationally defensible moral position and that the achievement of a truly socialist society—a genuine workers' democracy with full workers' control of the means of production and the conditions of their lives—is a desirable state of affairs, a morally worthwhile end to achieve.[1] Given these assumptions, I shall first, after

Copyright 1981 by Kai Nielsen. This is the first publication of this article.
[1] Tom Regan has convincingly argued both that pacifism cannot readily, if at all, be refuted on conceptual (logical) grounds alone and that pacifism is not a very compelling or plausible moral doctrine. Tom Regan, "A Defense of Pacifism," *Canadian Journal of Philosophy* 2 (September 1972): I have attempted to argue directly for socialism in my "A Defense of Radicalism," *Question* 7 (January 1974). For a sum-

some preliminary clarifications, attempt to show under what conditions violence, even in a democracy, is justified, and then I shall, with the minor adjustments necessary, apply this analysis specifically to the problem of terrorism. I shall close by returning to the cryptic remarks I have made above about terrorism as a tactical problem.

II

Let us compare "violence," "force," and "coercion." The OED characterizes them as follows:

1. *Violence:* The exercise of physical force so as to inflict injury on or damage to persons or property. (However, the OED to the contrary notwithstanding, violence can also take psychological forms as when someone so tortures one mentally as to drive one mad.)
2. *Force:* To exert physical or psychological power or coercion upon one to act in some determinate way.
3. *Coercion:* Government by force; the employment of force to suppress political disaffection.

It is often said that it is important to distinguish between force and violence. And it is indeed true that "violence" and "force" are often not substitutable terms. They have different referents and a different sense. The OED to the contrary notwithstanding, violence is not just physical or psychological force (direct or indirect) but, rather, is by definition illegal or unjustified force. Indeed, it is taken in many contexts to be the unauthorized or illegitimate use of force to effect decisions against the will of others. "Violence" generally has a negative emotive force. Indeed, it often functions normatively, expressing disapproval.

In the following sample utterances, if "force" were substituted for "violence," there would be a change both in emotive force and in meaning.

1. Bend every effort to prevent violence.
2. Do not allow well-considered goals to be obliterated by the passion of irrationality and violence.
3. There have been acts of violence against the administration.

Where "force" is substituted for "violence" in these sentences, there is a change in emotive force and in meaning. Moreover, with such substitutions, 1, 2, and 3 become to a certain extent conceptually problematic; that is, they would be rather indeterminate in meaning. Native speakers would balk at them and be in some perplexity as to what was being said.

In a similar vein, consider the fact that "legal coercion" is quite

---

marizing and synthesizing contemporary argument for socialism, see Michael P. Lerner, *The New Socialist Revolution* (New York: Dell Publishing, 1973).

unproblematic whereas "legal' violence" is not, although, where the law was being used in a certain very oppressive and unfairly discriminatory way, we could come quite naturally to speak in that way. Coercion, like force, is in a whole range of standard circumstances morally justified, but the very meaning of "violence"—"something that extremists do"— is such that there is a strong presumption that an act of violence is wrong. At least it is, like breaking a promise or lying, something that, everything else being equal, ought not to be done. And, while there are contexts in which "violence" is used in a commendatory way, we seldom employ "violence" in morally neutral descriptions.

Let us come at our distinction between "force" and "violence" in a somewhat different way. Anarchists apart, everyone agrees that in certain circumstances a state has not only *de facto authority* (essentially power) but also *de jure* (legitimate) authority to coerce one's behavior, to force one to comply with its laws. That is, states not only have a commanding position by virtue of their power and their ability to mold social opinion to get people within their territories to accept their authoritative claims— their laws, demands, and regulations—but they have—it is also generally believed—the *right* to command and to be obeyed. The claim to have a right to command and to be obeyed is the claim to have legitimate authority.

Where (if ever) a state uses *legitimate* authority and forces one to act in the ways prescribed by that authority, this use of force is plainly not violence. And the citizens of that state, committed to its fundamental principles, have a *prima facie* obligation to obey the laws of that state. I say *"prima facie* obligation," for no citizen has an absolute obligation to obey any law.[2] There may arise circumstances about particular laws or about the application of certain laws in certain circumstances in which obeying them would violate one's conscience or in which in some other way it would be plainly a grave mistake to obey the law. In such circumstances one's *prima facie* obligation—which is an *ever-present* but still *conditional* obligation—is overridden by more stringent moral considerations. But one always does have a *prima facie* obligation to obey the laws of the state if that state has established its legitimate as well as its *de facto* authority.

A central question in political philosophy—a question that I shall not try to answer here—is when, if ever, does a state have legitimate authority over us? *Assuming* that anarchism is mistaken and that in certain favored circumstances a state or authority has *legitimate* authority over us, the question then becomes, when does it have the right to exercise such authority? That is, when does it have the right to force our compliance and when has it exceeded its legitimate authority?

[2] Richard Wasserstrom, "The Obligation to Obey the Law," *U.C.L.A. Law Review* 10 (1963): 788–790; and Marshall Cohen, "Civil Disobedience," *The Great Ideas Today, 1971, Encyclopedia Britannica* (Chicago, 1971), pp. 239–278. Jeffrey H. Reiman, in his *In Defense of Political Philosophy* (New York: Harper & Row, 1972), in the context of developing a devestating critique of Robert Paul Wolff's "philosophical anarchism"— something that has only a slight resemblance to anarchism, convincingly develops this traditional notion that a citizen has no more than a *prima facie* obligation to obey the law.

When it has exceeded its legitimate authority and still exercises force on people, then that force is a form of violence. Thus, there is a legitimate point in speaking, as Marcuse does, of "institutionalized violence" to characterize the use of state force in such circumstances. Such violence, though it uses the coercive arm of the state, is also to be disparaged and to be called illegitimate. However, it is reasonable to maintain, as Marshall Cohen has, that, as citizens of constitutional democracy, we have a duty to support constitutional arrangements on which others in our society have relied "so long as it is reasonable to believe that these arrangements are intended to implement, and are capable of implementing, the principles of freedom and justice." [3] And it is reasonable to assert that such states have legitimate authority. But, when the state takes measures that repress the principles of freedom and social justice, it is engaging in institutional violence, and we have no obligation to follow such dictates, though prudence may require that we accept for the time being at least certain of its arrangements.

"Acts of violence" are acts that are usually taken by the people who *so label them* as both illegal and morally unjustified; but it does not follow that under all circumstances "acts of violence" are unjustified. Surely they are *prima facie* unjustified, for to inflict harm or injury to persons or their property always needs a careful, rational justification.

There are two diverse types of circumstances in which questions concerning the justification of violence need discussing. We need to discuss (1) revolutionary violence—the violence necessary to overthrow the state and to bring into being a new and better or at least putatively better social order—and (2) violence within a state when revolution is not an end but violence is only used as a key instrument of social change within a social system that as a whole is accepted as legitimate. It is often argued that, in the latter type of circumstance, a resort to violence is *never* justified when the state in question is a democracy.

Let us first try to ascertain whether this is so. Consider, first, the situation in which a democratic state is engaging in institutionalized violence. Suppose, for example, that there is heightened trouble in the black community. It takes the form of increased rioting in the black ghettos. And suppose further that it is not adequately contained within the ghettos but that sporadic rioting, not involving killing but some destruction of property, breaks out into white middle-class America. Suppose further that there are renewed ever more vigorous cries for "law and order" until finally a jittery, reactionary, but still (in the conventional sense) "democratically elected," government begins systematically to invade the black ghettos and haul off blacks in large numbers to concentration camps (more mildly "detention centers") for long periods of incarceration ("preventive detention") without attempting to distinguish the guilty from the innocent. Would not black people plainly be justified in resorting to violence to resist being so detained in such circumstances if (1) they had good reason to believe that their violent resistance might be effective and (2) they had good reason to believe that their counter-

[3] Marshall Cohen, "Civil Disobedience in a Constitutional Democracy," *The Massachusetts Rev.* 10 (Spring 1969): 218.

violence would not cause more injury and suffering all round than would simple submission or nonviolent resistance to the violence directed against them by the state?

Even in such vile circumstances, it could be claimed that the blacks should nonviolently resist and fight back only through the courts, through demonstrations, through civil disobedience, and the like. This is perhaps fair enough, but, if the counterviolence continues and the camps begin to fill up without the nonviolent efforts producing any effective countervailing forces, then the employment of violence against these repressive forces is morally justified.

In such circumstances there would be nothing unfair or unjust about violently resisting such detention. Violence, and not just force, has been instituted against the blacks—the state having exceeded its legitimate authority—and the blacks are not behaving unfairly or immorally in resisting an abuse of governmental authority—democracy or no democracy. In deliberation about whether or not to counter the institutional violence directed against them, the blacks and their allies should make tough and careful utilitarian calculations, for these considerations are the most evidently relevant considerations here. To utilize such calculations, they must try to ascertain as accurately as they can, both their chances of effectively resisting and the comparative amounts of suffering involved for them and for others from resistance as distinct from submission or passive resistance. If in resisting police seizure some police are likely to be injured or killed, and if this means massive retaliation, with the police gunning down large groups of blacks, and if the concentration camps are not modeled on Auschwitz but on American wartime camps for Japanese-Americans, it would seem to be better to submit and to live to fight another day. But, if instead the likelihood was that even in submitting to extensive brutalization and indeed death for many, if not at all, would be their lot, then violent resistance against such a "final solution" is in order, if that is the most effective way to lessen the chance of seizure. A clear understanding of what in each situation are the empirical facts is of central importance here. But what is evident— to put it minimally—is that there is no principled reason in such circumstances as to why even in a democracy counterviolence in response to institutionalized violence cannot be justified.

Suppose that a democratic superpower is waging a genocidal war of imperialist aggression against a small underdeveloped nation. Suppose that this superpower has invaded it without declaring war; suppose further that it pursues a scorched earth policy, destroying the land with repeated herbicidal doses, destroys the livestock, pollutes the rivers (killing the fish), and then napalms the people of this country, civilian and military alike. Suppose that repeated protests and civil disobedience have no effect on the policies of this superpower, which goes right on with its genocide and imperialist aggression. Suppose, further, that some conscientious and aroused—but still nonrevolutionary—citizens turn to acts of violence aimed in some small measure at disrupting and thus weakening this institutionalized violence. It does not at all seem evident to me (to put it conservatively) that they have done what in such circumstances they ought not to do, provided that the effects of their actions hold some reasonable promise of hampering the war effort. (Even if they were mainly symbolic and in reality did little to slow down the violent juggernaut, I would still find them admirable, provided that such actions did not in effect enhance the power of the juggernaut.)

If, on the one hand, only more suffering all round would result from such violence, then resort to violence is wrong; if, on the other hand, such acts of violence would likely lessen the sum total of human suffering and not put an unfair burden on some already cruelly exploited people, then such violence is justified.[4]

The agonizing and frightening thing is that in many situations it is exceedingly difficult even to make an educated guess concerning the probable consequences of such actions. But this is not always the case, and again it is evident that there is no principled reason as to why committed democrats in a state with a democratically elected government might not be justified in certain circumstances in engaging in violence even though no violence had been directed against them or their fellow citizens.

Let me now turn to a less extreme situation. Suppose that the members of a small, impoverished, ill-educated ethnic minority in some democratic society are treated as second-class citizens. They are grossly discriminated against in educational opportunities and jobs, segregated in specific and undesirable parts of the country, and not allowed to marry people from other ethnic groups or to mix socially with them. For years they have pleaded and argued their case but to no avail. Moreover, working through the courts has always been a dead end, and their desperate and despairing turn to nonviolent civil disobedience has been tolerated—as the powerful and arrogant can tolerate it—but utterly ignored. Their demonstrations have not been met with violence but, rather, have simply been nonviolently contained and then effectively ignored. And finally suppose that this small, weak, desperately impoverished minority has no effective way of emigrating. In such a circumstance, is it at all evident that they should not act violently in an attempt to attain what are in effect their human rights?

There is no principled reason as to why they should refrain from certain acts of violence. The strongest reasons for their not so acting are the prudential ones that, because they are so weak and their oppressors are so indifferent to their welfare and dignity, their chances of gaining anything by violent action is rather minimal. But again the considerations here are pragmatic and utilitarian. If there were good reason to think that human welfare—a justly distributed human happiness, the satisfaction of needs, and avoidance of suffering—would be enhanced by their acts of violence, then they would be justified in so acting.

We may conclude that, although violence ought *prima facie* to be avoided, a conscientious citizen committed to democracy and living in a

---

4 The relevant sense of "unfair" here and its role in ethical theory is captured by John Rawls in his "Justice as Fairness," *The Philosophical Review* 67 (1958): passim, and in his mammoth *A Theory of Justice* (Cambridge, Mass.: Harvard University Press, 1971).

democratic society need not always commit himself or herself to non-violent methods.

III

There are several quite perfectly natural objections to make at this juncture.

1. It might be objected that, where such situations as those characterized in my examples exist, the society in question would not be a democracy, but either a tyranny or something approximating a tyranny. However, such societies may well be democracies—democracies in bad shape, no doubt, but still democracies.

"Democracy," like "science," is frequently an honorific label, and where it is, we will be inclined to say that such societies are not *real* democracies. But democracies that are not "real democracies" are still democracies, just as women who, as sexists would have it, are not "real women" are still women. In utilizing such a manner of speaking, we are suggesting that they lack certain features that we regard as very precious and as crucial to a democracy. But "democracy" is also a descriptive, open-textured term with a range of different applications. And, within the range of such standard applications, societies with features such as I have described would be properly called "democracies." Finally, it is a moot question whether or not some industrial democracies of the recent past or the present actually have most of these features.

2. It is also natural to object that, while I may have shown that under some circumstances, even in a democracy violence would be justified, as a matter of fact, the consequences of acting violently in such circumstances would not be such as to justify violence of any sort.

Once this is admitted, there can no longer be any general, principled, moral objection to all acts of violence in a democracy. Rather, if the preceding claim is true, it only establishes that, even in those situations in which one would be tempted to resort to violence, without overriding considerations that one acknowledges to be moral, *in fact* it so turns out that violence would be counterproductive. But the facts—plain empirical facts—could well have turned out to be otherwise. And indeed in our complex changing world might have turned out to be otherwise.

If violence is threatened or engaged in routinely, human liberty and even minimal security would be undermined. In a genuinely democratic community, resort to violence can only be justified in extreme situations, and it can never be justified as something we should do as a matter of course, for it would be counterproductive.

However, in arguing that violence—including acts of terror—may sometimes be justified, it would not be reasonable to take the position that Sidney Hook arbitrarily sets up as a straw man and then proceeds—predictably enough—to demolish, namely, that "violence and the threat of violence are *always* effective in preparing the minds of men for change." [5] That is indeed not a reasonable position; but it does not at

[5] Sidney Hook, "The Ideology of Violence," *Encounter* 34 (April 1970): 34, italics mine.

all follow that violence is never justified in democracies. Nor is resort to violence in a democracy always or almost always counterproductive. Pointing out, as Hook does, that there have been many instances in which significant social changes have been gained without violence, the threat of violence, or even the fear of violence does little to establish that in a democracy violence is never, or even hardly ever, justified, either prudentially or morally. That would be like trying to establish that one was never justified in taking radiation treatment as a cure for cancer by pointing out that people had been cured of cancer by less drastic methods of treatment. That would only be a good argument if there were good reasons to believe that the kind of cancers that people have are all of a type. If Hook could show that there were significant similarities between the types of cases in which significant social changes occurred within a reasonable length of time without resort to violence and the cases I have described then his argument would be a strong one. But he has done nothing of the kind. What Hook needs to do is to show us that, in situations—such as the ones I described—in which violence appears at least to be required or appears at least to be the best alternative (the lesser evil), its employment in reality is always very likely to be counterproductive.

Chronic and pervasive violence is, of course, destructive of social stability and the fabric of confidence and trust essential for civilized society. But this is not the result of the kind of in-the-extreme-case utilization of violence of the committed democrat in an imperfectly democratic society.

If, by contrast, things have deteriorated to such an extent that people engage repeatedly in violence, the society in question would have already so badly crumbled—so rent in its social fabric—that talk of protecting social stability and orderly procedure would in effect come to a recommendation to support a rotten regime. Sane men will not lightly engage in violence, particularly when it is directed against the government. It grows out of a desperation after social tranquility and stability have already fled. In such a situation it is utterly mistaken to argue, as Hook does, that we must resist violence to promote stability and social harmony. It is more likely in such a chaotic and repressive situation that social stability and civilized life will return only after the social order has been transformed by a social revolution building on violence.

IV

I turn now to the justification of the use of violence to attain a revolutionary transformation of society. As Herbert Marcuse put it in "Ethics and Revolution," [6] "Is the revolutionary use of violence justifiable as a means for establishing or promoting human freedom and happiness?" The answer I shall give is that, under certain circumstances, it is.

To discuss this question coherently, we need first to make tolerably clear what we are talking about when we speak of "revolution." Revo-

6 Herbert Marcuse, "Ethics and Revolution," in Richard T. De George, ed., *Ethics and Society* (Garden City, N.Y.: Doubleday, 1966), pp. 133–147.

lution is "the overthrow of a legally established government and constitution by a social class or movement with the aim of altering the social
as well as the political structure." [7] Moreover, we are talking of a "left
revolution" and not of a "right revolution," in which the revolutionary
aim is to enhance the sum total of human freedom and happiness. (I
think in this context it is well to remind ourselves of a point made by
Marcuse in "Liberation from the Affluent Society" that "without an objectively justifiable goal of a better, a free human existence, all liberation
must remain meaningless." [8] If there are no objectively justifiable moral
principles, all talk of progress, justifiable revolution, and justifiable
revolutionary violence becomes senseless.)

Reasonable and humane persons will generally oppose violence, but
in some circumstances they may agree that violence is justified. However, to be justifiable the violence must be publicly defensible.

Violence admits of degrees and of kinds. It is, for example, extremely
important to distinguish between violence against property and violence
against persons. The sacking of a ROTC office is one thing; the shooting
of the ROTC officers is another. But it is surely evident that violence
of any considerable magnitude—particularly when it is against persons—
is not justified as a purely symbolic protest against injustice. (This is
even more evident when the persons in question are innocent persons.)
There must be some grounds for believing that this protest will have
an appropriate beneficial effect. It is—concentration camp-type circumstances apart—both immoral and irrational to engage in violence when
all is in vain, for this merely compounds the dreadful burden of suffering.
Bernard Gert is surely right in asserting that "neither purity of heart
nor willingness to sacrifice oneself justifies violence, and it is even clearer
that attempts to ease one's conscience do not do so." [9] For violence, revolutionary or otherwise, to be justified, the evil being prevented or eliminated must be significantly greater than the evil caused. As Marcuse
stresses, in advocating the use of violence, a revolutionary movement
must "be able to give rational grounds for its chances to grasp real possibilities of human freedom and happiness and it must be able to demonstrate the adequacy of its means for obtaining this end." [10] If there are
equally adequate alternative nonviolent means, it must use them. Surely
the American Marxist, Daniel De Leon, was plainly right in declaring
that, if it were possible, a peaceful and constitutional victory for socialism is preferable to a victory achieved through violence.

V

Marcuse remarks that traditionally the end of government "is not only
the greatest possible freedom, but also the greatest possible happiness of

[7] *Ibid.*, p. 134.
[8] Herbert Marcuse, "Liberation from the Affluent Society," in David Cooper, ed., *The
Dialectics of Liberation* (Harmondsworth, Middlesex, England: Penguin Books, 1968),
p. 175.
[9] Bernard Gert, "Justifying Violence," *The Journal of Philosophy* 66 (October 2, 1969):
627.
[10] Herbert Marcuse, "Ethics and Revolution," p. 135.

man, that is to say, a life without fear and misery, and a life in peace." [11] In asking whether the revolutionary use of violence is a justifiable means for establishing or promoting human freedom and happiness, we must, as Marcuse points out, ask whether or not there are "rational criteria for determining the possibilities of human freedom and happiness available to a society in a specific historical situation." [12] Can we ever establish in any historical situation that revolutionary violence would further more adequately human freedom and happiness than any of the other available alternatives? Given the technical and material progress at a particular time, what is the likelihood that the future society envisioned by the revolutionaries will come into being, sustain itself in a form that is distinct from the already existing society, and utilize the technical and material advances available or reasonably possible in such a way as to substantially increase human freedom and happiness? We must consider (1) "sacrifices exacted from the living generations on behalf of the established society"; (2) "the number of victims made in defense of this society in war and peace, in the struggle for existence, individual and national"; (3) the resources of the time—material and intellectual—that can be deployed for satisfying vital human needs and desires; and (4) whether or not the revolutionary "plan or program shows adequate promise of being able to substantially reduce the sacrifices and the number of victims." [13]

If we turn, with such considerations in mind, to the great revolutions of the modern period, keeping in mind that it would have been impossible for modern conditions to have come into existence without them, it is evident that "in spite of the terrible sacrifices exacted by them," they greatly enlarged the range of human freedom and happiness. As Marcuse well puts it;

> Historically, the objective tendency of the great revolutions of the modern period was the enlargement of the social range of freedom and the enlargement of the satisfaction of needs. No matter how much the social interpretations of the English and French Revolutions may differ, they seem to agree in that a redistribution of the social wealth took place, so that previously less privileged or underprivileged classes were the beneficiaries of this change, economically and/or politically. In spite of subsequent periods of reaction and restoration, the result and objective function of these revolutions was the establishment of more liberal governments, a gradual democratization of society, and technical progress.[14]

Moreover, as Marcuse continues;

> [T]hese revolutions attained progress in the sense defined, namely, a demonstrable enlargement of the range of human freedom; they thus

---

[11] *Ibid.*, p. 134. It should be remarked that here Marcuse makes a rather pardonable overstatement, for it is at least arguable that some kinds of fear give a certain spice and zest to life and thus might be desirable. What Marcuse has in mind is the persistent and massive kind of fear that goes with gross economic insecurity, powerlessness, and political repression.
[12] *Ibid.*, p. 135.
[13] *Ibid.*, p. 145.
[14] *Ibid.*, p. 143.

established, in spite of the terrible sacrifices exacted by them, an ethical right over and above all political justification.[15]

In sum, when the total of human misery and injustice has been diminished by a violent revolution more than it could have been in any other feasible way, then that revolution and at least some (though very unlikely all) of its violence was justified; if not, not.[16]

VI

In this context we should view terrorism as a tactical weapon in achieving a socialist revolution. "Terrorism" and "terrorist," we should not forget, are highly emotive terms. Burke referred to terrorists as hellhounds, and the word "terrorist" is often simply a term of abuse. A terrorist is one who attempts to further his or her political ends by means of coercive intimidation, and terrorism is a systematic policy designed to achieve that end. I shall view terrorism here in the context of socialist revolutionary activity and not consider it in the theoretically less interesting but humanly more distressing context of the truly massive terror and violence of conservative counterrevolutionary activity. I want, rather, to get clear about the place of terrorism in a socialist revolution.

Terrorist acts of assassination—as distinct from the massive acts of terroristic repression utilized by brutalitarian governments—rarely make any serious difference to the achievement of a revolutionary class consciousness and the achievement of a socialist society. Rather—as happened after the terrorist assassination of Tsar Alexander II in 1881— fierce reactions usually set in. In the abortive Russian revolution in 1905 terrorists took an active part. But they were hardly a major instrument of it; rather they were, in Rosa Luxemburg's apt phrase, merely some shooting flames in a very large fire. Their presence neither made nor broke the revolution. The terrorist acts of the Milan Anarchists in March

---

[15] *Ibid.*, pp. 143–144. It is not clear whether or not Marcuse recognizes that it is not enough to justify a revolution to establish that it produced desirable results; we must also show that without the revolution the desirable results would not have occurred as rapidly and with (everything considered) as little suffering and degradation. What I think he should be claiming is that when we examine the French and English revolutions that is just what we should conclude. In referring to the English Revolution, I am referring to a series of revolutionary happenings that went on in the seventeenth century.

[16] In the horrors of an extended civil war that might be linked with a revolution, it is very likely that on all sides there will develop indiscriminate and pointless terror. We need, in our historical calculations, to take account of these possibilities, but this does not at all give to understand that we are justifying them. We can accept their likelihood while condemning such acts and recognizing, as Marcuse does, that "there are forms of violence and suppression which no revolutionary situation can justify because they negate the very end for which the revolution is a means. Such are arbitrary violence, cruelty and indiscriminate terror." *Ibid.*, p. 141. I have developed my arguments about revolution in a more extended way in my "On the Choice Between Reform and Revolution," in Virginia Held, Kai Nielsen, and Charles Parsons, eds., *Philosophy and Political Action* (New York: Oxford University Press, 1972), pp. 17–51; and my "On the Ethics of Revolution," *Radical Philosophy* 6 (Winter 1973) : pp. 17–19.

of 1921, after the disillusioning failure of the general strike, are perhaps characteristic of the futility of many terrorist actions—actions that typically result from desperation and weakness. They bombed a theater, killing twenty-one people and injuring many more without achieving anything in the way of revolutionary or even progressive ends. Rather, this act alienated many workers from the anarchists and provided Mussolini's fascists with still a further excuse to take action against the Left.[17]

Like all acts of violence in a political context, terrorist acts must be justified by their political effects and their moral consequences. They are justified (1) when they are politically effective weapons in the revolutionary struggle and (2) when, everything considered, there are sound reasons for believing that, by the use of that type of violence rather than no violence at all or violence of some other type, there will be less injustice, suffering, and degradation in the world than would otherwise have been the case.

We must, however, be careful to keep distinct, on the one hand, individual or small-group acts of terror to provoke revolutionary action or to fight back against a vicious oppressor—the paradigm terrorist actions—and, on the other, terrorism as a military tactic in an ongoing war of liberation. For any army, vastly inferior in military hardware but with widespread popular support, terrorism in conjunction with more conventional military tactics might very well be an effective tactic to drive out an oppressor. It is in this context that we should view such acts in South Vietnam and in Algeria. Where we have—as in Rhodesia— a less extensive struggle, it may still very well be justified. But the terrorist tactics of the F.L.Q., the Weathermen, or (probably) the Irish Provisionals are something else again. They seem in the grossest pragmatic terms to have been counterproductive We have the horror and the evil of the killings without the liberating revolutionary effect—an effect that would be morally speaking justified, in which all human interests are considered and other viable alternatives are considered, if the likelihood would be of preventing on balance far more human suffering and opposition in the future. (In these last cases it is very unlikely.)

In making a similar point, the Marxist historian Eric Hobsbawm writes,

The epidemic of anarchist assassinations and bomb-throwings in the 1880's and 1890's, for instance, was politically more irrelevant than the big-game hunting of the period. In all likelihood, the last ten years' political killings and shootings in the U.S.A. have not substantially changed the course of American politics; and they include the two Kennedys, Martin Luther King, Malcolm X, the Nazi George Lincoln Rockwell and Governor Wallace. I don't claim that political assassination cannot possibly make a difference, only that the list of 20th century acts of this kind, which is by now extremely long and varied suggests that the odds against its doing so are almost astronomical. And if we take the case of the 250 or

---

[17] George Woodcock, *Anarchism* (Harmondsworth, Middlesex, England: Penguin Books, 1962), pp. 333–334.

so aircraft hijackings of recent years, what these have achieved is at most some financial extortion and the liberation of political prisoners. As a form of activity, hijacking belongs to the gossip column of revolutionary history, like "expropriation," as it's called—that is to say, political bank robbery. So far as I am aware, the only movements which have systematically used hijacking for political purposes are sections of the Palestine guerrillas: and it doesn't seem to have helped them significantly.[18]

The best case to be made for the effective use of terrorist tactics— apart from their use in an ongoing war of liberation in which there are actually opposed forces in the field—was in the latter part of the nineteenth century against tsarist autocracy. The Tsar had absolute power. Russian absolutism was vicious in the extreme, and some of the Tsar's ministers and police chiefs were particularly vicious. It was against this brutalitarianism that the Russian revolutionary anarchists directed their terror. One could see the point in assassinating the Tsar or his hangmen, but, even under such circumstances, terrorist activity did little to hasten the fall of Russian absolutism. Because terrorist activity must be judged by its consequences—the lessening of suffering, degradation, injustice, and the spread of liberty and a decent life for oppressed people—these Russian terrorist acts may not have been justified.

There is a sense of moral satisfaction—of justice having been done— when some thoroughly tyrannical brute has been gunned down by revolutionary terrorists or money for the poor has been extracted from the ruling class through political kidnappings; but, again, as Rosa Luxemburg coolly recognized, this sense of moral satisfaction tends to lull people into inaction. People are likely to be deceived into believing that something effective is being done and are thus less likely to come to see the absolute necessity of making a socialist revolution for attaining a mass proletarian base of class-conscious, committed workers.

We must be careful here not to overstate—as Hobsbawm is on the verge of doing—the case against revolutionary terrorism. Writing in 1905 and speaking of Russian terrorism, Rosa Luxemburg judiciously observed that, while terrorism could not by itself bring an end to Russian absolutism, it did not follow that it was a pointless and therefore a morally and pragmatically unjustified activity. It was necessary in Russia to attain bourgeois liberties to achieve a *Volksrevolution*. Without such a mass movement, the downfall of Russian autocracy would not have occurred. Terrorism can serve the rather minor role, once mass revolutionary activity has started, to fight back for the proletariat in their struggle with their oppressors, and, in such a situation, it may also be used appropriately as a tactic to force such a brutal absolutism into making concessions to the proletariat. It is a weapon in the struggle to meet the attempts to suppress "the revolution with blood and iron." [19] However, as Rosa Luxemburg goes on to say, as soon as absolutism recognizes the imbecility of such a use of force and, no matter

[18] Eric Hobshawm, "An Appraisal of Terrorism," *Canadian Dimension* 9 (October 1972): 11–12.
[19] Rosa Luxemburg, *Gesammelte Werke, Band I 1893 bis 1905, Zweiter Halbband* (Berlin: Dietz Verlag, 1972), p. 521.

how vacillatingly and indecisively, enters the road of constitutional concessions to the proletariat, then, just to that degree, terroristic tactics will lose their effectiveness and their rationale. Indeed, when considerable concessions are made, its role will be altogether finished and a second phase of the revolution will have begun.[20]

In sum, while Rosa Luxemburg recognizes that "the avenging hand of the terrorists can hasten the disorganization and demoralization of Absolutism, . . . to bring about the downfall of Absolutism and to realize liberty—with or without terror—can only be accomplished by the mass arm of the revolutionary working class." [21]

In an ongoing revolutionary struggle in which workers are already struggling against an overt and brutal oppressor who will not make significant concessions or give them any significant parliamentary rights, terrorism can be a useful and morally justified tactic. We can see this exemplified—as I have already noted—in Algeria and South Vietnam. But, once significant democratic concessions have been wrung from the ruling class, it is not only not a useful tactic, it is positively harmful to the cause of a socialist revolution, though it should also be recognized, as my hypothetical examples evidenced, that, where these democratic concessions are being seriously overridden, situations can arise in which a violent response on the part of the exploited and oppressed is justified.

VII

I recognize that arguments of the type I have been giving will with many people cut against the grain.[22] They will feel that somehow such calculative considerations conceptualize the whole problem in a radically mistaken way. They will say that we simply cannot—from a moral point of view—make such calculations when the lives of human beings are at stake.

My short answer is that we can and must. Not wishing to play God, we must sometimes choose between evils. In such circumstances, a rational, responsible, and humane person must choose the lesser evil. Sane people capable of making considered judgments in reflective equilibrium will realize that judgments about the appropriateness of the use of revolutionary violence are *universalizable* (generalizable) and that, without being moral fanatics, they will be prepared to reverse roles, though of course, a member (particularly an active member) of the ruling class, placed as he or she is in society and with the interests that he or she has, is in certain important respects one kind of person and a proletarian is another. (This, of course, is not to say that one is a "better person" than the other but, rather, that their positions in society are such that

---

20 *Ibid.*, p. 521.
21 *Ibid.*, pp. 521–522. In this context the balanced discussion of the activities of the Symbionese Liberation Army by the editors of *Ramparts* shows, much in the manner of Rosa Luxemburg, political good sense. See "Terrorism and the Left," *Ramparts* 12 (May 1974): pp. 21–27.
22 See my "On Terrorism and Political Assassination," in Harold Zellner, ed., *Political Assassination* (New York: Schenkman Publishing Company, 1974), Sections III and IV.

they will tend to see the world differently, live differently, relate to people differently, and have different values.)

The thing to keep vividly and firmly before one's mind is this: that, if anything is evil, suffering, degradation, and injustice are evil and that proletarians and the poor generally are very deeply afflicted with these evils. Some of them at least are avoidable; indeed some that we already know how to avoid flow from the imperialistic and repressive capitalist system and from its country cousin, state capitalism. If the use of revolutionary violence in the service of socialism were to lessen this suffering, degradation, and injustice more than would any other practically viable alternative, then it is justified, and if not, not.

In the past, revolutionary violence has been so justified, and in the future it may very well be justified again, even in what are formally democracies. Terrorism, by contrast, has a much more uncertain justifiable use. There are extreme cases—as with a charismatic leader such as Hitler—in which a terrorist assassination is very likely not only a good political tactic but, from a socialist and humanitarian point of view, morally desirable as well. More significantly and more interestingly, terrorist tactics may very well be justified in the liberation struggles in Chile, Angola, and Mozambique. Morally concerned rational human beings must go case by case. However, in the bourgeois democracies, in which concessions have been made and in which certain vital liberties exist, it is not a justifiable tactic but is rather a tactic that will harm the cause of revolutionary socialism.[23]

[23] I would like to thank Jack MacIntosh for his helpful comments on an earlier version of this essay.

ABRAHAM EDEL 30
NOTES ON TERRORISM

Because terrorism has become such a serious practical problem, a great deal of energy is today devoted to guarding against it. At every airport we are now aware of this. Journals carry articles on how negotiations were handled in specific cases of hijacking of planes or capture of hostages or how special police or army units are trained for dealing with terrorists. The psychology of the terrorist has been discussed as have the

Reprinted from Abraham Edel, *Exploring Fact and Value* (Transaction Books, 1980) by permission of the author and Transaction Books.

"Notes on Terrorism" is a revision of comments on Kai Nielsen's "Violence and Terrorism: Its Uses and Abuses" delivered in a session on terrorism at a conference on Morality and International Violence held at Kean College of New Jersey, Union, New Jersey, April 22–24, 1974. Reference is also made to a paper by Carl Wellman, "On Terrorism Itself," which was also read at the conference.

role of publicity in setting the stage for the terrorist's operations, the best way for a hostage to conduct himself or herself, and numerous other matters.

Obviously the terrorism envisaged is an evil, and concern with it is largely directed to preventing and eliminating it. But surprisingly there does not seem to be sufficient agreement on its interpretation for general legislation against terrorism, for it would not be wholly clear as to what was being banned. Even in the case of less than that—the hijacking of planes—there are political problems in securing international agreement for a universal ban. Could there possibly be any reservations about terrorism?

Perhaps among the contemporary inconveniences of terrorism we shall have to include theoretical burrowing into the concept of terrorism itself. The theoretical understanding is likely to have most practical bearings, indirectly if not directly.

PROBLEMS IN THE QUEST FOR A DEFINITION

We have plenty of clear-cut illustrations of the phenomenon: gangs terrorizing a trade into paying tribute, assassinations of government officials and leaders, Nazi tactics in an occupied town, wiping out of towns in war to intimidate the civilian population, hijacking planes and holding hostages, letter bombs, even retaliations to terrorism. Because it strikes us as a distinctive phenomenon, we begin to focus on it and think it deserves an essence of its own. This is prompted also by the natural tendency to straighten a bent stick by bending it in the opposite direction; for, as Carl Wellman has pointed out, terrorism has been treated largely as a footnote to the treatment of violence.

Certainly analysis of the concept of terrorism is prior to formulating or criticizing general conclusions about its use. Wellman, conjecturing as to what his hypothetical *New and Improved Dictionary for Philosophical Analysts* would say, defines terrorism as "the use or attempted use of terror as a means of coercion." This fits central clear cases of conspiratorial organization to terrorize a population by surprise violent actions. The fit is less neat for individual threats and actions or for situations in which general terror results without intentional "terrorism." As an example of the former, Wellman even includes threatening to fail students who hand in late papers. An example of the latter would be a community in a state of terror because of the frequency of muggings, so that scarcely any one dares to go out after dark. This is terror without terrorism. The individual mugger may not be interested in inspiring terror to achieve his or her end; cool prudence in the victim may be enough to make him or her freeze.

Perhaps we could go on to distinguish carefully among (1) a state of terror (which the appearance of a wild animal might inspire without its being a case of "use," though no doubt some evolutionary properties of inspiring terror might have accounted for the success of such animals), (2) the use of terror indifferently among a number of ways of securing one's end (the highwayman, like the mugger, does not care which feeling makes the victim hand over money or what the victim's affective structure may be), and (3) the deliberate or intentional use of terror as the sole or chief means. But perhaps the strength of the concept is wasted if we associate it with an isolated act rather than reserve it for a more systematic structure. And apart from all this we must recognize that even the success of one definition in opening up interesting questions does not mean that an alternative definition may not open up other serious questions.

To speak of wasting the strength of the concept expresses, perhaps, a different approach to the concept of terrorism and the problem of definition. Terrorism is an emerging concept rather than one endowed with an established essence, and what will emerge will be a quasi-technical usage on which will hang a variety of legal and moral consequences. Meanwhile, in the rich complex of phenomena there are different directions we can go in essence building, and, as we fix on one or another significant feature in a striking case, we may be carried at high speed past other possible turning points and find ourselves on a one-way highway. The legal and moral consequences may bring regret that the itinerary was not more cautiously experimental. For example, a definition might take as its point of departure that in terrorist phenomena all restraints are abandoned, any means being employed; when this is coupled with the recognition that morality involves some internal restraints, it follows that from the outset terrorism is immoral by its definition. Or by contrast, the point of departure may be the prevalence of violence in the phenomena of terrorism; this yields the familiar treatment of terrorism as a species of the genus violence, hence the debate over the types of conditions that would justify violence and even those which might justify terrorism. (Nielsen's analysis moves in this direction.) Or, again, the point of departure may be the psychological state of terror; this is Wellman's starting point, which he couples with the recognition that terror is induced in order to compel unwilling subjects to behave in a desired direction. Because terror may be induced in nonviolent ways—for example, by blackmail with a well-manipulated threat of exposure or in threats of loss of employment and ruin of careers as in McCarthyite charges of communism in the 1940s and 1950s—Wellman is led to exclude the reference to violence from the definition of terrorism while recognizing that violence stands out because it is a very effective means of inducing the terror that then has the coercive effect. Of course defining terrorism as a species of violence may take the saving move of extending the concept of violence itself to include institutional violence and psychological violence as well as physical force. (Of this, more later.) Again, a wholly different point of departure may be a focus on some classification of the ends for which the coercion is being exercised. In this vein, just as there are theoretical attempts to remove the taint of violence from legal use of sanctions involving force and limit it to the illegal, so inducing terror in the "criminal classes" to ensure legal observance (e.g., by high payment for informers, latitude for the police to use physical coercion, arming police with unusual weapons, quick convictions and stern sentences including physical and capital punishment) would not be taken to be terrorism.

Such varied handles for conceptualizing the phenomena suggest that our theoretical concern in definition is not with fitting a well-patterned set of current uses of the term, but with fashioning a concept that will bring the clearest understanding of the phenomena and give us the best handle for coming to grips with the social and human problems involved. To get such an investigation going comprehensively is more important at the present stage than a (possibly premature) formal definition; the latter can wait until we have more knowledge as an outcome of the investigation—if we turn out to need it then. Meanwhile, it will not matter much whether we think of terrorism as a species of the genus violence but with striking properties or as an independent genus whose most important species is differentiated by the use of violence (which as an empirical matter is probably the most effective means of inducing terror). Whichever definitional policy is ultimately decided on, there will have to be a host of contextual or nonformal qualifications. For example, minimally there has to be a certain degree of magnitude in various features: a certain degree of alarm, a certain temporal extent, a certain degree of organization or systematic structure in the process, and so on. The important thing at this point is to gather significant dimensions.

Several such obvious dimensions are here suggested. One is the *range of potential sufferers;* is it determinate, such as the wealthy or the officials who have behaved brutally to a designated race or ethnic group, or is it any random or chance collection? Certainly it is the high degree of randomness that is sometimes central in intensifying the atmosphere of terror. (A specific revengeful murder will not cause alarm, whereas random attacks will, even though less violent.) A second dimension is *motivation;* it is particularly significant whether the terrorism aims at monetary gain or is directed to advancing some cause. A third dimension is the *institutional setting;* does the terrorism come in peace or war, in prisons and police action, or is it prevalent even in education and family life? A fourth is the *cultural pattern* and the place of violence in it. A fifth is the specific *historical setting;* for example, whether terrorism occurs in the historical moment of a rising class or a declining class, in the context of a revolution or a reaction against it, in a period of self-indulgent prosperity or of deep economic depression. Doubtless many other significant dimensions are to be discerned.

Such dimensions could be of use in different ways to understand the phenomena of terrorism and to get a handle on coping with them. Certainly explorations along all these lines would be necessary in seeking a formal definition. For classification of types, perhaps the dimension of motivation (with some attention to institutional setting) would be the best preliminary basis; thus we shall distinguish later *terrorism in predatory crime, terrorism in war, and moralistic terrorism* (that is, terrorism in the service of a supposedly moral cause). But to see whether these involve different lessons and different principles for their understanding and handling or whether they are part of a common problem, we have to go beyond psychological motivation to the question of probably deep cultural roots. Again, in the frequent controversies as to whether violence in general and terrorism in particular are ever justified, we find arguments based on the particular historical situation and what it calls for. The remainder of this paper consists of reflections on some of these questions, beginning with controversies about justification, going on to cultural aspects, and then focusing on the different types of terrorism indicated.

THE QUESTION OF JUSTIFICATION

Because terrorist phenomena involve so much that is counter to human morality, a question of justification, if it is raised at all rather than a question of explanation, is formulated as a problem for the terrorist. We expect him or her—not the sufferer or the public—to say what are the reasons for such desperate action, what are the ends and means involved. In fact, terror is rarely seen as an end; it is more often proposed as a means and sometimes affirmed as a punishment. Each of these merits exploration. At some points the exploration can draw on the more familiar study of problems of justification for violence in general, as parallel issues are involved.

To terrorize people is rarely conceived as an end. Even a culture that makes a virtue of truculence and admires the bully probably has strength as the cultural goal and bullying as reliable evidence. Similarly, the joys of sadism, that perennial source of terrorizing others, have been sufficiently explored psychologically to be revealed as clinical symptoms rather than as an intrinsic value that happens to be socially dangerous. In the case of violence generally, particularly war as a seedbed of heroism, the claims for intrinsic value have been not infrequent in the past. But even in the *Iliad*, glory in violence was a fairly transparent avenue to status. And whatever the exaltation of war and the warlike in olden days, by the time of the world wars in our century prefascist and then fascist doctrines were clearly glorifying violence as an ideological weapon in the battle with a rationalistic liberalism. We may thus dismiss justification of violence as an end, not by stipulation but as the verdict of evidence about means and ends in human life.

The claim that terrorism is on occasion a justifiable means brings it into confrontation with a pacifist approach that rules it out on antecedent moral grounds and also with historical judgments about its efficacy. Because this is a separate problem, our comments here will be restricted to a few summary remarks.

The pacifist view applies to all violence and so *a fortiori* to terrorism: violence is not to be countenanced morally under any conditions. This has not, on the whole, won general acceptance as an absolute for action, though it is found in a "rather die than" attitude in some. But even those who reject it as such a categorical absolute can retain it as a universal principle in moral reckoning, a kind of aspect rule or "break only with regret" rule, to the effect that wherever violence is used it clearly diminishes greatly the value total of the situation. Nothing prevents such a rule from weighing universally, even though under certain conditions it is outweighed by other considerations of value. Such a universal formulation, however, is too wide a net to catch and hold back even the terrorist who freely admits the evil of what he or she is doing but claims that vastly greater evils are tolerated by his or her forebearing.

The general pacifist position in an instrumental mode—that nonviolence is a much more powerful means than violence—does seem to hold only for limited conditions. Consider, for example, the familiar case in the Indian nonviolent movement for independence, in which large masses of people sat down on the railroad tracks to stop the trains. What happened would depend on the character of the train engineer. The British engineer would tend to stop the train, but we may assume that a convinced Nazi would plow straight into the crowd. (There is the story of a Japanese engineer who slowed the train down to a crawl and then jumped off, leaving the demonstrators to make their own decision.) In the early phases of the civil rights movement in the United States, nonviolence expressed the highly moral tone among the participant youth; but this proved a passing phase in the move toward black nationalism. It is not therefore simply a question whether absolute pacifism is a rationally defensible moral position, but also whether nonviolence as a method is likely to be successful. It surely deserves the same kind of evaluation as a method that one gives to violence—especially as its intrinsic aspects of mutual respect are so clearly superior to the intrinsic evils of coercion in its opposite. Now, while it is empirically true that nonviolence is not a dependable instrument, it is equally the case that we have no really successful analyses of why it fails where it does and why it succeeds where it does. The question of its theoretical weight is therefore still unresolved, as are the assumptions underlying some of its forms. For example, there is the hypothesis found in Tolstoy and Gandhi that nonviolence releases a basic human drive. Whether it is thought of in religious or metaphysical terms as a love-force or in quasi-biological form as in the anarchist's faith in sympathy and mutual aid, it still remains one of the major theories about the human constitution. Our scientific psychologies have been too busy exploring guilt and aggression to take time to explore sympathy and mutuality, and only their occasional resurgence from the social depths reminds us that our theoretical picture is far from complete.

The claim that there are conditions under which the use of terror is justified is still left open by the confrontation of violence with pacifism, which we have considered, for it is possible that terrorism may be the only viable means in some limited and very unusual situations. In those cases it would have to face on its own the historical arguments already referred to, which were directed against violence generally but might seem to hold *a fortiori* for terrorism. Chief among these has been the view that resort to violence is a sign of weakness in social struggles. This need not, perhaps, apply to war, in which it has often been the excessive strength of a nation that prompted it to war against those who refused its demands and in the course of the war to employ terrorist tactics where popular resistance was strong. (Not to be able to win without terror here might, of course, be construed as *relative* weakness.) In the case of revolutions, confidence of strength has also played a part, though occasionally an uprising expresses suffering and despair. Nevertheless, the view that resort to violence is a sign of weakness has a certain plausibility. If you can win an election or have the army solidly behind you or (in the history of the labor movement) have an unchallenged and firm picket line, why use violence? The history of sabotage in labor struggles would seem to bear this out; often it appears as a rearguard action after a strike has been lost, expressing frustration or else a desperate attempt to keep the action going. Perhaps the qualification with respect to relative weakness should be extended here. It is not just weakness that is involved in the resort to violence, but sometimes the kind of relative weakness that is found in a precarious balance of strength. For example, a revolutionary terror may come from a governing group that fears a counterrevolution or a rightist terror from a governing group that is losing its grip. Terror in either case is directed toward preventing the consolidation of the opposition.

The view is sometimes urged that terrorism is not as effective as is often thought, that it is wasteful, that alternative methods for achieving a good end can usually be found, and so on. But there still remains the possibility that, although it expresses weakness, it may sometimes be the only available resort of those who are laboring under injustice and, hence, the only alternative to permanent resignation. Here the hope is that the instrument of terror will keep the issue alive and even serve to integrate the oppressed. But suppose it would, does that constitute a justification? And is it the same kind of justification that would be offered for a declaration of war?

There remains the element in terrorism that suggests the treatment is deserved. Terrorism then poses as an unusual form of punishment. Even where the terror is indiscriminate in its victims, it chooses them out of a certain class, as when public places in England have been bombed because the British do not withdraw from northern Ireland. If this is meant to be a mode of punishment, it clearly assumes collective responsibility; the morality of such an assumption would have to be considered. Or else it is punishment in the sense of deterrence—making one public suffer as, it is asserted, the other public has suffered—so that it will be stimulated to withdrawal. In any case, in specifying a reference class, it sets a limit to the indiscriminate character of the terrorism.

Despite such claims, the general moral objection remains that in terrorism people are being treated no longer as persons but as means. I do not know how far this will carry the argument; it is quite possible for the reflective terrorist to affirm his or her respect for the victims in the same sense as one side in a war respects the soldiers on the other side (though more often this has been explicit in the relations of opposing officers). Nietzsche, it will be recalled, wanted all crime treated as rebellion as it would respect the criminal, whereas a reformatory theory seemed to him to be manipulating the person. Presumably, an imaginative terrorist might declare a day of respectful mourning for the victims of his or her efforts, using it also to blame the reference group for these consequences of injustice.

In any case, terrorism is a great evil. From the terrorist's standpoint, it is a necessary evil. His or her task of attempted justification is harder than the justification of occasional violence: terroristic violence is not violence in resisting violence; it is not protective violence or ordinary deterrent violence or violence in the service of an established institution or of a revolutionary movement as such. It bears the stamp of a violence that is beyond the line of duty and beyond ordinary demands. It need not be controlled, and it can be duly measured; it need not be sadistic, and it probably loses its character if it is such. It has a kind of ultimate character. It deals in death, often in random surprise, in utter disrespect for the person in what seems like a calculated irrationality. When the terrorist undertakes to argue about it, his theme is that his end is good, that no lighter means are available, and that the means should be endured because, even with its evils, the net result of advancing the end is a better. The terrorist is likely to be dogmatic in his justification, not stressing the difficulties involved in judging nor making subtle differences of degree between violence against person and violence against property. Nor will the terrorist usually consider the possibility that the means have so high a cost to people that the end should rather be given up or left to a later period when more moral means become possible. Nor once embarked on terrorism is the terrorist likely to consider the moral need for less rather than greater violence.

Justification from the point of view of the terrorist has not carried us far enough into understanding what is going on. Perhaps the language of means and ends and that of cost–benefit analysis, and even that of respect for persons, misleads us in the situation under discussion. It talks as if terrorism were a mistake in calculation, or else perhaps a correct reckoning where it succeeds (something like deciding whether to use nuclear fission or coal for generating power to carry on the normal processes and achieve the normal ends of society), or else neglect of a proper interpersonal attitude. Now all these categories of analysis are perfectly proper but they are too general. The understanding of the specific phenomena that is needed for their evaluation may be more specifically cultural and social; and the broad philosophical attitude required for developing a normative policy, that is, asking what is to be done about terrorism, may come from looking at terrorism not only from the point of view of the terrorist's application for justificatory credentials, but also from the standpoint of the sufferer or patient.

CULTURAL BASIS OF TERRORISM

Terrorism gains wide currency usually in a society in which violence is an acceptable means. (Neither is an expression of human nature in the raw.) Philosophical controversies over what violence is legitimate and what is not, or even over what is and what is not violence, are indicative of a growing self-consciousness in the culture, though often in an oblique way; they are rarely simply verbal disputes to be resolved by linguistic analysis. This may be illustrated by taking two controversies—one old in political science, one new in sociology.

The first of these attempts to distinguish between force and violence. Force is declared a neutral term, be it the force of the police officer or of the burglar. Violence is the use of force that is not legitimate; it is used by the burglar, not the police officer. Such an analysis, however, merely passes the buck to the concept of legitimacy. If legitimacy has moral connotations, it is one thing. But if it is purely legal, then it raises all the questions of the Nuremberg trials about mass killings in accordance with law (similarly, about repressive violence by a government taking power through a coup, as in Chile, but also even about an established democratic government doing what the Americans did with napalm to intimidate civilian populations in Vietnam). Surely the use of napalm would have been violence (and terror) even if there had been prior and explicit congressional authorization for the use of this weapon. The attempt to limit "violence" to what those outside of an Establishment do, and to deny it of the behavior of Establishment figures and supporters, represents the efforts of the Establishment to take refuge in a moral garb, usually when it is under moral attack. How much of that garb covers real social needs or how much simply the nakedness of an order in trouble is precisely the issue that no linguistic legerdemain can dispose of.

The second controversy concerns the sociological use of the term "institutional violence." This is at the other end of the spectrum, for it extends the term "violence" to cover areas in which there may not even be overt force involved. It is warranted only if we exhibit continuities (often discovering them with the aid of theoretical advances) with the overt uses of force. No doubt this involves considerable analytic ordering in the nest of related concepts. The sense of "institutional violence" is both theoretical and moral. It is concerned with what actually goes on in prisons, in schools, in the very habits of male–female relations as well as parent–child relations. Take, for example, the time when spanking was an approved (legal and moral) procedure in dealing with children. It took a Plains Indian wholly outside our culture to recognize it as degrading violence—though perhaps our children sensed it too. It took the growth of psychological sophistication among adults to see it as their own aggression, not as a neutral instrument for the child's well-being in preserving a moral fiber. It took a wrench to see it from the child's point of view, much as photographers have sometimes tried to compose pictures from the child's perspective that would show the threatening look of the gigantic adult. Similarly, it has taken a whole liberation movement to uncover the character of male violence in relation to the female. If the concept becomes stretched when it is attached to the violent word as well as the violent deed, perhaps it nevertheless calls our attention to the common psychological essence. We must not be in a hurry to dismiss notions of psychological violence. In the current concern with what goes on in prisons, isolating a prisoner is none the less doing violence even without beatings. Whatever the conceptual outcome in the refinement of "violence," it should not be such as to obscure the theoretical findings nor sidetrack the moral critique.

Such illustrations show that our analysis of terrorism cannot stop with the first three dimensions of the list given earlier—the range of potential sufferers, the type of underlying motivation, and the institutional setting. To understand and evaluate for practical action, we have to go on to the cultural pattern and the specific historical setting. With respect to the first, it has been noted often that in the United States we have a violent culture, compared even with other branches of the Anglo–American tradition. Growing consciousness about the incidence of violence not merely in penal institutions but in familial institutions (studies of child-beating, for example) point in this direction, as do attitudes toward guns and their control. It is not a simple judgment, and we cannot here go into the many aspects that have to be explored both concerning practices and concerning attitudes. Its relevance to terrorism is simply this: to condemn terrorism taken as an isolated phenomenon may be simply to condemn a particularly aggravated symptom without understanding the human illness that underlies, produces, and supports it. This does not mean that the symptom should not be treated, but that the disease should also be diagnosed and understood.

The cultural dimension is not enough. We have to look to the specific historical setting. This is often indicated in the recognition that the Vietnam war had a particularly brutalizing effect; discussions of the My Lai episode made this very clear. In the other direction, television brought the horrors of the war into the home, though as a spectacle and interspersed with advertisements providing prescriptions for the body beautiful. But the Vietnam war was not itself an isolated historical incident. Its own analysis would carry us into the present state of world conflicts between the haves and the have-nots, the transition from colonialism to the problems of the developing countries, the relations of strength and belligerence in the advanced industrial powers. To take a recent analogy, we are no more likely to understand terrorism without such an in-depth analysis than we are to understand the recent revelations of bribery of government officials abroad by large American and multinational corporations without a full analysis of business motivations and business practices in the whole range of their operations. To keep to a purely general moralistic critique of terrorism would be like offering a critique of the bribing as simple individual dishonesty.

It does not follow from this that the vision of long-range understanding must stand in the way of short-range policies. They have to go hand in hand. We thus turn to the types of terrorism distinguished earlier, treating briefly predatory crime and terrorism in war and then the terrorism associated with social causes.

TERRORISM IN PREDATORY CRIME AND WAR

The finer distinctions that have to be made in types of terrorism can best be approached initially from the standpoint of the patient or sufferer, that is, not the immediate victim—unless he survives and his experience serves to intimidate him—but the group of potential victims whose intimidation by the act and the way it is done constitutes the agent's purpose. Now one thing is clear: Potential victims do not regard the contemplated suffering as merely chance misfortune, like discovering that one has cancer, or has caught a disease in an epidemic (where questions of blame for carelessness are not at issue), or for that matter being shot at by a deranged person firing from a tower at anyone coming into range. People may be alarmed in such cases, but they are not terrorized.

They can try to meet the dangers only by greater caution, systematic diagnosis of causes and probabilities, and research for preventive measures.

In predatory crime, any terrorism that occurs is carried out for gain. How will a shopkeeper look upon demands by a gang for payment for "protection"? Conceivably it could be seen as informal taxation or as part of the cost of production to be passed on to consumers. But more likely it will be seen as straight crime. Against such crime, the familiar policy is protection, deterrence, punishment. In extreme cases in which these are insufficient, people will be driven into a kind of garrison life. Only in very extreme cases will the relation of potential victims and criminals begin to resemble war. Usually it is something less: There are defensive acts that the potential victim cannot take—for example, to shoot to kill rather than wound, to gather evidence by unauthorized eavesdropping—and if the criminal is captured, the victim must allow him or her to be brought to fair trial.

Terrorism in war engenders different attitudes in the potential victims. It tends to be more indiscriminate, and with fewer restraints. War is an all-out affair; it is fighting to the death to win. (I am referring, of course, to the traditional conception; contemporary war is getting much more complicated, and third parties often try to get it ended as quickly as possible before it spreads and gets out of hand.)

Even in war there are differences in the kind of situation from the sufferer's point of view. There may in some cases, for example, be options. If the underground in an occupied country threatens assassination for brutality by occupying officials, the latter have the choice of not being brutal. Worst of all is the indeterminate war terror—wiping out whole villages to intimidate the civilian population, taking random hostages and shooting them, and so on. Whereas in the case of crime to obey the terrorist demand is often a viable option, in the war model it often amounts to surrender. The innocent victims, if they manage to survive, are drawn into the war on their side. Their suffering is now no different from that of the soldier who is shot at and hit; they have been conscripted by a different process.

It is important not to treat war as crime nor crime as war. There are times at which the concentration and organization of crime may approximate to war and there are kinds of actions in war that may, as in the Nuremberg trials, become identified as crimes and punished as such. But the categories remain distinct, as do the programs of action for overcoming each.

From the society's point of view, can moral demands be laid on the terrorist, whether in crime or in war, that limit the scope of his action? There is a type of moral rule that takes the form "Never do this, but if you do, observe such-and-such cautions." The sanctions involve, of course, adjusting punishment to the degree of conformity to the regulations. For violence in many of its forms, this is quite possible, as when crime and war are regarded as professions and are invited to work out the rules according to which their ends can be achieved with a minimum of suffering. (Highwaymen are gentlemen, jewel thieves never carry guns, murderers spare their victims' feelings, the enemy never tortures the prisoner for information when the prisoner refuses to give more than name, rank, and serial number.) The history of the rules of war shows the difficulties of such moral attempts to minimize suffering. We expect less is possible in the case of terrorism, but even here there is a difference between exploding a bomb in a crowded bar and exploding one in an empty building, or even a last-minute phone call to clear the building. The general difficulty with such attempted regulation of war and crime and terrorism, such attempts to domesticate them, is that too often the rules will begin to interfere wih achieving the end that the terrorist has in mind, for which he is engaging in the activity. Even in "normal" war, the pressure to use forceful methods to extract information from prisoners when it is believed that they can tell about an imminent and dangerous large-scale operation is tremendous, though sometimes inhibited by fear of like treatment of one's own captured soldiers. The moral issues are of course the familiar ones of ends justifying means in critical situations, and they cannot be discussed in abstraction as the answer to the general question whether the end justifies the means is obviously that some do and some do not, and in some kinds of cases for some kinds of means it never will. But which are which is precisely the question for the particular situation.

There is no point in pursuing this issue here. To attempt a moral regulation of terrorism that distinguishes the respectable from the disrespectable or the legitimate from the illegitimate in war warrants the description of "shuffling deck chairs for greater comfort on the Titanic." One cannot be sure that short-range goods will not be achieved, and certainly lives may be saved, but as a central direction of effort there is a danger that it will divert attention from tackling the underlying causes of the situation that begets terrorism. Within a clear perception of the whole it may be possible to isolate factors in terrorism and put obstacles in its path—for example, because much of it rests on publicity, to limit its advertisements in the media. If, however, terrorism is an expression of weakness or relative weakness, as suggested, the lessening of its effectiveness may, rather, lead to its escalation.

MORALISTIC TERRORISM

The most difficult type of terrorism to handle is that involving a cause, which we spoke of earlier as moralistic terrorism. In the old days, political prisoners were distinguished from and treated differently from ordinary predatory criminals. There was a time when even a foolish cause that was felt and followed as an ideal was taken to be ennobling. But the Nazi experience showed what depraved causes can invite and get people to sacrifice themselves. Even the potential victims of moralistic terror have therefore to ask themselves what is the underlying cause or ideal in the name of which they are likely to be victimized. And they have not merely to identify it but also to evaluate it if they are to form a sound policy for dealing with it.

Of course the various dimensions of terroristic action will make a difference in the public attitude. When an ROTC building was burned in the growing protest against the Vietnam war, it was specific and directed against part of the process of war making. When revolutionary groups in Argentina or Uruguay kidnapped executives of large corporations that they regarded as exploiting their people and asked for large ransoms to be distributed through some ameliorative social channels, the terror was still pointedly specific, though people now became its counters. Suppose that they had kidnapped any American and had made their demands against the American government? When a white man was shot at in the so-called Zebra cases in San Francisco, the terror (given that analysis of the incidents) was directed indiscriminately against a given broad class. The same was seen in the attack on Israeli athletes at Munich, or the shootings at European airports by Palestinian terrorists, or the capture of Dutch trains by South Moluccans.

It is possible, of course, to drop all differentiation and simply feel that we are back to the Hobbesian state of nature, the war of all almost against all. Although this reflects the general insecurity accurately at times, it is too general to provide guidance for what is to be done; or is the comparison to war helpful despite all the warring that may go on in many of these cases. Even though the black terrorist may regard it as a war, against all whites, or the Palestinian terrorists as a war against all Israelis and all whose activity may help the Israelis, it does not follow that the whites or the Israelis should regard it as a war. This need not inhibit protective action or even punitive action—that is a separate problem. But important differences in the long-range picture will flow from the attitude that is invoked.

Moralistic terror has then to be analyzed with attentiveness to the ideals or causes embodied in it. At the very least it is significant when a terrorist is ready to give up his own life to serve his cause. There are the familiar questions: Is the terrorist intellectually muddled about means? Is the terrorist mad? Is he expressing a frustration that has led to desperation? Is he just evil? I doubt that one can stop with the individual. As we have seen in identifying the cultural and historical dimensions, one has to look into the whole social background in which individuals come to take such a turn. Certainly there is enough familiarity by this time with the conditions of exploitation and oppression that give rise to racist and nationalist ideologies in the oppressed as well as the oppressors. And sometimes too it is not a question of oppressors and oppressed but the tragedy that lies in the conflict of opposing claims, where each is reasonable *if* taken alone. To use the analogy of war for the terrorism that grew from such a seedbed would be to be callous to the problems that generated them. It would thrust aside the responsibilities for allowing them to fester over generations of neglect and systematic turning aside, not to speak of the selfish gains that may have come from paying no attention to them. Indeed, for many types of moralistic terrorism, it would not be far amiss to feel them as an historical punishment for the callousness of people to the problems of people. The problems and attitudes of Job in his anguish may be more appropriate than ringing declarations of war. Of course some of the individuals who now suffer from the terrorism may not have shared in the callousness; they may even have spent years in less than successful struggles against the specific injustices. But many issues in the modern world assume wholesale proportions and may not be amenable to retail treatment.

If the act of moralistic terror thus becomes understandable, what can the potential victims do about it? Are they left with no resort but repression, care, protection, sometimes even acts of war and reprisal if not the full application of the war model? It would be too easy to say "Solve the underlying problems!" But at least harder work to open the channels is possible. There are parallel issues in human history that might point a direction. For example, when John Locke enunciated the right to revolution, he regarded it as an appeal to heaven when all appeals on earth had failed. But there is a sense in which this right was in part domesticated with the development of democracy so that the room for appeal to the electorate and the public was immeasurably broadened. And in our own time the increased recognition of individual conscience and the manifestations of civil disobedience gave greater social scope even to individually deviant commitments of deep intensity. Again, in the history of the labor movement, it was a long road from criminal syndicalism to collective bargaining. What is there to be learned about the ways in which threats of war were defused in such developments? Is there anything to parallel these stories for the areas that underlie today's major moralistic terrorisms?

A number of preliminary suggestions come to mind. Certainly there is the negative warning not to be distracted from the basic problems that generated the terroristic action. In this regard, the kind of liberalism that spends its best energies on opposing busing and affirmative action and has nothing to offer for advancing the liberation of blacks and women, or the conservatism that looks for strong men as dictators in Latin America, is heading for the war model and enshrining callousness. Moreover, even the means of repression of terrorism or of reprisal as deterrence have room for sensitivity. What, for example, are the components in Israeli attitudes to reprisal? Is the reprisal directed to destroying camps from which the terrorists emerge? Does it wipe out houses rather than people? Is it pressure on the government of a neighboring state to take a firmer line against terrorism? Is it needed as a channel for expressing popular Israeli feelings? The longer-run settlement has to solve the problem of the Palestinian Arabs, but the short-run character of action is of vital significance. Finally, there is the seriousness of attitude in seeking solutions to the problems that generated and support terrorism. This may be a long-run matter, but the short-range contribution lies in the authenticity of the present effort, the movement not "with all deliberate speed" but with effective immediate acceleration, the breaking through age-old ideological barriers to seeing the problems, and the movement toward cooperation in formulating solutions and projecting plans of action. It is true that Rome was not built in a day, but times have changed and construction workers know how fast a skyscraper can go up. Worse still, we all know that nowadays Rome can be destroyed in a day.

NICHOLAS FOTION
THE BURDENS OF TERRORISM
31

I

One might suppose, when first coming to think about acts of terrorism, that moralists could simply say that these acts are wrong. One might also be tempted to suppose that moralists who cannot show that such acts are wrong are not much good for anything. It is not as if in being expected to condemn terrists they were being asked to make close moral calls, as when in baseball the runner and ball arrive at first base within a fraction of a second of one another. Condemning terrorism, it would seem to the ethical novitiate, is like calling a runner out who is only halfway to first base when the ball has already settled into the first baseman's glove.

It is disturbing, therefore, to read an account of terrorism and violence that says, "Victimizing people is always at least *prima facie* wrong, indeed it is terribly wrong," that also urges a careful consideration of all moral options including terrorism but that, nonetheless, seems to open wider the door to terrorism and violence than these cautionary thoughts suggest it would.[1] It is also disturbing when this account is both biased in the direction of a particular political ideology and implies that terrorism is acceptable if it is successful.[2]

To be sure, I too will argue that victimizing people is always a *prima facie* wrong and that one ought to look at all the options as he or she should in theory in dealing with any moral issue—even terrorism. Nonetheless, I will go on to argue that the beginner in ethical theory is nearer the mark in condemning terrorism than are some sophisticated moralists who, in the end, permit more terrorism than they should. I will hedge a bit myself by permitting some forms of terrorism. It may be, for example, that certain forms are justified in dealing with an enemy in war who is himself engaged in terrorism. Further, there are many forms and degrees of terrorism, and it would be foolish in a *carte blanche* fashion to condemn them all for all possible settings. Nonetheless, if there are exceptions so that some forms of terrorism are justifiable, there are nevertheless other forms, especially those in which the terrorist directs his acts against innocent people, that should always be condemned.

Copyright 1981 by Nicholas Fotion. This article was especially written for this volume, and this is its first publication.

[1] Kai Nielsen, "Another Look at Terrorism and Violence: A Response to Professor Edel," unpublished manuscript.

[2] Kai Nielsen, "Violence and Terrorism: Its Uses and Abuses," this volume, pp. 435–449.

I will back my contention by focusing attention initially upon the recipients of the terrorist's activities rather than upon the actor himself. These recipients can be divided into those who are victims and those who are terrorized; and of these two, I will deal with the former first.

Terrorists do not have to have victims to do their work. It is possible for them to terrorize a population, a class of people, or a government simply by displaying their power in a threatening way. One can, for example, imagine a situation in which terrorists threaten to use an atomic weapon that everyone knows they have in their possession. However, in a vast majority of the cases familiar to us, some individuals will be victimized so as to make it clear that the terrorists mean to be taken seriously.

The terrorist's victims may not be, although they are often, terrorized in (and/or following) the process of being victimized. Yet, they must be hurt in some way if they are to have the status of victims. The victims can be robbed, tortured, raped, starved, killed, or abused in any number of other ways. They may also carry some guilt. When they do, we begin to hedge a bit by saying, "Of course terrorism is wrong. However, in cases such as these we can see why terrorism might be acceptable." But these are not the kinds of cases that disturb us the most. They should still disturb us if for no other reason than that the terrorist's victims should have been treated as if they were innocent until proved guilty. Thus, in killing an allegedly guilty person, the terrorist is, in effect, administering the death penalty without offering the victim due process of law.

Although the unilateral actions of the terrorist are bad enough when the victims chosen deserve (in some sense) the treatment they have received, the terrorist's actions cannot help but be seen in a worse light when the victims are innocent. There are, of course, degrees of innocence and guilt; but terrorists who choose their victims in a random or nearly-random fashion cannot help but victimize many people who are innocent of political or other wrongdoing. Think of a child, an uneducated peasant, a housewife, a white-collar worker, and even a person who shares the political views of the terrorist (but is against the tactics of terrorism) who may be randomly killed, maimed, or assaulted. Each is literally treated as an object to be used—we might even say used up—to further the terrorist's ends.

In fact, in being treated as an object, the innocent victim is worse off than the (alleged) guilty victim. Insofar as the latter is judged to have done a wrong, he is thought of as a human. After all, it is humans, not dogs and cats, who make political errors and commit moral wrongs. For the terrorist the innocent victim is neither a human in this judgmental sense nor a human in the sense of simply having value *as* a human being. Of course the terrorist needs to pick a human being as a victim. But he does this because choosing human victims brings about more terror than does choosing either dogs or cats for victims or inanimate objects for destruction. But this does not involve treating them *as* humans. Rather, they are victimized and thereby treated as objects *because* they are humans.

No doubt terrorists can reply to these accusations by saying that they regret all the death and suffering that they are causing; and, insofar as they do, they show at least some respect for their human victims. Further, we might contend that they do not consider the victims to be anything but objects. Rather, the terrorists find it necessary to sacrifice (valued) humans for some greater good.

But surely more than an expression of regret is required to establish that terrorists are treating their victims as humans and/or that they value them as humans. Minimally what would be required is a careful set of calculations showing us just how much value was placed on their victims and just how they made the calculations that resulted in their victims' losing out to the greater good. But even this is not enough. Without some behavioral consideration, some nonverbal gesture in the direction of showing that their victims actually received some consideration, it is tempting to say that the terrorists' regrets are insincere or simply represent so much rhetoric.[3] This is especially so if their victims are selected at random without regard to age, gender, biological and social status, past accomplishments, and failures and are chosen only with regard to their racial or ethnic status (i.e., because they are Jews, Chinese, etc.).

So the moral burden of terrorists who direct their harmful acts against innocent people is a heavy one. It is heavier still when we realize that their calculations ought to take account not only of the innocent people that they are victimizing as a type, but in terms of their numbers as well. How many will they "regretfully" sacrifice? Philosophers talk about the fallacy of the slippery slope, that is, of assuming that, when a person begins drinking, for example, that person will inevitably become an alcoholic. But surely some slopes are more slippery than others, and terrorists are on one of the most slippery of all. Because terrorists have a higher calling that allows them to victimize an individual, the very logic of their argument dictates that they find more victims to initiate and sustain terror. That their own argument greases the slope and thereby tempts them not to set a limit on the number of people that they will turn into victims on behalf of their higher good is, in fact, another indication of the object status to which they relegate their victims.

But the moral burden is heavier still. Not only are terrorists greasing the slope with a logic that allows them to create quantitatively an almost unlimited number of victims, but they are greasing it for quality as well. If mere bombings do not terrorize because they simply maim and kill, or because people have become inured to them, terrorist logic dictates a slight tactical change. Why not add rape and torture to the agenda? Why not concentrate on victimizing children? Surely, the terrorists might say to themselves, these "variations" will bring about more terror. Very likely they will, but they must also increase the terrorists' moral burden.

[3] Burton M. Leiser, *Liberty, Justice, and Morals: Contemporary Value Conflicts*, rev. ed. (New York: Macmillan, 1979). Professor Leiser focuses on the terrorist's rhetoric in a portion of his chapter (pp. 384–388) on terrorism.

II

Even if the terrorists admitted that they carry all these moral burdens, they have an effective counterargument available. They can say that in spite of its burdens, their tactics can and often do work. They succeed in terrorizing certain peoples and governments so that the "greater good" is brought about. Thus, insofar as terroristic tactics are successful, they are justified. It is as simple as that.

This argument is deceptively persuasive. However, when fully understood, although it may still persuade a few, I believe that most will not be moved by it. To show why, it is necessary to focus next upon the second group of people who receive the attentions of the terrorist, namely, the terrorized.

The first thing to note about those who are terrorized, obvious though it is, is that they are also harmed. To be terrorized is at least to suffer temporary emotional trauma and often permanent damage as well. More than that, terrorized persons may themselves harm others. In a terrorized condition, a person will often act violently while making demands on government officials, searching for food that others have, and seeking other things as well. In his irrational (terrorized) state, the terrorized person may even do things that will further harm himself.

The second thing to note, especially if the terrorism is aimed randomly at a general population, is that it will affect many innocent people. Again this may seem obvious; but, if the burdens of the terrorist are to be weighed, each harm that he does needs to be identified. So, to reach those people or officials who must in some sense capitulate to their demands, terrorists more than likely must harm two separate layers of innocent people (i.e., their victims and those terrorized)—actually three if one counts those harmed by the terrorized persons while they are in a terrorized condition. The terrorists destroy or very nearly destroy their victims and unhinge the terrorized. Along the way of getting what they consider to be the higher good, they are up to no good at all. Their means in fact are about as evil as their imaginations can conceive and their powers carry out. So *successfully* terrorizing people in and of itself counts heavily against an overall assessment of what the terrorists are up to. It is their "highest good" alone, when achieved, that sustains their argument, in theory at least, by counterbalancing the burdens of wrongdoing that they have committed against their victims and the terrorized.

Looking, then, at the "higher good" portion of the terrorists' argument, notice that even if the highest good is achieved and even if it truly is a higher good, that alone does not justify the terrorists' tactics. To do that, they must show us that no other tactical option is available that has a reasonable chance of bringing it about.[4] After all, because they chose morally the worst, or just about the worst, possible means, they owe us an explanation as to why just these means are chosen over all others. Why, for instance, did they not choose to terrorize the opponent's military establishment? Certainly, if the campaign against it

4 Nielsen, this volume, p. 440.

were pressed, that establishment might be significantly damaged. It is true that military people have an unpleasant habit of shooting back when attacked, and for that reason attacking them may be more dangerous than victimizing unarmed citizens. But this observation could hardly be turned into a morally convincing principle that, when revolutionary work becomes a bit hazardous, it is permissible to attack children, women, and other noncombatants. In fact, when one comes to think of it, the option of attacking the opponent's military establishment is always present. It is easy enough for the terrorist to say that there are not other options available but difficult to convince people that this is so. Indeed, people's feelings about this matter may be one key reason for its being so difficult to sympathize with terrorists. That is, the terrorist case is unconvincing, not just because the moral burden of attacking innocent people is so very heavy, but also because it is very difficult to show convincingly that there is no other way to get the revolutionary job done. Given different situations, different options will open up. Nonviolent resistance will work in some contexts; testing the laws to the limit will work in others. In still others, terrorizing the offending government officials directly may be an option that, for all its dangers, at least keeps innocent people from becoming victimized or terrorized. Still, the option of attacking the opponent's military establishment is always available; and because this is so, the terrorist tactics of attacking innocent people at random will seem intuitively to be morally wrong to most people.

It will do the terrorists little good to argue that when they talk about "having no other choice" they do not mean this literally but mean instead "having no other choice *as good as* killing innocent people." To clarify their meaning in this manner weakens their position considerably, for it is now obvious that the terrorists have a real choice. They cannot plead, after all, that the only choice that they have is to kill or be killed. Such an excuse would be sufficient in the case of one person who has killed another in self-defense, having no choice but to kill to save himself—even when the slain victim's threat was not malicious or deliberate. The terrorists' rhetorical claim that they have no choice but to kill their innocent victims is simply false. They are not *forced* to act as they do. Rather, it is their *decision* to adopt those tactics that both victimize and terrorize innocent people.

Further, now that it is obvious that their tactics are a matter of conscious and deliberate decision making, it makes sense to ask that public calculations be made to see if the terrorists have chosen well. To be sure, it is difficult to disprove their claim to have chosen well. But this is not so much because their position is so strong as because it is so difficult to imagine how *any* overall calculation can be made either of the position's strengths or of its weaknesses. Indeed, some calculations can be made; but they hardly help the terrorists to defend themselves against charges of gross immorality. It is the nature of the terrorists' tactics that some of their moral debts are calculable. We can count their victims and, in a crude fashion, measure some effects of their terror as these moral debts are so visible and are incurred by them in advance. In contrast, their credits tend to be promissory and/or often identified as credits by them in terms of their own ideological standards rather than in terms of the standards of a wide spectrum of people. The overall calculations (which could show that the moral costs of terrorism are less than the gains) are hard to produce. In addition, the terrorists must demonstrate that their form of behavior creates greater overall moral profit than does (1) terrorizing the opponent's military establishment and (2) any other option available. Such a demonstration would involve putting into a set of calculations not only the value of bringing about the higher good in the first place, but also such things as (1) the value of bringing it about a month (a year) sooner because terrorism was used rather than some other means, (2) the military and economic costs associated with terrorism as against the costs of using other means, and (3) the civilian costs associated with terrorism as against the costs of using other means. These and other difficult-to-come-by calculations leave terrorists in an awkward position, to say the least, as they need them to help justify their tactics.

The argument that put them in such a position can be summarized as follows: Given the high moral costs of their tactics, they can say that they have (literally) no choice if they are to act to bring about their "higher good." But what they say here is empirically false. The terrorists always do have another choice. They can choose, if no other option is available, to engage in a terroristic war against their opponent's military establishment. So they must admit that they are not literally forced to adopt the tactics that they do but, rather, that they choose to do so. But their choice, which victimizes and terrorizes innocent people and thereby carries a visibly heavy moral burden, becomes even more unattractive when we realize how difficult it is to prove that it is significantly better than other choices that could have been made. Thus, even if successful in bringing about their cherished goals and even if they come to us with claims of victory and success, it would not be inappropriate for us to withhold our moral congratulations. Instead we might ask them in their moment of triumph, "What assurances can you give us that some less bloody way was not better?"

III

Now there are many replies that terrorists can give to get out of these difficulties. I cannot, of course, deal with all of them, although I feel that all can be answered in such a way as to condemn all forms of terrorism of innocent people. I will, however, present three replies that they could give and deal briefly with each one.

First, they may argue that the argument against them places an undue burden of proof upon them. If they cannot prove that their tactics are the best of a bad lot, neither, they could argue, can the defenders of the other options prove that theirs are any better. However, in making this reply the terrorists forget that they carry a special burden of proof because they carry a special burden of wrongdoing. We do not ask people to justify their actions when they harm no one in the process of attempting to achieve a good or alleged good. If they fail, we say,

"Too bad," and perhaps urge them to try again. But the more their efforts harm others, the more we expect an accounting that makes sense. Thus, even if the terrorists are successful, it is difficult to make sense of tactics that involve such initial high costs and are difficult to assess. A related additional argument that puts the terrorists' tactics in a still worse light is that, if they fail, we are left with a heavy moral deficit with little or nothing on the positive side to counterbalance it.

The terrorists' second response is a desperate one at best. They can deny that the calculations needed to assess the merits of their position are difficult to make by claiming that calculations can be made because their victims and those that they terrorize count for nothing.[5] They are most likely to say this when those who are the objects of their attention belong to a hated ethnic (racial, national, etc.) group, so that it is at least possible for them to get support for their tactics among their own group.[6] But surely it will be difficult for them to get support for their discriminatory policies beyond their group if for no other reason than that they are violating the universalizability principle:

> As ethical judgements become more general, specific references to "me," "here" and "now," "them," "there" and "then" are eliminated and as long as any such references remain there is room for an appeal to a more general principle. The point at which the justification of a moral decision must cease is where the action under discussion has been unambiguously related to a current "moral principle," independent (in its wording) of person, place and time: e.g., where "I ought to take this book and give it back to Jones at once" has given way to "anyone ought always to do anything that he promises anyone else that he will do" or "It was a promise." If, in justifying an action, we can carry our reasons back to such universal principles, our justification has some claim to be called "ethical." But, if we cannot do so, our appeal is not to "morality" at all: if, for example, the most general principles to which we can appeal still contain some reference to us, either as individuals or as members of a limited group of people, then our appeal is not to "morality" but to "privilege."[7]

Morally, then, it is a bankrupt policy to turn the hated ethnics into worthless objects. It amounts to appealing to privilege rather than to ethics.

Somewhat less desperately the terrorists could claim that their victims and those that they terrorize count for something but that, in the sweep of history, the many good things produced by the revolution reduce its victims to insigificance. Aside from sounding both cavalier about other peoples' lives in saying this and also overly optimistic about the merits of the revolution, this reply is beside the point. The issue is,

[5] Thomas Sheehan, "Italy: Behind the Ski Mask," *The New York Review of Books*, August 16, 1979, pp. 20–26. See Sheehan's discussion of Antonio Negri's views.
[6] Michael Walzer, *Just and Unjust Wars* (New York: Basic Books, 1977), p. 203.
[7] Stephen Toulmin, *The Place of Reason in Ethics* (Cambridge: University Press, 1953), p. 168.

again, not just whether terrorist tactics have greater utility than doing nothing. Rather, it is whether they can be shown to be more beneficial than other options that have fewer initial moral costs.

The terrorists' third reply is not to deny the worth of those that they victimize and terrorize but to deny their innocence. Whole ethnic groups or classes of people can be said to share the guilt of some past deed or practice, they might argue. This being so, they claim that they bear virtually no moral burden for their actions.

In response, one may ask whether they are all *equally* guilty. Is the terrorist implying that the hated ethnic leader is no more guilty than a hated ethnic thirteen-year-old? Is the hated ethnic secret agent no more guilty than the hated ethnic athlete? Whatever guilt the athlete and the thirteen-year-old carry must certainly be so diluted as to pale into innocence. To claim that all of "them" are guilty equally, or even guilty enough so as to deserve becoming objects of the terrorists' attentions, is simply to be uttering half- (or quarter-) truths at best, or redefining "guilty" arbitrarily.

IV

My arguments against terrorism are really quite simple. They attempt to make explicit the reasons why people are instinctively repelled, especially by those forms of terrorism in which innocent people are the targets. Three basic arguments were presented.

The first is that terrorists take upon themselves a high initial burden of moral wrongdoing. It is a two-layered burden in that they victimize some and terrorize others. This burden might possibly be overcome if there were no other way to achieve the greater good that the terrorists want so badly. However, and this is the key premise in the second argument, there is always another way. Because there is and because the other way carries with it a lesser moral burden, the terrorists' position is now doubly unattractive morally.

The third argument is that more than any other tactician, terrorists need to show us how they figure that their way is superior to all others. But this showing is difficult to come by. The terrorists are left in limbo —needing to justify themselves but being unable to do so.

Of course, even if they could produce calculations that made sense to others (besides their most ardent followers), the others might show that there was a better way than the terrorists'. Consider whether it really makes a difference if the terror is applied *before* or *after* the terrorists come to power. Keep in mind that officials who use terror are also terrorists, even though they are sometimes called oppressors or tyrants instead. Whatever we may call them, we rightly feel that they do not deserve to stay in power if they resort to terrorism aimed at innocent people. By using such tactics they have morally disqualified themselves to rule, although in fact they do rule. Terrorists, having placed themselves in precisely the same moral position, have morally disqualified themselves from coming into positions of political authority.

1. Is Nielsen's use of Marcuse's phrase "institutionalized violence" helpful or misleading in the context in which it occurs? What is "institutionalized violence"?

2. It would seem that Machiavelli might approve of some aspects of Nielsen's approach, but he suggests in several places that potential terrorists make a hard-headed utilitarian calculation. Is it likely that John Stuart Mill or Jeremy Bentham would have approved of his approach?

3. To what principle does Nielsen appeal in opposing state violence and advocating terroristic or revolutionary violence?

4. How helpful is Nielsen's criterion for judging terrorist activity: that it must be "judged by its consequences—the lessening of suffering, degradation, and injustice, and the spread of liberty and a decent life for oppressed people." He finds, on this criterion, that the acts of the Russian terrorists may not have been justified. If one cannot be sure, more than a half-century later, whether a given terrorist act was justified, with all the developments that followed it plain for all to see, how can any potential terrorists, deliberating over their plans of action and striving mightily to do the right thing, make a rational judgment?

5. Nielsen argues that terrorism is justified when it is politically effective in the revolutionary struggle and when it leads to less injustice, suffering, and degradation than alternative forms of violence or no violence at all. Are his arguments in defense of this position persuasive? Are they sufficient to establish a moral justification for terrorism under certain circumstances?

6. Does Nielsen adequately consider the potential suffering of, say, the middle class, as opposed to the poor, in his analysis?

7. Abraham Edel, referring to some distinctions raised by Carl Wellman, suggests that terror may exist without terrorism. What exactly is the difference?

8. Are Edel's careful dissections of the concept, terrorism, mere exercises in semantics, or do they have some practical consequences? If so, what are they?

9. What assumptions must a pacifist make, and how do they relate to the problem of terrorism? Are those assumptions justified? How might they be justified by a dedicated pacifist?

10. Professor Edel gently takes scientific psychologists to task for their failure to explore sympathy and mutuality. If they were to do so, what do you suppose they might find, and what impact might those findings have upon the study of terrorism in particular and moral philosophy in general?

11. What is wrong (if anything) with a means–end, or cost–benefit analysis? What better form of analysis might there be of a moral or policy issue?

12. Edel discusses numerous forms of "violence" that seem, at least superficially, to stretch the use of that term. Has he adequately justified the use of such terms as *institutional violence, psychological violence,* and *male violence?* On further analysis, what do such terms mean? Are they merely emotive, condemnatory phrases; do they have some descriptive content; or is their use purely persuasive?

13. What exactly is moralistic terror and how is it distinguished, factually and morally, from other forms of terror?

14. Compare the arguments and the conclusions of Professors Nielsen and Edel. Where do they agree or disagree, and to what principles do they appeal, either in common or in opposition to one another? How well does each of them establish a groundwork for the principles to which he appeals?

15. Nicholas Fotion observes that terrorists choose their victims precisely because they are humans, and he suggests that they do not treat them *as* humans. What does this mean? Is it true?

16. Fotion takes terrorists to task for their willingness to sacrifice their victims for some allegedly higher good. But are their acts significantly different from those of governments that send their military forces into battle, knowing that many of them will never return? Or of governments sending their armed forces on raids designed to save hostages, such as the Israeli raid on Entebbe airport in Uganda, or the U.S. attempt in April 1980 to rescue from Iran American hostages being held at the American embassy in Tehran?

17. Fotion assumes that the terrorist's option is "morally the worst, or just about the worst, possible means" and that the burden of proof is therefore on the terrorist to demonstrate that the option chosen was indeed the best. *Why* is the terrorist's option the worst? If it is not to be judged on the terrorist's own terms, by results it is designed to effect, then what moral criteria *should* be applied to make such a judgment?

18. Fotion, like Edel and Nielsen, suggests that there is such a thing as official terrorism. If that is indeed the case, then why should there not also be small-scale terrorism, at least in those situations where it is designed to eliminate official terrorism? More importantly, what criteria might be offered to identify official terrorism? Is it anything other than a government policy, or a particular form of government, of which the potential terrorist strongly disapproves?

19. After reading the articles and cases that make up this book, have you made any progress toward resolving any of the difficult and complex issues explored in them? Do you feel that you are in a better position now than you were before to answer the questions raised by Professor Taylor? What, after all, *is* the meaning of life? Or is that question itself meaningless?

BIOGRAPHICAL NOTES

THE EDITOR:

BURTON M. LEISER received his degrees from the University of Chicago, Yeshiva University, and Brown University. His principal teaching positions have been at the State University College at Buffalo, Sir George Williams (now Concordia) University of Montreal, and Drake University, where he is Professor of Philosophy. His publications include *Custom, Law, and Morality: Conflict and Continuity in Social Behavior* (Doubleday Anchor, 1969), *Liberty, Justice, and Morals: Contemporary Value Conflicts* (Macmillan, Second Edition 1979), and articles in *Ethics, The Stanford Journal of International Studies, Archiv, Judaism, Barrister,* and other journals as well as in numerous anthologies. He has written and lectured widely on moral and legal issues.

THE CONTRIBUTORS:

WILLIAM AIKEN teaches philosophy at Chatham College. He has co-edited *World Hunger and Moral Obligation* and has published articles on a variety of social and political issues.

DIANA AXELSEN is Associate Professor and Chair of the Department of Philosophy of Spelman College, and also teaches a course on human values in medicine at the Morehouse College School of Medicine in Atlanta. Her degrees are from Stanford University. Her published work has included articles on ethical issues in human experimentation and on the care of handicapped newborns.

TOM L. BEAUCHAMP's degrees are from Southern Methodist University, Yale University, and the Johns Hopkins University. He is co-author of *Principles of Biomedical Ethics* (Oxford University Press, 1979) and has written articles covering a wide variety of philosophical concerns. He has also edited a number of volumes on ethics, on causation, and on Thomas Reid, is a general editor of *The Critical Edition and Collected Works of David Hume* (forthcoming) and is Professor of Philosophy and Senior Research Scholar at the Kennedy Institute-Center for Bioethics at Georgetown University.

HUGO ADAM BEDAU is Justin B. Fletcher Professor of Philosophy at Tufts University. He is the author of *The Courts, the Constitution, and Capital Punishment* (D.C. Heath, 1977), and editor of *Justice and Equality* (Prentice-Hall, 1971), *Civil Disobedience: Theory and Practice*

(Bobbs-Merrill, 1969), and *The Death Penalty in America* (Aldine, 1964). In addition, he has co-edited a book on capital punishment, co-authored a book on victimless crimes, and written widely on philosophical, legal, and political issues. He received his degrees from University of the Redlands, Boston University, and Harvard University.

RAY S. CLINE is Executive Director of World Power Studies at Georgetown University Center for Strategic and International Studies. He is also Adjunct Professor of International Relations in the School of Foreign Service, Georgetown, and Adjunct Professor at the Defense Intelligence School, an advanced study institute under the U.S. Department of Defense. During more than thirty years of service with the United States government, he has been Deputy Director for Intelligence of the Central Intelligence Agency and Director of the Bureau of Intelligence and Research in the State Department. He holds A.B., M.A., and Ph.D. degrees from Harvard, and also studied at Balliol College, Oxford University. Dr. Cline is author of a number of books, including *Secrets, Spies, and Scholars: A Blueprint of the Essential CIA* (Acropolis Books, 1976) and *World Power Trends and U.S. Foreign Policy for the 1980s* (Westview Press, 1980).

CARL COHEN, Professor (Residential College) at the University of Michigan, received his degrees from the University of Miami, the University of Illinois, and UCLA. He has held visiting appointments in New Zealand, Israel, Peru, and elsewhere. His books include *Communism, Fascism, and Democracy: The Theoretical Foundations* (Random House, 1972), *Civil Disobedience: Conscience, Tactics, and the Law* (Columbia University Press, 1971), and *Democracy* (The Free Press, 1973). His many articles reflect his interest in moral and political philosophy, civil liberties, jurisprudence, and the application of philosophical principles to contemporary public affairs.

RICHARD T. DE GEORGE, University Distinguished Professor of Philosophy and Co-Director for Humanistic Studies at the University of Kansas, is Past President of the American Section of the International Association for Philosophy of Law and Social Philosophy, a member of the Steering Committee of the International Federation of Philosophical Societies, and Chairman of the Steering Committee of the Conference of Philosophical Societies. He is the author or editor of twelve books, including *Ethics and Society* (Doubleday Anchor, 1963), *Soviet Ethics and Morality* (University of Michigan Press, 1969), and *Ethics, Free Enterprise, and Public Policy* (Oxford University Press, 1978).

ABRAHAM EDEL received his education at McGill, Oxford, and Columbia Universities. He taught philosophy at the City College of New York, served as Distinguished Professor of Philosophy at the Graduate School of the City University of New York, and as Research Professor of Philosophy at the University of Pennsylvania. He has also served as an Associate at the National Humanities Center, and has received numerous awards for his contributions to philosophy. His many publications on the relations of ethics and the social and humanistic disciplines include *Ethical Judgment: The Use of Science in Ethics* (Free Press, 1964),

Science and the Structure of Ethics (University of Chicago Press, 1961), *Analyzing Concepts in Social Science* (Transaction Books, 1979), and *Exploring Fact and Value* (Transaction Books, 1980).

JANE E. ENGLISH received her degrees at the University of Michigan and at Harvard University. In addition to a number of important articles in philosophical journals, she was editor of *Sex Equality* (Prentice-Hall, 1977). She was Associate Professor of Philosophy at the University of North Carolina at Chapel Hill when she died in 1978,

JOEL FEINBERG, whose degrees are from the University of Michigan, has taught philosophy at Brown University, Princeton University, U.C.L.A., and the Rockefeller University (where he was also Chairman of the Department), and is now Professor and Chairman of the Department of Philosophy at the University of Arizona. He has held numerous positions of responsibility in a variety of associations in the philosophical field, including the presidency of the Pacific Division of the American Philosophical Association. His many publications in ethics and philosophy of law include *Moral Concepts* (Oxford University Press, 1969), *Doing and Deserving: Essays in the Theory of Responsibility* (Princeton University Press, 1970), *Social Philosophy* (Prentice-Hall, 1973), *The Problem of Abortion* (Wadsworth Publishing Co., 1973), *Philosophy of Law* (Dickenson Publishing Co., 1977), *Philosophy and the Human Condition* (Prentice-Hall, 1980), and *Rights, Justice, and the Bounds of Liberty* (Princeton University Press, 1980).

PHILIPPA FOOT has taught in many American universities, including Cornell, Princeton, MIT, and the University of California at Berkeley. She has served as Fellow and Tutor of Somerville College, Oxford, and is now Senior Research Fellow there, as well as Professor of Philosophy at U.C.L.A. Her most recent book is *Virtues and Vices* (University of California Press, 1979), and she is editing a book of readings in medical ethics for the Oxford University Press.

NICHOLAS FOTION, Professor of Philosophy at Emory University, served for a number of years as Chairman of the Department of Philosophy at the State University of New York College at Buffalo. His articles have touched on such subjects as paternalism, medical ethics, conscience, wickedness, and the fact-value distinction, as well as the philosophy of language. His book, *Moral Situations,* was published by the Kent State University Press, (1964).

ANN GARRY, a graduate of Monmouth College, the University of Chicago, and the University of Maryland at College Park, is Associate Professor of Philosophy at California State University in Los Angeles. Her publications have been in the philosophy of mind, epistemology, and the philosophy of feminism.

YALE KAMISAR is Henry K. Ransom Professor of Law at the University of Michigan. He has written widely on criminal law and constitutional-criminal procedure. He is the author of *Police Interrogation and Confessions: Essays in Law and Policy* (University of Michigan Press, 1980), and co-author of two widely-used casebooks: *Constitutional Law:*

Cases, Comments, and Questions (West Publishing Co., 5th ed. 1980) and *Modern Criminal Procedure* (West Publishing Co., 5th ed. 1980). He is a graduate of New York University and Columbia Law School.

SAMUEL McCRACKEN, who is now Assistant to the President at Boston University, is a graduate of Drake University and the University of Connecticut. Prior to assuming his administrative position, he taught at Reed College and at Boston University. He has written extensively on current moral and political issues, on educational policies, and on nuclear energy. His book on nuclear power is scheduled for publication by Basic Books.

KAI NIELSEN is Professor of Philosophy at the University of Calgary. He has also taught at Amherst College, Brooklyn College of the City University of New York, York University, and the University of Ottawa. He is an editor of *The Canadian Journal of Philosophy* and is author of *Reason and Practice* (Harper & Row, 1971), *Contemporary Critiques of Religion* (Seabury Press, 1972), *Skepticism* (St. Martin, 1973), and many articles in various fields of philosophy.

RICHARD B. PARKER is a civil trial attorney. He has taught philosophy, law, or the philosophy of law at North Central College, the College of the University of Chicago, Harvard College, and Rutgers Law School. His degrees are from Harvard Law School and the University of Chicago.

DAVID A. J. RICHARDS received his undergraduate degree from Harvard College, his D. Phil. from Oxford University, and his J.D. from Harvard Law School. He is Professor of Law at New York University, specializing in criminal law, constitutional law, and jurisprudence. Among his publications are *A Theory of Reasons for Action* (Oxford University Press, 1971) and *The Moral Criticism of Law* (Dickenson, 1977).

JOHN A. ROBERTSON is Professor of Law in the Law School of the University of Wisconsin at Madison and in Medical Ethics in the Medical School of the University of Wisconsin.

FREDERICK SCHAUER teaches jurisprudence and constitutional law at the Marshall-Wythe School of Law, College of William and Mary, where he is Associate Professor of Law. He was educated at Dartmouth College and the Harvard Law School. In addition to lecturing widely in the United States, England, and Ireland on philosophical aspects of freedom of speech, he has written numerous articles on free speech and is the author of *The Law of Obscenity* (BNA Books, 1976).

RICHARD TAYLOR characterizes himself as a beekeeper and philosopher who lives in Trumanburg, New York. From other sources, however, I have learned that he received his degrees from the University of Illinois, Oberlin College, and Brown University. He has taught philosophy at Brown University, where he served as William Herbert Faunce Professor of Philosophy, at Columbia University, and at a number of other American colleges and universities prior to assuming his present post as Professor of Philosophy at the University of Rochester. His principal publications are *Metaphysics* (Prentice-Hall, 1973, rev. ed. 1974), *Action and Purpose* (Humanities Press), *Good and Evil* (Macmillan, 1970), *Freedom, Anarchy, and the Law* (Prentice-Hall, 1973), and *With Heart and Mind* (St. Martin's Press, 1973). His many articles cover a wide range of philosophical concerns, from philosophy of law and ethics to metaphysics and linguistic analysis.

MICHAEL TOOLEY, who has written on moral issues, has taught philosophy at Princeton University and at the Australian National University.

MARY ANNE WARREN received her Ph.D. from the University of California at Berkeley and has taught philosophy at Sonoma State University and at San Francisco State University. Her articles have been on the subjects of abortion, affirmative action, and population policy, and she is the author of a book on the philosophy of feminism, *The Nature of Woman: An Encyclopedia and Guide to the Literature* (Edgepress, 1979).

FRANCIS M. WILHOIT received his degrees from Harvard University. He is professor of Political Science at Drake University, and is the author of *The Politics of Massive Resistance* (Braziller, 1973) and *The Quest for Equality in Freedom* (Transaction Books, 1979).

AUTHORS OF JUDICIAL OPINIONS:

HARRY A. BLACKMUN, a graduate of Harvard College and Harvard Law School, was in private practice for 25 years before being appointed as judge on the Eighth Circuit Court of Appeals by President Eisenhower in 1959. He was appointed to the United State Supreme Court by President Nixon, and assumed his post as Associate Justice in 1970,

WILLIAM J. BRENNAN, JR. graduated from the Wharton School of Finance of the University of Pennsylvania and from the Harvard Law School. Before his appointment to the United States Supreme Court by President Eisenhower, he served as judge on the Superior Court of the State of New Jersey, on the Appellate Division of the Superior Court, and on the New Jersey Supreme Court.

ALBERT V. BRYAN, a graduate of the University of Virginia, has served as judge on the United States District Court for the Eastern District of Virginia and on the United States Circuit Court of Appeals, Fourth Circuit.

WARREN E. BURGER, a graduate of the St. Paul College of Law, has been active in Republican politics for many years. He was appointed Assistant Attorney General in charge of the Civil Division of the Justice Department by President Eisenhower, and to a judgeship on the U.S. Court of Appeals for the District of Columbia. President Nixon nominated him for the post of Chief Justice of the United States to fill the post being vacated by the retirement of Chief Justice Earl Warren, and he assumed the position in 1969.

PAUL J. LIACOS graduated from Boston University and from Howard University. He has served as Professor of Law at Boston University and as Adjunct Professor of Law at the same institution, as well as Distinguished Professor of Law at the United States Military Academy at West Point. He is the author of a *Handbook of Massachusetts Evidence* (Little, Brown, 1967), and of articles in legal journals, and has served as Justice on the Massachusetts Supreme Judicial Court since 1976.

ROBERT R. MERHIGE, JR. is judge of the United States District Court in Richmond and Adjunct Professor at the University of Richmond Law School, from which he received his degrees.

WILLIAM H. REHNQUIST graduated from Stanford University and from Stanford Law School. He served as law clerk to Supreme Court Justice Robert H. Jackson. He was appointed assistant attorney general in charge of the office of legal counsel by President Nixon, and was sworn in as Associate Justice of the United States Supreme Court in 1972 after being nominated by President Nixon and being confirmed by the Senate despite bitter opposition by civil rights, civil liberties, and labor groups who criticized his conservative record on issues of individual and minority rights.

POTTER STEWART graduated from Yale University and from Yale Law School. He was appointed by President Eisenhower to the Sixth Circuit Court of Appeals in 1954, and was appointed to the United States Supreme Court in 1958, despite opposition from Southern Democrats who disliked his stance on civil rights.

BYRON R. WHITE grew up in a small town in Colorado, and graduated from the University of Colorado, where he was an all-American football player. He played professional football for the Pittsburgh Steelers and the Detroit Lions, attended Oxford University as a Rhodes Scholar, graduated from Yale Law School, and served as a law clerk to Supreme Court Chief Justice Fred Vinson. He may be the only Supreme Court Justice to have been named to the Football Hall of Fame. He was named deputy attorney general by President Kennedy, and personally commanded more than 400 federal marshals assigned to protect the Freedom Riders, civil rights demonstrators led by Martin Luther King, Jr., who had been assaulted by mobs in Montgomery, Alabama. He was President Kennedy's first appointee to the United States Supreme Court, in 1962.